INTERNATIONAL WHITE COLLAR CRIME

Contemporary transnational criminals take advantage of globalization, trade liberalization, and emerging new technologies to commit a diverse range of crimes and to move money, goods, services, and people instantaneously for purposes of pure economic gain, political violence, or both. This book captures the importance of transnational business crime and international relations by examining the rise of international economic crime and recent strategies in the United States and abroad to combat it.

The book is organized into three main sections. The first part discusses substantive crimes, particularly tax, money laundering and counterterrorism financial enforcement, transnational corruption, transnational organized crime, and export control and economic sanctions. The second part discusses procedural aspects of international white collar crime, namely extraterritorial jurisdiction, evidence gathering, extradition, and international prisoner transfer. The third part discusses the role of international organizations, including the United Nations, the World Bank Group, INTERPOL, and economic integration groups.

Bruce Zagaris is a partner with the law firm of Berliner, Corcoran & Rowe, Washington, D.C. His practice includes criminal trial and appellate work. He has handled evidence gathering and extradition cases on both the interstate and international levels and cases involving prisoner transfer applications. He has consulted extensively for governments and international organizations. He has been an adjunct professor of law at several U.S. law schools. Since 1985, Zagaris has been the editor of the *International Law Enforcement Reporter*, which he founded. He has authored and edited several books and hundreds of articles on international law.

International White Collar Crime

CASES AND MATERIALS

Bruce Zagaris
Berliner, Corcoran & Rowe, LLP, Washington, D.C.

CAMBRIDGE
UNIVERSITY PRESS

CAMBRIDGE UNIVERSITY PRESS
Cambridge, New York, Melbourne, Madrid, Cape Town, Singapore,
São Paulo, Delhi, Dubai, Tokyo

Cambridge University Press
32 Avenue of the Americas, New York, NY 10013-2473, USA

www.cambridge.org
Information on this title: www.cambridge.org/9780521122993

First published 2010

Printed in the United States of America

A catalog record for this publication is available from the British Library.

Library of Congress Cataloging in Publication data

Zagaris, Bruce.
International white collar crime : cases and materials / Bruce Zagaris.
p. cm.
Includes bibliographical references and index.
ISBN 978-0-521-19468-6 (hardback) – ISBN 978-0-521-12299-3 (pbk.)
1. White collar crimes. 2. Transnational crime. 3. White collar
crimes – United States. I. Title.
K5215.Z34 2010
345′.0268 – dc22 2009028964

ISBN 978-0-521-19468-6 Hardback
ISBN 978-0-521-12299-3 Paperback

Contents

1 Introduction

I. Introduction

This book discusses the rise of international economic crime and recent U.S. and international strategies to combat such crime. It is organized into three main sections. The first discusses substantive crimes, particularly tax, money laundering and counterterrorism financial enforcement, transnational corruption, transnational organized crime, and export control and economic sanctions. The second part discusses procedural aspects of international white collar crime, namely extraterritorial jurisdiction, evidence gathering, extradition, and international prisoner transfer. The third part discusses the role of international organizations, including the United Nations, the World Bank Group, INTERPOL, and economic integration groups.

Although there is no recognized category of "business crimes" or white collar crimes,[1] this book includes within substantive white collar crimes those mentioned earlier. The term "white collar crime" was coined by Edwin Sutherland in a speech to the American Sociological Society in 1939. Subsequently, he stated that it "may be defined approximately as a crime committed by a person of respectability and high social status in the course of his occupation."[2] Thereafter, a variety of definitions have been applied to white collar crime.[3]

[1] Ellen S. Podgor & Roger S. Clark, Understanding International Criminal Law 37 (2d ed. 2008).

[2] Ellen S. Podgor, *Globalization and the Federal Prosecution of White Collar Crime*, 34 Am. Crim. L. Rev. 325, 327 (2007), citing Edwin H. Sutherland, White Collar Crime: The Uncut Version 7 (1983).

[3] Podgor, *id.*, citing David T. Johnson & Richard A. Leo, *The Yale White-Collar Crime Project: A Review and Critique*, 18 Law & Soc. Inquiry 63 (1993) (reviewing various definitions of white collar crime); Jerold H. Israel, Ellen S. Podgor, & Paul D. Borman, White Collar Crime: Law and Practice 1–11 (1996) (same).

II. Environment Giving Rise to International Economic Crimes

Contemporary transnational criminals take advantage of globalization, trade liberalization, and emerging new technologies to commit a diverse range of crimes and to move money, goods, services, and people instantaneously for purposes of pure economic gain, political violence, or both.[4] A key component facilitating international white collar or economic crime is trade liberalization, especially free trade agreements (FTAs). The problem is that the leadership of trade liberalization or FTAs and the politics do not allow negotiators to provide for comprehensive enforcement mechanisms. The politics of FTAs make ratification difficult, especially if costly regulatory or enforcement mechanisms are added since surely they are perceived politically as underserving sovereignty. Instead, such comprehensive enforcement mechanisms are completely omitted, or else only isolated subjects are treated.

For instance, in the North American Free Trade Agreement (NAFTA) there is a large section on intellectual property (IP) enforcement and only several provisions on customs cooperation and enforcement. Customs enforcement is a subject that FTAs normally cover. However, the extensive coverage of IP enforcement reflects the strong influence in the United States of intellectual property groups. As a result of failing to include comprehensive enforcement provisions in FTAs, individual criminals and criminal organizations are able to take advantage of FTAs to conduct their criminal activities. FTA members usually became aware of the growth of criminal problems arising out of FTAs several years after they are implemented. They then try to develop ad hoc enforcement agreements and arrangements. However, these agreements and arrangements usually have a narrower scope than the FTAs, usually lack institutional support, and sometimes overlap. As a result, the international enforcement architecture arising out of FTAs cannot sustain enforcement needs.

Transnational criminal groups and criminals live and operate in a borderless world. Increasingly, transnational criminals are diversifying their crimes, instrumentalities, markets, and networks. Their intelligence networks and the coincidence of economic and political power enable them to quickly transfer parts of their operations and enterprises to the territories that they can dominate (e.g., "gray areas" in which governments do not effectively control their territory – Afghanistan and parts of Pakistan and Yemen)[5] or to operate surreptitiously (e.g., with sleeper cells).[6] Although national governments have determined that transnational organized crime and terrorism are national security threats and have implemented various initiatives to combat those threats,[7] they are continuously and actively seeking more significant political and legal initiatives to establish

[4] Some of this introduction is adopted from Bruce Zagaris, *U.S. International Cooperation against Transnational Organized Crime*, 44 WAYNE L. REV. 1402–1405. 1–402–5 (1998). For additional background on globalization and international white collar crime, *see* Hervé Boullanger, LA CRIMINALITÉ ECONOMIQUE EN EUROPE (ECONOMIC CRIME IN EUROPE) 35–46 (2002).

[5] For a discussion of the gray area phenomena, whereby terrorists and criminals use portions of countries where the government does not effectively control its territory to hide and operate their enterprises, *see* GRAY AREA PHENOMENA: CONFRONTING THE NEW WORLD DISORDER (Max G. Manwaring ed., 1993).

[6] *See, e.g.*, Peter A. Lupsha, *Transnational Organized Crime versus the Nation-State*, 2 TRANSNAT'L ORG. CRIME 21–48 (1996).

[7] *See Interview with the Hon. Richard A. Clarke, Special Assistant to the President and Senior Director, Global Issues and Multinational Affairs, National Security Council, Nov. 30, 1995*, 1 TRENDS IN ORG. CRIME 5–9 (1996).

effective international enforcement regimes. Some policymakers believe that effectively combating new transnational crimes requires significant transformations in national legal systems.[8]

The international community and individual countries such as the United States have enacted a substantial amount of new legislation and developed initiatives to combat new transnational crimes, such as cybercrime, intellectual property and international tax crime, terrorism, and organized crime.[9] Yet, to a greater extent, globalization, free trade, and information technology have facilitated borderless transnational criminal operations. As transnational crime and especially terrorism increase and transnational criminal groups proliferate, national governments are challenged to prevent and combat transnational criminals operating in a borderless world.

Cybercrime exemplifies the difficulty whereby legal systems try to keep pace with the tremendous changes in technology that have enabled criminals to perpetrate diverse crimes, such as financial fraud, identity theft, pornography, hate crimes, and a vast range of other offenses. The international community is struggling to develop an enforcement regime that can use new technology to assist in the identification, investigation, and prosecution of cybercriminals. In this regard, the proposed Council of Europe Convention against Cybercrime provides a strong potential mechanism.

Intellectual property and counterfeiting crimes have grown tremendously in recent decades. Criminals counterfeit everything from software to cosmetics and clothing, indeed nearly every product that is sold internationally. The international community and governments have tried a combination of domestic criminal law and international trade law, such as Trade in Related Intellectual Property Services (TRIPS) and NAFTA, to criminalize violations of transnational intellectual property. For instance, in the United States trade associations such as the International Intellectual Property Association and the Motion Picture Society of America have pressured the U.S. government to bring an action against Mexico because of its government's alleged lack of criminal action against persons who intentionally violate IP law. Indeed, these same U.S. trade associations succeeded in persuading the NAFTA signatories to include provisions requiring criminal prosecution and civil action against violators of IP law – the only part of NAFTA that allows for criminal action to remedy IP crimes.

Money laundering is an example of the type of crime that governments and the international community have only criminalized since the mid-1980s. Through international conventions, such as the 1988 UN Convention against Illicit Traffic in Narcotic Drugs and Psychotropic Substances and the 1990 Council of Europe Convention on Laundering, Search, Seizure and Confiscation of the Proceeds from Crime, the international community has extended the use of a new anti-money laundering enforcement regime to

[8] *See, e.g.*, Senator John Kerry, The New War: The Web of Crime that Threatens America's Security 31 (1997).

[9] On Oct. 22, 1995, President Clinton used the occasion of his fourteen-minute speech before the fiftieth anniversary of the UN to announce a number of new initiatives against transnational organized crime, including the extension of economic sanctions against certain Colombian narcotics trafficking organizations. *See Remarks of President Clinton to the United Nations on the Occasion of the 50th Anniversary of the Creation of the United Nations*, Fed. News Service, Oct. 22, 1995, available in Lexis, Nexis Library, Curnws File. For the economic sanctions, *see* Exec. Order No. 12,978, 60 Fed. Reg. 54,579 (1995); for the text of Presidential Directive 42 on transnational crime, *see* White House, *Presidential Directive on International Organized Crime, Summary Sheet*, Oct. 22, 1995.

the entire world. Signatories are required to criminalize laundering offenses and initiate asset forfeiture and confiscation as remedies. These conventions require a broad range of international enforcement cooperation efforts, including evidence gathering and extradition, and also suggest a range of more customized bilateral cooperation agreements. Institutionally, the new crime of money laundering has spawned the establishment of financial investigative (or intelligence) units (FIUs) around the world, as well as the Egmont Group, an association of FIUs that meets regularly to facilitate cooperation among FIUs and develop uniform approaches to core issues. Anti-money laundering has given rise to new organizations and groups, such as the Financial Action Task Force on Anti-Money Laundering (FATF). Growing out of the industrial G8 meetings, FATF has developed cutting-edge requirements on legal, financial, and external relations with respect to anti-money laundering. Unfortunately, the erosion of bank and financial privacy has been among the many legal transformations brought about by anti-money laundering laws.

In the aftermath of the September 11, 2001, terrorist attacks, the emphasis of the U.S. government and the international community on counterterrorism financial enforcement has increased. The U.S. government has invoked a war paradigm and initiated a comprehensive financial strategy aimed at detecting, through financial movements, transnational terrorist movements and plans and preventing new terrorist attacks. The strategy is designed to investigate, prosecute, and seize terrorist assets by applying many of the anti-money laundering due diligence requirements commonly used by the private sector to counter terrorism. Simultaneously, the United States has applied its economic sanctions regime to terrorists. The U.S. strategy seeks to develop comprehensive international counterterrorism financial enforcement.

Although the international community has engaged in tax enforcement cooperation for many years through exchange of information provisions within income tax treaties and exchange of information agreements, many national courts have traditionally taken the position that one country will not help collect the taxes of another country. As a result, courts have refused to enforce foreign tax judgments and even requests for assistance. During the last two or three decades, the international community has developed multilateral conventions, such as the 1983 Council of Europe/OECD Convention on Mutual Administrative Assistance in Tax Matters, to overcome the traditional judicial reluctance to help foreign tax authorities. Increasingly, international organizations of tax authorities have met regularly to develop uniform approaches, networks, and conventions to reduce gaps in tax laws and strengthen enforcement cooperation. Additionally, national governments have criminalized tax fraud and evasion and required extensive and draconian reporting regimes that include administrative penal laws for noncompliance.

The international community has developed offshore blacklisting as a means to accelerate compliance with new "soft law." In 1999 and 2000, governments and international organizations continued their active efforts to increase regulatory and criminal enforcement of various laws to stem the tide of transnational crime. These efforts were reflected in the criminalization of various business and financial transactions, the imposition of new due diligence measures on the private sector and the concomitant weakening of privacy and confidentiality laws, strengthened penalties for noncompliance with regulatory efforts, and new law enforcement techniques. These techniques include undercover sting operations, wiretapping, expanded powers to search homes and businesses, and "controlled deliveries." The latter term signifies the technique whereby law enforcement allows the delivery of contraband to occur in order to identify and surveil the participants in the illegal transportation of the contraband. Law enforcement allows the delivery to occur in order to try to identify the leaders of the contraband delivery and criminal enterprises, penetrate and ultimately arrest and prosecute them.

A major development in 2000 was the almost simultaneous issuance by several international institutions of blacklists against noncompliant organizations. Within a one-month period, the Organization of Economic Cooperation and Development (OECD) issued its harmful tax competition initiative with a list of tax havens that did not agree to publicly commit to bring their practices into compliance; the Financial Stability Forum (FSF) now Financial Stability Board (FSB) issued its report on offshore financial centers (OFCs), classifying OFCs into three levels of compliance with international standards; and the Financial Action Task Force on Anti-Money Laundering (FATF) issued its list of fifteen noncomplying countries.

The simultaneous issuing of blacklists was an attempt to jumpstart the anti-money laundering enforcement regime and confer on soft laws a greater status in international law and politics. The October 2005 FATF decision to continue blacklisting fifteen noncooperative countries, together with the lack of any new commitments by the OECD harmful tax competition initiative and the decision by the International Monetary Fund (IMF) to take over the OFC work of the FSB, has meant that some companies, businesses, and investors are reconsidering the structure of their investments. On April 2, 2009, coincident to the G-20 meeting, the OECD issued a progress report on the harmful tax practices initiative, containing a more sophisticated group of white lists, gray lists, and black lists.

The convergence of the various initiatives shows a determination by intergovernmental organizations to combine development of an international financial enforcement subregime, which includes international tax and anti-money laundering policies, with the new international financial architecture, particularly the work of the FSF.

Countries such as Italy and the United States have pioneered national legislation to combat organized crime. On December 15, 2000, 124 countries signed the UN Convention on Transnational Organized Crime at a conference in Palermo, Italy, signifying the start of the construction of an international enforcement regime against transnational organized crime. The convention's three protocols (one to prevent, suppress, and punish trafficking in persons; a second against the smuggling of migrants by land, air, and sea; and a third on the illicit transfer of firearms) represent a new effort to attack transnational organized crime activity. The convention, effective as of the start of 2006, employs some of the same methods of the UN Counterdrug Convention, including using anti-money laundering and asset forfeiture efforts against transnational organized crime.

The challenges of transnational criminality at the millennium are substantial. Unless nation-states become better at networking and cooperating, they will lose power to transnational criminals who operate in a borderless world. To gain and maintain respect for their democracies, states must develop international enforcement regimes that are balanced and maintain fundamental and international human rights. To achieve success in combating transnational crime, criminal justice professionals must become more adept at working with noncriminal legal professionals, diplomats, international relations professionals, and a host of others. For instance, criminal justice professionals must study international organizational theory and chart the start, emergence, and evolution of international enforcement regimes. Indeed, new transnational crimes and responses in the context of globalization will continue to pose a mighty challenge to the legal and law enforcement professions.

This book examines recent approaches by the United States and the international community to combating the financing of international crime. In particular, it looks at organized crime, taxation, transnational corruption, securities and commodities futures enforcement, economic sanctions, and money laundering enforcement. Although the book discusses criminal and international law or international criminal law, as it is often called, it also focuses on the international aspects of administrative penal law. Focusing largely on U.S. laws and the U.S. legal perspective, this book discusses comparative and international law where relevant.

III. The Scope of International White Collar Crime

International white collar crime encompasses a number of problems in the areas where criminal, business and economic, and international law overlap and interact. Economic and financial crime refer to diverse activities that cannot be included under a homogeneous rubric. The newness of the field, the overlap of criminal and administrative penal law, the scope of economic and financial law, and divergences among legal systems make an accurate definition elusive.[10] The area is undergoing tremendous change and growth as a result of globalization and the increasing use of criminal and administrative penal sanctions to enforce international business norms.

This section divides international white collar crime into the following subareas: (1) substantive white collar crimes, (2) procedural aspects of white collar crimes, (3) the role of international organizations, and (4) the role of nongovernmental organizations.

International white collar crime may be thought to be intrinsic to the international economy. Such a perspective views international white collar crime not as forms of deviance from, but as rooted in the international economy itself. Hence, the market is the main source and mode of illegal conduct. Authors who emphasize the economic component of international white collar crime suggest that violations in the economic world are part and parcel of economic development. However, this perspective does not address the extent to which economic and financial crime data do or do not follow a precise pattern related to the economy, which is still an issue for criminological debate.[11] Although this book considers the economic component, it does not focus specifically on it.

One dynamic aspect of international white collar crime is that economic crime reacts to systemic economic changes caused by new combinations of productive factors. For example, the combination of banking and computers has led to cyberbanking and cyberfinancial products such as Internet gaming. Deviant entrepreneurs introduce new combinations of productive factors while devising deviant adaptations to economic changes, thereby pursuing legitimate goals through illegitimate means. White collar criminals also innovate by repelling the criminal label from their activity while directing it to

[10] Vincenzo Ruggiero, *Economic and Financial Crime in Europe*, LA CRIMINALITÉ ECONOMIQUE ET FINANCIERE EN EUROPE (ECONOMIC AND FINANCIAL CRIME IN EUROPE 19, 24 (Paul Ponsaers & Vincenzo Ruggiero eds., L'Harmattan, 2002).

[11] Ruggiero, *id.* at 20.

competitors. Hence, innovation in international white collar crime requires changes in the perception of business, whereby persons who innovate successfully claim their activities and practices to be ethical and those of competitors to be unethical.[12]

Some background in international criminal law (ICL) is required to understand international white collar crime. ICL is largely a mix of the penal aspects of international law and the international law aspects of criminal law. The international aspects of national criminal law consist of extraterritorial jurisdictional norms, conflicts of criminal jurisdiction between states and between a state and an international organization, and the international sources of law applicable to modalities of international cooperation in penal matters or the indirect enforcement system. The applicable international sources of law are found in multilateral and bilateral treaties, customary international law, and national norms applicable to national legal proceedings.[13]

The penal aspects of international law arise out of "conventions," "customs," and "general principles of law," all of which are among the sources of international law as set forth in Article 38 of the International Court of Justice's statute. However, the sources are subject to the principles of legality that derive from general principles of international law. The penal aspects of international law include the following: international crimes, elements of international criminal responsibility, the procedural aspects of the direct enforcement system of ICL, and certain aspects of the enforcement modalities of the indirect enforcement system of ICL. Increasingly the penal law aspects of international law have expanded and overlap with the international law aspects of national criminal law.[14]

A. *Substantive White Collar Crimes*

Substantive white collar crimes refer to legal areas of crime that national and international laws seek to prevent and punish. They can include fraud, computer crimes, securities, commodities futures, antitrust, intellectual property, customs, export control, environmental, money laundering, organized crime, transnational corruption, and taxation. This book necessarily covers only selected white collar crime areas.

B. *Procedural Aspects of White Collar Crimes*

The procedural aspects of international white collar crimes encompass all the national and international aspects of investigating, prosecuting, and then enforcing sanctions against white collar crimes. This book discusses jurisdiction, evidence gathering, asset freezes and forfeiture, gaining custody (i.e., extradition and alternatives), transfer of proceedings, recognition and enforcement of judgments, and transfer of prisoners.

C. *The Role of International Organizations*

The role of international organizations, also known as international governmental organizations (IGOs), is critical because these IGOs develop hard and soft law standards

[12] *Id.* at 26–27.
[13] M. Cherif Bassiouni, Introduction to International Criminal Law 5 (2003).
[14] *Id.* at 5.

in international white collar crime and help implement those standards. Some IGOs operate on a universal level, whereas other ones operate on a regional level. Some IGOs, such as banks, securities and commodities futures regulators, and financial intelligence units, have functional scopes.

Institutional responses to international white collar crime are triggered by diverse forces. First, international pressure demands that legislative loopholes be closed and approaches and laws be harmonized wherever possible. Second, the general awareness exists that this type of crime has a great impact on public finances. Third, the perception exists that international white collar crime encourages the development of more conventional forms of criminal activities that in some places are characterized with the synthetic name "organized crime."[15]

D. *The Role of Nongovernmental Organizations*

Increasingly, nongovernmental organizations (NGOs) are playing important roles in combating international white collar crime. Some NGOs, such as the International Committee of the Red Cross, Human Rights Watch, and Amnesty International, focus on international human rights and procedural aspects. Other NGOs include bar associations made up of lawyers; increasingly, these bar associations have committees on international criminal law that focus in part on white collar crime. Law enforcement professionals have their own NGOs, such as the International Association of Chiefs of Police and the International Association of Prosecutors. Other NGOs are business groups, such as the International Chamber of Commerce and various banking associations. Because efforts to combat international white collar crime emphasize the privatization of some of the prevention and related crime-solving roles, business groups have become important partners with governments and IGOs.

E. *Constructing International Enforcement Regimes*

One of the subjects discussed in this book is the effort to develop international enforcement regimes. International relations theory explains the manner in which international institutions affect collaboration among states by mediating and defining international relationships. Known as regime theory, this explanation has been an important focus of international relations study for the last twenty to twenty-five years. One of the main scholars of international regime theory, Stephen Krasner, defines international organizations or regimes "as sets of implicit or explicit principles, norms, rules, and decision-making procedures around which actors' expectations converge in a given area of international relations."[16] Regimes can take well-defined forms, such as the United Nations, or they can exist more informally, such as through networks. Regime theorists believe that regimes are common mechanisms of international cooperation whose importance is derived from their ability to shape the means through which states relate to one another in ways that

[15] Ruggiero, *supra* note 10, at 26.

[16] Stephen D. Krasner, *Structural Causes and Regime Consequences: Regimes as Intervening Variables, in* International Regimes 2, 2 (Stephen D. Krasner ed., 1983); David Zaring, *International Law by Other Means: The Twilight Existence of International Financial Regulatory Organizations*, 33 Tex. Int'l L.J. 281, 309.

theorists who examine states as autarchic entities in an anarchic international system cannot successfully explain.[17]

According to Robert O. Keohane, one of the important theorists of international regime theory, regimes attract the participation of states by reducing the transaction costs of mutually beneficial cooperation.[18] Regimes facilitate multilateral negotiations, legitimate and delegitimate different types of state action, enable the exchange of information, and promote the basis for enforcement of agreements.[19]

Professor Keohane defines international regimes both as "institutions with explicit rules, agreed upon by governments, that pertain to particular sets of issues in international relations" and more narrowly as "specific contractual solutions" to international problems.[20] Within a multilayered system, an important function of international regimes is to facilitate the making of specific agreements on matters of substantive importance within the issue-area encompassed by the regime – here international enforcement and specifically, in international enforcement subregimes, anti-money laundering and counterterrorism financial enforcement, anticorruption, and tax enforcement.[21] Hence, regime theory offers a useful mechanism to describe international enforcement cooperation, including efforts to build an enforcement regime against transnational crime or at least against various types of transnational crime.

Several chapters in this book discuss efforts to develop international enforcement subregimes. For instance, the establishment of the Egmont Group of Financial Intelligence Units, which has its headquarters in Canada, is an example of how governments are developing an international anti-money laundering enforcement and regulatory regime. The various international anticorruption conventions are how starting to develop an anticorruption enforcement subregime.

The efforts to develop international enforcement regimes for international white collar crime make the subject and this book of interest for international relations studies.

F. *The Role of International Enforcement Networks*

An important breakthrough in international enforcement has been the development, as part of regime enforcement, of governmental networks. The identification of governmental networks has arisen in part out of the emergence of a world politics paradigm that conceptualizes transnational relations as transcending the nation-state and broadening the conception of actions to include transnational actors, such as nongovernmental organizations.[22] Anne-Marie Slaughter has done much pioneering work in this field,

[17] Zaring, *id.*

[18] *Id.* Robert O. Keohane, AFTER HEGEMONY: COOPERATION AND DISCORD IN THE WORLD POLITICAL ECONOMY (hereafter AFTER HEGEMONY) 244 (1984). *See also* Robert O. Keohane, *The Demand for International Regimes, in* INTERNATIONAL REGIMES, 141, 141–72.

[19] Keohane, AFTER HEGEMONY, *supra* note 18, at 244–45.

[20] Robert Keohane, INTERNATIONAL INSTITUTIONS AND STATE POWER: ESSAYS IN INTERNATIONAL RELATIONS 3–4 (1989).

[21] Keohane, *The Demand for International Regimes, supra* note 18, at 150.

[22] *See, e.g.,* Joseph S. Nye, Jr. & Robert O. Keohane, *Transnational Relations and World Politics, in* TRANSNATIONAL RELATIONS AND WORLD POLITICS 371, 380, and 382 (Robert O. Keohane & Joseph S. Nye, Jr. eds., Harvard U. Press, 1971) (providing diagrams of the interactions among government, intergovernmental, and nongovernmental actors in world politics and bilateral interactions in world politics).

showing that each of the networks has specific aims and activities, depending on its subject area, membership, and history. Taken together, they also perform certain common functions. They expand regulatory and enforcement reach. Networks permit national government officials to keep up with other actors, such as corporations, civic organizations, and criminals. They build trust and establish relationships among their participants that then create incentives to establish a good reputation and avoid a bad one by implementing the obligations of the enforcement regime. These are the conditions essential for long-term cooperation. Networks also exchange regular information about their own activities and develop databases of best practices. They offer technical assistance and professional socialization to interested members from less developed nations, whether regulators, judges, or legislators.[23]

The concept of a "network" has many dimensions. A network includes all the different ways in which individual government institutions interact with their counterparts whether abroad or above them, alongside more traditional state-to-state interactions. Hence, a network is a pattern of regular and purposive relations among like government units working across the borders that divide countries from one another and that demarcate the "domestic" from the "international" sphere.[24]

Networks are an important form of global governance and foreign policy option. As a form of global governance, governmental networks are quite useful. Composed of national government officials, either appointed by elected officials or directly elected themselves, these networks can perform many of the functions of a world government – legislation, administration, and adjudication without the form of a government per se.[25]

Governmental networks facilitate compliance because, as noted earlier, international regimes promote the making of agreements. Governments' anticipation that international regimes will increase compliance motivates their making of such agreements. By creating incentives for compliance, regimes also make it more attractive for potential members to join. Social pressure, exercised through linkages among issues, provides the most compelling reasons for governments to comply with their commitments. Hence, governments may comply with rules because if they do not, other governments will observe their behavior, evaluate it negatively, and perhaps take retaliatory action.[26] Sometimes retaliation will be specific and authorized under the rules of a regime, such as blacklists in the context of the OECD harmful tax practices and the FATF initiative on Non-Compliant Countries and Territories (NCCT). In this connection, states and territories targeted by the OECD and FATF initiatives perceived that the costs of acquiring a bad reputation as a result of rule violations imposed on them as transgressors of international standards were not worth the conduct.[27] Hence, a number agreed to enact new laws, adopt new principles, and strengthen their enforcement cooperation in taxation in the context of the OECD harmful tax practices initiative and in anti-money laundering in the context of the FATF NCCT initiative. Similarly, signatories to the OECD anticorruption convention discussed in Chapter 4 are subject to periodic evaluations of their compliance. The evaluations are public and quickly reviewed by civil society groups, such as Transparency International. As a result, government members of the OECD

[23] Anne Marie Slaughter, A NEW WORLD ORDER 3–4 (2004). *See also* Keohane, *The Demand for International Regimes, supra* note 18, at 148–55.
[24] Slaughter, *id.* at 14.
[25] *Id.* at 4.
[26] Keohane, AFTER HEGEMONY, *supra* note 18, at 103.
[27] *Id.* at 105.

anticorruption convention encounter pressure to conform their laws and regulations and how they are implemented to their obligations under the convention.

Understood as a foreign policy option, a world of governmental networks, working alongside and even within traditional international organizations, should be particularly attractive to the United States. The United States has taken the lead in dealing with some problems multilaterally, such as international crime syndicates and transnational terrorism, rather than unilaterally, for reasons of legitimacy, burden sharing, and effectiveness.[28] Similarly, in the 1980s the United States exercised leadership in developing anti-money laundering and asset forfeiture enforcement subregimes. Governmental networks could provide multilateral support for domestic government institutions in failed, weak, or transitional states. They could play an instrumental role in supporting and reforming government institutions in countries that seek to meet new international enforcement regimes.[29] Indeed, the U.S. government during the Clinton administration announced a major initiative against transnational organized crime. At a speech during the UN General Assembly, President Clinton unveiled an initiative against transnational organized crime and urged the international community to join it.[30]

Understanding the roles and opportunities of governmental networks requires thinking about a world of governments, with all the different institutions that perform the basic functions of government – legislation, adjudication, implementation – interacting both with each other domestically and also with their foreign and supranational counterparts, such as the World Bank Group, the United Nations, INTERPOL, and economic integration groups. States still exist in this world; indeed, they are crucial actors. But they are "disaggregated." They relate to each other not only through their individual foreign affairs offices but also through regulatory, judicial, and legislative channels.[31] For instance, in the parlance of an international enforcement regime, viewing the government participants means realizing that they are more than the unitary state, as represented by their state's foreign affairs office (i.e., the U.S. Department of State). Instead, among the key government participants of international enforcement networking are the officials of the U.S. Department of Justice, the U.S. Department of Treasury, Customs Services, Immigration and Naturalization Service (the latter two as part of the Department of Homeland Security), and federal and state prosecutors.

Ms. Slaughter properly observes that viewing the world through the lens of disaggregated rather than unitary states permits leaders, policymakers, analysts, or simply concerned citizens to see features of the global political system that were previously hidden. Governmental networks suddenly are visible everywhere in international regulatory and enforcement systems.[32] Examples include the Financial Action Task Force, a network of finance ministers and other financial regulators taking charge of pursuing money launderers and financiers of terrorism, and the EU Council of Justice and Home Affairs, a network of ministers charged with applying and reforming laws interpreting the Single European Market. At the same time, it is possible to disaggregate international organizations (e.g., the UN, the World Bank Group, INTERPOL, and international courts),

[28] Joseph S. Nye, Jr., The Paradox of American Power 162 (Oxford 2002).

[29] Slaughter, *supra* note 23, at 4.

[30] For more on President Clinton's remarks, *see* "U.S. Initiatives against International Organized Crime." Remarks of William J. Clinton, President of the United States, at the 50th Anniversary Assembly of the United Nations, New York City, October 22, 1995.

[31] *Id.* at 6.

[32] *Id.*

as well as to see "vertical networks" between national regulators and judges and their supranational counterparts.[33] Examples include relations between national criminal justice professionals, say at the U.S. Department of Justice, and international organizations, such as the Inter-American Drug Abuse Commission (CICAD) at the Organization of American States (OAS),[34] the European national courts, and the European Court of Justice, or between national U.S., Mexican, and Canadian courts and the ad hoc international criminal tribunals (i.e., International Criminal Tribunal for the Former Yugoslavia) or the International Criminal Tribunal.[35]

The demand for conceptualizing and providing more opportunities for governmental networks arises out of the globalization paradox, whereby more government is needed, but at the same time is feared and believed to be dangerous, at least by a number of persons. In the 1990s, the conventional approach to achieving the goal of having more accountable international institutions was the championing of "global governance," a much looser and less threatening concept of collective organization and regulation without coercion. A major element of global governance has been the rise of global policy networks. These networks have a universal nature because they focus on global policy, such as anti-corruption, money laundering, and crimes against humanity. Necessarily they are composed of a broad spectrum of persons. They are celebrated for their ability to bring together all public and private actors on issues critical to the global public interest.

Global policy networks arise out of various "reinventing government" projects. These projects focus on the many ways in which private actors now can and do perform governmental functions, from providing expertise to monitoring compliance with regulations to negotiating the substance of those regulations, both domestically and internationally. The problem is ensuring that these private actors uphold the public trust.[36]

Although transgovernmental cooperation has expanded significantly during the last couple of decades, it is not a new phenomenon. For instance, the 1936 Convention for the Suppression of the Illicit Traffic in Dangerous Drugs required the establishment of new agencies to coordinate international efforts at drug control.[37] The communications were to occur directly between these agencies rather than through normal diplomatic

33 Slaughter, A NEW WORLD ORDER, *supra* note 23, at 6.

34 For a useful discussion of the networking within CICAD and between CICAD and the UN, *see, e.g.*, Irving Tragen, *World-Wide and Regional Anti-Drug Programs, in* DRUGS AND FOREIGN POLICY: A CRITICAL REVIEW 155–84 (Raphael F. Perl ed., 1994); and Abraham F. Lowenthal, *The Organization of American States and Control of Dangerous Drugs, in* DRUG POLICY IN THE AMERICAS 305–14 (Peter H. Smith ed., 1992).

35 In a speech to the ASIL, the president of the International Criminal Court (ICC) spoke of increasing relations and interactions between judges and professionals at the ICC and other international tribunals. A concrete example is the agreement between the ICC and the Special Tribunal for Sierra Leone to try Charles Taylor using the facilities of the ICC. *See also* Geert-Jan Alexander Knoops, AN INTRODUCTION TO THE LAW OF INTERNATIONAL CRIMINAL TRIBUNALS: A COMPARATIVE STUDY 157–78 (2003); FROM NUREMBERG TO THE HAGUE: THE FUTURE OF INTERNATIONAL CRIMINAL JUSTICE (Philippe Sands ed., 2003) (derived from a conference the book shows, *inter alia*, how criminal justice professionals have networked in developing international criminal justice principles).

36 *Id.* at 8–9. For more background on the emergence of calls for global governance, *see* David Held & Anthony McGrew, *Introduction*, in GOVERNING GLOBALIZATION 1, 1–21 (David Held & Anthony McGrew eds., 2002).

37 Kal Raustiala, *The Architecture of International Cooperation: Transgovernmental Networks and the Future of International Law*, 43 VA. J. INT'L L 1, 11–12 (2002), citing Convention of 1936 for the Suppression of the Illicit Traffic in Dangerous Drugs, June 16, 1936, 198 L.N.T.S. 4648; *see also* S. K. Chatterjee, LEGAL ASPECTS OF INTERNATIONAL DRUG CONTROL 168–85 (1981).

channels. Hence, the 1936 convention endeavored to establish a transgovernmental network for drug control.[38]

The governance dilemma becomes a trilemma: the international community needs global rules without centralized power but with government actors who can be held to account through a variety of political mechanisms. These government actors can and should interact with a wide range of NGOs, but their role in governance brings with it distinct and different responsibilities. They must represent all their different constituencies, at least those in a democracy. Corporate and civic actors that participate may be motivated by profits and noneconomic goals, respectively (depending on whether the civic actor is an organization whose work is humanitarian law or economic progress, such as the Chamber of Commerce, which was founded in 1919 and is one of the longest standing private networks representing private sector companies and associations in 130 countries).[39] Other examples of civil society participants in international enforcement networks are Transparency International, the International Association of Chiefs of Police, Amnesty International, and Doctors without Borders. However, "governance" must not become a cover for the blurring of these lines by collaboration among these various actors on common problems.[40]

Robert Keohane and Joseph Nye distinguish "transgovernmental" activity from the broader category of transnational activity. They define transgovernmental relations as "sets of direct interactions among sub-units of different governments that are not controlled or closely guided by the policies of the cabinets or chief executives of those governments." Moreover, governmental networks established for limited purposes, such as postal services and telecommunications, have existed for almost a century.[41]

What is new is the scale, scope, and type of transgovernmental ties. Links between government officials from two, four, or even a dozen countries have become extremely dense. Governmental networks, such as the G7, INTERPOL, the FATF, and the various organizations and groups of tax administrators and enforcement, have developed their own identity and autonomy in specific issue-areas. They perform more functions than in the past, from collecting and disseminating information on global or regional best practices to actively offering technical assistance to poorer and less experienced members. And they have spread far beyond regulators to legislators, judges, and enforcement officials.

Governmental networks have become recognized and semi formalized ways of doing business within loose international groupings like the Commonwealth and the Asian-Pacific Economic Cooperation (APEC) organization.[42] At the same time they have become one of the principal forms of governance for the EU, which itself is pioneering a new form of regional collective governance.[43]

[38] Raustiala, *supra* note 37, at 12.

[39] Ngaire Woods, *Global Governance and the Role of Institutions, in* GOVERNING GLOBALIZATION 25, 31.

[40] Slaughter, A NEW WORLD ORDER, *supra* note 23, at 10.

[41] *Id.* at 10, citing Robert O. Keohane & Joseph S. Nye, Jr., *Transgovernmental Relations and International Organizations*, WORLD POLITICS 27, 39 (1974); Keohane & Nye, *Transnational Relations and World Politics: An Introduction, in* TRANSNATIONAL RELATIONS AND WORLD POLITICS ix, xi (Robert O. Keohane & Joseph S. Nye, Jr. eds., 1970).

[42] *See, e.g.*, Robert S. Jordan et al., INTERNATIONAL ORGANIZATION: A COMPARATIVE APPROACH TO THE MANAGEMENT OF COOPERATION, at 85–132 (discussing institutional and bureaucratic developments) (2001).

[43] Slaughter, A NEW WORLD ORDER, *supra* note 23, at 10–11.

One of the weaknesses that critics have underscored about networks is that they reduce transparency and impede accountability.[44] The clublike, informal nature of networks often reinforces the dominance of major economic powers, especially the inequalities between the North and South. Networks may also offer an ultimately dangerous substitute for traditional multilateralism.[45] Consider the operation of the regulatory and enforcement aspects of the OECD and FATF. Critics have questioned the international politics underlying the elaboration and implementation of the new regulatory and enforcement regime and subregimes. For instance, the FATF initiative against noncooperative countries, the OECD harmful tax practices initiative, and FSF (now FSB) initiatives have suffered from the following: (1) exclusion from much of the decision-making process of the very countries that are the targets of the policy; (2) lack of adequate participation in policymaking and implementation by the private sector; (3) lack of transparency in the decision-making process; (4) the apparent use of economic sanctions and coercion through blacklists without binding hard law; (5) differential and favorable treatment of their own members whose inadequacies have not resulted in blacklisting; (6) apparent efforts to usurp critical policymaking responsibilities from democratically elected governments without adequate participation by such governments; and (7) questionable substantive policy design, especially in the case of the OECD harmful tax practices initiative.

IGOs have continued to advocate more democratic, transparent processes. For example, in issuing its Consultation Paper on revised recommendations on anti-money laundering and counterterrorism financing on May 30, 2002, FATF requested the views of all interested parties, including non-FATF members, the private sector, or any other interested persons. FATF also arranged two meetings to allow interested groups to provide oral comments. In addition, the IMF/WB is making efforts to improve transparency in preparing new anti-money laundering assessment methodology. Similarly, the OECD harmful tax practices initiative is striving to include so-called tax havens and other countries in its Global Forum.

The third part of this book on international organizations and several of the chapters on substantive international white collar crimes discuss international enforcement regimes and networks.

IV. *Additional Reading*

A. *U.S. White Collar Crime*

1. Books

American Bar Association, White Collar Crime National Institute (annual review of developments in white collar crime; has a number of chapters and materials on international issues).

Hervé Boullanger, La Criminalité Economique en Europe (Economic Crime in Europe) (2002).

Pamela H. Bucy, Bucy's White Collar Practice: Cases and Materials (3d ed., American Casebook Series®, 2004).

Jurg Gerber & Eric L. Jensen, Encyclopaedia of White Collar Crime (Greenwood Press, 2007).

[44] Kal Raustiala, *supra* note 37, at 5.

[45] Slaughter, A New World Order, *supra* note 23, at 5–6.

Julie R. O'Sullivan, O'Sullivan's Federal White Collar Crime: Cases and Materials (3d ed., American Casebook Series®, 2007).

Ellen S. Podgor & Jerold H. Israel, Podgor and Israel's White Collar Crime in a Nutshell (3d ed., Nutshell Series, 2004).

Ellen S. Podgor, Jerold H. Israel, Paul D. Borman, & Peter Henning, White Collar Crime, Law and Practice (2d ed., West/Thomson Publishing Co., 2003).

J. Kelly Strader, Irving D. Rosenberg, & Florence Rosenberg, White Collar Crime: Cases, Materials, and Problems (Matthew Bender, 2005).

2. Blogs

White Collar Crime Blog (http://lawprofessors.typepad.com/whitecollarcrime_blog/international).

3. Articles

Kumar Percy, *Features – Fighting Corporate and Government Wrongdoing: A Research Guide to International and U.S. Federal Laws on White – Collar, Law and Technology Resources for Legal Professionals*, http://www.llrx.com/features/whitecollarcrime.htm.

Ellen S. Podgor, *Globalization and the Federal Prosecution of White Collar Crime*, 34 Am. Crim. L. Rev. (2007).

B. International White Collar Crime

Ellen S. Podgor & Roger S. Clark, Understanding International Criminal Law (2d ed. Lexis-Nexis, 2008).

International Handbook of White-Collar and Corporate Crime (Henry N. Pontell & Gilbert L. Geis eds., Springer, 2007). (has a criminological perspective).

La Criminalité Economique et Financiere en Europe (Paul Ponsaers & Vincenzo Ruggiero eds., Economic and Financial Crime in Europe (L'Harmattan, 2002).

Edward M. Wise & Ellen S. Podgor, International Criminal Law: Cases and Materials (2d ed. Lexis Publishing, 2004) (Includes a number of chapters on white collar crime, such as on the Foreign Corrupt Practices Act, antitrust, export controls, and computer crimes).

2 Taxation

I. Extraterritorial Jurisdiction

A. *The U.S. Jurisdiction to Tax*

The limitations on the U.S. government's power to tax are contained in the Internal Revenue Code, which reflects the policy decisions of the U.S. Congress. These decisions are influenced by the need for revenue, administrative convenience, international politics, and macroeconomic policies.

Article I, § 8 of the Constitution of the United States delegates to Congress the "power to lay and collect taxes." The extent of Congress's power is "exhaustive," embracing "every conceivable power of taxation."[1]

Under the broad taxation powers of Congress, the U.S. Supreme Court has confirmed congressional authority to tax on various grounds, including citizenship, residence, situs of property, and source of income.

For instance, the U.S. Internal Revenue Code imposes tax on the foreign source income of a U.S. citizen, even if he or she has resided in a foreign country for the last ten or fifteen years and only receives dividends and interest from foreign income.

The United States asserts jurisdiction to tax the income of a foreign person only if there is some reasonable connection between the United States and that foreign taxpayer's source of income or his or her status. In this regard, citizens, resident aliens, and domestic corporations are subject to tax on their worldwide income, I.R.C. §§ 1 and 11(a). In addition, I.R.C. §§ 1(c), (d), and 11(a) impose an income tax on "every" individual and "every" corporation, respectively. I.R.C. §§ 2(d) and 11(d) exempt nonresident aliens and foreign corporations from that tax except to the extent of the tax imposed on U.S. source income by I.R.C. §§ 871, 877, and 882.

a. *Cook v. Tait*, 265 U.S. 47, 53 (1924)

The question in the case, and which was presented by the demurrer to the declaration is, as expressed by plaintiff, whether Congress has power to impose a tax upon income received by a native citizen of the United States who, at the time the income was received, was permanently resident and domiciled in the city of Mexico, the income being from real and personal property located in Mexico.

Plaintiff assigns against the power not only his rights under the Constitution of the United States but under international law, and in support of the assignments cites many cases. It will be observed that the foundation of the assignments is the fact that the citizen receiving the income and the property of which it is the product are outside of the territorial limits of the United States. These two facts, the contention is, exclude the existence of the power to tax. To view the contention another way, to the existence of the power and its exercise, the person receiving the income and the property from which he receives it must both be within the territorial limits of the United States and to be within the taxing power of the United States. The contention is not justified, and that it is not justified is the necessary deduction of recent cases.

The principle was declared that the government, by its very nature, benefits the citizen and his property wherever found, and therefore has the power to make the benefit complete. Or, to express it another way, the basis of the power to tax was not and cannot be made dependent upon the situs of the property in all cases, it being in or out of the United States, nor was not and cannot be made dependent upon the domicile of the citizen, that being in or out of the United States, but upon his relation as citizen to the United States and the relation of the latter to him as citizen. The consequence of the relations is that the native citizen who is taxed may have domicile, and the property from which his income is derived may have situs, in a foreign country and that the tax be legal – the government having power to impose the tax.

[1] *Brushaber v. Union Pacific RR*, 240 U.S. 1, 12, 36 S. Ct. 236, 60 L. Ed. 493 (1915).

b. *U.S. v. Bennett*, 232 U.S. 299, 306 (1914)

In *U.S. v. Bennett*, the Court upheld an excise duty on the use of a yacht owned by a U.S. citizen wholly outside the limits and territorial jurisdiction of the United States against his challenge that the tax violated the Fifth Amendment due process clause. The taxpayer asserted that case law limiting the power of the statutes to tax income and property outside the state also limited the U.S. government's power to levy taxes.

The Constitution imposes barriers on states and prevents them from transcending the limits of their authority. According to the majority decision in *Bennett* this destroys the rights of other states, and at the same time saves their rights from destruction by the other states. In other words, it maintains the rights of all the states. It affords no ground for constructing an imaginary constitutional barrier around the exterior confines of the United States for the purpose of shutting that government off from the exertion of powers that inherently belong to it by virtue of its sovereignty.

B. *The Exercise of Jurisdiction to Tax*

Pasquantino et al. v. United States, U.S. Supreme Court, No. 03–725

DECIDED APRIL 26, 2005. CERTIORARI FROM THE U.S. COURT OF APPEALS FOR THE FOURTH CIRCUIT

Petitioners carried out a scheme to smuggle large quantities of liquor into Canada from the United States to evade Canada's heavy alcohol import taxes. They were convicted of violating the federal wire fraud statute, 18 U.S.C. § 1343, for doing so. That statute prohibits the use of interstate wires to effect "any scheme or artifice to defraud, or for obtaining money or property by means of false or fraudulent pretenses." The Fourth Circuit affirmed its convictions, rejecting petitioners' argument that their prosecution contravened the common-law revenue rule, which bars courts from enforcing foreign sovereigns' tax laws. The Fourth Circuit also held that Canada's right to receive tax revenue was "money or property" within § 1343's meaning.

Held: A plot to defraud a foreign government of tax revenue violates the federal wire fraud statute. Pp. 3–21.

(a) Section 1343's plain terms criminalize a scheme such as petitioners'. Their smuggling operation satisfies both of the § 1343 elements that are in dispute here. First, Canada's right to uncollected excise taxes on the liquor petitioners imported into Canada is "property" within the statute's meaning. That right is an entitlement to collect money from petitioners, the possession of which is "something of value" to the Canadian Government. *McNally v. United States*, 483 U.S. 350, 358. Such valuable entitlements are "property" as that term ordinarily is employed. Second, petitioners' plot was a "scheme or artifice to defraud" Canada of its valuable entitlement to tax revenue, because petitioners routinely concealed imported liquor from Canadian officials and failed to declare those goods on customs forms. See *Durland v. United States*, 161 U.S. 306, 313. Pp. 3–7.

(b) The foregoing construction of § 1343 does not derogate from the common-law revenue rule. Pp. 8–21.

(1) Relying on the canon of construction that "[s]tatutes which invade the common law are to be read with a presumption favoring the retention of long-established and familiar principles, except where a statutory purpose to the contrary is evident," *United States v. Texas*, 507 U.S. 529, 534, petitioners argue that, to avoid reading § 1343 to derogate from the revenue

rule, the Court should construe the otherwise-applicable statutory language to except frauds directed at evading foreign taxes. Whether § 1343 derogates from the revenue rule depends on whether reading the statute to reach this prosecution conflicts with a well-established revenue rule principle. See *United States v. Craft*, 535 U.S. 274, 276. Thus, before concluding that Congress intended to exempt the present prosecution from § 1343's broad reach, the Court must find that the revenue rule clearly barred such a prosecution as of 1952, the year Congress enacted the wire fraud statute. See *Neder v. United States*, 527 U.S. 1, 22–23. Pp. 8–9.

(2) No common-law case decided as of 1952 clearly established that the revenue rule barred the United States from prosecuting a fraudulent scheme to evade foreign taxes. Pp. 9–17.

(i) The revenue rule has long been treated as a corollary of the rule that "[t]he Courts of no country execute the penal laws of another." *The Antelope*, 10 Wheat. 66, 123. It was first treated as such in cases prohibiting the enforcement of tax liabilities of one sovereign in the courts of another sovereign, such as suits to enforce tax judgments. The revenue rule's grounding in these cases shows that, at its core, it prohibited the collection of tax obligations of foreign nations. The present prosecution is unlike these classic examples of actions traditionally barred by the revenue rule. It is not a suit that recovers a foreign tax liability, but is a criminal prosecution brought by the United States to punish domestic criminal conduct. Pp. 9–11.

(ii) Cases applying the revenue rule to bar indirect enforcement of foreign revenue laws, in contrast to the direct collection of a tax obligation, cannot bear the weight petitioners place on them. Many of them were decided after Congress passed the wire fraud statute. Others come from foreign courts. And, significantly, none involved a domestic sovereign acting pursuant to authority conferred by a criminal statute to enforce the sovereign's own penal law. Moreover, none of petitioners' cases barred an action that had as its primary object the deterrence and punishment of fraudulent conduct – a substantial domestic regulatory interest entirely independent of foreign tax enforcement. The main object of the action in each of them was the collection of money that would pay foreign tax claims. The absence of such an object here means that the link between this prosecution and foreign tax collection is incidental and attenuated at best. Thus, it cannot be said whether Congress in 1952 would have considered this prosecution within the revenue rule. Petitioners answer unpersuasively that the recovery of taxes is indeed the object of this suit because restitution of Canada's lost tax revenue is required under the federal Mandatory Victims Restitution Act of 1996. Whether restitution is mandatory is irrelevant here because § 1343 advances the Government's independent interest in punishing fraudulent domestic criminal conduct. In any event, if awarding restitution to foreign sovereigns were contrary to the revenue rule, the proper resolution would be to construe the later enacted restitution statute not to allow such awards, rather than to assume that it implied repeal of § 1343 as applied to this prosecution. Pp. 11–14.

(iii) Also unavailing is petitioners' argument that early English common-law cases holding unenforceable contracts executed to evade other nations' revenue laws demonstrate that "indirect" enforcement of such laws is at the very core of the revenue rule, rather than at its margins. Those early cases were driven by an interest in lessening the commercial disruption caused by high tariffs. By the mid-twentieth century, however, that rationale was supplanted, and courts began to apply the revenue rule to tax obligations on the strength of the analogy between a country's revenue laws and its penal ones. Because the early English cases rested on a far different foundation from that on which the revenue rule came to rest, they say little about whether the wire fraud statute derogated from the revenue rule in its mid-twentieth century form. Pp. 14–15.

(iv) Petitioners' criminal prosecution "enforces" Canadian revenue law in an attenuated sense, but not in a sense that clearly would contravene the revenue rule. That rule never proscribed all enforcement of foreign revenue law. For example, at the same time they were enforcing domestic contracts that had the purpose of violating foreign revenue law, English courts also considered void foreign contracts that lacked tax stamps required under foreign revenue law. The line the revenue rule draws between impermissible and permissible "enforcement" of foreign revenue law has therefore always been unclear. The uncertainty persisted in American cases, which demonstrate that the extent to which the revenue rule barred indirect recognition of foreign revenue laws was unsettled as of 1952. Pp. 15–17.

Justice Ginsburg, with whom *Justice Breyer* joins, and *Justice Scalia* and *Justice Souter* join as to Parts II and III, dissenting.

> As I see it, and as petitioners urged, Reply Brief 17–19, the Court has ascribed an exorbitant scope to the wire fraud statute, in disregard of our repeated recognition that "Congress legislates against the backdrop of the presumption against extraterritoriality." . . . Notably, when Congress explicitly addressed international smuggling, see 18 U.S.C. § 546, it provided for criminal enforcement of the customs laws of a foreign nation only when that nation has a reciprocal law criminalizing smuggling into the United States. Currently, Canada has no such reciprocal law.

Of overriding importance in this regard, tax collection internationally is an area in which treaties hold sway. See *Attorney General of Canada v. R. J. Reynolds Tobacco Holdings, Inc.*, 268 F. 3d 103, 115119 (CA2 2001) (referencing tax treaties to which the United States is a party). There is a treaty between the United States and Canada regarding the collection of taxes, but that accord requires certification by the taxing nation that the taxes owed have been "finally determined." See Protocol Amending Convention with Respect to Taxes on Income and on Capital, September 26, 1980, S. Treaty Doc. No. 104–4, 2030 U. N. T. S. 236, Art. 15, 2 (entered into force Nov. 9, 1995) (hereinafter Protocol). Moreover, the treaty is inapplicable to persons, like petitioners in this case, who are United States citizens at the time that the tax liability is incurred. Art. 15, 8.

Today's novel decision is all the more troubling for its failure to take account of Canada's primary interest in the matter at stake. United States citizens who have committed criminal violations of Canadian tax law can be extradited to stand trial in Canada. Canadian courts are best positioned to decide "whether, and to what extent, the defendants have defrauded the governments of Canada and Ontario out of tax revenues owed pursuant to their own, sovereign, excise laws." 336 F. 3d 321, 343 (CA4 2003) (en banc) (Gregory, J., dissenting).

Notes and Questions

1. The United States has exercised its jurisdiction to tax more broadly and aggressively than many countries. For instance, U.S. citizens and residents are subject to taxation on "all income from what ever source derived."[2] Hence, a U.S. citizen who receives income exclusively from the foreign country of which he or she is a resident remains within the jurisdiction of the Internal Revenue Code and is liable for such taxes on that income as required under the Code. The Internal Revenue Service has wide authority to promulgate substantive and procedural rules.[3]

The Code imposes taxes on the nonresident alien and foreign corporation on income that has its source in the United States,[4] even if the nonresident alien or foreign corporation has never done business in the United States nor otherwise had any contact with the United States except as a source of income.

[2] I.R.C. § 61(a).

[3] Reg. § 1.1–1(b); Rev. Rul. 75–82, 1975–1 C.B.5.

[4] I.R.C. §§ 871 and 881.

2. Does the majority or dissenting opinion in *Pasquantino* seem more persuasive and on what basis?

3. In the prosecution of the Bank of New York for money laundering, Lucy Edwards and Peter Berlin pled guilty to money laundering. The underlying crime was wire fraud for helping Russian nationals defraud the Russian government of income tax.

4. In the third superseding indictment of Benjamin Kuehne, a prominent Miami defense counsel, the U.S. government charged him in the U.S. District Court, S.D. Florida with defrauding the Colombian government of income tax for violating currency control laws through using the Black Market Peso Exchange. See, e.g., *U.S. Grand Jury issues third superseding indictment against Miami Lawyer* v. Gloria Florez Velez et al., U.S. District Court S.D. Fla., Case No. 05-20770-Cr-CROOKE(s), third superseding indictment, at paragraphs 55 and 30–35. Bruce Zagaris, U.S. Grand Jury issues third superseding indictment against Miami Lawyer, 24 INTL ENFORCEMENT LAW REP. 259, 260 (July 2008).

C. *Choice of Law Issues*

Choice of law issues with respect to taxation often require the tax authority, taxpayer, tax counsel, and others involved to identify the nature of the taxpayer entity. For instance, the U.S. classification of an *anstalt* or *stiftung* as a corporation, trust, or other entity may determine its taxability and have numerous tax planning implications.

Notes and Questions

1. Mr. N. was a U.S. permanent resident from 1985 until 2001. He is a Dutch national and is married to a Dutch national. After his return to Holland in 2001, he and his wife surrendered their green card (U.S. permanent residency). He has received a notice from the IRS about a deficiency in tax from 2002–4 under the anti-expatriation law, whereby the United States reserves the right to tax former permanent residents. Is there any problem with the United States applying and enforcing its anti-expatriation law under 26 U.S.C. § 877?

2. A new client, a major Dutch Antillean fiduciary, seeks advice about problems in potential overlap of tax authority between the United States and Holland. Does the fiduciary have any useful mechanism to resolve the problem? What about the potential to use competent authority (or mutual assistance, as it is called in this treaty in Articles 29 and 34 of the U.S.-Netherlands income tax treaty) mechanisms? What if the fiduciary is doing business in a jurisdiction, such as Mauritius, with which the United States has no income tax treaty? Can the fiduciary possibly resort to other treaties, such as a bilateral investment agreement?

II. Substantive Criminal Tax Laws

For discussion purposes, this treatment of U.S. tax crimes examines both pure tax crimes and offenses related to tax crimes.[5] Although the Tax Division of the U.S. Department of Justice (DOJ) is responsible for authorizing prosecution in criminal proceedings under the income tax laws, U.S. Attorneys have the initial responsibility for trying criminal tax cases. However, depending on the resources and expertise of an individual U.S.

[5] For a useful discussion of tax crimes on which this section relies heavily, *see* Bruce I. Hochman et al., *Tax Crimes*, TAX MGMT PORTFOLIO 636–2nd, A-1–20 (1999). *See also* CRIMINAL TAX FRAUD (ABA 2000).

Attorney's Office, the prosecuting attorney may decide to use the resources of the DOJ Tax Division.[6]

One longstanding problem for practitioners has been the absence of a clear line between legitimate tax avoidance or minimization and unacceptable minimization or aggressive planning techniques, such as acquisition and use of holding companies and other entities for tax avoidance purposes, undercapitalization of corporate entities, and allocations of income and expenses between related taxpayers that do not reflect arm's-length transactions.[7] Recent trends toward penalizing and even criminalizing conduct in the gray area may sometimes motivate taxpayers and counsel[8] to toe the nonexistent line and will lead to more agonizing judgment calls for other professionals (e.g., courts and other revenue authorities affected by the U.S. penalization trends).

This discussion of tax crimes is limited to their substantive aspects. Successfully prosecuting or defending cross-border tax crimes and related offenses requires a consideration of tactical[9] and procedural elements, such as the ability to gather evidence in such cases through unilateral or cooperative methods,[10] the ability to obtain custody of the defendant(s), potential asset freezes and forfeiture aspects,[11] sentencing issues,[12] potential collateral consequences of tax investigations and convictions,[13] and a host of related issues.

A. *Tax Fraud (i.e., False Returns and Preparers of False Returns)*

26 U.S.C. § 7206 makes it a felony for any person to willfully make any document under the Internal Revenue Code that he or she does not believe to be true and correct. The law also applies to any person who willfully aids or assists in the preparation of any document under the tax laws that is fraudulent or false.

The elements of a prima facie offense under § 7206(1) are (1) a belief that the return, statement, or other document is not true and correct; (2) willfulness; (3) materiality; and (4) the making and subscribing of the document at issue under the penalty of perjury.

The potential punishment for violating § 7206(1) is a fine of up to $250,000 for individuals and $500,000 for corporations, imprisonment for not more than three years, and payment of the costs of prosecution.

B. *Tax Evasion*

Tax evasion, contained in IRC § 7201 (26 U.S.C. § 7201), is the most commonly charged tax crime in the United States. It is a willful attempt to evade or defeat any tax imposed

6 Department of Justice, *U.S. Attorneys Manual,* § 6–1.110 (Criminal Tax Cases).

7 Jon E. Bischel, Pamela B. Gann, & Susan F. Klein, *U.S. National Report,* in TAX AVOIDANCE/TAX EVASION, LXVIII A CAHIERS DE DROIT FISCAL INTERNATIONAL (Studies on International Fiscal Law) 333 (1983).

8 *See, e.g.,* the collection of articles in WHITE COLLAR CRIME 2001 (American Bar Association, 2001) (Sec. B Targeting Attorneys) for developments on the prosecution of attorneys in white collar cases.

9 For a useful review of tactical aspects from a defense perspective *see* John J. Tigue, Jr., *Representing the Client during a Criminal Investigation: Defense Tactics during IRS Administrative and Grand Jury Investigations,* in WHITE COLLAR CRIME 2001 at K-1–26 (2001).

10 *See, e.g.,* Bruce Zagaris, *U.S. Extends Its Reach for Evidence,* 15 CRIM. JUSTICE 4–55 (ABA Sec. of Crim. Just. 2001).

11 For code features and extraordinary IRS seizure remedies, *see* Ian Comisky, Lawrence S. Feld, & Steven M. Harris, 2 TAX FRAUD AND EVASION Chapter 12 (1994).

12 For sentencing issues pertaining to U.S. tax matters, *see* Ian M. Comisky, *Sentencing Guidelines Departure Update,* in CRIMINAL TAX FRAUD at G-1–21 (ABA Sec. Of Tax & Center for CLE 2000).

13 Ian M. Comisky, *Collateral Consequences of Criminal Investigations and Convictions,* in WHITE COLLAR CRIME 1999 at B-23–36 (1999).

under the Internal Revenue Code. The prosecutor must prove three elements of a prima facie case: (1) the existence of a tax deficiency, (2) an affirmative act constituting an evasion or attempted evasion of the tax, and (3) willfulness.[14]

The difference between a misdemeanor and felony tax evasion is that the felony offense involves some commission in additional to willful omission.[15] A willful, but passive neglect of statutory duty may constitute a misdemeanor; the presence of a willful and positive attempt will bring it to a felony.[16]

To convict under § 7201 requires an affirmative act showing an intent to conceal income from the imposition of tax. A defendant can assert as a defense a good faith misunderstanding of the law, which need not be objectively reasonable.[17] Negligence or gross negligence is insufficient to establish willfulness.[18]

Circumstantial evidence of willfulness is often used to prove tax evasion and may be inferred from, among other things, false account books and records, destruction of records, concealment of assets or income, avoidance of normal transactional records, and other means likely to mislead or conceal. An individual can be convicted for this offense by claiming false deductions[19] and false exemptions,[20] but not for making equivocal statements.[21] To assist revenue agents, the Internal Revenue Manual provides a list of potential "badges of fraud" that might be deemed to constitute a willful attempt.

Tax evasion may be punished by imprisonment of not more than five years and fines of up to $250,000 for individuals and $500,000 for corporations. Defendants convicted of tax fraud can be made to pay the costs of prosecution and any special assessments.

C. *Conspiracy to Engage in Tax Fraud, Evasion, and the Like: The Role of Offshore Banks*

One of the major investigations and prosecutions in 2008–9 was by the United States against UBS.

UBS Enters into Deferred Prosecution Agreement (Reprinted from 25 Int'l Enforcement L. Rep. 134 (Apr. 2009)).

by Bruce Zagaris

On February 18, 2009, UBS AG and the U.S. Department of Justice entered into a deferred prosecution agreement, which obligates UBS to pay $780 million and enter into various kinds of monitoring and due diligence arrangements with the U.S. government.[22]

[14] *Sansone v. U.S.*, 380 U.S. 343 (1965); *U.S. v. Koskerides*, 877 F.2d 1129 (2d Cir. 1989); *U.S. v. Stone*, 770 F.2d 842 (9th Cir. 1985).

[15] *Sansone v. U.S.*, *supra* note 14.

[16] *Spies v. U.S.*, 317 U.S. 492 (1943).

[17] *Cheek v. U.S.*, 498 U.S. 192 (1991), *on remand*, 931 F.2d 1206 (7th Cir. 1991).

[18] *U.S. v. Goichman*, 407 F. Supp. 980 (E.D. Pa. 1976), *aff'd per curiam*, 547 F.2d 778 (3d Cir. 1976).

[19] *Davis v. U.S.*, 226 F.2d 331 (6th Cir. 1955), *cert. den.*, 350 U.S. 965, *reh. denied*, 351 U.S. 915; *U.S. v. Schenck*, 126 F.2d 702 (2d Cir. 1942), *cert. denied*, 316 U.S. 705 (1942).

[20] *U.S. v. Williams*, 928 F.2d 145 (5th Cir. 1991), *cert. denied*, 502 U.S. 811.

[21] *U.S. v. Romano*, 938 F.2d 1569 (2nd Cir. 1991) (taxpayer trying to transport $359,5000 to Canada did not commit affirmative act required for conviction of tax evasion when he first admitted having only $30,000 to $35,000 in cash and only gradually admitting full amount).

[22] *United States of America v. UBS AG*, U.S. District Court, S.D. Florida, Case No. 09–60033-CR-COHN, Feb. 18, 2009, Deferred Prosecution Agreement.

On February 18, 2009, the U.S. government unsealed a criminal information in the U.S. District Court in the Southern District of Florida, charging UBS with one count of conspiring to defraud the United States by impeding the IRS in violation of 18 U.S.C. § 371. The information alleges that UBS performed cross-border banking services to approximately 20,000 clients in the United States with assets worth approximately $20 billion. The complaint alleges that about 17,000 of these clients concealed their identities and the existence of their UBS accounts from the IRS. The information alleges that many of the UBS clients willfully failed to pay tax to the IRS on income earned on their UBS accounts. UBS helped these U.S. clients conceal the income earned on UBS accounts by failing to report IRS Form 1099 information to the IRS. From 2002 through 2007, the information alleges the U.S. cross-border business produced about $200 million annually in revenue for UBS.[23]

The deferred prosecution agreement allocated $380 million toward the disgorgement of UBS's profits from the cross-border business during 2001 through 2008. $200 million will be paid to the Securities and Exchange Commission. $400 million of the settlement is for federal backup withholding tax UBS should have withheld with respect to disclosed accounts for the tax years at issue and for restitution for unpaid taxes for undeclared U.S. taxpayers who were actively assisted or facilitated by UBS private bankers.

One of the closely watched aspects of the agreement concerns the effort by the United States to force UBS to turn over the names of its U.S. taxpayer depositors. Although the Swiss Financial Market Supervisory Authority (FINMA) approved the disclosure of the client data, the U.S. government also seemed to acknowledge that UBS's cooperation could be limited by Swiss bank secrecy law.[24] The deferred prosecution announcement does not provide the exact number of UBS client names being turned over – the exhibit having been placed under seal – but a Swiss press report said that only 250 client names out of the 19,000 account holders were being passed along. According to an authoritative tax media report, a tax practitioner said that if true, that number may represent only those clients who were deemed to have committed tax fraud as defined by Swiss law. The identity of those clients would already be subject to disclosure under article 26 of the U.S.-Switzerland tax treaty.[25]

UBS must as part of the deferred prosecution provide periodic reports to the U.S. government on the exit of its illegal U.S. cross-border business. UBS must implement an effective program of internal controls with respect to compliance with UBS's obligations under the Qualified Intermediary (QI) Agreement and related rules or regulations. Additionally, UBS must implement a revised governance structure for the legal and compliance functions.[26]

UBS agrees to provide wide-ranging cooperation, including testimony or information in any criminal or other proceeding as requested by the government.[27] As a result, the U.S. government will be able to call on UBS in prosecuting or litigating cases against U.S. taxpayers with UBS accounts.

The deferred prosecution agreement requires the government to seek dismissal with prejudice as to UBS of the information filed against UBS if UBS is in compliance with all of

[23] *United States of America v. UBS AG*, U.S. District Court, S.D. Florida, Case No. 09–60038 Cr-MARRA, Information, paragraph 4.

[24] *United States of America v. UBS AG*, Deferred Prosecution Agreement, *supra* note 22, at para. 10

[25] Jeremiah Coder, *UBS Settles with U.S. Justice Department for $780 Million*, 2009 Worldwide Tax Daily 31–1 (Feb. 19, 2009).

[26] *United States of America v. UBS AG*, Deferred Prosecution Agreement, *supra* note 22, at paragraphs 5–6 and 8.

[27] *Id.* at paragraph 13.

its obligations under the Agreement. If UBS commits a material violation of the Agreement, gives false, incomplete, or misleading information or violates any U.S. federal criminal law or fails to comply with any directive or order issued by the Federal Reserve Board of Governors, it will in the government's sole discretion be subject to prosecution for any federal criminal violations of which the government has knowledge, including but not limited to a prosecution based on the information of the conduct described therein.[28]

The Agreement requires UBS to retain an independent accounting or other appropriate firm to conduct procedures testing, as agreed by the government.[29]

The Agreement is silent about the potential prosecution of UBS officials and private bankers. In November 2008, a federal grand jury indicted former UBS executive Raoul Weil, who is now a fugitive. In June 2008, UBS private banker Bradley Birkenfeld pleaded guilty to conspiring to defraud the United States for his role in overseeing the U.S. cross-border business. The information, Agreement, and the two previously mentioned indictments allege the wide involvement of UBS private bankers and other UBS officials. The U.S. voluntary disclosure program requires U.S. taxpayers to fully cooperate. Hence, the U.S. government has the potential of bringing more indictments against former UBS employees and such a tactic can increase its leverage against UBS. Nevertheless, the Agreement is an important milestone for UBS. The Agreement is just as significant for the U.S. government, both in ending the conspiracy that enabled so many taxpayers to evade taxes and in continuing its efforts to pressure those taxpayers and future ones to play by the rules.

Notes and Questions

1. On August 19, 2009, the U.S. and Swiss governments announced a settlement agreement to obtain 4,450 names of U.S. taxpayers with accounts in UBS pursuant to the U.S.-Swiss tax treaty. The case between the United States and UBS will be dismissed. An agreement establishes a rolling mechanism under which the UBS and Swiss governments will immediately start producing names and whereby the Swiss government will complete the production within 270 days of the requests. Is the settlement a victory for the U.S. or Swiss governments? The U.S. government heralded the settlement as a victory for tax authorities while the Swiss government said it was a victory for its sovereignty since the U.S. government agreed to use the treaty mechanism.

2. In the U.S. requests under the treaty, the U.S. did not specify the individual taxpayers and years under investigation. This is normally characterized as an impermissible "fishing expedition." Hence, the U.S. government has gained a short cut in obtaining information. Can the United States use this in cases other than UBS? In countries other than Switzerland?

3. What are the implications of the UBS settlement for bank secrecy in Switzerland and other countries with strong international financial service sectors.

4. On August 20, 2009, the U.S. District Court in Miami issued an indictment of a Swiss lawyer and banker involved in UBS. U.S. v. Hansruedi Shumacher and Matthias Rickenback, U.S. Dist. Ct., S.D. Fla., Case No. 09-60210, C. R. Hurley, Magistrate Judge Vitunac. Does the UBS case and subsequent prosecutions mean that financial institutions and practitioners must use more due diligence in the business dealings or risk criminal prosecutions?

[28] *Id.* at paragraph 16.

[29] *Id.* at paragraphs 21–2.

D. *Attempts to Obstruct or Interfere with Administration of Tax Laws*

Section 7212(a) criminalizes two related types of tax crimes. Part of § 7212(a) makes any threats or forcible effort designed to interfere with Internal Revenue employees felonies.[30] Another part of § 7212(a), the "omnibus clause," forbids any act that corruptly obstructs or impedes or tries to obstruct or impede the due administration of the Internal Revenue Code.[31]

Prosecutors have generally employed the omnibus clause to prosecute conduct occurring after the filing of a tax return, such as a taxpayer impeding or obstructing an audit or investigation.

Prosecutors must show three elements for a prima facie case with respect to the omnibus clause: (1) corrupt acts (2) attempting (3) to obstruct or impede the due administration of the income tax laws. Courts have construed "corruptly" as acting with the intent to obtain an unlawful advantage or benefit for onself or another party.[32] The corrupt conduct need not be aimed at individual officers or employees of the IRS and encompasses legal acts for a corrupt purpose. For example, an attorney was found to have acted corruptly when he formed a corporation expressly to enable a defendant to disguise the character of illegal income repatriated in a foreign bank.[33] Prosecutors are increasingly employing the omnibus clause to supplement substantive tax crimes charged against taxpayers and tax advisors.

E. *Offshore Tax Shelters*

IRS Notice 2004–45 on Meritless Filing Position

Based on Tax Code Sections 932(c) and 934(b)

This notice is scheduled to appear in Internal Revenue Bulletin 2004–28 dated July 12, 2004.

Part I – Income Taxes

Meritless Filing Position Based on Sections 932(c) and 934(b)

The Internal Revenue Service is aware that certain promoters are advising taxpayers to take highly questionable, and in most cases meritless, positions described below in order to avoid U.S. taxation and claim a tax benefit under the laws of the United States Virgin Islands (USVI). Promoters may also be advising taxpayers to take similar positions with respect to other U.S. possessions. This notice alerts taxpayers that the Service intends to challenge these positions in appropriate cases. The Service may impose civil penalties on taxpayers or persons who participated in the promotion or reporting of these positions. In addition to being subject to other penalties, any person who willfully attempts to evade or defeat tax by means of an arrangement such as the one described in this notice, or who willfully counsels or advises such evasion or defeat, may be guilty of a criminal offense under federal law . . .

30 *U.S. v. Przybyla*, 737 F.2d 828 (9th Cir. 1984), *cert. denied*, 471 U.S. 1099 (1995).

31 *U.S. v. Williams*, 644 F.2d 696, 699 (8th Cir.), *cert. denied*, 454 U.S. 841 (1981); *U.S. v. Popkin*, 943 F.2d 1535, 1539 (11th Cir. 1991), *cert. denied*, 1112 S.Ct. 1760 (1992).

32 *U.S. v. Popkin*, *supra* note 31, at 1540.

33 *Id.* at 1537.

Background

Section 934, which was enacted in 1960, provides that the USVI may reduce its territorial income tax only in certain limited cases. The USVI may not, however, reduce the tax liability of U.S. citizens or residents who are not bona fide residents of the USVI. In the case of U.S. citizens or residents who are bona fide residents of the USVI, it may reduce their tax liability only with respect to income from sources in the USVI or income effectively connected with the conduct of a trade or business within the USVI.

The legislative history of § 934 indicates that the statute was enacted in part because of concerns that certain local income tax programs, which were intended to provide incentives to corporations and USVI residents that made new investments in the USVI, were having the effect of reducing the tax liability attributable not only to income from sources within the USVI but also to income from sources within the United States. Although recognizing the goal of encouraging economic development in the USVI through appropriate income tax reductions, the legislative history to § 934 indicates that in no case should this [goal] be attained by granting windfall gains to taxpayers with respect to income derived from investments in corporations in the continental United States, or with respect to income in any other manner derived from sources outside of the Virgin Islands. S. Rep. No. 1767, 86th Cong., 2nd Sess. 4 (1960).

Typical Promotion

The highly questionable positions described in this notice may be promoted to taxpayers in a variety of forms. The Service is aware, however, that they have frequently been promoted in the following manner:

Promoters typically approach a taxpayer (Taxpayer) living and working in the United States and advise Taxpayer to (i) purport to become a USVI resident by establishing certain contacts with the USVI, (ii) purport to terminate his or her existing employment relationship with his or her employer (Employer), and (iii) purport to become a partner of a Virgin Islands limited liability partnership ("V.I.LLP") that is treated as a partnership for U.S. tax purposes. V.I.LLP then purports to enter into a contract with Employer to provide Employer with substantially the same services that were provided by Taxpayer prior to the creation of this arrangement. Typically, after entering into the arrangement, Taxpayer continues to provide substantially the same services for Employer that he or she provided before entering into the arrangement, but Taxpayer is nominally a partner of V.I.LLP instead of an employee of Employer.

Under this arrangement, Employer makes payments to V.I.LLP for Taxpayer's services and no longer treats the payments as wages paid to Taxpayer subject to the withholding and payment of employment taxes and reporting on Taxpayer's Form W-2. V.I.LLP, in turn, makes payments to Taxpayer for his or her services to Employer. V.I.LLP typically treats these payments for tax accounting purposes either as guaranteed payments for services or as distributions of Taxpayer's allocable share of partnership income. Under this arrangement, the promoter may be a general partner in V.I.LLP and may retain a percentage of the fees received from Employer.

V.I.LLP either has or secures a reduction, up to 90 percent, in USVI income tax liability under the Economic Development Program (EDP) of the USVI. Taxpayer takes the position that the EDP benefits granted to V.I.LLP provide a corresponding reduction in the income tax liability that Taxpayer reports on his or her USVI income tax return with respect to guaranteed payments from the partnership or distributive shares of the partnership's net income, or both.

Taxpayer pays tax to the USVI in an amount approximately equal to 10 percent of the U.S. income tax liability that otherwise would be imposed on Taxpayer's income from performing the services. Taxpayer claims that, for purposes of computing his or her U.S. income tax liability, gross income does not include guaranteed payments received from V.I.LLP or Taxpayer's distributive share, if any, of the partnership's net income, or both.

Positions Promoted

In situations such as those described previously, as well as in other situations, the following highly questionable positions are being promoted:

- **"You can continue to live and work in the United States and, nevertheless, be a bona fide resident of the USVI."** The concept of a "bona fide resident of the Virgin Islands" was an integral part of the predecessor to § 934(b), and as such, its meaning has been well established. *See* § 934(c) as enacted by P.L. 86–779, § 4(a) (1960). When Congress enacted the current versions of §§ 932 and 934(b), it retained this concept, but noted that Treasury has the authority to modify its meaning when necessary to prevent abuse. *See* H.R. Rep. No. 99–426 (1985) and General Explanation of the Tax Reform Act of 1986, JCS-10–87 (1987) ("Similarly, where appropriate, the Secretary may treat an individual as not a bona fide resident of the Virgin Islands.") The determination of whether an individual is a bona fide resident of the USVI turns on the facts and circumstances and, specifically, on an individual's intentions with respect to the length and nature of his or her stay in the USVI. *See* § 1.934–1(c)(2) (generally applying the principles of §§ 1.871–2 through 1.871–5). Promoters typically represent that a taxpayer need not make major lifestyle changes in order to become a bona fide resident of the USVI, and may represent that the taxpayer need only spend a few weeks or less out of the year in the USVI to become a resident for income tax purposes. These representations, however, have no basis in the well-established meaning of the term "bona fide resident of the Virgin Islands." Accordingly, a claim of USVI residency for income tax purposes may be considered without merit or fraudulent when the taxpayer continues to live and work in the United States.
- **"USVI source income includes income from services performed in the United States."** The principles that generally apply for determining gross and taxable income from sources within and without the United States (in particular, the rules of §§ 1.861–1 through 1.863–5) also generally apply in determining gross and taxable income from sources within and without a possession of the United States. *See* § 1.863–6 and *Francisco v. Commissioner*, 119 T.C. 317 (2002) aff'd, No. 03–1210 (D.C. Cir. June 18, 2004). With certain limited exceptions, compensation for labor or personal services performed in the United States is gross income from sources within the United States. *See* § 861(a)(3) and § 1.861–4(a)(1). The result does not change if the compensation is received in the form of a guaranteed payment from a partnership rather than in the form of a fee for services under an employment contract. *See Miller v. Commissioner*, 52 T.C. 752 (1969), acq. 1972–2 C.B. 2. Promoters typically claim that taxpayers are free to argue, under a variety of theories, that income from services performed in the United States constitutes income from USVI sources because "no rules exist under section 934" for determining whether income is from USVI sources. Based on the foregoing discussion, however, such arguments are without merit.
- **"For purposes of determining the source of income, USVI includes the United States."** Section 932 provides coordination rules for filing of returns for U.S. and USVI income

taxes by bona fide residents of the USVI and U.S. citizens and residents who have income derived from sources within the USVI or income effectively connected with the conduct of a trade or business within the USVI. To facilitate this coordination, § 932(c)(3) states that the USVI includes the United States for certain tax purposes. Section 932(c)(3) was modeled after § 935(c), which was enacted fourteen years earlier and which provides an equivalent rule with respect to Guam. For an illustration of the types of purposes for which these provisions apply, *see* § 1.935–1(c)(1)(ii). Notably, these provisions do not apply for purposes of determining the source of income. *See* H.R. Rep. No. 92–1479, 92d Cong., 2d Sess. 5 (Oct. 2, 1972) ("In determining the source of income for purposes of the special tax system provided in the bill (new code sec. 935), the principles contained in secs. 861–863 are to be applied without reference to sec. 935(c).") Based on an incorrect reading of § 932(c)(3), promoters may claim that compensation for services performed in the United States is considered for tax purposes to be compensation for services performed in the USVI. This claim is without merit. Section 932 does not apply to determine the source of income on which the USVI tax liability of bona fide residents may be reduced under § 934(b)(1). Thus, § 932(c)(3) does not operate to transform compensation from the performance of personal services in the United States into income from sources in the USVI.

- **"Non-USVI source income can be treated as effectively connected with the conduct of a trade or business within the USVI even if, under equivalent circumstances, such income would not be considered effectively connected with the conduct of a trade or business within the United States."** As noted above, § 934(b)(1) grants limited authority to the USVI to reduce the USVI tax liability with respect to income from USVI sources or income effectively connected with a trade or business within the USVI. The use of the term "effectively connected with the conduct of a trade or business" in § 934 indicates that Congress generally intended for the rules under § 934 to follow the well-established rules that apply for purposes of determining the taxation of nonresidents, such as the definition of effectively connected income under § 864(c). Section 934(b)(4), however, provides Treasury with the authority to issue regulations providing an alternative definition of the term. The legislative history of § 934 makes clear that this grant of regulatory authority was for the purpose of preventing abuse, and that Congress anticipated that it would be used to provide further limitations on the type of income that would be treated as from USVI sources or as effectively connected with the conduct of a trade or business within the USVI. S. Rep. No. 99–313, at 484, 1986–3 C.B. (vol. 3) 484. Taxpayers have no legal basis for claiming that the scope of the term "income effectively connected with the conduct of a trade or business" is broader under § 934 than it is under § 864. In particular, taxpayers have no legal basis for disregarding the rules of § 864(c)(4), which generally limit the amount of foreign source income that is treated as effectively connected with a U.S. trade or business to certain, very narrow categories of income. Accordingly, with the exception of those narrow categories, and in the absence of regulations to the contrary, income, gain, or loss from sources without the USVI cannot be treated as effectively connected with the conduct of a trade or business within the USVI for purposes of § 934. For example, income from the performance of personal services without the USVI cannot under any circumstances be treated as effectively connected with the conduct of a trade or business within the USVI. Promoters typically interpret the phrase "effectively connected to the conduct of a trade or business within the USVI" broadly, and inconsistently with § 864(c)(4), in order to claim a tax reduction with respect to income from non-USVI sources. As indicated above, however, these interpretations have no merit.

The IRS intends to challenge these positions and other similar claims that disregard the statutory and regulatory provisions concerning the limitations on the reduction of USVI income tax. Where taxpayers in order to make these claims enter into arrangements such as the one described in this notice, the Internal Revenue Service may disregard such arrangements on the grounds that they lack economic substance or that they have no purpose other than tax avoidance or evasion. The Service also may assert that the arrangement does not serve to terminate the employment relationship between a taxpayer and Employer for federal employment tax purposes, with the result that Employer remains liable for employment taxes and applicable penalties and interest.

In addition to liability for tax due plus statutory interest, taxpayers that claim to have no requirement to file a federal income tax return or pay federal income tax liability based on the positions described herein may be subject to penalties including, but not limited to, the accuracy-related penalty under § 6662, failure to file or pay penalties under § 6651, and civil fraud penalties under § 6663. Further, persons who participate in the promoting or reporting of these positions may be subject to aiding and abetting penalties under § 6701. In addition to other penalties, any person who willfully attempts to evade or defeat tax by taking the positions described in this notice, or who willfully counsels or advises such evasion or defeat, may be guilty of a criminal offense under §§ 7201, 7203, 7206, or 7212(a) or other provisions of federal law. Promoters and others who assist taxpayers in taking these positions also may be enjoined from doing so under § 7408.

U.S. Department of Justice Tax Div., Press Release, SUPERSEDING INDICTMENT OF 19 INDIVIDUALS FILED IN KPMG CRIMINAL TAX FRAUD CASE (Oct. 17, 2005)

WASHINGTON, D.C. – The Justice Department and Internal Revenue Service (IRS) today announced the filing of a superseding criminal indictment in the largest criminal tax case ever filed. Nineteen individuals were charged with conspiracy to defraud the IRS, tax evasion and obstruction of the Internal Revenue Laws arising out of illegal tax shelters that Big 4 accounting firm KPMG and others designed, marketed and implemented. According to the charges, the shelters generated at least $11 billion in fraudulent phony tax losses and resulted in at least $2.5 billion in tax evaded by wealthy individuals.

The indictment charges the former Deputy Chairman of KPMG; several former heads of KPMG's tax practice; the former CFO of KPMG; the former head of KPMG's Department of Professional Practice; a former KPMG Associate General Counsel; a former tax partner in the New York office of a prominent national law firm; and numerous other former KPMG tax partners. KPMG, headquartered in New York with offices in most major cities of the United States, acknowledged its criminal wrongdoing in a deferred prosecution agreement approved by the court on August 29, 2005. "The Department of Justice is committed to enforcing the tax laws to make certain all individuals comply with their tax obligations," said Acting Deputy Attorney General Robert McCallum. "To this end, the Department will vigorously prosecute any individual who makes false representations to the Internal Revenue Service. The prosecution of this case sends a strong message that tax professionals must be honest in their dealing with the IRS."

Among other charges, the indictment alleges that from 1996 to early 2004 the 19 defendants, KPMG, and others conspired to defraud the IRS by designing, marketing, and implementing illegal tax shelters, and focusing on four shelters known as FLIP, OPIS, BLIPS, and SOS. It is charged that this illegal course of conduct was approved and perpetrated at the highest levels of KPMG's tax management and involved numerous KPMG partners and other personnel. "The development and promotion of abusive tax shelters had a corrupting effect on the legal and accounting professions," said IRS Commissioner Mark Everson. "Tax professionals should help people pay what they owe – not more, not less."

According to the charges, the alleged conspirators designed, marketed, and implemented the shelters so that wealthy individuals who had large incomes or a large capital gain could eliminate all taxes on that income or gain by simply paying to KPMG all – in costs and fees of from 5–7 percent of the income or gain they wished to shelter. The shelters were marketed only to individuals who needed a minimum of $10 million or $20 million in losses, and according to the charges, the defendants and their co-conspirators filed and caused to be filed false and fraudulent tax returns that incorporated the phony tax losses. In addition, the defendants and their co-conspirators took specific steps to conceal the very existence of the shelters from the IRS and from IRS scrutiny – by among other things – failing to register the shelters with the IRS as required, and by fraudulently concealing the shelter losses and income on tax returns, according to the indictment.

The indictment also alleges that from 2002–2003, in response to the IRS examination of KPMG for failure to register tax shelters and related matters, certain of the defendants continued the fraud on the IRS by concealing KPMG's involvement and role in certain shelters; intentionally failing to produce documents that were called for by summonses issued by the IRS; and providing false and evasive testimony to the IRS regarding the nature and scope of KPMG's involvement with certain shelters. In addition, in connection with the investigation into tax shelters being conducted during the pendency of the IRS examination by a Senate Subcommittee, certain defendants provided false, misleading, and incomplete information and testimony at a hearing and a false response regarding documents that were called for in a subpoena issued by the Senate, relating to the personal use of tax shelters by KPMG and certain KPMG partners. "It is hard to imagine anything that can serve to undermine our voluntary system of taxation more than the crimes charged today, where so many professionals banded together with wealthy individuals to perpetrate this massive fraud on the tax system. This was an orchestrated case of deliberate tax evasion, and not legitimate tax planning. Professionals, including lawyers, accountants, bankers, so-called investment advisors and their firms – as well as taxpayers – should be on notice that the government will pursue even the most complicated tax fraud schemes designed to help the wealthy evade paying their fair share."

The investigation is ongoing. Assistant U.S. Attorneys Justin Weddle and Stanley J. Okula and Special Assistant U.S. Attorney Kevin M. Downing are in charge of the prosecution. Shirah Neiman, Chief Counsel to the U.S. Attorney, is supervising the investigation and prosecution.

The charges contained in the indictment are merely accusations, and the defendants are presumed innocent unless and until proven guilty.

Notes and Questions

1. One of the difficulties preventing the effective international enforcement of tax laws is the significant differences among the tax systems of international countries. For instance, although much of the world has value-added taxes (VAT), the United States does not have such taxes. For many countries, the extraterritorial scope of the U.S. tax system, coupled with its imposition of taxes on former citizens and former permanent

residents up to ten years after their expatriation, has posed significant enforcement difficulties.

2. In April 2004, the United States, the United Kingdom, Australia, and Canada announced they were planning the creation of a Joint International Tax Shelter Information Center (JITSIC), an international task force to combat abusive tax avoidance schemes. For more information *see* Sirena J. Scales, *Multination Task Force Created to Combat Abusive Tax Avoidance*, 2004 WORLDWIDE TAX DAILY, April 26, 2004, at 81–3. The four participating countries bring different specialized experience in fighting tax avoidance to the task force. The United Kingdom's expertise lies in identifying and uncovering avoidance schemes, especially concerning VAT, whereas the United States specializes in corporate and income tax avoidance and offshore tax shelters.

To execute the plan formally in 2004 those four countries (Australia, Canada, the United Kingdom, and the United States) signed a Memorandum of Understanding (MOU), by which the signatories agreed to form a Joint International Tax Shelter Information Center (JITSIC). Shortly after the signing of the MOU, the center became operational. Japan joined the group in 2007, China sent an observer in 2008, and South Korea is in the process of joining as an observer. JITSIC supplements the continuing work of tax administrations in identifying and stopping abusive tax avoidance transactions, arrangements, and schemes (which the MOU refers to as "abusive schemes").

On March 30, 2009, Director (International) Barry Shott, speaking at the Tax Executives Institute's 59th Midyear Conference, announced that JITSIC would expand to cover four new areas: offshore entities, high-wealth individuals, economic recovery coordination, and transfer pricing. Molly Moses, *Competent Authority to Add Fourth Group, Expand Tax Shelter Task Force, Shott Says*, DAILY REP. FOR EXEC., Mar. 31, 2009, at G-6.

As specified in the MOU, signatories will each appoint to JITSIC officials who are trained and experienced in tax examinations as they relate to abusive tax schemes. The headquarters of JITSIC will be in Washington, D.C. An Executive Steering Group will be established to coordinate, oversee, and evaluate its work, holding meetings periodically in different locations of the parties. Pursuant to the domestic procedures of the signatories, the members of JITSIC for that party will be delegated the ability to act as competent authorities for purposes of bilateral exchanges of information. After twelve months the signatories will conduct an initial review of JITSIC operations.

3. During the 1990s, attorneys and accountants developed and marketed a variety of offshore and other types of tax shelters to corporations and individuals with significant taxable income. Many of the tax avoidance schemes used offshore bank accounts and the Internet. The IRS and Department of Justice Tax Division have reacted to these developments in creative and proactive ways, including criminal prosecution such as the prosecution of KPMG partners described earlier.

KPMG itself reached a deferred prosecution agreement. *See* http://www.usdoj.gov/usao/nys/pressrelease2005.html. The provisions of the agreement include the following: KMPG relinquishes its high net worth individual practice and its compensation and benefits practice; KPMG agrees permanently to standards for tax opinions and tax return preparation that differ markedly from the standards applicable to the remainder of the industry, including KPMG will not give "covered" tax opinions to individuals or small private entities unless it can reach a "should" threshold and KPMG will not prepare tax returns for individuals or small private entities that include a transaction unless that position is "more likely than not"; a waiver of the privilege (subject to a couple of limited carve-outs); and the appointment of an independent monitor.

On August 28, 2008, the U.S. Court of Appeals for the second Circuit in *United States v. Stein*, No. 07–3042—cr (2d Cir. Aug. 28, 2008) upheld the dismissal of criminal charges against thirteen former executives at KPMG, saying prosecutors violated the defendants' rights by pressuring the accounting firm not to pay their legal bills (Reuters, "Court upholds dismissal of charges in KPMG case," Aug. 28, 2008). The dismissal sent a strong message that courts will not tolerate aggressive tactics that trample attorney-client relationships, and it was a setback to the tax shelter prosecutions.

In 2000, the IRS and DOJ started a campaign to obtain information regarding accounts issued by banks in tax-haven jurisdictions. They succeeded in obtaining court orders issuing John Doe Summonses of international affiliates of MasterCard, Visa, and American Express, with respect to accounts held by taxpayers in various jurisdictions. The IRS developed the Offshore Credit Card Project (OCCP) to address this problem and made it a strategic priority for FYs 2003–4. The OCCP uses information from the transactions of credit cards issued from offshore banks to identify taxpayers evading taxes and the promoters of this type of scheme.

In early 2003, the IRS started the Offshore Voluntary Compliance Initiative (OVCI), a limited amnesty. The OVCI allowed individuals who had participated in offshore financial arrangements that were not properly reflected on their tax returns to come forward and disclose this information to the IRS through April 15, 2003. In return the IRS would agree to limit the potential penalty exposure only to the accuracy and delinquency penalties (foregoing fraud).

These and other initiatives have targeted promoters of offshore and abusive tax shelters and tax avoidance transactions and promoters. For a useful account of the IRS and DOJ initiatives against tax shelters, including offshore ones, *see* Darrell D. Hallett, John M. Colvin, & Stephen E. Silver, *Tax Shelters – Entering the Era of the Billion Dollar Tax Loss*, American Bar Association, CRIMINAL TAX FRAUD 2005, Section B.

4. For additional background on tax crimes, *see* Bruce I. Hochman et al., Tax Crimes, Tax Mgmt. Portfolios 636–2nd; Ian M. COMISKY, LAWRENCE S. FELD, & STEVEN M. HARRIS, TAX FRAUD AND EVASION (Warren, Gorham & Lamont updated annually), American Bar Association, CRIMINAL TAX FRAUD (yearly CLE programs) (www.abanet.com).

5. On March 5, 2009, a jury in St. Croix acquitted four partners of Kapok Management of numerous federal charges of tax evasion, conspiracy, and fraud. In May 2003, federal agents raided Kapok's offices in St. Croix. In March 2007, a grand jury issued a twenty-one-count indictment. Prosecutors argued that the defendants conspired to defraud a legitimate Economic Development Authority program and evaded taxes by engaging in sham financial transactions to create the illusion of a management consulting business. Treasury issued final regulations establishing bona fide residency in January 2006 and final regulations on source of income in April 2008. *See* Jeremiah Coder, *U.S.V.I. Criminal Tax Case Part of Growing Trend, Practitioners Say*, 2009 WORLDWIDE TAX DAILY 48–2, Mar. 16, 2009.

F. *Intercompany Pricing*

Pursuant to Section 482 of the Internal Revenue Code the Internal Revenue Service has broad powers to allocate income and deductions among taxpayers, as follows:

26 U.S.C. § 482 Allocation of Income and Deductions among Taxpayers

In any case of two or more organizations, trades, or businesses – regardless of incorporation status, U.S. organization, and affiliation – owned or controlled directly or indirectly by the same interests, the Secretary may distribute, apportion, or allocate gross income, deductions, credits, or allowances between or among such organizations, trades, or businesses, if he determines that such distribution, apportionment, or allocation is necessary in order to prevent evasion of taxes or clearly to reflect the income of any of such organizations, trades, or businesses. In the case of any transfer (or license) of intangible property (within the meaning of section 936(h)(3)(B)), the income with respect to such transfer or license shall be commensurate with the income attributable to the intangible.

Can intercompany pricing violations be prosecuted as crimes? Consider the case of Marc Rich.

U.S. House of Representatives Committee on Government Reform, February 8, 2001, 21–2 (footnotes omitted)

In September of 1983, a federal grand jury in New York returned a 51-count indictment against Marc Rich, Pincus Green, and their companies. The original indictment was restructured into a 65-count indictment in March of 1984. All of the counts were charged against Marc Rich, Pincus Green, Clyde Melzer, A.G., and Marc Rich + Co, International Ltd. The superseding indictment was arranged to include in counts 1 through 23 the scheme to defraud the IRS. These charges were brought pursuant to 18 USC § 1343, the federal statute prohibiting wire fraud. These charges related to the fraudulent transactions among WTM and Marc Rich's companies discussed above. Counts 24 through 38 included the scheme to defraud the Department of Energy, and were brought pursuant to 18 USC § 1341, prohibiting mail fraud. Counts 39 and 40 were racketeering charges brought under the RICO Act. Marc Rich + Co. International's 1980 and 1981 tax returns, cover an amount totaling over $100 million in unreported income, which was concealed by the efforts of Rich, Green, Meltzer, and Rich's two companies. As stated in the indictment, International was able to evade more than $49 million in taxes. These counts were also brought against Marc Rich and Pincus Green personally. The tax and racketeering counts were approved and authorized by the Department of Justice. Counts 43 through 57 alleged that Rich defrauded the Department of Treasury for his transactions with the Iranians during the oil embargo and the American hostage crisis. Finally, Counts 57 through 65 charged Rich with "trading with the enemy" for Rich's secret deals with the Iranians. In the superseding indictment, these charges were not leveled against the companies. As a letter accompanying the indictment states, "[t]he primary focus of those counts has always been the activities of the American individuals, Marc Rich and Pincus Green."

For the indictment *see U.S. v. Marc Rich, Pincus Green et al.* (S.D.N.Y. Mar. 6, 1984) (S 83 Cr. 579) (Exhibit 4 to the Committee report); see http://news.findlaw.com/cnn/docs/marcrich/usrichindict.pdf

During congressional hearings, Jack Quinn, former White House counsel, and Marc Rich, lobbyist, testified that he took the pardon request to the Clinton Administration because he believed that the prosecution case against Rich was a "legal house of cards." "The case was based on a meritless tax charge, which formed the basis for the fraud charge, which was the predicate for the RICO," Quinn testified. "It was a misuse of RICO on top of misuse of

RICO predicates and underlying it all, a tax and energy case with no merit. The case was flawed." RICO refers to the Racketeer Influenced and Corrupt Organizations Act. *See House committee investigates Rich pardon*, CNN, February 8, 2001.

Notes and Questions

1. State and local governments often have stakes in major tax cases. Hence, the pardon of Mr. Rich did not resolve his State and City of New York tax cases. In this regard, on March 1, 2001, New York State Commissioner of Taxation and Finance Arthur J. Roth announced that the state had commenced legal action seeking $137 million from Rich for personal income taxes on money he accrued from fraudulent business activities during the early 1980s. On March 1, 2001, the State Department of Taxation and Finance filed a jeopardy assessment and issued a tax warrant against Rich personally, allowing the state to immediately place a lien on and begin collection against any assets held by Rich in New York State. *See State: Fugitive Financier Rich Owes $137 Million in Back Taxes*, N.Y. State Department of Taxation and Finance, Mar. 1, 2005.

2. From the start of the indictment until his pardons, many counsel, both representing Rich and neutral commentators, opined that the tax evasion counts of the indictment were questionable and difficult to sustain. *See*, e.g., *Law Professors Concluded Marc Rich Companies Did Not Evade Income Tax*, TAX ANALYSTS Doc 2001–5331 (Dec 7, 1990) (memorandum by Professors Bernard Wolfson and Martin Ginsburg on behalf of Marc Rich); *GOP lawyer: Facts 'misconstrued' in Rich case*, CNN, Mar. 2, 2001 (discussing the testimony before a House Committee of Lewis Libby, then White House counsel and former Rich counsel). However, *see* Morris "Sandy" Weinberg Jr., *Marc Rich Prosecutor Rebuts Clinton's Pardon Arguments*, DETROIT NEWS, March 5, 2001; Morris Weinberg, *Your Case Has No Merit, Mr. Clinton*, WASH. POST, February 25, 2001.

3. For additional reading *see* John P. Warner, *Transfer Pricing: Introductory Materials*, TAX MGMT. FOREIGN INCOME PORTFOLIOS #886; John P. Warner & Harrison B. McCawley, *Transfer Pricing: The Code and the Regulations*, TAX MGMT. FOREIGN INCOME PORTFOLIOS #887.

G. *Reporting*

Increasingly, the IRS and tax authorities around the world require taxpayers and tax advisors to report transactions and activities that are believed to be problematic or emblematic of tax crimes and tax violations.

26 U.S.C. § 6038A. Information with Respect to Certain Foreign-Owned Corporations

(a) Requirement – If, at any time during a taxable year, a corporation (hereinafter in this section referred to as the "reporting corporation") –

(1) is a domestic corporation, and
(2) is 25 percent foreign-owned,

such corporation shall furnish, at such time and in such manner as the Secretary shall by regulations prescribe, the information described in subsection (b) and such corporation shall maintain (in the location, in the manner, and to the extent prescribed in regulations) such records as may be appropriate to determine the correct treatment of transactions with related parties as the Secretary shall by regulations prescribe (or shall cause another person to so maintain such records).

(b) Required information – For purposes of subsection (a), the information described in this subsection is such information as the Secretary may prescribe by regulations relating to

(1) the name, principal place of business, nature of business, and country or countries in which organized or resident, of each person which

(A) is a related party to the reporting corporation, and

(B) had any transaction with the reporting corporation during its taxable year,

(1) the manner in which the reporting corporation is related to each person referred to in paragraph (1), and

(2) transactions between the reporting corporation and each foreign person that is a related party to the reporting corporation.

The Internal Revenue Code imposes financial penalties (i.e., $10,000 for each taxable year and $10,000 for each thirty-day period during which failure continues after the IRS mails notice of failure to report. In addition, § 6038A(e)(3) applies procedural disabilities to persons who do not comply.

26 U.S.C. § 6050I requires businesses that receive cash in excess of $10,000 in one transaction (or two or more related transactions) to file Form 8300 (Cash Payments Over $10,000 Received in a Trade or Business) with the IRS, and to provide a related statement to the payment. Hence, a tax practitioner can be required to file Form 8300 if he receives cash of more than $10,000 either for client fees, for the account of a client, or as an agent for a client.

31 U.S.C. § 5314 provides that "the Secretary of the Treasury shall require a resident or citizen of the United States or a person in, and doing business in, the United States, to keep records, file reports, or keep records and file reports, when the resident, citizen, or person makes a transaction or maintains a relation for any person with a foreign financial agency." A willful failure to file is a crime under 31 U.S.C. § 5322.

Form TD F 90.22.1 and instructions require each person subject to U.S. jurisdiction with a "financial interest in, or signature or other authority over, a bank, securities or other financial account in a foreign country" to file a foreign bank account report (FBAR), which is a Treasury Form, TD F 90–22.1. The form is required in addition to the reporting obligations with respect to foreign accounts on Form 1040.

Notes and Questions

1. Paragraph XXVIII of the 1992 understanding to the Netherlands-U.S. income tax treaty provides that where a U.S. taxpayer that is a reporting corporation under Code § 6038A does not have access to relevant records but the records are controlled by a foreign-related party that is a Dutch resident, the IRS must generally request such records from the Netherlands under Article 30 of the treaty before issuing a summons to the U.S. taxpayer. These provisions illustrate how some U.S. treaty partners have successfully required the resort to treaty requests as superseding unilateral evidence gathering provisions.

For background reading *see* Institute for International Research, MANAGING THE TAX COMPLIANCE BURDEN OF SEC. 6038A (Sept. 26–27, 1991).

H. *Efforts of International Organizations to Combat Harmful Tax Practices*

Starting in 1998, The Organization of Economic Cooperation and Development (OECD) actively promoted strengthened tax enforcement cooperation, including tax information exchange through its harmful tax practices (HTP) initiative. The OECD has requested all countries to pledge to abide by the initiative's principles and participate in the initiative. The OECD has done this through its reports on obstacles to obtaining bank information and transparency in corporate vehicles and through its initiative on harmful tax practices. Participation in the initiative requires transparency of country's tax system and an effective tax information exchange regime. The OECD has threatened countries outside the OECD, warning that unless they improve the transparency of their tax and commercial systems and conclude tax information exchange agreements, the OECD would consider imposing countermeasures. Targeted countries have responded by forming their own organization, the International Tax and Investment Organization (ITIO), and making their agreement to participate in the HTP initiative contingent on the OECD and other countries agreeing to take the same steps so that the competitiveness in financial services of the targeted countries is not compromised and there is a "level playing field." The OECD has formed a Global Forum on Taxation, which has broad membership of countries including many non-OECD members, in part to review whether the participating countries have reached the level playing field required to trigger compulsory participation.

The Global Forum and its Subcommittee on Transparency met in Melbourne, Australia, in November 2005 to discuss these matters. The results of the Melbourne meeting show a crack in the unified stance taken by the international financial centers, partly because the Isle of Man and Bermuda have started concluding Tax Information Exchange Agreements (TIEAs). However, the international financial centers may argue that the TIEAs have provided some of the incentives they have sought and demanded in exchange for such TIEAs. In any event, in spite of the EU pledge announced in Melbourne to provide technical assistance to countries wanting help in negotiating TIEAs and continued dialogue, the controversy about whether a level playing field exists is not over. In addition, efforts of the G7 Finance Ministers, the Financial Action Task Force, the World Bank Group, and other international organizations and groups have strengthed international cooperation against money laundering, counterterrorist financial enforcement, anticorruption, and international tax crimes.

Notes and Background

1. The OECD harmful tax practices initiative has given rise to a growth of blacklists against so-called tax havens, even after the blacklisted jurisdictions have fulfilled the conditions for removal from the blacklists. Jason Sharman & Gregory Rawlings, *Deconstructing National Tax Blacklists: Removing Obstacles at Cross-Border Trade in Financial Services* (Society of Trust and Estate Practitioners, Sept. 19, 2005, www.step.org).

2. For additional background and reading *see* TIM BENNETT, INTERNATIONAL INITIATIVES AFFECTING FINANCIAL HAVENS (Tolley's Int'l Series, 2001); OECD, HARMFUL TAX COMPETITION: AN EMERGING GLOBAL ISSUE (1998); INTERNATIONAL TAX COMPETITION: GLOBALISATION AND FISCAL SOVEREIGNTY (Rajiv Biswas ed., Commonwealth Secretariat, 2002); ANDREAS ANTONIOU, INTERNATIONAL FINANCIAL SERVICES SECTORS IN SMALL VULNERABLE ECONOMIES; CHALLENGES AND PROSPECTS (Commonwealth Secretariat, 2004); TOWARDS A LEVEL PLAYING FIELD: REGULATING CORPORATE VEHICLES

in Cross-Border Transactions (STEP 2003); Bruce Zagaris, *Symposium Focuses on Groups' International Initiatives*, 40 Tax Notes Int'l 138 (Oct. 10, 2005) (discussing the OECD, FATF, and other international organizations' initiatives).

3. On April 2, 2009, the G20 members in a Communiqué agreed to act against noncooperative jurisdictions, including tax havens, and to impose sanctions to protect public finances and financial systems, end bank secrecy, and promote the international exchange of tax information. Simultaneously, the OECD released a "progress report on the jurisdictions surveyed by the OECD Global Forum in Implementing the Internationally Agreed Tax Standard." (London summit-leaders' statement 2 April 2009, http://www.wcoomd.org/files/1.public files/PDFandDocuments/Highlights/G20_Final_London_communique.pdf; accessed Aug 25, 2009.)

III. Evidence Gathering

A. *Unilateral Measures*

In criminal tax cases the United States has used at least ten different methods of coercion to obtain documentary information or evidence situated abroad, to obtain testimony from witnesses resident or located abroad, and to secure the transfer of private assets to the United States.[34]

(1) Since 1926, federal courts have been able to issue a subpoena directing a U.S. citizen or resident in a foreign country to return to the United States and appear as a witness before the issuing court. The court can impose penalties for failure to appear.

(2) In transnational criminal cases involving transactions between a U.S. corporation or person and a related corporation in a foreign country, in which records are located in the foreign country and the laws of such country protect the records from disclosure usually because of confidentiality, the United States will resort to coercive measures such as subpoenas to obtain evidence located abroad when (a) the documents or other tangible evidence is in the possession, custody, or control of the alleged wrongdoer or a related entity; (b) the United States has personal jurisdiction over the alleged wrongdoer; and (c) the production of the evidence is not protected by an evidentiary privilege. Most cases have upheld such coercive measures on a U.S. entity and reject the argument that the production of documents by a related foreign entity would violate the laws of the country where the documents were located.[35]

(3) U.S. prosecutions have successfully compelled documents from abroad when the documents have been in the possession of a third party that was not a target of the investigation or a defendant in the prosecution; for example, documents of foreign banks or corporations or of foreign branches of U.S. banks or corporations with which the target or defendant did business.[36]

[34] For a discussion generally of coercive means used by the United States to obtain information in international criminal cases, *see* M. Abbell, Obtaining Evidence Abroad in Criminal Cases (Martinus Nijhoff Publ., 2008) Chapter 5, especially § 5-2, on which this discussion relies.

[35] *Marc Rich & Co., A.G. v. United States*, 707 F.2d 663 (2d Cir.), *cert. denied*, 463 U.S. 1215 (1983); *United States v. Vetco, Inc.*, 644 F.2d 1234 (9th Cir.), *cert. denied*, 454 U.S. 1098 (1981).

[36] *See, e.g.*, *Re Sealed* 825 F.2d 494 (D.C. Cir. 1987); *In re Grand Jury Proceedings of Nova Scotia*, 740 F.2d 817 (11th Cir.), *cert. denied*, 469 U.S. 1006 (1984).

(4) U.S. prosecutors can subpoena persons who are transiting to or from the United States to testify in a criminal trial or grand jury.[37]

(5) Assuming the United States has personal jurisdiction over an entity, U.S. prosecutors can subpoena the production of records of foreign entities from a custodian or agent of the records over whom the United States has personal jurisdiction.[38]

(6) To circumvent foreign bank secrecy laws, prosecutors have persuaded U.S. courts to issue an order directing the account holder to tell the bank to provide the records of any account in the bank, on which the signatory is authorized to draw, to the designated governmental recipient.[39]

(7) Sometimes U.S. prosecutors have obtained orders from federal courts directing targets of U.S. criminal investigations and defendants in U.S. criminal cases not to take action abroad to block the efforts of U.S. prosecutors from obtaining evidence.[40]

(8) Compelling the repatriation of assets to pay a fine or taxes or for purposes of forfeiture: In cases in which a person, over whom a U.S. court has personal jurisdiction and who has substantial assets abroad, is subject to a civil or criminal fee or tax jurisdiction and lacks sufficient U.S. assets to satisfy the fine or judgment, the U.S. court can issue a judgment[41] directing that assets in another country belonging to the person be forfeited to the United States. In at least one case a U.S. district court upheld its power under 26 U.S.C. § 7402(a) to compel a person against whom it had imposed a valid, final tax judgment to repatriate sufficient assets from abroad to satisfy the judgment.[42]

(9) Imposing a tax levy on a bank in the United States for funds of a taxpayer located in a foreign branch: The U.S. Internal Revenue Service has authority to collect a jeopardy assessment against a taxpayer by filing a notice of levy on the headquarters or branch of a bank in the United States, under circumstances in which the taxpayer/customer had an account at a branch or headquarters of the bank in a foreign country. Through the levy, the IRS has looked to force the bank to transfer the assets to the United States to satisfy a tax levy. Funds deposited by a customer in an account in a foreign bank are an obligation of that bank and not of its U.S. headquarters or branch. Hence, such a levy may be of questionable validity, especially if the U.S. office of the bank did not participate in the transactions by which the funds were deposited in the foreign branch or headquarters.

(10) A variation on the above mechanisms of issuing subpoenas to third-party recordholders is the use of John Doe Subpoenas. In an order that significantly assisted law enforcement efforts in combating tax avoidance, money laundering, and organized crime, as well as strengthening future relations between the United States and strong offshore jurisdictions, U.S. District Court Judge D. Lowell

37 *United States v. Field*, 532 F.2d 404 (5th Cir.), *cert. denied*, 429 U.S. 940 (1976); *Re Grand Jury Proceedings* (Bowe), 694 F.2d 1256 (11th Cir. 1982). *See also Re Sealed Case*, 825 F.2d 494 (D.C. Cir. 1987).

38 *Re Sealed Case*, 832 F.2d 1268 (D.C. Cir. 1987); *Re Grand Jury Proceedings (Bowe)*, 694 F.2d 1156 (11th Cir. 1982).

39 *Doe v. United States*, 101 L.Ed2d 184 (1988).

40 *United States v. Davis*, 767 F.2d 1025, 1036–40 (2d Cir. 1985); *see also*, *Garpeg, Ltd. v. United States*, 583 F.Supp. 789, 797–99 (S.D.N.Y. 1984).

41 The court uses its authority under 18 U.S.C. § 1963 or 21 U.S.C. § 853.

42 *United States v. McNulty*, 446 F. Supp. 90 (N.D. Cal. 1978).

Jensen upheld a broad June 14, 1988, subpoena requiring the Bank of America to produce.

> all records . . . which reflect . . . transfers of a minimum total of $9,500 during any 90 day period in 1986 and/or 1987 . . . by any person by any means, including [wire transfers by telephone or private network. . . .] to or from the Bahamas, the Cayman Islands, Hong Kong, the Netherlands Antilles, and Panama.

The subpoena requested records maintained at or originating from "Bank of America or any of its branches, subsidiaries or correspondent bank[s]" and did not distinguish between Bank of America's domestic and overseas operations. The IRS was fortunate in this case to have as the federal judge the very person who was Assistant Attorney General in the mid-1980s when the U.S. Attorney General was enforcing its subpoenas against foreign banks. In particular the famous case of the *Bank of Nova Scotia II* was litigated during Judge Jensen's tenure as Assistant Attorney General.[43]

Judge William Schwarzer, who issued the subpoena on June 14, 1988, ordered that if Bank of America objected to the summons, "or any part of it," it should appear before the court and show cause why the summons should not be enforced on or before September 2, 1988. In a bad tactical move, the bank, rather than entering an objection or appearing before the court, entered into discussions with the IRS regarding its compliance with the subpoena. Although disagreement exists about whether Bank of America was fully cooperative, there was no dispute that the discussions resulted in the production of records generated and maintained by Bank of America's domestic offices. However, in its meetings and correspondence with the IRS, the bank challenged the validity of the subpoena as it applied to overseas offices and questioned its ability to respond to the subpoena given the banking secrecy laws of "haven" countries.

As of April 5, 2009, a remaining important unresolved issue in the UBS case (discussed earlier) was whether UBS must comply with the John Doe Summons, which UBS argues is precluded by Swiss financial confidentiality law and the need to give priority to requesting evidence under the tax information exchange provisions of the U.S.-Swiss income tax treaty.

B. *International Agreements for Evidence Gathering in Tax Cases*

1. Bilateral Conventions

United States Model Income Tax Convention of September 20, 1996

Article 26: Exchange of Information and Administrative Assistance

1. The competent authorities of the Contracting States shall exchange such information as is relevant for carrying out the provisions of this Convention or of the domestic laws of the Contracting States concerning taxes covered by the Convention insofar as the taxation

[43] United States v. The Bank of Nova Scotia, 722 F.2d 657 (9th Cir. 1983), *cert. denied* 84–329, 53 L.W. 3472 (Jan. 8, 1985); B. Zagaris, *Judge Paine Socks it to the Bank of Nova Scotia – The Continuing Saga of the Bank of Nova Scotia Case*, 54 TAXES INT'L 12–20 (1984).

thereunder is not contrary to the Convention, including information relating to the assessment or collection of, the enforcement or prosecution in respect of, or the determination of appeals in relation to, the taxes covered by the Convention. The exchange of information is not restricted by Article 1 (General Scope). Any information received by a Contracting State shall be treated as secret in the same manner as information obtained under the domestic laws of that State and shall be disclosed only to persons or authorities (including courts and administrative bodies) involved in the assessment, collection, or administration of, the enforcement or prosecution in respect of, or the determination of appeals in relation to, the taxes covered by the Convention or the oversight of the above. Such persons or authorities shall use the information only for such purposes. They may disclose the information in public court proceedings or in judicial decisions.

2. In no case shall the provisions of paragraph 1 be construed so as to impose on a Contracting State the obligation:

a) to carry out administrative measures at variance with the laws and administrative practice of that or of the other Contracting State;
b) to supply information that is not obtainable under the laws or in the normal course of the administration of that or of the other Contracting State;
c) to supply information that would disclose any trade, business, industrial, commercial, or professional secret or trade process, or information the disclosure of which would be contrary to public policy (*ordre public*).

3. Notwithstanding paragraph 2, the competent authority of the requested State shall have the authority to obtain and provide information held by financial institutions, nominees or persons acting in an agency or fiduciary capacity, or respecting interests in a person, including bearer shares, regardless of any laws or practices of the requested State that might otherwise preclude the obtaining of such information. If information is requested by a Contracting State in accordance with this Article, the other Contracting State shall obtain that information in the same manner and to the same extent as if the tax of the first-mentioned State were the tax of that other State and were being imposed by that other State, notwithstanding that the other State may not, at that time, need such information for purposes of its own tax. If specifically requested by the competent authority of a Contracting State, the competent authority of the other Contracting State shall provide information under this Article in the form of depositions of witnesses and authenticated copies of unedited original documents (including books, papers, statements, records, accounts, and writings), to the same extent such depositions and documents can be obtained under the laws and administrative practices of that other State with respect to its own taxes.

4. Each of the Contracting States shall endeavor to collect on behalf of the other Contracting State such amounts as may be necessary to ensure that relief granted by the Convention from taxation imposed by that other State does not inure to the benefit of persons not entitled thereto. This paragraph shall not impose upon either of the Contracting States the obligation to carry out administrative measures that would be contrary to their sovereignty, security, or public policy.

5. For the purposes of this Article, the Convention shall apply, notwithstanding the provisions of Article 2 (Taxes Covered), to taxes of every kind imposed by a Contracting State.

6. The competent authority of the requested State shall allow representatives of the applicant State to enter the requested State to interview individuals and examine books and records with the consent of the persons subject to examination.

b. U.S. Procedure for Obtaining and Disclosing TIEA Information

To understand the application of the new tax information exchange agreements requires a detailed consideration of the different examination procedures [including the circumstances under which the types of information exchanges are started, continued, and terminated (and/or expanded)]. In addition, an understanding of the new TIEA program requires a detailed consideration of mutual assistance procedures, assistance in collection, and how the new information exchange procedures fit into these elements. One consideration, for instance, is whether the IRS or its tax treaty partner may find an alternative procedure or treaty more effective and expeditious than a TIEA. Although that discussion is beyond the scope of this chapter, a review of the salient points of U.S. procedure on obtaining and exchanging information follows.

I.R.C. Sec. 6103(k)(4) authorizes disclosure of information with foreign countries. In particular, it states: "A return or return information may be disclosed to a competent authority of a foreign government which has an income tax or gift and estate tax convention or other convention relating to the exchange of tax information, with the United States but only to the extent provided in, and subject to the terms and conditions of, such convention." The tax information exchange agreements are treated as income tax conventions for purposes of § 6103(k)(4) under IRS § 274(h)(6)(C). The U.S. "Competent Authority" is the Associate Commissioner (Operations). The authority to act as U.S. Competent Authority was redelegated for administering most of the international exchange and examination programs to the Associate Commissioner (Operations).

i. Receipt of Information from Foreign Tax Authorities (U.S.) as Requesting Country

If the IRS requires information from a country with which it has a tax treaty, it will submit a request.[44] Internally, the Assistant Commissioner (International) staff reviews the request. If appropriate, a staffer drafts a letter of request for the signature of the Assistant Commissioner (International) for transmission to the foreign tax authority. In the case of the Simultaneous Examination Program or an Industry-wide Exchange of Information, the Assistant Commissioner (International), will send the request to the treaty partners' competent authority upon receiving it from the field. In the case of Spontaneous Exchanges of Information, the Assistant Commissioner (International) will transmit foreign-initiated exchanges to the Assistant Regional Commissioner (Examination) for forwarding to the applicable District Director.

Information that the IRS receives from a foreign tax authority is subject to secrecy clauses contained in the specific tax treaty. To the extent the information relates to the liability or possible liability for tax of a U.S. taxpayer or otherwise is within the definition of return information in I.R.S. § 6103(b)(2), it is return information subject to the restrictions on disclosure imposed by I.R.C. § 6103 as well as the restrictions contained in the treaty clauses. The secrecy clauses prevent tax treaty information from being disclosed to State tax agencies under I.R.C. § 6103(d), the Department of Justice, or other Federal agencies under I.R.C. § 6103(i), allowing disclosure for non-Federal tax administration purposes. Disclosure Officers have the responsibility to ensure that information disclosed for non-Federal tax

[44] I.R.M. (25)00 Disclosure to Foreign Countries Pursuant to Tax Treaties, MT 1272–166.

administration purposes is reviewed and tax treaty information is removed prior to disclosure. Information obtained under a tax treaty is often stamped to indicate that it is tax treaty information.

Tax treaty information received from a foreign tax authority may be disclosed to the U.S. taxpayer to whom it relates pursuant to I.R.C. § 6103(e). The taxpayer in this case is deemed to be concerned with assessment, collection, enforcement, or prosecution with respect to the taxes that are the subject of the tax treaty. However, disclosure will not be made to the taxpayer if the IRS or the foreign tax authority providing the information objects to disclosure or if disclosure would seriously impair Federal tax administration.[45]

ii. Disclosure of Information to Foreign Tax Authorities (U.S. as Requested State)

When the U.S. receives a request from a foreign country with which it has a tax treaty, the request is transmitted to the U.S. Competent Authority.[46] The Assistant Commissioner (International) or the Associate Commissioner (Operations) in sensitive cases authorizes the exchanges. The Philadelphia Service Center handles certain automatic or "routine" exchanges (i.e., reports of taxes withheld from income paid to nonresident aliens).

The Assistant Commissioner (International) usually forwards requests for information to the appropriate IRS offices. When the Assistant Commissioner receives the requested information, he/she prepares a response for the signature of the Assistant Commissioner (International), transmitting the information to the foreign Competent Authority. The Assistant Commissioner (International) will authorize any disclosure for requests pertaining to the Simultaneous Criminal Investigation Program.

For treaty partner requests under the Simultaneous Examination Program or Industry-wide Exchange of Information, the Assistant Commissioner (International) or the Associate Commissioner (Operations) in sensitive cases will forward the request to the District Director for action; and when the information is received, transmit it to the treaty partner Competent Authority.

In the case of Spontaneous Exchanges of Information, the Assistant Commissioner (International) or the Associate Commissioner (Operations) in sensitive cases will forward a U.S.-initiated exchange to the treaty partner Competent Authority.

Normally, the United States does not furnish returns to foreign tax authorities pursuant to tax treaties.

If the U.S. Competent Authority needs to issue a summons in order to obtain the requested information, it will prepare and forward the summons to Branch 1, Associate Chief Counsel (International) for review prior to issuance.

The U.S. Competent Authority exempts from the exchange of information provisions of the treaties and hence from their transmission pursuant to requests information that would reveal business or trade secrets.

The Competent Authority must account pursuant to I.R.C. § 6103(p)(3) and the Privacy Act of 1974 for disclosures to foreign tax authorities made pursuant to tax treaties. The Competent Authority (U.S. Treasury) must disclose requests for taxpayer information and responses to such requests to the Joint Committee on Taxation.

[45] For further background on this section *see* I.R.M. (25)20, Information Received from Foreign Tax Authorities, MT 1272–166 from which this account draws heavily.

[46] For a discussion of these provisions, *see* I.R.C. § 6103(e)(7).

iii. Nontreaty Disclosure to Foreign Countries

In addition to the authority for disclosure of return information to foreign tax authorities in I.R.S. § 6103(k)(4), other provisions of sec. 6103 allow limited disclosures to foreign countries or individuals of foreign countries in certain situations.[47] Such disclosures can be made regardless of whether the United States has a tax treaty with the country. However, the U.S. exchanges information under a tax treaty, when one is in effect, to the extent possible. Return information may be disclosed by IRS employees to individuals of foreign countries pursuant to I.R.C. § 6103(k)(6). Returns and return information may also be disclosed to individuals of foreign countries designated in writing by a U.S. taxpayer to receive such information in accordance with I.R.C. § 6103(c) and (e). For instance, if a taxpayer has made a written request and signed a consent for disclosure, the IRS can certify to a tax treaty country that taxes were paid in the United States to enable the taxpayer to receive a credit for the taxes on a foreign return.

2. Multilateral Conventions

Binding Convention: Convention on Mutual Assistance in Tax Matters

In 1988, the Council of Europe and the OECD concluded the Convention on Mutual Administrative Assistance in Tax Matters (Tax Convention),[48] a multilateral convention that affects the ability of the United States and the other parties to obtain information regarding investors in those countries.[49]

On June 28, 1989, the United States signed it. On September 18, 1990, the U.S. Senate approved the treaty, and it entered into force with respect to the United States on April 1, 1995. Countries that are members of the Council of Europe, OECD, or both are eligible parties to the treaty. As of April 5, 2009, the treaty is in force in the following twelve countries: Azerbaijan, Belgium, Denmark, Finland, France, Iceland, Italy, the Netherlands, Norway, Poland, Sweden, and the United States. Canada and the Ukraine signed the Convention in 2004, but have not yet ratified it.[50]

The parties began negotiating the Tax Convention to improve cooperation in tax matters, reduce the incidence of tax evasion, and otherwise enhance tax administration. It substantially affects investor confidentiality because of its provisions for multilateral administrative assistance with respect to income, capital (wealth), social security, and other taxes.[51] Administrative assistance includes exchanges of information and simultaneous

[47] For further background on this section *see* I.R.M. (25)(30), Disclosure of Information to Foreign Tax Authorities, MT 1272–66 from which this account draws heavily.

[48] Convention on Mutual Administrative Assistance in Tax Matters, opened for signature Jan. 25, 1988, I.L.M. 1160 (1988) [hereinafter Tax Convention] reprinted in R. Rhoades and M. Langer, 5 INCOME TAXATION OF FOREIGN RELATED TRANSACTION ch. 85 (1989).

[49] *Id., passim.* For a current perspective on the Tax Convention, *see* Bruce Zagaris, *Exchange of Tax Information Policies at the Millennium: Balancing Enforcement with Due Process and International Human Rights*, prepared for the International Platform Association Annual Convention Roundtable on International Bureaucratic Lawmaking, Is Big Brother the Taxpayer's Friend of Foe? Or When Taxmen Are Allowed to Dictate the Law: OECD Harmful Tax Competition, FATF, and Other Anti-Privacy Initiatives Endanger Markets, Tax Reform and the U.S. Economy, available at http://www.solami.com/13September.htm.

[50] For a current list of the signatories and ratifications, *see* the Council of Europe Web site, http://conventions.coe.int/Treaty (accessed September 25, 2005).

[51] *Id.*, art. 1.

tax service of documents.[52] The Tax Convention should eventually result in standardized procedures for information exchanges and enhanced worldwide cooperation in tax matters.

The Tax Convention provides for the exchange of tax information on request, automatically, or spontaneously.[53] Two or more parties can examine the tax liabilities of a taxpayer simultaneously, and examinations can occur abroad.[54] However, the Tax Convention allows signatory countries, through reservations, to limit its applicability to certain types of taxes (e.g., social security or local taxes) and to limit the duty to assist either in collecting taxes or serving tax documents.[55] A party may also refrain from actions that are at a variance with its own public policy or laws and decline to furnish information regarding trade secrets or processes.[56] Information obtained through the Tax Convention may be used only for tax enforcement purposes and must be treated as a secret according to the most restrictive secrecy laws among the particular countries exchanging information.[57]

The Tax Convention covers a broad variety of taxes – far beyond the extent of bilateral tax treaties – including income, capital gains, net wealth, state and local social security contributions, and estate, inheritance, gift, and other taxes.[58] Its scope is not restricted by the residence or nationality of the taxpayer.[59] The potentially intrusive results of its broad scope have engendered the opposition of many business groups, including International Chamber of Commerce (ICC) member groups.[60] ICC member groups also have criticized the Tax Convention because it fails to distinguish adequately between tax evasion and legitimate tax avoidance.[61] Another criticism is that only national, and not state, governments are involved in tax cooperation under the Tax Convention. Some European nations have objected to the possibility of American states participating in tax information exchanges themselves and with the federal government in the United States concerning matters such as unitary taxation, and so have declined to sign the Tax

[52] *Id.*, art. 28(2).
[53] *Id.*, arts. 5, 8–9.
[54] *Id.*, art. 30(1).
[55] *Id.*, art. 21.
[56] *Id.*, art. 21.
[57] *Id.*, art. 22.
[58] *Id.*, art. 2(1)(a)–(b).
[59] *Id.*, art. 1(3).
[60] *See International Chamber of Commerce Seeks to Re-Open Debate on Multilateral Tax Accord*, BNA DAILY TAX REP. No. 189 at G-3 (Oct. 1, 1987) (reporting that ICC member organizations have lobbied against the Tax Convention for several years). The American Bar Association has also argued that individual taxpayers should be notified regarding requests for information under the Tax Convention. *See Practitioners Call for Protection of Taxpayer Rights under OECD Treaty*, BNA DAILY TAX REP. No. 194 (Oct. 6, 1988).
[61] *Id.* The ICC also argued that the Tax Convention is superfluous in light of existing treaties and that it "lacks clear standards for information." *Id. See also* Zagaris, *OECD Convention on Mutual Assistance Opened for Signature while ICC and Others Oppose Its Ratification*, 3 INT'L ENFORCEMENT L. REP. 337, 338 (1987) (reporting on ICC objections). The Business and Industry Advisory Committee opposed the Tax Convention on the ground that it would increase the risk that taxpayer confidentiality might be compromised – "without the knowledge of affected taxpayers." *International Chamber of Commerce Seeks to Re-Open Debate on Multilateral Tax Accord, supra* note 60. However, policy representatives of the Treasury Department have indicated strong support for the convention and have alleged that such exchanges of taxpayer information proceed with "extreme sensitivity." *See Multilateral Treaty Includes Adequate Confidentiality Provisions, Treasury Official States*, BNA DAILY TAX REP. No. 90 at G-4 (May 12, 1987).

Convention.[62] On January 20, 1987, even before the convention was initially opened for signature, U.S. Assistant Treasury Secretary for Tax Policy, O. Donaldson Chapoton, said he hoped it would go into effect that year.[63] Although the United States had not formally decided to sign, Mr. Chapoton reportedly stated that he was optimistic the convention would receive a positive recommendation and would be signed later in the year. He signaled that the convention would be particularly important for tax cooperation among governments without bilateral treaties.[64]

On May 13, 1988, Charles Triplett, Deputy Associate IRS Chief Counsel (International), and William Roth, director of the IRS Office of International Programs, said that as a result of the OECD Draft Convention, the IRS and Treasury were considering whether to notify taxpayers and allow them to appeal foreign governments' request for information.[65] In particular, Article 21 of the OECD Convention provides limits to the obligation of the requested state to provide assistance. For instance, the requested state need not supply information that is not obtained under its own laws or its administrative practice or that would disclose any trade, business, industrial, commercial, or professional secret; trade process; or other information whose disclosure would contravene public policy. The requested state need not provide administrative assistance if such assistance would lead to discrimination between a national of the requested state and nationals of the applicant state in the same circumstances. The Commentary to the Article explains that if a requested state has no power to take measures of conservancy it could decline to take such measures on its behalf, or if seizure of goods to satisfy a tax claim is not allowed in the applicant state, the requested state is not obliged to seize goods when providing assistance in collection. As a result of these provisions, a requested state is only obliged to implement the powers and practices that it has in common with the requesting treaty state.

Article 23(1) provides that proceedings relating to measures taken under the convention by the requested state will be brought only before the appropriate body of that state. The OECD Commentary to the Article specifies that the Article confers powers on the authority, and the question arises where the individual is entitled to require the tax authority to exercise those powers, especially where the failure to do so violates a right guaranteed by the national law of the tax authority in question. Specifically, when a taxpayer wants to resist the recovery of a tax or the enforcement of the tax laws, two grounds for that resistance normally exist in the laws of a treaty country. Either the taxpayer can contest the existence of the enforceability of the claim, or he or she can try to contest the enforcement measures themselves.

In 1988, the U.S. government announced that it had decided to reserve recovery of taxes because the provisions on assistance in collecting taxes in the current U.S. treaties

[62] E.g., Switzerland, Luxembourg, and Portugal. *See OECD Opens Information Exchange Convention to Signature by U.S. and Other Countries*, BNA DAILY TAX REP. No. 195 at G-2 (Oct. 9, 1987) [hereinafter OECD Open Convention]. Austria, Australia, Germany, and the UK declined to decide whether to sign when the Tax Convention was first opened for signature. *Id.*

[63] This discussion of the U.S. ratification process is taken from Bruce Zagaris, *Exchange of Tax Information Policies at the Millennium, supra* note 40, at 20–4.

[64] *OECD Convention for Mutual Assistance Opens for Signature*, 4 INT'L ENFORCEMENT L. REP. 9 (Jan. 1987).

[65] Bruce Zagaris, *IRS Contemplates Taxpayer Rights under OECD Assistance Convention*, 4 INT'L ENFORCEMENT L. REP. 158 (May 1988).

are not used and cooperation in the collection of taxes tends to be controversial in the United States.

OECD Agreement on Exchange of Information in Tax Matters

I. Introduction

1. The purpose of this Agreement is to promote international cooperation in tax matters through exchange of information.
2. The Agreement was developed by the OECD Global Forum Working Group on Effective Exchange of Information ("the Working Group"). The Working Group consisted of representatives from OECD Member countries as well as delegates from Aruba, Bermuda, Bahrain, Cayman Islands, Cyprus, Isle of Man, Malta, Mauritius, the Netherlands Antilles, the Seychelles, and San Marino.
3. The Agreement grew out of the work undertaken by the OECD to address harmful tax practices. *See* the 1998 OECD Report "Harmful Tax Competition: An Emerging Global Issue" (the "1998 Report"). The 1998 Report identified "the lack of effective exchange of information." The Agreement represents the standard of effective exchange of information for the purposes of the OECD's initiative on harmful tax practices.
4. This Agreement is not a binding instrument but contains two models for bilateral agreements drawn up in the light of the commitments undertaken by the OECD and the committed jurisdictions. In this context, it is important that financial centers throughout the world meet the standards of tax information exchange set out in this document. As many economies as possible should be encouraged to cooperate in this important endeavor. It is not in the interest of participating economies that the implementation of the standard contained in the Agreement should lead to the migration of business to economies that do not cooperate in the exchange of information. To avoid this result requires measures to defend the integrity of tax systems against the impact of a lack of cooperation in tax information exchange matters. The OECD members and committed jurisdictions have to engage in an ongoing dialogue to work towards implementation of the standard. An adequate framework will be jointly established by the OECD and the committed jurisdictions for this purpose particularly because such a framework would help to achieve a level playing field where no party is unfairly disadvantaged.
5. The Agreement is presented as both a multilateral instrument and a model for bilateral treaties or agreements. The multilateral instrument is not a "multilateral" agreement in the traditional sense. Instead, it provides the basis for an integrated bundle of bilateral treaties. A party to the multilateral agreement would only be bound by the Agreement vis-à-vis the specific parties with which it agrees to be bound. Thus, a party wishing to be bound by the multilateral Agreement must specify in its instrument of ratification, approval, or acceptance the party or parties which it wishes to be so bound. The Agreement then enters into force, and creates rights and obligations, only as between those parties that have mutually identified each other in their instruments of ratification, approval, or acceptance that have been deposited with the depositary of the Agreement. The bilateral version is intended to serve as a model for bilateral exchange of information agreements. As such, modifications to the text may be agreed in bilateral agreements to implement the standard set in the model.

6. As mentioned above, the Agreement is intended to establish the standard of what constitutes effective exchange of information for the purposes of the OECD's initiative on harmful tax practices. However, the purpose of the Agreement is not to prescribe a specific format for how this standard should be achieved. Thus, the Agreement in either of its forms is only one of several ways in which the standards can be implemented. Other instruments, including double taxation agreements, may also be used provided both parties agree to do so, given that other instruments are usually wider in scope.
7. For each Article in the Agreement there is a detailed commentary intended to illustrate or interpret its provisions. The relevance of the Commentary for the interpretation of the Agreement is determined by principles of international law. In the bilateral context, parties wishing to ensure that the Commentary is an authoritative interpretation might insert a specific reference to the Commentary in the text of the exchange instrument, for instance in the provision equivalent to Article 4, paragraph. 2.

IV. Recent Changes in Exchange of Information under Tax Treaties

Recent changes in the OECD Tax Convention and upcoming revisions to the UN Model Treaties enable broader exchanges of information. The 2005 OECD Article 26 covers "information as is necessary for carrying out the provisions of this Convention or of the domestic laws concerning taxes of every kind and description imposed on behalf of the Contracting States, or of their political subdivisions or local authorities, insofar as the taxation thereunder is not contrary to the Convention." Article 26(1) substitutes the right to request and the obligation to provide tax information when it becomes "forseeably relevant" rather than "necessary." Another change made in Article 26(1) is to expand the possible use of exchanged information to include the oversight of tax matters, so that information exchanged can be made available to oversight bodies that supervise tax administration and enforcement authorities, such as legislatures.

There is a new Article 26(4), which provides that, notwithstanding the exceptions in 2005 OECD Article 26(3), a domestic tax interest requirement does not limit the obligation to exchange information. Article 5(1) and paragraph 43 of the Commentary to the OECD Model TIEA also provide that a domestic tax interest does not limit the obligation to exchange information.

Article 26(5) of the 2005 OECD provides for an "override" of bank secrecy laws. The Commentary (paragraph 19.11) about the 2005 Article 26(5) explains that the change is pursuant to the international trend as set forth in the OECD Model TIEA and is discussed in the OECD report, "Improving Access to Bank Information for Tax Purposes." The report explained that, although access to information held by banks or other financial institutions may be by direct means or indirectly through a judicial or administrative process, the procedure for indirect access should not be so burdensome and time-consuming as to act as an obstacle to access to bank information.

Paragraph 19.12 of the Commentary about the 2005 OECD Article 26 broadly defines "fiduciary" and "agency" and provides that a requested state must not decline to furnish information solely because the information is held by persons acting in an agency or fiduciary capacity. In addition, Paragraph 19.24 of the Commentary about 2005 OECD Article 26(5) prevents the use of the attorney-client privilege when a person is acting as an agent or fiduciary as opposed to an attorney.

New tax treaties of the United States and other countries are likely to have these more ample tax information exchange provisions.

Notes and Questions

1. The 2005 OECD Model Income Tax Treaty has expanded the right of a signatory to obtain tax information. Article 26 added a new Article 26(4) providing that, notwithstanding the exceptions in 2005 OECD Article 26(3), a domestic tax interest requirement does not limit the obligation to exchange information. Article 5(1) and paragraph 43 of the Commentary to the OECD Model TIEA also provide that a domestic tax interest does not limit the obligation to exchange information.

2. *Hypothetical* – You are an Assistant U.S. Attorney and are investigating U.S. tax crimes of X company, a company registered in Barbados, and/or Mr. X., a Swiss and Greek dual national. Many records, including bank records, are in the Bahamas. Can you issue a subpoena on Mr. X. and X company, demanding that they turn over the documents in Barbados? What are the salient considerations?

3. *Hypothetical*: A magistrate may charge individuals with, *inter alia*: narcotics violations, money laundering, and tax crimes. More than likely, the individuals also have some legal entities through which they are conducting business (i.e., selling automobiles, airplanes, arms, and narcotics). Although the Mexican government can seek much of the information needed through a letters rogatory, it would be able to obtain the information faster through a request for assistance under the TIEA. For instance, if the Mexican authorities know that Juan Suarez, a Mexican resident and delinquent U.S. taxpayer, has extensive dollar holdings in the Chase Manhattan Bank in Manhattan, it would provide such information and the bank account number (if known) to the IRS, along with a description of the tax years and tax issues at stake. The IRS, assuming it is a case fulfilling the requirements of the TIEA, would then send this request to the treaty persons to prepare a summons, after which it would go to Branch 1, Office of International Tax Counsel. This office tries to issue a summons within five days to a revenue agent to serve. Once the summons is served on a bank or other third-party record keeper, the taxpayer would have notice. The taxpayer can then intervene and object. However, if Mexico merely wants confirmation that Juan Suarez still has a condominium on Calle Cinco or Biscayne Boulevard in Miami, the IRS will not notify Mr. Suarez. Under the Mutual Legal Assistance Treaty between Mexico and the United States, Mexico can transmit a letter of request for the same documents and simultaneously ask the United States to freeze the Chase Manhattan Bank account.[66]

U.S. counsel may be retained by a target of the investigating magistrate or by a third-party intermediary, such as a financial institution or professional from whom documents are subpoenaed. U.S. counsel should immediately try to learn as much as possible about the investigation in Mexico. For instance, counsel should try to ascertain which agency actually started the investigation, whether the investigation has met the legal requirements of at least Mexican law (i.e., search and seizure), and the bases for potentially challenging the request. Some cases of first impression under the treaty are now pending.

[66] For a discussion of the proposed MLAT between the United States and Mexico and other forms of bilateral criminal cooperation between the two countries, *see* Zagaris (ed.), Developments in Mexican-U.S. Law Enforcement Cooperation: What the Practitioner Needs to Know (American Bar Assoc. Sec. of Crim. Justice 1990).

Counsel could especially focus on the limitations imposed in the TIEA. Both governments must use all legal means and best efforts to execute a request. All requests that comply with the TIEA must be executed. However, a requested state is not required to comply with a request in the following situations: where compliance would require the disclosing country to exceed its legal authority; if the requested state determines that compliance with the request would be contrary to its national security or public policy; if compliance would disclose a trade, industrial, or commercial secret; or where the information furnished will be used to administer a provision of the tax law that would discriminate against a national of the requested state. A law is considered discriminatory if it is more burdensome with respect to a national of the requested state than to a similarly situated national of the requesting state. Although a requested state is not bound to provide the information in these circumstances, it may do so at its discretion. Such information may include information obtained in violation of its own laws. Questions of privilege that arise under the requesting state's law are to be resolved by the requesting state. (*See* also the earlier discussion of limitations on the requirement of the requested state to comply.)

Counsel for the target would want to make as many of these arguments and any other applicable arguments as possible. It may also be possible to argue that the request be denied because the information will be used in connection with nontax matters or will not be kept secret in the same manner as if the requested state had obtained the information under its own laws. For instance, perhaps an official or an alleged collaborator of an official in Mexico has threatened to use the information in nontax matters.

4. As a policy matter, can small offshore financial centers (SOFCs) require some quid pro quo for concluding tax information exchange agreements? What are the precedents, if any, that they can cite? Whether it is useful or desirable for developed countries to provide incentives, such as sharing withholding tax (e.g., the EU Savings Directive and the Caribbean Basin Economic Recovery Act of 1983, 19 U.S.C. § 2701–2707, esp. § 2702) to developing countries that agree to conclude TIEAs or to expanded information exchange, mutual assistance, and collection of tax debts in an income tax treaty depend on whether the international community or individual countries believe that it is useful macroeconomic policy and equity to provide such incentives. *See*, e.g., Bruce Zagaris, *The Procedural Aspects of U.S. Tax Policy towards Developing Countries: Too Many Sticks and No Carrots?* 35 GEO. WASH. INT'L L.REV. 331, 383–88 (2003).

5. For background on evidence gathering for tax offenses, *see* James P. Springer, Charles W. Blau, & Roger M. Olsen, *Obtaining Evidence Abroad for Criminal and Civil Tax Matters*, Sec. D., CRIMINAL TAX FRAUD 2005 (ABA CLE); Bruce Zagaris, *Obtaining Evidence in International Criminal Tax Cases*, Sec. D., CRIMINAL TAX FRAUD 2005 (ABA CLE).

V. Assistance in Collecting Taxes

Art. 31 of the U.S.-Netherlands Income Tax Treaty: Assistance and Support in Collection

1. The States undertake to lend assistance and support to each other in the collection of the taxes which are the subject of the present Convention, together with interest, costs, and additions to the taxes and fines not being of a penal character.

2. In the case of applications for enforcement of taxes, revenue claims of each of the States which have been finally determined may be accepted for enforcement by the other State and collected in that State in accordance with the laws applicable to the enforcement and collection of its own taxes. The State to which application is made shall not be required to enforce executory measures for which there is no provision in the law of the State making the application.
3. Any application shall be accompanied by documents establishing that under the laws of the State making the application the taxes have been finally determined.
4. The assistance provided for in this Article shall not be accorded with respect to the citizens, corporations, or other entities of the State to which application is made, except in cases where the exemption or reduced rate of tax granted under the Convention to such citizens, corporations, or other entities has, according to mutual agreement between the competent authorities of the States, been enjoyed by persons not entitled to such benefits.

Notes and Questions

1. Some of the more recent income tax treaties have a provision requiring assistance in collection. Such provisions are found either in the exchange of information article or in a separate article on assistance in the collection of taxes. Most of these provisions are limited and provide that each of the signatory countries will endeavor to collect on behalf of the other signatory country amounts equal to such taxes imposed by the other state as will ensure that any exemption or reduction in the rate of tax granted under this convention by that other state will not be enjoyed by persons not entitled to such benefits.[67] Some recent U.S. tax treaties, such as those with Canada and the Netherlands, have expanded the types of assistance rendered in the collection of taxes.

Although assistance in collection in tax matters has not traditionally been rendered, a significant departure from the tradition is occurring. Presumably, if the facts of a case do not fall within the assurance that the relief and/or exemptions of the treaty are not enjoyed by persons not entitled to such benefits, then most likely such a case will not be covered and assistance in collecting U.S. taxes will not be given. A number of U.S. treaties (i.e., the Canadian, Danish, French, Dutch, Netherlands Antilles, and Swedish) have a broader scope and will have a higher likelihood of applying to a given case.

2. *Hypothetical* – In the earlier discussed claim by the state and local tax authorities of New York against Marc Rich, can the United States on behalf of such authorities assert a claim against Mr. Rich in Switzerland, Israel, or other jurisdictions, such as the Netherlands, where it may either find him or his assets?

3. I have helped initiate a proposed resolution before the American Bar Association, urging the U.S. Treasury to promulgate regulations that would require the United States, as a requested state, to notify interested taxpayers of any request concerning them or their returns and offering them an opportunity to object to some or all of the requests. *See*, e.g., Bruce Zagaris, *U.S. Bar Association Withdraws Taxpayer Notification Resolution*, 40 Tax Notes Int'l 37 (Oct. 3, 2005). What are the arguments for and against such regulations?

[67] *See, e.g.*, U.S.-Australia, Art. 25(5).

VI. Extradition and Gaining Custody

U.S. House of Representatives Committee on Government Reform, February 8, 2001, at 24–25 (footnotes omitted)

After Rich and Green fled the country in anticipation of their indictment, the Southern District of New York unsuccessfully sought their extradition a number of times. On July 20, 1984, the United States requested extradition of Rich and Green from Switzerland. That request was rejected by the Swiss government in September of 1984 on the basis that the offenses charged against Rich and Green were "fiscal violations" and violations of "provisions concerning currency, trade policy, and economic policy" and that the government of Switzerland did not recognize the charges against Rich and Green as extraditable crimes. In June of 1994, the Justice Department attempted to extradite Rich and Green from Israel, but the Israeli government also turned down the request. Israel's Attorney General, Michael Ben-Ya'ir, told the U.S. Government that the extradition treaty between the two governments did not include fiscal offenses. And even though Rich had become a citizen of Spain, prosecutors could not extradite him because, like Switzerland and Israel, Spain does not extradite its citizens for tax evasion.

On January 20, 2001, Mr. Rich's life as a fugitive ended when President Clinton pardoned Rich during Clinton's last day in office.

Notes and Questions

1. Traditionally, extradition treaties have not included fiscal offenses. In part, countries omitted fiscal offenses because of the chaotic and divergent state of their fiscal and economic structures prior to the twentieth century. The divergence in economic systems continued after World War II with the emergence of socialism and communism in Eastern and Central Europe. Most governments perceived a lack of acceptance of fiscal violations and hence did not want to agree to extradite except between compatible economic systems.[68]

Only since the 1970s has the United States begun to include fiscal offenses in extradition treaties. The U.S. extradition treaties in the 1970s and 1980s that use dual criminality to define extraditable offenses authorize extradition from the United States for fiscal offenses to the extent that the requested offense satisfies the dual criminality requirement. Additionally, in many of the extradition treaties that use the list method for state offenses, along with the straight dual criminality method for federal offenses, willful tax evasion is an extraditable offense. Clearly a trend exists both on the part of the United States and other countries to include fiscal offenses as an extraditable offense.

Money movement offenses are closely related. For instance, a related but separate offense may be exchange control. In some countries this offense is a fiscal offense, whereas in others it is a customs offense. In recent years, the rise of money laundering offenses has led to their inclusion in bilateral and multilateral (e.g., the Vienna UN Drug Convention of 1988).

One problem that may affect the extraditability of a tax case is whether the signatory countries criminalize the same types of tax offenses. The substantive distinctions between

[68] *See, e.g., Sack, Non-Enforcement of Foreign Revenue Laws in International Law and Practice,* 81 U. Pa. L.R. 559 (1933).

tax evasion and tax fraud may enable defense counsel to successfully argue that the crimes are sufficiently distinguishable that extradition should not be granted.[69]

2. A trend is to include tax crimes in international criminal cooperation agreements. For instance, Article 1 of the Optional Protocol related to the Inter-American Convention on Mutual Assistance in Criminal Matters provides that the signatories to the Protocol shall not exercise the right provided for in Article 9f of the Convention to refuse a request for assistance solely on the ground that the request concerns a tax crime in any case in which the request is from another state party to this Protocol. Article 2 provides that the State parties to this Protocol, when acting as a requested state under the Convention, shall not decline assistance that requires the measures referred to in Article 5 of the Convention, if the act specified in the request corresponds to a tax crime of the same nature under the laws of the requested state. The Protocol is already in effect between Ecuador and the United States.

3. The best chance to compel extradition for tax offenses is with crimes involving tax fraud. In some extradition treaties coverage may include tax offenses and offenses "connected with" tax offenses. Offenses that may be connected with tax offenses include false statements, obstruction of justice, Continuing Criminal Enterprise (CCE), RICO, wire fraud, and mail fraud.

4. *Hypothetical* – Gide Flemant, a Belgian citizen who currently resides in Belgium, has extensive business dealings in the United States. Many of these business dealings involve transactions through a Canadian corporation in which he is a minority shareholder. Mr. Flemant learns that the IRS is auditing his returns for potential criminal violations. Until recently, he would not have had to worry about U.S. information gathering, let alone criminal cooperation between the two countries. However, the Mutual Legal Assistance Treaty (MLAT) signed on January 28, 1988, and now in force between Belgium and the United States, will be available to, *inter alia*, locate or identify persons, information, documents, and evidence, execute requests for search and seizure; and locate, trace, immobilize, seize, and forfeit proceeds of crime.

Under the U.S.-Belgian Tax Treaty of 1970, the U.S. government can request assistance relating to assessment, collection, enforcement, or prosecution of taxes that are the subject of the treaty. Fortunately for Mr. Flemant the two governments do not yet have a simultaneous examination program or a simultaneous criminal investigation program. Article 27 of the same treaty provides for assistance in collection. It requires that a requested state must try to collect on behalf of the requesting state such taxes imposed by that other requesting state as will ensure that any exemption or reduced rate of tax granted under the treaty will not be enjoyed by such persons not entitled to such benefits.

If the criminal investigation progresses, Gide will be sad to learn that the proposed Belgium-U.S. extradition treaty, signed on April 27, 1987, makes an offense extraditable if it is punishable under the laws of both signatory countries by deprivation of liberty for a maximum period of more than one year or by a more severe penalty. Article 20 provides that the treaty applies to offenses committed before as well as after it enters into force. The fact that Gide did business in Canada is not good for Gide, because Canada

[69] For a discussion of these differences and the impact of international criminal cooperation, *see* Bruce Zagaris & Fantauzzi, *The Application of Foreign Criminal Laws to U.S. Businesses Abroad,* 1 Int'l Quarterly 124, 134–42 (Oct. 1989); Bruce Zagaris, *The Defense of Transnational Tax and Money Laundering Offenses* 2–10, The Alleged Transnational Criminal (Int'l Bar Assoc. Paper July 4–6, 1991 Munich).

and the United States also have a new MLAT, have simultaneous civil and criminal tax programs, and have concluded a protocol to their extradition treaty that specifically includes fiscal offenses.

5. In a few treaties tax charges are not specifically covered (e.g., Greece, Luxembourg, and Portugal) and extradition for such offenses is only discretionary (e.g., Germany and Switzerland). It also appears that, notwithstanding the obligation to extradite under the treaty, Irish law may possibly override the treaty and prevent extradition. The trend is for modern treaties to specifically require extradition for tax and related crimes and for governments to extend international tax cooperation generally and specifically on extradition for tax crimes. As a result, prospects for the U.S. government's success in extradition for tax crimes are becoming more favorable.

6. On July 19, 2003, the European Union published in the *EU Official Journal* the texts of the EU-U.S. Agreements on extradition and mutual assistance that were signed on June 25, 2003, in Washington, D.C., during the most recent EU-U.S. summit. (Council Decision of 6 June 2003 concerning the signature of the agreements between the European Union and the United States of America on extradition and mutual legal assistance in criminal matters, O.J.E.U.L. 181). For a text of the agreements, *see* http://europa.eu.int/eur-lex/en/oj/2003/l_18120030719en.html. Although these agreements were concluded in the context of counterterrorism enforcement efforts in the aftermath of the terrorist incidents of September 11, 2001, they have enormous implications for the investigation and prosecution of tax cases.

The extradition agreement has a number of provisions that will facilitate extradition for tax and related crimes where the participating countries could not previously obtain extradition (Agreement on Extradition between the European Union and the United States of America, O.J.E.U. L181.27; July 19, 2003). Article 5 of the European Extradition Convention permits extradition if parties so decide among themselves, provided that extradition meets the standard requirements, including the dual criminality rule. Fiscal crimes encompass tax, duty, customs, and exchange offenses. As of April 5, 2009, the EU-U.S. extradition treaty was not yet in force.

7. For additional background on extradition generally *see* Michael Abbell, Extradition to and from the United States (2001); M. Cherif Bassiouni, International Extradition: United States Law and Practice (2002). For background on extradition for tax offenses, *see* Bruce Zagaris, *U.S. Efforts to Extradite Persons for Tax Offenses*, 25 Loy. L.A. Int'l. & Comp. L. Rev. 653 (2003).

VII. *Additional Reading*

A. *Books*

Andreas Antoniou, International Financial Services Sectors in Small Vulnerable Economies; Challenges and Prospects (Commonwealth Secretariat, 2004).

Tim Bennett, International Initiatives Affecting Financial Havens (Tolley's Int'l Series, 2001).

International Tax Competition: Globalisation and Fiscal Sovereignty (Rajiv Biswas, ed.) (Commonwealth Secretariat, 2002).

OECD, Harmful Tax Competition: An Emerging Global Issue (1998).

Bruce I. Hochman et al., Tax Crimes, Tax Mgmt Portfolio 636–2nd, A-1–20 (1999).

Ian M. Comisky, Lawrence S. Feld, & Steven M. Harris, Tax Fraud and Evasion (Warren, Gorham, & Lamont updated annually).

J. C. Sharman, HAVENS IN A STORM: THE STRUGGLE FOR GLOBAL TAX REGULATION (Cornell U. Press 2006).

TOWARDS A LEVEL PLAYING FIELD: REGULATING CORPORATE VEHICLES IN CROSS-BORDER TRANSACTIONS (STEP 2003).

B. Articles

C. Namorato & S. Michel, *International Criminal Tax Cases*, 50 U. MIAMI L. REV. 617 (1996).

James P. Springer, *An Overview of International Evidence and Asset Gathering in Civil and Criminal Tax Cases*, 22 GEO. WASH. J. INT'L L. & ECON. 277 (1988).

James P. Springer, Charles W. Blau, & Roger M. Olsen, *Obtaining Evidence Abroad for Criminal and Civil Tax Matters*, Sec. D., CRIMINAL TAX FRAUD 2005 (ABA CLE).

Bruce Zagaris, *Obtaining Evidence in International Criminal Tax Cases*, Sec. D., CRIMINAL TAX FRAUD 2005 (ABA CLE).

Bruce Zagaris, *U.S. Efforts to Extradite Persons for Tax Offenses*, 25 LOY. L. A. INT'L & COMP. L. REV. 653 (2003).

3 Money Laundering and Counterterrorism Financial Enforcement

I. International Politics of Anti-Money Laundering Regulations and Enforcement

One way to view the web of international agreements and arrangements governing anti-money laundering (AML) regulations is to consider the international political overlay. This is best done by considering the international regulatory and enforcement agreements and arrangements on the universal and regional levels developed to construct AML regulatory and enforcement regimes.

A. *Universal Organizations*

Universal organizations refer to international organizations whose membership is universally based.

1. The United Nations

The United Nations pioneered international AML cooperation with the 1988 Vienna Convention against Illicit Traffic in Narcotic Drugs and Psychotropic Substances, which requires signatories to criminalize money laundering and immobilize the assets of persons involved in illegal narcotics trafficking.[1] Because this convention was an initial effort and the participating governments were so diverse, there are differences in each country's criminalization of money laundering, extent of scienter required, enforcement methods, number of convictions, and range of punishments.[2] Nevertheless, subsequent efforts have drawn from the Vienna Convention and wherever possible use the same terminology and systematic approach.

The 1999 International Convention for the Suppression of the Financing of Terrorism prohibits direct involvement or complicity in the international and unlawful provision or collection of funds, attempted or actual, with the intent or knowledge that any part of the funds may be used to carry out any of the offenses described in the convention, such as acts intended to cause death or serious bodily injury to any person not actively involved in armed conflict in order to intimidate a population, and any act intended to compel a government or international organization to take action or abstain from taking action.[3] Offenses are deemed to be extraditable crimes, and signatories must establish their jurisdiction over the offenses, make them punishable by appropriate penalties, take alleged offenders into custody, prosecute or extradite violators, cooperate in preventive measures and countermeasures, and exchange information and evidence needed in related criminal proceedings.

The International Convention for the Suppression of the Financing of Terrorism requires each signatory to take appropriate measures, in accordance with its domestic legal principles, for the detection, freezing, seizure, and forfeiture of any funds used or

[1] Convention against Illicit Traffic in Narcotic Drugs and Psychotropic Substances, Dec. 19, 1988, Sen. Treaty Doc. No. 101–4 (1989), 28 I.L.M. 47 (1989) (entered into force Nov. 11, 1990).

[2] *See* United Nations Office on Drugs and Crime Global Programme against Money Laundering, Model Legislation on Laundering, Confiscation and International Cooperation in Relation to the Proceeds of Crime (1999).

[3] International Convention for the Suppression of the Financing of Terrorism, Dec. 9, 1999, 39 I.L.M. 270 (2000) (entered into force Apr. 10, 2002).

allocated for the purposes of committing the listed offenses.[4] Article 18(1) requires signatories to subject financial institutions and other professionals to "Know Your Customer" requirements and to file suspicious transaction reports. Additionally, Article 18(2) requires signatories to cooperate in preventing the financing of terrorism through the licensing of money service businesses and other measures to detect or monitor cross-border transactions.

Another UN treaty with important AML/counterterrorism financial enforcement (CTFE) provisions is the 2000 Palermo Convention against Transnational Organized Crime,[5] which contains three supplementary protocols: one to prevent, suppress, and punish trafficking in persons, especially women and children; another to stop the smuggling of migrants by land, sea, and air; and a third to stop the illicit manufacturing of and trafficking in firearms, their parts, components, and ammunition.

This convention seeks to strengthen the power of governments to combat serious crimes by providing a basis for stronger common action against money laundering through synchronized national laws, so that no uncertainty exists as to whether a crime in one country is also a crime in another. Signatory countries pledge to (1) criminalize offenses committed by organized crime groups, including corruption and corporate or company offenses; (2) combat money laundering and seize the proceeds of crime; (3) accelerate and extend the scope of extradition; (4) protect witnesses testifying against criminal groups; (5) strengthen cooperation to locate and prosecute suspects; (6) enhance prevention of organized crime at the national and international levels; and (7) develop a series of protocols containing measures to combat specific acts of transnational organized crime. The signatories must establish regulatory regimes to deter and detect all forms of money laundering, including customer identification, recordkeeping, and reporting of suspicious transactions.[6] In these respects, the convention's provisions are similar to those found in the Forty Recommendations of the Financial Action Task Force on Money Laundering.[7]

In addition to conventions, the UN Office on Drugs and Crime has drafted model laws such as the Model Legislation on Laundering, Confiscation, and International Cooperation in Relation to the Proceeds of Crime[8] and, in response to its expansion into the realm of CTFE, the Model Money-Laundering, Proceeds of Crime and Terrorist Financing Bill.[9] The Office on Drugs and Crime provides technical assistance on legislative drafting, financial intelligence, capacity building, and a range of services to help governments and law enforcement agencies implement their obligations under the Vienna Convention and related AML initiatives.[10]

[4] *Id.*

[5] Convention against Transnational Organized Crime, Dec. 12, 2000 (entered into force Sept. 29, 2003).

[6] *Id.*

[7] Paul Allan Schott, Reference Guide to Anti-Money Laundering and Combating the Financing of Terrorism III-3, III-4 (2002).

[8] U.N. Office on Drugs and Crime, Model Legislation on Laundering, Confiscation and International Cooperation in Relation to the Proceeds of Crime (1999).

[9] U.N. Office on Drugs and Crime, Model Money-Laundering, Proceeds of Crime and Terrorist Financing Bill (2003).

[10] U.N. Office on Drugs and Crime, Global Programme against Money Laundering, *at* http://www.unodc.org/unodc/en/money_laundering.html (n.d.).

2. The Financial Action Task Force

In response to mounting concern over money laundering, the 1989 Paris G7 Summit established the Financial Action Task Force on Money Laundering (FATF). Recognizing the threat posed to the banking system and to financial institutions, the G7 (now G8) Heads of State of Government and President of the European Commission convened the task force from the G7 member states, the European Commission, and eight other countries.

The G7 Summit conferred on FATF the responsibility to examine money laundering techniques and trends, review actions that had already been taken at a national or international level, and establish measures needed to combat money laundering. In April 1990, less than one year after its creation, the FATF issued a report containing a set of Forty Recommendations, which provide a comprehensive plan of action to fight money laundering.

In 1991 and 1992, the FATF expanded its membership from the original sixteen to twenty-eight members. Since then FATF has continued to examine the methods used to launder criminal proceeds and has completed two rounds of mutual evaluations of member countries and jurisdictions. In 2004, FATF updated the Forty Recommendations to reflect changes in money laundering, and the group has sought to encourage other countries around the world to adopt AML measures.

In June 2000, the FATF began an initiative against noncooperative countries and territories (NCCTs) that were not following the minimum international AML standards. It issued a list of twenty-three countries that were considered as not meeting international AML standards. However, the FATF does not maintain a list of "restricted" countries.

The FATF has indicated that, for all jurisdictions on the NCCTs list, FATF Recommendation 21 applies. Recommendation 21 indicates that financial institutions should give special attention to business relations and transactions with persons, companies, and financial institutions from jurisdictions that do not adequately apply the FATF Recommendations. But it is up to individual jurisdictions to determine specifically how to apply this recommendation (such as whether or not to process a transaction or report it as a suspicious transaction). Many countries have issued specific guidance; interested persons would therefore need to consult their regulator to determine which precise rules apply in their situation.

The process of selecting countries and jurisdictions as not meeting the minimum international standards was quite controversial, as was the process to delist them once they met those standards. Since 2005, FATF has not listed any new country or territory, and as of October 6, 2008, there were no countries on the NCCT list. The last countries removed from the list were Myanmar and Nigeria.[11]

In 2001, the FATF's mission was expanded to include the development of standards in the fight against terrorist financing. As a result, FATF issued an additional Nine Terrorist Financial Recommendations.

Each year FATF issues a report on its AML work and a typologies report discussing current trends in money laundering.

[11] FATF, Non–Cooperative Countries and Territories http://www.fatf–gafi.org/document/4/0,3343,en_32250379_32236992_33916420_1_1_1_1,00.html. The current Web site says that "as of 13 October 2006, there are no Non–Cooperative Countries and Territories."

Although FATF is discussed as a universal organization, among its limitations are that it is not a formal organization and it has limited membership and limited permanent staff. FATF's limitations affect its legitimacy and its ability to make and implement policies, both with governments and the private sector.

3. The International Monetary Fund/World Bank Group

Until 2001, the International Monetary Fund (IMF) resisted proactive involvement in anti-money laundering and counterterrorist financial enforcement, perceiving its role as helping with financial regulation but not enforcement of criminal law. More recently, its large shareholders have demanded that it become more actively involved in the AML and counterterrorism financial (CTF) regulatory and enforcement regimes.[12] In this new political climate, the IMF has become more involved in AML/CFT policy due to prudential and macroeconomic effects of money laundering on national and international financial systems. In particular, the IMF has been concerned that money laundering and large-scale criminal organizations would undermine, corrupt, and destabilize markets and even smaller economies. Signs of the corrosive effects of money laundering include inexplicable changes in money demand, greater prudential risks to bank soundness, contamination effects on legal financial transactions, and greater volatility of international capital flows and exchange rates due to unanticipated cross-border asset transfers.[13]

The IMF's AML unit has between twenty to thirty staff members, many with short-term contracts. Its limited budget and its lack of permanent staff reflect a lack of long-term commitment to AML policy and have limited its ability to attract top professionals.

a. *Promoting the AML/CFTE regime*

The IMF is contributing to the efforts of the Financial Action Task Force on Money Laundering (FATF) in several important ways, consistent with its core areas of competence. As a collaborative institution with near-universal membership, the IMF is a natural forum for sharing information, developing common approaches to issues, and promoting the AML and CTF regulatory and enforcement policies and standards developed by FATF. In addition, the IMF has unique expertise derived from its broad experience in conducting financial sector assessments, providing technical assistance in the financial sector and exercising surveillance over members' exchange systems.[14]

After September 11, 2001, the IMF identified new ways to advance its contribution to international efforts to combat money laundering and terrorist financing. In cooperation with the World Bank, it took three steps:

1. It added the FATF Forty Recommendations and Nine Special Recommendations on Terrorist Financing to the list of areas and associated standards and codes

[12] For an early justification of IMF's role in AML policy, *see* Michael Camdessus, Managing Director of the International Monetary Fund, at the Plenary Meeting of the Financial Action Task Force on Money Laundering, "Money Laundering: the Importance of International Countermeasures," February 10, 1998, http://www.imf.org/external/np/speeches/1998/021098.htm.

[13] *Id.*

[14] For background *see IMF, The IMF and the Fight against Money Laundering and the Financing of Terrorism*, IMF Factsheet (Sept. 2004).

for which Reports on the Observance of Standards and Codes (ROSCs) can be prepared.

2. In partnership with the World Bank, the FATF, and the FATF-Style Regional Bodies (FSRBs), the IMF participated in a twelve-month pilot program of AML/CFT assessments of forty-one jurisdictions, completed in October 2003. Additional assessments have been completed since then.
3. Working with the World Bank, the IMF substantially increased technical assistance to member countries to help them strengthen financial, regulatory, and supervisory frameworks for AML/CFT. In 2002–3, there were 85 country-specific technical projects benefiting 63 countries, and 32 regional projects reaching more than 130 countries. Since 2004, the pace of technical assistance has intensified.

After a March 2004 review of the pilot program, the IMF Executive Board agreed to make AML/CFT assessments a regular part of IMF work. It also endorsed the revised FATF Forty Recommendations as the standard for which AML/CFT ROSCs will be prepared, as well as a revised methodology to assess compliance with that standard. Drawing on the positive experience under the twelve-month pilot program, the Executive Board decided to expand IMF's AML/CFT assessments and technical assistance work to cover the full scope of the expanded FATF recommendations.

AML/CFT assessments are usually prepared within the framework of the Financial Sector Assessment Program (FSAP), another joint IMF/World Bank initiative, which is specifically designed to assess the strengths and weaknesses of financial sectors. The IMF conducts the AML/CFT assessments with the FSAP as part of voluntary assessments of offshore financial centers.[15]

b. *Technical assistance*

The goals of the IMF technical assistance, as described in its Articles of Agreement, are "to contribute to the development of the productive resources of member countries by enhancing the effectiveness of economic policy and financial management." In practice, the IMF fulfills this objective by helping countries develop their human and institutional capacity to design and implement effective macroeconomic and structural policies and put in place reforms that strengthen their financial sectors and reduce their vulnerability to crises.[16] By helping countries reduce their economic weaknesses and vulnerabilities, the IMF's technical assistance also contributes to a more robust and stable global economy.

Technical assistance is one of the benefits of IMF membership. The IMF normally provides such assistance free of charge to any requesting member country, within resource constraints. Approximately three-quarters of IMF technical assistance goes to low and lower middle income countries, particularly in sub-Saharan Africa and Asia. Postconflict countries are also major beneficiaries, with Timor-Leste, the Democratic Republic of Congo, and Afghanistan among the top ten recipients in recent years. A wide range of other countries seek technical assistance to strengthen their capacities.

The IMF has increasingly adopted a regional approach to the delivery of technical assistance and training. It operates four regional technical assistance centers: in the

[15] *Id.*
[16] IMF, *Technical Assistance*, IMF Factsheet (Sept. 2004).

Pacific, the Caribbean, and in East and West Africa. A fifth center is planned for the Middle East, and the IMF intends to establish three more centers to cover all of sub-Saharan Africa over the medium term. In addition, the IMF provides training for officials at its headquarters in Washington, D.C., at the IMF Institute, as well as through a network of six regional training centers, operating in collaboration with various cosponsors.

The IMF provides technical assistance in various ways, including through short staff missions and the placement of experts or resident advisors for periods ranging from a few weeks to a few years. (If the intention is to field a long-term advisor, countries may be asked to make a financial or in-kind contribution). Assistance might also be provided in the form of technical and diagnostic reports, training courses, seminars, workshops, and online advice and support.

IMF technical assistance is financed from both internal and external sources. The IMF directly finances technical assistance delivery, supervision, and administrative and other overhead costs; these expenses account for about one-fifth of the IMF's total net administrative budget. The IMF also administers funding provided by bilateral and multilateral donors. Such cooperation and resource sharing have two benefits: leveraging the resources available for technical assistance and helping avoid duplication of advice.

c. *IMF surveillance*

Understanding the importance of the Financial Sector Assessment Program (FSAP) requires a consideration of IMF surveillance because the FSAP arises from the surveillance role. A core responsibility of the IMF is to promote a dialogue among its member countries on the national and international consequences of their economic and financial policies. This process of monitoring and consultation, normally referred to as "surveillance," has rapidly evolved as the world economy has changed. IMF surveillance has also become increasingly open and transparent in recent years.[17]

Recent financial crises and their contagion effect have underscored the importance of effective surveillance. In response, the IMF has undertaken many initiatives to strengthen its capacity to detect vulnerabilities and risks at an early stage, to help member countries strengthen their policy frameworks and institutions, and to improve transparency and accountability.[18]

Under Article IV of its Articles of Agreement, the IMF has a mandate to exercise surveillance over the exchange rate policies of its members to ensure the effective operation of the international monetary system. In 1977, an Executive Board decision recognized that the IMF's appraisal of exchange rate policy requires a comprehensive analysis of the general economic situation and policy strategy of each member country. The decision also emphasized that the ultimate goal of surveillance is to help member countries achieve financial stability and sustainable economic growth.

Financial sector issues have received increasing emphasis in IMF surveillance after a series of banking crises in both industrial and developing countries in the 1990s. In 1999, the IMF and the World Bank created the joint Financial Sector Assessment Program (FSAP) to assess the strengths and weaknesses of countries' financial sectors. In

[17] IMF, *IMF Surveillance*, IMF Factsheet (Sept. 2004).

[18] For instance, as a result of the contagion effect of financial crises, the Financial Stability Forum was formed outside of the IMF and issued its report on offshore financial centers (OFCs), classifying them into three levels of compliance with international standards. *See* Financial Stability Forum, Report of the Working Group Offshore Centres (Apr. 2, 2000), available at http://www.fsforum.org/Reports/RepOFC.pdf.

those countries that have participated, FSAP findings provide important inputs into IMF surveillance.

Institutional issues – such as central bank independence, financial sector regulation, corporate governance, policy transparency, and accountability – have also become increasingly important to IMF surveillance in the wake of financial crises and some member countries' transition from planned to market economies. In recent years, the IMF and the World Bank have taken a central role in developing, implementing, and assessing internationally recognized standards and codes in areas that are crucial for the efficient functioning of a modern economy.[19]

An example of the contribution of IMF surveillance in AML/CFT policy is the IMF study on financial intelligence units (FIUs), tracing their development over ten years.[20] With more than eighty FIUs having gained admission into the Egmont Group, the informal international association of FIUs established in 1995,[21] and many more countries planning to establish an FIU or improve the effectiveness of existing ones, the IMF/World Bank foresaw the need for an overall discussion of FIUs as a guide for authorities who want to establish such organizations (see the next section on the Egmont Group). It also publishes cutting-edge literature on FIUs.[22]

The initiative taken by the IMF has catapulted multilateral development banks (MDBs) into the business of providing technical assistance and surveillance with respect to AML/CFT regulatory and enforcement regimes. For instance, the Inter-American Development Bank has provided substantial technical and financial assistance to its members in establishing FIUs.

The universal membership of countries in the IMF and regional MDBs has minimized some of the more controversial aspects of the FATF standards. The fact that small countries have a seat at the table lends the AML/CFT policymaking and implementation processes more legitimacy than they might otherwise enjoy. Nevertheless, even in the IMF and MDBs small countries believe the processes do not afford adequate opportunities for them to present their views.

4. The Egmont Group

To combat money laundering, governments have created agencies to analyze information submitted by financial institutions to meet money laundering reporting requirements. These agencies are commonly known as financial intelligence units (FIUs). They serve as the focal point for national AML programs, because they provide for the exchange of information between financial institutions and law enforcement.

In 1995, a number of FIUs began working together and formed the Egmont Group (named for the location of its first meeting at the Egmont-Arenberg Palace in Brussels). The purpose of the group is to provide a forum for FIUs to enable them to better support each of their national AML programs and to coordinate AML initiatives. This support includes expanding and systematizing the exchange of financial intelligence information,

[19] IMF, *IMF Surveillance, supra*.

[20] International Monetary Fund/World Bank, Financial Intelligence Units: An Overview (133 pp., 2004, ISBN 1–58906-349-X).

[21] The Egmont Group Financial Intelligence Unit (FIUs), at www.egmontgroup.org/about_egmont.pdf.

[22] In addition to the IMF book on FIUs, *see* Paul Allan Schott, Reference Guide to Anti-Money Laundering and Combating the Financing of Terrorism (2003); IMF, Suppressing the Financing of Terrorism: A Handbook for Legislative Drafting (2003).

improving expertise and capabilities of personnel, fostering better communication among FIUs through technology, and helping develop FIUs worldwide.[23]

To join the Egmont Group, a country's FIU must meet the Egmont definition of an FIU: "a central, national agency responsible for receiving (and, as permitted, requesting), analyzing and disseminating to the competent authorities, disclosures of financial information: (i) concerning suspected proceeds of crime, or (ii) required by national regulation, in order to counter money laundering." A member must also commit to act in accordance with the Egmont Group's Principles for Information Exchange between Financial Intelligence Units for Money Laundering Cases.[24]

More than seventy countries belong to the Egmont Group. Members have access to a secure, private Web site to exchange information.

5. The Basel Committee on Banking Regulations and Supervisory Practices

The Basel Committee on Banking Regulations and Supervisory Practices (Basel Committee) has been active in promulgating soft law recommendations. For example, in 1988, it adopted a statement of principles entitled "Prevention of Criminal Use of the Banking System, Draft Code of Conduct." The statement requires banks to know their customers, spot suspicious transactions, and fully cooperate with law enforcement authorities.

B. *Regional Level*

Regional organizations refer to international organizations whose membership is regionally based.

1. FATF-Style Regional Bodies (FSRBs)

The FATF-Style Regional Bodies (FSRBs) are important in the promotion and implementation of AML/CFT standards within their respective regions. FSRBs are modeled after FATF and, like FATF, have AML/CFT efforts as their sole goals. They encourage the implementation and enforcement of FATF's Forty Recommendations on Money Laundering and Nine Special Recommendations on Terrorist Financing. They also administer mutual evaluations of their members, which are intended to identify weaknesses so that members may take remedial action. Finally, the FSRBs provide information to their members about trends, techniques, and other developments in money laundering in their typology reports, which are usually produced on an annual basis.

The FSRBs are voluntary and cooperative organizations. Membership is open to any country or jurisdiction within the given geographic region that is willing to abide by the rules and goals of the organization. Some members of FATF are also members of an FSRB. Nonvoting observer status is available to jurisdictions and organizations that want to participate in the activities of the organization.

The following FSRBs are now in operation:

a. Asia/Pacific Group on Money Laundering (APG)
b. Caribbean Financial Action Task Force (CFATF)

[23] *See* Statement of Purpose, Egmont Group, at http://www1.oecd.org/fatf/pdf/Egstat-200106_em.pdf.
[24] *Id.*

c. Council of Europe – MONEYVAL
d. Eastern and Southern Africa Anti-Money Laundering Group (ESAAMLG)
e. Financial Action Task Force on Money Laundering in South America (GAFISUD)

2. The European Union

The EU's June 10, 1991, anti-money laundering directive was an important early step toward an international AML regime. The directive, which has been supplemented by a second directive and superseded by a third one, requires EU members to criminalize the laundering of illegal proceeds, abolish anonymous bank accounts, and abide by most of the FATF AML/CFT due diligence requirements. When an EU member (e.g., Austria in the case of anonymous savings accounts) has not implemented the directives, the EU has brought an enforcement action against it in the European Court of Justice in Luxembourg.

Because the members of the EU have a common foreign policy and enormous influence in most international organizations and groups that make AML policy, the EU AML policy has importance beyond the EU.

3. The Council of Europe

The main goals of the Council of Europe, which was established in 1949, are to promote European unity, foster social and economic progress, and protect human rights. Until relatively recently, its membership was limited to the countries of western Europe. However, with the demise of communist rule and the end of the Cold War, the Council of Europe has played a key role in embracing the countries of central and eastern Europe.

For many years the Council of Europe has prioritized its activities in the legal sphere. Its efforts to promote modernization of the law and closer cooperation among its members have resulted in the conclusion of more than 160 international treaties and conventions. More than twenty of these concern criminal law.

Multilateral international criminal cooperation conventions, including the 1957 European Convention on Extradition and the European Convention on Mutual Assistance in Criminal Matters, have been among its most significant achievements. In addition, its Transfer of Prisoners Convention has been important. Many governments outside the Council of Europe, including the United States and the Bahamas, rely on the Transfer of Prisoners Convention to administer applications for transfer of prisoners.

The European Committee on Crime Problems has regularly prepared and recommended the adoption of international treaties, harmonized criminal laws, and regulations. In several ways, the 1990 Council of Europe Convention on Laundering, Search, Seizure and Confiscation of the Proceeds from Crime goes further than the UN Counterdrug Convention of 1988. First, the obligation to criminalize money laundering is not restricted to drug trafficking offenses; instead, it extends to any "predicate offense." The legislative history explains that such measures should at least be made applicable to serious crimes and to offenses that generate huge profits.[25] Second, paragraph 3 of Article 6 of the 1990 Convention allows, but does not require, the criminalization of

[25] Explanatory Report on the Convention on Laundering, Search, Seizure and Confiscation of the Proceeds from Crime 204.

certain acts, including negligent laundering, in addition to those contained in the 1988 UN Convention. Such an approach to negligent conduct in this context is compatible with Recommendation 6 of the FATF and finds expression in the domestic legislation of several European countries, including the Netherlands, Norway, and Sweden.

The 1990 Council of Europe Convention was revised in 2005, and the new agreement is the first international treaty covering both the prevention and the control of money laundering and the financing of terrorism. The most significant change is the recognition that it is vital to gain access to the financial information of criminal organizations and terrorist groups in order to suppress them. The new convention came into force on May 1, 2008, after it was ratified by six signatories. As of October 23, 2008, the ratifying nations are Albania, Armenia, Bosnia and Herzegovina, Croatia, Malta, Moldova, Montenegro, the Netherlands, Poland, Romania, and Slovakia.[26]

4. The Organization of American States (OAS)

In 1992, the Organization of American States adopted Model Regulations Concerning Laundering Offenses Connected to Illicit Drug Trafficking and Related Offenses, which were prepared by the Inter-American Drug Abuse Commission (CICAD).[27] The Model Regulations follow the Vienna UN Drug Convention mentioned earlier and incorporate, whenever possible, the FATF recommendations. The OAS has also elaborated an Inter-American Convention on Corruption and the Inter-American Convention against Terrorism.

Notes and Questions

1. For a discussion of efforts to construct an international AML enforcement regime, *see* Bruce Zagaris & Sheila M. Castilla, *Constructing an International Financial Enforcement Regime: The Implementation of Anti-Money-Laundering Policy*, 19 Brook. J. Int'l L. 871 (1993); Bruce Zagaris, *International Money Laundering, Managing the Interdependence of IOs Subnational, Transnational, and Transborder Entities, in* International Organizations: A Comparative Approach to the Management of Cooperation 138–150 (Robert Jordan ed., 4th ed. 2001) (discussing the evolution of the international money movement enforcement regime and how, although starting as an integral component of international counterdrug policy, it has rapidly gathered its own momentum by expanding to encompass other forms of criminal activity). *See also* William C. Gilmore, Dirty Money: The Evolution of Money Laundering Counter-measures (Council of Europe Press, 1995).

2. The listed NCCT jurisdictions complained about the small size of FATF's membership (e.g., thirty countries) and their inability to participate in shaping policy (e.g., the AML/CFT Recommendations) and implementing it. The NCCTs argued that the list targeted only the small jurisdictions and the process was inherently unfair. Do you think these arguments have merit?

[26] For a current list of the signatories and ratifications, *see* the Council of Europe Web site, http://conventions.coe.int/Treaty (accessed October 23, 2008).

[27] Model Regulations Concerning Laundering Offenses Connected to Illicit Drug Trafficking and Related Offenses, Inter-American Drug Abuse Control Commission, adopted at the OAS General Assembly, May 18–22, 1992, Bahamas.

3. One criticism of the effort to build an international AML regulatory and enforcement regime is the lack of a universal institution whose purpose is to make and implement AML policy. Because there is no such institution, there are efforts to have FATF make and implement policy and to transfer some of its evaluation and policy functions to the IMF. What do you think about the institutional architecture of AML policy and the politics of AML regulatory enforcement regimes? How can small governments and the private sector become better integrated into the process so that they feel ownership and will enthusiastically implement the soft law AML policies?

II. Substantive Components of Anti-Money Laundering Law

As a result of the work of the international organizations, the AML requirements of international conventions, and the FATF Recommendations, *inter alia*, a uniform substantive AML law has started to be developed. Although important differences remain, the international institutionalization of AML efforts through FIUs, the Egmont Group, and international organizations promotes the uniform development of substantive AML law. This section illustrates some of these substantive components.

A. *Life-Cycle of Money Laundering*

To understand the substantive components of anti-money laundering requires a consideration of the life-cycle of money laundering. It has three stages.

1. Placement

The initial stage of the process involves placement of illegally derived funds into the financial system, such as through a financial institution. Countries develop record keeping for financial transactions and currency transaction reports to create an audit trail to facilitate financial investigations. Criminals try to adjust to those efforts to establish an audit trail by circumventing the patterns that will trigger reporting and using intermediaries to shield the names of the actual principals.

2. Layering

The second money laundering stage occurs after the illegal proceeds have entered the financial system. Launderers create layers between the illegal proceeds so that they become difficult to trace. Layering is accomplished by engaging in transactions with different persons and jurisdictions.

3. Integration

The third stage involves the integration of funds into the legitimate economy. A launderer can accomplish integration through the use of a series of transactions, jurisdictions, and persons, often within an overall business plan. For instance, an imports-export business may be used to disguise and, by creating more layers, legitimize various international transfers. Once a criminal achieves integration, the illegal source of the funds cannot be ascertained.

B. *Methods and Typologies*

Money can be laundered in diverse ways. The balloon effect principle means that, each time law enforcement authorities succeed in developing mechanisms to stop or make more difficult certain routes and methods for laundering, criminals find new methods; that is, each time law enforcement chokes off a method of laundering, the "balloon" is squeezed and becomes smaller in that place, but is enlarged elsewhere in the balloon.

The various ways by which money is laundered are referred to as methods or typologies. The terms "methods" or "typologies" may be used interchangeably, without any distinction between the two. Money laundering methods usually differ from country to country because of characteristics or factors unique to each country, including its economy, complexity of financial markets, AML regime, enforcement efforts, and international cooperation. These methods are continually evolving.

Various international organizations and countries regularly produce reference works on money laundering methods and techniques. Such studies help financial institutions be aware of evolving methods.

Notes and Questions

1. For useful background on the money laundering industry *see* JEFFREY ROBINSON, THE LAUNDRYMEN: INSIDE MONEY LAUNDERING, THE WORLD'S THIRD LARGEST – BUSINESS (Arcade Publishing, 1996); ROBERT E. POWIS, THE MONEY LAUNDERERS: LESSONS FROM THE DRUG WARS – HOW BILLIONS OF ILLEGAL DOLLARS ARE WASHED THROUGH BANKS AND BUSINESS (Probus Publishing Co., 1992); INGO WALTER, THE SECRET MONEY MARKET: INSIDE THE DARK WORLD OF TAX EVASION, FINANCIAL FRAUD, INSIDER TRADING, MONEY LAUNDERING, AND CAPITAL FLIGHT (Harper & Row, 1990).

C. *Anti-Money Laundering Prevention Programs*

A key element of AML substantive law is that governments must require financial institutions and certain nonfinancial businesses and professionals to develop and implement AML prevention programs.

FATF R.15 Financial institutions should develop programs against money laundering and terrorist financing. These programs should include:

a) The development of internal policies, procedures, and controls, including appropriate compliance management arrangements and adequate screening procedures to ensure high standards when hiring employees.
b) An ongoing employee training program.
c) An audit function to test the system.

1. Extending AML to Designated Nonfinancial Businesses and Professionals

In 2004 the FATF extended many AML prevention programs (i.e., AML due diligence) to designated nonfinancial businesses and professions (NFBPs). They are defined as follows:

a) Casinos.
b) Real estate agents.
c) Dealers in precious metals.

d) Dealers in precious stones.
e) Lawyers, notaries, other independent legal professionals and accountants – this refers to sole practitioners, partners, or employed professionals within professional firms. It is not meant to refer to "internal" professionals who are employees of other types of businesses, nor to professionals working for government agencies, who may already be subject to measures that would combat money laundering.
f) Trust and Company Service Providers refers to all persons or businesses that are not covered elsewhere under these Recommendations and that as a business, provide any of the following services to third parties:

- acting as a formation agent of legal persons;
  - acting as (or arranging for another person to act as) a director or secretary of a company, a partner of a partnership, or similar position in relation to other legal persons;
  - providing a registered office; business address or accommodation, correspondence or administrative address for a company, a partnership, or any other legal person or arrangement;
  - acting as (or arranging for another person to act as) a trustee of any express trust;
  - acting as (or arranging for another person to act as) a nominee shareholder for another person.

SEC. 352 of the USA PATRIOT ACT amended Section 5318(h) of title 31, United States Code

(H) ANTI-MONEY LAUNDERING PROGRAMS

(1) IN GENERAL In order to guard against money laundering through financial institutions, each financial institution shall establish anti-money laundering programs, including, at a minimum

(A) the development of internal policies, procedures, and controls;
(B) the designation of a compliance officer;
(C) an ongoing employee training program; and
(D) an independent audit function to test programs.

(2) REGULATIONS

The Secretary of the Treasury, after consultation with the appropriate federal functional regulator (as defined in section 509 of the Gramm-Leach-Bliley Act), may prescribe minimum standards for programs established under paragraph (1) and may exempt from the application of those standards any financial institution that is not subject to the provisions of the rules contained in part 103 of title 31, of the Code of Federal Regulations, or any successor rule thereto, for so long as such financial institution is not subject to the provisions of such rules.

Notes and Questions

1. On April 29, 2002, the U.S. Department of Treasury issued the first in a series of interim final rules implementing Section 352 of the USA PATRIOT ACT by requiring

banks, savings associations, credit unions, registered brokers and dealers in securities, futures commission merchants, and casinos to establish AML programs.

Section 352 adds new 31 U.S.C. § 5318(h)(1) of the Bank Secrecy Act (BSA) to require all financial institutions to establish an AML program that includes, at a minimum (i) the development of internal policies, procedures, and controls; (ii) the designation of a compliance officer; (iii) an ongoing employee training program; and (iv) an independent audit function to test the effectiveness of the institution's AML program. Related rules impose similar requirements on money services businesses, operators of credit card systems, mutual funds and futures, and commission merchants.

2. The extension of AML due diligence to lawyers, accountants, and others is known as the gatekeeper initiative because attorneys and accountants are viewed as gatekeepers for clients and persons. Notwithstanding the FATF gatekeeper initiative embodied in the FATF 2004 revised recommendations, the recommendations are primarily carried out in the EU, where the Revised Money Laundering Directive applies to lawyers. *See, e.g.*, Proceeds of Crime Act 2002 (POCA) and Money Laundering Regulations (MLRs); H.M. Treasury, *Paper for the Money Laundering Advisory Committee on Guidance*, 21st November 2003; Law Society of England and Wales, Annex 3B Money Laundering Guidance. The duty to report money laundering has been clarified by the Court of Appeal in *Bowman v. Fels*. The Law Society of England and Wales has finalized the *Bowman v. Fels* money laundering guidance, which supersedes various other previously issued guidance. *See* http://www.lawsociety.org.uk/professional/conduct/guideonline.

3. In response to the EU Money Laundering Directive, the Canadian government enacted legislation that brings lawyers within the category of persons required to record and report information relating to "suspicious transactions" and "large cash transactions" to the Financial Transactions and Reports Analysis Centre (FINTRAC).

The implementing regulations provide that lawyers are subject to Part 1 of the act when they engage in the following activities on behalf of another person: (a) receiving or paying funds (with certain exceptions); (b) purchasing or selling securities, real property, or business assets or entities; and (c) transferring funds or securities by any means. The legislation requires lawyers to report financial transactions that are "suspicious" and prohibits counsel from disclosing to their clients that they have made such a suspicious transaction report. There are also significant penalties for violations of these requirements.

On November 8, 2001, when certain provisions of the act came into force requiring lawyers secretly to report suspicious transactions of their clients to the FINTRAC, the Federation of Law Societies of Canada (FLSC) filed a petition in the Supreme Court of British Columbia, requesting that the court declare certain provisions of the act and implementing regulations unconstitutional. The petition also requested interlocutory relief exempting lawyers from complying with the regulations until there is a decision on the merits.

On November 20, 2001, the British Columbia Supreme Court ruled in favor of petitioners and granted lawyers an exemption from the application of Section 5 of the regulations, pending a full hearing on the merits.

In considering whether the independence of the bar may rise to the level of a right protected by the Constitution Act, 1867 and the Charter, the court acknowledged that neither document contains an express provision in this regard. The court, however, restated the general principle that the Canadian Constitution "embraces unwritten, as well as written rules." It further recognized that, although the independence of the bar is not an enumerated right in the Charter, the Supreme Court has often "looked beyond the rights expressed in the Charter to protect the principles that underlie that right." Based on these principles and given the fundamental role that solicitor–client confidentiality plays in a democratic country like Canada, the court agreed with petitioners that the protection of the independence of the bar could be found to be an unwritten principle of the Constitution and that this independence, together with solicitor–client confidentiality, may be found to underlie the rights guaranteed by sections 7, 8, and 10(b) of the Charter.

The court also found that if the independence of the bar was determined to be a constitutionally protected right, the challenged portions of the act could be found to violate that right, given that lawyers would be placed in conflict between their duty of confidentiality and their duty to comply with the new law, given the serious penalties for noncompliance. Thus, the court concluded that petitioners had successfully met the first prong of the test for interlocutory relief on a constitutional challenge. The court further concluded that petitioners had satisfied the second and third prongs of the test, that is, they had established that they would suffer irreparable harm if the interlocutory relief were not granted and that the balance of convenience, taking into account the public interest, weighed in favor of granting such relief.

Finally on May 15, 2002, the FLSC and the Attorney General of Canada reached an agreement that exempts all lawyers in Canada from the recording and reporting provisions of Part 1 of the act, including those concerning suspicious transactions and large cash transactions, until the FLSC constitutional challenge is heard by the British Columbia Supreme Court and the Court makes a decision on the merits. The agreement provides that if the FLSC is successful in its challenge, all lawyers in all provinces and territories will be exempt from these provisions unless a subsequent appeal provides otherwise.

As stated by the FLSC in its Notice to the Law Societies and the Legal Profession of August 16, 2002, "the principles of the independence of the bar and solicitor-client confidentiality are therefore preserved at least until the hearing of the constitutional challenge." For more information *see* Federation of Law Society of Canada and Attorney General of Canada, Supreme Court of British Columbia, Vancouver Registry, May 13, 2005, No. L013117. Chronology and court orders available on the FLSC Web site, http://www.flsc.ca/en/committees/moneylaundering.asp#news

4. In July 2004, the Brussels Bar sued the Belgian government for a declaration that the Belgian money laundering law, which was enacted on January 12, 2004, to implement the European Money Laundering Directive 2001, is unconstitutional. The suit challenges the law, which updates a 1993 law to include lawyers among the persons regulated in anti-money laundering. In particular, the law extends the requirement to lawyers to identify and report suspicious transactions.

The suit argues that the law violates lawyers' obligations of professional confidentiality and independence. Under the law, Belgian lawyers have to report suspicious transactions not to the financial intelligence unit, but to the batonnier (the Bar). The batonnier then must decide whether to override professional confidentiality. In addition, the law forbids the batonnier and the lawyer from warning the client that the lawyer has filed a Suspicious Activity Report (SAR).

The Brussels Bar argues that the new law improperly contravenes professional confidentiality and the rights of a defense, two important rights recognized by the European Community Court and the European Human Rights Court. On July 13, 2005, the Belgian court referred the matter to the European Court of Justice. For a copy of the decision to refer the case, *see* http://www.ccbe.org/doc/Fr/court_decision_fr.pdf.

The European Court of Justice issued its opinion on June 26, 2007. It determined that, because the EU directive in question distinguished between the lawyer acting in financial transactions and the lawyer acting as a litigator, it did not violate professional confidentiality. For the decision in English *see* http://eur-lex.europa.eu/LexUriServ/LexUriServ.do?uri=CELEX:62005J0305:EN:HTML.

5. For a discussion of American Bar Association (ABA) policies and materials, *see* http://www.abanet.org. For the ABA resolution on anti-money laundering, lawyers, and the gatekeeper initiative, *see* http://www.abanet.org/leadership/recommendations03/104.pdf. For background discussion of policy issues *see* Bruce Zagaris, *Gatekeepers Initiative: Seeking Middle Ground between Client and Government*, 18 CRIM. JUSTICE MAG. (Winter 2002); Kevin L. Shepherd, *USA PATRIOT Act and the Gatekeeper Initiative: Surprising Implications for Transactional Lawyers*, SECTION OF REAL PROPERTY, PROBATE, AND TRUST LAW, PROBATE & PROPERTY (September/October 2002); Bruce Zagaris, *The Gatekeeper Initiative: An Emerging Challenge for International Financial Advisors*, 2001 WORLDWIDE TAX DAILY 82–2, 22 TAX NOTES INT'L 2293–98 (May 7, 2001); Edward J. Krauland & Stephane Lagonico, *Lawyers and Anti-Money Laundering: The Gatekeeper Initiative*, 31 INT'L LAW NEWS (Fall 2002); James Roselle, *Combating Money Laundering and Terrorist Activity: The Lawyers' Role and Recent SILP/ABA Initiatives*, 31 INT'L LAW NEWS (Fall 2002). As of April 3, 2009, the ABA had circulated a draft good practices guide for lawyers.

6. For European lawyers' perspectives *see* Ramon Mullerat, "Lawyers: Between Maintaining Trust, Keeping Gates and Blowing Whistles," Dec. 29, 2004 http://www.abanet.org/buslaw/attorneyclient/materials/027/027.pdf; Council of the Bars and Law Societies of Europe (CCBE) position on the requirements on a lawyer to report suspicions of money laundering and on the European Commission Proposal for a Third EU Directive on Money Laundering (November 2004); CCBE Response to the Financial Action Task Force (FATF) Consultation Paper. (September 2002); http://www.ccbe.org/en/comites/money_laundering_en.htm#positions.

7. For other bar positions and for a *see* IBA Money Laundering Forum, http://www.anti-moneylaundering.org.

D. *Overriding Bank Secrecy*

FATF Recommendation 4. Countries should ensure that financial institution secrecy laws do not inhibit implementation of the FATF Recommendations. International conventions such as the Vienna Drug Convention, the Palermo Convention on Transnational Organized Crime, the anticorruption conventions, and the Council of Europe Anti-Money Laundering Convention require signatories to establish gateways to overcome secrecy in order to comply to AML requirements.

E. *Customer Due Diligence and Recordkeeping*

Subtitle A – International Counter-Money Laundering and Related Measures

SEC. 311. SPECIAL MEASURES FOR JURISDICTIONS, FINANCIAL INSTITUTIONS, OR INTERNATIONAL TRANSACTIONS OF PRIMARY MONEY LAUNDERING CONCERN.

(a) IN GENERAL – Subchapter II of chapter 53 of title 31, United States Code, is amended by inserting after section 5318 the following new section:

Sec. 5318A. Special measures for jurisdictions, financial institutions, or international transactions of primary money laundering concern

(a) INTERNATIONAL COUNTER-MONEY LAUNDERING REQUIREMENTS –

(1) IN GENERAL – The Secretary of the Treasury may require domestic financial institutions and domestic financial agencies to take 1 or more of the special measures described in subsection (b) if the Secretary finds that reasonable grounds exist for concluding that a jurisdiction outside of the United States, 1 or more financial institutions operating outside of the United States, 1 or more classes of transactions within, or involving, a jurisdiction outside of the United States, or 1 or more types of accounts is of primary money laundering concern, in accordance with *subsection (c)*.

(2) FORM OF REQUIREMENT – The special measures described in

(A) subsection (b) may be imposed in such sequence or combination as the Secretary shall determine;

(B) paragraphs (1) through (4) of subsection (b) may be imposed by regulation, order, or otherwise as permitted by law; and

(C) subsection (b)(5) may be imposed only by regulation.

(3) DURATION OF ORDERS; RULEMAKING – Any order by which a special measure described in paragraphs (1) through (4) of subsection (b) is imposed (other than an order described in section 5326)

(A) shall be issued together with a notice of proposed rulemaking relating to the imposition of such special measure; and

(B) may not remain in effect for more than 120 days, except pursuant to a rule promulgated on or before the end of the 120-day period beginning on the date of issuance of such order.

(4) PROCESS FOR SELECTING SPECIAL MEASURES – In selecting which special measure or measures to take under this subsection, the Secretary of the Treasury

(A) shall consult with the Chairman of the Board of Governors of the Federal Reserve System, any other appropriate Federal banking agency, as defined in section 3 of the Federal Deposit Insurance Act, the Secretary of State, the Securities and Exchange Commission, the Commodity Futures Trading Commission, the National Credit Union Administration Board, and in the sole discretion of the Secretary, such other agencies and interested parties as the Secretary may find to be appropriate; and

(B) shall consider

(i) whether similar action has been or is being taken by other nations or multilateral groups;

(ii) whether the imposition of any particular special measure would create a significant competitive disadvantage, including any undue cost or burden associated with compliance, for financial institutions organized or licensed in the United States;

(iii) the extent to which the action or the timing of the action would have a significant adverse systemic impact on the international payment, clearance, and settlement system, or on legitimate business activities involving the particular jurisdiction, institution, or class of transactions; and

(iv) the effect of the action on United States national security and foreign policy.

(5) NO LIMITATION ON OTHER AUTHORITY – This section shall not be construed as superseding or otherwise restricting any other authority granted to the Secretary, or to any other agency, by this subchapter or otherwise.

(b) SPECIAL MEASURES – The special measures referred to in subsection (a), with respect to a jurisdiction outside of the United States, financial institution operating outside of the United States, class of transaction within, or involving, a jurisdiction outside of the United States, or 1 or more types of accounts are as follows:

(1) RECORDKEEPING AND REPORTING OF CERTAIN FINANCIAL TRANSACTIONS –

(A) IN GENERAL – The Secretary of the Treasury may require any domestic financial institution or domestic financial agency to maintain records, file reports, or both, concerning the aggregate amount of transactions, or concerning each transaction, with respect to a jurisdiction outside of the United States, 1 or more financial institutions operating outside of the United States, 1 or more classes of transactions within, or involving, a jurisdiction outside of the United States, or 1 or more types of accounts if the Secretary finds any such jurisdiction, institution, or class of transactions to be of primary money laundering concern.

(B) FORM OF RECORDS AND REPORTS – Such records and reports shall be made and retained at such time, in such manner, and for such period of time, as the Secretary shall determine, and shall include such information as the Secretary may determine, including

(i) the identity and address of the participants in a transaction or relationship, including the identity of the originator of any funds transfer;
(ii) the legal capacity in which a participant in any transaction is acting;
(iii) the identity of the beneficial owner of the funds involved in any transaction, in accordance with such procedures as the Secretary determines to be reasonable and practicable to obtain and retain the information; and
(iv) a description of any transaction.

(2) INFORMATION RELATING TO BENEFICIAL OWNERSHIP – In addition to any other requirement under any other provision of law, the Secretary may require any domestic financial institution or domestic financial agency to take such steps as the Secretary may determine to be reasonable and practicable to obtain and retain information concerning the beneficial ownership of any account opened or maintained in the United States by a foreign person (other than a foreign entity whose shares are subject to public reporting requirements or are listed and traded on a regulated exchange or trading market), or a representative of such a foreign person, that involves a jurisdiction outside of the United States, 1 or more financial institutions operating outside of the United States, 1 or more classes of transactions within, or involving, a jurisdiction outside of the United States, or 1 or more types of accounts if the Secretary finds any such jurisdiction, institution, or transaction or type of account to be of primary money laundering concern.

(3) INFORMATION RELATING TO CERTAIN PAYABLE-THROUGH ACCOUNTS – If the Secretary finds a jurisdiction outside of the United States, 1 or more financial institutions operating outside of the United States, or 1 or more classes of transactions within, or involving, a jurisdiction outside of the United States to be of primary money laundering concern, the Secretary may require any domestic financial institution or domestic financial agency that opens or maintains a payable-through account in the United States for a foreign financial institution involving any such jurisdiction or any such financial institution operating outside of the United States, or a payable-through account through which any such transaction may be conducted, as a condition of opening or maintaining such account

(A) to identify each customer (and representative of such customer) of such financial institution who is permitted to use, or whose transactions are routed through, such payable-through account; and

(B) to obtain, with respect to each such customer (and each such representative), information that is substantially comparable to that which the depository institution obtains in the ordinary course of business with respect to its customers residing in the United States.

(4) INFORMATION RELATING TO CERTAIN CORRESPONDENT ACCOUNTS – If the Secretary finds a jurisdiction outside of the United States, 1 or more financial institutions operating outside of the United States, or 1 or more classes of transactions within, or involving, a jurisdiction outside of the United States to be of primary money laundering concern, the Secretary may require any domestic financial institution or domestic financial agency that opens or maintains a correspondent account in the United States for a foreign financial institution involving any such jurisdiction or any such financial institution operating outside of the United States, or a correspondent account through which any such transaction may be conducted, as a condition of opening or maintaining such account

(A) to identify each customer (and representative of such customer) of any such financial institution who is permitted to use, or whose transactions are routed through, such correspondent account; and

(B) to obtain, with respect to each such customer (and each such representative), information that is substantially comparable to that which the depository institution obtains in the ordinary course of business with respect to its customers residing in the United States.

(5) PROHIBITIONS OR CONDITIONS ON OPENING OR MAINTAINING CERTAIN CORRESPONDENT OR PAYABLE-THROUGH ACCOUNTS – If the Secretary finds a jurisdiction outside of the United States, 1 or more financial institutions operating outside of the United States, or 1 or more classes of transactions within, or involving, a jurisdiction outside of the United States to be of primary money laundering concern, the Secretary, in consultation with the Secretary of State, the Attorney General, and the Chairman of the Board of Governors of the Federal Reserve System, may prohibit, or impose conditions upon, the opening or maintaining in the United States of a correspondent account or payable-through account by any domestic financial institution or domestic financial agency for or on behalf of a foreign banking institution, if such correspondent account or payable-through account involves any such jurisdiction or institution, or if any such transaction may be conducted through such correspondent account or payable-through account.

(c) CONSULTATIONS AND INFORMATION TO BE CONSIDERED IN FINDING JURISDICTIONS, INSTITUTIONS, TYPES OF ACCOUNTS, OR TRANSACTIONS TO BE OF PRIMARY MONEY LAUNDERING CONCERN

(1) IN GENERAL – In making a finding that reasonable grounds exist for concluding that a jurisdiction outside of the United States, 1 or more financial institutions operating outside of the United States, 1 or more classes of transactions within, or involving, a jurisdiction outside of the United States, or 1 or more types of accounts is of primary money laundering concern so as to authorize the Secretary of the Treasury to take 1 or more of the special measures described in subsection (b), the Secretary shall consult with the Secretary of State and the Attorney General.

(2) ADDITIONAL CONSIDERATIONS – In making a finding described in paragraph (1), the Secretary shall consider in addition such information as the Secretary determines to be relevant, including the following potentially relevant factors:

(A) JURISDICTIONAL FACTORS – In the case of a particular jurisdiction

(i) evidence that organized criminal groups, international terrorists, or both, have transacted business in that jurisdiction;

(ii) the extent to which that jurisdiction or financial institutions operating in that jurisdiction offer bank secrecy or special regulatory advantages to nonresidents or nondomiciliaries of that jurisdiction;
(iii) the substance and quality of administration of the bank supervisory and counter-money laundering laws of that jurisdiction;
(iv) the relationship between the volume of financial transactions occurring in that jurisdiction and the size of the economy of the jurisdiction;
(v) the extent to which that jurisdiction is characterized as an offshore banking or secrecy haven by credible international organizations or multilateral expert groups;
(vi) whether the United States has a mutual legal assistance treaty with that jurisdiction, and the experience of United States law enforcement officials and regulatory officials in obtaining information about transactions originating in or routed through or to such jurisdiction; and
(vii) the extent to which that jurisdiction is characterized by high levels of official or institutional corruption.

(B) INSTITUTIONAL FACTORS – In the case of a decision to apply 1 or more of the special measures described in subsection (b) only to a financial institution or institutions, or to a transaction or class of transactions, or to a type of account, or to all 3, within or involving a particular jurisdiction

(i) the extent to which such financial institutions, transactions, or types of accounts are used to facilitate or promote money laundering in or through the jurisdiction;
(ii) the extent to which such institutions, transactions, or types of accounts are used for legitimate business purposes in the jurisdiction; and
(iii) the extent to which such action is sufficient to ensure, with respect to transactions involving the jurisdiction and institutions operating in the jurisdiction, that the purposes of this subchapter continue to be fulfilled, and to guard against international money laundering and other financial crimes.

1. Politically Exposed Persons (PEPs)

FATF Recommendation 6. Financial institutions should, in relation to politically exposed persons, in addition to performing normal due diligence measures:

a) Have appropriate risk management systems to determine whether the customer is a politically exposed person.
b) Obtain senior management approval for establishing business relationships with such customers.
c) Take reasonable measures to establish the source of wealth and source of funds.
d) Conduct enhanced ongoing monitoring of the business relationship.

Notes and Questions

1. Countries apply the requirements concerning PEPs differently. For instance, Canada applies them to both domestic and foreign PEPs, whereas the United States applies them only to foreign PEPs. In addition, the definition of PEPs varies.

2. Note that most of the recent international criminal conventions, such as those relating to anticorruption and transnational organized crime, have provisions targeting political corruption and money laundering.

2. Correspondent Accounts

FATF R.7 Financial institutions should, in relation to cross-border correspondent banking and other similar relationships, in addition to performing normal due diligence measures:

a) Gather sufficient information about a respondent institution to understand fully the nature of the respondent's business and to determine from publicly available information the reputation of the institution and the quality of supervision, including whether it has been subject to a money laundering or terrorist financing investigation or regulatory action.
b) Assess the respondent institution's anti-money laundering and terrorist financing controls.
c) Obtain approval from senior management before establishing new correspondent relationships.
d) Document the respective responsibilities of each institution.
e) With respect to "payable-through accounts," be satisfied that the respondent bank has verified the identity of and performed ongoing due diligence on the customers having direct access to accounts of the correspondent and that it is able to provide relevant customer identification data upon request to the correspondent bank.

SEC. 312. SPECIAL DUE DILIGENCE FOR CORRESPONDENT ACCOUNTS AND PRIVATE BANKING ACCOUNTS

(a) IN GENERAL – Section 5318 of title 31, United States Code, is amended by adding at the end the following:

(I) DUE DILIGENCE FOR UNITED STATES PRIVATE BANKING AND CORRESPONDENT BANK ACCOUNTS INVOLVING FOREIGN PERSONS

(A) IN GENERAL – Each financial institution that establishes, maintains, administers, or manages a private banking account or a correspondent account in the United States for a non-United States person, including a foreign individual visiting the United States, or a representative of a non-United States person shall establish appropriate, specific, and, where necessary, enhanced due diligence policies, procedures, and controls that are reasonably designed to detect and report instances of money laundering through those accounts.

(B) POLICIES, PROCEDURES, AND CONTROLS – The enhanced due diligence policies, procedures, and controls required under paragraph (1) shall, at a minimum, ensure that the financial institution in the United States takes reasonable steps

(i) to ascertain for any such foreign bank, the shares of which are not publicly traded, the identity of each of the owners of the foreign bank, and the nature and extent of the ownership interest of each such owner;
(ii) to conduct enhanced scrutiny of such account to guard against money laundering and report any suspicious transactions under subsection (g); and

(iii) to ascertain whether such foreign bank provides correspondent accounts to other foreign banks and, if so, the identity of those foreign banks and related due diligence information, as appropriate under paragraph (1).

(3) MINIMUM STANDARDS FOR PRIVATE BANKING ACCOUNTS – If a private banking account is requested or maintained by, or on behalf of, a non-United States person, then the due diligence policies, procedures, and controls required under paragraph (1) shall, at a minimum, ensure that the financial institution takes reasonable steps

(A) to ascertain the identity of the nominal and beneficial owners of, and the source of funds deposited into, such account as needed to guard against money laundering and report any suspicious transactions under subsection (g); and

(B) to conduct enhanced scrutiny of any such account that is requested or maintained by, or on behalf of, a senior foreign political figure, or any immediate family member or close associate of a senior foreign political figure that is reasonably designed to detect and report transactions that may involve the proceeds of foreign corruption.

F. *Identification and Reporting of Suspicious Transactions and Other Reporting Requirements*

31 Code of Federal Regulations Sec. 103.18 Reports by Banks of Suspicious Transactions

(a) General.

(1) Every bank shall file with the Treasury Department, to the extent and in the manner required by this section, a report of any suspicious transaction relevant to a possible violation of law or regulation. A bank may also file with the Treasury Department by using the Suspicious Activity Report specified in paragraph (b)(1) of this section or otherwise, a report of any suspicious transaction that it believes is relevant to the possible violation of any law or regulation but whose reporting is not required by this section.

(2) A transaction requires reporting under the terms of this section if it is conducted or attempted by, at, or through the bank, it involves or aggregates at least $5,000 in funds or other assets, and the bank knows, suspects, or has reason to suspect that:

(i) The transaction involves funds derived from illegal activities or is intended or conducted in order to hide or disguise funds or assets derived from illegal activities (including, without limitation, the ownership, nature, source, location, or control of such funds or assets) as part of a plan to violate or evade any federal law or regulation or to avoid any transaction reporting requirement under federal law or regulation;

(ii) The transaction is designed to evade any requirements of this part or of any other regulations promulgated under the Bank Secrecy Act, Pub. L. 91–508, as amended, codified at 12 U.S.C. 1829b, 12 U.S.C. 1951–1959, and 31 U.S.C. 5311–5330; or

(iii) The transaction has no business or apparent lawful purpose or is not the sort in which the particular customer would normally be expected to engage, and the bank knows of no reasonable explanation for the transaction after examining the available facts, including the background and possible purpose of the transaction.

Notes and Questions

1. 31 U.S.C. 5311 states that the purpose of the Bank Secrecy Act (BSA)'s requirement of filing SARs is to require financial institutions to keep certain records and file reports that the Secretary of the Treasury determines have a high degree of utility in criminal, tax, and regulatory matters or in the conduct of intelligence or counterintelligence activities to guard against international terrorism. In addition, Sec. 103.15 states that the Treasury has determined that required reports have a high degree of usefulness in criminal, tax, or regulatory investigations or proceedings. An identical determination is contained in Section 103.21 for records that are required to be kept. Pursuant to the USA PATRIOT ACT, Sec. 103.19 extends the SAR requirement to brokers or dealers, Sec. 103.20 extends the requirement to money services businesses, and Sec. 103.20 extends the SAR requirement to casinos.

2. In 1974, the U.S. Treasury also required financial institutions to file Currency Transaction Reports (CTRs) (IRS Form 4789) for deposits of $10,000 or more. The United States is the only country to require the filing of CTRs, a process that is quite burdensome and costly for banks and financial institutions. Critics of national and international AML regimes have focused on the lack of hard data on the costs of filing these reports. Former U.S. Treasury Secretary Paul O'Neill unsuccessfully raised this issue. *See* PETER REUTER & EDWIN M. TRUMAN, CHASING DIRTY MONEY: THE FIGHT AGAINST MONEY LAUNDERING 191 (2004). The authors also argue for a microeconomic research agenda that examines such elements of money laundering analysis as the market model for laundering services, as well as how the activity might respond to different kind of regulations and other interventions. Do you think cost-benefit analyses and a microeconomic research agenda for AML laws and regulations are needed?

3. In addition, the Treasury requires businesses to file IRS Form 8300 whenever they receive $10,000 or more in cash.

4. Sec. 103.23 requires that each person who physically transports, mails, or ships or causes to be physically transported, etc. or attempts to cause to be physically transported, etc. an aggregate amount exceeding $10,000 at one time from the United States to any place outside the United States, or into the United States from any place outside the United States, file a report thereof. Reporting is required on U.S. Customs Form 4790, the "Report of International Transportation or Currency or Monetary Instruments," commonly known as the CMIR. The funds that must be reported include currency, traveler's checks, and unrestricted monetary instruments (i.e., those in bearer form).

Failure to report the transportation of currency and instruments can result in civil and criminal penalties, as well as seizure and forfeiture of some or all of the assets that were subject to the reporting requirement. The U.S. Customs Service investigates violations of the CMIR reporting requirement.

5. Sec. 103.24 requires that persons subject to U.S. jurisdiction (except a foreign subsidiary of a U.S. person but including a U.S. citizen or permanent resident residing abroad) having a financial interest in, or signature or other authority over, a bank, securities, or other financial account in a foreign country, and the aggregate value of these exceed $10,000, must report such relations to the Commissioner of the Internal Revenue for each year in which such a relationship exists, and must provide such information in a reporting form prescribed by the Treasury: the "Report of Foreign Bank and Financial

Accounts, or FBAR, Treasury Form TD F 90–22.1. The FBAR requirement arises from 31 U.S.C. § 5314. *See* discussion of the FBAR in Chapter 2, on Taxation.

G. *Institutional and Other Measures to Combat Money Laundering and Terrorist Financing*

FATF R. 26 Countries should establish an FIU that serves as a national center for the receiving (and, as permitted, requesting), analysis and dissemination of STR and other information regarding potential money laundering or terrorist financing. The FIU should have access, directly or indirectly, on a timely basis to the financial, administrative, and law enforcement information that it requires to properly undertake its functions, including the analysis of STR.

FATF R. 27 Countries should ensure that designated law enforcement authorities have responsibility for money laundering and terrorist financing investigations. Countries are encouraged to support and develop, as far as possible, special investigative techniques suitable for the investigation of money laundering, such as controlled delivery, undercover operations, and other relevant techniques. Countries are also encouraged to use other effective mechanisms such as the use of permanent or temporary groups specialized in asset investigation, and cooperative investigations with appropriate competent authorities in other countries.

Notes and Questions

1. The IMF/World Bank group has published Financial Intelligence Units: An Overview (2004). In establishing FIUs, governments should undertake consultations with the private sector. Considerations in establishing an FIU are how to finance its establishment and operations and the various forms an FIU can take in a government structure. For instance, a wide variety of arrangements have been undertaken for FIUs: the administrative-type FIU; the law-enforcement-type FIU, the judicial- or prosecutorial-type FIU, and the "mixed" or "hybrid" FIU. The three core functions shared by all FIUs are to receive, analyze, and disseminate information to combat money laundering and terrorist financing, on both a domestic and international basis.

2. Multilateral development banks, such as the IMF/World Bank, and regional development banks, such as the Inter-American Development Bank and the Asian Development Bank, have provided technical and financial assistance to governments to form and help develop FIUs.

3. A key aspect of the international anti-money laundering regime has been the establishment of FIUs; the establishment of a headquarters and secretariat for the Egmont Group, which serves as the Secretariat for FIUs, is significant.

H. *Criminalizing Money Laundering*

Scope of the Criminal Offense of Money Laundering

FATF R. 1. Countries should criminalize money laundering on the basis of the United Nations Convention against Illicit Traffic in Narcotic Drugs and Psychotropic Substances, 1988 (the Vienna Convention) and the United Nations Convention against Transnational Organized Crime, 2000 (the Palermo Convention).

Countries should apply the crime of money laundering to all serious offenses, with a view to including the widest range of predicate offenses. Predicate offenses may be described by reference to all offenses, or to a threshold linked either to a category of serious offenses or to the penalty of imprisonment applicable to the predicate offense (threshold approach), or to a list of predicate offenses, or a combination of these approaches.

Where countries apply a threshold approach, predicate offenses should at a minimum comprise all offenses that fall within the category of serious offenses under their national law or should include offenses punishable by a maximum penalty of more than one year of imprisonment or for those countries that have a minimum threshold for offenses in their legal system, predicate offenses should comprise all offenses, which are punished by a minimum penalty of more than six months imprisonment.

Whichever approach is adopted, each country should at a minimum include a range of offenses within each of the designated categories of offenses.

Predicate offenses for money laundering should extend to conduct that occurred in another country, which constitutes an offense in that country, and which would have constituted a predicate offense had it occurred domestically.

Countries may provide that the offense of money laundering does not apply to persons who committed the predicate offense, where this is required by fundamental principles of their domestic law.

FATF R. 2. Countries should ensure that:

a) The intent and knowledge required to prove the offense of money laundering is consistent with the standards set forth in the Vienna and Palermo Conventions, including the concept that such mental state may be inferred from objective factual circumstances.
b) Criminal liability, and, where that is not possible, civil or administrative liability, should apply to legal persons. This should not preclude parallel criminal, civil or administrative proceedings with respect to legal persons in countries in which such forms of liability are available. Legal persons should be subjective to effective, proportionate and dissuasive sanctions. Such measures should be without prejudice to the criminal liability of individuals.

TITLE 18 > PART I > CHAPTER 95 > UNITED STATES CODE § 1956

Section 1956. Laundering of monetary instruments

(a)

(1) Whoever, knowing that the property involved in a financial transaction represents the proceeds of some form of unlawful activity, conducts or attempts to conduct such a financial transaction which in fact involves the proceeds of specified unlawful activity

(A)

(i) with the intent to promote the carrying on of specified unlawful activity; or
(ii) with intent to engage in conduct constituting a violation of section 7201 or 7206 of the Internal Revenue Code of 1986; or

(B) knowing that the transaction is designed in whole or in part

(i) to conceal or disguise the nature, the location, the source, the ownership, or the control of the proceeds of specified unlawful activity; or
(ii) to avoid a transaction reporting requirement under State or Federal law,

shall be sentenced to a fine of not more than $500,000 or twice the value of the property involved in the transaction, whichever is greater, or imprisonment for not more than twenty years, or both.

(2) Whoever transports, transmits, or transfers, or attempts to transport, transmit, or transfer a monetary instrument or funds from a place in the United States to or through a place outside the United States or to a place in the United States from or through a place outside the United States

(A) with the intent to promote the carrying on of specified unlawful activity; or

(B) knowing that the monetary instrument or funds involved in the transportation, transmission, or transfer represent the proceeds of some form of unlawful activity and knowing that such transportation, transmission, or transfer is designed in whole or in part

(i) to conceal or disguise the nature, the location, the source, the ownership, or the control of the proceeds of specified unlawful activity; or
(ii) to avoid a transaction reporting requirement under State or Federal law,

shall be sentenced to a fine of not more than $500,000 or twice the value of the monetary instrument or funds involved in the transportation, transmission, or transfer, whichever is greater, or imprisonment for not more than twenty years, or both. For the purpose of the offense described in subparagraph (B), the defendant's knowledge may be established by proof that a law enforcement officer represented the matter specified in subparagraph (B) as true, and the defendant's subsequent statements or actions indicate that the defendant believed such representations to be true.

(3) Whoever, with the intent

(A) to promote the carrying on of specified unlawful activity;

(B) to conceal or disguise the nature, location, source, ownership, or control of property believed to be the proceeds of specified unlawful activity; or

(c) to avoid a transaction reporting requirement under State or Federal law, conducts or attempts to conduct a financial transaction involving property represented to be the proceeds of specified unlawful activity, or property used to conduct or facilitate specified unlawful activity, shall be fined under this title or imprisoned for not more than twenty years, or both. For purposes of this paragraph and paragraph (2), the term "represented" means any representation made by a law enforcement officer or by another person at the direction of, or with the approval of, a Federal official authorized to investigate or prosecute violations of this section.

(b) Penalties.

(1) In general – Whoever conducts or attempts to conduct a transaction described in subsection (a)(1) or (a)(3), or section 1957, or a transportation, transmission, or transfer described in subsection (a)(2), is liable to the United States for a civil penalty of not more than the greater of

(A) the value of the property, funds, or monetary instruments involved in the transaction; or

(B) $10,000.

(2) Jurisdiction over foreign persons – For purposes of adjudicating an action filed or enforcing a penalty ordered under this section, the district courts shall have jurisdiction over any foreign person, including any financial institution authorized under the laws of a foreign country, against whom the action is brought, if service of process upon the foreign person is made under the Federal Rules of Civil Procedure or the laws of the country in which the foreign person is found, and

(A) the foreign person commits an offense under subsection (a) involving a financial transaction that occurs in whole or in part in the United States;

(B) the foreign person converts, to his or her own use, property in which the United States has an ownership interest by virtue of the entry of an order of forfeiture by a court of the United States; or

(c) the foreign person is a financial institution that maintains a bank account at a financial institution in the United States.

(3) Court authority over assets – A court described in paragraph (2) may issue a pretrial restraining order or take any other action necessary to ensure that any bank account or other property held by the defendant in the United States is available to satisfy a judgment under this section.

Section 1957. Engaging in monetary transactions in property derived from specified unlawful activity

(a) Whoever, in any of the circumstances set forth in subsection (d), knowingly engages or attempts to engage in a monetary transaction in criminally derived property of a value greater than $10,000 and is derived from specified unlawful activity, shall be punished as provided in subsection (b).

(b)(1) Except as provided in paragraph (2), the punishment for an offense under this section is a fine under title 18, United States Code, or imprisonment for not more than ten years or both.

(2) The court may impose an alternate fine to that imposable under paragraph (1) of not more than twice the amount of the criminally derived property involved in the transaction.

(c) In a prosecution for an offense under this section, the Government is not required to prove the defendant knew that the offense from which the criminally derived property was derived was specified unlawful activity.

(d) The circumstances referred to in subsection (a) are –

(1) that the offense under this section takes place in the United States or in the special maritime and territorial jurisdiction of the United States; or

(2) that the offense under this section takes place outside the United States and such special jurisdiction, but the defendant is a United States person (as defined in section 3077 of this title, but excluding the class described in paragraph (2)(D) of such section).

(e) Violations of this section may be investigated by such components of the Department of Justice as the Attorney General may direct, and by such components of the Department of the Treasury as the Secretary of the Treasury may direct, as appropriate and, with respect to offenses over which the United States Postal Service has jurisdiction, by the Postal Service. Such authority of the Secretary of the Treasury and the Postal Service shall be exercised in accordance with an agreement which shall be entered into by the Secretary of the Treasury, the Postal Service, and the Attorney General.

(f) As used in this section

(1) the term "monetary transaction" means the deposit, withdrawal, transfer, or exchange, in or affecting interstate or foreign commerce, of funds or a monetary instrument (as defined in section 1956(c)(5) of this title) by, through, or to a financial institution (as defined in section 1956 of this title), including any transaction that would be a financial transaction under section 1956(c)(4)(B) of this title, but such term does not include any transaction necessary to preserve a person's right to representation as guaranteed by the sixth amendment to the Constitution;

(2) the term "criminally derived property" means any property constituting, or derived from, proceeds obtained from a criminal offense; and

(3) the term "specified unlawful activity" has the meaning given that term in section 1956 of this title.

Notes and Questions

1. Should 18 U.S.C. § 1956(a)(2)(A), the promotion provision, be construed to criminalize the transfer of funds that is merely incidental to the commission of specified unlawful activity or, instead, be limited to conduct intended to reinvest monetary instruments or funds into the criminal enterprise? Which interpretation of the statute is more consistent with the congressional intent in enacting the Money Laundering Control Act?

2. How might substantial differences in definitions and concepts in money laundering laws affect efforts to render international enforcement cooperation (e.g., mutual assistance or extradition)?

I. *Transparency of Legal Persons and Arrangements*

FATF R. 33. Countries should take measures to prevent the unlawful use of legal persons by money launderers. Countries should ensure that there is adequate, accurate, and timely information on the beneficial ownership and control of legal persons that can be obtained or accessed in a timely fashion by competent authorities. In particular, countries that have legal persons that are able to use bearer shares should take appropriate measures to ensure that they are not misused for money laundering and be able to demonstrate the adequacy of those measures. Countries could consider measures to facilitate access to beneficial ownership and control information to financial institutions undertaking the requirements set out in Recommendation 5.

Notes and Questions

1. Improving the transparency of corporate vehicles has been one of the OECD's major initiatives. The OECD has published standards on transparency of corporate vehicles, for which it strives to obtain pledges from countries to adhere to such standards, and provides the framework for peer review of fulfilling the standards. There is much interaction among transparency efforts for AML, tax, and anticorruption laws. *See, e.g.*, OECD Committee on Fiscal Affairs, Improving Access to Bank Information for Tax Purposes (Mar. 24, 2000); OECD, Harmful Tax Competition: An Emerging Global Issue (1998), esp. 28–30, 33; c.f., Stikeman Elliott, Towards a Level Playing Field: Regulating Corporate Vehicles in Cross-Border Transactions (I.T.I.O. and STEP); STEP, Beyond the Level Playing Field? Lowering Barriers to Trade in Financial Services between International Financial Centres and OECD States (2006).

J. *Asset Forfeiture*

1988 U.N. Convention against Illicit Traffic in Narcotic Drugs and Psychotropic Substances, Art. 5

Confiscation

1. Each Party shall adopt such measures as may be necessary to enable confiscation of:

a. Proceeds derived from offenses established in accordance with Article 3, paragraph 1, or property the value of which corresponds to that of such proceeds;

b. Narcotic drugs and psychotropic substances, materials and equipment or other instrumentalities used in or intended for use in any manner in offenses established in accordance with Article 3, paragraph 1.

2. Each Party shall also adopt such measures as may be necessary to enable its competent authorities to identify, trace, and freeze or seize proceeds, property, instrumentalities or any other things referred to in paragraph 1 of this article, for the purpose of eventual confiscation.

3. In order to carry out the measures referred to in this article, each party shall empower its courts or other competent authorities to order that bank, financial or commercial records be made available or be seized. A Party shall not decline to act under the provisions of this paragraph on the ground of bank secrecy . . .

5. a. Proceeds or property confiscated by a Party pursuant to paragraph 1 or paragraph 4 of this article shall be disposed of by that Party according to its domestic law and administrative procedures.

6. a. If proceeds have been transformed or converted into other property, such property shall be liable to the measures referred to in this article instead of the proceeds.

b. If proceeds have been intermingled with property acquired from legitimate sources, such property shall, without prejudice to any powers relating to seizure of freezing, be liable to confiscation up to the assessed value of the intermingled proceeds . . .

7. Each Party may consider ensuring that the onus of proof be reversed regarding the lawful origin of alleged proceeds or other property liable to confiscation, to the extent that such action is consistent with the principles of its domestic law and with the nature of the judicial and other proceedings.

8. The provisions of this article shall not be construed as prejudicing the rights of *bona fide* third parties.

FATF R. 3 Provisional Measures and Confiscation. Countries should adopt measures similar to those set forth in the Vienna and Palermo Conventions, including legislative measures, to enable their competent authorities to confiscate property laundered, proceeds from money laundering or predicate offenses, instrumentalities used in or intended for use in the commission of these offenses, or property of corresponding value, without prejudicing the rights of bona fide third parties.

Such measures should include the authority to: (a) identify, trace, and evaluate property which is subject to confiscation; (b) carry out provisional measures, such as freezing and seizing, to prevent any dealing, transfer or disposal of such property; (c) take steps that will prevent or void actions that prejudice the State's ability to recover property that is subject to confiscation; and (d) take any appropriate investigative measures.

Countries may consider adopting measures that allow such proceeds or instrumentalities to be confiscated without requiring a criminal conviction, or which require an offender to demonstrate the lawful origin of the property alleged to be liable to confiscation, to the extent that such a requirement is consistent with the principles of their domestic law.

Notes and Questions

1. Confiscation of criminal proceeds is a useful tool enabling law enforcement to pay for itself; it can both reinforce the effectiveness of existing AML and other criminal programs and permit initiatives to occur that might not otherwise have been possible. *See* William C. Gilmore, Dirty Money: The Evolution of Money Laundering Counter-Measures 73 (1995). For a discussion of the political dimension of forfeiture, *see* Bruce Zagaris, *Constructing a Financial Enforcement Regime to Reallocate Assets*

from the "Bad Guys" to the "Good Guys," in Gray Area Phenomenon: Confronting the New World Disorder 93, 39–108 (Max G. Manwaring ed., 1993).

2. The U.S. approach to asset forfeiture has been the most aggressive, providing for forfeitures in both criminal and civil proceedings. Seizures in either type of proceeding depend on a final determination that seizure is warranted. Otherwise these proceedings differ significantly. Jurisdiction for civil forfeiture rests on the property's location; it is an *in rem* procedure, and the property must be seized in order to obtain jurisdiction. Civil forfeiture also carries a lower burden of proof to obtain a forfeiture order. Once the government shows probable cause to believe that the property is subject to forfeiture, the burden shifts to the defendant to show that the property should not be forfeited. Criminal forfeiture's jurisdiction is *in personam*; the defendant must be within the court's jurisdictional reach. The burden of proof to obtain a forfeiture order in a criminal proceeding is also more rigorous and so more difficult to obtain. Accordingly, a criminal conviction is not required to forfeit assets in the United States; civil forfeiture orders do not rest on a conviction, only on a showing that the preponderance of the evidence indicates that the property is related to the predicate crime. *See* Elizabeth Kingma, *The Emerging Regime of Asset Forfeiture, in* International Handbook on Drug Control 45, 55–6 (Scott B. MacDonald & Bruce Zagaris eds., 1992). For a useful discussion of the procedural differences between U.S. civil and criminal forfeiture, *see* Robert Luskin, *Forfeiture Statutes: A Brief Survey and History*; Michael Zeldin & Roger G. Weiner, *Forfeiture and Third Party Rights: The Rights and Scope of Recovery of Innocent Third Parties*; Michael Goldsmith & Mark Jay Linderman, *Asset Forfeiture and Third Party Rights: The Need for Further Law Reform*, all *in* Forfeitures and Asset Freezes: A Comprehensive Survey of Asset Forfeiture, Restraints and Third-Party Rights (A.B.A. Nat'l Institute, Criminal Justice Sec., Dec. 3–4, 1990).

3. One concern about asset forfeiture is its potential adverse impact on the fairness of the criminal justice system, because law enforcement's ability to use the proceeds of predicate offenses and instrumentalities give it a stake in ensuring the forfeiture of property, notwithstanding the link with the illicit proceeds or instrumentalities. *See* Gilmore, *supra* note 1, at 73.

4. On November 20, 2008, the European Commission issued a Communication on the need and recent efforts to strengthen the confiscation and recovery of the proceeds of crime in the EU. It calls for the establishment of uniform and effective asset recovery offices and extending the EU confiscation regime, including facilitating civil confiscation, creating a new criminal offense for owning "unjustified" assets, expanding the scope of mandatory confiscation, enforcing the obligation to provide information on bank accounts, and requiring strengthened cooperation among national authorities. *See*, European Commission, Ensuring That Crime "Does Not Pay." Commission Proposes Ten Strategic Priorities on Confiscation and Recovery of Criminal Proceeds, 18/8/1748. Nov. 20, 2008.

III. Substantive Components of Counterterrorism Financial Enforcement

Article 2 of the International Convention for the Suppression of the Financing of Terrorism (1999)

1. Any person commits an offense within the meaning of this Convention if that person by any means, directly or indirectly, unlawfully and willingly, provides or collects funds with the

intention that they should be used or in the knowledge that they are to be used, in full or in part, in order to carry out:

(a) An act which constitutes an offense within the scope of and as defined in one of the treaties listed in the annex, or
(b) Any other act intended to cause death or serious bodily injury to a civilian, or to any other person not taking an active part in the hostilities in a situation of armed conflict when the purpose of such act, by its nature or context, is to intimidate a population, or to compel a government or international organization to do or abstain from doing an act.

3. For an act to constitute an offense set forth in paragraph 1, it shall not be necessary that the funds were actually used to carry out an offense referred to in paragraph 1, subparagraph (a) or (b).

Unfortunately, the countries that have adopted the convention have yet to agree on a consensus definition of terrorism. Because significant political, religious, and national implications vary among countries, the meaning of terrorism is not universally accepted.

The substantive components of counterterrorism financial enforcement (CTFE) include FAFT's Nine Special Recommendations (SR) on Terrorist Financing:

FAFT Special Recommendation I. Ratification and implementation of UN instruments. Each country should take immediate steps to ratify and to implement fully the 1999 United Nations International Convention for the Suppression of the Financing of Terrorism.

Countries should also immediately implement the United Nations resolutions relating to the prevention and suppression of the financing of terrorist acts, particularly United Nations Security Council resolution 1373.

SR II Criminalizing the financing of terrorism. Each country should criminalize the financing of terrorism, terrorist acts, and terrorist organizations. Countries should ensure that such offenses are designated as money laundering predicate offenses.

SR III. Freezing and confiscating terrorist assets. Each country should implement measures to freeze without delay funds or other assets of terrorists, those who finance terrorism and terrorist organizations in accordance with the United Nations resolutions relating to the prevention and suppression of the financing of terrorist acts.

Each country should also adopt and implement measures, including legislative ones, which would enable the competent authorities to seize and confiscate property that is the proceeds of, or used in, or intended or allocated for use in, the financing of terrorism, terrorist acts or terrorist organizations.

SR VIII. Nonprofit organizations. Countries should review the adequacy of laws and regulations that relate to entities that can be abused for the financing of terrorism. Nonprofit organizations are particularly vulnerable, and countries should ensure that they cannot be misused:

i. by terrorist organizations posing as legitimate entities;
ii. to exploit legitimate entities as conduits for terrorist financing, including for the purposes of escaping asset freezing measures; and
iii. To conceal or obscure the clandestine diversion of funds intended for legitimate purposes to terrorist organizations.

The USA PATRIOT ACT has expanded the ability of the U.S. government to seize foreign assets and give assistance to foreign governments wanting to seize assets in the U.S.

Section 319 amends U.S. asset forfeiture law. In particular, it amends 18 U.S.C. §981 to treat funds deposited by foreign banks in interbank accounts with U.S. banks as having been deposited in the United States for purposes of the forfeiture rules. It grants the Attorney General authority, in the interest of justice consistent with the United States' national interest, to suspend a forfeiture proceeding, based on that presumption (that such interbank accounts are deposited in the United States and hence subject to U.S. jurisdiction). U.S. financial institutions must request information from a U.S. regulator relating to anti-money laundering compliance within 120 days receipt of such a request, and requires foreign banks that maintain correspondent accounts in the United States to appoint agents for service of process within the United States. The Attorney General and Secretary of the Treasury are authorized to issue a summons or subpoena to any such foreign bank, seeking records, wherever located, relating to such a correspondent account, and it requires U.S. banks with correspondent arrangements with foreign banks that do not either comply with or contest any subpoenas to provide to appropriate federal banking agencies information and account documentation for any account opened, maintained, administered, or managed in the United States by the financial institution. U.S. courts are given authority to order a convicted criminal to return property located abroad and to order a civil forfeiture defendant to return property located abroad pending trial on the merits.

Section 320 of the USA PATRIOT ACT amends 18 U.S.C. §981 to allow the United States to institute forfeiture proceedings against the proceeds of foreign predicate offenses found in the United States.

Section 323 allows the government to seek a restraining order to preserve the availability of property subject to a foreign forfeiture confiscation judgment.

Notes and Questions

1. The UN and regional (i.e., OAS) counterterrorist conventions and UN Security Council resolutions all reinforce the obligations of governments to adopt laws criminalizing terrorist financing violations, requiring financial institutions and other covered persons to take preventive (i.e., due diligence) measures and to provide international and judicial assistance to other governments in counterterrorist investigations and prosecutions.

2. In the United States President Bush issued the Executive Order on asset forfeiture under the International Emergency Economic Powers Act (IEEPA),[28] section 5 of the United Nations Participation Act of 1945, as amended (UNPA),[29] and section 301 of title 3, U.S. Code. President Bush also cited as legal bases UN Security Council Resolution (UNSCR) 1214 of December 8, 1998; UNSCR 1267 of October 15, 1999; UNSCR 1333 of December 19, 2000, and multilateral sanctions contained therein; and UNSCR 1363 of July 30, 2001, establishing a mechanism to monitor the implementation of UNSCR 1333.

Because many of the terrorist groups and individuals operate primarily overseas or have little money in the United States, the U.S. government has notified foreign governments that do not freeze or block terrorists' ability to access their foreign funds and share information that it has the authority to freeze their banks' U.S. assets and transactions. Legally the Executive Order authorizes this action by empowering "persons determined by the Secretary of the Treasury, in consultation with the Secretary of State and the

[28] 50 U.S.C. § 1701 et seq.
[29] 22 U.S.C. § 287c.

Attorney General," and "after such consultation, if any, with foreign authorities as the Secretary of State, in consultation with the Secretary of the Treasury and the Attorney General, deems appropriate, in the exercise of his discretion."

The following persons are subject to the blocking order:

(1) foreign persons determined by the Secretary of State to have committed, or to pose a significant risk of committing, acts of terrorism that threaten the security of U.S. nationals or the national security, foreign policy, or economy of the United States; (2) persons determined by the Secretary of Treasury to be owned or controlled by, or to act for or on behalf of any persons listed under the Order or any other persons determined to be subject to it; (3) persons determined by the Secretary of Treasury to assist in, sponsor, or provide financial, material, or technological support for, or financial or other services to or in support of, such acts of terrorism or those persons listed under the Order or determined to be subject to it; (4) persons determined by the Secretary of Treasury to be otherwise associated with those persons listed under the Order or determined to be subject to it.[30]

The Executive Order's other principal prohibitions include (1) no transaction or dealing by U.S. persons (including their overseas branches, but not their foreign subsidiaries) or within the United States in blocked property; (2) prohibition against U.S. persons or persons in the United States from evading or avoiding, or attempting to evade or avoid any of the Order's prohibitions; (3) prohibition against any conspiracy to violate any of the Order's prohibitions; and (4) prohibition against donations intended to relieve human suffering to persons listed under the Order or determined to be subject to it.[31]

Practically speaking, the new terrorist sanctions largely overlap existing U.S. terrorist sanctions administered by the Office of Foreign Assets Control (OFAC); that is, the Terrorism Sanctions Regulations (31 CFR Part 595) and the Foreign Terrorist Organizations Regulations (31 CFR Part 597). Under the Terrorism Sanctions Regulations, OFAC has blocked the property of persons posing a significant risk of disrupting the Middle East peace process. Under the Foreign Terrorist Organizations Regulations, U.S. financial institutions must block all funds in which foreign terrorist organizations have an interest. Most of the persons listed in President Bush's September 23, 2001, Executive Order are already listed as Specially Designated Terrorists under Part 595 or as Foreign Terrorist Organizations under Part 597.

The new sanctions significantly enlarge existing sanctions. First, they are broader than the Terrorism Sanctions Regulations because they extend beyond terrorists who pose a significant risk of disrupting the Middle East peace process. Second and most important they are broader than the Foreign Terrorism Organization Regulations in that they require blocking actions against all U.S. persons, not just U.S. financial institutions. Third, the new sanctions make it easier to designate terrorists because anyone "associated" with terrorists can be listed. As mentioned above, the Bush administration intended to block the U.S. assets of and bar U.S. market access to foreign banks that could be linked to terrorists in any way and that refused to freeze terrorists' assets. Previously, the United

[30] Ben H. Flowe, Jr. & Ray Gold, *President Bush Waives Glenn Amendment Sanctions against India and Pakistan and Imposes Additional Sanctions against Terrorists, Export Licensing Client Memo*, Sept. 24, 2001 (available by subscription from RayGold@bcr-dc.com).

[31] *Id.*

States has had difficulty in convincing its allies and foreign banks to impose sanctions on terrorists.

Foreign subsidiaries of U.S. companies will now deal with terrorists at their peril. Although they appear to be beyond the scope of the Executive Order, any link between a foreign subsidiary and a terrorist could be treated as an "association" warranting sanctions.[32]

3. For an excellent background and reference guide to AML/CTFE, *see* PAUL ALLAN SCHOTT, REFERENCE GUIDE TO ANTI-MONEY LAUNDERING AND COMBATING THE FINANCING OF TERRORISM (2004 World Bank).

4. On the overall AML policy, *see* PETER REUTER & EDWIN M. TRUMAN, CHASING DIRTY MONEY: THE FIGHT AGAINST MONEY LAUNDERING (2004 Instit. for Int'l Economics). They describe the activity of money laundering and provide an overview of the global AML regime as it has evolved over the past fifteen years. The authors assess the regime's effectiveness in addressing three underlying goals: reducing crime, protecting the integrity of the core financial system, and controlling three types of global "public bads" – terrorism, corruption, and failed states. The authors conclude with recommendations for improvement in the U.S. and global AML regime during its next phase, which will probably be one of consolidation after the rapid expansion of the regime to date. They argue that the global AML regime needs to be strengthened through development of a systematic research program using economic tools, starting with more sophisticated assessment of its costs. Another important research-related activity is the creation of a database of existing cases that provides a detailed description of the prices, methods, and predicate crimes involved. This would represent a first step in analyzing the existence and mechanisms of the market for money laundering services.

5. For background and legislative draft guidance on CTFE, *see* IMF LEGAL DEPARTMENT, SUPPRESSING THE FINANCING OF TERRORISM: A HANDBOOK FOR LEGISLATIVE DRAFTING (2003 IMF); Criminal Law Unit, Legal and Constitutional Affairs Division, Commonwealth Secretariat, REPORT OF EXPERT WORKING GROUP ON LEGISLATIVE AND ADMINISTRATIVE MEASURES TO COMBAT TERRORISM (Feb. 2002).

6. To protect against nonprofit organizations' facilitation of terrorism financing, international organizations and governments have issued regulations and guidelines for due diligence in dealing with such organizations. *See, e.g.*, FATF, Combating the Abuse of Non-Profit Organizations (international best practices at http://www.fatg-gafi.org/pd/SR8-NPO_en.pdf (11 Oct. 2002); European Commission, Draft Recommendations to Member States Regarding a Code of Conduct for Non-Profit Organizations to Promote Transparency and Accountability Best Practices, (JLS/D2/DB/NSK D92005) 8208, July 22, 2005, discussed in Bruce Zagaris, *EU Issues Draft Recommendations on Code of Conduct for Non-Profit Organizations*, 21 INT'L ENFORCEMENT L. REP. 433 (Nov. 2005); U.S. Department of Treasury, *Protecting Charitable Organizations* (it contains various individual discussions of nonprofit organizations and terrorism financing), http://www.treas.gov/offices/enforcement/key-issues/protecting/charities_exec-orders.shtml.

6. Several periodicals discuss money laundering laws and policies, including MONEY LAUNDERING ALERT; LAVADODINERO.COM (Spanish language), KYC NEWS, and the ABA's MONEY LAUNDERING AND TERRORISM ISSUES UPDATE (the American Bankers Association newsletter).

[32] *Id.*

7. For background information on U.S. AML laws *see* PETER G. DJINIS & CHARLES A. INTRIAGO, ABC'S OF THE UNITED STATES ANTI-MONEY LAUNDERING REGULATIONS AND LAW (Alert Global Media, 1st ed. 2003).

8. For a discussion of comparative and international money laundering laws, *see* GUY STESSENS, MONEY LAUNDERING A NEW INTERNATIONAL LAW ENFORCEMENT MODEL (2000 Cambridge U. Press) (analyzing the legal issues raised by international anti-money laundering, especially comparative criminal and preventive law aspects from an international perspective).

9. For a discussion of Latin American AML laws *see* RICARDO M. ALBA, PROGRAMA Y MANUAL UNIFORME PARA LA PREVENCIÓN Y CONTROL DEL LAVADO DE ACTIVOS EN AMÉRICA LATINA (2004–2005).

Hypotheticals

1. Mr. B. is retired from a Big Four Accounting Firm, where he was the head of the firm's Latin American practice. He retired to the Bahamas where he still consults for clients. He also has a flat in London, where he works periodically. He was approached by Mr. A., the advisor of Mr. Rodriquez, a high-net-worth individual who currently lives in Lebanon. The individual also has ranches in Colombia, currency exchange shops on the Brazilian-Paraguayan border, export-import businesses throughout the world, and restaurants and entertainment venues. Mr. A. originally wanted to visit Mr. B. when he heard Mr. B. would be in London, especially because Mr. A. and his wife wanted to attend the theater there. However, when Mr. B. heard of the nature of the consulting, he said he would prefer to defer the meeting to when he returned to the Bahamas, because it could be more leisurely and face fewer potential regulatory issues.

Mr. A. requests help in structuring about $10 million worth of investments, including some U.S. investments. He is very concerned about financial privacy. In particular, he notes that he is accustomed to using multitiered corporations in jurisdictions like the Bahamas that have traditionally protected privacy; he is also accustomed to using bearer shares. He also expresses an interest in minimizing taxes and avoiding the bureaucractic hassle of filing reports to governments. In particular, he says he needs privacy because he is a prominent entrepreneur and is active politically in Lebanon, his son was kidnapped last year by Israeli security or intelligence sources, and he is estranged from his wife but not yet divorced. Mr. A. promises that, because Mr. Rodriquez and his cohorts are "cash cows," there will be many more investments and much more money if Mr. A. is successful, at least in protecting his privacy.

Because Mr. Rodriquez is originally from Colombia, he has been confused with someone else who is on an OFAC list. Because he comes from Lebanon, he is concerned about potential discrimination against persons from the Middle East. Additionally the kidnapping of his son together with the OFAC issue has made him ask Mr. A. for a referral to a U.S. lawyer familiar with the operation of U.S. law enforcement and financial intelligence.

Mr. A. heard that in the 1970s Mr. B. structured a trust in the Bahamas, using an accommodation settlor. The trust required a Bahamian trustee and protectors. The trust held shares of a Bahamian company that invested successfully in some very profitable ventures and simultaneously maintained the anonymity of the investors. The trustees even refused the requests of the settlor and others for information when tax authorities demanded information from the settlors.

Mr. B. says he can help. He contacts his longstanding friend at one of the leading investor advisor firms and seeks help with investment documentation and asset management.

Mr. B. also consults his longstanding friend at a U.K. law firm to advise on some aspects of the deal. Because Mr. A. wants some U.S. investments and has asked for legal advice on the intelligence issues, Mr. B. calls a friend at a U.S. law firm to advise about structuring U.S. investments. Please discuss the privacy, anti-money laundering, ethical, and related issues of this hypothetical.

2. The ABC Law Firm is a small general practice firm in the Midwest. It is in a county seat of a rural area. Mr. X., a U.S. client, requests tax planning advice from one of the ABC attorneys whose practice includes tax. Mr. X. has not been a client of the firm, but his restaurant is a client. It offers Lebanese cuisine and has done well over the last ten years. Mr. X. and his family have been model citizens in the community. He wants to minimize his tax base by making some charitable donations, including some appreciated stock. One of the potential donees is the Islamic Foundation in Houston, Texas, to which he wants to make a large donation (e.g., $100,000). The other donees are family members, including his parents in Lebanon. Mr. X. asks for advice on tax and business planning aspects. Mr. X. does not want the ABC Law Firm to spend much time on this request and specifically asks for a quote before ABC starts to bill. Should any of these facts require anti-money laundering due diligence and, if so, what kinds? Should the circumstances constitute "suspicious circumstances?"

3. Later Mr. X. returns to the ABC Law Firm and requests the attorney who specializes in international business to review arrangements for an exchange program whereby his two sons will study abroad in Lebanon for one year. As part of the program, Mr. X. has to sign some agreements on housing and the contract for enrollment in the school in Lebanon. Should any of these actions require anti-money laundering (AML) due diligence? What if the school is in Pakistan? Or Saudi Arabia? Or Yemen? Or Egypt? Does the ABC Law Firm have to inquire about the type of study? Does it matter if the school is a strictly religious school?

IV. *Additional Reading*

A. *Books*

Stefan D. Cassella, Asset Forfeiture Law in the United States (JurisNet, LLC, 2007).

Dee R. Edgeworth, Asset Forfeiture Practice and Procedure in State and Federal Courts (ABA Criminal Justice Section, 2d ed. 2008).

William C. Gilmore, Dirty Money: The Evolution of Money Laundering Counter-measures (Council of Europe Press, 1995).

Jimmy Gurulé, Unfunding Terror: The Legal Response to the Funding of Global Terrorism (Edward Elgar 2008).

IMF, Suppressing the Financing of Terrorism: A Handbook of Legislative Drafting (2003).

IMF/World Bank Group, Financial Intelligence Units: An Overview (2004).

Jeffrey Robinson, the laundrymen: Inside money laundering, the World's Third Largest Business (Arcade Publishing, 1996).

Robert E. Powis, the Money Launderers: Lessons from the Drug Wars – How Billions of Illegal Dollars are Washed through Banks and Business (Probus Publishing Co., 1992).

Peter Reuter & Edwin M. Truman, Chasing Dirty Money: The Fight against Money Laundering (Institute for International Economics 2004).

Paul Allan Schott, Reference Guide to Anti-Money Laundering and Combating the Financing of Terrorism III-3, III-4 (2002).

Guy Stessens, Money Laundering: A New International Law Enforcement Model (Cambridge Univ. Press 2000).

INGO WALTER, THE SECRET MONEY MARKET: INSIDE THE DARK WORLD OF TAX EVASION, FINANCIAL FRAUD, INSIDER TRADING, MONEY LAUNDERING, AND CAPITAL FLIGHT (Harper & Row, 1990).

B. Articles

Edward J. Krauland & Stephane Lagonico, *Lawyers and Anti-Money Laundering: The Gatekeeper Initiative*, 31 INT'L. LAW NEWS (Fall 2002).

Kevin L. Shepherd, *USA PATRIOT Act and the Gatekeeper Initiative: Surprising Implications for Transactional Lawyers*, Section of Real Property, Probate, and Trust Law PROBATE & PROPERTY (September/October 2002).

Bruce Zagaris, *Gatekeepers Initiative: Seeking Middle Ground between Client and Government*, 18 CRIM. JUSTICE MAG. (Winter 2002).

Bruce Zagaris, *The Gatekeeper Initiative: An Emerging Challenge for International Financial Advisors*, 2001 Worldwide Tax Daily 82–2, 22 TAX NOTES INT'L 2293–98 (May 7, 2001).

Bruce Zagaris & Sheila M. Castilla, *Constructing an International Financial Enforcement Regime: The Implementation of Anti-Money-Laundering Policy*, 19 BROOK. J. INT'L L. 871 (1993).

4 Transnational Corruption

I. Introduction[1]

In 1977, Congress enacted the Foreign Corrupt Practices Act (FCPA). For many years, as a result of the FCPA, the United States was the only country with laws actively prohibiting its citizens, nationals, businesses, and, in some circumstances, foreign companies that participate in its capital markets from bribing foreign officials.

Since the passage of the FCPA, a number of international initiatives and conventions have resulted in widespread laws prohibiting bribery and improper inducement of foreign officials in connection with business transactions. Beginning in 1995, several international conventions addressing transnational corruption have entered into force. As a result, the hard law requirements preventing and criminalizing participation in transnational corruption have greatly multiplied. In addition, international organizations and civil society groups have joined to require corporate governance initiatives focusing on antibribery and anticorruption measures.

In recent years, corruption scandals have contributed to the downfall of governments in Ecuador, Brazil,[2] Italy, Trinidad and Tobago,[3] and India. They have weakened long-entrenched ruling parties, including Japan's Liberal Democratic Party and Mexico's

[1] The author is grateful to Michael McCullough, Director of the Latin America and Caribbean Division, American Bar Association, for his comments and suggestions on this chapter.

[2] Corruption and Political Reform in Brazil: The Impact of Collor's Impeachment (Keith S. Rosenn & Richard Downes eds.), (1999).

[3] Bruce Zagaris, *Trinidad Energy Minister Resigns due to Bribery Charges*, 22 Int'l Enforcement L. Rep. 102 (Mar. 2006).

Institutional Revolutionary Party. In the United States, two decades after the Watergate scandals prompted new rules concerning political contributions and the enactment of FCPA, campaign finance reform has reemerged as a major political issue.[4]

The number and variety of countries facing corruption scandals highlight the complexity and prominence of corruption as a global issue. Pervasive and uncontrolled corruption thwarts economic development and undermines political legitimacy. Less pervasive corruption results in wasted resources, increased inequity in resource distribution, diminished political competition, and greater distrust of government. Establishing and exploiting opportunities for bribery at high levels of government can also increase the cost of government, distort the allocation of government spending, and dangerously lower the quality of infrastructure. Even relatively petty or routine corruption can deprive a government of revenues, distort economic decision making, and impose negative externalities such as increased pollution on society.[5] Increasingly anticorruption interacts with many other international white collar crime subject areas, such as money laundering, taxation, and organized crime.

This chapter is divided into three parts: the first, focusing on U.S. law, and the second, covering international conventions and standards. The third presents a series of hypothetical problems.

II. U.S. Law and the Foreign Corrupt Practices Act

The FCPA has two principal mechanisms addressing inducements to foreign officials concerning business activities. One is a prohibition on payments to foreign officials that is applicable to U.S. nationals, U.S. businesses, publicly held companies, many foreign companies with links to the United States, and, in certain circumstances, almost anyone, provided the United States has jurisdiction. As mentioned in Chapter 7, U.S. asserts very broad extraterritorial jurisdiction. The second mechanism imposes accounting and recordkeeping requirements on the domestic and foreign operations of publicly held companies.

The FCPA, which was initially enacted in 1977, was amended in 1988 and 1998. Although its purpose and language seem uncomplicated, the act's scope and means of application present complex questions for practitioners.

A. *The Antibribery Provisions of the FCPA*

§ 78DD-1. Prohibited Foreign Trade Practices by Issues

(A) Prohibition

It shall be unlawful for any issuer which has a class of securities registered pursuant to section 78l of this title or which is required to file reports under section 78o(d) of this title, or for

[4] Kimberly Ann Elliott, *Corruption as an International Policy Problem: Overview and Recommendations in*, Corruption and the Global Economy 175 (Kimberly Ann Elliott ed., 1997). R. Jeffrey Smith, *DeLay Indicted in Texas Finance Probe*, Wash. Post, Sept. 29, 2005, at A1; Susan Schmidt & James V. Grimaldi, *Abramoff Pleads Guilty to 3 Counts*, Wash. Post, Jan. 4, 2006, at A1.

[5] *Id.* at 175–76. Sahr J. Kpundeh & Irene Hors, *Overview, in* Corruption & Integrity Improvement Initiatives in Developing Countries 7, 11(UNDP, 1998).

any officer, director, employee, or agent of such issuer or any stockholder thereof acting on behalf of such issuer, to make use of the mails or any means or instrumentality of interstate commerce corruptly in furtherance of an offer, payment, promise to pay, or authorization of the payment of any money, or offer, gift, promise to give, or authorization of the giving of anything of value to

(1) any foreign official for purposes of

(A) (i) influencing any act or decision of such foreign official in his official capacity (ii) inducing such foreign official to do or omit to do any act in violation of the lawful duty of such official, or (iii) securing any improper advantage; or

(B) inducing such foreign official to use his influence with a foreign government or instrumentality thereof to affect or influence any act or decision of such government or instrumentality,

in order to assist such issuer in obtaining or retaining business for or with, or directing business to, any person;

(2) any foreign political party or official thereof or any candidate for foreign political office for purposes of

(A) (i) influencing any act or decision of such party, official, or candidate in its or his official capacity, (ii) inducing such party, official, or candidate to do or omit to do an act in violation of the lawful duty of such party, official, or candidate, or (iii) securing any improper advantage; or

(B) inducing such foreign official, political party, party official, or candidate to use influence with a foreign government or instrumentality thereof to affect or influence any act or decision of such government or instrumentality,

in order to assist such issuer in obtaining or retaining business or with, or directing business to, any person; or

(3) any person, while knowing that all or a portion of such money or thing of value will be offered, given, or promised, directly or indirectly, to any foreign official, to any foreign political party or official thereof, or to any candidate for foreign political office, for purposes . . .

(b) Exception for Routine Governmental Action

Subsections (a) and (g) of this section shall not apply to any facilitating or expediting payment to a foreign official, political party, or party official the purpose of which is to expedite or to secure the performance of a routine governmental action by a foreign official, political party or party official.

(c) Affirmative Defenses

It shall be an affirmative defense to actions under subsection (a) or (g) of this section that

(1) the payment, gift, offer, or promise of anything of value that was made, was lawful under the written laws and regulations of the foreign official's, political party's, party official's, or candidate's country; or

(2) the payment, gift, offer, or promise of anything of value that was made, was a reasonable and bona fide expenditure, such as travel and lodging expenses, incurred by or on behalf of a foreign official, party, party official, or candidate and was directly related to:

(A) the promotion, demonstration, or explanation of products or services; or
(B) the execution or performance of a contract with a foreign government or agency thereof.

1. Essential Elements of the Antibribery Provisions of the FCPA

The essential elements of the FCPA's antibribery provisions are as follows:

- A payment, offer, or promise of
- Anything of value
- To any
  - foreign official
  - foreign political party or party official,
  - candidate for foreign political office, or
  - other person while knowing that all or part of the payment or promise to pay will be passed on to one of the foregoing;
- With corrupt intent;
- For the purpose of
- influencing an official act or decision of the person
  - inducing that person to do or omit to do any act in violation of his or her lawful duty;
  - inducing that person to use his influence with a foreign government
  - to affect or influence any government act or decision; or
  - to assist in obtaining or retaining business for or with, or directing business to any person.

2. Jurisdiction

The jurisdiction of the FCPA's antibribery provisions is quite extensive. The provisions apply to "domestic concerns" and "issuers," and to any person, including foreign individuals and entities, acting in furtherance of the improper inducement of a foreign public official while in U.S. territory. Application of the U.S. territorial principle requires some connection to U.S. territory for the prohibited activity to be subject to U.S. laws. For instance, any matter involving U.S. interstate or foreign commerce gives rise to U.S. jurisdiction.

In 1998, Congress extended the FCPA to include the nationality principle as a basis for jurisdiction. As a result, jurisdiction can be based solely on the status of an individual as a U.S. national or when an entity is established under U.S. laws or has its principal place or business in the United States. Hence, the United States can assert the FCPA on the basis of the principles of nationality or territoriality or both.

The antibribery provisions address a separate category of inducers: issuers, domestic concerns, and any individual or entity acting within the territory of the United States in furtherance of a prohibited inducement.

3. Payment, Offer, or Promise: A Hypothetical

Mr. X., a U.S. businessman, visits Assistant Deputy Minister (ADM) from Country Y with which X.'s company has had a contract for five years. The contract is expiring. He brings the ADM some company products, namely a corporate pen, t-shirt, and mouse pad. Mr. X. tells the ADM that he wants his company to win the contract again, when it is relet. In fact, because Mr. X.'s children and ADM's children have become well acquainted, he promises, if he is able to visit Country Y again to attend the ceremony of the announcement of the new contract, he will take both his own and ADM's children on a skiing trip they have discussed for some months. Is that promise proscribed by the FCPA? Why? Is bringing the ADM products of the company proscribed by the FCPA? Why?

4. Anything of Value

The FCPA construes very broadly the definition of "anything of value." Value can include scholarships for family members, upgrades to first-class or business airfare, trips to resorts, employing a family member for an internship, and allowing an official to designate to whom charitable contributions are directed, especially if the official has a connection to the charity. Indeed, value will often depend on the particular circumstances. In some impoverished countries a token gift may be enough to influence decision making. It is important to observe that the FCPA has no *de minimis* exception.

5. Foreign Officials

The prohibitions against making or offering inducements to foreign officials apply to all branches of government as well as to all units of governments, including the civil service and political functions in countries where they are separated. It makes no difference whether the public official is paid or unpaid. The pivotal question is whether the inducement is in any way connected with the individual's power to exert influence in an official capacity.

Hypothetical: Ms. A., an agent of a U.S. Company, offers an inducement to the assistant treasurer of Party A, which has a fighting chance to win the national election, in exchange for consideration on some energy concession contracts. Does this action pose any problem under the FCPA? Does it make any difference whether Ms. A. offers an inducement to Party A through a person not officially connected to it, such as a cousin or friend of the assistant treasurer or of a campaign worker without any title?

The FCPA's prohibition of inducing foreign officials extends to political parties, party officials, or any candidate for political office.

The antibribery provisions include "instrumentalities" of foreign governments, such as parastatals or state-owned enterprises. Hence, a foreign official can include someone who is employed by a commercial enterprise that is government-owned or operated. The inclusion of an enterprise may depend on how the government characterizes the enterprise and whether it prohibits and prosecutes bribery of the employees of state-owned enterprises as public corruption. The degree of control exercised by the government over the enterprise may also be important.

Are inducements to officials of international organizations covered? The United States accords immunity to such organizations and their officials under the International Organizations Immunities Act (IOMA).[6] If international organizations and their officials have immunity under the IOMA, are they nonetheless covered by the FCPA?

[6] 22 U.S.C. § 288.

6. Corrupt Intent

The FCPA punishes conduct only when a payment or offer of payment is made to induce the intended beneficiary to misuse his or her official position. This requirement is analogous to U.S. domestic bribery law, which requires that the inducement be offered in exchange or return for some official action, inaction, or violation of some official duty to be impartial.

The determination of culpability arises from the intent of the person making the inducement, as opposed to the official's action, inaction, or capacity. The bribe need not be paid for a person to violate the FCPA. In fact, a person making an inducement can violate the FCPA even if the recipient or intended beneficiary does not at the relevant time have the actual authority to make or influence the official decision.

7. Obtain or Retain Business

A company that induces a foreign official to engage in conduct to assist in obtaining, retaining, or directing business to the company violates the FCPA. Hence, the briber must intend to induce the official to act on the briber's behalf to assist him or her in obtaining or retaining business. From a practical standpoint, prosecutors have difficulty since such prosecutions frequently are filed years after the fact, in which case prosecutors have difficulty establishing that an inducement had a business purpose.

The term "assist" in the antibribery provisions is interpreted quite broadly. Actions can assist a particular goal by facilitating achievement of the goal. For instance, payments or gifts to a government official to circumvent quotas, bypass licensing requirements, or reduce or forgive proposed taxes or penalties can all constitute business purposes.

An important case used to interpret the element that the bribe must be to "obtain or retain business" is *U.S. v. Kay*, 359 F.3d 738 (5th Cir. 2004), affirmed, 513 F.3d 423 (5th Cir. 2007), rehearing denied by 513 F.3d 461 (5th Cir. 2008). The appellate court concluded that making payments to foreign officials to reduce customs duties and taxes may constitute payments made to "obtain or retain business" within the meaning of the FCPA. The defendants were charged with bribing Haitian customs officials to accept false bills of lading and other documentation that understated by about one-third the quantity of rice shipped to Haiti by the Rice Corporation of Haiti, a wholly owned subsidiary of the Houston-based public company, American Rice, Inc. The district court dismissed the indictment, holding that "as a matter of law, bribes paid to obtain favorable tax treatment are not payments made to 'obtain or retain business' within the intendment of the FCPA, and thus are not within the scope of that statute's proscription of foreign bribery." 359 F.3d at 740. The Fifth Circuit reversed and remanded the case to the district. The court explained that, although not every bribe for reduced taxes is a violation of the FCPA, the bribery intended to produce an effect that would "assist in obtaining or retaining business" is a violation. *Id.* at 756. After a trial on the merits, both defendants were convicted and then appealed. The Fifth Circuit rejected the defendants' arguments on appeal that the FCPA provision failed to give fair notice and that the jury instructions were insufficient. 513 F.3d at 423 (5th Cir. 2007).

In the Matter of Bristow Group, Inc., Exchange Act Release 56533 (September 26, 2007; available at http://www.sec.gov/litigation/admin/2007/34–56533.pdf), addressed the requirement that the bribe must be made to "obtain or retain business." In this settled administrative proceeding, the Order for Proceedings alleged that a Nigerian affiliate of the Bristow Group made improper payments to Nigerian state government officials in return for a reduction in employment taxes. The Order also alleged books and records and internal controls violations. The Respondent consented to an order directing that it cease and desist from violations of the antibribery, books and records, and internal control provisions.

8. Exceptions and Affirmative Defenses

The antibribery provisions have one category of exceptions and two categories of affirmative defenses. Each is linked to circumstances in which the inducements are made, creating in effect a safe harbor.

a. *Facilitating payments*

The antibribery provisions allow "facilitating," "expediting," or "grease" payments. They are limited to payments made "to expedite or to secure the performance of a routine governmental action by a foreign official, political party, or party official."[7] Facilitating payments are made to obtain or accelerate performance of a nondiscretionary act that an official is already obligated to perform. Examples are the issuance of a permit that is automatic or will be granted in only a matter of time. The payment only accelerates the act, such as obtaining the installation of telephone service. The "routine governmental action" exception is limited to any facilitating or expediting payment, the purpose of which is to expedite or to secure the performance of a routine governmental action that is ordinarily and commonly performed by a foreign official.[8]

Such facilitation payments are often payments to obtain permits, licenses, or other official documents or to obtain services such as police protection, mail delivery, telephone service, utilities, cargo handling, and protection of perishable products. They may encompass payments including for processing of governmental papers, including visas and work orders; scheduling of inspections associated with contract performance or the transit of goods across country; and expediting of shipments through customs.

Notwithstanding their protection facilitation payments pose a hidden risk to those who engage in them. Because such payments are rarely countenanced by the written law of a host country, they are rarely recorded. If they are not properly recorded, however, these otherwise legal payments can constitute violations of the accounting and recordkeeping provisions of the FCPA. In addition, facilitating payments of sufficient frequency may eventually cross a threshold and constitute an improper relationship with government officials that does in fact violate the FCPA.

b. *Bona fide business expenses*

The antibribery provisions allow, as an affirmative defense, reasonable "and bona fide expenditures."[9] Such expenditures must be directly related to the promotion, demonstration, or explanation of products or services or to the execution or performance of a contract with a foreign government or agency.

7 15 U.S.C. §§ 78dd-1(b), -2(b), -3(b).
8 *Id.*, §§ 78dd-1(f)(3)(A), -2(h)(4)(A), -3)(f)(4)(A).
9 *Id.*, §§ 78dd-1(c)(2), -2(c)(2), -3(c)(2).

A company must determine whether a government official or agency can lawfully receive payment or reimbursement for expenses before such a payment can qualify as a bona fide business expense. Many countries limit the amount of such payments as well as manner of making them (e.g., such payments may require prior approvals by the host government).

Trips for the promotion, demonstration, or explanation of products sometimes violate the antibribery provisions when they involve unnecessary diversions to resorts or travel upgrades to first class. Such payments must be necessary business expenditures and must be reasonable under the circumstances. An expense that is out of proportion or unrelated to a legitimate business purpose can serve as a basis for concern.

Proper corporate governance helps ensure that offers to pay or reimburse reasonable expenses are carefully documented and vetted as part of an entity's compliance program. The business compliance unit should determine whether the expenditures are reasonable in terms of purpose and amount, are made in good faith, and relate directly to (1) the promotion, demonstration, or explanation of products or services or (2) the execution or performance of a contract with a foreign government or agency.

9. Local Law

A business can raise an affirmative defense under the antibribery provisions for payments or offers that are lawful under the written laws and regulations of the country of the foreign official, political party, party official, or candidate.[10] Most governments do not as an official act allow payments or offers to violate a lawful duty. A person cannot assert a recognized custom or practice within a particular country as an affirmative defense. Affirmative defenses are ordinarily limited to situations in which contributions to political parties or candidates for public office are at issue.

10. Opinion Procedure

The Department of Justice (DOJ) has an FCPA Opinion Procedure that allows an issuer or a domestic concern to request an advisory opinion concerning proposed business conduct.[11] Where subsequent conduct conforms to a prior advisory opinion authorizing such conduct, the defendant has a rebuttable presumption that the conduct is lawful. A written opinion binds only the Justice Department and the parties to a request – it is nonbinding for other parties.

Although the SEC does not have an equivalent procedure, it does not take civil enforcement action against a party that has obtained a favorable opinion from the DOJ.[12]

Because the opinion process can be lengthy and costly, Justice Department officials recommend that prospective requestors meet informally with them before they make a formal request. These informal meetings can help determine whether a company should formally request an opinion and, if so, how to properly construe the request.

The information provided in an opinion request is exempt from disclosure under the Freedom of Information Act. However, the Justice Department has the right to make a public release describing the requestor, identifying the country, summarizing

[10] *Id.*, §§78dd-1(c)(1), -2(c)(1), -3(c)(1).
[11] *Id.*, §§ 78dd-1(e), -2(f); 28 C.F.R. §§ 80.1-.16.
[12] Exchange Act Release No. 34–18255, 4 FED. SEC. L. REP. (CCH) 26,629 (Nov. 12, 1981).

the proposed conduct, and announcing its action. The Justice Department posts the opinion procedure releases on its Web site, which is a source of useful guidance on structuring transactions and in determining how the Justice Department may respond to certain factual situations.[13]

11. Statute of Limitations

a. *Criminal cases*

The general federal criminal five-year statute of limitations in 18 U.S.C. § 3292 applies to FCPA criminal prosecutions. The prosecutor can request a court order tolling the statute of limitations for up to three years when necessary evidence is sought from abroad. The provisions only apply when a federal grand jury is impaneled and has not returned an indictment and a prosecutor requests the suspension of the statute before a district court, which must find by a preponderance of the evidence that an official request has been made for the evidence and it reasonably appears at the time that the evidence is in the foreign country. *See, e.g., U.S. v. Miller,* 830 F.2d 1073 (9th Cir. 1987).

In *U.S. v. Kozeny,* 493 F. Supp. 2d 518 (S.D.N.Y.), 2008 US. App. LEXIS 18523 (Aug. 29, 2008), two defendants, Messrs. Bourke and Pikerton, moved to dismiss as time barred the indictment against them for conspiracy to bribe government officials in Azerbaijan to ensure that the state-owned oil company would be privatized. Although the DOJ had previously received a court order tolling the statute of limitations and filed the request for assistance with the governments of the Netherlands and Switzerland within the five-year statute of limitations, it did not obtain the §3292 order until after the five-year period had expired. The court concluded that, although the statutory text was ambiguous, the legislative history of § 3292, the structure of the provisions, the policy rationale behind statutes of limitations, and the doctrine of constitutional avoidance all pointed toward an interpretation of § 3292 that does not allow the government to apply to suspend a statute of limitations after the limitations period has expired. The Second Circuit Court of Appeals affirmed, concluding that the text of § 3292 is not ambiguous. It found that the plain language of the provisions, and the structure and content of the law by which it was enacted, required the government to apply for a tolling of the statute of limitations before the limitations period expired.

b. *SEC actions*

No express statute of limitations is applicable to injunctive actions brought by the SEC. Similarly, courts have traditionally refused to apply the equitable doctrine of latches. *See, e.g., SEC v. Rind,* 991 F.2d 1486 (9th Cir. 1993); *SEC v. Lorin,* 869 F. Spp. 1117 (S.D.N.Y. 1994); *SEC v. Williams,* 884 F. Supp. 28 (D. Mass 1995); *SEC v. Toomey,* 866 F. Supp. 719 (S.D.N.Y. 1992). However, when the equitable relief sought can be perceived as punitive, the general five-year federal statute of limitations applicable to all federal civil enforcement actions seeking a penalty, fine, or forfeiture in 28 U.S.C. §2462 may apply. *SEC v. Thomas W. Jones and Lewis E. Daidone,* No. 05–7044 (S.D.N.Y. Feb. 26, 2007).

c. *Public authority defense*

In *U.S. v. Giffen,* 473 F.2d 30 (2nd Cir. 2007), the court held that it did not have jurisdiction to hear an appeal from a district court order concerning a defendant's notice

[13] Department of Justice, FCPA Opinion Procedure Releases, http://www.usdoj.gov/criminal/fraud/fcpa/opiindx.htm.

that a "public authority" defense would be raised as premature because the district court had not ruled squarely on the issue. The public authority defense has two aspects. The first is premised on the actual authority, whereas the second is premised on estoppel.

The actual authority defense "exists where a defendant has in fact been authorized by the government to engage in what would otherwise be illegal activity." *Id.* at 39. When the proffer does not disclose either express or implied authorization by the government to commit the criminal acts that are charged, the court found it is not a "public authority" defense.

A defendant can establish the entrapment by estoppel defense without the defendant having received actual authorization. "It depends on the proposition that the government is barred from prosecuting a person for his criminal conduct when the government, by its own actions, induced him to do those acts and led him to rely reasonably on his belief that this action would be lawful by reason of the government's *seeming* authorization." *Id.* at 41. (Emphasis original). Because the defendant did not disclose to the government an intention to commit the bribe and fraud crimes changed against him, he would not be entitled to assert the defense in the case.

A related doctrine of negation of intent is not an affirmative defense. Rather, it is an effort to rebut the government's proof of intent by showing that the defendant acted in the good faith belief that he was authorized to act by the government. Only the Eleventh Circuit has adopted this position. The court explained it had great difficulty with the proposition. However, the court observed that "we assume for purpose of argument... that, at least in some circumstances, a defendant may offer evidence that he lacked the intent essential to the offense charged because of his good faith belief that he was acting on behalf of the government." *Id.* at 43.

B. *Accounting and Recordkeeping Provisions of the FCPA*

§ 78m. Periodical and Other Reports

(a) Reports by Issuer of Security; Contents

Every issuer of a security registered pursuant to section 78l of this title shall file with the Commission, in accordance with such rules and regulations as the Commission may prescribe as necessary or appropriate for the proper protection of investors and to insure fair dealing in the security

(1) such information and documents (and such copies thereof) as the Commission shall require to keep reasonably current the information and documents required to be included in or filed with an application or registration statement filed pursuant to section 78l of this title, except that the Commission may not require the filing of any material contract wholly executed before July 1, 1962.
(2) such annual reports (and such copies thereof), certified if required by the rules and regulations of the Commission by independent public accountants, and such quarterly reports (and such copies thereof), as the Commission may prescribe.

Every issuer of a security registered on a national securities exchange shall also file a duplicate original of such information, documents, and reports with the exchange.

(b) **Form of Report; Books, Records, and Internal Accounting; Directives**

(2) Every issuer which has a class of securities registered pursuant to section 78l of this title and every issuer which is required to file reports pursuant to section 78o(d) of this title shall

(A) make and keep books, records, and accounts, which, in reasonable detail, accurately and fairly reflect the transactions and dispositions of the assets of the issuer; and
(B) devise and maintain a system of internal accounting controls sufficient to provide reasonable assurances that –

(i) transactions are executed in accordance with management's general or specific authorization;
(ii) transactions are recorded as necessary (i) to permit preparation of financial statements in conformity with generally accepted accounting principles or any other criteria applicable to such statements, and (ii) to maintain accountability for assets;
(iii) access to assets is permitted only in accordance with management's general or specific authorization; and
(iv) the recorded accountability for assets is compared with the existing assets at reasonable intervals and appropriate action is taken with respect to any differences.
(v) No person shall knowingly circumvent or knowingly fail to implement a system of internal accounting controls or knowingly falsify any book, record, or account described in paragraph (2).

1. Scope

The accounting and recordkeeping provisions, which are more limited than the antibribery provisions, only apply to issuers. Officers, directors, employees, and stockholders or agents of the issuer acting on its behalf are subject to the terms of the accounting and recordkeeping provisions. Individuals and entities may also be subject to these provisions if they are accomplices to a violation of those provisions.

Because the accounting and recordkeeping provisions require issuers to maintain accurate records of their transactions and of the disposition of their assets, these provisions apply without regard to whether foreign conduct, foreign officials, or improper inducements are involved. The provisions apply to an issuer's domestic and foreign operations, including domestic reporting and disclosure practices as well as practices involving foreign payments. They create an affirmative duty on the part of issuers and their officers, directors, employees, and agents or stockholders acting on their behalf.

The accounting and recordkeeping provisions do not apply to foreign subsidiaries if the U.S. issuer holds an interest of 50 percent or less in the foreign entity. However, the issuer still must "proceed in good faith to use its influence to the extent reasonable under the circumstances to cause [the affiliate] to devise and maintain a system of internal accounting controls" consistent with the requirements of the accounting and recordkeeping provisions.[14] The interpretation of "reasonable" in context depends mainly on the practices governing the affiliate in the country where it is located. An issuer

[14] 15 U.S.C. § 78m(b)(6).

showing good faith efforts to use its influence will be "conclusively presumed" to have fulfilled its statutory obligation.[15]

The 1983 case of *SEC v. World-Wide Coin Investment, Ltd.* is one of the few cases that litigated the accounting provisions of the FCPA, providing the only example of judicial interpretation of the FCPA prior to its 1988 amending.[16] Most other cases on the accounting provisions were resolved before trial by consent decree or other settlement.[17]

How do the scope of the FCPA's accounting and recordkeeping provisions compare with the counterpart provision at the international anticorruption conventions?

2. Recordkeeping Provisions

Under the recordkeeping provisions an issuer must "make and keep books, records, and accounts which, in reasonable detail, accurately and fairly reflect the transactions and dispositions of the assets of the issuer."[18] An issuer's records must show transactions in conformity with accepted accounting standards and should be designed to prevent off-the-books transactions such as kickbacks and bribes. "Reasonable detail" is "such level of detail and degree of assurance as would satisfy prudent officials in the conduct of their own affairs."[19]

An important feature of the provisions is that they apply to all payments, not just to sums that would be material in the traditional financial context. Traditionally, except for disclosures as to certain aspects of an issuer's activities, materiality has been the overriding determining factor as to what required disclosure and what constituted a violation.

a. *Falsification of books and records*

An issuer's management must ensure that its books and records are accurate so that the entity can prepare financial statements in conformity with accepted procedures. The SEC has issued two rules to ensure that the accounting books of original entry, ledgers, and other accounting data are maintained to the extent reasonably necessary to support the financial statements and to allow independent auditors to apply accepted audit procedures.

Rule 13b2–1 forbids the falsification of books and records that must be kept under the recordkeeping provisions.[20] It applies to "any person" and is not limited to officers and directors of an issuer. Rule 13b2–1 has no materiality requirement. Additionally, books and records are defined broadly to include "accounts, correspondence, memoranda, tapes, discs, papers, books, and other documents or transcribed information of any type, whether expressed in ordinary or machine language."[21]

Manipulating books or records to mask transactions by obliquely characterizing or actually falsifying them can lead to serious legal exposure for an issuer and those

[15] *Id.*
[16] *SEC v. World-Wide Coin Investments, Ltd.*, 567 F.Supp. 724 (N.D. Ga. 1983).
[17] Kathleen A. Lacey & Barbara Crutchfield George, *Expansion of SEC Authority into Internal Corporate Governance: The Accounting Provisions of the Foreign Corrupt Practices Act*, 7 J. TRANSNAT'L L. & POL'Y 119, 121–22 (1998).
[18] *Id.*, § 78m(b)(2)(A).
[19] *Id.*, § 78m(b)(7).
[20] 17 C.F.R. § 240.13b2–1.
[21] 15 U.S.C. § 78c(a)(37).

individuals involved. For instance, concealing a transaction may subject the issuer and other responsible persons to enforcement action for violating Rule 13b2–1. In recent years, the SEC has emphasized that it has "zero tolerance" for the falsification of records relating to an improper payment.

b. *Misrepresentations to auditors*

Rule 13b2–2 prohibits any officer or director from making materially false or misleading statements or failing to state any material facts in the preparation of filings required by the Exchange Act. Although the rule applies to officers and directors, it also applies both to internal auditors and outside auditors and covers "causing another person to make a material misstatement or make or cause to be made a materially false or misleading statement."[22]

After enactment of the Sarbanes-Oxley Act of 2002, the SEC broadened Rule 13b2–2. As a result, officers and directors of an issuer, or anyone acting on their behalf, are prohibited from "taking any action to fraudulently influence, coerce, manipulate, or mislead any independent public or certified accountant engaged in the performance of an audit of the financial statements of that issuer for the purpose of rendering such financial statements materially misleading."[23]

3. Internal Accounting Controls Provisions

The accounting provisions of the FCPA seek to prevent the improper use of an issuer's assets. They require issuers to develop and maintain internal accounting controls that provide reasonable assurance that transactions are executed in accordance with management's general or specific authorization; that transactions are recorded as necessary to allow the preparation of financial statements in conformity with generally accepted accounting principles or any other criteria applicable to such statements, and to maintain accountability for assets; that access to company assets is allowed only in accordance with management's general or specific authorization; and that records are compared with existing assets at reasonable intervals and appropriate action is taken with respect to any differences.

The SEC has construed "reasonable assurance" of management control over an issuer's assets as "such level of detail and degree of assurance as would satisfy prudent officials in the conduct of their own affairs."[24] The "prudent man" standard is analogous to management's expectations concerning its oversight obligations under U.S. law and does not require any specific type of internal accounting controls. The standard for compliance is whether a system, taken as a whole, reasonably fulfills the statute's goals.

The SEC has identified elements of an adequate system of internal controls, which it looks for when considering specific systems. Such criteria include *inter alia*: the board of directors must oversee the establishment and maintenance of strong internal accounting controls; the board must identify a method of analyzing the system of accounting controls that is effective within the context of each entity; and management must have reasonable assurance that the system of internal accounting is functioning as designed. An effective

[22] 17 C.F.R. § 240.13b2–2.
[23] 15 U.S.C. §7242; 17 C.F.R. § 240.13b2–2(b).
[24] *Id.*, §78m(b)(7).

system of internal accounting controls has a range of review and approval guidelines designed to detect and deter questionable payments. The planning, implementation, and monitoring of an issuer's compliance program should be closely connected, if not intertwined, with its system of internal accounting controls.

In *World-Wide Coin*, the Court's greatest concern was that the company's independent auditors had alerted it to serious weaknesses in its internal controls that constituted potential FCPA violations, including no adequate segregation of duties, no documentation to support transactions, and inadequate and improperly filed accounting records. Although notified of these deficiencies and possible FCPA violations by the auditor's opinion letter, World-Wide Coin management took no corrective action. The Court later found World-Wide Coin in violation of Section 13(b)(2) of the FCPA and ordered a full fraud accounting and disgorgement of wrongfully received benefits by defendant Hale.[25]

How effective do you think is the fact that the SEC has responsibility for the FCPA's accounting and recordkeeping provisions while the DOJ has responsibility for the enforcement of other aspects? How do other countries argue the regulation and enforcement of transnational corruption laws?

4. Siemens Anticorruption Case

Effective International Enforcement Cooperation Results in Largest Penalties of $1.6 Billion as Siemens Pleads Guilty of Corruption Violations

REPRINTED FROM 25 INT'L ENFORCEMENT L. REP. 75 (FEB. 2009)

by Bruce Zagaris

On December 15, 2008, Siemens Aktiengesellschaft (Siemens AG), a German corporation, and three of its subsidiaries pleaded guilty to violations of and charges related to the Foreign Corrupt Practices Act (FCPA) in the U.S. District Court for Washington D.C. Siemens agreed to penalties of $1.6 billion, including penalties assessed by the Securities and Exchange Commission. The combined U.S. penalties are the largest monetary sanction ever imposed in an FCPA case.[26]

Siemens AG pleaded guilty to a two-count information charging criminal violations of the FCPA's internal controls and books and records provisions. Siemens S.A.-Argentina pleaded guilty to a one-count information charging conspiracy to violate the books and records provisions of the FCPA. Siemens Bangladesh and Siemens Venezuela each pleaded guilty to separate one-count information charging conspiracy to violate the anti-bribery and books and records provisions of the FCPA. Siemens AG agreed, as part of the plea agreements, to pay a $448.5 million fine; and Siemens Argentina, Bangladesh, and Venezuela each agreed to pay a $500,000.00 fine, for a combined total criminal fine of $450 million.

Court documents revealed that starting in the mid-1990s Siemens AG engaged in systematic efforts to falsify its corporate books and records and knowingly failed to implement and circumvent existing internal controls. From March 12, 2001, when it was listed on the New York Stock Exchange, through approximately 2007, Siemens AG made payments totaling

[25] *World-Wide Coin*, 567 F. Supp. at 751–52, 760; Lacey & George, *supra* note 16 at 141.

[26] U.S. Department of Justice, *Siemens AG and Three Subsidiaries Plead Guilty to Foreign Corrupt Practices Act Violations and Agree to Pay $450 Million in Combined Criminal Fines*, Press Release, Dec. 15, 2008.

approximately $1.36 billion through various mechanisms. $805.5 million was intended as corrupt payments to foreign officials through the payment mechanisms.[27]

From 2000 to 2002, four Siemens AG subsidiaries were awarded 42 contracts with a combined value of more than $80 million with the Ministries of Electricity and Oil of the government of the Republic of Iraq under the United Nations Oil for Food Program. To obtain these contracts, the Siemens subsidiaries paid a total of at least $1,736,076.00 in kickbacks to the Iraqi government, and they collectively earned more than $38 million in profits.[28]

The violations by Siemens executives included using off-the-books slush fund accounts and shell companies to facilitate bribes, making false entries on the company's books and records by, for example, falsely recording bribes as consulting fees; and by accumulating profit reserves as a liability on company books, and then using these funds to facilitate bribe payments. The violations also included short-changing audits that might have gotten too close to so-called "business consultants," who were de facto conduits for illicit payments; using removable post-it notes in order to conceal the identity of executives who had authorized illicit payoffs; and carrying cash in suitcases.[29]

The press releases, press conferences, and court documents underscore that the coordinated efforts of U.S. and German law enforcement authorities in the case set the standard for multi national cooperation in the fight against corrupt business practices. Also proactively participating in the case were the Financial Services Authority in the U.K. and the Hong Kong Securities and Futures Commission.[30] In addition, Siemens has taken extraordinary steps to reveal its long-standing, systemic criminal conduct and it has fundamentally restructured its operations to make them transparent.

Linda Chatman Thomsen, Director of the SEC's Division of Enforcement, characterized the Siemens pattern of bribery as "unprecedented in scale and geographic reach." The corruption involved more than $1.4 billion in bribes to government officials in Asia, Africa, Europe, the Middle East, and the Americas.[31]

The resolution of the U.S. criminal investigation of Siemens AG and its subsidiaries resulted to a large extent from the actions of Siemens AG and its audit committee in disclosing potential FCPA violations to the Department after the Munich Public Prosecutors Office initiated searches of multiple Siemens AG offices and homes of Siemens AG employees. Siemens AG and its subsidiaries disclosed these violations after initiating an internal FCPA investigation of unprecedented scope; shared the results of that investigation with the Department efficiently and continuously; cooperated extensively and authentically with the Department in its ongoing investigation; took appropriate disciplinary action against individual wrongdoers, including senior management with involvement in or knowledge of the violations; and took remedial action, including the complete restructuring of Siemens AG and the implementation of a sophisticated compliance program and organization.[32]

The plea agreement requires Siemens AG to retain an independent compliance monitor for a four-year period to oversee the continued implementation and maintenance of a robust

[27] *Id.*
[28] *Id.*
[29] *U.S. v. Siemens Aktiengesselschaft, et al.*, U.S. Dist. Court for D.C., Case No. 1:08-cr-00367-RJL, Department's Sentencing Memorandum, Dec. 12, 2008, at 4–5.
[30] U.S. Department of Justice, *Transcript of Press Conference Announcing Siemens AG and Three Subsidiaries Plead Guilty to Foreign Corrupt Practices Act Violations*, Dec. 15, 2008, www.usdoj.gov.
[31] U.S. Department of Justice, *Siemens AG and Three Subsidiaries Plead Guilty, supra* note 25.
[32] *Id.*

compliance program and to make reports to the company and the Department of Justice. Siemens AG also agreed to continue fully cooperating with the Department in ongoing investigations of corrupt payments by company employees.

Siemens AG agreed also to a disposition resolving an ongoing investigation by the Munich Public Prosecutor's Office of Siemens AG's operating groups other than Telecommunications. In October 2007, in connection with charges related to corrupt payments to foreign officials by Siemens AG's Telecommunications operating group, the Munich Public Prosecutor's Office announced a settlement with Siemens AG under which Siemens AG agreed to pay €201 million, or approximately $287 million, under a €1 million fine and €200 million in disgorgement of profits.[33]

Although Siemens faced fines under the Federal Sentencing Guidelines of up to $2.7 billion, its conduct resulted in the DOJ's prosecuting asking for a penalty reduced to $450 million. Additionally, because of Siemens conduct, DOJ decided not to charge Siemens under the FCPA's anti-bribery provisions. As a result, it will probably not be barred from U.S. government contracts. The DOJ has said it views as exceptional Siemens' wide-ranging cooperation efforts throughout the investigation, which included a sweeping internal investigation, the creation of innovative and effective amnesty and leniency programs, and exemplary efforts with respect to preservation, collection, testing, and analysis of evidence.[34]

German prosecutors initially opened the Siemens case in 2005. U.S. authorities became involved in 2006 because Siemens' shares are traded on the New York Stock Exchange. The involvement of Siemens in bribery is perhaps explained by the fact that before 1999, bribes were deductible as business expenses under the German tax code. Giving gratuities to a foreign official was not a crime. However, in February 1999, Germany joined the OECD Convention against Transnational Bribery. By 2000, Austrian and Swiss authorities started having suspicions about Siemens payments to offshore bank accounts, especially to Liechtenstein and the British Virgin Islands. Typically, a number of Siemens business units budgeted substantial amounts of money for bribery payments that ranged from 5 percent to 6 percent of a contract's value.[35]

Once the U.S. started investigating, Siemens engaged David Polk & Wardwell to represent the Company, and engaged Debevoise & Plimpton LLP, a U.S. law firm to conduct an internal investigation for the Audit Committee. Debevoise then hired Deloitte & Touche GmbH, translators, computer experts, litigation support firms, and other third parties to assist in the investigation, and work with federal investigators.[36] Debevoise had more than 300 lawyers, forensic analysts and staff members to uncover the extent of the misconduct. Debevoise lawyers conducted more than 1,700 interviews in 34 countries, collected more than 100 million documents, creating special facilities in China and Germany to keep records from that single investigation. Debevoise and an outside auditor had 1.5 million billable hours. Siemens has said that the internal inquiry and related responses have cost it more than $1 billion.[37]

The U.S. government told the court Siemens "has provided extraordinary cooperation in connection with the investigation of its past corporate conduct, and has undertaken

[33] *Id.*

[34] *U.S. v. Siemens Aktiengesselschaft, et al., supra* note 28.

[35] Siri Schubert & T. Christian Miller, *At Siemens, Bribery Was Just a Line Item*, N.Y. Times, Dec. 20, 2008, http://www.nytimes.com/2008/.

[36] *U.S. v. Siemens Aktiengesselschaft, et al., supra* note 28.

[37] Schubert and Miller, *supra* note 34.

uncommonly sweeping remedial action in response to the discovery of its prior misconduct. Siemens also provided "substantial and timely assistance in the investigation of other persons and entities."[38]

Analysis

The size of the penalties and the amount of involvement by foreign enforcement agencies show the heightened attention to the investigation and prosecution of transnational corruption cases. From 2001 to 2004, the Justice Department resolved or charged seventeen FCPA cases. For the period of 2005 to 2008, the number grew to forty-two resolutions, representing an increase of more than 200 percent. Large transnational corruption cases have been brought successfully by foreign governments.[39]

The Siemens case is a fascinating illustration of the enormous scope of the culture of transnational bribery by multinationals. The extent of internal investigation, cooperation, and remediation also provides a remarkable example of how a business should admit and act to change its corporate misconduct and culture. So vast is the scope of misconduct, the effort to investigate and prosecute, especially the international cooperation, and the action to come to grips with and remedy its wrongdoing that the saga merits many professional studies. The case should send a wake-up call to other businesses involved in the global market.

C. *Vicarious Liability*

An individual or entity can suffer vicarious liability for the conduct of a third party when the third party is acting for or on behalf of the individual or entity. Actions by an agent, consultant, or representative can subject an individual or entity to liability. Despite a third party's exemption from the FCPA, an individual or entity can become subject to vicarious liability if the individual or entity authorizes, directs, or in some way ratifies activity that is prohibited by the FCPA. The knowledge requirement for establishing vicarious liability is important and varies according to whether the antibribery or the accounting or recordkeeping provisions are involved and whether criminal or civil charges are brought.

One basis of liability occurs when express provisions exist for vicarious liability as part of the statutory mandate. Both the FCPA criminal and civil antibribery provisions establish vicarious liability. Implicitly, the accounting and recordkeeping civil provisions establish vicarious liability. A second basis for vicarious liability is the general one in all U.S. statutory provisions for accomplices, aiders, and abettors.

1. Antibribery Provisions

Offers or payments are expressly prohibited to "any person, while knowing that all or a portion of such money or things of value will be offered, given, or promised, directly or indirectly, to any foreign official, to any foreign political party or official thereof, or to any candidate for foreign political office."[40] These provisions apply to anyone in the

[38] *U.S. v. Siemens Aktiengesselschaft, et al., supra* note 28.
[39] U.S. Department of Justice, *Transcript of Press Conference, supra* note 29.
[40] 15 U.S.C. §§ 78dd-1(a)(3), -2(a)(3), -3(a)(3).

United States or abroad who acts on behalf of an individual or entity subject to the terms of antibribery provisions – encompassing consultants, distributors, joint venture partners, foreign subsidiaries or affiliates, contractors, or subcontractors.

An offender can be vicariously liable under the antibribery provisions with respect to improper payments made by or through a third party to obtain or retain business when anything of value is offered or paid to a third party where the offeror knows that all or a portion of such value is or will be offered, given, or promised, directly or indirectly, to a foreign official. Vicarious liability also exists where a third party is authorized to offer or pay anything of value to a foreign official.

The only difference in terms of vicarious liability between criminal and civil enforcement actions is that the standard of proof is a preponderance of evidence in a civil context and beyond a reasonable doubt in a criminal context.

a. *The knowledge requirement*

The antibribery provisions prohibit promising or giving benefits to a third party when the offeror knows that the benefits will be passed on by the third party to a foreign official. An individual or entity is responsible for the conduct of a third party when it "knows" that the money or thing of value given to the third party would be used, directly or indirectly, to make an improper payment.

If an individual or entity "is aware of a high probability of the existence of" activity prohibited by the antibribery provisions but does not have actual knowledge of the circumstance, the individual or entity is still deemed to "know" of the existence of the circumstance.[41] The FCPA deems an individual or entity to have the requisite knowledge of any activity of a third party if the individual or entity (1) "is aware that such person is engaging in such conduct, that such circumstance exists, or that such result is substantially certain to occur" or (2) "has a firm belief that such circumstance exists or that such result is substantially certain to occur."

In a trial, knowledge can be inferred under the antibribery provisions when facts show that the act occurs with conscious disregard of or willful blindness to the evident purpose of the offer or payment. Prosecutors try to establish the existence of such knowledge when they show circumstances that should raise suspicions or red flags. In such cases knowledge on the part of an individual or entity will most likely be established – for instance, making a payment to someone who did not appear to perform a service or making a payment grossly disproportionate to the value of the services to be delivered. A payor telling a recipient that he will never need to know how the services for which he is paying are rendered raises another red flag.

In 1988, amendments to the FCPA removed the "reason to know" standard, which, albeit never applied by the Justice Department, was perceived as possibly including situations where an individual or entity negligently disregarded the risk that a sales agent might use payments made to bribe a foreign official by an individual or entity subject to the antibribery provisions. However, there is little practical difference between the current "knowledge" standard and the former "reason to know" standard.

Knowledge is imputed under the antibribery provisions to an individual or entity that has information indicating a "high probability" that prohibited conduct may result. Knowledge can also be established if an individual or entity consciously disregards or

[41] *Id.*, §§ 78dd-1(f)(2)(B); -2(h)(3)(B); -3(f)(3)(B).

deliberately ignores circumstances that should reasonably have alerted the individual or entity to a high probability of a violation. Hence, if an individual or entity becomes aware of questionable circumstances concerning the activities of a third party with whom a relationship may exist, diligence must be exercised in undertaking an inquiry, at the risk that an individual or entity could be found to have consciously disregarded information that could have served as notice of the likelihood of a violation.

b. *Authorization*

In addition to prohibiting an inducement to a foreign official, the antibribery provisions also prohibit the "authorization" of an improper inducement to be made by another.[42] Such prohibitions apply to, among others, sales representatives, consultants, and foreign subsidiaries.

Although the antibribery provisions do not define the standard for authorization, legislative history shows that authorization can be either explicit or implicit. Authorization appears to mean approval or direction to carry out the conduct. Because implicit authorization is proscribed, when an individual or entity becomes aware of possible improper payments to third parties, he or it should establish a record to show that such conduct was not authorized and should document explicit objection to such improper conduct, if possible.

Authorization may include knowing acquiescence or tacit approval by individuals or entities that could have prevented the conduct leading to the making of an improper inducement.

c. *Control*

If a foreign corporation is not an issuer subject to the FCPA, the antibribery provisions generally do not apply, even to a controlled foreign affiliate of a U.S. entity that is subject to the FCPA. If a foreign subsidiary makes an improper inducement, this action is not in itself a violation of the antibribery provisions unless an act in furtherance of the improper inducement occurs within U.S. territory. Hence, officers, directors, employees, and agents of foreign affiliates are not subject to the antibribery provisions if these individuals or entities are neither domestic concerns nor issuers. However, an issuer of a domestic concern can be vicariously liable for the conduct of its foreign subsidiary if the issuer directs, authorizes, or knowingly acquiesces to the foreign subsidiary's prohibited conduct in some way.

2. Accounting and Recordkeeping Provisions

Issuers may be held strictly liable in a civil enforcement case for the actions of controlled subsidiaries or foreign affiliations that violate the accounting and recordkeeping provisions. The SEC need not prove that an issuer knew or even suspected wrongful conduct on the part of its controlled subsidiary or affiliate to establish civil liability.

The 1988 FCPA amendments narrowed the knowledge requirement under the accounting and recordkeeping procedures. Criminal liability can be established if an individual or entity subject to the accounting and recordkeeping provisions knowingly

[42] 15 U.S.C. §§ 78dd-1(a), -2(a), -3(a).

circumvents or fails to implement a system of internal accounting controls or knowingly falsifies any book, record, or account.[43]

An individual or entity can be criminally liable for acts of third parties if an individual or entity had knowledge that the third party has circumvented the internal controls or falsified books and records. Deliberate ignorance or knowing disregard can establish the requisite knowledge, especially if an individual or entity becomes aware of questionable circumstances.

3. Vicarious Liability for Accomplices

Individuals and entities may also be secondarily criminally liable under the federal conspiracy and aiding and abetting statutes for violations of the antibribery or the accounting and recordkeeping provisions. The prosecutor must show that the individual's or entity's knowledge is coupled either with a conspiratorial agreement[44] or actions that aid or abet[45] a violation in connection with prohibited conduct on the part of a third party.

Notes and Questions

1. U.S. prosecutors and law enforcement have reemphasized the reinvigorated enforcement of the FCPA. The thirty-eight FCPA enforcement cases brought by the DOJ and SEC in 2007 more than doubles the fifteen cases brought in 2006. In addition, there reportedly are more than 100 open investigations. *See, e.g., Lawyer Says Variability in DOJ Agreements to Defer Prosecution Makes for Uncertainty*, 39 Sec. Reg. L. Rep. (BNA), at 1570 (Oct. 15, 2007).

2. At the time of the enactment of the FCPA in 1977, most other countries did not criminalize foreign bribery. In fact, many countries allowed tax deductions for such payments. The uncompetitive position of U.S. businesses made them exert pressure on the U.S. government and intersectorial organizations to level the playing field through negotiating international anticorruption agreements and soft law anticorruption requirements.

3. With the proliferation of anticorruption conventions, these have developed divergencies in the requirements of the FCPA and those of the anticorruption conventions. For instance, the definition of prohibited conduct differs. Many conventions criminalize illicit enrichment. The U.S. has had to declare that it cannot create an illicit enrichment offense because this would violate the overall presumption of innocence guaranteed under the U.S. Constitution. Similarly, the FCPA allows facilitating payments whereas some anticorruption conventions do not. The scope of persons covered differs in the FCPA and some international conventions. If you are the U.S. law enforcement authorities with responsibility to enforce the FCPA, the U.S. business community, and U.S. civil society, how should you treat these differences?

III. International Antibribery Initiatives

Although the U.S. government first raised its anticorruption initiatives in the U.N. general assembly in 1975 disagreements with developing countries precluded agreement on the U.N. Economic and Social Committee in 1981. Philippa Webb, United Nations

[43] *Id.*, § 78m(b)(4)-(5).
[44] 18 U.S.C. § 371.
[45] *Id.* at § 2.

Convention against Corruption: Global Achievement or Missed Opportunity, 8.1 Journal of International Economic Law 191–229 (2005).

The United States then focused on the OECD for anticorruption efforts; the OECD is a much smaller and more homogeneous set of countries. Hence, the United States, which in the largest contributor to the OECD budget, could persuade OECD members more easily of the utility of tackling transnational corruptions. The Directorate for Financial and Economic affairs established the working group on Bribery. The latter issued a set of recommendations in 1994. It recommended in 1996 that bribes no longer be tax deductible.

A. *OECD Convention on Combating Bribery of Foreign Officials in International Business Transactions*

Article 1 The Offense of Bribery of Foreign Public Officials

1. Each Party shall take such measures as may be necessary to establish that it is a criminal offense under its law for any person internationally to offer, promise or give any undue pecuniary or other advantage, whether directly or through intermediaries, to a foreign public official, for that official or for a third party, in order that the official act or refrain from acting in relation to the performance of official duties, in order to obtain or retain business or other improper advantage in the conduct of international business.
2. Each party shall take any measures necessary to establish that complicity in, including incitement, aiding and abetting, or authorisation of an act of bribery of a foreign public official shall be a criminal offense. Attempt and conspiracy to bribe a foreign public official shall be criminal offenses to the same extent as an attempt and conspiracy to bribe a public official of that Party.
3. The offenses set out in paragraphs 1 and 2 above are hereinafter referred to as "bribery of a foreign public official".
4. For the purpose of this Convention:

a. "foreign public official" means any person holding a legislative, administrative or judicial office of a foreign country, whether appointed or elected; any person exercising a public function for a foreign country, including for a public agency or public enterprise; and any official or agent of a public international organisation;
b. "foreign country" includes all levels and subdivisions of government, from national to local;
c. "act or refrain from acting in relation to the performance of official duties" includes any use of the public official's position, whether or not within the official's authorised competence.

Article 2 Responsibility of Legal Persons

Each Party shall take such measures as may be necessary, in accordance with its legal principles, to establish the liability of legal persons for the bribery of a foreign public official. . . .

Article 7 Money Laundering

Each Party which has made bribery of its own public official a predicate offense for the purpose of the application of its money laundering legislation shall do so on the same terms for the bribery of a foreign public official, without regard to the place where the bribery occurred.

Article 8 Accounting

1. In order to combat bribery of foreign public officials effectively, each party shall take such measures as may be necessary, within the framework of its laws and regulations regarding the maintenance of books and records, financial statement disclosures, and accounting and auditing standards, to prohibit the establishment of off-the-books accounts, the making of off-the-books or inadequately identified transactions, the recording of nonexistent expenditures, the entry of liabilities with incorrect identification of their object, as well as the use of false documents, by companies subject to those laws and regulations, for the purpose of bribing foreign public officials or of hiding such bribery.
2. Each Party shall provide effective, proportionate and dissuasive civil, administrative or criminal penalties for such omissions and falsifications in respect of the books, records, accounts and financial statements of such companies.[46]

Notes and Questions

1. Background, Status of Ratifications, Scope, and Jurisdiction

The OECD Convention on Combating Bribery of Foreign Public Officials in International Business Transactions was signed on December 17, 1997, and entered into force on February 15, 1999. It was the first modern international antibribery convention.

As of March 12, 2008, forty-one countries had ratified this convention, including countries that are not members of the OECD.

Article 3(1) of the convention requires signatories to establish jurisdiction over offenses that are committed in whole or in part by "any person" acting within a party's territories.[47]

2. Foreign Officials

The convention extends to officials of any branch of government, including part-time or unpaid officials, private individuals carrying out official functions, and officials of parastatals. It defines a "public official" as any person exercising a public function. A "public function" is any activity in the public interest delegated by a foreign country, such as a delegated task connected to public procurement. Individuals who may not be considered public officials under the law of the country where the inducement is directed can still be treated as public officials under the terms of the OECD Convention.

3. Transfers of Value

Like the FCPA, the OECD Convention applies to transfers other than pecuniary payments and does not provide for a *de minimis* amount. Although the convention does not expressly exclude facilitating or expediting payments, the OECD Commentaries show that small facilitation payments are not proscribed.

[46] OECD/C(996)27/FINAL (1996), reprinted in 35 I.L.M. 1311 (1996).
[47] OECD Antibribery Convention, Art. 3,1.

4. Intent and Knowledge

The OECD Convention prohibits cover payments to obtain or retain business and those made to secure any "other improper advantage in the conduct of international business."[48] Its prohibitions cover procurements, licenses, permits, and incentives.

The convention covers both indirect and direct payments to public officials. Its anti-bribery offense is an "intent" crime. However, the OECD Convention's standard is not clear as to whether intent will be found and liability vicariously imposed for payments by third parties in cases of "willful blindness" or in the circumstances of knowledge of "red flags" or similar "suspicious circumstances." The standard may depend on national criminal law standards.

5. Sanctions and Corporate Criminal Responsibility

Under the convention, parties must impose criminal penalties on violators comparable to those applicable to public officials in their respective jurisdictions. If a party's legal system does have criminal sanctions against entities, then it must apply "effective, proportionate and dissuasive" noncriminal penalties, such as monetary sanctions.[49] Parties must adopt measures that would allow the confiscation or forfeiture of an improper payment as well as the proceeds of an improper inducement. The proceeds can include the profits and other benefits derived by the individual or entity making the improper inducement.

6. International Cooperation

The OECD Convention requires parties to provide "prompt and effective" legal assistance to other parties making bribery investigations and proceedings.[50] As a result of these provisions, a requested state cannot deny to a requesting state assistance due to the dual criminality requirement. A requested state cannot assert bank secrecy to avoid giving assistance. The OECD Convention provides the treaty basis for extradition where a party from which extradition is sought conditions assistance on a treaty being in force with the requesting party. It requires that parties comply with the "extradite or prosecute" principle, including with their own nationals. These provisions follow and build on a series of UN international criminal conventions, including the 1988 UN Vienna Counterdrug Convention and the 2000 Palermo Convention against Transnational Organized Crime.

7. Monitoring and Follow-Up

The OECD Convention requires that parties participate in a follow-up program to monitor and promote full implementation and consistent enforcement of the convention's provisions. The monitoring process, which started in April 1999, assesses implementation and enforcement components meant to ensure active and consistent implementation and enforcement by parties to the OECD Convention. The monitoring includes a system of self- and mutual evaluation by the Working Group on Bribery, on the basis

48 *Id.*, Art. 1, 1.
49 OECD Convention, Art. 3, 2.
50 *Id.*, Art. 9, 1.

of which a report will provide an objective assessment of the progress of the participating country in implementing the convention's provisions. The monitoring process includes providing information regularly to the public on its work and activities and on implementation of the monitoring process.

The Working Group on Bribery meets four to five times a year at the Paris Headquarters of the OECD to monitor compliance with the convention. The monitoring process, which is based on peer review, is divided into two examination phases. Phase 1 is a comprehensive assessment of the conformity of the country's antibribery laws with the OECD Convention. Phase 2 involves one week of intensive meetings in the examined country with key actors from government, law enforcement authorities, business, trade unions, and civil society. With input from these actors, the Working Group assesses how effective that country's antiforeign bribery laws are in practice. Phase 1 of the OECD review process examined the legislation of Convention signatories. Phase 2 focuses on the implementation of the convention. The Working Group on Bribery, also known as the peer review mechanism, is considered by some commentators as the most valuable aspect of the convention. The Working Groups reports have focused on the inability of governments to use suspicious activities reports to detect and investigate corruption. In contrast, a weakness of the UNCAC is its lack of a comparable mechanism. Chaikin and Sherman, CORRUPTION AND MONEY LAUNDERING, *supra*, at 34–36. In addition, the desire of governments to avoid an adverse report and public criticism motivates them to meet international anticorruption standards. *Id.* at 37. Civil society and media groups have become aware of and criticized the signatories' lack of political commitment to their obligations in the OECD Convention as a result of their review of mutual evaluations by the Working Group on Bribery.[51]

8. Scope and Limitations

The target of the OECD Convention is "active" bribery or the offering side of the bribery bargain. It is directed to stop the "supply" of bribes to foreign officials, with each country taking responsibility for the activities of its companies and what occurs on its own territory. The OECD Convention is not directed at the foreign officials who may take the bribes. This is left to the responsibility of the home country of the official. It also does not cover private sector bribery or bribery for reasons not related to business. How does the scope compare with the scope of the Council of Europe and UN Conventions? Despite the limited scope of the coverage of the OECD Anti-Bribery Convention are their advantages to developing countries acceding to the convention? The OECD convention has been enlarged because it does not address domestic corruption, private sector corruption, embezzlement, and passive corruption. Are the criticisms of its limitations valid?

9. Remaining Issues

The negotiators left several issues to be resolved by the OECD Working Group on Bribery, including whether acts of bribery should include bribes paid to foreign political parties and candidates, whether to expand accounting and recordkeeping procedures

[51] See, e.g., Tetsuya Morimoto, *OECD Criticized Japan for its Laxness in Implementing the Anti-Bribery Convention*, 21 INT'L ENFORCEMENT L. REP. 249 (June 2005).

to include independent external audits, and whether to impose required internal controls.

A success of the OECD convention has resulted from its regional outreach networks dedicated to combating corruption. The OECD since 1998 has had an Anti-Corruption Network for Eastern Europe and Central Asia and more recently with the OAS with which it signed a memorandum of undestanding in 2007. OECD has also started to cooperate with the Asian Development Bank on anticorruption. Chaikin and Sherman, CORRUPTION AND MONEY LAUNDERING, *supra* 1, at 38.

B. OAS *Inter-American Convention against Corruption*

Article VI Acts of Corruption

1. This Convention is applicable to the following acts of corruption:
   a. The solicitation or acceptance, directly or indirectly, by a government official or a person who performs public functions, of any article or monetary value, or other benefit, such as a gift, favor, promise, or advantage for himself or for another person or entity, in exchange for any act or omission in the performance of his public functions.
   b. The offering or granting, directly or indirectly, to a government official or a person who performs public functions, of any article of monetary value, or other benefit, such as a gift, favor, promise or advantage for himself or for another person or entity, in exchange for any act or omission in the performance of his public functions;
   c. Any act or omission in the discharge of his duties by a government official or a person who performs public functions for the purpose of illicitly obtaining benefits for himself or for a third party.
   d. The fraudulent use or concealment of property derived from any of the acts referred to in this article; and
   e. Participation as a principal, co-principal, instigator, accomplice, or accessory after the fact, or in any other manner, in the commission or attempted commission of, or in any collaboration or conspiracy to commit, any of the acts referred to in this article.
2. This Convention shall also be applicable by mutual agreement between or among two or more States parties with respect to any other act of corruption not described herein.

Article VII Domestic Law

The States Parties that have not yet done so shall adopt the necessary legislative or other measures to establish as criminal offenses under their domestic law the acts of corruption described in Article VI(1) and to facilitate cooperation among themselves pursuant to this Convention.

Article VIII Transnational Bribery

Subject to its Constitution and the fundamental principles of its legal system, each State Party shall prohibit and punish the offering or granting, directly or indirectly by its nationals, persons having their habitual residence in its territory, and businesses domiciled there, to a government official of another State, of any article of monetary value, or other benefit, such as a gift, favor, promise, or advantage, in connection with any economic or commercial transaction in exchange for any act or omission in the performance of that official's public functions.

Among those States parties that have established transnational bribery as an offense, such offense shall be considered an act of corruption for the purposes of this Convention.

Any State Party that has not established transnational bribery as an offense shall, insofar as its laws permit, provide assistance and cooperation with respect to this offense as provided in this Convention.

Article IX Illicit Enrichment

Subject to its Constitution and the fundamental principles of its legal system, each State Party that has not yet done so shall take the necessary measures to establish under its laws as an offense a significant increase in the assets of a government official that he cannot reasonably explain in relation to his lawful earnings during the performance of his functions.

Among those States parties that have established illicit enrichment as an offense, such offense shall be considered an act of corruption for the purposes of this Convention.

Any State Party that has not established illicit enrichment as an offense shall, insofar as its laws permit, provide assistance and cooperation with respect to this offense as provided in this Convention.

Notes and Questions

1. Background

In 1994, the General Assembly of the OAS adopted a resolution condemning corruption in international trade. The resolution led to other initiatives, culminating in the 1996 approval of the Inter-American Convention against Corruption.[52] The convention entered into force on March 6, 1997. As of April 12, 2009, thirty-three countries have deposited their instruments of ratification of accession to the Inter-American Convention against Corruption. What is the practical significance, if any, of the adoption by the OAS General Assembly of resolutions, such as the one condemning corruption in international trade?

The Inter-American Convention is broader in scope than the OECD Convention in that it also criminalizes the "demand" side of corruption; that is, "passive" corruption. It also provides for the development of institutions to combat corruption and to implement mechanisms to facilitate the enforcement of anticorruption measures. To what, if any extent, may the Inter-American Convention affect the future of international anticorruption conventions?

2. Public Official

The Inter-American Convention covers all levels of civil servants, whether they are "governmental officials," "public servants," elected officials, appointed officials or employees, or others carrying out "public" functions.

[52] The convention is reprinted in 35 I.L.M. 724 (1996). It is also available on the OAS Web site. For current information on signatories, accession, ratification, and reservations to the convention see http://www.oas.org/juridico/english/Sigs/b-58.html.

The definition of public officials is more limited in the Inter-American Convention than under the OECD Convention. The former does not include officials or agents of a public international organization nor officials or employees of parastatals covered by the OECD Convention. Do you think a more limited definition of public officials as in the Inter-American Convention, is the best approach? Why?

3. Passive Bribery

The Inter-American Convention targets the direct or indirect solicitation or acceptance by a public official of any article of monetary value or other benefit, whether for the pubic official or for another individual or entity, in exchange for any act or omission in the performance of his or her official functions. It includes acts or omissions by a public official or by a person who performs a public function in order to obtain benefits. The Inter-American Convention also includes participation in a corrupt act and the fraudulent use or concealment of property derived from a corrupt act. Do you think the inclusion of passive bribery as one of the crimes covered by the Convention influenced the coverage of corruption crimes in any of the subsequent conventions, that is, the Council of Europe Criminal Convention and the UN Convention against Corruption, especially because the latter were adopted after the OAS Convention?

4. Transnational Bribery

A separate article of the Inter-American Convention addresses bribery of foreign officials. Although the convention does not expressly provide an exception for facilitating payments, the OAS Juridical Committee's report on model elements for inclusion in domestic implementing legislation implicitly recognizes that parties can exclude facilitating payments from their legislation.

5. Illicit Enrichment

Parties are required to make illicit enrichment an offense under their laws unless doing so would contravene fundamental principles of their legal systems. Because of the constitutional need to guarantee the presumption of innocence in criminal cases, the United States and Canada have appended an understanding or declaration in their instruments of ratification to the effect that they are not obligated to establish illicit enrichment as a crime in implementing the Inter-American Convention.

6. Cooperation

Parties are required to cooperate, and to the extent permitted by their laws, provide mutual legal assistance to combating crimes covered by the convention – such as illicit enrichment – provided that such acts are crimes under domestic law. As in a series of international enforcement conventions starting from the 1988 Vienna Counterdrug Convention, bank secrecy cannot be asserted as a reason to avoid international cooperation. Neither can the political offense exception be a reason to refuse to cooperate. Extradition treaties are expanded to include criminal offenses covered by the Inter-American Convention and provide a basis for extradition between parties that do not have extradition treaties. How can governments try to ensure extradition for anticorruption offenses, especially because the Inter-American Convention and other anticorruption conventions require extradition for containing transnational corruption offenses? See, for example, the role of MESICIC, discussed immediately below.

7. Monitoring

In June 2001, the OAS adopted the Mechanism for Follow-Up of Implementation of the Inter-American Convention against Corruption (MESICIC), which serves as an evaluation mechanism.[53] MESICIC goals are to help with the implementation of the convention; review, with the input of civil society, the manner in which the states parties are meeting their obligations; and facilitate activities of technical cooperation, the exchange of information, experiences and best practices, and the harmonization of states parties' legislation.[54] The first round of review of states parties' implementation of the convention was concluded in March 2006.

The MESICIC consists of two bodies: the Conference of States Parties, composed of representatives of all of the states, which has the authority and responsibility of supervising its implementation (the political body); and the Committee of Experts, composed of experts designated by each state party, which is responsible for the technical review of the implementation of the convention by the states parties (technical body). The General Secretariat of the OAS acts as Technical Secretariat of MESICIC.

C. *Council of Europe Conventions*

The Council of Europe has two conventions – one on criminal law and one on civil law.

1. The Criminal Law Convention on Corruption

On June 15, 1994, justice ministers from the Council of Europe adopted a program to combat corruption. The program established a multidisciplinary group on corruption (GMC) to address issues such as public and private codes of conduct, fines for illegal payments, means to prevent corruption by foreign officials, and extradition and international cooperation when corruption is involved.

In 1998, on the recommendations of the GMC, the Criminal Law Convention was negotiated by the member states of the Council of Europe with the participation of observers, including the United States. In 1998, the Council of Ministers adopted it.[55] On July 1, 2002, the CoE Criminal Law Convention entered into force. As of April 13, 2009, it had forty-one ratifications and eight signatories not followed up by ratifications. The United States and Mexico are among the nonmembers of the Council of Europe in the latter category.[56]

[53] For current information on the parties that have adopted the Evaluation Mechanism, *see* OAS, Follow-up Signatories, Evaluation Mechanism, at http://www.oas.org/juridico/english/followup_sigs.htm.

[54] *See* OAS Web site for a discussion of MESICIC http://www.oas.org/juridico/english/faq_ac.htm#1, accessed Apr. 11, 2009.

[55] ETS No. 173, *reprinted in* 38 I.L.M. 5050 (1999).

[56] For current information as to signatories and ratifications to the CoE Criminal Law Convention, *see* CoE at http://conventions.coe.int, then go to "Full List" then to No. "173," then to "Chart of signatures and ratifications."

The CoE Convention addresses both the supply and demand side of corruption, requiring parties to criminalize both the act of bribery – active bribery – and the act of soliciting or receiving a bribe, passive bribery. It also addresses a broader range of corrupt activities than the OECD and Inter-American Conventions by encompassing private sector bribery and "trading in influence."

The CoE Convention requires parties to criminalize active and passive bribery regardless of whether the inducer's purpose relates to obtaining or retaining business. The range of public officials is more limited than in the other anticorruption conventions. Rather than having a single definition of public official, it allows a party's national law to determine who is a public official. The convention requires the prohibition of bribery of officials of public international organizations and members of international assemblies only when the intended recipient is an official or contracted employee of an organization or assembly of which the prosecuting party is also a member. Bribery of judges and officials of international courts is prohibited only for courts whose jurisdiction has been accepted by a prosecuting party.

The convention does not have a specific exception for facilitating payments.

Parties must criminalize the active and passive bribery of private individuals and entities "in the course of business activity."[57] This is known as commercial bribery.

Parties must enact laws criminalizing the giving or receiving of "any undue advantage" in exchange for "improper influence" over the decisions of domestic or foreign officials, legislators, judges, or employees of international organizations. This forbids direct and indirect promises of "undue advantage" by an individual who "asserts or confirms" an ability to exert improper influence over a public official's decision-making function, even if the individual does not actually have the ability to do what is asserted or confirmed.[58]

Parties are required to criminalize money laundering of proceeds from corruption offenses[59] and "account offenses," such as creating or using an invoice or any other accounting document or record containing false or incomplete information or unlawfully omitting the making of a record of a payment.[60]

Parties must establish corporate liability, whether in a criminal, civil, or administrative context, for offenses committed for or on behalf of the entity by an individual with a "leading position" within the organization based on "a power of representative of the legal person; or an authority to take decisions on behalf of the legal person; or an authority to exercise control within the legal person; as well as for involvement of such a natural person as accessory or instigator."[61]

The convention requires parties to furnish broad international cooperation. Neither dual criminality nor bank secrecy can be used to refuse cooperation. The convention can substitute for bilateral conventions as the basis of cooperation if parties have not entered into the same.[62] A party may spontaneously transmit information to another party when it believes that the disclosure of such information might assist the receiving party in investigating crimes covered by the convention.[63]

[57] CoE Criminal Law Convention, Art. 8.
[58] *Id.*, Art. 12.
[59] *Id.*, Art. 13.
[60] *Id.*, Art. 14.
[61] *Id.*, Art. 18.
[62] *Id.*, Articles 25 to 31.
[63] *Id.*, Art. 28.

In 1997, the Council of Europe established a monitoring mechanism called the Group of States against Corruption (GRECO). GRECO uses firsthand evaluations by peer-review investigation teams similar to the OECD. However, unlike the OECD, which publishes the country reports, GRECO has confidential reporting.[64]

The convention allows up to five reservations with respect to some of its more controversial aspects, such as trading in influence, some forms of passive bribery, and private sector bribery.[65]

In May 2003, the Council of Europe adopted the Additional Protocol to the Criminal Law Convention. It entered into force on January 2, 2005. It expands the scope of the convention to arbitrators and to jurors.[66]

2. The Civil Law Convention on Corruption

In 1999, the Committee of Ministers of the Council of Europe adopted the CoE Civil Law Convention on Corruption. It entered into force on November 1, 2003. As of April 7, 2006, it had forty signatories, including one nonmember state (Belarus) and twenty-five ratifications. It constitutes the first effort to provide an international mechanism to respond to corruption by means of civil legal measures. The parties to the convention must provide in their domestic law "for effective remedies for persons who have suffered damage as a result of acts of corruption, to enable them to defend their rights and interests, including the possibility of obtaining compensation for damage."[67]

The convention requires each party to provide for a private right of action for "full compensation" against an individual or entity that has committed or authorized an act of corruption or failed to take reasonable steps to prevent an act of corruption.[68] Each party must provide a private right of action for persons suffering damage as a result of an action of corruption by its public officials in the exercise of their functions to claim compensation from the state or, in the case of a nonstate party, from that party's appropriate authorities.[69] Compensation may cover material damage, lost profits, and nonpecuniary losses.[70]

A party must provide for contributory negligence, if shown, as a means to reduce or disallow liability or compensation.[71]

The statute of limitation that applies to any action brought under the convention is at least three years from knowledge of the act of corruption or knowledge of damage from the act of corruption and knowledge of the identity of the responsible individual or entity. No action is allowed ten years after the act of corruption.[72]

64 For more information on monitoring, *see* the GRECO Web site at http://www.greco.coe.int.

65 CoE Criminal Law Convention, Art. 37.

66 For information on parties and the status of their ratification to the Additional Protocol, *see* Council of Europe at http://conventions.coe.int, then go to "full List", then to No. "191," then to "Chart of signatures and ratifications."

67 CoE Civil Law Convention, Art. 1.

68 *Id.*, Art. 3, 1.

69 *Id.*, Art. 5.

70 *Id.*, Art. 3, 2.

71 *Id.*, Art. 6.

72 *Id.*, Art. 7.

A party must include provisions in its domestic law to nullify "any contract or clause of a contract providing for corruption."[73]

To encourage whistleblowers, a party must incorporate into domestic law protection against any unjustified sanction for employees who have reasonable grounds to suspect corruption and who report in good faith their suspicions to responsible persons or authorities. Such reporting should not be considered a breach of the duty of confidentiality.[74]

The convention requires parties to implement measures requiring that "companies" prepare "annual accounts" that provide a "true and fair view" of a company's financial position.[75] An entity must have an auditor confirm the annual accounts.[76]

The convention requires parties to provide in their domestic law for effective procedures for the acquisition of evidence in civil proceedings from the act of corruption and to provide other types of cooperation, such as serving documents, jurisdiction, and recognition and enforcement of foreign judgments.[77]

The convention does not allow reservations.[78] It must be implemented by each of the parties, and GRECO is responsible for monitoring its implementation. As of July 6, 2004, thirty-eight states including the United States had joined GRECO. Membership in the GRECO overlaps, but is not identical to, membership in the CoE Convention. Although a state party automatically joins GRECO when it ratifies the CoE Convention, the reverse is not true; a state party may choose to participate only in GRECO, but not accede to the CoE Convention.

Notes and Questions

1. What do you think are the advantages and disadvantages of confidential reporting?
2. How significant do you think allowing the five reservations has been in persuading countries to join the Criminal Convention?
3. How important are the potential civil legal measures for victims of transnational corruption? What if anything, should civil society and businesses do to effectively use the civil legal measures allowed under the CoE Civil Law Convention?
4. What are some difficulties of taking action if a business believes it may have lost a contract due to bribery?
5. Are there differences in how the criminal and civil legal proceedings on an anticorruption case interact in common law and civil law countries? If so, now should the differences potentially impact strategies in bringing proceedings relating to anticorruption matters?
6. One of the processes of the Council of Europe agreements is the peer review process.
7. One of the problems revealed during its implementation reports is the political discretion over corruption prosecutions. Politically appointed prosecutor generals in civil law countries often have wide discretion in deciding to initiate, continue, or stop prosecutions. GRECO has stressed the need for a transparent, objective, and merit-based system for the appointment, promotion, and disciplining of prosecutors in order to avoid

[73] *Id.*, Art. 8.
[74] *Id.*, Art. 9.
[75] *Id.*, Art. 10, 1.
[76] *Id.*, Art. 10, 2.
[77] *Id.*, Art. 13.
[78] *Id.*, Art. 17.

political interference. DAVID CHAIKAN AND J. C. SHARMAN, CORRUPTION AND MONEY LAUNDERING: A SYMBIOTIC RELATIONSHIP 74 (Palgrave MacMillan 2009).

D. United Nations Convention against Corruption

Article 5 Preventive Anti-Corruption Policies and Practices

1. Each State Party shall, in accordance with the fundamental principles of its legal system, develop and implement or maintain effective, coordinated anti-corruption policies that promote the participation of society and reflect the principles of the rule of law, proper management of public affairs and public property, integrity, transparency and accountability.
2. Each State Party shall endeavor to establish and promote effective practices aimed at the prevention of corruption.
3. Each State Party shall endeavor to periodically evaluate relevant legal instruments and administrative measures with a view to determining their adequacy to prevent and fight corruption.
4. States Parties shall, as appropriate and in accordance with the fundamental principles of their legal system, collaborate with each other and with relevant international and regional organizations in promoting and developing the measures referred to in this article. That collaboration may include participation in international programmes and projects aimed at the prevention of corruption.

Article 6 Preventive Anti-Corruption Body or Bodies

1. Each State Party shall, in accordance with the fundamental principles of its legal system, ensure the existence of a body or bodies, as appropriate, that prevent corruption by such means as:
   (a) Implementing the policies referred to in article 5 of this Convention and, where appropriate, overseeing and coordinating the implementation of those policies;
   (b) Increasing and disseminating knowledge about the prevention of corruption.
2. Each State Party shall grant the body or bodies referred to in paragraph 1 of this article the necessary independence, in accordance with the fundamental principles of its legal system to enable the body or bodies to carry out its or their functions effectively and free from any undue influence. The necessary material resources and specialized staff, as well as the training that such staff may require to carry out their functions, should be provided.
3. Each State Party shall inform the Secretary-General of the United Nations of the name and address of the authority or authorities that may assist other States Parties in developing and implementing specific measures for the prevention of corruption.

Article 10 Public Reporting

Taking into account the need to combat corruption, each State Party shall, in accordance with the fundamental principles of its domestic law, take such measures as may be necessary to enhance transparency in its public administration, including with regard to its organization, functioning and decision-making processes, where appropriate. Such measures may include, *inter alia*:

(a) Adopting procedures or regulations allowing members of the general public to obtain, where appropriate, information on the organization, functioning, and decision-making processes of its public administration and, with due regard for the protection of privacy and personal data, on decisions and legal acts that concern members of the public;
(b) Simplifying administrative procedures, where appropriate, in order to facilitate public access to the competent decision-making authorities; and
(c) Publishing information, which may include periodic reports on the risks of corruption in its public administration.

Article 12 Private Sector

1. Each State Party shall take measures, in accordance with the fundamental principles of its domestic law, to prevent corruption involving the private sector, enhance accounting and auditing standards in the private sector and, where appropriate, provide effective, proportionate and dissuasive civil, administrative, or criminal penalties for failure to comply with such measures.

3. In order to prevent corruption, each State Party shall take such measures as may be necessary, in accordance with its domestic laws and regulations regarding the maintenance of books and records, financial statement disclosures and accounting and auditing standards, to prohibit the following acts carried out for the purpose of committing any of the offences established in accordance with this Convention:
(a) The establishment of off-the-books accounts;
(b) The making of off-the-books or inadequately identified transactions;
(c) The recording of non-existent expenditure;
(d) The entry of liabilities with incorrect identification of their objects;
(e) The use of false documents; and
(f) The international destruction of bookkeeping documents earlier than foreseen by the law.

Article 13 Participation of Society

1. Each State Party shall take appropriate measures, within its means and in accordance with fundamental principles of its domestic law, to promote the active participation of individuals and groups outside the public sector, such as civil society, non-governmental organizations, and community-based organizations, in the prevention of and the fight against corruption and to raise public awareness regarding the existence, causes and gravity of, and the threat posed by corruption. The participation should be strengthened by such measures as:
(a) Enhancing the transparency of and promoting the contribution of the public to decision-making processes;
(b) Ensuring that the public has effective access to information;

(c) Undertaking public information activities that contribute to non-tolerance of corruption, as well as public education programmes, including school and university curricula;

(d) Respecting, promoting, and protecting the freedom to seek, receive, publish, and disseminate information concerning corruption. That freedom may be subject to certain restrictions, but these shall only be such as are provided for by law and are necessary:

  (i) For respect of the rights or reputations of others;

  (ii) For the protection of national security or *ordre public* or of public health or morals.

2. Each State Party shall take appropriate measures to ensure that the relevant anti-corruption bodies referred to in this Convention are known to the public and shall provide access to such bodies, where appropriate, for the reporting including anonymously, of any incidents that may be considered to constitute an offense established in accordance with this Convention.

Chapter III Criminalization and Law Enforcement

Article 15 Bribery of National Public Officials

Article 16 Bribery of Foreign Public Officials and Officials of Public International Organizations

Article 17 Embezzlement, Misappropriation, or Other Diversion of Property by a Public Official

Article 18 Trading in Influence

Article 19 Abuse of Functions

Article 20 Illicit Enrichment

Article 21 Bribery in the Private Sector

Article 22 Embezzlement of Property in the Private Sector

Article 23 Laundering of Proceeds of Crime

Article 24 Concealment

Article 25 Obstruction of Justice

Article 26 Liability of Legal Person

Article 27 Participation and Attempt

Article 28 Knowledge, Intent, and Purpose as elements of an offense: Knowledge, intent, or purpose required as an element of an offense established in accordance with this convention may be inferred from objective factual circumstances.

Article 29 Statute of Limitations

Article 30 Prosecution, Adjudication, and Sanctions

Article 31 Freezing, Seizure, and Confiscation

Article 32 Protection of Witnesses, Experts, and Victims

Article 33 Protection of Reporting Persons

Article 34 Consequences of Acts of Corruption: With due regard to the rights of third parties acquired in good faith, each State Party shall take measures, in accordance with the fundamental principles of its domestic law to address consequences of corruption. In this context, States Parties may consider corruption a relevant factor in legal proceedings to annul or rescind a contract, withdraw a concession or other similar instrument or take any other remedial action.

Article 35 Compensation for Damage: Each State Party shall take such measures as may be necessary, in accordance with principles of its domestic law, to ensure that entities or persons who have suffered damage as a result of an act of corruption have the right to initiate legal proceedings against those responsible for that damage in order to obtain compensation.

Notes and Questions

1. Overview

The Convention against Corruption, which entered into force on December 14, 2005, had 140 signatories and 133 parties as of February 15, 2007. The United States became a party on April 30, 2006. The convention arises out of initiatives in the United Nation's Commission on International Trade Law and the work of the UN Crime Committee on Narcotics Control (the 1988 Vienna Counterdrug Convention) and the 2000 Palermo Convention against Transnational Organized Crime.[79]

The convention has several unique provisions focusing on the public and private sector: requirements to criminalize derivative crimes to corruption, preventive obligations, and language on technical assistance. Many of the convention's provisions are optional and some are hortatory in nature.

2. Public Official

The convention uses three factors in determining who is a public official. One factor is a semiautonomous standard based on traditional considerations as to whether an individual holds a legislative, executive, administrative, or judicial office of a party.[80] Each party will interpret who is a member of those categories and how each category is to be applied.[81] A public official can include a person in a temporary or unpaid position, irrespective of the seniority of the position.[82] The convention's commentaries explain that it also does not matter what unit or subunit of the government is involved.

A second factor is a semiautonomous standard associated with determining whether an individual has a public function, including for a public agency or enterprise, or provides a public service.[83] The domestic law of a party will determine what is a public function or a public service. A third factor is whether an individual is otherwise defined as a "public official" under a party's domestic law.[84]

3. Corruption Offenses

Parties must criminalize certain offenses and consider adopting other corruption-related offenses. In particular, parties must criminalize active and passive bribery, embezzlement of public funds, laundering the proceeds of crime, and obstruction of justice.[85]

[79] As of April 9, 2006, the U.S. government had signed, but not ratified the Convention against Corruption.
[80] UN Convention, Art 2, a (I). The term "executive" includes the military branch.
[81] For interpretation and reservations to the UN Convention, see http://www.unodc.org/unodc/en/crime_signatures_corruption.html.
[82] *Id.*, Art. 2, a.
[83] UN Convention, Art. 1. a (ii).
[84] *Id.*, Art. 2, a (iii).
[85] UN Convention, Arts. 15–17, 23, 25.

Parties must consider criminalizing trading in influence, abuse of public functions, illicit enrichment, private sector or commercial bribery, the embezzlement of private property, and concealment of property.[86]

Although it follows the OECD Convention, the Inter-American Convention, and the FCPA's antibribery provisions by requiring a commercial nexus to the prohibition against inducements to foreign officials, the UN Convention expands the traditional view of "international business" to include "the provision of international aid" within the meaning of conducting business.

Unlike the active component of transnational bribery, the UN Convention does not require a commercial nexus for the passive component of transnational bribery concerning foreign or international officials.[87] The convention follows the international and comparative law trend in that a commercial nexus requirement does not apply to active or passive domestic bribery.[88] How important do you think the commercial nexus is in successfully prosecuting or obtaining civil law remedies against corruption?

The UN Convention and interpretative notes are silent on the issue of facilitating payments. If you are defending a person for alleged corruption under the UNCAC, how easy will it be to assert the defense that the payment was in fact a facilitating act? Do you think the laws of the best country and the other countries with jurisdiction may be important?

The UN Convention has an article requiring the adoption of legislation and other measures to criminalize laundering of the proceeds of corruption and requires a much broader basis to invoke a party's money laundering statutes than does the Council of Europe Criminal Law Convention.

The UN Convention allows the inference of knowledge or intent of an offense from objective factual circumstances.[89]

It requires parties to establish the liability of legal or juridical persons for offenses established in accordance with the UN Convention. Their liability need not be criminal as long as they are "subject to effective, proportionate, and dissuasive criminal or non-criminal sanctions."[90]

The convention requires each party, where appropriate, to establish a long statute of limitations period in which to start proceedings for any offense established in accordance with it and to establish a longer statute of limitations period or provide for the suspension of the statute of limitations when the alleged offender has evaded the administration of justice.[91]

4. Private Sector

The UN Convention focuses on many aspects of private sector corruption. It seeks to enhance accounting and auditing standards through the establishment of business codes of conduct, to prevent conflicts of interest, to promote transparency among private entities, and to ensure that private entities have adequate internal auditing controls.[92]

86 *Id.*, Arts. 18–22, 24.
87 *Id.*, Art. 16, 2.
88 *Id.*, Art. 15.
89 *Id.*, Art. 28.
90 *Id.*, Art. 27, 4.
91 *Id.*, Art. 29.
92 *Id.*, Art. 12, 1–2.

The parties must prohibit various accounting and recordkeeping practices that make possible any of the offenses established in accordance with Article 12(3) of the UN Convention.

Similar to the CoE Civil Law Convention, the UN Convention establishes a private right of action for states and legal and natural persons against "those responsible for damage in order to obtain compensation."[93] In addition and as with the CoE Civil Law Convention, the UN Convention provides that, in the context of civil proceedings, parties may "consider corruption a relevant factor in legal proceedings to annul or rescind a contract, withdraw a concession or other similar instrument, or take any other remedial action."[94] As a result, corruption increasingly serves as a legal basis to refuse to enforce or even invalidate a contract. Should the legal departments of governments responsible for anticorruption take action to organize their staff to take advantage of the private right of action afforded persons under the UN and other Conventions? If you can, give some example of how governments try to take advantage of the right of private action?

5. Preventive Measures

Chapter 2 of the UN Convention requires parties to take a host of measures to promote integrity, honesty, and responsibility among public officials and prevent corruption. These measures include developing and implementing or maintaining effective, coordinated anticorruption policies that promote the participation of society and, *inter alia*, reflect integrity, transparency, and accountability.[95] Each party has the obligation to ensure the existence of a body or bodies, as appropriate, to prevent corruption.[96] It is quite possible that this obligation, together with other anticorruption prevention responsibilities, will result in the establishment of uniform anticorruption agencies. This would be similar to what has happened in the counterdrug and anti-money laundering fields; in the latter area, such agencies are referred to as financial intelligence units (FIUs) and are linked together by the Egmont Group, which is discussed in the chapter on money laundering and is the organization representing FIUs.

The goal of the preventive measures is to strengthen systems for the recruitment, hiring, retention, promotion, and retirement of civil servants and, where appropriate, other nonelected public officials.[97] Parties are required to promote codes of conduct for public officials, such as the International Code of Conduct for Public Officials contained in the annex to UN General Assembly Resolution 51/59 of December 12, 1996.[98] Under this code of conduct, parties agree to establish appropriate procurement systems, based on transparency, competition, and objective criteria in decision making that are effective in preventing corruption.[99] Parties must take measures to enhance transparency in public administration, including publishing information on the risks of corruption in their public administration.[100] They must require the private sector to

[93] *Id.*, Art. 35.
[94] *Id.*, Art. 34.
[95] *Id.*, Art. 5.
[96] *Id.*, Art. 6.
[97] *Id.*, Art. 7.
[98] *Id.*, Art. 8.
[99] *Id.*, Art. 9.
[100] *Id.*, Art. 10.

take preventive measures and allow the participation of individuals and groups outside the public sector, such as civil society, NGOs, and community-based organizations involved in anticorruption.[101] Parties must take specific anti-money laundering measures, especially where the measures are related to corruption.[102]

Many countries restrict Politically Exposed Persons to cover only foreign officials and not domestic ones. Exceptions include Brazil, Canada, Belgium and Mexico. Art. 52(1) does not distinguish between foreign and domestic public officials. Are signatories that have not conformed their laws to their obligations in breach? If so, what if anything should the UN and interested persons do? Commentaries argue that this legal gap hinders effective implementation of the UNCAC. See, e.g., Chaikan and Sherman, CORRUPTION AND MONEY LAUNDERING at 84(2009).

6. Asset Recovery

Chapter 5 of the UN Convention provides that the return of assets is a fundamental principle and that parties must render one another the widest measure of cooperation and assistance in this regard.[103] Parties must allow other states parties to initiate civil action in their courts to establish title to or ownership of property acquired through the commission of a corruption offense within the scope of the UN Convention.[104] They must adopt mechanisms for recovering property through international cooperation in confiscation. Parties are to try to adopt special cooperation measures[105] and establish an FIU for purposes of receiving, analyzing, and disseminating to the competent authorities reports of suspicious financial transactions.[106] Property confiscated by a party must be disposed of, including by return to its prior legitimate owners, by the party in accordance with the provisions of the convention and its domestic law.[107] A number of countries, particularly in Africa, have complained that many countries have not cooperated to help return assets looted from the government. These complaints about the unsatisfying experience repatriating illicit assests resulted in a change of approach in the UNCAC. Unlike prior multilateral treaties and bilateral MLATs, under which the ownership of confiscated property belongs to the requested state where the property is located, the UNCAC requires requested states to return the illicit assets to the requesting states insofar as this is consistent with the convention's principles. In addition to providing detailed processes and conditions for asset recovery (Chapter V), the UNCAC (Art. 57) requires states to retrun illicit assets to the rightful owner. It foresees three situations for assets recovery, depending on the nature of the corruptions offense, the strength of the evidence and claims of ownership of property, the rights of prior legitimate owners of property, as well as the entitlement of other victims of corruption offenses. CHAIKIN & SHERMAN, supra, at 141, citing UNODC, Legislative Guide for the Implementation of the United Nations Convention against corruptions 264 (Vienna, 2006).

101 *Id.*, Art. 13.
102 *Id.*, Art. 14.
103 *Id.*, Art. 51.
104 *Id.*, Art. 53.
105 *Id.*, Art. 56.
106 *Id.*, Art. 58.
107 *Id.*, Art. 57.

The first situation, Article 57(3)(a), provides that where public funds are embezzled or laundered, so that they clearly belong to the requesting states, the requested state must return the confiscated property to the requesting state. The second concerns proceeds of any other corruption offense under the convetion, which does not involve embezzlement. In these cases, the requested state may or may not be the owner of those funds [Art. 57(3)(b)]. In such a case the requested state must return the confiscated property to the requesting state when the requesting state "reasonably establishes its prior ownership of such confiscated property," or when the requested state "recognizes damages" to the requesting state as a basis for returning the confiscated property. Third, Article 57(3)(c) provides in all other cases that the requested state must give priority to returning confiscated property to the requesting state, or to its prior legitimate owners, or compensating the victims of the crime. CHAIKIN AND SHERMAN, *supra*, at 140–41.

7. Cooperation

The UN Convention includes detailed and comprehensive provisions requiring parties to provide mutual legal assistance, extradition, and other forms of international cooperation.[108] Parties must take such measures as may be necessary to allow authorities to employ and use evidence from controlled delivery and other special investigative techniques, including electronic surveillance and undercover operations.[109]

8. Monitoring

To facilitate its implementation, the UN Convention establishes a Conference of the States Parties that is to meet regularly.[110] The Conference is to provide a mechanism to review the status of implementation by the parties and facilitate the progress of other obligations under the convention.[111] It can also establish another mechanism, as appropriate, to help implement the convention.[112] The success of the convention may well depend on how effectively the Conference of the States Parties carries out its obligations. Indeed, a shortcoming of the UNCAC is the lack of a peer review process. The challenge for UNCAC is to ensure countries meet the standards to which they have committed. Should the UNCAC have peer review process as a long-term goal? Developing the requested trust among members will take time. In the interim, UNCAC may have to take intermediate steps, such as self-assessment or private or informal peer reviews. NGOs such as transparency International or The International Chamber of Commerce can play important roles CHAIKIN AND SHERMAN, supra, at 192–193.

9. Technical Assistance

Article 60 provides for training and technical assistance. In this regard, in October 2008, INTERPOL arranged, in cooperation with the UNODC, for the establishment in Laxemburg, Austria, of an academy to train officials in investigating and prosecuting

[108] *Id.*, Chapter IV (Articles 43 to 50).
[109] *Id.*, Art. 51.
[110] *Id.*, Art. 63.
[111] *Id.*, Art. 63, 4.
[112] Id., Art. 63, 7.

corruption. The academy opened in the fall of 2009 and offers classes, conferences, and seminars as well as publishing materials on combating corruption. On July 1, 2009, the Austrian federal member of the Interior Ministry, Dr. Maria Fekter, visited INTERPOL's General Secretariat to sign a memorandum of understanding between INTERPOL and Austria on the establishment of the Academy. (See INTERPOL Austria member of interior's visit to INTERPOL seals agreement on landmark International Anti-Corruption Academy, Interpol Press Release, July 1, 2009, Interpol Web site).

Lesotho Charges Top Water Boss, Deputy with Bribery in Katse Dam Project

(REPRINTED FROM 22 INT'L ENFORCEMENT L. REP. 141 APRIL 2006

by Bruce Zagaris

On February 12, 2006, media sources disclosed that prosecutors probing bribery in connection with the Katse Dam Project had charged Reatile Mochebelele, the former top Lesotho official on the Highlands Water Commission and now an influential adviser on water matters with The New Partnership for Africa's Development, and Letlafuoa Molapo, his deputy on the commission and current deputy, with bribery.[113]

Until his appearance in court for a preliminary hearing, Mochebelele had been helping the prosecution. Lahmeyer International, Germany's largest engineering consultancy, had been charged with bribing Mochebelele while he was still Lesotho's top representative on the commission.

Now the prosecution has withdrawn charges against Lahmeyer and instead charged Mochebelele and Molapo. The implication is that the officials at Lahmeyer have decided to give evidence against Mochebelele. One of the bail conditions of the accused is that they may not contact several Lahmeyer officials listed as state witnesses.[114]

As the head of the Lesotho Highlands Water Commission between 1998 and 2001, Mochebelele represented Lesotho on a joint permanent commission, holding a position higher than the CEO of the project.

According to Borotho Matsoso, the Director-General of the Directorate on Corruption and Economic Offenses and the former deputy commissioner of police, the investigations into the activities of the two accused started in 2004 and involved follow up in Belgium, Germany, and South Africa.[115]

Until Lahmeyer officials agreed to aid the prosecution, prosecutors had not been able to obtain cooperation from any of the defendants.[116]

A turning point in the case came in early 1999 when the Swiss authorities provided the bank records of Mr. Sole's Swiss bank accounts to the Lesotho Ambassador, despite resistance by all the contractors and consultants working in Lesotho who also had Swiss accounts.[117]

In May 2002, prosecutors obtained the conviction of Masuphe Sole, the CEO of the Lesotho Highlands Water project. He was convicted on 13 counts of bribery.[118] On June 4, 2002,

[113] Carmel Rickard, *Top Lesotho Water Boss Charged*, SUNDAY TIMES, Feb 12, 2006 (www.sundaytimes.co.za).

[114] *Id.*

[115] *Id.*

[116] *Id.*

[117] *Lesotho Case Study – At Goliath's Feet: The Lesotho Highlands Water Scheme Corruption & Bribery Trials.*

[118] *See Lesotho Corporate Bribe-Taker Jailed*, BBC NEWS, June 4, 2002.

Mr. Sole was sentenced to 18 years in jail, 12 of those years for taking U.S. $265,531 in bribes from the local representative of Acres International, a prominent Canadian engineering firm.[119] Appointed as chief executive of the Lesotho Highlands Development Authority in 1986 when the dam project started, Sole's primary responsibility was to award contracts worth hundreds of millions of pounds to foreign construction companies. Sole allegedly maintained at least three Swiss bank accounts.[120]

An investigation into Acres' bribery allegations by American law firm Arnold and Porter concluded that there is "reasonably sufficient" evidence that Acres engaged in a corrupt practice by paying monies to Sole, through Z. M. Bam, to influence Sole in connection with work performed by Acres for the Lesotho Highlands Water Project. The World Bank Sanctions Committee later announced there was "insufficient evidence" to debar Acres from future contracts, but warned Acres that this was an interim decision the Committee would revisit after examining the evidence produced during the Lesotho criminal proceedings.[121]

Mr. Matsoso has stated that "it was obvious that Sole was not the only one.... We suspected that there were others who we had not yet touched. As we went along with his case we found payments that had been made and at that stage we were not sure who had got the money." Mr. Matsos worked during the investigation with Guido Penzhorn SC and his junior, Hhjalmar Woker, both South African advocates who have been prosecuting corruption cases on behalf of Lesotho for a number of years.

They discovered that Mochebelele had bought several properties in South Africa between 2001 and 2003, in Umhlanga Rocks, Bloemfontein, and Pretoria. The matter has been postponed until April 4, 2005, when it is expected to be transferred to the High Court for hearing.[122]

Mr. Sole allegedly maintained at least three Swiss bank accounts. According to the prosecution, the companies were linked by a web of corruption and collusion and that graft was commonly used in awarding contracts for the Lesotho dams. The Lesotho Highlands Project consortium allegedly paid the largest bribes, in which Balfour Beatty, a British Company, was a partner. The consortium is accused of depositing more than $1 million in Mr. Sole's accounts over three years. In 1991, the first payment, occurred weeks after it won a contract worth $135 million. About two weeks later it won another contract, for $41 million, and another large deposit occurred.[123]

Another consortium, Highlands Water Venture, which includes two other British firms – Kier International and Stirling International – allegedly paid Mr. Sole $250,000. Sir Alexander Gibb and Co. is accused of paying $51,478.01. Canadian, French, German, Italian, Swiss, and South African companies are also charged. The companies allegedly used middlemen – two South Africans and a Frenchman – to move the money through Panamanian front companies.[124]

The companies and their alleged intermediaries will be tried once Mr. Sole's case has concluded. All parties have strenuously denied paying bribes.

The prosecution says the onus is on the accused to establish that the transfers were not bribes. The prosecution points out that it was illegal for Mr. Sole to hold the Swiss accounts

[119] *See* Probe International, *Lesotho: Odious Debts*, http://www.odiousdebts.org.

[120] Chris McGreal, *Lesotho: Foreign Contractors Put on Trial for Bribery*, CorpWatch, June 2001 (http://corpwatch.org).

[121] Probe International, *supra* note 118.

[122] Rickard, *supra* note 112.

[123] Chris McGreal, *supra* note 119.

[124] *Id.*

and a breach of contract by the accused companies to make payments to Lesotho officials connected with the project.[125]

The way in which the Lesotho prosecutor has shouldered much of the effort to prosecute the case shows that, notwithstanding comparatively small resources, prosecutors in small countries can successfully litigate against multinational companies. The case is likely to increase the pressure on European countries and international financial organizations to enforce international antibribery conventions and their own anticorruption rhetoric. For instance, already the evaluation by the Organization for Economic Cooperation and Development of the British implementation of its anticorruption convention indicated serious gaps.[126]

E. *World Bank Anticorruption Initiatives*

International organizations, particularly the World Bank Group and international financial institutions, play an important role in anticorruption because of their procurement rules, the enormous amount of funds they control, and their ability to disburse money in conjunction with rules designed to prevent corruption in the procurement and disbursement processes.

World Bank Stops Chad Loan Disbursements amidst Corruption Controversy

REPRINTED FROM 22 INT'L ENFORCEMENT L. REP. 100 (MAR. 2006)

by Bruce Zagaris

On January 6, 2006, World Bank President Paul D. Wolfowitz announced the suspension of all of the aid from the World Bank to Chad in a dispute over anti-corruption mechanisms.[127] The World Bank's decision follows Chad's violation of its agreement to put oil revenues in a fund in London for poverty reduction. The decision affects $124 million in eight projects for Chad as well as an estimated $20 million in new grants or credits that were under preparation.[128]

On December 29, 2005, Mr. Wolfowitz warned that the World Bank would consider legal remedies for a violation of its 1999 loan agreement with Chad if amendments to the petroleum law were adopted.

The new law reduces a poverty reduction program that was a precondition for World Bank support for the Chad-Cameroon pipeline project. Although Mr. Déby had not yet signed into law the revisions to the Petroleum Revenue Management Law (PRML) passed by the National Assembly when the World Bank acted, he had initiated the amendments. The revisions to the PRML would eliminate the "future generations fund," part of the bank's agreement with Chad which was designed to ensure benefits to the population when the oil reserves are exhausted. The amendments also expand the definition of "priority sectors" to include security and territorial administration and double the share of royalties and dividends that

[125] *Id.*
[126] *Id.*
[127] Paul Blustein, *World Bank Cuts Off Aid to Chad in Oil Dispute*, WASH. POST, Jan. 7, 2006, at A1, col. 6.
[128] Diana I. Gregg, *World Bank Halts Disbursements to Chad, Says Oil Revenue Law Breached Pipeline Pact*, DAILY REP. FOR EXEC., Jan. 9, 2006, at A-12.

can be allocated to "non-priority sectors." In addition the new law increases the government's unsupervised share of revenues from 13.5 to 30 per cent, and widens the rules to cover new oil fields, in line with international partners' wishes. Since the World Bank has disbursed the loans for that project, the decision only affects other existing loans for Chad.[129]

Wolfowitz explained he took the decision after two conversations with Chad's president, Idriss Déby, lasting two hours and 45 minutes. Wolfowitz said the dialogue between the World Bank and Chad is continuing.[130]

Chad tied with Bangladesh for the worst corruption rating among countries in a 2005 survey by Transparency International, which monitors corruption worldwide.[131]

World Bank support for the $4.2 billion investment, including a 1,070 km pipeline through neighboring Cameroon, was important for the consortium of ExxonMobil, ChevronTexas and Petronas of Malaysia to proceed with the project, especially since Chad has experienced decades of civil war and poor governance.[132]

Suspending loans to Chad is a dicey initiative for the World Bank since it could cause a collapse of the government and result in a failed state which could become a haven for terrorists.[133] The dispute escalates a growing threat to the Déby administration from breakaway army groups and a clash with its eastern neighbor Sudan, which it accuses of backing and arming rebels.[134]

Déby's presidential aide, Mahamat Saleh Annadif, characterized the World Bank's position as blackmail and warned that Chad was preparing to withstand further measures such as accelerated credit repayments. He suggested that Chad might respond by stopping oil sales or seeking direct access to its share of revenues.[135]

The Chad government's refusal to adhere to the conditions in the World Bank loans and the link of the conditions to anti-corruption efforts presented the World Bank with a difficult choice. Indeed, the formation of Transparency International by Peter Eigen, a former World Bank professional, arose out of his perception of the World Bank's failure to adhere to anti-corruption and integrity principles and the importance of the World Bank's leadership due to its large role in financing major projects and setting goals in developing countries. Because many other developing countries depend on the World Bank and the IMF for financial and technical assistance, the ability of the World Bank Group to implement effectively anti-corruption and integrity principles has major importance.

(At press time, the FINANCIAL TIMES has run two extensive stories on this issue, one of which links the Chad controversy to Paul Wolfowitz's controversial efforts to reform the World Bank.[136] A second article notes that as a result of the World Bank's actions, Citibank is now blocking further transfers to Chad.[137]).

[129] *Id.* David White, *Chad Defies World Bank over Use of Oil Revenues*, FIN. TIMES, Jan. 13, 2006, at 4, col. 1.

[130] Blustein, *supra* note 126.

[131] *Id.*

[132] White, *supra* note 128.

[133] Blustein, *supra* note 126.

[134] White, *supra* note 128.

[135] *Id.*

[136] Andrew Balls & Edward Alden, *Wolfowitz Anti-Graft Mission Triggers World Bank Strife*, FIN. TIMES, Jan. 23, 2006.

[137] David White, *The 'Resource Curse' Anew: Why a Grand World Bank Oil Project Has Fast Run into the Sand*, FIN. TIMES, Jan. 23, 2006.

F. *Efforts by Developing Countries to Bring Criminal Cases in Developed Countries*

Increasingly, NGOs and citizens are bringing criminal cases in developed countries. For example on December 2, 2008, Transparency International France, the SHERPA Association, other nongovernmental organizations, and a Gabonese citizen announced the filing of a complaint with a "civil party petition" against three African presidents – Omar Bongo Ondimba of Gabon, Denis Sassou-Nguesso of the Congo Republic, and Teodoro Obiang of Equatorial Guinea – and several of their associates, alleging them of acquiring luxury homes in France with embezzled public money. The goal of the action is to freeze, seize, and forfeit those assets and to force the defendants to make restitution of the stolen assets, as required by the UN Convention against Corruption, which France ratified in 2005. An additional goal is to raise the awareness of the authorities and public opinion on stolen assets.[138]

G. *Need to Attack Corruption and Money Laundering in Tandem*

A recent book as observed that corruption and money laundering are closely interrelated and mutually reinforcing. The book argues success in preventing and prosecuting corruption and money laundering requires a more integrated approach to these related crimes. The book argues that money laundering laws are underutilized in fighting corruption. The potential of using anti-money laundering (AML) laws, regulations and institutions, especially the gathering of financial intelligence enhancing international cooperations and recovering assets laundered and hidden in other countries, is often overlooked due to an excessively rigid bureaucratic separation of roles between different agencies. See David Chaikin and J. C. Sharman, Corruption and Money Laundering: A Symbiotic Relationship 6 (Palgrave MacMillan 2009). What do you think of this thesis? Can a similar argument on thesis be applied to the interaction, of other transnational white collar crime areas such as tax and money laundering and tax and corruption, or export control and corruption? How can national governments, international organizations, and civil society develop more integrated approaches to different transnational crimes?

IV. Hypotheticals

1. A U.S. company wants to sell products to a foreign state enterprise. However, properly demonstrating the production process and after-sale services requires bringing the key decision makers to the U.S. plant. The U.S. company does not have a plant abroad. The government officials do not have a budget for travel, and it is considering products from a foreign competitor who have wined and dined government officials in its country. What, if anything, can a U.S. company do?

A U.S. company can arrange for foreign government officials to visit to demonstrate its product. The Foreign Corrupt Practices Act (FCPA) creates an affirmative defense to antibribery liability for payments that are "reasonable and bona fide expenditure(s),

[138] Bruce Zagaris, *Anti-Corruption Complaint Brought against Three African Presidents in France*, 25 Int'l Enforcement L. Rep. 73 (Feb. 2009).

such as travel and lodging expenses, incurred by or on behalf of a foreign official" that are "directly related" to (A) "the promotion, demonstration or explanation of products or services;" or (B) "the execution or performance of a contract with a foreign government or agency thereof." The defense clarifies that bona fide expenses connected with promotional activities are lawful.

Because the tentative visit will take the group to Atlanta and they expressed great interest in visiting Disney World, one of the company marketing people suggests routing the group through Orlando and paying their way to Orlando. Is this a violation of the FCPA? It does seem to go beyond a bona fide expense and may be deemed as an improper payment.

What if the company schedules two meetings over breakfast and lunch in Orlando to discuss the operation of its products? This would also seem to violate the bona fide requirement unless there is an overriding business reason to meet in Orlando.

What if the company wants to take the officials to lunch or dinner in or both Atlanta to explain the products and services? This should be proper.

If the company learns that the government officials like to have the company of "loose women" when they go abroad, can the company arrange to provide some prostitutes for them? Absolutely not – these expenses clearly would not be bona fide. If a company official volunteers that his niece or niece's friend loves foreigners, especially from the foreign officials' country, can the company official arrange for the niece or niece's friend to accompany the foreign officials? This arrangement should be appropriate, especially if no arrangement is made for sex or any favors of this kind. However, it would clearly be a violation of the FCPA if the company or anyone associated with the company paid the niece or niece's friend any money to accompany the foreign officials. Company policy may be to avoid even the appearance of impropriety and so may advise against the arrangement.

The company produces pens and t-shirts and a variety of consumer (e.g., food and beverages) and entertainment products, which it is trying to sell to the foreign government. When the foreign government officials visit, the marketing department has suggested they should be given company pens, t-shirts, food, and beverages and CDs and DVDs of the famous and current movies and albums produced by the U.S. company. Is this a violation of the FCPA? A gift of those products that relate to the proposed sales, especially if they promote, demonstrate, or explain the products or services, is proper.

The company should carefully consider and document that the products and services meet the statutory requirements.

2. A U.S. company that would like to do business in Hungary has arranged an appointment with some high-level Hungarian officials to discuss sales of some new products. The U.S. company is told that it is customary to bring gifts to such meetings and that it will be difficult to do business without gifts. The general counsel consults you about purchasing a gift. Is it appropriate to bring some nominal gift?

This is a gray area. Congress has clarified that if a payment or gift is "corruptly made, in order to obtain an official act or omission," then "it cannot be bona fide, good-faith payment, and this defense would not be available." Hence, this exception is in a certain sense not a true affirmative defense because it does not apply where the basic elements of the antibribery prohibition have been fulfilled.

As noted above, because the FCPA has no *de minimus* rule, if the U.S. company brings a gift that has any value, such that it may be considered to influence Hungarian officials to make a decision about the U.S. company's products, then it may be a violation of the FCPA. To be on the safe side, the U.S. company would have to bring a gift that is so nominal that it would be questionable what, if any value, it would have. The safest course of action legally would be not to bring a gift unless it is a company product that is brought for demonstration and marketing purposes.

What would happen if the U.S. company brings the gift and shortly thereafter wins a new no-bid contract worth $1 million a year for the next five years? In that situation, you are approached by a Czech company that believes it has lost the contract because of those gifts, which it heard about through personal connections subsequent to the contract award. What, if any, rights might the Czech company have?

3. When a U.S. company receives information that it is customary to bring some gifts for meetings with government officials, is there any way to verify the information and also determine whether such conduct is permitted under local law? Yes. U.S. or foreign counsel can try to ascertain what the local laws on procurement and bribery state. Increasingly, the OECD and similar international organizations interested in anticorruption maintain Web sites covering antibribery laws. Another useful source of information is Transparency International (TI). In a consultation in which I was involved, the U.S. company's counsel went to the TI Web site to contact the organization's local chapter in Hungary, which is at the Chamber of Commerce. Within twenty-four hours, we received an answer that Hungary has no custom requiring visitors to bring gifts to government officials. Local counsel is also a good resource.

Hypotheticals 4 through 7 concern XYZ Widget Co., a Delaware corporation, which has targeted the Kingdom of Ebenezer as a new export market. The kingdom is starting its transition to a modern market economy, but the ruling family still controls the government. Widgets are critical to the infrastructure projects that the kingdom is considering.

4. XYZ has sent Mr. J., a marketing representative, to the kingdom and has given him an overall budget to open XYZ's office there. When he seeks to open that office, he finds that all of his computer and communications equipment, as well as corporate samples and literature – worth more than $20,000 – are being held at the airport by customs officials. Although he specifically checked and ascertained that no duties are applied to such corporate equipment, the customs official informs him that he must make a cash payment of $50 to receive the equipment. Would it matter if the cash payment were $500 or $1,000?

What should Mr. J. do?

- Pay the money and record the expense as "miscellaneous"?
- Pay the money and record the expense as a "facilitating payment"?
- Intervene with the host government?

It seems that Mr. J. should inquire further about the reason for the refusal to release the equipment. If the customs official is overwhelmed with responsibilities and $50 is needed to prioritize the processing of the equipment, then $50 is probably an appropriate "facilitating payment" to have the customs official perform a "routine governmental action," which is one of the exceptions to an improper payment. However, it is important that the payment be accurately reflected on the books and records of XYZ. A payment of $500 or $1,000 is more difficult to justify because of the relationship to the value of the merchandise – in this case, more than $20,000).

5. Mr. J. decides to recommend the hiring of a local representative as an agent. He learns that other foreign companies use members of the ruling family who have no "official" role but market themselves as "consultants" who can provide access to the high-level procurement decision makers within the government. One of Mr. J.'s contacts recommends Mr. A., the son of the Director of Procurement for Ebenezer's Ministry of Public Works. What should Mr. J. do about the recommendation?

Hiring Mr. A., the son of the Director of Procurement for a ministry with which XYZ Co. is likely to do business, would be a red flag and should be avoided, if possible, or scrutinized very carefully. Hiring a family member or a relative of a high-level official or official who will make procurement decisions is an indication that payments may actually go to the decision maker or may influence improperly his decision because of the direct or indirect benefit he would receive from them (*see* the earlier discussion of a due diligence program). Mr. J. may want to perform more investigation, obtain a World Trader Data Report, and check any references with the U.S. embassy in Ebenezer or any local organizations (e.g., Chamber of Commerce) and trade associations (e.g., American-Ebenezer Chamber of Commerce) in Ebenezer. Before hiring any agent, Mr. J. may want to develop a checklist of duties and obligations along with compliance obligations for the prospective agent and interview personally any likely candidates for the job. He may want to visit the offices and meet the staff of likely candidates to ascertain whether they have adequate resources to perform the job. Mr. J. may want to hire an investigative firm in Ebenezer to ascertain the background and reputation of any final candidate(s) and follow other guidelines of the due diligence program.

6. In negotiating the commission rate, the proposed local agent asks for a commission of 15 percent on all sales. Mr. J. learns that commissions in XYZ's widget sector in this geographical area range from 7.5 percent to 10 percent. Should Mr. J. agree to pay 15 percent?

Mr. J. should confront the proposed local agent with the information about the normal commission range. Unless the proposed local agent can provide an explanation detailing how market difficulties justify the higher rate, Mr. J. should refuse to pay it. Mr. J. should also note that payment of almost double the normal commission may indicate a bad economic arrangement for XYZ Co. and consider the possibility that the proposed local agent may be contemplating some unusual activity – such as bribery – to perform the job.

Mr. J. should document his negotiations with the agent regarding the commission rate, the amount XYZ ultimately pays the agent, and why he believes the amount is reasonable and consistent with the market in Ebenezer.

7. In negotiating the agreement with the proposed local agent, the local agent requests all commissions in cash. What should Mr. J. do? Cash payments are a red flag and should be avoided (*see* the discussion of the due diligence program). Mr. J. should ascertain the reason for the agent's preference for cash payments and explain that any payments will be accurately recorded on the books and records of XYZ according to the requirements of U.S. and Ebenezer laws, especially their respective income tax laws. Mr. J. should also inquire about the laws and practices of Ebenezer with as many as possible of the sources mentioned earlier.

What if the proposed local agent requests that all payments be made to a numbered account in an offshore bank in Antigua? Such a request would be a red flag because companies should avoid paying consultants outside of the country where services are rendered, unless local counsel has provided an opinion that such conduct is legal in the jurisdiction in question. Additionally, the request to pay commissions into a numbered account in an offshore bank in Antigua is suspect because since 1999 the U.S. and U.K. governments have warned their banks about doing business with Antiguan financial institutions because of their insufficient supervision. Mr. J. should ascertain the reason for preference for payments into a numbered account in Antigua and explain that any payments will be accurately recorded on the books and records of XYZ and according to the requirements of U.S. and Ebenezer laws, especially their respective income tax laws.

8. A developing country hires you to review its anticorruption laws. It also asks you to advise on whether it needs some type of anticorruption agency. Please describe the advantages and disadvantages of an anticorruption agency. What institutions in a government may be involved in anticorruption work?

V. *Additional Reading*

A. *Books and Guides*

ANTI-CORRUPTION CONVENTIONS IN THE AMERICAS: WHAT CIVIL SOCIETY CAN DO TO MAKE THEM WORK (Transparency International, 2006).

Vinay Bhargava and Emily P. Bolongaita (eds.), CHALLENGING CORRUPTION IN ASIA: CASE STUDIES AND A FRAMEWORK, FOR ACTION. WASHINGTON, D.C.: World Bank, 2003.

H. LOWELL BROWN, BRIBERY IN INTERNATIONAL COMMERCE (2003 & Supp. 2004).

DAVID CHAIKIN AND J.C. SHARMAN, CORRUPTION AND MONEY LAUNDERING: A SYMBIOTIC RELATIONSHIP (Palgrave MacMillan 2009).

COMBATING CORRUPTION: A COMPARATIVE REVIEW OF SELECTED LEGAL ASPECTS OF STATE PRACTICE AND MAJOR INTERNATIONAL INITIATIVES (W. Paatii Ofosu-Amaah et al. eds., World Bank, 1999).

Commonwealth and Chatman House. Anti-Corruption Conference: The UN Convention Against Corruption Implementation and Enforcement: Meeting the Challenges. London: Commonwealth Secretariat and Chatman House, 2006.

CORRUPTION AND INTEGRITY IMPROVEMENT INITIATIVES IN DEVELOPING COUNTRIES (UNDP/OECD Development Centre, 1998).

STUART H. DEMING, THE FOREIGN CORRUPT PRACTICES ACT AND THE NEW INTERNATIONAL NORMS (American Bar Assoc. 2005).

INSTITUTIONAL ARRANGEMENTS TO COMBAT CORRUPTION – A COMPARATIVE STUDY (UNDP).

UNITED NATIONS DEVELOPMENT PROGRAMME, DEMOCRATIC GOVERNANCE PRACTICE TEAM (UNDP Regional Centre in Bangkok, 2005).

SUSAN ROSE-ACKERMAN, CORRUPTION AND GOVERNMENT: CAUSES, CONSEQUENCES AND REFORM. Cambridge: Cambridge Univ. Press, 1999.

TRANSPARENCY INTERNATIONAL, MONITORING UNCAC. POSITION PAPER 2008. Berlin: Transparency International, 2008.

UNITED NATIONS OFFICE ON DRUGS AND CRIME, AN ANTI-CORRUPTION TOOLKIT, third edition, Vienna: UNODC, 2004.

UNITED NATIONS OFFICE ON DRUGS AND CRIME, LEGISLATIVE GUIDE FOR THE IMPLEMENTATION OF THE UNITED NAMES CONVENTION AGAINST CORRUPTION. VIENNA: UNODC, 2006.

UNITED NATIONS OFFICE ON DRUGS AND CRIME/WORLD BANK, STOLEN ASSETS RECOVERY (STAR) INITIATIVES: CHALLENGES, OPPORTUNITIES AND ACTION PLAN. WASHINGTON, D.C.: UNODC, 2007.

WORLD BANK, LITERATURE SURVEY ON CORRUPTION 2000–2005. Washington, D.C.: World Bank, 2006.

WORLD BANK, STRENGTHENING BANK GROUP ENGAGEMENT ON GOVERNANCE AND ANTI-CORRUPTION. Washington, D.C.: World Bank, 2007.

ROGER M. WITTEN, COMPLYING WITH THE FOREIGN CORRUPT PRACTICES ACT (2003).

DON ZARIN, DOING BUSINESS UNDER THE FOREIGN CORRUPT PRACTICES ACT (Practising Law Institute's Corporate and Securities Law Libr., 2004).

B. *Articles*

Pamela Karten Bookman, Solving the Extraterritoriality Problem: Lessons from the Honest Services Statute, 92 Virginia L.R. 749–91 (2006).

Michael R. Geroe, *Complying with U.S. Antibribery Laws*, 31 INT'L LAW. 1037 (1997).

Richard W. Grime & Alison Fischer, *Obvious and Not-So-Obvious Consequences from the Rise in FCPA Enforcement*, WHITE COLLAR CRIME 2008 R-1 (ABA-CLE publication).

Stanley Sporkin, *The Worldwide Banning of Schmiergeld: A Look at the FCPA on its Twentieth Birthday*, 18 N.W. J. INT'L L. & BUS. 269 (1998).

U.S. Department of Justice, *Lay Persons Guide to the FCPA*, http://www.usdoj.gov/criminal/fraud/docs/dojdocb.html.

5 Transnational Organized Crime

I. Introduction

Organized crime is difficult to define. In 1919, the Chicago Crime Commission began referring to certain patterns of behavior as "organized crime,"[1] and in 1929, U.S. President Herbert Hoover talked about the concept.[2]

In 1975, the United Nations Crime Prevention and Criminal Justice Branch invoked the term "transnational crime" to identify certain criminal phenomena transcending international borders, transgressing laws of several states, or having an international impact. Until the 2000 passage of the Palermo Convention, "transnational crime" and "transnational organized crime" (TOC) were largely criminological terms used to discuss a crime with different definitions in different states, but that transcended the jursidiction of a given state.

In 1994, the UN Secretariat, as part of the Fourth UN Survey of Crime Trends and Operations of Criminal Justice Systems,[3] identified eighteen categories of transnational – and mostly organized – criminality: money laundering; illicit drug trafficking and corruption and bribery of public officials; infiltration of legal business; bankruptcy fraud; insurance fraud; computer crime; theft of intellectual property; illicit traffic in arms; terrorist activities; aircraft hijacking; sea piracy; hijacking on land; trafficking in persons; trade in human body parts; theft of art and cultural objects; environmental crime; and other offenses committed by organized criminal groups.[4]

On December 15, 2000, the U.S. National Security Council issued a report outlining the impact of transnational crime on U.S. and international strategic interests. According to the report, international criminal networks – including traditional organized crime groups and drug traffickers – have exploited dramatic changes in technology, international politics, and the global economy to operate in a more sophisticated, flexible fashion. Globalization has given rise to more professional criminals who quickly adapt to market changes. Criminal organizations are networking and cooperating, merging their expertise, and widening the scope of their activities. By cooperating, many criminal organizations reduce the risks and costs of pursuing criminal opportunities.

In addition, insurgent, paramilitary, and extremist groups, whose crimes are primarily violent attacks against the state, are increasingly involved in traditional organized crime and drug trafficking syndicates. For example, both Marxist insurgents and right-wing groups in Colombia generate revenue by taxing, protecting, and even participating in the cocaine trade. In Africa, formerly warring groups such as Angola's UNITA and Sierra Leone's Revolutionary United Fund (RUF) sell diamonds to support their causes. The growth and spread of transnational crime have also been facilitated by institutional shortcomings in smaller jurisdictions. Many countries' criminal justice systems cannot cope with sophisticated criminal organizations because of inadequate resources, limited

[1] Rodrigo Labardini, *Mexico's Federal Organized Crime Act*, 11 U.S.-Mexico L.J. 133 (2003), citing Klaus von Lampe, *The Concept of Organized Crime in Historical Perspective* (http://people.freenet.de/kvlampe/lauhtm01.htm).

[2] *Rival Views of Organized Crime*, ISS, monograph no. 77, http//www.iss.co.za/Pubs/Monographs/no.77/content/html.

[3] A.CONF.169/15/Add.1, 4 April 1995.

[4] Gerhard O. W. Mueller, *Transnational Crime: Definitions and Concepts*, 4 Transnat'l Org. Crime – Special Issue Combating Transnational Crime: Concepts, Activities, and Responses 13, 14, and 20 (Phil Williams & Dimitri Vlassis eds., 1998).

investigative authorities, and problems with corruption. Countries also suffer from outdated or nonexistent laws addressing offenses associated with transnational organized crime, such as corruption, money laundering, financial and high-tech crimes, piracy, white collar crime, and human trafficking.[5]

Failing to manage the challenges presented by transnational organized crime has serious consequences. The international community has been forced to prioritize the struggle against TOC, in terms of both resource allocation and the development of appropriate strategies. A comprehensive international approach to TOC requires a sustained and consistent commitment, especially in the realm of criminal justice systems and international enforcement cooperation.[6]

II. U.S. Law and Transnational Organized Crime (TOC)

A. *RICO*

In the United States, the federal Racketeer Influenced and Corrupt Organizations (RICO) statute, 18 U.S.C. § 1961, has been one of the main mechanisms used by prosecutors to prosecute organized crime. This statute defines "racketeering activity" very broadly: "any act or threat involving murder, kidnapping, gambling, arson, robbery, bribery, extortion, dealing in obscene matter, or dealing in a controlled substance or listed chemical which is chargeable under State law and punishable by imprisonment for more than one year" or more than eighty federal crimes referred to in § 1961(1)(B). § 1961(4) defines "enterprise" to include "any individual, partnership, corporation, association, or other legal entity, and any union or group of individuals associated in fact although not a legal entity."[7]

Under § 1961(5) RICO provides that a "pattern of racketeering activity" requires "at least two acts of racketeering activity, one of which occurred after the effective date of this chapter and the last of which occurred within ten years (excluding any period of imprisonment) after the commission of a prior act of racketeering activity."

U.S. prosecutors often employ the concept "continuing criminal enterprise" under 21 U.S.C. § 848(c)(2). It defines a Continuing Criminal Enterprise (CCE) as "any group of six or more people, where one of the six occupies a position of organizer, a supervisory position, or any other position of management with respect to the other five, and which generates substantial income or resources, and is engaged in a continuing series of violations" of specified federal crimes.

Under § 848(a) a defendant convicted of CCE faces a heavy potential sentence:

> Any person who engages in a continuing criminal enterprise shall be sentenced to a term of imprisonment which may not be less than 20 years and which may be up to life imprisonment, to a fine not to exceed the greater of that authorized in accordance with

[5] *See* White House, *International Crime Threat Assessment* (Dec. 2000), http://www.whitehouse.gov/WH/EOP/NSC/html/documents/pub45270/pub45270intro.html; *U.S. Issues Report on Transnational Organized Crime*, 17 Int'l Enforcement L. Rep. 170 (Apr. 2001); *see also* Phil Williams & Dimitri Vlassis, *Introduction and Overview*, 4 Transnat'l Organized Crime – Special Issue Combating Transnational Crime: Concepts, Activities, and Responses 1 (Phil Williams & Dimitri Vlassis eds., 1998).

[6] Williams & Vlassis, *supra* note 5.

[7] Professor Lynch observes that RICO is one of the most controversial statutes in the federal criminal code. Gerard E. Lynch, *RICO: The Crime of Being a Criminal, Parts I & II*, 87 Colum. L. Rev. 661, 661 (1987).

the provisions of title 18 or $2,000,000 if the defendant is an individual or $5,000,000 if the defendant is other than an individual, and to the forfeiture prescribed in section 853 of this title; except that if any person engages in such activity after one or more prior convictions of him under this section have become final, he shall be sentenced to a term of imprisonment which may not be less than 30 years and which may be up to life imprisonment, to a fine not to exceed the greater of twice the amount authorized in accordance with the provisions of title 18 or $4,000,000 if the defendant is an individual or $10,000,000 if the defendant is other than an individual, and to the forfeiture prescribed in section 853 of this title.

B. *Individual Liability for the Conduct of Others*

The federal government and most states have abandoned the common law distinction among the four categories in a participant's role in an offense, imposing liability on all participants equally. Although the accomplice's liability derives from the liability of the primary actor, no distinction exists between them for purposes of punishment. The law of complicity is quite flexible in holding liable persons who provide even minimal assistance in committing a crime. The crime of conspiracy is very broadly construed, both in its scope and as a means for holding participants liable for the underlying offenses committed in furtherance of the conspiracy.[8] Many of the contemporary prosecutions of organized crime figures rely on conspiracy law, thereby extending the potential for imposing criminal liability far beyond that of most other crimes.[9]

C. *Presidential Decision Directive* 42 1995

U.S. Initiatives against International Organized Crime

REMARKS OF WILLIAM J. CLINTON, PRESIDENT OF THE UNITED STATES, AT THE 50TH ANNIVERSARY ASSEMBLY OF THE UNITED NATIONS, NEW YORK CITY, OCTOBER 22, 1995

To stem the flow of narcotics and stop the spread of organized crime, we are cooperating with many nations, sharing information, providing military support, initiating anticorruption efforts. And results are coming. With Colombian authorities, we have cracked down on the cartels that control the world's cocaine market. Two years ago, they lived as billionaires, beyond the law; now many are living as prisoners behind bars. . . .

First, the steps we will take: Yesterday I directed our government to identify and put on notice nations that tolerate money laundering. Criminal enterprises are moving vast sums of ill-gotten gains through the international financial system with absolute impunity. We must not allow them to wash the blood off profits from the sale of drugs from terror or organized crimes. Nations should bring their banks and financial systems into conformity with the international anti-money laundering standards. We will work to help them to do so. And if they refuse, we will consider appropriate sanctions.

[8] *See, e.g.*, Peter J. Henning, *Individual Liability for Conduct by Criminal Organizations in the United States*, 68 INT'L REV. PENAL L. 751, 752–755 (NOS. 3–4 1997).

[9] *Id.* at 756; Phillip E. Johnson, *The Unnecessary Crime of Conspiracy*, 61 CAL. L. REV. 1137, 1143 (1973) (pointing out that conspiracy is a mechanism to expand the substantive criminal law and to enhance punishment).

Next, I directed our government to identify the front companies and to freeze the assets of the largest drug ring in the world, the Cali Cartel – to cut off its economic lifelines and stop our own people from dealing unknowingly with its companies.

Finally, I have instructed the Justice Department to prepare legislation to provide our other agencies with the tools they need to respond to organized criminal activity. But because we must win this battle together, I now invite every country to join in negotiating and endorsing a declaration on international crime and citizen safety; a declaration which would first include a no sanctuary pledge, so that we could say together to organized criminals, terrorists, drug traffickers and smugglers, you have nowhere to run and nowhere to hide.

Second, a counterterrorism pact, so that we would together urge more states to ratify existing antiterrorism treaties, and work with us to shut down the gray markets that outfit terrorists and criminals with firearms and false documents.

Third, an antinarcotics offensive. The international drug trade poisons people, breeds violence, tears at the moral fabric of our society. We must intensify action against the cartels and the destruction of drug crops. And we, in consumer nations like the United States, must decrease demand for drugs.

Fourth, an effective police force partnership. International criminal organizations target nations whose law enforcement agencies lack the experience and capacity to stop them. To help police in the new democracies of Central Europe, Hungary and the United States established an international law enforcement academy in Budapest. Now we should consider a network of centers all around the world to share the latest crime-fighting techniques and technology.

Fifth, we need an illegal arms and deadly materials control effort that we all participate in. . . .

This is a full and challenging agenda, but we must complete it and we must do it together.

President Clinton, in his address to the United Nations General Assembly on its fiftieth anniversary, called for international cooperation to address the threat posed by money laundering, narcotics trafficking, and terrorism, noting that the forces of international crime "jeopardize the global trend toward peace and freedom, undermine fragile democracies, sap the strength from developing countries, (and) threaten our efforts to build a safer, more prosperous world." Declaring international crime a threat to the national security interest of the United States in Presidential Decision Directive (PDD) 42, the president ordered the Departments of Justice, State, and Treasury; the Coast Guard; National Security Council; the intelligence community; and other federal agencies to step up and integrate their efforts against international crime syndicates and money laundering.

A key component of PDD-42 was the imposition of sanctions under the International Emergency Economic Powers Act (IEEPA), blocking the assets of the leaders, cohorts, and front companies of identified Colombian narcotics traffickers in the United States and in U.S. banks overseas. The directive requires any U.S. person who receives assets or property of any listed person to immediately block such property and report them to the U.S. Treasury's Office of Foreign Asset Control (OFAC). IEEPA authorizes the Secretary of the Treasury to impose sanctions, including freezing assets held in U.S. financial institutions, against nations and entities deemed to pose a threat to the national security, foreign policy, or economy of the United States. Executive Order 12978, signed by President Clinton on October 21, 1995, under the authority of IEEPA, finds that the activities of significant foreign narcotics traffickers centered in Colombia and the unparalleled violence, corruption, and harm that they cause constitute an unusual and extraordinary threat to the United States' national security and economy. In addition, U.S. individuals and companies are barred from engaging in financial transactions or trade with those identified individuals or enterprises linked to the Colombian Cali cartel.

On January 15, 1997, the Treasury Department identified an additional twenty-one businesses and fifty-seven individuals determined to be directly involved with illegal traffickers and their so-called legitimate business fronts. This brought to a total of 359 the number of businesses and individuals whose assets have been blocked between 1995 and January 15, 1997, under authority of the president's Executive Order. As part of the PDD 42 process an interagency group is reviewing whether measures can be taken against other international criminal cartels.

In his UN address, President Clinton also stated that the United States was moving to take extraordinary steps against money launderers. To implement PDD 42, U.S. agencies identified nations where money laundering has important implications for U.S. national security and where expanded cooperation would significantly strengthen U.S. anti-money laundering efforts. Several of these nations have been approached by U.S. interagency teams in an effort to increase cooperation bilaterally as well as multilaterally and to reduce the threat posed by money laundering.

In response to the president's directive a comprehensive package of legislation was formulated to substantially assist U.S. law enforcement agencies in their efforts against drug traffickers, terrorists, and other international crime syndicates as well as to counter money laundering. The International Crime Control Act of 1996 (ICCA) was sent to the U.S. Congress on September 27, 1996. The ICCA was devised to enhance the U.S. ability to go after violent international criminals by "vigorously investigating and prosecuting them, taking their money, and depriving them of their ability to cross America's borders and strike at its domestic institutions."[10]

D. *Bilateral Enforcement Mechanisms*

The U.S. government has included anti-TOC initiatives in its bilateral enforcement agreements. For example, in the U.S.-Swiss Mutual Legal Assistance Treaty (MLAT), the United States was able to convince the Swiss government to override its financial confidentiality rules in cases involving organized crime figures. In some U.S. MLATs – such as those with Italy, Switzerland, and Mexico – the United States and its treaty partners have formed special TOC working groups. These groups meet periodically to share information and strategic planning. Thereafter, they jointly target and investigate certain TOC groups.

E. *Law Enforcement Response to Ethnic Organized Crime Groups*

Ethnic TOC groups can be difficult to penetrate because they often form alliances centered around families or tribes from specific provinces or ethnicities. For example, the Chechens, Chinese, Albanians, Nigerians, Russians, Colombians, and Sicilians each

[10] U.S. Department of State, Bureau for International Narcotics and Law Enforcement Affairs, International Narcotics Control Strategy Report, 1996 (Mar. 1997).

have their own close-knit groups.[11] Law enforcement and academics refer to some of these groups, *inter alia*, as the Japanese Yakuza, Chinese Triads, the Italian Cosa Nostra and 'Ndrangheta, and the American La Cosa Nostra. Penetrating these groups requires law enforcement personnel who understand their culture, including their language and ethnic dialects.

National law enforcement groups such as the FBI, as well as state and local law enforcement agencies, have established specialized units to deal with these TOC groups.[12] The FBI periodically meets with its international counterparts to share trends and strategies. For instance, law enforcement agencies throughout the world have established programs targeting Nigerian advance fee fraud.[13] International organizations facilitating criminal cooperation, such as INTERPOL, have units specializing in TOC that monitor groups and trends and exchange information.

F. *Money Laundering and Organized Crime*

The U.S. government has pioneered the use of anti-money laundering and asset forfeiture laws against organized crime. The Bank Secrecy Act introduced these reporting forms: the Currency Transaction Report (CTR), Currency or Monetary Instrument Report (CMIR), and Foreign Bank Account Report (FBAR).[14] Subsequently, in 1986, legislation criminalizing money laundering and providing for asset forfeiture was enacted. The U.S. approach has significantly influenced international and comparative approaches, which have emulated many U.S. efforts.[15]

G. *U.S. Contemporary Efforts to Combat Drug Kingpin Groups*

U.S. Indicts 50 Colombian FARC Leaders for Cocaine Trafficking

REPRINTED FROM 22 INT'L ENFORCEMENT L. REP. 211–214 (MAY 2006)

by Bruce Zagaris

On March 22, 2006, the United States announced a federal grand jury indictment against 50 leaders of the Fuerzas Armadas Revolucionarias de Colombia (Revolutionary Armed Forces of Colombia, usually known by its Spanish acronym FARC), Colombia's largest Marxist rebel group, accusing them of operating an extensive cocaine trafficking cartel and killing persons and shooting down U.S. plans seeking to fumigate coca crops.[16] In October 1997 and again

[11] *See, e.g.*, Ko-Lin Chin, Sheldon Zhang, & Robert J. Kelly, *Transnational Chinese Organized Crime Activities: Patterns and Emerging Trends*, 4 TRANSNAT'L ORG. CRIME SPECIAL ISSUE COMBATING TRANSNATIONAL CRIME: CONCEPTS, ACTIVITIES AND RESPONSES 127 (Nos. 3 & 4 1998).

[12] For background *see* Frank Bovenker, *Organized Crime and Ethnic Minorities: Is There a Link*, 4 TRANSNAT'L ORG. CRIME 109 (Nos. 3 & 4 1998). Letzia Paoli, *Criminal Fraternities or Criminal Enterprises?*, 4 TRANSNAT'L ORG. CRIME 88 (Nos. 3 & 4 1998).

[13] U.S. White House, International Crime Control Strategy of the United States, May 12, 1998, in SPECIAL ISSUE: INTERNATIONAL CRIME CONTROL STRATEGY OF THE UNITED STATES, 4 TRENDS ORG. CRIME 1, 33–34 (No. 1 1998).

[14] *See, e.g.*, President's Commission on Organized Crime, *The Cash Connection: Organized Crime, Financial Institutions, and Money Laundering* (Oct. 1984).

[15] *See, e.g.*, Peter J. Henning, *supra* note 8 at 751, 763–66, 767–72.

[16] *United States v. Pedro Antonio Marin*, U.S. Dist. Ct. For D.C., Crim. No. 04–446 (TFH).

on October 2, 2003, the U.S. Secretary of State designated the FARC as a foreign terrorist organization pursuant to 8 U.S. Code § 1189.[17]

At the time the indictment was announced, 47 of the 50 commanders were free in Colombia. U.S. prosecutors said they had requested the extradition of three of the suspects who are in custody in Colombia. The U.S. State Department is offering $75 million in rewards for the arrest of the other 47 suspects, all of whom prosecutors want to try in U.S. courts. U.S. Justice Department spokesman Bryan Sierra is quoted as saying, "We're hoping the amounts being offered, up to $5 million each for some of the suspects, result in some arrests and in us being able to request further extraditions."[18]

The indictment discusses in detail the structure of FARC. The organization is led by the Secretariat, the top seven leaders who are the ultimate decision makers. Members of the Secretariat also serve as advisors to different regions of the FARC. The FARC has a central governing body – the Estado Mayor, or general counsel – which is directly under the Secretariat. It is comprised of the seven members of the Secretariat and approximately 20 others. The Estado Mayor membership, although it changes, draws its members from Bloc Commanders, senior Front Commanders, and other individuals who have attained leadership positions within the FARC.[19]

The indictment describes how the FARC is made up of approximately 77 Fronts and Mobile Columns. They are designated by number (e.g., the " 16th Front") or by name (such as "Teofilo Forero Castro Mobile Column"). Each Front has primary responsibility for all activities in the geographic area which it controls, including all activities relating to cocaine and cocaine paste manufacturing and distribution. Each Front is led by a Front Commander, who is primarily responsible for everything that occurs in the geographic area controlled by the Front.[20]

According to the indictment the FARC has approximately 12,000 to 18,000 members. Some members join voluntarily while others are allegedly forced to join under threat to them or members of their families, or are kidnapped.[21]

The FARC initially imposed a "tax" on individuals involved in every aspect of cocaine and cocaine paste production occurring within its territory, including coca farmers, cocaine lab operators, cocaine traffickers receiving the finished cocaine for distribution, and individuals who operated clandestine air strips through which the cocaine was transported. In return, the FARC protected the drug traffickers from theft, assisted the movement of cocaine paste within areas it controlled, and escorted loads of cocaine as they were transported out of the Colombian jungles to shipment points on the way to the U.S. and elsewhere.[22]

The indictment relates that in approximately the 1990s and continuing to the present, the FARC took a more active role in the production of cocaine paste and cocaine, increasing its income from the manufacture and distribution of cocaine. The FARC developed into a broker between the cocaine-paste-producing *campesinos* and the cocaine transportation infrastructure, eventually increasing its role to become the sole buyer of cocaine paste in

[17] *Id.* at para. 7.

[18] Chris Kraul, U.S. *Indicts Colombian Guerrillas*, L.A. Times, Mar. 23, 2006; DEA Public Affairs, *United States Charges 50 Leaders of Narco-Terrorist FARC in Colombia with Supplying More than Half of the World's Cocaine*, Mar. 22, 2006.

[19] *Id.* at para. 10.

[20] *Id.* at para. 12.

[21] *Id.* at para. 16.

[22] *Id.*, at para. 17.

the areas it controlled.[23] The FARC allegedly imposed a series of often lethal punishments, termed "Revolutionary Justice," on those who violated its cocaine policies. FARC ordered vast numbers of *campesinos* murdered for selling cocaine paste to non-FARC buyers and for diluting the purity of the cocaine paste, or for other violations of FARC policies. Some *campesinos* were shot, stabbed, or dismembered alive; bodies were found cut open, filled with rocks, and sunk in nearby rivers.[24]

The FARC leadership ordered its members to take countermeasures against fumigation, including shooting down fumigation aircraft; forcing *campesinos* to publicly rally against fumigation; and attacking Colombian infrastructure to force the Colombian government to divert resources from fumigation. The Secretariat and Estado Mayor allegedly ordered FARC members to kidnap and murder U.S. citizens to dissuade the U.S. from its continued efforts to fumigate and disrupt the FARC's cocaine and cocaine paste manufacturing and distribution activities.[25]

The indictment alleges that the FARC and the 50 named leaders engaged in a conspiracy to distribute huge amounts of cocaine into the U.S. in violation of 21 U.S.C. §§ 952, 959, 960, and 963.[26] The indictment claims the right to forfeit an amount of money equal to $25 billion under 21 U.S.C. §§ 853(a) and 963, representing the amount of proceeds obtained as a result of the offense. The indictment states that the U.S. intends to also forfeit substitute assets under 21 U.S.C. § 853(p), in the event some of the $25 billion is no longer available, has been placed beyond the jurisdiction of the court, transferred or sold to, or deposited with, a third party, has been commingled with other property which cannot be divided without difficulty, or has been substantially diminished in value.[27]

The media raised questions about the timing of the announcement of the indictments, since it came before the Bush Administration was expected to release annual figures for coca cultivation in Colombia that showed only slight reductions in 2003 and 2004 despite expanded spraying. Some people believe it could have been timed to strengthen support and reassure supporters of Plan Colombia, the U.S. military aid and eradication program, which has toted $4 billion in subsidies since 1999.[28]

Sabas Pretelt, the Colombian Minister of Interior, said that if the FARC enters into a peace accord, it would probably result in the suspension of the extradition requests. Pretelt continued that the indictment and extradition requests do not close the doors to a dialogue between the Uribe administration in Colombia and the FARC. She said the FARC must cease its activities, deliver its illicit proceeds, and collaborate with justice and the dismantling of the FARC.[29] The Justice and Peace Law, enacted in July of 2005, provides a legal mechanism for individuals in illegal armed groups to demobilize with certain legal protections and assurance. The new law has greatly accelerated the demobilization of the paramilitary United Self Defence Forces (AUC) groups involved in narcotics trafficking.[30]

[23] *Id.* at paras. 19–24.
[24] *Id.* at paras. 27–28.
[25] *Id.* at para. 31.
[26] *Id.* at para. 35.
[27] *Id.* at para. 38.
[28] Chris Kraul, *supra* note 18.
[29] AFP, *Pedidos de extradición contra jefes de las Farc se suspenderían si hay un acuerdo de pax (Extradition requests against FARC leaders would be suspended if there is a peace accord)*, El Tiempo, Mar. 23, 2006.
[30] U.S. Department of State, International Narcotics Control Strategy Rep., Vol. I, 101 (Mar. 2006).

Some of the FARC leaders, such as "Mono Joyoy," have already been indicted in the U.S. in 2002. Other FARC members have been extradited, such as "Simón Trinidad" and Nayibe Rojas Valderama (aka "Comandante Sonia," whose cases should be resolved this year). In Colombia the indictment is also significant because it brands FARC a cocaine cartel, a shift from its classification as a Marxist revolutionary force seeking social change.[31]

After 15 years and billions of dollars in U.S. resources to support the Colombian military's counternarcotics efforts, the results include the decapitation of the Medellin and Cali cartels and many arrests, extraditions, and convictions, including long sentences in U.S. jail. Now the AUC and FARC groups are major forces with trafficking interests reaching high into the political and military establishment.[32] The FARC and AUC territories are de facto countries within a country. With their own law, economy, and infrastructure, they have become territories where the controlling authority sustains itself in large part from the drug trade.[33]

The FARC indictment is unprecedented in its sweep and political significance. Its importance may be as much political as it is legal, since it may provide support to the Uribe administration at a critical time, pressuring FARC leaders and possibly depriving them of some of their legitimacy.

Notes and Questions

1. The United States has been deporting large numbers of members of gangs to Central America and the Caribbean. In some cases they arrive without any warning and with little preparation by the countries that must absorb them. Some of the deportees have been gone since they were infants and have few if any family members or relatives in the countries to which they are deported. Generally, the criminal justice systems and the societies in these countries do not have the capacity to absorb them. In addition, the deportees often transfer their know-how and skills in committing crimes to others. In many cases the target of the criminal activities remains in the United States, because the deportees still have knowledge of the United States and criminal contacts there. *See, e.g.*, Victoria Gotsch, *Central America Increasingly Overwhelmed by U.S. Deportation of Criminal Aliens*, 22 INT'L ENFROCEMENT L. REP. 364 (Sept. 2006) (responding to increased criminal activities among immigrant gangs, in 1996 the U.S. Congress passed the Illegal Immigration Reform and Immigrant Responsibility Act (PL 104–208), implementing an aggressive immigration strategy to deport criminal noncitizens back to their home countries without warning local law enforcement in the receiving country). Bruce Zagaris, *Central American Gangs Continue to Plague Both the U.S. and Home Countries*, 21 INT'L ENFORCEMENT L. REP. 4 Pg. 167 (Apr 2005) (on February 21, 2005, the U.S. Federal Bureau of Investigation (FBI) and representatives of police organizations of Central America met in San Salvador, El Salvador, and started an initiative to analyze combating gangs known as "maras," whose violent attacks have plagued the region).

2. What are some ways to develop policies on the deportation of felons in a way to reduce the impact of transnational organized crime both in the receiving countries

[31] Sergio Gómez Maseri, *Estados Unidos abrió proceso contra las Farc como el cartel de droga más grande de Colombia (United States opened process against the FARC as the largest drug cartel in Colombia)*, EL TIEMPO, Mar. 22, 2006.

[32] Moisés Naim, ILLICIT: HOW SMUGGLERS, TRAFFICKERS, AND COPYCATS ARE HIJACKING THE GLOBAL ECONOMY 70 (2005).

[33] *Id.* at 84.

and in the United States itself? In 1997, the U.S. government made an agreement with twenty-four countries within Central America and the Caribbean obligating it to provide the receiving countries at least three days notice of the intended removal of criminal aliens and escorted noncriminal aliens. Under the agreement, the Office of Detention and Removal (DRO) notifies the receiving country of all aliens being removed. Once the removal is scheduled via commercial or charter aircraft or the Justice Prisoner and Alien Transportation System (JPATS), a cable notification is prepared indicating the name, date of birth, and alien registration number of the deportee; the reason for removal; any special notes regarding the deportee; and the itinerary. The United States sends the cable through the Department of State cabling system to the U.S. Embassy in the receiving country. When there is an Immigration and Customs Enforcement (ICE) attaché in the country, the attaché informs the local immigration and law enforcement authorities of the impending arrival. In the case of JPATS flights, the names are included in a manifest and transmitted to the local immigration and/or law enforcement officials. If the United States does not have an attaché in the country in question, the cable is routed to the Regional Security Office in the U.S. Embassy, which informs the receiving country of the impending arrival of the flight.

The Electronic Travel Document System (ETDS) allows DRO to work with cooperating foreign governments to electronically process and obtain travel documents required for removal, avoiding the need for slower, less efficient, mail-based correspondence. This system has decreased the processing times for travel document issuance from weeks to days and in some cases to just a few hours. Additionally, the ETDS gives foreign law enforcement agencies immediate access to valuable biometric information about deportees through the travel document issuance process. At present, the governments of El Salvador, Guatemala, and Honduras are participating in the ETDS. DRO plans for all countries to participate in the program, especially those in the Western Hemisphere, which want more information on the criminal records of deportees, if any, and assistance in reintegrating deportees into their home country.

In response to concerns raised by the Caribbean Community and Common Market (CARICOM) leaders, ICE offered to provide CARICOM members the ETDS computer hardware and software that have already been shown to be successful in Central America. With the support of the Department of State, the Department of Homeland Security has begun to brief individual governments on the system. The United States hopes to have the first agreement to implement the system in a CARICOM country in place within the next two years. It was partly implemented in some countries in CARICOM at the end of 2007.

The UNDP-funded $1 million International Organization for Migration (IOM) project in Haiti provides deportee reintegration services, including counseling, vocational training, skills development, and microcredit lending. The United States has started giving financial and technical assistance to Haiti to help it absorb its deportees as well. *See* Bruce Zagaris, *U.S. Congress Holds Hearings on Deportees in Latin America and the Caribbean*, 10 INT'L ENFORCEMENT L. REP. 392 (Oct. 2007).

3. On July 18, 2007, Assistant Secretary of State for the Western Hemisphere Shannon announced the Strategy to Combat Criminal Gangs from Central America, Mexico, and the United States through both prevention and enforcement. It is designed to prevent youth from entering gangs and to strengthen the fight against gang-related violence and other crimes.

4. On April 23, 2008, after almost seven years of relative inactivity on TOC, U.S. Attorney General Michael B. Mukasey announced a new strategy to combat international organized crime (IOC). It followed an October 2007 International Organized Crime Threat Assessment. The Law Enforcement Strategy to Combat International Crime consists of nine strategic goals addressing programmatic areas cutting across all IOC threats. Although some goals propose new tools and capabilities required to combat IOC, others enhance or improve existing tools and capabilities. The strategy establishes an investigation and prosecution framework that stresses four priority areas of action against IOC:

- marshal information and intelligence through collecting, synthesizing, and timely disseminating the best available information and intelligence from multiple sources, including law enforcement, the intelligence community, foreign partners, and the private sector, to optimize law enforcement's ability to identify, assess, and draw connections among nationally significant IOC threats;
- prioritize and target the most significant IOC threats by selecting and targeting for high-impact law enforcement action the IOC figures and organizations that pose the greatest threat to the United States, and ensure the national coordination of investigations and prosecutions involving these targets;
- attack from all angles by employing all available law enforcement and nonlaw enforcement tools – including drawing upon the unique expertise of every participating U.S. law enforcement agency in domestic operations, partnering with foreign counterparts to pursue cases at home and abroad, and employing U.S. government sanctions and advisories – all in a crosscutting effort to disrupt IOC activity; and
- enterprise theory by developing aggressive strategies for dismantling entire criminal organizations, especially their leadership, by using proactive investigative techniques and multilayered prosecutions.

The strategic goals are to (a) prioritize and target IOC figures and organizations for concerted, high-impact law enforcement action; (b) pursue concerted, high-impact domestic law enforcement operations against IOC targets; (c) team with foreign counterparts to pursue domestic, foreign, and joint law enforcement operations against IOC threats; (d) employ nonlaw enforcement measures to prevent international organized criminals from operating in the United States; (e) collect and synthesize critical information on IOC targets for law enforcement action; (f) develop and retain skilled and knowledgeable analysts, investigators, and prosecutors to fight IOC; (g) provide law enforcement with updated legislation and operational procedures needed to combat international organized crime; (h) raise awareness and leverage resources in combating IOC through outreach to public and private institutions; and (i) reconvene the Attorney General's Organized Crime Council to provide direction on policy and resources and ensure accountability in the IOC program.

The announcement was significant for what it did not propose as well. For instance, Mukasey acknowledged that no legislation would be proposed nor significant new funds sought. Indeed, unveiling an IOC strategy when an administration has been in office for more than seven years and has only eight months left and at a time when it had very low political capital with the U.S. Congress and foreign allies necessarily constrained its potential maneuverability. For more background *see* U.S. Department of Justice, *Overview of the Law Enforcement Strategy to Combat International Organized Crime*

5–6 (April 2008); Bruce Zagaris, *U.S. Attorney General Announces Initiative against International Organized Crime*, 24 INT'L ENFORCEMENT L. REP. 242 (June 2008).

5. Many foreign governments have tried unsuccessfully to use RICO laws to sue smugglers of cigarettes who have imported cigarettes without paying excise taxes. The cases have alleged that major tobacco companies operate a "smuggling enterprise" and effectively manage the black market for their products. The European Commission and ten member states had brought cases against Philip Morris and R. J. Reynolds – it was thought that British American Tobacco would be added to this case once the technicalities had been pleaded. A separate case had also been brought by state governors of Colombia against British American Tobacco and Philip Morris, making similar allegations. *See, e.g., European Union v. RJR Nabisco, Inc.*, 355 F.3d 123 (2d Cir. 2004). *Separation of Powers. Foreign Affairs. Second Circuit Holds That the Revenue Rule Bars a Foreign Sovereign's Civil RICO Suit for Tax Revenue. Attorney General of Canada v. R. J. Reynolds Tobacco Holdings, Inc.*, 268 F.3d 103 (2d Cir. 2001), Note, HARV. L. REV., 115, No. 8 (Jun. 2002), pp. 2333–2340. *Supreme Court Refuses to Hear Cigarette Smuggling Case*, BUS. J., Jan. 13, 2004 (the U.S. Supreme Court declined to review a decision of the Eleventh Circuit Court of Appeals affirming the dismissal of civil RICO cases filed by the Republics of Honduras, Ecuador, and Belize, seeking taxes and revenues allegedly lost as a result of cigarette smuggling). The suits alleged that cigarette companies created a circuitous and clandestine distribution chain for the sale of cigarettes in order to facilitate smuggling within various foreign countries.

6. Until now the U.S. government has not been able to persuade other countries to impose economic sanctions against various TOC groups or individuals, such as designated narcotics kingpins, as President Bill Clinton implored in his address to the UN General Assembly. Why do you think the United States has not succeeded in persuading other counties to join in the imposition of economic sanctions against such alleged TOC persons?

7. One of the ways that the United States and other countries have attacked TOC is to form organized strike forces targeting various forms of ethnic organized crime groups. The strike forces rely heavily on persons from the country targeted because they know the language, culture, and how to best penetrate ethnic crime cells. *See*, e.g., Bruce G. Ohr, *Effective Methods to Combat Transnational Organized Crime in Criminal Justice Processes*, U.S. ATTORNEYS' MANUAL, Chapter 9 (discussing the various task forces, such as the Russian, Korean, Japanese, etc.).

8. One of the success stories of the U.S. government in combating Italian organized crime is the establishment of the Italian-American Working Group under the U.S.-Italian MLAT. An impetus for its formation was the coinciding of numerous appeals from within the Justice and State Departments for high-level intervention to take advantage of the cooperative relationships forged at the working level. Regular meetings among prosecutors and investigators led to sharing of information about their common discoveries. The U.S. goals of the Working Group were to streamline the exchange of information relating to narcotics trafficking and money laundering; gain assistance identifying Mafia members and associates; and obtain the results of Italian investigative files and wiretaps. The Working Group meetings concluded with a declaration of achievements and identification of future goals. These goals were translated into specific objectives to be pursued and reported on at the next meeting. The Working Group established a subcommittee on narcotics and organized crime and one on terrorism, both of which reviewed specific

issues and reported back to the Working Group. The Working Group studied the use of DNA evidence, crime-scene recovery techniques, terrorist profiles, laboratory analyses, witness protection programs, fugitive relocation methods, policies on immigration and their relation to organized crime, and the link between narcotics trafficking and terrorism. Occasionally it invited the Royal Canadian Mountain Police and Spanish authorities to participate. *See*, e.g., Richard A. Martin, *The Italian American Working Group: Why It Worked*, U.S. Working Group on Organized Crime National Strategy Information Center, esp. 16 (1998). Can the model of the Italian-American Working Group be applied to Mexico and Colombia? What are some of the elements that are needed for it to be successful? *Id.* at 23–25.

9. A difficulty in combating TOC is that significant elements in the security services of many countries are colluding with these criminal enterprises so that it is not always possible to distinguish between the criminals and the government personnel who supposedly are fighting them. Governments themselves have difficulties countering collusion between TOC and their security services, which provide information to the TOC groups about what means the state is employing to defeat them. Some TOC groups, such as the Colombian cartels, have successfully defended themselves by using the arsenal of weapons, wiretaps, and other surveillance tools routinely employed by national intelligence services. For instance, the Cali cartel, with the assistance of Israeli experts, established an organization for technical surveillance in Colombia that controlled about two million telephone lines, including those of the U.S. Embassy and the Colombian security services. *See* Volker Foertsch, Former Director, (West) German Clandestine Intelligence Service, *The Role of Counterintelligence in Countering Transnational Organized Crime* 5 (U.S. Working Group on Organized Crime, National Strategy Information Center 2000), citing Peter A. Lupsha, *Transnational Organized Crime versus the Nation-State*, 2 Transnat'l Org. Crime (No. 1, Spring 1996). Counterintelligence (CI) – the concept, approach, and methodology of countering hostile intelligence and hostile influences, CI sometimes emanating from foreign intelligence services – is needed to fight TOC. It has both offensive and defensive objectives, using measures against adversarial activities of any kind, such as hostile intelligence, subversion, disinformation and deception, covert action, and terrorism. CI methods range from doubling foreign agents and controlling and penetrating adversarial organizations to paralyzing and destroying hostile structures. CI also involves measures taken to protect one's own security structures. Foertsch, *id.* at 6.

III. International Organizations

Several international organizations are involved in TOC issues, including the UN, International Monetary Fund and the World Bank, INTERPOL, the World Customs Organization (WCO), and the International Organization for Migration (IOM).[34] A number of regional organizations and ad hoc bodies, without special status or authority, also deal with TOC.

[34] For an annotated list of international organizations dealing with transnational crime and TOC, *see* G7-PE-Senior Experts Group on Transnational Organized Crime, *Inventory of International Organizations Dealing with Transnational Crime, Annex* 3, Paris, Apr. 12, 1996, 2 Trends Org. Crime 81 (1997).

A. *The United Nations and the Palermo Convention against Transnational Organized Crime*

The United Nations has been the key international organization in the fight against TOC. Its Crime Prevention and Criminal Justice Division (UNCPCJD), International Drug Control Program (UNDCP), and International Narcotics Control Board (INCB) have all been instrumental in anti-TOC efforts.

On December 15, 2000, 124 countries signed the United Nations Convention on Transnational Organized Crime during a four-day high-level signing conference in Palermo, Italy.[35] The convention has 147 signatories and is currently in effect in 149 nations. It entered into force on September 23, 2003. During the same conference, two protocols – one to prevent, suppress, and punish trafficking in persons, especially women and children, and the other against the smuggling of migrants by land, sea, and air – were opened for signature as well.

United Nations Convention against Transnational Organized Crime

Article 1: Statement of Purpose

The purpose of this Convention is to promote cooperation to prevent and combat transnational organized crime more effectively.

Article 2: Use of Terms

For the purposes of this Convention:

(a) "Organized criminal group" shall mean a structured group of three or more persons, existing for a period of time and acting in concert with the aim of committing one or more serious crimes or offenses established in accordance with this convention, in order to obtain, directly or indirectly, a financial or other material benefit;
(b) "Serious crime" shall mean conduct constituting an offense punishable by a maximum deprivation of liberty of at least four years or a more serious penalty;
(c) "Structured group" shall mean a group that is not randomly formed for the immediate commission of an offense and that does not need to have formally defined roles for its members, continuity of its membership or a developed structure; . . .

Article 3: Scope of Application

1. This Convention shall apply, except as otherwise stated herein, to the prevention, investigation and prosecution of:
   (a) The offenses established in accordance with articles 5, 6, 8 and 23 of this Convention; and
   (b) Serious crime as defined in article 2 of this Convention;

[35] *More Than 120 Nations Sign New UN Convention on Transnational Organized Crime, as High-Level Meeting Concludes in Palermo*, United Nations, L/PMO/12, December 15, 2000 (http://www.odccp.org/palermo/sum1.html; for additional background *see* Alessandra Stanley, *Palermo Shows Off as a Cleaned-Up Mafia Capital*, N.Y. Times, Dec. 13, 2000, at A3, col. 1.

where the offense is transnational in nature and involves an organized criminal group.

2. For the purpose of paragraph 1 of this article, an offense is transnational is nature if:
   (a) It is committed in more than one State;
   (b) It is committed in one State but a substantial part of its preparation, planning, direction or control takes place in another State;
   (c) It is committed in one State but involves an organized criminal group that engages in criminal activities in more than one State; or
   (d) It is committed in one State but has substantial effects in another State.

Article 4: Protection of Sovereignty

1. States Parties shall carry out their obligations under this Convention in a manner consistent with the principles of sovereign equality and territorial integrity of States and that of non-intervention in the domestic affairs of other States.
2. Nothing in this Convention entitles a State party to undertake in the territory of another State the exercise of jurisdiction and performance of functions that are reserved exclusively for the authorities of that other State by its domestic law.

Article 5: Criminalization of Participation in an Organized Criminal Group

1. Each State Party shall adopt such legislative and other measures as may be necessary to establish as criminal offenses, when committed intentionally:
   (a) Either or both of the following as criminal offenses distinct from those involving the attempt or completion of the criminal activity:
      (i) Agreeing with one or more other persons to commit a serious crime for a purpose relating directly or indirectly to the obtaining of a financial or other material benefit and, where required by domestic law, involving an act undertaken by one of the participants in furtherance of the agreement or involving an organized criminal group.
      (ii) Conduct by a person who, with knowledge of either the aim and general criminal activity of an organized criminal group or its intention to commit the crimes in question, takes an active part in:
         a. Criminal activities of the organized criminal group;
         b. Other activities of the organized criminal group in the knowledge that his or her participation will contribute to the achievement of the above-described criminal aim;
         c. Organizing, directing, aiding, abetting, facilitating or counselling the commission of serious crime involving an organized criminal group.
2. The knowledge, intent, aim, purpose or agreement referred to in paragraph 1 of this article may be inferred from objective factual circumstances.
3. States parties whose domestic law requires involvement of an organized criminal group for purposes of the offenses established in accordance with paragraph 1 (a) (i) of this article shall ensure that their domestic law covers all serious crimes involving organized criminal groups. Such States Parties, as well as States Parties whose domestic law requires an act in furtherance of the agreement for purposes of the offenses established in accordance with paragraph 1 (a) (i) of this article, shall so inform the

Secretary-General of the United Nations at the time of their signature or of deposit of their instrument of ratification, acceptance or approval of or accession to this Convention.

Article 6: Criminalization of the Laundering of Proceeds of Crime

1. Each State Party shall adopt, in accordance with fundamental principles of its domestic law, such legislative and other measures as may be necessary to establish as criminal offenses, when committed intentionally:
   (a) (i) The conversion or transfer of property, knowing that such property is the proceeds of crime, for the purpose of concealing or disguising the illicit origin of the property or of helping any person who is involved in the commission of the predicate offense to evade the legal consequences of his or her action;
   (ii) The concealment or disguise of the true nature, source, location, disposition, movement or ownership of or rights with respect to property, knowing that such property is the proceeds of crime;
   (b) Subject to the basic concepts of its legal system:
   (i) The acquisition, possession or use of property, knowing, at the time of receipt, that such property is the proceeds of crime;
   (ii) Participation in, association with or conspiracy to commit, attempts to commit and aiding, abetting, facilitating and counseling the commission of any of the offenses established in accordance with this article.
2. For purposes of implementing or applying paragraph 1 of this article:
   (a) Each State Party shall seek to apply paragraph 1 of this article to the widest range of predicate offenses;
   (b) Each State Party shall include as predicate offenses all serious crime as defined in article 2 of this Convention and the offenses established in accordance with articles 5, 8 and 23 of this Convention. In the case of States Parties whose legislation sets out a list of specific predicate offenses, they shall, at a minimum, include in such list a comprehensive range of offenses associated with organized criminal groups;
   (c) For the purposes of subparagraph (b), predicate offenses shall include offenses committed both within and outside the jurisdiction of the State Party in question. However, offenses committed outside the jurisdiction of a State Party shall constitute predicate offenses only when the relevant conduct is a criminal offense under the domestic law of the State where it is committed and would be a criminal offense under the domestic law of the State Party implementing or applying this article had it been committed there;
   (d) Each State Party shall furnish copies of its laws that give effect to this article and of any subsequent changes to such laws or a description thereof to the Secretary-General of the United Nations;
   (e) If required by fundamental principles of the domestic law of a State Party, it may be provided that the offenses set forth in paragraph 1 of this article do not apply to the persons who committed the predicate offense;
   (f) Knowledge, intent or purpose required as an element of an offense set forth in paragraph 1 of this article may be inferred from objective factual circumstances.

Article 7: Measures to Combat Money-Laundering

1. Each State Party:
   (a) Shall institute a comprehensive domestic regulatory and supervisory regime for banks and non-bank financial institutions and, where appropriate, other bodies particularly susceptible to money-laundering, within its competence, in order to deter and detect all forms of money-laundering, which regime shall emphasize requirements for customer identification, record-keeping and the reporting of suspicious transactions;
   (b) Shall, without prejudice to articles 18 and 27 of this Convention, ensure that administrative, regulatory, law enforcement and other authorities dedicated to combating money-laundering (including, where appropriate under domestic law, judicial authorities) have the ability to cooperate and exchange information at the national and international levels within the conditions prescribed by its domestic law and, to that end, shall consider the establishment of a financial intelligence unit to serve as a national center for the collection, analysis and dissemination of information regarding potential money-laundering.
2. States Parties shall consider implementing feasible measures to detect and monitor the movement of cash and appropriate negotiable instruments across their borders, subject to safeguards to ensure proper use of information and without impeding in any way the movement of legitimate capital. Such measures may include a requirement that individuals and businesses report the cross-border transfer of substantial quantities of cash and appropriate negotiable instruments.
3. In establishing a domestic regulatory and supervisory regime under the terms of this article and without prejudice to any other article of this Convention, States Parties are called upon to use as a guideline the relevant initiatives of regional, interregional and multilateral organizations against money-laundering.
4. States Parties shall endeavour to develop and promote global, regional, subregional and bilateral cooperation among judicial, law enforcement and financial regulatory authorities in order to combat money-laundering.

Article 8: Criminalization of Corruption

1. Each State Party shall adopt such legislative and other measures as may be necessary to establish as criminal offenses, when committed intentionally:
   (a) The promise, offering or giving to a public official, directly or indirectly, of an undue advantage, for the official himself or herself or another person or entity, in order that the official act or refrain from acting in the exercise of his or her official duties;
   (b) The solicitation or acceptance by a public official, directly or indirectly, of an undue advantage, for the official himself or herself or another person or entity, in order that the official act or refrain from acting in the exercise of his or her official duties.
2. Each State Party shall consider adopting such legislative and other measures as may be necessary to establish as criminal offenses conduct referred to in paragraph 1 of this article involving a foreign public official or international civil servant. Likewise, each State Party shall consider establishing as criminal offenses other forms of corruption.

3. Each State Party shall also adopt such measures as may be necessary to establish as a criminal offense participation as an accomplice in an offence established in accordance with this article.
4. For the purposes of paragraph 1 of this article and article 9 of this Convention, "public official" shall mean a public official or a person who provides a public service as defined in the domestic law and as applied in the criminal law of the State Party in which the person in question performs that function.

Article 9: Measures against Corruption

1. In addition to the measures set forth in article 8 of this Convention, each State Party shall, to the extent appropriate and consistent with its legal system, adopt legislative, administrative or other effective measures to promote integrity and to prevent, detect and punish the corruption of public officials.
2. Each State Party shall take measures to ensure effective action by its authorities in the prevention, detection and punishment of the corruption of public officials, including providing such authorities with adequate independence to deter the exertion of inappropriate influence on their actions.

Article 10: Liability of Legal Persons

1. Each State Party shall adopt such measures as may be necessary, consistent with its legal principles, to establish the liability of legal persons for participation in serious crimes involving an organized criminal group and for the offences established in accordance with articles 5, 6, 8 and 23 of this Convention.
2. Subject to the legal principles of the State Party, the liability of legal persons may be criminal, civil or administrative.
3. Such liability shall be without prejudice to the criminal liability of the natural persons who have committed the offenses.
4. Each State Party shall, in particular, ensure that legal persons held liable in accordance with this article are subject to effective, proportionate and dissuasive criminal or non-criminal sanctions, including monetary sanctions.

Article 11: Prosecution, Adjudication and Sanctions

1. Each State Party shall make the commission of an offence established in accordance with articles 5, 6, 8 and 23 of this Convention liable to sanctions that take into account the gravity of that offense.
2. Each State Party shall endeavour to ensure that any discretionary legal powers under its domestic law relating to the prosecution of persons for offenses covered by this Convention are exercised to maximize the effectiveness of law enforcement measures in respect of those offences and with due regard to the need to deter the commission of such offences.
3. In the case of offenses established in accordance with articles 5, 6, 8 and 23 of this Convention, each State Party shall take appropriate measures, in accordance with its domestic law and with due regard to the rights of the defense, to seek to ensure that conditions imposed in connection with decisions on release pending trial or appeal

take into consideration the need to ensure the presence of the defendant at subsequent criminal proceedings.

4. Each State Party shall ensure that its courts or other competent authorities bear in mind the grave nature of the offences covered by this Convention when considering the eventuality of early release or parole of persons convicted of such offenses.
5. Each State Party shall, where appropriate, establish under its domestic law a long statute of limitations period in which to commence proceedings for any offense covered by this Convention and a longer period where the alleged offender has evaded the administration of justice.
6. Nothing contained in this Convention shall affect the principle that the description of the offenses established in accordance with this Convention and of the applicable legal defenses or other legal principles controlling the lawfulness of conduct is reserved to the domestic law of a State Party and that such offenses shall be prosecuted and punished in accordance with that law.

Article 12: Confiscation and Seizure

1. States Parties shall adopt, to the greatest extent possible within their domestic legal systems, such measures as may be necessary to enable confiscation of:
   (a) Proceeds of crime derived from offenses covered by this Convention or property the value of which corresponds to that of such proceeds;
   (b) Property, equipment or other instrumentalities used in or destined for use in offences covered by this Convention.
2. States Parties shall adopt such measures as may be necessary to enable the identification, tracing, freezing or seizure of any item referred to in paragraph 1 of this article for the purpose of eventual confiscation.
3. If proceeds of crime have been transformed or converted, in part or in full, into other property, such property shall be liable to the measures referred to in this article instead of the proceeds.
4. If proceeds of crime have been intermingled with property acquired from legitimate sources, such property shall, without prejudice to any powers relating to freezing or seizure, be liable to confiscation up to the assessed value of the intermingled proceeds.
5. Income or other benefits derived from proceeds of crime, from property into which proceeds of crime have been transformed or converted or from property with which proceeds of crime have been intermingled shall also be liable to the measures referred to in this article, in the same manner and to the same extent as proceeds of crime.
6. For the purposes of this article and article 13 of this Convention, each State Party shall empower its courts or other competent authorities to order that bank, financial or commercial records be made available or be seized. States Parties shall not decline to act under the provisions of this paragraph on the ground of bank secrecy.
7. States Parties may consider the possibility of requiring that an offender demonstrate the lawful origin of alleged proceeds of crime or other property liable to confiscation, to the extent that such a requirement is consistent with the principles of their domestic law and with the nature of the judicial and other proceedings.
8. The provisions of this article shall not be construed to prejudice the rights of bona fide third parties.

9. Nothing contained in this article shall affect the principle that the measures to which it refers shall be defined and implemented in accordance with and subject to the provisions of the domestic law of a State Party.

Article 15: Jurisdiction

1. Each State Party shall adopt such measures as may be necessary to establish its jurisdiction over the offences established in accordance with articles 5, 6, 8 and 23 of this Convention when:
   (a) The offense is committed in the territory of that State Party; or
   (b) The offense is committed on board a vessel that is flying the flag of that State Party or an aircraft that is registered under the laws of that State Party at the time that the offence is committed.
2. Subject to article 4 of this Convention, a State Party may also establish its jurisdiction over any such offense when:
   (a) The offense is committed against a national of that State Party;
   (b) The offense is committed by a national of that State Party or a stateless person who has his or her habitual residence in its territory; or
   (c) The offense is:
      (i) One of those established in accordance with article 5, paragraph 1, of this Convention and is committed outside its territory with a view to the commission of a serious crime within its territory;
      (ii) One of those established in accordance with article 6, paragraph 1 (b) (ii), of this Convention and is committed outside its territory with a view to the commission of an offense established in accordance with article 6, paragraph 1 (a) (i) or (ii) or (b) (i), of this Convention within its territory.
3. For the purposes of article 16, paragraph 10, of this Convention, each State Party shall adopt such measures as may be necessary to establish its jurisdiction over the offenses covered by this Convention when the alleged offender is present in its territory and it does not extradite such person solely on the ground that he or she is one of its nationals.
4. Each State Party may also adopt such measures as may be necessary to establish its jurisdiction over the offenses covered by this Convention when the alleged offender is present in its territory and it does not extradite him or her.
5. If a State Party exercising its jurisdiction under paragraph 1 or 2 of this article has been notified, or has otherwise learned, that one or more other States Parties are conducting an investigation, prosecution, or judicial proceeding in respect of the same conduct, the competent authorities of those States Parties shall, as appropriate, consult one another with a view to coordinating their actions.
6. Without prejudice to norms of general international law, this Convention does not exclude the exercise of any criminal jurisdiction established by a State Party in accordance with its domestic law.

Article 23: Criminalization of Obstruction of Justice

Each State Party shall adopt such legislative and other measures as may be necessary to establish as criminal offenses, when committed intentionally:

(a) The use of physical force, threats or intimidation or the promise, offering or giving of an undue advantage to induce false testimony or to interfere in the giving of testimony or the production of evidence in a proceeding in relation to the commission of offences covered by this Convention;

(b) The use of physical force, threats or intimidation to interfere with the exercise of official duties by a justice or law enforcement official in relation to the commission of offences covered by this Convention. Nothing in this subparagraph shall prejudice the right of States Parties to have legislation that protects other categories of public officials.

Article 24: Protection of Witnesses

1. Each State Party shall take appropriate measures within its means to provide effective protection from potential retaliation or intimidation for witnesses in criminal proceedings who give testimony concerning offenses covered by this Convention and, as appropriate, for their relatives and other persons close to them.
2. The measures envisaged in paragraph 1 of this article may include, *inter alia*, without prejudice to the rights of the defendant, including the right to due process:
   (a) Establishing procedures for the physical protection of such persons, such as, to the extent necessary and feasible, relocating them and permitting, where appropriate, non-disclosure or limitations on the disclosure of information concerning the identity and whereabouts of such persons;
   (b) Providing evidentiary rules to permit witness testimony to be given in a manner that ensures the safety of the witness, such as permitting testimony to be given through the use of communications technology such as video links or other adequate means.
3. States Parties shall consider entering into agreements or arrangements with other States for the relocation of persons referred to in paragraph 1 of this article.
4. The provisions of this article shall also apply to victims insofar as they are witnesses.

Article 25: Assistance to and Protection of Victims

1. Each State Party shall take appropriate measures within its means to provide assistance and protection to victims of offenses covered by this Convention, in particular in cases of threat of retaliation or intimidation.
2. Each State Party shall establish appropriate procedures to provide access to compensation and restitution for victims of offenses covered by this Convention.
3. Each State Party shall, subject to its domestic law, enable views and concerns of victims to be presented and considered at appropriate stages of criminal proceedings against offenders in a manner not prejudicial to the rights of the defense.

Article 27: Law Enforcement Cooperation

1. States Parties shall cooperate closely with one another, consistent with their respective domestic legal and administrative systems, to enhance the effectiveness of law enforcement action to combat the offenses covered by this Convention. Each State Party shall, in particular, adopt effective measures:
   (a) To enhance and, where necessary, to establish channels of communication between their competent authorities, agencies and services in order to facilitate the secure and rapid exchange of information concerning all aspects of the offences covered

by this Convention, including, if the States Parties concerned deem it appropriate, links with other criminal activities;

(b) To cooperate with other States Parties in conducting inquiries with respect to offences covered by this Convention concerning:

(i) The identity, whereabouts and activities of persons suspected of involvement in such offenses or the location of other persons concerned;

(ii) The movement of proceeds of crime or property derived from the commission of such offences;

(iii) The movement of property, equipment or other instrumentalities used or intended for use in the commission of such offenses;

(c) To provide, when appropriate, necessary items or quantities of substances for analytical or investigative purposes;

(d) To facilitate effective coordination between their competent authorities, agencies and services and to promote the exchange of personnel and other experts, including, subject to bilateral agreements or arrangements between the States Parties concerned, the posting of liaison officers;

(e) To exchange information with other States Parties on specific means and methods used by organized criminal groups, including, where applicable, routes and conveyances and the use of false identities, altered or false documents or other means of concealing their activities;

(f) To exchange information and coordinate administrative and other measures taken as appropriate for the purpose of early identification of the offences covered by this Convention.

2. With a view to giving effect to this Convention, States Parties shall consider entering into bilateral or multilateral agreements or arrangements on direct cooperation between their law enforcement agencies and, where such agreements or arrangements already exist, amending them. In the absence of such agreements or arrangements between the States Parties concerned, the Parties may consider this Convention as the basis for mutual law enforcement cooperation in respect of the offenses covered by this Convention. Whenever appropriate, States Parties shall make full use of agreements or arrangements, including international or regional organizations, to enhance the cooperation between their law enforcement agencies.
3. States Parties shall endeavour to cooperate within their means to respond to transnational organized crime committed through the use of modern technology.

Article 28: Collection, Exchange and Analysis of Information on the Nature of Organized Crime

1. Each State Party shall consider analysing, in consultation with the scientific and academic communities, trends in organized crime in its territory, the circumstances in which organized crime operates, as well as the professional groups and technologies involved.
2. States Parties shall consider developing and sharing analytical expertise concerning organized criminal activities with each other and through international and regional organizations. For that purpose, common definitions, standards and methodologies should be developed and applied as appropriate.
3. Each State Party shall consider monitoring its policies and actual measures to combat organized crime and making assessments of their effectiveness and efficiency.

Article 31: Prevention

1. States Parties shall endeavour to develop and evaluate national projects and to establish and promote best practices and policies aimed at the prevention of transnational organized crime.
2. States Parties shall endeavour, in accordance with fundamental principles of their domestic law, to reduce existing or future opportunities for organized criminal groups to participate in lawful markets with proceeds of crime, through appropriate legislative, administrative or other measures. These measures should focus on:
   (a) The strengthening of cooperation between law enforcement agencies or prosecutors and relevant private entities, including industry;
   (b) The promotion of the development of standards and procedures designed to safeguard the integrity of public and relevant private entities, as well as codes of conduct for relevant professions, in particular lawyers, notaries public, tax consultants and accountants;
   (c) The prevention of the misuse by organized criminal groups of tender procedures conducted by public authorities and of subsidies and licences granted by public authorities for commercial activity;
   (d) The prevention of the misuse of legal persons by organized criminal groups; such measures could include:
      (i) The establishment of public records on legal and natural persons involved in the establishment, management and funding of legal persons;
      (ii) The introduction of the possibility of disqualifying by court order or any appropriate means for a reasonable period of time persons convicted of offenses covered by this Convention from acting as directors of legal persons incorporated within their jurisdiction;
      (iii) The establishment of national records of persons disqualified from acting as directors of legal persons; and
      (iv) The exchange of information contained in the records referred to in subparagraphs (d) (i) and (iii) of this paragraph with the competent authorities of other States Parties.
3. States Parties shall endeavour to promote the reintegration into society of persons convicted of offenses covered by this Convention.
4. States Parties shall endeavour to evaluate periodically existing relevant legal instruments and administrative practices with a view to detecting their vulnerability to misuse by organized criminal groups.
5. States Parties shall endeavour to promote public awareness regarding the existence, causes and gravity of, and the threat posed by transnational organized crime. Information may be disseminated where appropriate through the mass media and shall include measures to promote public participation in preventing and combating such crime.
6. Each State Party shall inform the Secretary-General of the United Nations of the name and address of the authority or authorities that can assist other States Parties in developing measures to prevent transnational organized crime.
7. States Parties shall, as appropriate, collaborate with each other and relevant international and regional organizations in promoting and developing the measures referred to in this article. This includes participation in international projects aimed at the prevention of transnational organized crime, for example by alleviating the circumstances that render socially marginalized groups vulnerable to the action of transnational organized crime.

Article 32: Conference of the Parties to the Convention

1. A Conference of the Parties to the Convention is hereby established to improve the capacity of States Parties to combat transnational organized crime and to promote and review the implementation of this Convention.
2. The Secretary-General of the United Nations shall convene the Conference of the Parties not later than one year following the entry into force of this Convention. The Conference of the Parties shall adopt rules of procedure and rules governing the activities set forth in paragraphs 3 and 4 of this article (including rules concerning payment of expenses incurred in carrying out those activities).
3. The Conference of the Parties shall agree upon mechanisms for achieving the objectives mentioned in paragraph 1 of this article, including:
   (a) Facilitating activities by States Parties under articles 29, 30 and 31 of
   (b) this Convention, including by encouraging the mobilization of voluntary contributions;
   (c) Facilitating the exchange of information among States Parties on patterns and trends in transnational organized crime and on successful practices for combating it;
   (d) Cooperating with relevant international and regional organizations and non-governmental organizations;
   (e) Reviewing periodically the implementation of this Convention;
   (f) Making recommendations to improve this Convention and its implementation.
4. For the purpose of paragraphs 3 (d) and (e) of this article, the Conference of the Parties shall acquire the necessary knowledge of the measures taken by States Parties in implementing this Convention and the difficulties encountered by them in doing so through information provided by them and through such supplemental review mechanisms as may be established by the Conference of the Parties.
5. Each State Party shall provide the Conference of the Parties with information on its programmes, plans and practices, as well as legislative and administrative measures to implement this Convention, as required by the Conference of the Parties.

B. *Protocols of the Palermo Convention*

1. Protocol to Prevent, Suppress, and Punish Trafficking in Persons

This protocol has 117 signatories and 130 parties and entered into force on December 25, 2003. It "prevents and combats" trafficking in persons and facilitates international cooperation against such trafficking. It also criminalizes human trafficking and requires international cooperation, victim protection, and victim assistance. "Trafficking in persons" includes a range of offenses in which organized criminal groups exploit human beings, such as the movement of people across borders or their exploitation within a country by a TOC group. Drafters had difficulty incorporating the wide range of coercive means used by organized crime – including, among others, abduction, force, fraud, and deception – and distinguishing between consensual acts or criminal treatment.

Signatories must implement security measures to prevent trafficking, such as strengthening border controls, requiring commercial carriers to check passports and visas (Art. 8), setting standards for the technical quality of passports and travel documents (Art. 9), and cooperating to verify their own documents when used abroad [Art. 6, para. (3)]. The protocol also provides for other methods of prevention, such as research, advertising, and social or economic support, both by governments and in collaboration (Art. 10).

2. Protocol against the Smuggling of Migrants by Land, Air, and Sea

This protocol has 112 signatories and 119 parties and entered into force on January 28, 2004. It seeks to combat migrant smuggling and to safeguard the human rights of smuggled migrants by promoting international cooperation. However, it only deals with activities involving an "organized criminal group." States parties must criminalize migrant smuggling, including the procurement of illegal entry or illegal residence in order to obtain any financial or other benefit, whether direct or indirect (Arts. 2, 4). They must criminalize the procurement, provision, possession, or production of a fraudulent travel or identity document where this occurred for the purpose of smuggling migrants (Art. 4). The protocol excludes illegal migrants from liability "for the fact of having been smuggled," but does not exclude liability for the smuggling of others or other offenses, even where the accused is also a migrant.

Part II of the protocol gives states that encounter ships believed to be smuggling migrants authority to arrest the migrants and smugglers and preserve evidence, while respecting the sovereignty of the states in which the ships are flagged or registered. These provisions emulate those of the UN Convention on the Law of the Sea (1982), the UN Convention against the Illicit Traffic in Narcotic Drugs and Psychotropic Substances (1988), and interim measures prepared by the International Maritime Organization (IMO). In many cases ships used for smuggling are decrepit or unsound, and delays in boarding them due to procedural requirements may endanger the lives of migrants or crew members.

Signatories must take preventive measures against migrant smuggling (Art. 11), establishing or strengthening public education about smuggling and sharing information required by law enforcement or immigration officials to act against smugglers.

Articles 12 and 13 address document (passport) security. Signatories must develop documents that cannot easily be used by a person other than the legitimate holder. Documents must be of good enough quality that they cannot easily be falsified, altered, or replicated, subject to the availability of the necessary means in developing countries. Signatories must have adequate security precautions against theft of materials, blank documents, and issuance of fraudulent documents. Signatories must establish that travel documents purported to have been issued by them are genuine and valid.

3. Protocol against Illicit Manufacturing of or Trafficking in Firearms

This protocol has fifty-two signatories and seventy-nine parties and entered into force on July 3, 2005. Its purpose is to combat the illicit transfer of firearms from one country to another. Signatories must (1) pass new laws to eradicate the illegal manufacturing of firearms, to track existing illicit weapons, and to prosecute offenders; (2) cooperate to prevent, combat, and eliminate the illegal manufacturing and trafficking of firearms; (3) tighten controls on the export and import of firearms; and (4) exchange information about illicit firearms.

To bridge gaps in import-export controls, signatories must adopt new controls that: (1) establish an effective system for the international transit licensing of firearms (i.e., licensing firearms to pass through countries); (2) confirm that firearms are licensed or authorized by importing countries before granting export licences; (3) deny the transit, reexport, retransfer, or transhipment of firearms to any destination without written approval from the exporting country and licenses from receiving countries; and (4) strengthen controls at export points for firearms.

This protocol requires international cooperation in the tracing of firearms [Art. 14(3)], the sharing of information about offenders and their methods [Art. 14(1)], and in more general scientific or forensic matters related to firearms [Art. 14(2)]. Specific bilateral or regional cooperation agreements are encouraged (Art. 15), and more general forms of mutual legal assistance and investigative cooperation are covered by the relevant provisions of the Palermo Convention itself. The protocol requires the establishment of a contact body in each state to implement it and be a liaison with other countries (Art. 15 *bis*), the exchange of experience and training (Art. 16), and the provision of technical assistance to/an enforcement and other government officials (Art. 18). Signatories must seek cooperation from manufacturers, dealers, importers, exporters and commercial carriers of firearms.

C. *Relationship between the Convention and Its Protocols*

Article 37 of the Convention requires states to ratify the convention before they can be party to any protocols. Hence, each protocol must be read and applied in conjunction with the main convention. The various articles of all four instruments take into consideration this relationship. The main convention has general provisions dealing with such matters as cooperation, technical assistance, and legal assistance. Each protocol has more specific provisions supplementing and adapting these rules for application to the specific problems associated with trafficking in persons, smuggling migrants, and trafficking in firearms.

Countries involved with cases under one of the protocols may rely on the general provisions of the convention where the offense involved is established by the convention or is a "serious crime " as defined by the convention, and the offense is "transnational in nature and involves an organized criminal Group," or where the offense is established by the Protocol and the text of the protocol specifically states that some or all of the general provisions of the convention apply.

Notes and Questions

1. *Convention against TOC*. The convention seeks to strengthen the power of governments to combat serious crimes by providing the basis for stronger common action against money laundering, simplifying extradition, enhancing witness protection programs, and augmenting judicial cooperation.[36] It also creates a funding mechanism to help countries

[36] For background to the draft of the Palermo Convention, *see* Dimitri Vlassis, *Drafting the United Nations Convention against Transnational Organized Crime*, COMBATING TRANSNATIONAL CRIME: CONCEPTS, ACTIVITIES, AND RESPONSES, 4 TRANSNATIONAL ORGANIZED CRIME 356 (Phil Williams & Dimitri Vlassis, eds., Nos. 3 & 4 1998).

implement the convention. More broadly, the convention helps countries synchronize their national laws, reducing uncertainty about whether a crime in one country is a crime in another.[37]

Signatory countries to the Convention against TOC undertake a number of commitments, agreeing (1) to criminalize offenses committed by organized crime groups, including corruption and corporate crime; (2) to combat money laundering of the proceeds of crime; (3) to accelerate and extend the scope of extradition; (4) to protect witnesses who testify against criminal groups; (5) to strengthen cooperation to locate and prosecute suspects; (6) to enhance prevention of organized crime at the national and international levels; and (7) to develop a series of protocols containing measures to combat specific acts of transnational organized crime.[38]

The provisions of the instruments can be divided into seven categories:

2. *Definitions.* The initial articles of each instrument define the important terms, provide for the elements of offenses that must be established pursuant to the instruments, and determine the circumstances in which the provisions of the respective instruments apply. The definitions serve to standardize terminology among countries that act against transnational organized crime.

3. *Requirements to criminalize.* The convention creates four specific crimes: participation in the activities of an "organized criminal group" and "organizing, directing, aiding, abetting, facilitating or counseling" serious crimes involving organized criminal groups, Art. 5; money laundering, Art. 6; corruption where a link exists to transnational organized crime, Art. 8; and obstruction of justice, including the use of corrupt (e.g., bribery) or coercive means (physical force, threats, or intimidation) to influence testimony, other evidence, or the actions of any law enforcement or other justice official, to combat areas of crime that are commonly used in support of transnational organized crime activities, Art. 23. In addition, the three protocols create additional crimes that deal with their basic subject matter: trafficking in persons, smuggling of migrants, and smuggling or illicit manufacture of firearms.

Most countries punish crimes falling within the convention definition of "serious crimes" with at least four years' imprisonment. The protocols also create more minor offenses, such as falsification of travel documents and defacement of firearm serial numbers, that support their basic policy goals. The convention only applies to these offenses where the protocol so provides. Countries that ratify the instruments must enact legislation making these activities domestic offenses if such laws do not already exist.

4. *Domestic measures to combat organized crime.* Signatories must adopt domestic laws and practices that would prevent or suppress certain types of organized-crime-related activities. For example, to combat money laundering, signatories must require their banks to maintain accurate records and have them available for inspection by domestic law enforcement officials. Signatories cannot allow anonymous bank accounts, and bank secrecy cannot be used to shield criminal activities. Additional domestic offenses, such as failing to keep or produce bank records, must be established to support these

[37] *More Than 120 Nations Sign New UN Convention on Transnational Organized Crime, supra* note 35; for additional background *see* Alessandra Stanley, *Palermo Shows Off as a Cleaned-Up Mafia Capital, supra* note 35.

[38] *After Palermo: An Overview of What the Convention and Protocols Hope to Accomplish,* United Nations Web site (http://www.odccp.org/palermo/sum1.html).

measures. Trafficking in persons and the smuggling of migrants are combated by the relevant protocols that contain minimum standards for the manufacture, issuance, and verification of passports and other international travel documents. Although some of the measures are mandatory, others have greater flexibility as to whether states will implement a measure and, if so, how.

5. *International cooperation obligations*. To facilitate the necessary international cooperation against transnational organized crime, signatories have agreed to assist one another in dealing with TOC as a general problem and to assist in dealing with specific cases. Cooperation under the convention includes mutual legal assistance and extradition (Arts. 16 and 18), as well as specific measures, such as law enforcement cooperation and collection and exchange of information. Although these provisions are similar to ones already in place in many regional or bilateral agreements, the large number of countries that have ratified the convention will facilitate broader legal assistance and extradition than presently exist. These provisions are intended to set minimum standards only, and signatories are encouraged to extend cooperation in bilateral or regional arrangements. A requested state cannot refuse assistance on the basis of bank secrecy [Art. 18(8)] or because the alleged offense also involves "fiscal matters" [Art. 18(22)].

The convention also provides the general basis for joint investigations (Art. 19), cooperation involving special investigative procedures such as electronic surveillance, and general law enforcement cooperation (Arts. 20 and 27). The protocols provide for additional, more specific types of cooperation, such as assistance with the tracing of firearms or with the identification of nationals who are found in other countries as smuggled migrants.

6. *Training and technical assistance*. Several articles require signatories to maintain national expertise and adequate training facilities to deal with TOC problems. Given the resource limitations of developing countries, the convention and protocols provide for technical assistance projects in which developed countries help with technical expertise, resources, or both. For instance, Article 30(2)(b) requires signatories to strengthen financial and material assistance to support the efforts of developing countries to combat TOC and to implement the convention. Art. 30(2)(c) requires "adequate and regular voluntary contributions to . . . an account specifically designated for that purpose in a UN funding mechanism" to support such efforts. Art. 14(3) and Art. 30(2)(c) require the use of confiscated proceeds of crime for this purpose, subject to domestic legal restrictions. According to paragraph 6 of the draft resolution, the General Assembly is to adopt the convention and operate a designated account mentioned in Art. 30 within the UN Crime Prevention and Criminal Justice Fund. Art. 30 also encourages signatories to start making contributions immediately in order to help developing countries prepare to implement the convention.

7. *Prevention*. Art. 31 of the Convention against TOC and the protocols require signatories to adopt measures to prevent various types of transnational organized crime, including security precautions, training, recordkeeping on arms transfers, and verification of travel documents.

8. *Technical and other provisions*. The concluding provisions of each instrument provide for technical and procedural matters such as the procedures for signing, ratification, and coming into force. Pursuant to Art. 36(1), the convention opened at a signing ceremony at Palermo, Italy, on December 12–15, 2000, and thereafter at the UN headquarters in New York until December 12, 2002. Instruments certifying the ratification by

signatories were filed thereafter at UN headquarters, and the convention entered into force on September, 29, 2003, in accordance with Article 38.

The Anti-Organized Crime and Law Enforcement Unit of the United Nations Office on Drugs and Crime (UNODC) assists states in taking effective, practical steps in line with the provisions of the convention to fight organized crime.

An example of practical assistance to member states is the project, Assistance to the Signatories of the United Nations Convention against Transnational Organized Crime and its related Protocols. It provides technical assistance to support the implementation of the convention, with key outputs to facilitate the assessment and revision of national legislation to ensure compliance with the convention and its protocols; to strengthen the institutional and operational capacity of law enforcement and judicial bodies to investigate, prosecute, and adjudicate serious crimes, including organized crime; to enhance international cooperation between criminal justice practitioners; and to collect, assess, and disseminate best practices in combating organized crime.

9. *Drug trafficking.* The United Nations Office on Drugs and Crime works closely with national governments, NGOs, and civil society to enhance international cooperation to counter the pervading influence of organized crime and drug trafficking. UNODC has initiated and oversees numerous counternarcotics and anti-organized crime projects, thereby assisting member states in the ratification and implementation of the TOC convention. It monitors the implementation of the convention; develops and promotes best practices in countering organized crime across the globe; improves the exchange of information; enhances judicial cooperation and mutual legal assistance between law enforcement officials; determines the most effective method for collecting information on organized crime from a regional and global perspective; and ensures that such information is available to policymaking and technical assistance projects. *See UNODC and Organized Crime*, http://www.unodc.org/unodc/en/organized-crime/index.html, accessed Oct. 26, 2008.

10. *Assessing organized crime trends.* Accurate information that provides a detailed overview of organized crime and state attempts to counter it is an essential prerequisite for designing appropriate responses to TOC, including UNODC technical assistance interventions with respect to cross-border cooperation.

UNODC has carried out two regional assessment surveys on organized crime. The first covers the Central Asia region, with a particular focus on the states of Kazakhstan, Tajikistan, Uzbekistan, and the Kyrgyz Republic. The second covers the West Africa region, specifically Cote d'Ivoire, Senegal, Ghana, Nigeria, and Sierra Leone. Assessments for East Africa and South Asia are planned. *See UNODC and Organized Crime, id.*

11. *Kidnapping and organized crime.* The increasing involvement of organized crime groups in kidnapping for ransom has raised serious concern. In the most severely affected countries, TOC groups conduct several hundred kidnappings each year. The Anti-Organized Crime and Law Enforcement Unit has developed a UN Counter-Kidnap Manual to include best practices for law enforcement authorities to combat kidnapping.

The manual is a constructive tool for policymakers, law enforcement officers, and criminal justice practitioners that provides national authorities with guidelines on how to deal with a kidnapping case in a practical and effective manner. Although it covers legislative and national policies that target kidnapping, the manual is primarily devoted to the key responses needed for success in prevention and investigation. It arose from a series of working groups, in which regional experts participated. The manual was made available to member states in all the official languages of the United Nations in early 2006.

In addition, information regarding kidnapping received from member states can be found in a report submitted in six languages at the twelfth session of the Commission on Crime Prevention and Criminal Justice.

12. Does a "structured group" mean a hierarchical or other elaborate structure, or can it embrace nonhierarchical groups in which roles of the members of the group are not formally defined? The interpretative notes provide that the term should be used broadly to include all these groups.

13. What about terrorism and TOC? The interpretative notes on Article 3 (scope of application) indicate that all states participating in the negotiations expressed the determination to deny safe havens to terrorists.

14. If a foreign state or international organization is participating in TOC, is its property subject to confiscation and seizure? The *travaux préparatoires* indicate that Article 12, on confiscation and seizure, should take into account the international law principle that property belonging to a foreign state and used for noncommercial purposes may not be confiscated without consent of the foreign state. Additionally, the *travaux préparatoires* indicate that it is not the convention's intention to restrict the rules that apply to diplomatic or state immunity, including that of international organizations.

15. The Palermo Convention, like the UN Vienna Counterdrug Convention, the UN Convention to Suppress Terrorist Financing, and the UN Convention against Corruption, contains several articles on international enforcement cooperation, such as Article 16 (extradition), Article 17 (transfer of sentenced person), Article 18 (mutual legal assistance), (Article 19) joint investigations, Article 20 (special investigative techniques), Article 21 (transfer of criminal proceedings), Article 22 (establishment of a criminal record), and Article 26 (measures to enhance cooperation with law enforcement authorities).

D. *European Union*

The European Union has worked to implement the Palermo Convention as part of its efforts against transnational organized crime. On December 14, 1996, the (EU's) European Council created a High Level Group to prepare specific recommendations and timetables for combating TOC. On April 28, 1997, it proposed an Action Plan to combat organized crime, including collection and analysis of data, coordination with then-candidate countries of Central and Eastern Europe, a Pre-accession Pact on cooperation against organized crime, closer cooperation with other countries and international organizations and bodies, a cross-pillar study on high-technology crime and its use and links with organized crime, joint action establishing a specific multiyear program to combat organized crime, including fraud against the financial interests of the European union, and measures to shield certain vulnerable professionals from the influence of organized crime, such as through the adoption of codes of conduct.[39] The Action Plan also recommends detailed legal instruments and measures to strengthen practical

[39] *Action Plan of 28 April 1997 to Combat Organised Crime*, Gert Vermeulen, International and European Criminal Law Essential Texts on International and European Criminal Law 187–212 (Gert Vermeulen ed., 1st ed., Oct. 2000).

cooperation among police, judicial authorities, and customs officials in combating organized crime. Under the Action Plan, the EU would extend the mandate and tasks of Europol, taking various measures to improve money laundering and confiscation.

1. Framework Decision of 2005 to Combat Organized Crime

On November 25, 2002, at a conference in London the European Union and the countries of southeastern Europe announced an initiative to combat organized crime in southeastern Europe. In particular, they announced their commitment to cooperate to fight crime at the source by targeting criminals on their home territory, to fight crime in transit by disrupting and ending networks that cut across Europe and beyond and tracking illicit money, to fight crime at its destination by targeting criminals operating on foreign territory and confiscating the proceeds of crime, and to fight corruption.

Under this initiative the international community was to continue to assist countries with regional commitments; in return, regional governments were to maintain domestic efforts to meet their commitments. International and regional efforts were to concentrate on technical and operational initiatives against the most important aspects of organized crime, especially illegal immigration and human trafficking, drug and arms trafficking, corruption, and other major transnational crimes.

The EU was to use the review mechanisms within the stabilization and association process (SAP) framework to achieve its commitments and coordinate its work against organized crime, ensuring coherence with the EU and assistance from EU members.[40]

On January 19, 2005, the European Commission adopted a proposal for a Framework Decision to Combat Organized Crime. Its goals are to ensure severe penalties for persons involved in criminal organizations, harmonize EU law, and improve international cooperation in line with the UN Convention against Transnational Organized Crime.[41]

Article 1(1) provides a definition of "criminal organization." It is defined as a "structured association," established over a period of time, of more than two persons, acting in concert with a view to committing offenses that are punishable by deprivation of liberty or a detention order of a maximum of at least four years or by a more serious penalty. A "structured association" means an association that is not randomly formed for the immediate commission of an offense and that does not need to have formally defined roles for its members, continuity of its membership, or a developed structure.[42]

The goal of a criminal organization is to obtain financial or other material benefits. The aim of participating in an organized criminal group is assumed to be to commit a "serious offense" – an offense punishable by deprivation of liberty for at least four years. This definition corresponds to the one used by the Palermo Convention and is deemed preferable to preparing a list of specific offenses.

Article 2 requires each EU member to take action to ensure that the following are regarded as offenses: (a) directing a criminal organization and (b) conduct by a person

40 Bruce Zagaris, *EU Initiative on Fighting Organized Crime in South Eastern Europe*, 20 INT'L ENFORCEMENT L. REP. (Jan. 2005).

41 Bruce Zagaris, *European Commission Adopts Proposed Framework Decision to Combat Organized Crime*, 20 INT'L ENFORCEMENT L. REP. 162 (Apr. 2005); European Union, *Commission Adopts a Proposal for a Framework Decision on Combating Organized Crime*, Memo/05/25, Jan. 27, 2005.

42 Commission of the European Communities, *Proposal for a Council Framework Decision on the Fight against Organized Crime*, 2005/003 (CNS), COM(2005) 6 final, Jan. 19, 2005.

who, with intent and with knowledge of either the aim and general activity of the organization or its intention to commit the offenses in questions, actively participates in the organization's criminal activities, including by the provision of information or material means, the recruitment of new members, and all forms of financing of its activities, knowing that such participation will contribute to the achievement of the organization's criminal activities.

Article 3(1) requires each EU member to act to ensure that the offense of directing a criminal organization contained in Article 2(a) has a maximum term of imprisonment not less than ten years and that the offense of participating in a criminal organization referred to in Article 2(b) has a maximum term of imprisonment not less than five years.

Article 3(2) requires each EU member to act to ensure that the offenses referred to in Article 1, when committed within the framework of a criminal organization, incur longer terms of imprisonment than are provided for by national law for such offenses, except where the penalties provided for are already the longest terms of imprisonment provided by national law.

Unlike the Joint Action Plan, which only required EU members to provide for effective, proportional, and dissuasive criminal penalties, EU members must now go further and establish minimum thresholds for prison sentences to reflect the degree of participation in the criminal organization.

Article 4 permits EU members to take measures to ensure that penalties set forth in Article 3 may be reduced if an offender renounces criminal activity and provides administrative or judicial authorities with information not otherwise available that helps prevent or mitigate the effects of the offense, identifies other offenders, finds evidence, deprives a criminal organization of illicit resources or proceeds of criminal activities, or prevents further Article 2 offenses.[43]

Article 5(1) requires each EU member to take measures to ensure that legal persons can be held liable for any of the organized crime offenses mentioned in Article 2 committed for their benefit by any person, acting either individually or as part of an organ of the legal person, who has a leading position within the legal person, based on one of the following: (a) power of representation of the legal person, (b) authority to take decisions on behalf of the legal person, and (c) authority to exercise control within the legal person.

Article 5(2) also requires EU members to ensure that legal persons can be held liable where the lack of supervision or control by a person in a criminal organization has made possible the commission of any of the offenses relating to participation in a criminal organization mentioned in Article 2 for the benefit of that legal person by a person under his authority.

According to Article 5(3) the liability of legal persons must not exclude criminal proceedings against natural persons who are perpetrators of or accessories to any of the offenses relating to participation in a criminal organization.

Article 6 requires each EU member to ensure that a legal person held liable is punishable by effective, proportionate, and dissuasive penalties, which must include criminal or noncriminal fines and may include other penalties, such as (a) exclusion from entitlement to public benefits or aid, (b) temporary or permanent disqualification from certain commercial activities, (c) judicial supervision, (d) a judicial winding-up

[43] *Id.*

order, and (e) temporary or permanent closure of establishments used for committing the offense.

Article 7 concerns jurisdiction, requiring EU members to ensure that their jurisdiction covers at a minimum cases in which any of the offenses of participating in a criminal organization were committed in whole or in part in its territory, wherever the organization is based or conducts its criminal activities.

When an offense of participating in a criminal organization is within the jurisdiction of more than one EU member and when any one of the EU members concerned can validly prosecute on the basis of the same facts, the EU members concerned must cooperate to decide which state will prosecute the offenders, with the goal of centralizing proceedings in a single EU member. To accomplish this objective, EU members can, if necessary, have recourse to Eurojust, which is a mechanism consisting of investigating magistrates and judges who work on joint investigations.

In considering whether to exercise jurisdiction, an EU member must take into account the following factors: (a) the EU member in whose territory the acts were committed, (b) the EU member of which the offender is a national or resident, (c) the EU member of origin of the victims; and (d) the member in whose territory the offender was found.

Article 8 provides for protection of, and assistance to, victims. Article 8(1) requires EU members to ensure that investigations into, or prosecution of, offenses covered by this Framework Decision are not dependent on testimony from a person subjected to the offense, at least if the acts were committed in the territory of the EU member.

Article 8(2) requires that, in addition to the measures set forth in Council Framework Decision 2001/220/JHA of March 15, 2001, on the standing of victims in criminal proceedings, each EU member must, if necessary, act to ensure appropriate assistance for victims' families.

Article 9 repeals Joint Action 98/733/JHA. Article 10(1) provides for implementation and reports. Once adopted, EU members will have a precise date by which to act. Article 10(2) requires each EU member to transit to the General Secretariat of the Council and Commission, by a date to be prescribed, the provisions transposing into their national law the obligations imposed on them by the Framework Decision. The Council, acting on a report derived from information and reports from the Commission, will assess the extent to which EU members have complied with the Framework Directive.

2. Analysis and Prospects

The proposal for a Framework Directive illustrates the EU's engagement in supranational law through uniform legislation on a broad range of offenses. The directive requires detailed action to adopt uniform legislation on all aspects of combating organized crime, including definitions, penalties, and victim assistance. The new arrangements proposed by the Commission indicate that effective harmonization of relevant criminal legislation in the EU is a prerequisite for any meaningful effort to eliminate criminal organizations. Most importantly, the EU has and does exercise the power to enact such legislation and policy. For instance, the EU does not hesitate to bring enforcement actions in the European Court of Justice against EU members that refuse or are tardy in fulfilling their obligations to adopt measures.

The proposed Framework Directive incorporates the substantive elements of the Palermo Convention. The EU, a signatory to the convention, has an obligation to meet its requirements. The EU is using its power over criminal justice to carry out its responsibilities.

Article 8 provisions ensure that cases can be prosecuted even if victims have not filed a complaint or statement, which is an effort to allow prosecutions when victims are afraid of reprisals by Mafia-type organizations.

In November 2004, the European Council adopted the Hague Program, a five-year (2005–2010) program to enhance cooperation among European states on justice and home affairs. It assessed the Hague Program progress during the second half of 2006. It found that although the EU members made good progress in meeting the program's goals, additional work was needed to meet the program's goals.

The European Council implemented a strategic plan to address cross-border organized crime. Proposals were received for criminal legislation to combat counterfeiting and piracy and to strengthen witness protection efforts.

Within the EU, Europol continues to facilitate strategy and share intelligence on transnational organized crime.[44]

E. *Council of Europe*

At the third summit of the Council of Europe, in May 2005, heads of state and governments expressed their determination to combat organized crime, including money laundering and financial crimes, human trafficking, and cybercrime. Since 1996, the Council of Europe has prepared annual reports on organized crime, based on a questionnaire sent to Council of Europe member states, situation reports, and threat analyses.[45]

F. *Organization of American States*

In accordance with conclusions and recommendations adopted at the meeting of the Ministers of Justice and Attorneys General for the OAS (REMJA-V), who met on April 28–30, 2004, the OAS General Assembly adopted a resolution instructing its Permanent Council to convene a group of experts through its Committee on Hemispheric Security to study how to implement the obligations contracted by the states parties to the UN Convention against TOC and its three protocols. The group's mission was "to consider the advisability of drawing up a Hemispheric Plan of Action against Transnational Organized Crime, as an integrated plan that brings together the efforts being made by each OAS area on diverse aspects of the problem, with the participation of the various OAS bodies that have been working in this area, in accordance with the Declaration on Security in the Americas."[46]

On June 7, 2006, the OAS General Assembly adopted a resolution on "fighting transnational organized crime in the Hemisphere."[47] The resolution invites OAS members

[44] See, e.g., Emanuele Marotta, *Responding to Transnational Crime – The Role of Europol*, Special Issue Combating Transnational Crime: Concepts, Activities and Responses 4 Transnat'l Org. Crime 303 (Phil Williams & Dimitri Vlassis eds., Nos. 3 & 4 1998).

[45] Council of Europe, *Organized Crime in Europe: The Framework* (Council of Europe Web site, accessed on May 8, 2006).

[46] OAS, AG/RES. 2026 (XXXIV – O/04), *Fighting Transnational Organized Crime in the Hemisphere* (resolution adopted at the fourth plenary session, held on June 8, 2004).

[47] OAS, AG/RES (XXXV-O/05), *Fighting Transnational Organized Crime in the Hemisphere*, Washington, D.C., June 7, 2005.

that have not already done so to consider signing and ratifying, or acceding, to the Palermo Convention and three supplementary protocols as soon as possible. The resolution urges OAS members to adopt or strengthen legislation and hemispheric cooperation against TOC. It also asks the Permanent Council to submit the Draft Hemispheric Plan of Action against TOC to the Sixth Meeting of the Ministers of Justice or of the Ministers or Attorneys General of the Americas (REMJA-VI) and for the Secretariat to develop a Hemispheric Plan of Action against TOC, using the Palermo Convention and its three protocols as the framework for strengthening international cooperation against TOC.

G. *Informal International Groups – The G8*

The Group of 8 (G8) has helped fight TOC by prioritizing the issue at its meetings, formulating strategy, and monitoring implementation. The strategy has targeted TOC generally[48] and various types of crimes, such as alien smuggling and the use of fraudulent documents.[49]

Notes and Questions

1. To what extent has the EU accession process helped accession states fight organized crime? The EU continues to require progress to prevent and combat organized crime as a core criterion for accession.[50]

2. How successful are national governments and international organizations in conceptualizing and developing measures to combat TOC?

3. Examine how one or more countries have implemented international conventions or measures (e.g., the EU Framework Directive and Action Plan) to combat TOC. Has the country been successful?

IV. Approaches of Non-U.S. Countries

A. *Italy*

The Italian approach to transnational organized crime is rooted in the realization that organized crime is both a law enforcement challenge and a cultural phenomenon in that country.[51] Because both the United States and Italy contend with serious organized crime problems, the two countries have developed similar law enforcement strategies despite differences between their civil and common law legal systems.

[48] G7-P8 – Senior Experts Group on Transnational Organized Crime, *G7-P8, Senior Experts Group Recommendations*, Annex 4, Paris, April 12, 1996, in 2 Trends Org. Crime 72 (No. 4 1997).

[49] G7-P8 – Senior Experts Group on Transnational Organized Crime, *Implementation of Recommendations 35, 36 and 37, Alien Smuggling and Fraudulent Documents, Project Based Action, Follow-up of Lyons Summit, Lyon, France, October 16, 1996*, 2 Trends Org. Crime 76 (No. 4 1997).

[50] *See, e.g.*, Bruce Zagaris, *European Commissioner Encourages Bulgarian Parliament Accession Work*, 22 Int'l Enforcement L. Rep. 138 (Apr. 2006) (discussing a speech to the Bulgarian parliament in which the European Commissioner responsible for Justice, Freedom and Security encouraged Bulgaria to make a high-level political commitment to fight corruption and organized crime as part of its efforts to qualify to join the EU in January 2007 as planned).

[51] Sergio Moccia, *Le Système Pénal à l'Épreuve du Crime Organisé*, Int'l Rev. Penal L. 68 (September 1997) 853.

U.S. law aggressively criminalizes behaviors associated with organized crime through RICO, whereas Italian law criminalizes four types of organized crime: association for the purposes of committing offenses, association for the purposes of terrorism or subversion, Mafia-type association, and association for the purposes of illicit trafficking of narcotic or psychotropic substances.[52] Under Italian law, a suspect found to have taken part in a criminalized association, irrespective of other illegal acts, can face a prison term.[53] As in the United States, the criminalization of association offers prosecutors an easier route in winning convictions against defendants with ties to organized crime.

Italy has also strengthened its asset forfeiture laws, most notably with the 1982 passage of Article 240 of the Italian penal code. Article 240, which allows prosecutors to confiscate "the proceeds of any crime," has been a valuable tool for Italian law enforcement in prosecuting organized crime.[54]

B. *Mexico*

On October 18, 1996, Mexico enacted an organized crime law, the *Ley Federal Contra la Delincuencia Organizada* (LFDO) or the Federal Organized Crime Act. Among other changes, it authorized the use of wiretapping,[55] plea bargaining,[56] anonymous informants, undercover operations to gather intelligence,[57] witness concealment,[58] witness protection,[59] and rewards for criminals who cooperate with authorities.[60]

The LFDO defines organized crime as three or more individuals organized to permanently or repeatedly try to commit one of the following eleven crimes: terrorism, drug trafficking, counterfeiting, money laundering, arms trafficking, trafficking of migrants, trafficking of organs, robbery, kidnapping, trafficking of minors, and car theft.[61]

Only a *ministerio público*, or federal prosecutor, working with the *Unidad Especializada contra la Delincuencia Organizada*, Specialized Unit against Organized Crime, can request a wiretap.[62] Constitutional law precludes a judge from authorizing a wiretap for matters related to electoral, fiscal, commercial, civil, labor, or administrative issues, as well as communications between counsel and client.[63]

[52] Franco Roberti, *Effective Methods to Combat Transnational Organized Crime in Criminal Justice Processes*, 113–14, in United Nations Asia and Far East Institute for the Prevention of Crime and Treatment of Offenses, Resource Material Series No. 58, December 2001.

[53] *Id.*

[54] M. Cherif Bassiouni, *Effective National and International Action against Organized Crime and Terrorist Criminal Activities*, 4 EMORY INT'L L. REV. 9 (1990). For a longer discussion of Italian asset forfeiture laws, *see* Alexander Cain, *Section 1963(A)(1) of RICO and Article 240 of the Italian Penal Code: Two Potential Weapons against Russian Organized Crime*, NEW ENG. INT'L & COMP. L. ANN. 1996.

[55] Rodrigo Labardini, *supra* note 1 at 133, 140, citing Mex. Const. available at www.cddhcu.gob.mex/leyinfo/pdf/1.pdf, art. 16(9), and LFDO, published in the *Diario Oficial de la Federación* (DOF) on Nov. 7, 1997, as amended, available at http://www.cddhcu.gob.mex/leyinfo/pdf/101.pdf.

[56] LFDO, art. 35 (II).

[57] *Id.* at art. 38.

[58] *Id.* at art. 14.

[59] *Id.* at art. 34.

[60] *Id.* at arts. 35–39.

[61] Labardini, *supra* note 55 at 140.

[62] LFDO, arts. 8(4) and 15–28.

[63] Labardini, *supra* note 55 at 141, citing Mex. Const. at art. 16.

On June 25, 2002, the *Suprema Corte de Justicia de la Nación* (the Supreme Court of Mexico) ruled that LFDO is constitutional.[64]

The LFDO has brought important conceptual changes to Mexican law and facilitates cooperation with the United States on organized crime investigations. However, it remains to be seen whether Mexico will fully fund and implement its new organized crime units, thereby allowing the new law to realize its potential.[65]

V. Hypotheticals

A. The mythical country of Guatahondurica is experiencing serious violence and crime because of gang activities. Many of the leaders come from Mara and other gangs and are deported by the U.S. government. You have been hired by the country's National Security Director to develop a plan to overcome the violence and criminal activities of the gangs. Would your plan be different if you were hired by the Attorney General or Minister of Foreign Affairs? To what extent should you involve other internal agencies? To what extent should you involve U.S. or international organizations?

B. You are an Assistant U.S. Attorney in the District of Columbia. You have information about the persons responsible for kidnapping American government employees and private contractors working on counternarcotics activities in Colombia and then holding them for years in the jungle. The narcotics cartel for which the peoples' responsible work is involved in multiton shipments of cocaine to North America and Europe. In the boats they use to transport the cocaine, they sometimes transport smuggled aliens into the United States. On the return trip they bring small arms and cash. Please advise on the preparation of an indictment, the potential charges, and the potential use of any multilteral or bilateral conventions to obtain evidence or extradite the potential defendants.

VI. *Additional Reading*

A. *Internet Resources*

James J. Na, *Resources on Transnational Organized Crime on the World Wide Web*, 2 TRANSNAT'L ORG. CRIME 81 (Spring 1996).

Resources on the Internet on Organized Crime, 1 Trends in Organized Crime 126 (No. 1 Fall 1995) (http://www.law.ubc.ca/centres/icclr.html).

B. *Periodicals*

For corruption and organized crime, see *Special Section: Corruption and Organized Crime*, 2 TRENDS ORG. CRIME 4–68 (No. 4 1997).

Two periodicals that monitor TOC trends are: *Transnational Organized Crime* and *Trends in Organized Crime*.

67 INT'L REV. PENAL L. The Criminal Justice Systems Facing the Challenge of Organised Crime, Preparatory for the XVI International Congress of Penal (Nos. 3–4 1996).

[64] *Id.*, at 145, citing Suprema Corte de Justicia de la Nación, *Versión Taquigráfica de la Sesión Pública Ordinaria del Pleno de la Suprema Corte de Justicia de la Nación, Celebrada el martes 25 de junio de dos* mil dos, Mexico City, June 25, 2002.

[65] *Id.*, at 148.

68 INT'L REV. PENAL L. The Criminal Justice Systems Facing the Challenge of Organised Crime, Topic I, General Part (Nos. 3 & 4 1997).
69 INT'L REV. PENAL L. The Criminal Justice Systems Facing the Challenge of Organised Crime, Topic II, Procedural Part (Nos. 3 & 4 1998).
70 INT'L REV. PENAL L. The Criminal Justice Systems Facing the Challenge of Organised Crime, Topic IV International Criminal Law (Nos. 1 & 2 1999).

C. *Books*

M. CHERIF BASSIOUNI, ORGANIZED CRIME: A COMPILATION OF U.N. DOCUMENTS 1975–1998, (Transnational Publishers, 1998).
PATRICK L. CLAWSON & RENSSELAER W. LEE III, THE ANDEAN COCAINE INDUSTRY (1996).
THE ILLICIT GLOBAL ECONOMY AND STATE POWER (Richard R. Friman & Peter Andreas eds., Rowman & Littlefield, 1999).
Gray Area Phenomena: CONFRONTING THE NEW WORLD DISORDER (Max Manwaring ed., Westview Press, 1993).
STEPHEN HANDELMAN, COMRADE CRIMINAL: RUSSIA'S NEW MAFIYA (Yale U. Press, 1995).
ORGANIZED CRIME: A GLOBAL PERSPECTIVE (Robert J. Kelly ed., Rowman & Littlefield, 1986).
SIDNEY R. KIRKPATRICK, LORDS OF SIPAN: A TRUE STORY OF PRE-INCA TOMBS, ARCHAEOLOGY, AND CRIME (Henry Holt and Co., 1992).
ROBERT LACEY, LITTLE MAN: MEYER LANSKY AND GANGSTER LIFE (Little Brown & Co., 1991).
ORGANIZED CRIME, DEMOCRATIC GOVERNABILITY: MEXICO AND THE U.S.-MEXICAN BORDERLANDS (John Bailey & Roy Godson eds., University of Pittsburgh Press, 2001).
JEFFREY ROBINSON, THE MERGER: THE CONGLOMERATION OF INTERNATIONAL ORGANIZED CRIME (Overlook Press, 2000).
RUSSIAN ORGANIZED CRIME: THE NEW THREAT (Phil Williams ed., Frank Cass Publishers, 1997).
CLAIRE STERLING, OCTOPUS: THE LONG REACH OF THE SICILIAN MAFIA (W. W. Norton, 1990).
FRANCISCO THOUMI, ECONOMÍA, POLÍTICA Y NARCOTRÁFICO (ECONOMY, POLICY, AND NARCOTRAFFICKING (Tercer Mundo, 1994).
ARKADY VAKSBERG, THE SOVIET MAFIA (St. Martin's Press, 1991).

6 Export Control and Economic Sanctions

I. Introduction[1]

Export controls and related rules and restrictions, especially those imposed by the United States, create a "frightful labyrinth" for practitioners.[2] In the United States, several agencies issue regulations and licenses to control exports based on different statutes. These regulations then interact with numerous free-standing pieces of legislation, many of

[1] The author is grateful to Ray Gold, Esq., Berliner, Corcoran & Rowe, LLP, for his review and comments on this chapter.

[2] Cecil Hunt & Thomas M. DeButts, *Overview of U.S. Export Controls*, Coping with U.S. Export Controls 23, 17 (Evan R. Berlack & Christopher R. Wall eds., Practising Law Instit. 2005).

which are not enacted as amendments to basic statutes or codified. As a result, it can be hard to find and understand the various applicable laws. In addition, the objectivity and transparency one finds in other regulatory areas are often missing from the export control area. Finally, practitioners working in the export control field often find that limitations on judicial review and judicial deference to the executive branch on matters related to foreign policy or national security result in relatively little oversight of official actions.[3]

Economic sanctions are even broader than export controls, encompassing the imposition by governmental or international organizations of economic sanctions for noneconomic foreign policy reasons. Examples include a variety of trade and investment sanctions against apartheid-era South Africa; financial and other sanctions against Panama; measures against Libya, especially after the bombing of Pan Am Flight 103; UN sanctions against Sudanese leaders and against former Liberian head of state Charles Taylor; U.S. sanctions targeting narcotics traffickers and kingpins; and U.S. and international sanctions against persons engaged in transnational terrorism.[4]

Sanctioning parties have three possible mechanisms by which to inflict costs on targeted countries: limiting exports, restricting imports, and impeding finances, including reducing aid. Trade sanctions involve costs to the target country in terms of lost export markets, denial of critical imports, lower prices for embargoed exports, and higher domestic prices for substitute imports. In cases where only export or import controls have been invoked, the targeting countries generally prefer export controls to restrictions on imports.[5]

Economic sanctions, first used in ancient Greece, have a long history. The most celebrated case was Pericles' Megarian decree, enacted in 432 BC in response to the kidnapping of three Aspasian women.[6] In U.S. colonial history, colonies boycotted English goods in 1765 in response to the Stamp Act, which was repealed the following year. From 1767–70, the colonies boycotted English goods in response to the enactment of the Townshend Acts, which raised money to cover salaries of judges and officials. Britain subsequently repealed the Townshend Acts, except on tea. The continued tea tax was the pretext for the Boston Tea Party in 1774 and the calling of the Continental Congress.[7]

This chapter provides an overview of U.S. export controls and U.S. and international economic sanctions and discusses their impact on international law enforcement. Export controls and economic sanctions are considered in the context of international criminal and enforcement cooperation.

II. U.S. (and National Government) Issues

Although the U.S. export control regime includes many of the same items found on lists maintained by other countries participating in multilateral control regimes, U.S. businesses and their foreign counterparts operate in different export control environments.

[3] *Id.*

[4] Barry E. Carter, International Economic Sanctions: Improving the Haphazard U.S. Legal Regime 1 (1989).

[5] Gary Clyde Hufbauer, Jeffrey J. Schott, & Kimberly Ann Elliott, Economic Sanctions Reconsidered: History and Current Policy 36 (1990).

[6] *Id.* at 4. *See also* Charles Fornara, *Plutarch and the Megarian Decree*, 24 Yale Classical Stud. 13–28 (1975).

[7] Hufbauer et al., *supra* note 5 at 28.

U.S. companies must contend with more rigorous and more complicated restrictions. Some U.S. controls are completely unilateral, and U.S. licensing policies under multilateral controls are often more strict than those maintained by other regime member nations. Violations of U.S. controls often result in severe monetary and other penalties in both criminal and administrative enforcement cases, whereas most foreign governments pursue criminal prosecution in a significantly smaller number of cases.[8]

A. *Structure of the U.S. Export Control System*

A number of U.S. government agencies are involved in the export licensing process. The roles of the Bureau of Industry and Securities, the U.S. Department of State's Directorate of Defense Trade Controls, the U.S. Department of the Treasury's Office of Foreign Assets Control, and other key agencies are discussed in this section.

The Bureau of Industry and Security (BIS) of the Department of Commerce administers controls over most exports pursuant to the Export Administration Regulations [15 C.F.R. §§ 730–774 (EAR)]. The Export Administration Act (EAA) (50 U.S.C. app. §§ 2401–2420) is the normal statutory basis for the EARs, but it is temporary legislation that is periodically renewed. Presidential orders issued under the International Emergency Economic Powers Act (IEEPA) are issued to maintain the EAR when the EAA lapses.[9]

The EAR often apply to "dual-use" items suitable for military and nonmilitary uses. However, some items subject to the EAR have no military use. The EAR include controls imposed for a variety of purposes, such as the cold war emphasis on denying Warsaw Pact countries and the People's Republic of China access to certain strategically significant items. Today, the EAR reflect a new emphasis on stopping the proliferation of weapons of mass destruction and limiting the ability of certain countries to support international terrorism or pursue destabilizing military efforts.[10]

EAR violators can incur severe criminal and administrative penalties. BIS or Bureau of Customs and Border Protection special agents investigate criminal cases, which are prosecuted by the U.S. Attorneys' Office, part of the Department of Justice. The BIS, through charges filed with an administrative law judge by BIS counsel, may impose civil fines or administrative sanctions, although it generally imposes penalties through settlements. Such sanctions include subjecting the offender and related persons to a "denial order." This order not only bars exports by such persons but also bars others from furnishing such persons with items that have been exported from the United States. The Assistant Secretary for Export Enforcement can impose a denial order temporarily on an *ex parte* basis without a finding of a violation, if he or she believes such a measure is necessary to prevent an imminent violation. In addition, a party may be denied export privileges if convicted of violating the EAA or other export control or national security laws.[11]

The Directorate of Defense Trade Controls (DDTC) of the Department of State administers controls over exports of "defense articles" and "defense services." Pursuant to the Arms Export Control Act (AECA),[12] the International Traffic in Arms Regulations

[8] Hunt & DeButts, *supra* note 2 at 17–18.
[9] IEEPA, 50 U.S.C. §§ 1701–1706; see Exec. Order No. 13222, Aug. 17, 2001, 66 Fed. Reg. 44205, Aug. 22, 2001, as extended by the Notice of Aug. 2, 2005, 70 Fed. Reg. 45273 (Aug. 5, 2005).
[10] Hunt and DeButts, *supra* note 2 at 18–19.
[11] *Id.* at 29.
[12] 22 U.S.C. §§ 2778–2994.

(ITAR), which include the U.S. Munitions List (USML),[13] control the export of defense articles and services, temporary imports, transfers, and persons engaged in defense-related brokering activities.

The AECA imposes criminal and civil penalties for ITAR violations. The penalties are made by reference to the penalties in the EAA of 1979, as amended, except that the maximum civil penalty is $500,000 per violation, rather than $100,000. In addition, the AECA incorporates by reference certain EAA provisions concerning investigation of possible offenses, the administrative imposition of civil penalties, and forfeiture.[14] The DDTC relies upon Customs and the Defense Investigative Service to conduct investigations. The ITAR have procedures for administrative enforcement proceedings analogous to those in the EAR.

The AECA bars, with provision for review and exceptions, the issuance of licenses to export USML items to a person convicted of violating specified export control and security-related statutes or debarred by another export control agency. Additionally, the ITAR allow for administrative debarment based upon an administratively determined ITAR violation that DDTC believes shows lack of future compliance reliability. Normally violators receive a three-year debarment.[15]

The Office of Foreign Assets Control (OFAC) controls exports to countries, such as Iran, Cuba, and Sudan, that are subject to broad trade embargoes and economic sanctions covering more than just exports. The U.S. president and delegates issue most OFAC regulations when the president declares an emergency and invokes presidential authority under the IEEPA.

OFAC administers civil penalties under procedures in Subpart G of the various OFAC regulations. OFAC sends a violator a prepenalty notice and gives him or her the opportunity to file a written response. However, OFAC does not accord a hearing or use an administrative law judge. If a violator does not pay a penalty, OFAC refers the matter to the Department of Justice for recovery action. OFAC's enforcement division refers cases to Customs or the Federal Bureau of Investigation.

OFAC regulations are based on different statutes, and the applicable penalties vary with the statutory provision involved. Civil penalties are set forth in the IEEPA, Trading with the Enemy Act, the Iraq Sanctions Act of 1990, and the Foreign Narcotics Kingpin Designation Act. Each of these statutes has criminal penalties as well. Sections 303 and 321 of the Antiterrorism and Effective Death Penalty Act (18 U.S.C. §§ 2332d and 2339B) have penalties with respect to a person engaging in a transaction with the government of a designated country or providing material support to a designated foreign terrorist organization.[16]

B. *Terrorist-Supporting Countries*

Certain aspects of the controls on each of the terrorist-supporting or embargoed countries are multilateral in nature, based primarily on international export regimes such as the Wassenaar Arrangement, the Australia Group, the Missile Technology Control Regime, or the Nuclear Suppliers Group. Additionally, certain trade sanctions arise from UN Security Council mandates. Still, export controls on terrorist-supporting or embargoed

[13] 22 C.F.R. parts 120 through 130.
[14] 22 U.S.C. § 2278(e).
[15] Hunt & DeButts, *supra* note 2 at 20–21.
[16] *Id.* at 28–29.

countries are primarily unilateral. U.S. policy is usually more strict than that of other regime partners. In general, the United States has a licensing policy of denial to these destinations for multilaterally controlled items. Additionally, the U.S. has license requirements for exporting many widely available industrial and consumer items, which are not found on any multilateral regime list, to target countries, such as Cuba, Iran, Sudan, and Syria. Unless an exception applies, which is rare, the United States applies a policy of denial for these exports.[17]

Under section 6(j) of the EAA, the executive branch must notify the House Foreign Affairs Committee and the Senate Banking Committee before approving a license for the export of goods or technology valued at $7 million or more if the Secretary of State determines (1) that the country supports international terrorism and (2) that the items in question would significantly contribute to the military potential or would enhance the terrorist-supporting capability of the designated country.[18] In the International Security and Development Cooperation Act of 1980, the Senate Foreign Relations Committee was added to the list of committees to be notified.[19]

In 1989, the Anti-Terrorism and Arms Export Amendments Act expressly required a validated license for items that the Secretary of State determined met the criteria of Section 6(j)(1)(B).[20] Under these amendments the dollar value threshold for congressional notification was removed. In its place alternative criteria were added to remove a country from the terrorist list. The legislative history shows Congress's intent "to capture within the requirements of Section 6(j)(1)(B) a wide range of goods and technology" that could reasonably be determined to significantly contribute to the military potential or terrorist-supporting capability of a 6(j) country.[21]

In December 1993, the Department of State issued a determination with respect to all terrorist-supporting countries announcing that all items subject to national security controls (except computers with an MTOPS level under 500); all items subject to chemical and biological weapons controls, missile proliferation controls, and nuclear weapons proliferation controls; and all military-related items are controlled under EAA Section 6(j), if they are destined to the military, police, intelligence entities, or other sensitive end-users in terrorist-supporting countries. The determination required that the Departments of State and Commerce notify Congress when the administration intends to approve such exports. If any item is removed from one or more of the multilateral control lists, it will no longer be controlled under EAA Section 6(j), but will continue to be controlled for antiterrorism (AT) reasons under EAA Section 6(a).[22]

The State Department will continue to review the proposed export of any item to a terrorist-supporting country, such as Iran and Syria, under EAA Section 6(a) to determine, if, under the particular circumstances of the case, it could significantly contribute to the military potential or could improve its terrorist-supporting capability. The State and Commerce Departments must notify Congress of intended approval of an item with such potential consequences.

[17] Philip K. Ankel & Glenn H. Kaminsky, *Exporting to Special Destinations and Persons: Terrorist-Supporting and Embargoed Countries, Designated Terrorists and Sanctioned Persons*, Coping with U.S. Export Controls 2005 271, 281.

[18] Pub. L. 96–72, Sept. 29, 1979.

[19] Pub. L. 96–533, December 16, 1980.

[20] *See* Pub. L. 101–222, December 12, 1989.

[21] Cong. Rept. 101–296 at 13; *See also* 130 Cong. Rec. 7351 October 23, 1989.

[22] Ankel & Kaminsky, *supra* note 17.

The determination has established two tiers of antiterrorism controls. The first tier, embracing almost all items on multilateral export lists destined to military, police, intelligence, or other sensitive end-users, is controlled under EAA Section 6(j) and requires a report to the Congress before a license is approved for export. The second tier, including all multilateral list items to civilian end-users, as well as all other items controlled unilaterally for antiterrorism reasons, is controlled under the general authority of EAA Section 6(a) and may require a report to Congress prior to approval of a license.[23]

Under the Anti-Terrorism Arms Export Amendments Act of 1989, the Secretary of State must publish each new country designation in the Federal Register and must simultaneously provide the complete list of terrorist-supporting countries.[24]

Notes and Questions

1. There are a number of parallels between the motives for sanctions and the three basic purposes of criminal law: to punish, to deter, and to rehabilitate. Countries that impose sanctions, like states that punish criminals, may find goals of rehabilitation unrealized while goals of punishment and deterrence are achieved. *See* Hufbauer et al., *supra*, at 11.

2. What are the limitations on the use of sanctions? One study has suggested that sanctions do not succeed when the goals are too elusive, the means too gentle, or the necessary cooperation from other countries not sufficiently robust. Sanctions can fail for a variety of reasons. First, they can create their own antidotes; for example, by unifying a target country in support of its government and in search of commercial alternatives. Second, sanctions may prompt powerful or wealthy allies of the target country to assume the role of a "black knight," as in U.S. sanctions against the Soviet Union, Cuba, and Nicaragua, and Soviet sanctions against Yugoslavia and Albania. For instance, Canada and the EU have served as black knights to Cuba when they believed U.S. unilateral extraterritorial sanctions violated international law (i.e., *see* role of U.K. and French governments with respect to U.S. sanctions against the Soviet Union's natural gas pipline on p. 412 following) Third, economic sanctions may alienate international allies and domestic business interests. For instance, in reaction to sanctions, allies may enact national antisanctions laws, such as the U.S. antiboycott provisions[25] and the British Protection of Trading Interests Act, which are designed to counteract the impact of others' sanctions on foreign policy and economic interests. Business firms at home may experience severe losses when sanctions interrupt trade and financial contacts. In addition to the immediate loss of sales, businesses and countries may lose their reputation for reliability because of sanctions. *See* Hufbauer et al., *supra*, at 12–13. For instance, countries and businesses may buy high-tech and energy equipment of inferior quality from a non-U.S. business because they may not want to risk that the enormous breadth of U.S. sanctions may deprive them of the ability to sell to a number of markets because of the number of countries subject to U.S. unilateral sanctions.

3. Given the limitations of economic sanctions, why do countries such as the United States employ them so frequently? On balance, sanctions can be useful, whereas the most obvious alternative to economic sanctions – military action – is often unsatisfactory. Hufbauer, *supra*, at 13. Indeed, one of the central elements in the debate surrounding

[23] *Id.*, at 282. Categories of items controlled under EAA Section 6(a) are identified in 15 C.F.R. Part 742, Supplement 2.

[24] *See* Pub. L. 101–222, Sec. 4.

[25] For a discussion of the U.S. antiboycott laws, *see* Carter, *supra* note 4 at 175–79; S. Marcus, *The Antiboycott Law: The Regulation of International Business Behavior*, 8 GA. J. INT'L COMP. L. 559 (1978).

the Bush administration's invasion of Iraq was whether international economic sanctions had effectively constrained Iraq and Saddam Hussein. *See, e.g.*, Homer E. Moyer, Jr. & Linda A. Mabry, *Export Controls as Instruments of Foreign Policy: The History, Legal Issues, and Policy Lessons of Three Recent Cases*, 15 LAW POL'Y INT'L BUS. 1–171 (1983).

4. Most governments other than the United States give broad authority to chief executives to control imports, exports, and private financial transactions. Hence, the mechanisms for imposition of economic sanctions in other countries tend to be simpler than those in the United States. For a broad but abbreviated view of the comparative implementation of economic sanctions, *see* B. CARTER, INTERNATIONAL ECONOMIC SANCTIONS: IMPROVING THE HAPHAZARD U.S. LEGAL REGIME, *supra*, at 219–32.

5. What recommendations help maximize the effectiveness of sanctions in coercing change in the policies of a target country? *See* the nine commandments applied to case studies in Hufbauer et al., *supra*, at 94–107. In summary they are (1) arrange your sanctions narrowly initially until you see that your country and others affected can cope with the trade-offs; (2) do not exaggerate the importance of international cooperation with your policies, but don't underestimate the role of international assistance to your target; (3) target the weak and helpless; (4) target, if necessary, allies and trading partners, but remember that strong allies sometimes take decades to cultivate and should not be taken for granted; (5) impose the maximum cost on your target; (6) minimize the cost of sanctions on yourself; (7) apply sanctions decisively and with resolution; (8) do not expect sanctions to work right away, and do not jump to implement covert maneuvers of military action too soon; and (9) plan carefully, because economic sanctions may exacerbate a bad situation.

C. *Customs Export Enforcement*

The Department of Homeland Security, through the U.S. Customs and Border Protection (CBP) along with U.S. Immigration and Customs Enforcement (ICE), enforces various laws at the border, including for various government agencies. In general, CBP is responsible for inspection and interdiction, whereas ICE is responsible for investigation. Their goal is to ensure that illegal trade is deterred, stopped, and punished.

Customs authorities work principally with three agencies in enforcing export controls: the Bureau of Industry and Security (formerly the Bureau of Export Administration), the Office of Defense Trade Controls, and the Office of Foreign Assets Control. CBP and ICE have enforcement authority under the laws and regulations administered by these agencies and cooperate with each in the development of enforcement actions. Customs authorities closely cooperate with U.S. Attorneys, the Justice Department, and other government agencies in criminal prosecutions and civil actions.[26]

1. Investigation

ICE special agents have extensive law enforcement powers. They have authority to carry weapons, make arrests, and obtain search warrants. Customs special agents often work with cooperating individuals and companies, examining records and reviewing paper trails to follow illegal exports or profits from illegal activity.

[26] W. Alexander Daman, *Coping with U.S. Export Controls: A Survey of Customs Export Enforcement*, COPING WITH U.S. EXPORT CONTROLS 2005, *supra* note 2 at 497–98.

Customs officers maintain information-sharing relationships with other customs services around the world, often pursuant to Customs Mutual Assistance Agreements and pursuant to 19 U.S.C. § 1628. Even in the absence of an agreement, an illegal import into one country can be an illegal export from the United States.

ICE can issue an export subpoena to obtain records concerning exports.[27] Customs officers can obtain records required pursuant to the EAR[28] and ITAR.[29]

An ICE agent involved in a criminal investigation with an Assistant U.S. Attorney can serve a grand jury subpoena to obtain information. Special agents can also apply for wiretap orders for certain export violations.[30] Customs officers have authority to recruit and pay informants or to pay cooperating individuals or corporations for their expenses in assisting the government, and under certain circumstances they can use forfeiture funds to finance enforcement actions.[31]

2. Detention and Seizure

CBP can initially detain a shipment whereas CBP, ICE, and the appropriate licensing agencies investigate the possible legal basis for seizure as evidence in an investigation, as subject to forfeiture, or as both. Under the EAR and 22 U.S.C. § 401, Customs officers and OFAC may take various actions to detain a shipment to examine it for a longer period of time.

When CBP detains a shipment, inspectors and agents usually obtain information concerning the merchandise to determine whether there exists evidence that the shipment should be seized. They review shipment documentation, obtain technical information about the cargo, and coordinate with the Exodus Command Center for advice from the licensing agencies and experts. If special agents have probable cause to believe that the shipment is being exported in violation of the EAR or ITAR, CBP, and ICE, they may seize the shipment.[32]

3. Fines, Penalties, and Forfeitures

If CBP finds a licensable export at the border, without a license, it can take several courses of action: seize or forfeit the shipment, permit the exporter to apply for a license while the shipment remains in CBP custody, or permit the exporter to retrieve the shipment.

Customs laws control forfeiture proceedings in illegal export cases.[33] If items are valued at $500,000 or less, CBP issues potential claimants a notice of seizure and intent to forfeit through its Office of Fines, Penalties, and Forfeitures.[34] Claimants can have the claim decided administratively by CBP or judicially in a U.S. District Court.[35] A claimant who

[27] See 15 C.F.R. § 762.7 (authority to subpoena records relating to exports).
[28] *See* 15 C.F.R. §§ 762.2–762.3 (records to be kept).
[29] *See* 22 C.F.R. § 127.4(c).
[30] *See* 18 U.S.C. § 2516.
[31] *See* U.S.C. § 401(b) (incorporating Customs laws regarding informants); 19 U.S.C. § 619 (authority for moiety payments to informants); 31 U.S.C. § 9703 (authority for Treasury Forfeiture Fund).
[32] *See* 15 C.F.R. § 758.7(b)(6); 22 U.S.C. § 401.
[33] 22 U.S.C. § 401(b); *see also* 18 U.S.C. § 983(i).
[34] 19 U.S.C. § 1607; 19 C.F.R. § 162.31.
[35] 19 U.S.C. § 1608; 19 C.F.R. § 162.31.

wants a judicial decision must file a claim with CBP within twenty days of the first date of publication of the seizure and post a bond of $5,000 or 10 percent of the value of the merchandise, whichever is lower.[36] Items valued at more than $500,000 can only be forfeited judicially.[37] Claimants who decide to proceed administratively may file a petition for remission or mitigation, essentially seeking administrative clemency from the seizure.[38]

4. Prosecution

In serious cases Customs authorities work with U.S. Attorneys' offices to criminally prosecute export control cases. Criminal cases normally start before the pursuit of civil sanctions and may include separate criminal forfeiture proceedings. If an investigation establishes a criminal violation of export control laws, other violations of law can be implicated and charged, such as false statements to government officials or money laundering.[39]

D. *Use of Undercover Sting Operations*

Law enforcement personnel investigating export control violations involving overseas purchasers, funds, or witnesses sometimes encounter problems when foreign law enforcement officials are unwilling to assist investigators. This is particularly likely to occur when the conduct at issue is not illegal in the foreign jurisdiction or when foreign officials view the export control laws as assertions of extraterritorial jurisdiction. For example, U.S. sanctions against Cuba have been quite controversial abroad. As a result, foreign prosecutors have refused to assist and sometimes have taken action to inhibit U.S. enforcement. Some foreign governments have enacted legislation to block U.S. prosecution of unilateral export controls. Other governments have even prosecuted compliance with U.S. export controls – for example, Mexico's recent prosecution of the Mexican subsidiary of Sheraton Hotels (see the article reprinted later in this chapter).

Prosecution of Wheeler for Supercomputer Exports to Bulgaria Overturned and Dismissed

REPRINTED FROM 16 INT'L ENFORCEMENT L. REP. 874 (AUG. 2000)

On October 5, 1999, U.S. District Judge in the Southern District of Florida, Miami Division, William M. Hoeveler dismissed the indictment against Robert Wheeler in connection with charges that he helped export a supercomputer to Bulgaria in violation of U.S. export control laws, thereby ending his odyssey with the U.S. criminal justice system of almost eighteen years.[40] The case shows the methods of export control enforcement operations, including the

[36] 19 U.S.C. § 1608; *see* 19 C.F.R. § § 171.11, 171.12.

[37] 19 U.S.C. § 1610.

[38] *See* 19 U.S.C. § 1618; 19 C.F.R. Part 171 (procedures for petitions for remission or mitigation).

[39] *See e.g.*, 18 U.S.C. §§ 1001 (false statements), 1956(c)(7)(D) (money laundering "specified unlawful activities" include IEEPA, AECA, and EAA).

[40] Order for Dismissal of the Indictment, *United States of America v. Robert Wheeler*, U.S. District Court S.D.Fl. Miami Div., Case No. 90–448-Cr-Hoeveler (Oct. 1999).

use of undercover sting operations and confidential informants, and the never-ending operation of the law enforcement process against certain targets.

On August 1, 1991, Wheeler was found guilty of conspiracy to export and attempted exportation of a supercomputer to Bulgaria. 18 U.S.C. § 371; 50 U.S.C. § 2304(a). Defense counsel did not timely file a motion for a new trial. Still the court granted a new trial despite defense counsel's failure to file a timely request, because of the inability of Wheeler to call as a witness his codefendant Nicolas Spiliotis as a witness due to the latter's privilege against self-incrimination.[41]

Prior to the trial, the Magistrate Judge recommended denial of Wheeler's motion for severance in order to have Spiliotis testify that Wheeler had no knowledge that the supercomputer was intended for shipment to Bulgaria, a prohibited destination without a license. Procedurally, Wheeler's counsel failed to ask the court to review the Magistrate Judge's decision prior to trial. When Wheeler's counsel renewed the motion at the close of evidence in the case, the court denied the motion due to the near-conclusion of the trial. The jury convicted both Spiliotis and Wheeler. After Wheeler's counsel's failure to file a motion for new trial, Judge Hoeveler issued his order of June 29, 1993, granting Wheeler a new trial.

The Court of Appeals overturned the court's order based on a writ of error *coram nobis* and remanded the case to Judge Hoeveler on August 3, 1994.[42]

On December 1, 1995, Wheeler's counsel filed a Motion for New Trial Based on Newly Discovered Evidence, namely an affidavit from Eddie Haak, the confidential informant in Belgium, admitting that he lied about telling Wheeler the supercomputer was going to Bulgaria. The court denied the motion on the basis that the false testimony was known at the time of trial and hence not newly discovered.

In January 1997, Wheeler was sentenced to a period of incarceration of eighteen months. On January 21, 1997, his counsel filed a direct appeal, which the Court of Appeals dismissed with prejudice. Wheeler's counsel then filed a *habeas corpus* petition while the direct appeal was pending.

Judge Hoeveler granted the *habeas* petition based on ineffective assistance of counsel due to his counsel's failure to renew the severance motion at the start of trial and failure to timely file a motion for a new trial or request an extension of time for the same. Judge Hoeveler found that Wheeler was deprived of his Sixth Amendment right of effective assistance of counsel, including on appeal. Essentially, Wheeler was deprived of Spiliotis' testimony that the confidential informant Haak never told Wheeler in his presence that the computer was going to Bulgaria and Spiliotis never informed Wheeler that Bulgaria was the intended destination of the supercomputer.

Judge Hoeveler explained that Haak testified he was wired with a two-hour time when he spoke during the undercover meeting with Wheeler. Although they discussed a lot, they never discussed that the computer in question was going to an end-user in Bulgaria. Near the conclusion of his testimony, Haak testified that after the tape expired, Haak advised Wheeler of Bulgaria as the ultimate destination of the computer. Judge Hoeveler found Haak's questionable testimony provided an additional reason for Hoeveler's conclusion that Wheeler suffered prejudice from the joinder with Spiliotis.[43]

[41] Order Granting Motion for New Trial, *U.S.A. v. Wheeler*, June 29, 1993.

[42] *United States v. Wheeler*, 66 F.3d 340 (11th Cir. 1995).

[43] Order Granting Motion to Vacate Conviction, *Robert Wheeler v. U.S.A.*, Case No. 97–1124-CIV-Hoeveler, 90–0448-CR-Hoeveler, Feb. 25, 1999.

After relentlessly pursuing Wheeler, the U.S. Government finally decided not to appeal the Hoeveler order. However, Wheeler's company was still denied the right to export for ten years starting June 25, 1995.

The role of the confidential informant, Eddie Haak, was critical in the case. His lack of credibility at trial, his affidavit admitting unethical conduct, and the failure of U.S. law enforcement authorities to supervise him and then take responsibility for his efforts and the unfair nature of the prosecution against Wheeler raises important questions about public accountability of U.S. law enforcement authorities in general and the U.S. Customs Service in particular. The case also illustrates Customs' frequent use of undercover sting operations, often with a convicted person serving as the lead sting operator.[44]

Press Release, "Sigma-Aldrich Pays $1.76 Million Penalty to Settle Charges of Illegal Exports of Biological Toxins"

U.S. Department of Commerce (Nov. 4, 2002)

For Immediate Release

The Commerce Department announced today that Sigma-Aldrich Corporation of St. Louis, Missouri, and two of its subsidiaries have agreed to pay a $1,760,000 fine to settle charges involving illegal exports of biological toxins. The settlement was reached after a significant legal ruling in the Commerce Department's favor by an administrative law judge adjudicating the dispute.

The penalty is the largest imposed by the Commerce Department in a case involving biological toxins, and one of the largest penalties ever paid to the Department for export control violations. The Department had instituted administrative enforcement actions against the Sigma-Aldrich companies alleging that a company they had acquired in 1997 had made unauthorized exports of controlled biological toxins to Europe and Asia on numerous occasions prior to the acquisition and had continued the unlicensed exports for more than a year after the acquisition. In a fifteen-page opinion, an administrative law judge held that companies can be held liable for export control violations that have been committed by firms that they acquire.

Commenting on the cases, Under Secretary of Commerce for Industry and Security Kenneth I. Juster stated: "This settlement, and the administrative law judge ruling upon which it is based, make two things quite clear. First, this Commerce Department will vigorously enforce our export control laws to prevent the spread of biological toxins and other substances that can be used for weapons purposes. Second, corporations will be held accountable for violations of U.S. export control laws committed by companies that they acquire."

Assistant Secretary of Commerce for Export Enforcement Michael J. Garcia issued an Order to implement the settlement. The Order is based on 318 charges, including 268 charges of unlicenced exports of biological toxins. The penalty was mitigated because the evidence available to the Department indicated that none of the exports in question was destined for biological weapons-related uses.

[44] For a discussion of the case of Hossein Alikhani, an Iranian and Cypriot who was lured to the Bahamas by an undercover operative to purchase natural gas equipment in violation of the U.S. Libyan sanctions, *see* HOSSEIN ALIKHANI, IN THE CLAW OF THE EAGLE: A GUIDE TO U.S. SANCTONS AGAINST LIBYA Chapter 7 (359–406) (1995) (discussing his case).

In issuing the Order, Assistant Secretary Garcia explained: "These cases set the important precedent that when acquiring another firm, a company should scrutinize the export control practices of the acquired company in order to avoid the risk of incurring substantial liability along with the assets of the company. In this case, the acquiring companies not only failed to discover the prior unlicenced exports, they allowed them to continue for more than one year after the acquisition."

Assistant Secretary Garcia commended the efforts of Special Agent Michael Imbrogna from the Office of Export Enforcement's field office in Boston for his investigation of the case.

Notes and Questions

1. Prior to the agreement to settle and pay penalties, Sigma-Aldrich unsuccessfully challenged the BIS complaint. The administrative law judge explained that successor liability applied under the export control regulations to the case at hand. *See In the Matter of Sigma-Aldrich Business Holdings, Inc.*, U.S. Department of Commerce, Bureau of Industry and Security, Case No. 01-BXA-06 et al, Order Denying Respondents' Motion for Summary Judgment, Aug. 29, 2002, reprinted in COPING WITH U.S. EXPORT CONTROLS 2005, at 859.

2. What is the best strategy to avoid entanglement in an export control enforcement action? A business should have an effective internal control system to monitor compliance with all applicable export control laws and regulations. The system must have the continuing support of top management, who must devote sufficient personnel and resources to its implementation. *See, e.g.*, Donald W. Smith & Christopher E. Dominguez, *Defense of Export Control Enforcement Actions*, COPING WITH U.S. EXPORT CONTROLS 2005, *supra*, at 547; Peter L. Flanagan, *Key Elements of an Effective U.S. Foreign Trade Controls Compliance Program*, COPING WITH U.S. EXPORT CONTROLS 2005, *supra*, at 437–60. For a discussion of internal controls with respect to exporting technology and software, *see, e.g.*, Benjamin H. Flowe, *Exporting Technology and Software, Particularly Encryption*, COPING WITH U.S. EXPORT CONTROLS 2005, *supra* at 331, 348–50.

3. Given the breadth of the delegation to the executive branch in making and enforcing export control policies and the lack of effective congressional oversight, Congress has not provided much judicial review of administrative actions under the EAA. As a result, the administrative process is quite undisciplined and often overreaching. Businesses subject to enforcement actions sometimes challenge the failure of the Commerce Department to adhere to statutory deadlines for processing license applications, actions allegedly exceeding the Secretary's authority, and constitutional challenges. Grant D. Aldonas & Frances J. Henderson, *Judicial Review under the Export Administration Act: Section 13 and the Cost of Unreviewable Regulation*, LAW AND POLICY OF EXPORT CONTROLS: RECENT ESSAYS ON KEY EXPORT ISSUES 137, 142–47, 162.

4. Most investigations of export violations are ultimately resolved without formal action by the investigating agency or by issuance of a warning letter. Often the settlements between the government agency and the private parties involve only monetary penalties. Exporting companies generally prefer to resolve enforcement actions quickly because of the costs and risks associated with litigation, including the lack of effective judicial review. Smith & Dominguez, *supra*, at 571–72.

5. One challenge in strengthening international cooperation with export controls and economic sanctions is the lack of a uniform agency. For instance, in the international

effort to combat narcotics and money laundering, most governments have formed an agency whose competence and jurisdiction relate to only one crime (a drug enforcement agency for narcotics enforcement, a tax or revenue authority for tax crimes, and a financial intelligence unit for money laundering). In contrast, in the United States and some other countries, several agencies have overlapping authority to regulate and enforce economic sanctions and export controls. The involvement of multiple agencies can make networking and cooperation in the international sphere more difficult.

6. On September 8, 2008, OFAC issued a revised set of Economic Sanctions Enforcement Guidelines. 73 *Fed. Reg.* 51933 (Sept. 8, 2008). The new guidelines took effect when issued, although Treasury solicited written comments on them until November 7, 2008. The new guidelines reflect continuing efforts to impose regularity on an area of sanctions enforcement that is often criticized as unpredictable. They mark the first published effort at broad revision since the publication, in January 2003, of "proposed rules" that, though never formally adopted, were viewed informally as a guide to sanctions penalty practice. They also take the place of interim final rules issued in 2006, which were addressed to and limited to banking institutions.

According to OFAC, the new guidelines were prompted by enactment of the Emergency Economic Powers Enhancement Act (IEEPA Enhancement Act) in October 2007, which substantially increased penalties in the IEEPA-based sanctions programs, although of course the "proposed rules" predated that by four years. Under the IEEPA Enhancement Act, the statutory maximum penalty for IEEPA violations can climb to as high as twice the total transaction value of $250,000 per violation. The aim of the new guidelines is to identify factors and considerations that will go into establishing what, if any, penalties are appropriate.

7. Because of the obscure laws and decisions on export control matters, attorneys in the Washington, D.C., area have formed an informal group, the OFAC Practitioners Forum. It meets every few months to discuss OFAC developments, as well as export control developments of agencies such as the Departments of State and Commerce, and how practitioners can best respond to them.

III. State Responses to Unilateral Extraterritorial Export Control Enforcement

Government responses to unilateral extraterritorial export control enforcement vary. In many cases, governments, especially intelligence agencies, try to support unilateral extraterritorial enforcement. However, depending on the facts of a case and the extent to which government agencies have been notified of, approved, or participated in the law enforcement operation, governments can be supportive of, neutral, or opposed to it. The responses of different agencies within the same government can conflict, again depending on the facts and the participation and interests of each agency. The involvement of a country's nationals or companies and their respective levels of political influence can also influence the positions and responses of foreign governments.

In terms of bilateral enforcement, foreign governments may not have laws that criminalize unilateral export controls, such as trading with certain embargoed countries – Cuba, for example. The U.S. government's efforts to apply its laws to other sovereign states are always controversial and frequently considered offensive or even intolerable by those states. The extraterritorial application of U.S. export controls has sometimes resulted in direct conflict between U.S. and foreign laws. In fact, foreign governments, including the closest U.S. allies, such as Canada, have sometimes opposed the extraterritorial reach of U.S. export controls.[45]

For example, reacting to the unprecedented jurisdictional reach of U.S. pipeline sanctions in 1981 and 1982 to delay completion of the Soviet Union's natural gas pipeline to Western Europe, the UK and French governments acted to block application of the U.S. controls. Other European governments openly opposed and urged action against the application of the sanctions.[46]

In response to the military rule in Poland, on June 18, 1982, President Reagan announced that prior Commerce Department oil and gas export controls would be broadened to include foreign subsidiaries and licensees of U.S. companies.[47] These measures were unprecedented in two respects. First, they were the first use of EAA authority to prohibit foreign subsidiaries of U.S. firms from exporting wholly foreign-origin nonstrategic equipment and technology. Second, the measures banned unaffiliated foreign companies from exporting foreign-origin products made with technology acquired from licensing agreements with U.S. companies, irrespective of whether the U.S. technology had been subject to controls at the time of export from the United States.

Several European countries encouraged and even ordered companies subject to the controls to perform their contractual obligations with the Soviets in spite of the U.S. ban. In turn, the United States promptly penalized the companies for violating U.S. law. The U.S. Commerce Department added several foreign companies to a "temporary denial" list and revoked all of their outstanding validated export licenses, effectively precluding them from participating in any transactions involving controlled U.S.-origin oil and gas equipment or technology. However, European companies continued to ship pipeline equipment to the Soviets and challenged U.S. controls and enforcement actions in administrative and judicial proceedings.[48] While the challenges were pending, on November 13, 1982, President Reagan announced that, as a result of an agreement between the United States and its allies to discuss East-West trade issues, the United States was revoking the pipeline controls.[49]

Some governments and businesses affected by unilateral export controls have challenged the application of extraterritorial jurisdiction. Foreign governments angered by the assertion of U.S. extraterritorial jurisdiction have used diplomatic means to express their views, including through formal diplomatic protests and negotiations. Although the United States has tried to avoid the extremes of extraterritorial reexports in foreign-policy-based imposed controls and has appeared more willing to rely on multilateral agreements, it has not renounced its position on extraterritoriality. Clearly,

[45] Joseph P. Griffin & Michael R. Calabrese, *Coping with Extraterritoriality Disputes in*, Law and Policy of Export Controls: Recent Essays on Key Export Issues 329 (Homer E. Moyer Jr. et al., eds., 1989); *see, e.g.*, Fred Abbott, *Defining the Extraterritorial Reach of American Export Controls: Congress as Catalyst*, 17 Cornell Int'l L.J. 79, 81 (1984).

[46] Griffin & Calabrese, *supra* note 45.

[47] Edward L. Rubinoff, *Exports of Oil and Gas Equipment and Technology to the Soviet Union: A Case Study in the Use of Export Controls as Instruments of U.S. Foreign Policy*, Law and Policy of Export Controls, 417, 420, citing Statement on Extension of U.S. Sanctions on the Export of Oil and Gas Equipment to the Soviet Union, June 18, 1982, 18 Weekly Com. Pres. Doc. 820 (June 21, 1982).

[48] *Id.* at 421, citing 47 Fed. Reg. 51, 463 (Nov.15, 1982) (Dresser); *Dresser Industries v. Baldridge*, No. 82–2385 (D.D.C., filed Aug. 23, 1982).

[49] *Id.* at 421, citing *East-West Trade Relations and the Soviet Pipeline Sanctions*, 18 Weekly Comp. Pres. Doc. 1475 (Nov. 19, 1982).

extraterritorial export controls create political costs for the nation imposing them and for affected third countries, and they impose extreme economic costs on businesses caught in the middle.[50]

Mexico Punishes U.S. Hotel for Expelling Cuban Officials to Comply with U.S. Embargo

(REPRINTED FROM 22 INT'L ENFORCEMENT L. REP. 231 (JUNE 2006))

On March 24, 2006, the Mexican government announced that it would fine Hoteles Sheraton SA 1,216,750 pesos (U.S. $111,186.52) for violating Mexican law when it expelled a group of Cuban officials.[51] The company is a subsidiary of New York-based Starwood Hotels & Resorts Worldwide.

The Mexican Foreign Ministry issued a resolution as part of the administrative procedure against the Sheraton Hotel company for violations to the law that protects trade and investment from foreign laws that violate international law. The fine, determined by the circumstances of the case, is equal to 25,000 days of the minimum daily wage in Mexico City.

The resolution concludes a procedure that started with the events that occurred in the Maria Isabel Sheraton Hotel on February 3, 2006, when Hotel Maria Isabel Sheraton ejected 16 Cuban officials who were meeting with U.S. energy executives.[52] Starwood had been advised by U.S. Treasury officials that it was violating U.S. law by providing services to Cuban officials.

On March 22, 2006, Mexican Foreign Minister Luis Ernesto Derbez explained that because the Mexican government does not accept the application of foreign laws in Mexico, the Sheraton case was being treated on its merits as it corresponded to Mexican national legislation.

Mexico sanctioned Starwood under its Law of Protection to Trade and Investment from Foreign States that Contravene International Law. The law permits fines as high as $444,000, or 100,000 times the current Mexico City daily minimum wage of 48.67 pesos (U.S. $4.44). (Legal fines in Mexico are calculated as multiples of the minimum wage.) The 1996 law was enacted in response to U.S. enactment of the Helms-Burton Act, which tightened restrictions on trade and foreign investment in Cuba.[53]

Following the hotel's expulsion of the Cuban nationals, local officials inspected the hotel and cited violations of local building codes, including operating a bar without a proper license and failing to provide a menu in Braille. Local authorities closed the hotel, which appealed the ruling, and eventually fined Starwood $15,000.[54]

Meanwhile, in Washington, D.C., State Department spokesman Sean McCormack said the Sheraton in Mexico City was a subsidiary of a U.S.-owned hotel group and hence subject to U.S. laws and regulations.[55]

[50] *Id.* at 343–44.

[51] Michael O'Boyle, *Mexico Fines U.S.-Owned Hotel for Expelling Cuban Officials to Comply with U.S. Embargo*, DAILY REP. FOR EXEC., Mar. 28, 2006, at A-13.

[52] Ministry of Foreign Affairs, Mexican Government, *The Foreign Ministry Penalizes the Sheraton Hotel, Press Release # 64*, Mar. 24, 2006.

[53] O'Boyle, *supra* note 51.

[54] *Mexico Fines US Hotel in Cuba Row: Hotel Maria Isabel Sheraton in Mexico City*, BBC NEWS, Mar. 6, 2006.

[55] *Id.*

Treasury said answering such questions is the most challenging part of OFAC's enforcement program. Although the department is required by statute to enforce all transactions regardless of size, the Treasury official said, OFAC is mainly interested in pursuing large financial transactions. "We don't expect coffee houses overseas to start checking passports," the Treasury official said. He added, however, that businesses where checking identification is a standard practice, such as hotels, may be expected to take extra care to ensure that they are complying with U.S. law.

The law does not exempt businesses or individuals who engaged in trade with Cuban nationals just because they did so unknowingly, but it does take criminal penalties off the table, he said. The maximum civil penalty for a violation of Cuba sanctions is $65,000. There is also no lower limit for the value of the transaction that would be considered illegal and enforceable, meaning transactions valued at $10 or $10,000 could both end in fines.

A key determinant in whether OFAC will pursue an enforcement action, however, is whether a transaction did "damage" to the sanctions policy. An illegal transaction that was stopped by the bank would be treated differently than a completed illegal transaction giving money directly to Cuban President Fidel Castro, the official said.

A more difficult situation for both companies and Treasury is when complying with U.S. sanctions law will cause a company to violate the local laws of the country in which it is doing business, as was the case with the Sheraton in Mexico City. "We expect businesses to follow the U.S. law requirements. That's our position. To the extent they're between a rock and a hard place, if there's anything we can do, we'll try to help them out," the Treasury official said.[56]

Some commentators have observed that the Starwood incident highlights the unintended consequences of unilateral U.S. sanctions. In this case, application of U.S. sanctions to a foreign corporation has strained U.S.-Mexican relations, undermining official cooperation on security issues and damaging the U.S.'s image abroad. As Treasury noted, application of these sanctions also put U.S. companies and their foreign subsidiaries between a rock and a hard place as they attempt to comply with conflicting laws.[57]

Notes and Questions

1. The success of export controls and economic sanctions often depends on international cooperation. In high-profile cases, such as during the two world wars, the League of Nations action against Italy, the series of U.S. sanctions against the Soviet Union, and the 1990 sanctions against Iraq, parties focused on achieving international cooperation to deny the target country access to the supplies or markets of principal trading partners. The extent of cooperation obtained has often disappointed the lead country. There is generally a range of cooperation that goes from (1) no cooperation, in which a single sender country imposes sanctions and usually does not seek cooperation (i.e., the U.S. campaign against Brazil to destabilize President João Goulart in 1962–64); (2) minor cooperation, in which the sender country enlists verbal support and possibly token restraints from other countries (i.e., U.S. sanctions imposed on the Soviet Union in part for its support of repressive measures in Poland); (3) modest cooperation, in which the sender country obtains meaningful restraints, but limited in time and coverage (i.e., U.S. sanctions against Iran during the hostage crisis); and (4) significant cooperation, in which

56 For additional background *see* Brett Ferguson, *OFAC Says Action on Mexico City Sheraton Not Signal of New Cuba Sanctions Strategy*, Daily Rep. For Exec., Apr. 10, 2006, at A-13.

57 Jack Colvin, *Cuba Policy, Sanctions Can Alienate Allies*, Miami Herald, Feb. 17, 2006.

the important trading partners make a major effort to limit trade, although leakages may still occur through neutral countries (i.e., the recent U.S. and UN sanctions against Iraq).[58]

2. Some governments have enacted laws to retaliate against the imposition by foreign governments of economic sanctions against them. *See*, e.g., Bruce Zagaris, *Panama Enacts Law to Retaliate against Discriminatory Foreign Enforcement Measures*, 18 INT'L ENFORCEMENT L. REP. 339 (Aug. 2002). Tax, trade, and investment policies can be a source of friction, as discussed in further detail later. On May 28, 2002, reacting to continued friction over these issues, the Panamanian legislature enacted Law No. 85, which permits Panamanian authorities to take reciprocal action against countries imposing restrictive measures on Panama. The legal instrument authorizes the president of Panama to apply measures of reciprocity against a country that has adopted discriminatory provisions against Panama if, after bilateral negotiations, the offending country does not revoke the same action within forty-five calendar days. The law states that any country that discriminates against "any Panamanian source natural or corporate person, good, service, public work, lease, security, title, or fund in their laws, regulations, practices, resolutions, judgments, or sentences" is eligible for reciprocal treatment by the Republic of Panama as well as the specific retaliatory measures in the new law, without prejudice to the Republic of Panama being able to take in turn additional measures required to object to such discriminatory measures before the World Trade Organization (WTO) and/or any other appropriate international organizations.

IV. Multilateral Regimes and Memberships

Countries that want to impose economic sanctions and export control measures try to persuade allies to participate. In some cases they even use international organizations, such as the United Nations, or international financial institutions (IFIs), such as the World Bank Group to impose sanctions. In other cases, they form informal fora to cooperate in determining export controls and sanctions.

A. *The Australia Group*

The Australia Group (AG) is an informal forum of industrialized countries that have agreed to cooperate in curbing the proliferation of chemical and biological weapons (CBW). This is accomplished through harmonization of export controls, the exchange of information on CBW-related activities of concern, and other diplomatic channels. The AG was formed in 1985 when the United States and fifteen other nations joined in imposing export controls on a number of chemicals that could be used to produce chemical weapons.

Since 1985, the AG has expanded its export control list to cover other CBW-related items. Based on this harmonized list, export controls are applied by each member on a national basis. The United States requires license for exports to certain destinations of the following:

- chemical and toxic chemical agents that are precursors in the production of chemical weapons;

[58] Hufbauer et al., *supra* note 5 at 44.

- microorganisms and toxins that can be used in the production of biological weapons;
- chemical manufacturing facilities and equipment that can be used in the production of precursor chemical weapons agents;
- equipment that can be used in the production of biological agents; and
- related chemical/biological technology.

Commerce Department regulations governing the export of these goods and technologies may be found in Part 742 of the Export Administration Regulations.

Current members include Argentina, Australia, Austria, Belgium, Bulgaria, Canada, Cyprus, Czech Republic, Denmark, Estonia, Finland, France, Germany, Greece, Hungary, Iceland, Ireland, Italy, Japan, Latvia, Lithuania, Luxembourg, Malta, Netherlands, New Zealand, Norway, Poland, Portugal, Romania, Slovakia, Slovenia, South Korea, Spain, Sweden, Switzerland, Turkey, Ukraine, United Kingdom, and the United States.

B. *Missile Technology Control Regime*

U.S. export controls on goods and technology that could contribute to missile proliferation are consistent with the controls of thirty-three other countries in the multilateral Missile Technology Control Regime (MTCR). The MTCR was created on April 16, 1987, by the United States, Canada, France, Germany, Italy, Japan, and the United Kingdom to limit the proliferation of missiles "capable of delivering nuclear weapons." An informal group whose members coordinate their national export controls based on consensus, the regime was extended to include missile systems capable of delivering all types of weapons of mass destruction (WMD): nuclear, chemical, and biological.

The United States implements its export control policies based on two MTCR documents: the Guidelines and the Equipment and Technology Annex. The Guidelines provide licensing policy, procedures, review factors, and standard assurances. The Annex is divided into two categories and lists twenty subcategory "items" of missile-related commodities.

(1) Category I covers missile systems (including ballistic and cruise missiles, space launch vehicles, and other unmanned air vehicles) capable of delivering 500-kg payload to at least a 300-km range. It also covers the major subsystems, production facilities, and production equipment for such missiles;

(2) Category II covers materials, components, and production and test equipment. All missile systems with a 300-km range are controlled, regardless of payload, to cover WMD-capable missiles, their major subsystems, production facilities, and production equipment.

The Commerce Department administers controls on approximately 120 missile entries on the Commerce Control List, such as the manufacturing equipment for Category I items and the dual-use items in Category II. The licensing policy and procedures for items controlled for missile technology reasons are found in Part 742 of the Export Administration Regulations.

Current MTCR members include Argentina, Australia, Austria, Belgium, Bulgaria, Brazil, Canada, Czech Republic, Denmark, Finland, France, Germany, Greece, Hungary, Iceland, Ireland, Italy, Japan, Luxembourg, New Zealand, Netherlands,

Norway, Poland, Portugal, Russia, South Africa, South Korea, Spain, Sweden, Switzerland, Turkey, Ukraine, United Kingdom, and the United States.

C. *The Nuclear Suppliers Group*

Consistent with the Nuclear Suppliers Group (NSG) Dual Use Regime, the Bureau of Industry and Security (BIS) administers export controls on goods and technology that could contribute to nuclear weapons development. The NSG, formed on March 31, 1992, is an informal group whose forty members agree to multilaterally control exports of dual-use commodities that have nuclear weapons utility.

BIS implements nuclear export control policies based on two NSG documents, the Guidelines and the Annex. The Guidelines provide the underlying precepts of the regime and contain the basic principles under which members agree not to authorize transfers of equipment, material, or related technology identified in the Annex –

- for use in a non-Nuclear Weapon State;
- a nuclear explosive activity;
- an unsafeguarded nuclear fuel-cycle activity;
- in general, where there is an unacceptable risk of diversion to such an activity; or
- when the transfers are contrary to the objective of averting the proliferation of nuclear weapons

The Annex designates seventy categories of dual-use equipment and material with nuclear weapons utility. It also contains a General Technology Note that ensures that exports of technology directly associated with listed items will be subject to the same degree of scrutiny and control as the items themselves.

Commerce Department regulations governing the export of nuclear goods and technologies may be found in Part 742 of the Export Administration Regulations.

Current members of the NSG include Argentina, Australia, Austria, Belgium, Belarus, Brazil, Bulgaria, Canada, China, Czech Republic, Cyprus, Denmark, Estonia, Finland, France, Germany, Greece, Hungary, Ireland, Italy, Japan, Kazakhstan, Latvia, Lithuania, Luxembourg, Malta, Netherlands, New Zealand, Norway, Poland, Portugal, Romania, Russia, Slovak Republic, Slovenia, South Korea, South Africa, Spain, Sweden, Switzerland, Turkey, Ukraine, United Kingdom, and the United States.

D. *The Wassenaar Arrangement on Export Controls for Conventional Arms and Dual-Use Goods and Technologies*

Compliance with U.S. Reexport Controls

REPRINTED FROM INTERNATIONAL CORPORATE COMPLIANCE, 6, JAN. 19, 2006, 5–7

by Benjamin H. Flowe Jr.

COCOM [Coordinating Committee for Multilateral Export Controls] was formed as a classified agreement among NATO Member countries, less Iceland, plus Japan, to control exports to Warsaw Pact countries during the Korean War and the Cold War. COCOM operated on a principle of tight export controls on transfers of military critical technologies in an effort to maintain NATO's technological lead time advantage to counterbalance the Warsaw Pact's advantage in military personnel and weapons. At the time of its demise on March 31, 1994, COCOM also included Australia, and many other countries had agreed to adopt COCOM-like controls (Austria, Finland, Hong Kong, Ireland, New Zealand, Switzerland, Sweden, and South Korea). COCOM operated by agreeing on three basic lists of controlled products and technologies: the International Munitions List, the Atomic Energy List, and the International List of Dual-Use items that could have a military use as well as a predominantly civilian use. The latter was the principal focus of COCOM and debate therein. COCOM member representatives working in Paris reviewed export license cases submitted to them by the members under a rule of unanimity, which allowed one country to veto many export license cases at high technical levels.

Technological innovations far outpaced the bureaucracies, as did the thawing of the Cold War with German unification, the breakup of the U.S.S.R., and heightened concerns over non-proliferation as a result of the First Persian Gulf War with Iraq. In the meantime, the United States continued to veto many significant license applications to modernize U.S.S.R. telecommunications infrastructure in the early 1990s, and warming of East-West relations eroded the consensus upon which COCOM was built. U.S. industry demonstrated in foreign availability cases that computer and telecommunications products for which licenses were being denied were freely available to COCOM and other U.S. target destinations from other countries, rendering the lower level COCOM controls futile and anti-competitive. Also, Russia and other Commonwealth of Independent States nations complained that COCOM was a barrier to new good relations. COCOM members agreed to include the former Warsaw Pact countries in a vaguely defined COCOM Forum discussion group commencing in June 1991. This Forum encouraged Russia and other newly independent states to develop export control regimes and qualify to become members of a COCOM successor. COCOM members agreed to disband as of the end of March 1994 and to negotiate to develop a successor regime, with Russia to be a founding member.

Although COCOM indeed disbanded, problems in forming its successor delayed formal establishment of the new regime for over two years. The new regime was implemented by all member nations except the United States on November 1, 1996. The focus of the successor regime, named the Wassenaar Arrangement ("WA") for a small town in the Netherlands where it was founded, is to contribute to regional and international security and stability by promoting transparency and responsibility in transfers of conventional arms and related dual-use items. More specifically, but not stated squarely, it is to deny conventional weapons and related dual-use items to certain rogue countries and to regions of instability. It does not (as yet) incorporate the other non-proliferation regimes discussed below. Although that would seem to be a logical long-term goal, it has not been pursued given the clearer focus of the other regimes. The United States proposed and most nations informally agreed at the creation of the WA on an unofficial target list proposal to address terrorist supporting nations and the four rogue states of Iran, Iraq, Libya, and North Korea, but there were and remain no clear targets. There are no veto rights of members, only reporting requirements and loose agreements as described below. The focus of the regime still remains fuzzy, but the United States and others are pressing for increased precision as WA operates over time.

The WA consists of 33 member states. It is twice the size of COCOM, its predecessor regime, because it has many new members (including former COCOM targets such as Russia, Ukraine, Bulgaria, Poland, Hungary, and the Czech Republic). The two most difficult problems of formation were the inclusion of Russia and other former Warsaw Pact allies and control over conventional weapons, especially to Iran. Russia agreed several times publicly to halt new arms sales to Iran and to wind down current contracts, but implementation has been fraught with disagreements. Allies also have had difficulty with U.S. proposals to control conventional weapons given that the United States is the world's biggest arms exporter and is proposing to cut off markets of other traditional customer countries. Russia and other newly independent states are being aided by former COCOM members in developing export control regimes and have become members since they are a supplier nation of weapons and other items of concern. The People's Republic of China ("the PRC") is unlikely to qualify for some time, if ever, unless it begins to engage in developing effective export controls of its own. China has recently enacted regulations to control chemical, biological, and missile [weapons], in accordance with its participation in the non-proliferation regimes discussed below, but its controls for Wassenaar items and the effectiveness of the implementation of these other controls are still of primary concern to U.S. policymakers.

The members agreed on a basic list of items to be controlled at the national discretion level by individual member states, a subset of that list as a sensitive list with more restrictive review and scrutiny, and a smaller subset of the latter as a very sensitive list. The list was comprised from the current COCOM Industrial List, plus the COCOM International Munitions List and parts of COCOM's Atomic Energy List to fill certain gaps in the nonproliferation regimes. Members also agreed that controls will be on a national discretion basis, with no COCOM veto rights. Consensus is required to change the list.

1. Participating States

Participating states include Argentina, Australia, Austria, Belgium, Bulgaria, Canada, Croatia, Czech Republic, Denmark, Estonia, Finland, France, Germany, Greece, Hungary, Ireland, Italy, Japan, Latvia, Lithuania, Luxembourg, Malta, Netherlands, New Zealand, Norway, Poland, Portugal, Republic of Korea, Romania, Russian Federation, Slovakia, Slovenia, South Africa, Spain, Sweden, Switzerland, Turkey, Ukraine, United Kingdom, and the United States.

2. Guidelines and Procedures

I. Purposes

As originally established in the Initial Elements adopted by the Plenary of 11–12 July 1996 and as exceptionally amended by the Plenary of 6–7 December 2001.

1. The Wassenaar Arrangement has been established in order to contribute to regional and international security and stability, by promoting transparency and greater responsibility in transfers of conventional arms and dual-use goods and technologies, thus preventing destabilizing accumulations. Participating States will seek, through their national policies, to ensure that transfers of these items do not contribute to the development or enhancement of military capabilities which undermine these goals, and are not diverted to support such capabilities.
2. It will complement and reinforce, without duplication, the existing control regimes for weapons of mass destruction and their delivery systems, as well as other internationally recognized measures designed to promote transparency and greater responsibility, by

focusing on the threats to international and regional peace and security which may arise from transfers of armaments and sensitive dual-use goods and technologies where the risks are judged greatest.

3. This Arrangement is also intended to enhance co-operation to prevent the acquisition of armaments and sensitive dual-use items for military end-uses, if the situation in a region or the behavior of a state is, or becomes, a cause for serious concern to the Participating States.
4. This Arrangement will not be directed against any state or group of states and will not impede bona fide civil transactions. Nor will it interfere with the rights of states to acquire legitimate means with which to defend themselves pursuant to Article 51 of the Charter of the United Nations.
5. In line with the paragraphs above, Participating States will continue to prevent the acquisition of conventional arms and dual-use goods and technologies by terrorist groups and organisations, as well as by individual terrorists. Such efforts are an integral part of the global fight against terrorism.

II. Scope

1. Participating States will meet on a regular basis to ensure that transfers of conventional arms and transfers in dual-use goods and technologies are carried out responsibly and in furtherance of international and regional peace and security.
2. To this end, Participating States will exchange, on a voluntary basis, information that will enhance transparency, will lead to discussions among all Participating States on arms transfers, as well as on sensitive dual-use goods and technologies, and will assist in developing common understandings of the risks associated with the transfer of these items. On the basis of this information they will assess the scope for co-ordinating national control policies to combat these risks. The information to be exchanged will include any matters which individual Participating States wish to bring to the attention of others, including, for those wishing to do so, notifications which go beyond those agreed upon.
3. The decision to transfer or deny transfer of any item will be the sole responsibility of each Participating State. All measures undertaken with respect to the Arrangement will be in accordance with national legislation and policies and will be implemented on the basis of national discretion.
4. In accordance with the provisions of this Arrangement, Participating States agree to notify transfers and denials. These notifications will apply to all non-participating states. However, in the light of the general and specific information exchange, the scope of these notifications, as well as their relevance for the purposes of the Arrangement, will be reviewed. Notification of a denial will not impose an obligation on other Participating States to deny similar transfers. However, a Participating State will notify, preferably within 30 days, but no later than within 60 days, all other Participating States of an approval of a licence which has been denied by another Participating State for an essentially identical transaction during the last three years.
5. Participating States agree to work expeditiously on guidelines and procedures that take into account experience acquired. This work continues and will include, in particular, a continuing review of the scope of conventional arms to be covered with a view to extending information and notifications beyond the categories described in Appendix 3.

Participating States agree to discuss further how to deal with any areas of overlap between the various lists.

6. Participating States agree to assess, on a regular basis, the overall functioning of this Arrangement.
7. In fulfilling the purposes of this Arrangement as defined in Section I, Participating States have, *inter alia*, agreed to the following guidelines, elements and procedures as a basis for decision making through the application of their own national legislation and policies:
   - "Elements for Objective Analysis and Advice Concerning Potentially Destabilizing Accumulations of Conventional Weapons" – adopted by the December 1998 Plenary;
   - "Statement of Understanding on Intangible Transfers of Software and Technology" – adopted December 2001;
   - "Best Practice Guidelines for Exports of Small Arms and Light Weapons (SALW)" – adopted December 2002;
   - "Elements for Export Controls of Man-Portable Air Defense Systems (MANPADS)" – adopted December 2003;
   - "Elements for Effective Legislation on Arms Brokering" – adopted December 2003;
   - "Statement of Understanding on Control of Non-Listed Dual-Use Items" – adopted December 2003.

III. Control Lists

1. Participating States will control all items set forth in the Lists of Dual-Use Goods and Technologies and in the Munitions List [2] (see Appendix 5), with the objective of preventing unauthorized transfers or re-transfers of those items.
2. The List of Dual-Use Goods and Technologies (Dual-Use List) has two annexes: 1) sensitive items (Sensitive List) and 2) very sensitive items (Very Sensitive List).
3. The lists will be reviewed regularly to reflect technological developments and experience gained by Participating States, including in the field of dual-use goods and technologies which are critical for indigenous military capabilities. In this respect, studies shall be completed to coincide with the first revision to the lists to establish an appropriate level of transparency for pertinent items.

IV. Procedures for the General Information Exchange

1. Participating States agree to exchange general information on risks associated with transfers of conventional arms and dual-use goods and technologies in order to consider, where necessary, the scope for co-ordinating national control policies to combat these risks.
2. In furtherance of this objective, and in keeping with the commitment to maximum restraint as a matter of national policy when considering applications for the export of arms and sensitive dual-use goods to all destinations where the risks are judged greatest, in particular to regions where conflict is occurring, Participating States also agree to exchange information on regions they consider relevant to the purposes of the Arrangement. These Regional Views should be based on, but not limited to, Section 2 of

the "Elements for Objective Analysis and Advice Concerning Potentially Destabilizing Accumulations of Conventional Weapons" (adopted by the 1998 Plenary*).

3. A list of possible elements of the general information exchange on non-participating states is contained in Appendix 1.

V. Procedures for the Exchange of Information on Dual-Use Goods and Technology

1. Participating States will notify licences denied to non-participants with respect to items on the List of Dual-Use Goods and Technologies, where the reasons for denial are relevant to the purposes of the Arrangement.
2. For the Dual-Use List, Participating States will notify all licences denied relevant to the purposes of the Arrangement to non-participating states, on an aggregate basis, twice per year. The indicative content of these denial notifications is described in Appendix 2.
3. For items in the Sensitive List and Very Sensitive List, Participating States will notify, on an individual basis, all licences denied pursuant to the purposes of the Arrangement to non-participating states. Participating States agree that notification shall be made on an early and timely basis, that is, preferably within 30 days but no later than within 60 days, of the date of the denial. The indicative content of these denial notifications is described in Appendix 2.
4. For items in the Sensitive List and Very Sensitive List, Participating States will notify licences issued or transfers made relevant to the purposes of the Arrangement to non-participants, on an aggregate basis, twice per year. The indicative content of these licence/transfer notifications is described in Appendix 2.
5. Participating States will exert extreme vigilance for items included in the Very Sensitive List by applying to those exports national conditions and criteria. They will discuss and compare national practices at a later stage.
6. Participating States agree that any information on specific transfers, in addition to that specified above, may be requested *inter alia* through normal diplomatic channels.

VI. Procedures for the Exchange of Information on Arms

1. Participating States agree that the information to be exchanged on arms will include any matters which individual Participating States wish to bring to the attention of others, such as emerging trends in weapons programmes and the accumulation of particular weapons systems, where they are of concern, for achieving the objectives of the Arrangement.
2. As an initial stage in the evolution of the new Arrangement, Participating States will exchange information every six months on deliveries to non-participating states of conventional arms set forth in Appendix 3, derived from the categories of the UN Register of Conventional Arms. The information should include the quantity and the name of the recipient state and, except in the category of missiles and missile launchers, details of model and type.
3. Participating States agree that any information on specific transfers, in addition to that specified above, may be requested *inter alia* through normal diplomatic channels.

VII. Meetings and Administration

1. Participating States will meet periodically to take decisions regarding this Arrangement, its purposes and its further elaboration, to review the lists of controlled items, to consider ways of co-ordinating efforts to promote the development of effective export control systems, and to discuss other relevant matters of mutual interest, including information to be made public.
2. Plenary meetings will be held at least once a year and chaired by a Participating State on the basis of annual rotation. Financial needs of the Arrangement will be covered under annual budgets, to be adopted by Plenary Meetings.
3. Working Groups may be established, if the Plenary meeting so decides.
4. There will be a secretariat with a staff necessary to undertake the tasks entrusted to it.
5. All decisions in the framework of this Arrangement will be reached by consensus of the Participating States.

VIII. Participation

The new Arrangement will be open, on a global and non-discriminatory basis, to prospective adherents that comply with the agreed criteria in Appendix 4. Admission of new participants will be based on consensus.

IX. Confidentiality

Information exchanged will remain confidential and be treated as privileged diplomatic communications. This confidentiality will extend to any use made of the information and any discussion among Participating States.

Appendix 1 General Information Exchange

Indicative Contents

The following is a list of possible principal elements of the general information exchange on non-participating states, pursuant to the purposes of the agreement (not all elements necessarily applying to both arms and dual-use goods and technology):

1. Acquisition Activities

- Companies/organizations
- Routes and methods of acquisition
- Acquisition networks inside/outside the country
- Use of foreign expertise
- Sensitive end-users
- Acquisition patterns
- Conclusions.

2. Export Policy

- Export control policy
- Trade in critical goods and technology
- Conclusions.

3. Projects of Concern

- Description of the project
- Level of technology
- Present status of development
- Future plans
- Missing technology (development and production)
- Companies/organisations involved, including end-user(s)
- Diversion activities
- Conclusions.

4. Other Matters

Appendix 2 Specific Information Exchange on Dual-Use Goods and Technologies

Indicative Content of Notifications

The content of denial notifications for tier 1 will be based on, but not be limited to, the following indicative or illustrative list:

From (country)

Country of destination

Item number on the Control List

Short description

Number of licences denied

Number of units (quantity)

Reason for denial.

Denial notification for items in the second tier and its sub-set of very sensitive items will be on the basis of, but not be limited to, the following indicative or illustrative list:

From (country)

Item number on the Control List

Short description

Number of units (quantity)

Consignee(s)

Intermediate consignee(s) and/or agent(s):

Name

Address

Country

Ultimate consignee(s) and/or end-user(s):

Name

Address

Country

Stated end-use

Reason for the denial

Other relevant information.

The content of notifications for licences/transfers in the second tier will be based on, but not be limited to, the following indicative or illustrative list:

From (country)

Item number on the Control List

Short description

Number of units (quantity)

Destination (country)

Appendix 3 Specific Information Exchange on Arms – Content by Category

1. Battle Tanks

Tracked or wheeled self-propelled armored fighting vehicles with high cross-country mobility and a high level of self-protection, weighing at least 16.5 metric tonnes unladen weight, with a high muzzle velocity direct fire main gun of at least 75 mm caliber.

2. Armored Combat Vehicles

2.1 Tracked, semi-tracked or wheeled self-propelled vehicles, with armored protection and cross-country capability designed, or modified and equipped:
   2.1.1 to transport a squad of four or more infantrymen, or
   2.1.2 with an integral or organic weapon of at least 12.5 mm caliber, or
   2.1.3 with a missile launcher.

2.2 Tracked, semi-tracked or wheeled self-propelled vehicles, with armored protection and cross-country capability specially designed, or modified and equipped:
   2.2.1 with organic technical means for observation, reconnaissance, target indication, and designed to perform reconnaissance missions, or
   2.2.2 with integral organic technical means for command of troops, or
   2.2.3 with integral organic electronic and technical means designed for electronic warfare.

2.3 Armored bridge-launching vehicles. (*) footnote

3. Large Caliber Artillery Systems

3.1. Guns, howitzers, mortars, and artillery pieces combining the characteristics of a gun or a howitzer capable of engaging surface targets by delivering primarily indirect fire, with a caliber of 100 to 155 mm, inclusive.

3.2. Guns, howitzers, mortars, and artillery pieces combining the characteristics of a gun or a howitzer capable of engaging surface targets by delivering primarily indirect fire, with a caliber above 155 mm.
3.3. Multiple-launch rocket systems capable of engaging surface targets, including armor, by delivering primarily indirect fire with the caliber of 100 mm and above.
3.4. Gun-carriers specifically designed for towing artillery. (*) footnote

4. Military Aircraft/Unmanned Aerial Vehicles

4.1 Military Aircraft: Fixed-wing or variable-geometry wing aircraft which are designed, equipped or modified:
4.1.1 to engage targets by employing guided missiles, unguided rockets, bombs, guns, machine guns, cannons, or other weapons of destruction.
4.1.2 to perform reconnaissance, command of troops, electronic warfare, electronic and fire suppression of air defense systems, refueling or airdrop missions.
4.2 Unmanned Aerial Vehicles: Unmanned aerial vehicles, specially designed, modified, or equipped for military use including electronic warfare, suppression of air defense systems, or reconnaissance missions, as well as systems for the control and receiving of information from the unmanned aerial vehicles.

"Military Aircraft" does not include primary trainer aircraft, unless designed, equipped, or modified as described above.

5. Military and Attack Helicopters

Rotary-wing aircraft which are designed, equipped, or modified to

5.1 engage targets by employing guided or unguided, air-to-surface, anti-armor weapons, air to sub-surface or air-to-air weapons, and equipped with an integrated fire-control and aiming system for these weapons.
5.2 perform reconnaissance, target acquisition (including anti-submarine warfare), communications, command of troops, or electronic warfare, or mine laying missions.

6. Warships (**) footnote

Vessel or submarines armed and equipped for military use with a standard displacement of 150 metric tonnes or above, and those with a standard displacement of less than 150 metric tonnes equipped for launching missiles with a range of at least 25 km or torpedoes with a similar range.

7. Missiles or Missile Systems

Guided or unguided rockets, ballistic or cruise missiles capable of delivering a warhead or weapon of destruction to a range of at least 25 km, and means designed or modified specifically for launching such missiles or rockets, if not covered by categories 1 to 6.

This category:

7.1 also includes remotely piloted vehicles with the characteristics for missiles as defined above;
7.2 does not include ground-to-air missiles.

Footnotes

* This Appendix 3, which contains a modified category 6, represents a further revision to the original Appendix 3 to the Wassenaar Arrangement Initial Elements adopted on 12 July 1996, and as amended at the 1999 and 2001 Plenaries.
** The standard displacement parameter in this Category was modified from 750 to 150 metric tonnes by decision of the December 2002 Plenary.

Appendix 4 – Participation Criteria

When deciding on the eligibility of a state for participation, the following factors, *inter alia*, will be taken into consideration, as an index of its ability to contribute to the purposes of the new arrangement:

- Whether it is a producer/exporter of arms or industrial equipment respectively;
- Its non-proliferation policies and its appropriate national policies, including:
- Adherence to non-proliferation policies, control lists and, where applicable, guidelines of the Nuclear Suppliers Group, the Missile Technology Control Regime and the Australia Group; and through adherence to the Nuclear Non-Proliferation Treaty, the Biological and Toxicological Weapons Convention, the Chemical Weapons Convention and (where applicable) START I, including the Lisbon Protocol;
- Its adherence to fully effective export controls.

Public Statement 2005 Plenary Meeting of the Wassenaar Arrangement on Export Controls for Conventional Arms and Dual-Use Goods and Technologies

The eleventh Plenary meeting of the Wassenaar Arrangement (WA)[1] was held in Vienna, 13–14 December 2005, and was chaired by Ambassador Dorothea Auer (Austria). The meeting reviewed the accomplishments of the year and considered further export control measures.

The Plenary welcomed the participation of Croatia, Estonia, Latvia, Lithuania, Malta, and Slovenia in the Plenary for the first time, and admitted South Africa as the first African state to join the Arrangement. The Plenary reiterated that the WA is open, on a global and non-discriminatory basis, to prospective adherents that comply with the agreed criteria, and noted that membership applications would continue to be examined on a case-by-case basis.

The WA continues to keep pace with advances in technology, market trends, and international security developments, such as the threat of terrorist acquisition of military and dual-use goods. The Plenary agreed to a number of amendments to the control lists, including in relation to items of potential interest to terrorists such as jamming equipment and unmanned aerial vehicles. The Plenary agreed to keep under review other items that could pose a threat if acquired by terrorists.

The WA considered growing international concerns about unregulated "intangible" transfers, such as by oral or electronic means, of software and technology related to conventional weapons and dual-use items.

In view of the threat posed by terrorist acquisition of manned-portable air defense systems (MANPADS), the Plenary welcomed practical steps by a number of Participating States in implementing Wassenaar Elements for Export Controls of MANPADS, for example through the destruction of stockpiles of such weapons. The Plenary especially encouraged Participating States to promote the Wassenaar Elements on MANPADS to non-WA States.

Following a survey conducted over the past year, the Plenary approved an indicative list of end-use assurances that Participating States commonly require as a condition for export of controlled items. The Plenary agreed to make the list public via the WA website: www.wassenaar.org.

The WA continues to place a high priority on transparency and outreach to non-Participating States and international organizations, with the aim of promoting the objectives of the Arrangement. Over the past year, the WA conducted outreach to South Africa and China, and further built upon last year's Outreach Seminar by focusing on outreach to industry in WA Participating States, where participants recognized the need for greater engagement with industry. Participating States undertook outreach to other countries in their national capacities.

Vienna, 14 December 2005

E. *Financial Action Task Force Initiative against Noncooperative Countries*

Although this chapter focuses on economic sanctions in the context of export controls and security policy, economic sanctions are also used as a tool of economic policy. One of the most controversial examples of the use of economic sanctions in this domain is the Financial Action Task Force initiative against noncooperative countries.

One of the goals and challenges of international organizations is ensuring compliance with and enforcement of international regulatory standards. An example is the effort of the Financial Action Task Force (FATF), which the G8 countries created in 1989, to set international anti-money laundering standards. The FATF promulgated a set of Forty Recommendations, supplemented in 2003 by Nine Special Recommendations with respect to counterterrorism financial regulation. One of the first mechanisms designed to motivate countries to comply with the standards was publishing a mutual evaluation. FATF established regional bodies that conducted country evaluations as well.

In 1998, to further motivate countries to comply with the "soft law" mandates of the FATF recommendations, FATF announced an initiative against noncooperative countries and territories (NCCT). The principal objective of the NCCT initiative is to reduce the vulnerability of the financial system to money laundering by ensuring that all financial centers adopt and implement measures for the prevention, detection, and punishment of money laundering according to internationally recognized standards.

The FATF remains committed to the NCCT process and welcomes the continued progress by the jurisdictions on the list in addressing identified deficiencies. The FATF continues to review the situation of listed countries at each plenary meeting and closely monitors developments in countries that are removed from the list. All decisions on NCCTs are taken only by the FATF Plenary.

The February 2000 NCCT report laid out the basic procedure for reviewing countries and territories as part of this initiative. The FATF has established four regional review groups (Americas, Asia/Pacific, Europe, Africa/Middle East) consisting of representatives from the FATF member governments that serve as the main points of contact with the reviewed country or territory.

Based on FATF members' experiences, countries were selected for review on a priority basis. The jurisdictions to be reviewed were informed of the work to be carried out by the FATF. The review groups gathered relevant laws, regulations, and other relevant information; analyzed this information against the twenty-five anti-money laundering criteria, and drafted a report that was sent to the jurisdictions for comment. Each reviewed jurisdiction provided its comments on its respective draft report. These comments and the draft reports themselves were discussed during a series of face-to-face meetings. Subsequently, the FATF Plenaries discussed and adopted the draft reports.

Forty-seven countries or territories were examined in two rounds of reviews (in 2000 and 2001). Of these, twenty-three were listed as NCCTs – fifteen in 2000 and eight in 2001. The FATF has not reviewed any new jurisdictions since 2001.

There are two consequences of being on the list, as detailed in Recommendation 21:

> "Financial institutions should give special attention to business relationships and transactions with persons, including companies and financial institutions, from countries which do not or insufficiently apply the FATF Recommendations. Whenever these transactions have no apparent economic or visible lawful purpose, their background and purpose should, as far as possible, be examined, the findings established in writing, and be available to help competent authorities. Where such a country continues not to apply or insufficiently applies the FATF Recommendations, countries should be able to apply appropriate countermeasures.

In accordance with Recommendation 21, the FATF recommends that financial institutions give special attention to business relations and transactions with persons, including companies and financial institutions, from NCCTs and in so doing take into account issues raised in relevant summaries of the annual NCCT reports and any progress made by these jurisdictions since being listed as NCCTs.

The FATF itself does not determine what specific measures financial institutions must take. It is up to each country to issue its own specific guidance or regulations with which financial institutions must comply.

Another potential consequence of being listed as an NCCT is being subjected to countermeasures. In jurisdictions that have failed to make adequate progress in addressing the serious deficiencies identified by the FATF, in addition to the application of Recommendation 21, the FATF recommends the application of further countermeasures that should be gradual, proportionate, and flexible and taken in concerted action toward a common objective. These countermeasures include the following: stringent requirements for identifying clients; enhancement of advisories, including jurisdiction-specific financial advisories, to financial institutions for identification of the beneficial owners before business relationships are established with individuals or companies from these countries; enhanced reporting mechanisms or systematic reporting of financial transactions on the assumption that financial transactions with such countries are more likely to be suspicious; in considering requests for approving the establishment in FATF member countries of subsidiaries or branches or representative offices of banks, taking into account the fact that the relevant bank is from an NCCT; and warning nonfinancial sector businesses that transactions with entities within the NCCTs might run the risk of money laundering.

As with Recommendation 21, the FATF itself does not determine what specific measures financial institutions and nonfinancial businesses must take. It is up to each country to specifically determine how to apply the countermeasures.[59]

Notes and Questions

1. The legitimacy of FATF's mandate is often questioned by critics of the organization. The legitimacy problem arises from FATF's small size – thirty-three full member countries – and its creation by the G8. FATF is an informal group without legal personality, domiciled in the offices in Paris of another Western elite club, the OECD.

Critics also note that FATF's procedures do not bear the hallmarks of the usual democratic governance mechanisms recommended for governments and lawmaking bodies. Instead of relying on thorough, reliable studies to define problems, FATF seems to favor anecdotal typologies. It then proposes solutions, often in the way of recommendations. Until 2002, FATF did not invite or allow private sector groups to participate in its decision-making processes. Thereafter, it devised procedures to allow private sector groups affected by FATF proposed policies to make written and oral submissions. However, FATF policymakers deliberated in secret and then issued amended and new recommendations without any account of their deliberations. Hence, this process undermines the legitimacy of its actions.

2. *Hypothetical*: You work for the U.S. Treasury Department or National Security Council. You are instructed to develop a plan to increase the effectiveness of U.S. anti-money laundering initiatives against NCCTs. Please discuss, *inter alia*, the implications for the U.S. government's own flexibility of implementing such standards, especially in view of gatekeeper standards that require the United States to make lawyers and other gatekeepers identify and report suspicious transactions and not "tip off" their clients by informing them when they make such reports.

3. How can governments such as the U.S. government effectively apply economic sanctions and other policies through international organizations, such as international financial institutions (IFIs)? The IFIs include the International Monetary Fund and the four multilateral development banks (MDBs): the World Bank Group, the Inter-American Development Bank, the Asian Development (ADB), and the African Bank (AFDB). All have nonpolitical objectives and multilateral decision-making processes. Does the United States encounter problems when it seeks to use the IFIs for its own foreign policy purposes (e.g., to cut off aid to Chile in 1970–73 because of its distaste for the Allende administration and to cut off aid to Nicaragua in the late 1970s due to its dislike for the Sandinista policies)? *See* Barry E. Carter, International Economic Sanctions 158, 161–63.

4. Does it matter that most decisions on loan requests in IFIs are made by the executive boards through informal consensus rather than through formal voting procedures? If you are representing one of the countries targeted by the FATF's NCCT initiative, what can you argue if the United States or other governments succeed in having IFIs implement the FATF's NCCT program? What is the impact, if any, of IFI application of U.S. (and

[59] FATF, *NCCT Initiative* (http://fatf-gafi.org).

other government) anti-money laundering and other policies (i.e., human rights and democracy)?

V. Hypotheticals

A. You serve as counsel for the Ministry of International Business in the country of Caribebana. The OECD has targeted you and ten other jurisdictions for not fulfilling obligations under its harmful tax practices initiative. In particular, the OECD is targeting Caribebana for not having concluded enough Tax Information Exchange Agreements (TIEAs). In fact, Caribebana has concluded several TIEAs but only as part of income tax treaties. Caribebana's position is that it will negotiate TIEAs either as part of an income tax treaty or as part of another arrangement whereby Caribebana obtains economic benefits. Advise Caribebana of its legal and diplomatic moves in response to the OECD initiative.

B. You advise an insurance company that is considering an acquisition of a U.S. insurance company. In the due diligence process prior to the acquisition, it appears that the U.S. insurance company was insuring some transactions in Cuba, even though Cuba is one of the countries to which the OFAC sanctions apply. Advise the acquiring company of its options in dealing with the proposed acquisition, especially in terms of complying with OFAC sanctions.

VI. Additional Reading

A. U.S. Export Controls

Kenneth W. Abbott, *Linking Trade to Political Goals: Foreign Policy Export Controls in the 1970s and 1980s*, 65 MINN. L. REV. 739–889 (1981).

Coping with U.S. Export Controls 2005 (Evan R. Berlack & Christopher R. Wall eds., Practising Law Instit. 2005).

BENJAMIN H. FLOWE, EXPORT COMPLIANCE GUIDE (Export Practitioner 1995).

ERIC L. HIRSCHHORN, THE EXPORT CONTROL AND EMBARGO HANDBOOK (2000).

Judicial Review Commission on Foreign Asset Control, FINAL REPORT TO CONGRESS (3 Volumes) (Jan. 2001).

LAW AND POLICY OF EXPORT CONTROLS: RECENT ESSAYS ON KEY EXPORT ISSUES (Homer E. Moyer Jr. et al., ed., Sec. of Int'l Law & Practice, Amer. Bar Assoc., 1993).

WILLIAM A. ROOT & JOHN R. LIEBMAN, UNITED STATES EXPORT CONTROLS (3rd ed. 1996 Supplement).

B. Economic Sanctions

C. LLOYD BROWN-JOHN, MULTILATERAL SANCTIONS IN INTERNATIONAL LAW: A COMPARATIVE ANALYSIS (1975).

BARRY E. CARTER, INTERNATIONAL ECONOMIC SANCTIONS: IMPROVING THE HAPHAZARD U.S. LEGAL REGIME (1989).

MARGARET P. DOXEY, INTERNATIONAL SANCTIONS IN CONTEMPORARY PERSPECTIVE (1987).

ECONOMIC COERCION AND U.S. FOREIGN POLICY: IMPLICATIONS OF CASE STUDIES FROM THE JOHNSON ADMINISTRATION (Sidney Weintraub ed., 1982).

Peter L. Fitzgerald, *Pierre Goes Online: Blacklisting and Secondary Boycotts in U.S. Trade Policy*, 31 VAND. J. TRANSNAT'L L. 1 (1998).

Peter L. Fitzgerald, *"If Property Rights Were Treated like Human Rights, They Could Never Get Away with This:" Blacklisting and Due Process in U.S. Economic Sanctions Programs*, 51 HASTINGS L.J. 73 (1999).

PETER L. FITZGERALD, *Managing "Smart Sanctions" against Terrorism Wisely*, 36 NEW ENG. L. REV. 957 (2002).

GARY CLYDE HUFBAUER, JEFFREY J. SCHOTT, & KIMBERLY Ann ELLIOTT, ECONOMIC SANCTIONS RECONSIDERED: HISTORY AND CURRENT POLICY (2d ed. 1990).

MICHAEL P. MALLOY, U.S. ECONOMIC SANCTIONS: THEORY AND PRACTICE (Kluwer Law International, 2001).

MICHAEL P. MALLOY, *Economic Sanctions and Trade Regulation*, 4 CHI. J. INT'L L. 371 (2003).

NATIONAL INSTITUTE ON ECONOMIC SANCTIONS (American Bar Association Section of International Law 2005).

U.S. Library of Congress, Congressional Research Service, *U.S. Economic Sanctions Imposed against Specific Foreign Countries: 1979 to the Present*. CRS Report for Congress, 88–612 F, rvd. September 9, 1988.

C. *Web Sites*[60]

U.S. Government Departments and Agencies with Export Control Responsibilities

Department of Commerce, Bureau of Industry and Security: Regulates the export of dual-use goods and technologies, including enforcing export controls, antiboycott, and public safety laws. http://www.bis.doc.gov/.

Department of State, Directorate of Defense Trade Controls: Enforces defense trade controls and formulates defense trade policy. http://www.pmdtc.org/.

Department of Defense, Defense Threat Reduction Agency-Technology Security: Responsible for the development and implementation of policies on international transfers of defense-related technology, and reviews certain dual-use export license applications referred by Commerce. http://www.dtra.mil/.

Department of the Treasury, Office of Foreign Assets Control (OFAC): Administers and enforces economic and trade sanctions against targeted foreign countries, terrorism-sponsoring organizations, and international narcotics traffickers. http://www.treas.gov/offices/enforcement/ofac/.

Department of Homeland Security, Bureau of Customs and Border Protection: Responsible for regulating and enforcing controls over imports of goods into and exports of goods from the United States. http://www.cbp.gov/.

U.S. Nuclear Regulatory Commission, Office of International Programs: Licenses the imports and exports of nuclear material and equipment. http://www.nrc.gov/.

Office of Defense Nuclear Nonproliferation, National Nuclear Security Administration: Provides support for U.S. export control compliance and seeks to improve foreign export control practices. http://www.nnsa.doe.gov/na-20/.

Department of Energy, Office of Fossil Energy: Responsible for regulating natural gas imports and exports. http://www.fe.doe.gov/.

Department of the Interior, U.S. Fish and Wildlife Service, International Affairs Office: Controls the export of endangered fish and wildlife species. http://www.fws.gov/international/.

Drug Enforcement Administration: Controls the import and export of controlled substances. http://www.dea.gov/.

Food and Drug Administration: Issues "Certificates of Export" for regulated products and oversees the export of medical devices and medical drugs. http://www.fda.gov/.

Patent and Trademark Office: Oversees patent filing data sent abroad. http://www.uspto.gov/.

Environmental Protection Agency, International Affairs: Regulates toxic waste exports. http://www.epa.gov/international/.

International Organizations and Groups

World Trade Organization: Global international trade organization dealing with the rules of trade among nations. http://www.wto.org/.

[60] These addresses are from *Useful Export Control Websites*, COPING WITH U.S. EXPORT CONTROLS 2005, *supra* note 2, 1019–20.

Wassenaar Arrangement: Multilateral agreement for the control of exports of conventional arms and dual-use goods. http://www.wassenaar.org/.

Australia Group: Arrangement seeking to reduce the risk that exporting or transshipping countries will allow chemical and biological weapon proliferation. http://www.australiagroup.net/.

Missile Technology Control Regime: Association of countries seeking to coordinate national export licensing efforts to prevent the proliferation or weapons of mass destruction. http://www.mtcr.info/.

Financial Action Task Force: An informal group of countries created by the G8 Summit in 1989 to develop anti-money laundering policies. http://www.fatf-gafi.org.

7 Extraterritorial Jurisdiction

I. Introduction and Hypotheticals

Globalization, the information revolution, and the proliferation of free trade have facilitated the spread of transnational crime, including white collar crime. As the geographical reach of crime has expanded, so too have the efforts of governments to expand jurisdiction over crimes with international elements. This chapter examines the bases for extraterritorial jurisdiction, especially as they relate to white collar crime, and various mechanisms used to limit the inevitable conflicts that arise from concurrent assertions of jurisdiction.[1] This chapter also discusses limitations on the power to enforce and adjudicate related to the immunities of states, diplomats, consuls, international organizations, and their officials.

National criminal law is based on the principle of territorial sovereignty of the state. This principle requires courts within a particular state to apply its criminal law, whereas in civil or commercial cases domestic courts sometimes apply foreign laws. The inability of domestic courts to apply foreign law in criminal cases makes jurisdictional conflicts more important and more difficult to resolve. In the same vein, the potential for diplomatic conflicts when other states are denied the ability to assert their criminal jurisdiction is much greater than in civil cases.[2]

When analyzing trends in national criminal jurisdiction, it is useful to distinguish among the following categories: (1) jurisdiction to prescribe (also referred to as legislative jurisdiction), (2) jurisdiction to enforce (or executive or enforcement jurisdiction), and (3) jurisdiction to adjudicate.[3]

Hypothetical 1: You are an Assistant District Attorney in New York City. The District Attorney has asked you to advise on jurisdictional issues related to a series of transactions involving the family that owns Banco Grande (BG), a prominent financial institution in the Latin American state of Venecolomador. The family has prominent political connections with the government of Venecolomador. The District Attorney has received evidence suggesting that, between January 2002 and December 2004, BG helped high-net-worth individuals evade currency exchange controls and move money out of Venecolomador using BG branches in the Bahamas and the Cayman Islands. In addition, the District Attorney believes that BG paid off officials in the Venecolomador government to ensure that bank inspectors would not uncover irregularities. The illicit payments may have been approved at a BG board meeting in Venecolomador, in which Mr. Executivo, a board member, participated by phone from his office in New York. In addition, BG cleared many of the illicit payments through the New York Clearing Exchange.

The District Attorney has learned that one year ago BG whistleblowers unsuccessfully approached the government of Venecolomador and urged officials to prosecute. Four months ago the same whistleblowers approached the U.S. Attorney in Miami. Although initially interested, he declined to prosecute after a preliminary investigation.

Please advise the New York District Attorney of the potential jurisdiction to prosecute. Would the situation be different if you were advising a prosecutor in Berlin or Paris? Would it matter if some of the bribe payments were made from the United States? Does it matter whether Venecolomador considered bringing the case? If the District Attorney in New York learns that whistleblowers approached the U.S. Attorney in Miami, does he have any legal or ethical obligation to contact the U.S. Attorney in Miami? The Department of Justice?

[1] Some of this chapter is based on an earlier article by Bruce Zagaris & Jay Rosenthal, *United States Jurisdictional Considerations in International Criminal*, 15 Cal. W. L.J. 305 (1985).

[2] *See, e.g.*, Szaszy, *Conflict-of-Laws Rules in International Criminal Law and Municipal Criminal Law in Western and Socialist Countries*, *in* A Treatise on International Criminal Law 135–68 (M. Bassiouni & V. Nanda eds., 1973).

[3] 1 Restatement (3rd) of Foreign Relations of the United States (hereafter Restatement (3rd), § 401 (1987).

Hypothetical 2: You are a high-level Department of Justice (DOJ) official. The U.S. Attorney in the District of Columbia is investigating the use of technology sold to a prohibited government by a Dutch company. The Dutch company and its executives have pleaded guilty in the United States and have been sentenced. In the Netherlands, three midlevel officials have pleaded guilty and have been sentenced. Now, the Dutch Attorney General has formally requested that the U.S. Department of Justice dismiss the indictment against the three midlevel officials because they have already been prosecuted in the Netherlands. At DOJ, the Assistant Attorney General is pressing to at least ensure that he or one of his assistants can interrogate the three midlevel officials to determine whether they were truthful in their discussion of the events and whether the Office of the U.S. Attorney in Washington, D.C., should pursue any other persons. How should you advise the Attorney General?

Efforts by some states, especially the United States, to apply their laws based on broad conceptions of territoriality or nationality have resulted in resentment and conflicting assertions of the rules of international law. Diplomatic relations between the United States and its allies have been strained by U.S. efforts to implement economic sanctions through restraints, administrative penal actions, and even prosecutions of foreign subsidiaries of corporations based in the United States. Efforts by U.S. regulatory agencies, such as the Federal Maritime Commission and the Civil Aeronautics Board, to exercise jurisdiction over international transport conferences, especially to secure information from conference members located abroad, have encountered resistance in the form of blocking legislation from many important trading partners and allies of the United States. *See* RESTATEMENT (3RD), § 442, Reporters' Notes 1 and 4. Additionally, the extraterritorial application of antitrust and securities laws has periodically been viewed by other states as illegal. *See* RESTATEMENT (3RD), §§ 415 and 416. As a result of the adverse reactions of other states, the United States has modified its assertions of jurisdiction in some areas. *See*, e.g., RESTATEMENT (3RD), § 315, Comment b and Reporters' Notes 7 and 8.

II. Jurisdiction to Prescribe

Jurisdiction to prescribe is the authority of a state to make and apply its law to things, or to the conduct, relations, status, or interests of persons via legislation, executive act or order, administrative rule, or court action.[4] According to the Restatement and subject to certain limitations, under international law the United States may exercise jurisdiction to prescribe and apply its law with respect to

1. a. conduct, a substantial part of which occurs within its territory;
   b. the status of persons, or interests in things, present within its territory;
   c. conduct outside its territory which has or is intended to have substantial effect;
2. the conduct, status, interests or relations of its nationals outside as well as within its territory; or
3. certain conduct outside its territory by persons not its nationals, which is directed against the security of the state or certain other state interests.[5]

[4] RESTATEMENT (3RD), § 402. Not all commentators agree on the categories of jurisdiction or the parameters of each category. *See, e.g.*, Christopher Blakesley, *United States Jurisdiction over Extraterritorial Crime*, 73 J. CRIM. L. & CRIMINOLOGY 1109 (1982); S. Z. Feller, *Jurisdiction over Offenses with a Foreign Element*, in M. Bassiouni & V. Nanda, *supra* note 2, vol. II at 9–10 (1973).

[5] *Id*. 402.

A. *Bases of Jurisdiction to Prescribe*

Criminal jurisdiction in the United States and in other countries is primarily based on five principles: (1) territorial, (2) protective, (3) nationality, (4) passive personality, and (5) universal.[6] Federal and state court decisions in the United States, as well as most textbooks and treatises, adopt these bases.[7]

1. The Territorial Principle

Generally speaking, territoriality is the typical and nationality the exceptional basis for the exercise of jurisdiction. Both bases of jurisdiction may be relevant in some circumstances. For example, jurisdiction based on effects in a specific territory is more easily used when applied to nationals of the state exercising the jurisdiction.[8]

Historically, three different practices have arisen concerning claims of extraterritorial criminal jurisdiction. One group of states, which includes the United States and the United Kingdom, emphasizes the territorial nature of a criminal act. Countries in this group do not believe that a state can punish an alien for a breach of criminal law where the act is committed outside its territory.[9] A second group, which includes France, Germany, and the majority of states, also asserts jurisdiction on a territorial basis. Additionally, these states permit the assertion of jurisdiction where acts are directed against the security of the state or its financial credit.[10] A third group, which includes Turkey and Italy, does not limit the exercise of jurisdiction by territorial factors. They assert their jurisdiction when the crime, wherever committed, is a social evil that all civilized countries have an interest in suppressing. This jurisdictional principle is known as universality. However, in practice these states assert jurisdiction only for acts of foreigners committed abroad when the "crimes" are prejudicial to the state or one of its nationals.[11]

Objective and subjective territoriality are closely related and often occur simultaneously. Subjective territoriality requires an element of the case to occur within the asserting state. Objective territoriality exists when the effect or result of the criminal conduct affects the asserting state, but the other elements of the offense occur wholly beyond the territorial boundaries.[12]

Traditionally, the United States and United Kingdom have at least theoretically denied the ability of a state to assert criminal jurisdiction outside of its territory against a nonnational. However, they believe that in certain circumstances a crime may be committed within the territory of a state and hence be justifiable by its criminal courts, even though the actor is physically outside the territory. Moreover, these states assert jurisdiction when an act is committed physically outside their territory but injures, harms, or affects its citizens or interests located within its territory. In such cases the basis for jurisdiction is often referred to as "objective territorial jurisdiction." Recently, U.S.

[6] Harvard Research in International Law, *Jurisdiction with Respect to Crime*, 29 Am. J. Int'l L. 435 (Supp. 1935).

[7] Blakesley, *supra* note 4, at 2, n. 5.

[8] Restatement (3rd), § 402, Comment (a).

[9] *Id.*, § 402, Reporters' Note 1.

[10] Feller, *supra* note 4, at 26–28.

[11] 6 M. Whiteman, Digest of International Law 94–95 (1970).

[12] Christopher Blakesley, *Extraterritorial Jurisdiction, in* International Criminal Law: Procedural and Enforcement Mechanisms 33, 47 (M. Cherif Bassiouni ed., 2d. ed. 1999).

prosecutors and courts have increasingly relied on objective territorial jurisdiction – also called the effects doctrine.[13]

United States of America, Plaintiff-Appellee, v. Jerry D. Mitchell, Defendant-Appellant

UNITED STATES COURT OF APPEALS FOR THE FIFTH CIRCUIT, 553 F.2D 996; 1977 U.S. APP. LEXIS 12970; 10 E.C. (BNA) 1177; 43 A.L.R. FED. 585; 7 EAR 20484, LEXSEE 553 F.2D 996 (JUNE 13, 1977)

This appeal turns on whether the Marine Mammal Protection Act of 1972 (MMPA), *16 U.S.C. § 1361 et seq.*, and related regulations, *50 C.F.R. § 216.11 (1974)*, apply to an American citizen taking dolphins within the territorial waters of a foreign sovereign state. The defendant-appellant, Jerry Mitchell, is an American citizen convicted of violating the Act by capturing 21 dolphins within the three-mile limit of the Commonwealth of the Bahamas. We hold that the criminal prohibitions of the Act do not reach conduct in the territorial waters of a foreign sovereignty. We reverse the conviction.

The parties stipulated that Mitchell had a Bahamian work permit to capture the dolphins (Atlantic Bottlenose Dolphins). He admits taking them during 1974 while employed by George Curtis Johnson, the owner of Seafloor Aquarium, a marine attraction in Nassau, Bahamas. Johnson, a Bahamian citizen, obtained Mitchell's permit from the Bahamian government with the intention of exporting dolphins to Great Britain. Seafloor paid the defendant $800 for each captured dolphin. None of the dolphins were imported into the United States.

The Government's evidence as to its practices in issuing permits applicable to American citizens in foreign territorial waters suffers from a lack of clarity. According to government witnesses, in March 1973 the National Marine Fisheries Service of the Department of Commerce (NMFS) learned of Mitchell's plan to establish a dolphin-capturing business. Charles Fuss, Chief of Law Enforcement for the Service, and another agent met with Mitchell and an Englishman to discuss the proposed venture, which at that time was to be based in Haiti. Fuss testified that he cautioned Mitchell that the moratorium provision of MMPA prohibited American citizens from capturing marine mammals anywhere, and he advised Mitchell to seek legal advice, both from a lawyer and from the Service's Washington office. Fuss stated that Seafloor would not be granted a United States permit to capture dolphins because "that facility is located in a foreign country." . . .

In a 32-count indictment, the Government charged Mitchell with taking four dolphins on May 11, 1974, nine in June or July, and two on August 9, all in violation of the NMFS regulation. Stated without a geographical restriction, the regulation purports to prohibit all unauthorized takings of marine mammals by United States citizens. The indictment also charged that Mitchell possessed these same dolphins in violation of another regulation and that he transported and sold the animals in violation of the same provision. The jury found Mitchell guilty of these twenty-three counts, as well as of one count of conspiracy to violate the Act and the regulations. The jury acquitted the defendant of eight counts of taking, possessing, transporting, and selling six dolphins in violation of the MMPA sections prohibiting takings on the high seas, possession of illegally taken mammals, and transport or sale of such mammals. (Footnotes omitted). . . .

[13] RESTATEMENT (3RD), § 402, Comment (d).

Mitchell argues that Congress did not intend to exercise its legislative authority to establish subject matter jurisdiction over takings, possessions, and sales of marine mammals in foreign countries. He concedes, as he must, that Congress has the power to control the conduct of American citizens overseas. The Supreme Court has held repeatedly that the legislative authority of the United States over its citizens extends to conduct by Americans on the high seas and even within the territory of other sovereigns. In *Blackmer v. United States*, 1932, 284 *U.S.* 421, 52 *S. Ct.* 252, 76 *L. Ed.* 375, for example, the Court held that a district court had subject matter jurisdiction to hold an American citizen residing in Paris in criminal contempt for failure to return to the United States in reply to a subpoena. More recently, this Court relied on *Blackmer* to uphold the power of a district court to try for criminal contempt a prospective witness who refused to return from Israel to testify. *United States v. Lansky*, 5 *Cir.* 1974, 496 *F.2d* 1063, 1067, *rehearing denied en banc*, 502 *F.2d* 1168. As the Restatement explains, international law principles do not constrain this legislative authority, because citizenship alone is generally recognized as a relationship sufficient to justify the exercise of jurisdiction by a state. Restatement (Second) of the Foreign Relations Law of the United States § 30 (1965). *See also United States v. Black*, S.D.N.Y. 1968, 291 *F. Supp.* 262, 266. Consequently, Mitchell poses a question not about the authority of Congress but instead about the congressional purposes embodied in the statute.

Two principles of statutory construction must be considered in determining whether Congress intended to apply the criminal prohibitions of the MMPA extraterritorially. First, *United States v. Bowman*, 1922, 260 *U.S.* 94, 43 *S. Ct.* 39, 67 *L. Ed.* 149, requires us to examine the nature of the law:

[Some laws] are such that to limit their *locus* to the strictly territorial jurisdiction would be greatly to curtail the scope and usefulness of the statute and leave open a large immunity for frauds as easily committed by citizens on the high seas and in foreign countries as at home. In such cases, Congress has not thought it necessary to make specific provision in the law that the *locus* shall include the high seas and foreign countries, but allows it to be inferred from the nature of the offense. *Id. at* 98, 43 *S. Ct. at* 41, *quoted in Stegeman v. United States*, 9 *Cir.* 1970, 425 *F.2d* 984, 986 (en banc), *cert. denied*, 400 *U.S.* 837, 91 *S. Ct.* 74, 27 *L. Ed. 2d* 70. Second, if the nature of the law does not mandate its extraterritorial application, then a presumption arises against such application. *Bowman*, 260 *U.S. at* 98, 43 *S. Ct.* 39, 67 *L. Ed.* 149; *accord Steele v. Bulova Watch Co.*, 1952, 344 *U.S.* 280, 285, 73 *S. Ct.* 252, 97 *L. Ed.* 319; *Foley Bros. v. Filardo*, 1949, 336 *U.S.* 281, 285, 69 *S. Ct.* 575, 93 *L. Ed.* 680; *Airline Stewards and Stewardesses Ass'n v. Trans World Airlines*, 2 *Cir.* 1959, 273 *F.2d* 69, 70, *cert. denied*, 362 *U.S.* 988, 80 *S. Ct.* 1075, 4 *L. Ed. 2d* 1021. To overcome the presumption and to apply the statute beyond the territory of the United States, the Government must show a clear expression of congressional intent. *Steele*, 344 *U.S. at* 285, 73 *S. Ct.* 252, 97 *L. Ed.* 319; *Foley Bros.*, 336 *U.S. at* 285, 69 *S. Ct.* 575, 93 *L. Ed.* 680....

The Restatement (Second) of the Foreign Relations Law of the United States § 38 (1965) (Reporters' Note 1) states in part:

Federal legislation is usually construed to apply only to conduct taking place within the territory of the United States unless otherwise provided....

Federal statutes designed to be applied to conduct taking place outside the United States usually expressly so provide....

In summary, then, the Act and its legislative history do not demonstrate the clear intent required by *Bowman* and its progeny to overcome the presumption against extraterritorial extension of American statutes. Congress did extend the force of the MMPA to the high seas, but any further extension to regulate the taking of marine mammals in the territory of other sovereign states is not justified by the Act. The legislative scheme requires the State Department to pursue international controls by the usual methods of negotiation, treaty, and convention. Without a clearer expression from Congress to the contrary, we must presume that United States jurisdiction under the Act ceases at the territorial waters and boundaries of other states.

Ford v. United States, 273 U.S. 593 (1927)

Mr. Chief Justice TAFT delivered the opinion of the Court.

This is a review by *certiorari* of the conviction of George Ford, George Harris, J. Evelyn, Charles H. Belanger, and Vincent Quartararo, of a conspiracy, contrary to section 37 of the Criminal Code (Comp. St. 10201), to violate the National Prohibition Act, title 2, 3 and 27 (41 Stat. 305, 308, 316, c. 85 (Comp. St. 10138½ aa, 10138½ p)), and the Tariff Act of 1922, 593(b) being 42 Stat. 858, 982, c. 356 (Comp. St. 5841h13). The trial and conviction resulted largely from the seizure of the British vessel Quadra, hovering in the high seas off the Farallon Islands, territory of the United States, 25 miles west from San Francisco. The ship, her officers, her crew, and cargo of liquor were towed into the port of San Francisco. The seizure was made under the authority of the treaty between Great Britain and the United States, proclaimed by the President May 22, 1924 (43 Stat. 1761), as a convention to aid in the prevention of the smuggling of intoxicating liquors into the United States.

The main questions presented are, first, whether the seizure of the vessel was in accordance with the treaty; second, whether the treaty prohibits prosecution of the persons, subjects of Great Britain, on board the seized vessel brought within the jurisdiction of the United States upon the landing of such vessel, for illegal importation of liquor; third, whether the treaty authorizes prosecution of such persons not only for the substantive offense of illegal importation or attempt to import but also for conspiracy to effect it; and, fourth, whether such persons [273 U.S. 593, 601] without the United States conspiring and co-operating to violate its laws with other persons who are within the United States, and to commit overt acts therein, can be prosecuted therefor when thereafter found in the United States.

The petitioners and 55 others were indicted in November, 1924, for carrying on a continuous conspiracy at the bay of San Francisco in the jurisdiction of the United States, from January 1, 1924, to November of that year, the date of the indictment, to commit offenses against the laws of the United States, first, by introducing into and transporting in the United States intoxicating liquor in violation of the National Prohibition Act; second, by importing liquor into the United States in violation of section 593, subdivision (b) of the Tariff Act of 1922, making it a penal offense to introduce merchandise into the United States in violation of law; and, third, by violation of the terms of the treaty. It charged as overt acts the loading of 12,000 cases of liquor on the Quadra at Vancouver, British Columbia, her proceeding on September 10, 1924, to a point less than 12 miles from the Farallon Islands, a distance which could be traversed in less than an hour by the Quadra and by the motorboats, the 903-B, C-55, Marconi, California, Ocean Queen, and divers others, by which the liquor was then delivered from her and imported into the United States; that on the 29th of September, 1924, the defendants landed from the steamer Quadra a barrel containing 100 gallons of whisky, and at another time on October 11, 1924, a large variety of alcohol, gin, brandy, whisky, and vermouth; and that at another time, on October 12th, the day of the seizure, they attempted to land 89 sacks of whisky, but that two of the defendants, who were on the small craft C-55, were arrested and were prevented from carrying out their purpose. Two defendants pleaded guilty. Of 29 defendants tried, 19, including all the crew of [273 U.S. 593, 602] the Quadra, were acquitted, and 10, including the captain and the first and second officers of the Quadra, were convicted. Of these 10, 5, including the three officers, are now before the court as petitioners. The convictions were affirmed by the Circuit Court of Appeals of the Ninth Circuit. 10 F. (2d) 339.

The next objection of the defendants taken from the Quadra is that on all the evidence they were entitled to a directed verdict of not guilty. They argue that they are charged with a conspiracy illegally to import or to attempt to import liquor into the United States, when they were corporeally at all times during the alleged conspiracy out of the jurisdiction of the United States, and [273 U.S. 593, 620] so could commit no offense against it. What they are charged with is conspiring "at the Bay of San Francisco" with the defendants Quartararo and Belanger illegally to import liquor, and the overt acts of thus smuggling and attempting to smuggle it. The conspiracy was continuously in operation between the defendants in the United States and those on the high seas adjacent thereto, and of the four overt acts committed in pursuance thereof, three were completed and took effect within the United States, and the fourth failed of its effect only by reason of the intervention of the federal officers. In other words, the conspiring was directed to violation of the United States law within the United States, by men within and without it, and everything done was at the procuration and by the agency of each for the other in pursuance of the conspiracy and the intended illegal importation. In such a case all are guilty of the offense of conspiring to violate the United States law whether they are in or out of the country. . . .

It will be found among the earlier cases that the principle is sometimes qualified by saying that the person out of the state cannot be held for a crime committed within the state by his procuration, unless it is done by an innocent agent or a mechanical one; but the weight of authority is now against such limitation. Generally the [273 U.S. 593, 622] cases show that jurisdiction exists to try one who is a conspirator, whenever the conspiracy is in whole or in part carried on in the country whose laws are conspired against. In *Hyde v. United States*, 225 U.S. 347, 32 S. Ct. 793, Ann. Cas. 1914A, 614, and *Brown v. Elliott*, 225 U.S. 392, 32 S. Ct. 812, the question was whether a conspiracy could be tried not where it was carried on, but in a place where only an overt act under it was performed by one conspirator. There was strong diversity of opinion among the justices, though a majority sustained the venue following the Court of King's Bench in *Rex v. Brisac and Scott*, 4 East, 164. But we have no such ground for difference here, for the conspiracy was being carried on all the time by communications exchanged between the conspirators in San Francisco and on the high seas just beyond the 3-mile limit near San Francisco Bay, and the overt acts were in both places.

The whole question was fully considered from the international standpoint in a learned opinion by John Bassett Moore, now Judge of the Permanent Court of International Justice, while he was Assistant Secretary in the State Department, to be found in Moore's *International Law Digest*, vol. 2, p. 244. The report was made in view of controversy between this government and the government of Mexico in reference to the arrest and imprisonment of one Cutting for libel charged to have been committed by Cutting in the publication of an article in a newspaper in the state of Texas. The prosecution was under article 186 of the Mexican Penal Code. That Code provided that penal offenses committed in a foreign country against a Mexican might be punished in Mexico. Our government maintained that it could not recognize the validity of a prosecution in Mexico of an American citizen, who happened thereafter to be there, for an offense committed in the United States, merely because it was committed against a Mexican. In the course of the examination [273 U.S. 593, 623] of this question, Mr. Moore, recognizing the principle already stated, said:

"The principle that a man, who outside of a country willfully puts in motion a force to take effect in it, is answerable at the place where the evil is done, is recognized in the criminal jurisprudence of all countries. And the methods which modern invention has furnished for the performance of criminal acts in that manner has made this principle one of constantly growing importance and of increasing frequency of application. . . .

The overt acts charged in the conspiracy to justify indictment under section 37 of the Criminal Code were acts within the jurisdiction of the United States, and the conspiracy charged, although some of the conspirators were corporally on the high seas, had for its object crime in the United States, and was carried on partly in and partly out of this country, and so was within its jurisdiction under the principles above settled. . . ."

The judgment of conviction of the Court of Appeals is Affirmed.

Chua Han Mow, Petitioner-Appellant, v. United States of America

UNITED STATES COURT OF APPEALS FOR THE NINTH CIRCUIT, 730 F.2D 1308; 1984 U.S. APP. LEXIS 23623, LEXSEE 730 F.2D 1308

On May 16, 1973, Chua Han Mow, a Malaysian citizen, was charged along with six others with violating United States laws against importation and distribution of controlled substances. Chua was in Malaysia at this time. Two of Chua's codefendants who were in the United States were arrested and eventually pled guilty to one count each. They each received a 10-year sentence, and they each served approximately three years before being deported.

On August 4, 1975, Chua was arrested by Malaysian authorities and incarcerated in Malaysia until October 1, 1977, pursuant to the Malaysian Emergency Ordinance of 1969. On November 2, 1977, a superseding indictment in the United States was returned against Chua and others. Chua was charged with violating *21 U.S.C. §§* 846 and 963 (Count I – conspiracy to import heroin) and *21 U.S.C. §* 959 (Counts II and III – distribution of heroin). Chua was arrested by Malaysian authorities a second time on December 21, 1977. He remained incarcerated in Malaysia until he was extradited to the United States on November 28, 1979.

Mr. Chua eventually challenged the jurisdiction through a petition for writ of habeas corpus in the District Court of the District of Kansas. From a denial of his motion he appealed.

Chua argues that the United States lacked subject-matter jurisdiction to prosecute him because all the unlawful acts he committed were done in Malaysia. We disagree. There is no constitutional bar to the extraterritorial application of penal laws. *United States v. King, 552 F.2d 833, 850 (9th Cir. 1976), cert. denied, 430 U.S. 966, 52 L. Ed. 2d 357, 97 S. Ct. 1646 (1977)*. Although courts have been reluctant to give extraterritorial effect to penal statutes, they have done so when congressional intent to give extraterritorial effect is clear. *United States v. Bowman, 260 U.S. 94, 98, 67 L. Ed. 149, 43 S. Ct. 39 (1922)*. Section 959 specifically states that it is intended to reach prohibited acts committed outside the territorial jurisdiction of the United States. Sections 846 and 963, the statutory basis for the conspiracy count in this case, do not specifically provide for extraterritorial application. This court, however, has regularly inferred extraterritorial reach of conspiracy statutes on the basis of a finding that the underlying substantive statutes reach extraterritorial offenses. *E.g.*, *United States v. Cotten*, "objective" territorial principle, 471 *F.2d* 744, 750 (9th Cir.), *cert. denied*, 411 *U.S.* 936, 36 *L. Ed.* 2d 396, 93 *S. Ct.* 1913 (1973); *Brulay v. United States*, 383 *F.2d* 345, 350 (9th Cir.), *cert. denied*, 389 *U.S.* 986, 19 *L. Ed.* 2d 478, 88 *S. Ct.* 469 (1967). *See also United States v. Layton*, 509 *F. Supp.* 212, 225 (N.D. Cal.), *appeal dismissed*, 645 *F.2d* 681 (9th Cir. 1981). Thus, the inference that Congress intended sections 846 and 963 to have extraterritorial application is readily made.

Before giving extraterritorial effect to penal statutes, courts have considered whether international law permits the exercise of jurisdiction. *E.g.*, *United States v. Schmucker-Bula*, 609 *F.2d* 399, 402–403 (7th Cir. 1980); *King*, 552 *F.2d at* 851; *Rivard v. United States*, 375 *F.2d* 882, 885 (5th Cir. 1967).... Many cases involve the prosecution of United States citizens for acts committed abroad, but extraterritorial authority is not limited to cases involving the nationality principle....

In *King*, this court upheld the authority of the United States to prosecute United States citizens for distribution of heroin in violation of section 959, the same statute involved in the present case. The distribution occurred in Japan, but the heroin was intended for importation into the United States. The court noted that the nationality principle applied because the appellants were United States citizens. However, the court stated that "appellants' prosecution for violating § 959 could also be justified under the territorial principle, since American courts have treated that as an 'objective' territorial principle." *Id. at* 851.

Under the "objective" territorial principle, Acts done outside a jurisdiction, but intended to produce and producing detrimental effects within it, justify a State in punishing the cause of the harm as if he had been present at the effect, if the State should succeed in getting him within its power. *Strassheim v. Daily*, 221 *U.S.* 280, 285, 55 *L. Ed.* 735, 31 *S. Ct.* 558 (1911). This rule applies to nations as well as states. *Rocha v. United States*, 288 *F.2d* 545, 549 (9th Cir. 1961). In the present case, Chua intended to create a detrimental effect in the United States and committed acts which resulted in such an effect when the heroin unlawfully entered the country. Chua's section 959 prosecution is therefore justified under the "objective" territorial principle. *See Rivard*, 375 *F.2d at* 887.

Other courts have relied on the protective principle to justify jurisdiction over extraterritorial crimes involving the unlawful importation of controlled substances. *See United States v. Newball*, 524 *F. Supp.* 715, 720 (E.D. N.Y. 1981); *United States v. Egan*, 501 *F. Supp.* 1252, 1258 (S.D. N.Y. 1980). Noting that drug smuggling compromises a sovereign's control of its own borders, the Seventh Circuit has suggested that it might uphold extraterritorial criminal jurisdiction over alien drug smugglers even if the territorial principle did not apply. *Schmucker-Bula*, 609 *F.2d at* 403. We are persuaded that the protective principle also justifies Chua's section 959 prosecution.

The objective territorial principle and the protective principle are equally applicable to the conspiracy count. Furthermore, the Supreme Court has held that extraterritorial jurisdiction over aliens exists when a conspiracy had for its object crime in the United States and overt acts were committed in the United States by co-conspirators. *Ford v. United States*, 273 *U.S.* 593, 624, 71 *L. Ed.* 793, 47 *S. Ct.* 531 (1927). *See also United States v. Winter*, 509 *F.2d* 975, 982 (5th Cir.), *cert. denied*, 423 *U.S.* 825, 96 *S. Ct.* 39, 46 *L. Ed.* 2d 41 (1975). In the present case, Chua's co-conspirators committed acts in furtherance of the conspiracy inside the United States. Co-conspirator Tang was arrested at the San Francisco Airport as he attempted to retrieve suitcases containing heroin. Therefore, the United States does have jurisdiction to prosecute Chua.

Notes and Questions

1. Over the last twenty years, some U.S. courts have applied the objective territorial theory more expansively, including in situations where there is no more than intent to affect U.S. territory. *See, e.g.*, Christopher Blakesley, *Extraterritorial Jurisdiction, in* INTERNATIONAL CRIMINAL LAW: PROCEDURAL AND ENFORCEMENT MECHANISMS, fn. 99, citing and discussing *U.S. v. Wright-Barker*, 784 F.2d 161 (3d Cir. 1986) (conspiracy of at least eight persons to import narcotics – twenty-three tons of marijuana – into the United States from a vessel on the high seas, 200 miles off the New Jersey coast) cited and discussed in Cecil J. Olmstead, *Restatement: Jurisdiction, Symposium on the* RESTATEMENT (THIRD), 14 YALE J. INT'L L. 468, 471, n. 19 (1989); *see also U.S. v. Stuart*, 109 S.Ct. 1183, 1197 (1989) (Scalia, J., concurring); *U.S. v. Marino-Garcia*, 679 F. 2d 1373, 1380–81 (applying a "nexus" theory along with the objective territorial theory and the protective principle), *reh'g denied*, 685 F. 2d 1389 (11th Cir. 1982), *cert. denied*, 459 U.S. 1114 (1982); *U.S. v. Convoy*, 589 F.2d 1258 (5th Cir. 1979); *U.S. v. Postal*, 589 F.2d 862 (5th Cir. 1979); *U.S. v. Cadena*, 585 F.2d 1252 (5th Cir. 1979); *King*, 552 F.2d 833, *cert. denied*, 430 U.S. 966 (combining nationality principle with the intent to cause an effect theory).

2. Similarly, in recent years the U.S. government and U.S. courts have tended to expand jurisdiction over extraterritorial crime in a way that is inconsistent with fundamental principles of international law. Some U.S. court decisions have broadened the objective and subjective territoriality theories beyond any actual effect upon or connection with U.S. territory. For instance, the territorial theory has been applied to thwart extraterritorial narcotics or other conspiracies, as mentioned earlier, even when no overt act, element, or any effect has occurred there.[14] According to Professor Blakesley, the courts have not distinguished between the protective and objective territoriality principles. The cases and the Restatement (Third)[15] expand the objective territorial principle, providing in section 402(1)(c) that jurisdiction over an extraterritorial crime will obtain when the crime "has or is intended to have substantial effect within [U.S] territory."[16]

According to Professor Blakesley, the application of objective territoriality in this manner is incorrect. In some cases other theories would have been appropriate. Jurisdiction over thwarted extraterritorial conspiracies is proper, but not on the basis of objective territoriality. A thwarted extraterritorial conspiracy does not trigger jurisdiction on the basis of objective or subjective territoriality unless the coconspirators worked in the United States or the goods involved entered the United States.

Professor Blakesley points out that this trend in U.S. courts began with the Supreme Court's incorrect statement in *Ford v. U.S.*, discussed earlier, that objective territoriality applied to circumstances in which no territorial effects had occurred. In making this statement, the Court misused objective territoriality in circumstances in which subjective territoriality would have applied. The British subjects who were convicted of conspiracy to violate U.S. liquor laws were on board a British vessel on the high seas. The conspiracy itself had its situs within U.S. territory. Conspirators were within and outside of U.S.

[14] *See, e.g.*, Blakesley, *Extraterritorial Jurisdiction, supra* note 4, at 82, fn. 263 and cases cited therein.

[15] RESTATEMENT (3RD), §§ 402(1)(c), 403.

[16] Blakesley, *Extraterritorial Jurisdiction, supra* note 4 at 82, citing RESTATEMENT (3RD), §§ 402(1)(c), 403. Reporter's 8, following § 403, incorrectly relies on some of the cases discussed therein (e.g., those on the territoriality theories) to promote the notion that objective territorial jurisdiction obtains when there exists simply an intent to have an impact on U.S. territory.

borders, and four overt acts occurred in the United States.[17] By definition, a fully thwarted extraterritorial conspiracy has no effect within the territory; rather, it is an inchoate offense and has no effects until the substantive offense to which the parties were conspiring is accomplished. The goal of criminalizing conspiracy is to prevent the effects from occurring by attaching a sanction to undesirable collaboration early in its development. Although conspiracy laws attempt to prevent potential effects, the objective territorial theory is not the correct mechanism for this purpose. It strains credulity and the objective territoriality theory to say that the harm has had an impact on the intended state the moment the agreement is made outside the territory. In spite of this, U.S. courts have subsequently used the erroneous *Ford* dicta and its confused analysis as authority for the proposition that objective territorial jurisdiction applies to extraterritorial conspiracies in which no element nor any harmful effects have been caused.[18]

3. What happens if a Canadian spouse poisons her husband in New York, he subsequently dies in Canada, and she is arrested in the United States? Should the United States extradite her to Canada? *See Sternamen v. Peck*, 83 F. 690 (2d Cir. 1897).

4. Many difficult territorial cases involve intended but unrealized effect. When the intent to commit a proscribed act – for example, securities fraud or export control violations – is clear and shown by some activity, and the effect to be produced by the activity is substantial and foreseeable, the fact that a plan or conspiracy was stopped does not deprive the target state of jurisdiction to make its law applicable. *See* RESTATEMENT (3RD), § 402, Comment d. The territorial theories are not sufficient for jurisdiction over wholly extraterritorial offenses such as narcotics trafficking or money laundering. When the offense occurs totally abroad and no effect actually occurs within the territory, territoriality cannot apply. *See* Christopher Blakesley, *Extraterritorial Jurisdiction*, *in* INTERNATIONAL CRIMINAL LAW: PROCEDURAL AND ENFORCEMENT MECHANISMS, at 53. European jurisprudence does not provide jurisdiction over thwarted extraterritorial attempts or conspiracy. *Id.* C.f., *Liangsiriprasert v. United States Government*, [1990] All E.R. 866 (English court-based jurisdiction on a conspiracy entered into abroad with no overt act in the United Kingdom).

5. Some experts have questioned whether broad exercises of territorial jurisdiction should not be subjected to the traditional conditions that exist in relation to extraterritorial jurisdiction, such as dual criminality or a request to prosecute coming from the state on whose territory the extraterritorial conduct was committed. From a human rights perspective, such experts wonder whether such assertions of jurisdiction should be subjected to the *ne bis in idem* principle, requiring that states take into account foreign judgments rendered with respect to the facts for which they wish to apply such broad assertions of jurisdiction. Such experts point out that the international protection of the individual is inadequate. First, no international *ne bis in idem protection* exists.[19] Additionally, the

[17] *Ford*, 273 U.S. at 630.

[18] Blakesley, *Extraterritorial Jurisdiction*, *supra* note 4, at 83–84.

[19] Christine van den Wyngaert, *General Report, Topic IV International Criminal Law, The Criminal Justice Systems Facing the Challenge of Organized Crime*, 70 INT'L REV. OF PENAL LAW 133, 166 (No. 1–2 1999). In particular, Article 14 para. 7 of the International Covenant on Civil and Political Rights states, "No one shall be liable to be tried or punished again for an offense for which he has already been finally convicted or acquitted in accordance with the law and penal procedure of each country." The article has a very limited application. It only applies to decisions made within one state, not to foreign judgments. As a result, Art. 14, para. 7 does not give rise in positive international human rights law to imposing an obligation on statutes

few international conventions dealing with the problem carve out an exception where the jurisdiction of the state that prosecutes a second time is based on the territoriality principle.[20] Such an exception constitutes an important limitation in international human rights protection. The legitimate interest of states to expand the reach of their laws in the fight against complex transnational business crimes should be balanced with an equally legitimate interest of individuals not to be punished twice or more for the same conduct.

6. In hypothetical 2 in section 1 above, can a defendant argue that exercise of jurisdiction by a state of the United States violates international law? Can a defendant contend that the supremacy clause of the Constitution precludes an exercise of jurisdiction by a state that contravenes the limitations of the Restatement (3rd), §§ 402–403? See RESTATEMENT (3RD), § 111 and Comment d to that section.

7. The effects principle has especially invoked controversy when it has been used to support regulation of activities abroad by foreign nationals because of the economic impact of those activities in the regulating state. Within the European Community and some of its member states the effects doctrine is being increasingly used to regulate restrictive business practices. *See, e.g.*, § 98 of the Law against Restraints on Competition (GWB) of Germany, quoted in § 415, Reporters' Note 9, and the Decision of the European Court of Justice in *Imperial Chemical Industries, Ltd. v. Commission*, Case 4869 [1972] E.C.R. 619 (the Dyestuffs case) 11 COMMON MKT. L.R. 557 (Ct. of Justice 1972).

2. The Protective Principle

U.S. v. BOWMAN, 260 U.S. 94 (1922), Argued Oct. 17, 1922, Decided Nov. 13, 1922

MR. CHIEF JUSTICE TAFT DELIVERED THE OPINION OF THE COURT

This is a writ of error under the Criminal Appeals Act (34 Stat. c. 2564, p. 1246 [Comp. St. 1704]) to review the ruling of the District Court sustaining a demurrer of one of the defendants to an indictment for a conspiracy to defraud a corporation in which the United States was and is a stockholder, under section 35 of the Criminal Code, as amended October 23, 1918 (40 Stat. 1015 [Comp. St. Ann. Supp. 1919, 10199]).

During the period covered by the indictment, i.e., between October, 1919, and January, 1920, the steamship Dio belonged to the United States. The United States owned all the stock in the United States Shipping Board Emergency Fleet Corporation. The National Shipping Corporation agreed to operate and manage the Dio for the Fleet Corporation, which under the contract was to pay for fuel, oil, labor, and material used in the operation. The Dio was on a voyage to Rio de Janeiro under this management. Wry was her master, Bowman was her engineer, Hawkinson was the agent of the Standard Oil Company at Rio de Janeiro, and Millar was a merchant and ship repairer and engineer in Rio. Of these four, who were the defendants in the indictment, the first three were American citizens, and Millar was a British

to recognize convictions or acquittals by foreign courts. The Human Rights Committee has explicitly acknowledged this in its decision in the case of *A.P. v. Italy* (July 16, 1986). It held that the guarantee of *ne bis in idem* does not apply with respect to the national jurisdictions of two or more states. Instead, it explained that the provision prohibits double jeopardy only with regard to a crime adjudicated in one state.

20 *Id.*

subject. Johnston & Co. were the agents of the National Shipping Corporation at Rio. The indictment charged that the plot was hatched by Wry and Bowman on board the Dio before she reached Rio. Their plan was to order, through Johnston & Co., and receipt for, 1,000 tons of fuel oil from the Standard Oil Company, but to take only 600 tons aboard, and to collect cash for a delivery of 1,000 tons through Johnston & Co., from the Fleet Corporation, and then divide the money paid for the undelivered 400 tons among the four defendants. This [260 U.S. 94, 96] plan was to be, and was, made possible through the guilty connivance of the Standard Oil agent, Hawkinson, and Millar, the Rio merchant, who was to, and did, collect the money. Overt acts charged included a wireless telegram to the agents, Johnston & Co., from the Dio while on the high seas ordering the 1,000 tons of oil. The Southern District of New York was the district into which the American defendants were first brought and were found, but Millar, the British defendant, has not been found.

The first count charged a conspiracy by the defendants to defraud the Fleet Corporation, in which the United States was a stockholder, by obtaining and aiding to obtain the payment and allowance of a false and fraudulent claim against the Fleet Corporation. It laid the offense on the high seas, out of the jurisdiction of any particular state, and out of the jurisdiction of any district of the United States, but within the admiralty and maritime jurisdiction of the United States. The second count laid the conspiracy on the Dio on the high seas and at the port of Rio de Janeiro, as well as in the city. The third count laid it in the city of Rio de Janeiro. The fourth count was for making and causing to be made in the name of the Standard Oil Company, for payment and approval, a false and fraudulent claim against the Fleet Corporation in the form of an invoice for 1,000 tons of fuel oil, of which 400 tons were not delivered. This count laid the same crime on board the Dio in the harbor of Rio de Janeiro. The fifth count laid it in the city, and the sixth at the port and in the city.

The sole objection was that the crime was committed without the jurisdiction of the United States or of any state thereof and on the high seas or [260 U.S. 94, 97] within the jurisdiction of Brazil. The District Court considered only the first count, which charged the conspiracy to have been committed on the Dio on the high seas, and, having held that bad for lack of jurisdiction, a *fortiori* it sustained the demurrer as the others.

The court in its opinion conceded that under many authorities the United States as a sovereign may regulate the ships under its flag and the conduct of its citizens while on those ships, and cited to this point (references omitted). The court said, however, that while private and public ships of the United States on the high seas were constructively a part of the territory of the United States – indeed, peculiarly so, as distinguished from that of the States – Congress had always expressly indicated it when it intended that its laws should be operative on the high seas. The court concluded that, because jurisdiction of criminal offenses must be conferred upon United States courts and could not be inferred, and because section 35, like all the other sections of chapter 4 (Comp. St. 10191–10252), contains no reference to the high seas as a part of the locus of the offense defined by it, as the sections in chapters 11 and 12 of the Criminal Code (Comp. St. 10445–10483a) do, section 35 must be construed not to extend to acts committed on the high seas. It confirmed its conclusion by the statement that section 35 had never been invoked to punish offenses denounced, if committed on the high seas or in a foreign country.

We have in this case a question of statutory construction. The necessary locus, when not specially defined, depends upon the purpose of Congress as evinced by the description and nature of the crime and upon the territorial limitations upon the power and jurisdiction of a [260 U.S. 94, 98] government to punish crime under the law of nations. Crimes against private individuals or their property, like assaults, murder, burglary, larceny, robbery, arson, embezzlement, and frauds of all kinds, which affect the peace and good order of the community must, of course, be committed within the territorial jurisdiction of the government where it may properly exercise it. If punishment of them is to be extended to include those committed outside of the strict territorial jurisdiction, it is natural for Congress to say so in the statute, and failure to do so will negative the purpose of Congress in this regard. We have an example of this in the attempted application of the prohibitions of the antitrust law to acts done by citizens of the United States against other such citizens in a foreign country. *American Banana Co. v. United Fruit Co.*, 213 U.S. 347, 29 Sup. Ct. 511, 16 Ann. Cas. 1047. That was a civil case, but as the statute is criminal as well as civil, it appears an analogy.

But the same rule of interpretation should not be applied to criminal statutes which are, as a class, not logically dependent on their locality for the government's jurisdiction, but are enacted because of the right of the government to defend itself against obstruction, or fraud wherever perpetrated, especially if committed by its own citizens, officers, or agents. Some such offenses can only be committed within the territorial jurisdiction of the government because of the local acts required to constitute them. Others are such that to limit their locus to the strictly territorial jurisdiction would be greatly to curtail the scope and usefulness of the statute and leave open a large immunity for frauds as easily committed by citizens on the high seas and in foreign countries as at home. In such cases, Congress has not thought it necessary to make specific provision in the law that the locus shall include the high seas and foreign countries, but allows it to be inferred from the nature of the offense. Many of these occur in chapter 4, which bears the title 'Offenses [260 U.S. 94, 99] against the Operation of the Government.' Section 70 of that chapter (Comp. St. 10238) punishes whoever as consul knowingly certifies a false invoice. Clearly the locus of this crime as intended by Congress is in a foreign country, and certainly the foreign country in which he discharges his official duty could not object to the trial in a United States court of a United States consul for crime of this sort committed within its borders. Forging or altering ship's papers is made a crime by section 72 of chapter 4 (Comp. St. 10240). It would be going too far to say that because Congress does not fix any locus it intended to exclude the high seas in respect of this crime. The natural inference from the character of the offense is that the sea would be a probable place for its commission. Section 42 of chapter 4 (Comp. St. 10206) punishes enticing desertions from the naval service. Is it possible that Congress did not intend by this to include such enticing done aboard ship on the high seas or in a foreign port, where it would be most likely to be done? Section 39 (Comp. St 10203) punishes bribing a United States officer of the civil, military, or naval service to violate his duty or to aid in committing a fraud on the United States. It is hardly reasonable to construe this not to include such offenses when the bribe is offered to a consul, ambassador, and army or a naval officer in a foreign country or on the high seas, whose duties are being performed there, and when his connivance at such fraud must occur there. So, too, section 38 of chapter 4 (Comp. St. 10202) punishes the willfully doing or aiding to do any act relating to the bringing in, custody, sale or other disposition of property captured as prize, with intent to defraud, delay or injure the United States or any captor or claimant of such property. This would naturally often occur at sea, and Congress could not have meant to confine it to the land of the United States. Again, in section 36 of chapter 4 (Comp. St. 10200), it is made a crime to steal, embezzle, or knowingly apply to his own use ordinance, arms, ammunition, clothing, subsistence stores, money or other property of the United [260 U.S. 94, 100] States furnished or to be used for military or naval service. It would hardly be reasonable to hold that if any one, certainly if a citizen of the United States, were to steal or embezzle such property which may properly and lawfully be in the custody of army or naval officers either in foreign countries, in foreign ports or on the high seas, it would not be in such places an offense which Congress intended to punish by this section.

What is true of these sections in this regard is true of section 35, under which this indictment was drawn. We give it in full in the margin. 1 [260 U.S. 94, 101] It is directed generally against whoever presents a false claim against the United States, knowing it to be such, to any officer of the civil, military or naval service or to any department thereof, or any corporation in which the United States is a stockholder, or whoever connives at the same by the use of any cheating device, or whoever enters a conspiracy to do these things. The section was amended in 1918 to include a corporation in which the United States owns stock. This was evidently intended to protect the Emergency Fleet Corporation or any corporation in which the United States of America is a stockholder, or willfully to conceal such money or other property, shall deliver or cause to be delivered to any person having authority to receive the same amount of such money or other property less than that for which he received a certificate or took a receipt; or whoever, being authorized to make or deliver any certificate, voucher, receipt, or other paper certifying the receipt of arms, ammunition, provisions, clothing, or other property so used or to be used, shall make or deliver the same to any other person without a full knowledge of the truth of the facts stated therein and with intent to defraud the United States, or any department thereof, or any corporation in which the United States of America is a stockholder, shall be fined not more than $10,000 or imprisoned not more than ten years, or both. And whoever shall purchase, or receive in pledge, from any person any arms, equipment, ammunition, clothing, military stores, or other property furnished by the United States, under a clothing allowance or otherwise, to any soldier, sailor, officer, cadet, or midshipman in the military or naval service of the United States or of the National Guard or Naval Militia, or to any person accompanying, serving, or retained with the land or naval forces and subject to military or naval law, having knowledge or reason to believe that the property has been taken from the possession of the United States or furnished by the United States under such allowance, shall be fined not more than $500 or imprisoned not more than two years, or both. [260 U.S. 94, 102] United States was the sole stockholder, from fraud of this character. That corporation was expected to engage in, and did engage in, a most extensive ocean transportation business, and its ships were seen in every great port of the world open during the war. The same section of the statute protects the arms, ammunition, stores, and property of the army and navy from fraudulent devices of a similar character. We cannot suppose that when Congress enacted the statute or amended it, it did not have in mind that a wide field for such frauds upon the government was in private and public vessels of the United States on the high seas and in foreign ports and beyond the land jurisdiction of the United States, and therefore intended to include them in the section. . . .

The three defendants were found in New York, were citizens of the United States, and were certainly subject to such laws as it might pass to protect itself and its property. Clearly it is no offense to the dignity or right of sovereignty of Brazil to hold them for this crime against the government to which they owe allegiance. The other defendant is a subject of Great Britain. He has never been apprehended, and it will be time enough to consider what, if any, jurisdiction the District [260 U.S. 94, 103] Court below has to punish him when he is brought to trial.

The judgment of the District Court is reversed, with directions to overrule the demurrer and for further proceedings. (Footnotes are omitted.)

Notes and Questions

1. The protective principle gives a state the right to exert jurisdiction over a certain class of limited offenses that are committed outside its territory by nonnationals. This claim can be invoked to assert jurisdiction when the offenses are directed against the security of the state or against important state interests or functions.[21] Representative offenses include espionage, counterfeiting of the state's seal or currency, the falsification of official documents, perjury before consular officials, and conspiracies to violate immigration and customs law. Although the United States does not often invoke the protective principle, it has used it to establish jurisdiction over nonnationals who make false statements on visa applications at U.S. consulates.[22] Some U.S. courts have asserted the protective principle simultaneously with the objective territoriality principle to support criminal jurisdiction.[23]

2. The *Bowman* case illustrates both the protective and territorial principles (e.g., private and public ships of the United States on the high seas are constructively a part of the territory of the United States).

3. The Nationality (or Active Personality) Principle

The United States rarely bases extraterritorial jurisdiction on the nationality of the offender. This jurisdictional basis, which is called the nationality or active personality principle, is most often applied in cases that involve subsidiaries of U.S. corporations rather than individual citizens.

The nationality principle arises from the notion of state sovereignty under which nationals are entitled to their state's protection even while outside its territorial boundaries. These individuals have a corresponding obligation of allegiance to national laws even when outside of the state of which they are citizens.[24] Although the nationality principle is widely recognized in international law, its precise definition and application differ widely.[25]

U.S. federal criminal legislation, in comparison with other national penal codes such as the German Penal Code or the Japanese Draft Penal Code, is not expressly based on nationality. However, prosecution for treason in the United States is a longstanding example of criminal jurisdiction based on the nationality principle. The implication of treason cases, specifically *Kawakita v. United States* (see excerpt in this section) is that treason can only be committed by one who is a citizen.[26] In contrast with decisions of

[21] RESTATEMENT (3RD), § 402(3) and § 402(3), Comment (f); *Harvard Research in International Law, the Draft Convention With Respect to Crime*, arts. 7, 8, 29 AM. J. INT'L L. 435 (Supp. 1935); M. WHITEMAN, *supra* note 11, at 95–100.

[22] 18 U.S.C. § 1546. *See, e.g., United States v. Pizzarusso*, 388 F.2d 8 (2d Cir. 1968), *cert. denied*, 392 U.S. 936 (1968); *United States v. Rodriguez*, 182 F. Supp. 479 (S.D. Cal. 1960); *United States v. Archer*, 51 F. Supp. 708 (C.D. Cal. 1943).

[23] *See, e.g., Rocha v. United States*, 288 F.2d 545 (9th Cir. 1961), *cert. denied*, 366 U.S. 948 (1961). *See also* Blakesley, TERRORISM, DRUGS, INTERNATIONAL LAW, AND THE PROTECTION OF HUMAN LIBERTY 113–17 (Transnational Publishers 1992).

[24] *Joyce v. Director of Public Prosecutions*, 62 T.L.R. 208 (1946); M. Bassiouni, INTERNATIONAL EXTRADITION AND WORLD PUBLIC ORDER 251 (1974); 1 L. Oppenheim, INTERNATIONAL LAW 290, 686–89 (8th ed. 1955).

[25] M. Bassiouni, INTERNATIONAL EXTRADITION AND WORLD PUBLIC ORDER, *supra* note 24, at 250–51.

[26] *Kawakita v. United States*, 343 U.S. 717 (1952). *See also Gillars v. United States*, 182 F.2d 962 (D.C. Cir. 1950); *Chandler v. United States*, 171 F.2d 921 (1st Cir. 1948), *cert. denied*, 336 U.S. 918 (1949).

courts in other countries, U.S. courts base jurisdiction in treason cases solely on the nationality principle.[27] Other states often assert jurisdiction in such cases based on the protective principle.

The nationality principle has also been used to enjoin trademark infringement outside the United States.[28] However, most of the traditional applications of the nationality principle concern national security. Such traditional applications include failure of U.S. citizens to comply with selective service law,[29] the Logan Act,[30] and export controls laws such as the Trading with the Enemy Act.[31]

In *Blackmer v. United States*,[32] the U.S. Supreme Court upheld the issuance of a subpoena, pursuant to statute, to a U.S. citizen residing abroad. The subpoena required his attendance in a U.S. court as a witness. In upholding the subpoena, the Supreme Court commented, "The jurisdiction of the United States over its absent citizen, so far as the binding effect of its legislation is concerned, is a jurisdiction in personam, as he is personally bound to take notice of the laws that are applicable to him and obey them."[33]

Some commentators have correctly criticized jurisdiction based on nationality alone where the crime over which jurisdiction is asserted is not also a crime where it is committed.[34] In practice, the attempt to prosecute a person solely on the nationality principle necessitates cooperation from another state. In the absence of an extradition treaty, the willingness of the country to extradite may depend in part on the political relations of the United States vis-à-vis the other state and in part on the exercise of restraint by the United States in extraterritorial enforcement of its criminal laws. Of course, choice of law and other policy considerations also come into play.[35]

Kawakita v. United States, 343 U.S. 717 (1952)

At petitioner's trial for treason, it appeared that originally he was a native-born citizen of the United States and also a national of Japan by reason of Japanese parentage and law. While a minor, he took the oath of allegiance to the United States; went to Japan for a visit on an American passport; and was prevented by the outbreak of war from returning to this country. During the war, he reached his majority in Japan; changed his registration from American to Japanese; showed sympathy with Japan and hostility to the United States; served as a civilian employee of a private corporation producing war materials for Japan; and brutally abused American prisoners of war who were forced to work there. After Japan's surrender, he registered as an American citizen; swore that he was an American citizen and had not done

[27] *See, e.g.*, *Joyce v. Director of Public Prosecutions*, [1946] Q.B. 347; *Rex v. Neumann*, [1949] 3 S. Afr. L.R. 1238.

[28] *Steele v. Bulova Watch Co.*, 344 U.S. 280 (1952).

[29] 50 U.S.C. § 453 (Supp. III 1979) (this act requires every male U.S. citizen to register for military service).

[30] 18 U.S.C. § 953 (this act prohibits any U.S. citizen wherever located from carrying on any correspondence or intercourse with any foreign government in its relations with the United States).

[31] 31 C.F.R. § 500.329(a)(1).

[32] *Blackmer v. United States*, 284 U.S. 421 (1932).

[33] *Id.* at 438.

[34] Epstein, *The Extraterritorial Reach of Proposed Criminal Justice Reform Act of 1975-S.1*, 4 Am. J. Crim. L. 275, 284–85 (1976). *See, e.g.*, Note, *Extraterritorial Jurisdiction: Criminal Law*, 13 Harv. Int'l L.J. 346, 363 (1972).

[35] M. Bassiouni, International Extradition and World Public Order, *supra* note 24, at 252–55.

various acts amounting to expatriation; and returned to this country on an American passport. Held: His conviction for treason is affirmed.

MR. JUSTICE DOUGLAS delivered the opinion of the Court.

Petitioner contends that a person who has a dual nationality can be guilty of treason only to the country where he resides, not to the other country which claims him as a national. More specifically, he maintains that while petitioner resided in Japan he owed his paramount allegiance to that country and was indeed, in the eyes of our law, an alien enemy.

The argument in its broadest reach is that treason against the United States cannot be committed abroad or in enemy territory, at least by an American with a dual nationality residing in the other country which [343 U.S. 717, 733] claims him as a national. The definition of treason, however, contained in the Constitution contains no territorial limitation. "Treason against the United States, shall consist only in levying War against them, or in adhering to their Enemies, giving them Aid and Comfort . . ." Art. III, 3. A substitute proposal containing some territorial limitations was rejected by the Constitutional Convention. *See* 2 Farrand, The Records of the Federal Convention, pp. 347–348. The Act of April 30, 1790, 1 Stat. 112, which was passed by the first Congress defining the crime of treason likewise contained no territorial limitation; and that legislation is contained in substantially the same form in the present statute. 18 U.S.C. (Supp. IV) 2381. 7 We must therefore reject the suggestion that an American citizen living beyond the territorial limits of the United States may not commit treason against them. *See Chandler v. United States*, 171 F.2d 921, 929–930; *Burgman v. United States*, 88 U.S. App. D.C. 184, 185, 188 F.2d 637, 640.

One who has a dual nationality will be subject to claims from both nations, claims which at times may be competing or conflicting. . . .

Circumstances may compel one who has a dual nationality to do acts which otherwise would not be compatible with the obligations of American citizenship. An American with a dual nationality who is charged with playing the role of the traitor may defend by showing that force or coercion compelled such conduct. The jury rejected that version of the facts which petitioner tendered. He is therefore forced to maintain that, being a national and a resident of Japan, he owed no allegiance to the United States even though he was an American citizen. That proposition we reject.

Notes and Questions

1. With some types of white collar crime, such as taxation, corruption, and export control, the United States does not hesitate to impose criminal liability based on nationality and residency.

2. Many states allow their nationals to be prosecuted for all crimes – or at least all serious crimes – regardless of where the crimes are committed. Note that many exercises of jurisdiction on the basis of nationality could also be supported on other bases, especially the effects principle. In fact, prosecutions on the basis of nationality are infrequent. RESTATEMENT (3RD), § 403, Reporters Notes 1, citing Henkin, Pugh, Schachter, & Smit, INTERNATIONAL LAW 835–36 (2d ed. 1987) for French, German, and British statutes and codes applicable on the basis of nationality.

3. What happens if a person expatriates and surrenders his or her U.S. nationality or permanent residency prior to the circumstances giving rise to the alleged crime? For instance, on July 20, 2006, the U.S. Attorney's Office for the District of Columbia agreed to drop an indictment against Sabri Yakou for violating the U.S. embargo against Iraq. The court ruled that, because Sabri left the United States a decade earlier, he

had effectively abandoned his permanent-resident status in the United States, thereby depriving the U.S. government of jurisdiction to prosecute him as a "U.S. person" under the criminal statutes prohibiting arms sales to the Iraqi government. Prosecutors unsuccessfully argued that he had never officially revoked his permanent-resident status when he moved to London in 1993 and later to Iraq, and had used his green card on several occasions to reenter the United States. In this case, the court was persuaded that a permanent resident could involuntarily lose permanent-resident status by leaving the United States for an extended period of time. *See* Jason McLure, *Iraq Arms Dealer Case Collapses*, Legal Times, July 31, 2006, at 1, col. 1.

4. The Passive Personality Principle

The passive personality principle allows a state, in certain circumstances, to apply its criminal law to an act committed outside its territory by a nonnational because the victim of the act was its national. The principle is normally applied only in instances where terrorist or other organized attacks are made against a state's nationals because of their nationality. It also is applied when a state's ambassadors or government officials are assassinated.[36]

This principle has been applied in U.S. counterterrorism efforts. For instance, the United States applied the "passive personality" principle in § 1202 of the Omnibus Diplomatic Security and Antiterrorism Act of 1986, 18 U.S.C. § 2231. This act makes it a crime to kill, or attempt or conspire to kill, or to cause serious bodily injury, to a national of the United States outside the territory of the United States. However, unless the Attorney General or his or her delegate certifies that in their judgment the offense was intended to coerce, intimidate, or retaliate against a government or a civilian population, prosecution cannot be brought.

Another example of the use of the passive personality principle for counterterrorism is Article 5(1)(c) of the Convention against Torture, and Other Cruel, Inhuman or Degrading Treatment or Punishment. The Introductory Note to Part VII authorizes a state party to exercise jurisdiction "when the victim is a national of that State if that State considers it appropriate."[37]

5. Universal Jurisdiction

The principle of universal jurisdiction enables a State to exercise jurisdiction to prescribe for a class of offenses known as *delicta juris gentium* or certain crimes under international law. These acts constitute crimes under international law that the community of nations recognizes as warranting universal concern.[38] Such crimes by their very nature threaten to undermine the very foundations of the enlightened international community.[39] Each state has the right to exercise jurisdiction over the offender, even where the other jurisdictional bases are not present. However, to exercise universal

[36] *See Case of the S.S. Lotus (Fr. v. Turkey)*, 1927 P.C.I.J., ser. A, No. 10 (Judgment of Sept. 7); Restatement (3RD), § 402(2), Comment (g); Reporters' Note 3.

[37] Restatement (3RD), § 402, Reporters' Note 3.

[38] Restatement (3rd), § 404.

[39] H. Jescheck, *Crimes du droit des gens*, 26 R. Int'l Dr. Penal 503–544 (1965).

jurisdiction, the offender must be in the prescribing state's territory. The nexus between the offender and the *lex loci deprehensionis*[40] is considered the injury that the offense causes to the foundation and security of the entire community. As such, each state has the power to exercise criminal jurisdiction.[41] The offenses for which universal jurisdiction may be exercised include piracy, slave trade, attacks on or hijacks of aircraft, genocide, war crimes, and perhaps certain acts of terrorism.[42] Some of the international agreements providing for universal criminal jurisdiction are set forth in the Restatement 3rd.[43]

Compared to the principles of extraterritorial criminal jurisdiction, universal jurisdiction is likely to be used less for white collar or business crimes. One exception to this approach, however, is the use of universal jurisdiction to prosecute arms traffickers. In recent years, governments have increasingly targeted businesses and individuals supplying arms and materials to warlords and former heads of state for use in civil wars. For example, a number of people who sold weapons to Charles Taylor, former head of state for Liberia, are being prosecuted for their roles in these conflicts.[44] Under this approach, a business or individual's knowledge of and role in an alleged crime for which universal jurisdiction can be asserted may expose the business or individual to criminal liability.

6. The Representation Principle

In addition to the five traditional principles discussed above, states may resort to the representation principle to assert jurisdiction. A state may employ this residuary doctrine when faced with punishing an offender who is physically present in its territory for acts committed outside its territory. These illegal acts are typically of such a nature that the offender is not eligible for extradition to the other state. A jurisdictional problem of this nature usually arises when (1) there is no mutual extradition agreement between the two countries, (2) the offender is a national of the extraditing state, or (3) extradition is not worthwhile considering the *de minimis* nature of the offense.[45] In such cases, the state in whose territory the act was committed will request the state with custody to bring an action against the offender. A prerequisite for establishing this jurisdiction is that the

40 That is, the law of the place in which an offense is committed.

41 Feller, *supra* note 4, at 32–34.

42 RESTATEMENT (3RD), § 404.

43 *Id.*, § 404. For instance, the agreements include the Hague Convention for the Suppression of Unlawful Seizure of Aircraft, 22 U.S.T. 1641, T.I.A.S. 7192 (1971); the Montreal Convention for the Suppression of Unlawful Acts against the Safety of Civil Aviation, 24 U.S.T. 565, T.I.A.S. 7570, 974 U.N.T.S. 178 (1973); the Convention on the Prevention and Punishment of Crimes against Internationally Protected Persons including Diplomatic Agents, 28 U.S.T. 1975, T.I.A.S. 8532, 1035 U.N.T.S. 167 (1977); and the International Convention against the Taking of Hostages, G.A. Res. 146 (XXXIV), U.N. GAOR, 34th Sess., Supp. No. 46, at 245, U.N. Doc. A/34/46, 1316 UNTS 205; TIAS No. 11081; 18 ILM 1456 (1979). These agreements include an obligation on the parties to punish or extradite offenders, even when the offense was not committed within their territory or by a national.

44 *See* Jason McClurg, *Appeals Chambers Paves Way for Taylor Trial in The Hague; Pressure Intensifies on Taylor's Inner Circle*, 22 INT'L ENFORCEMENT L. REP. 325, 326–27 (Aug. 2006), discussing a Dutch court conviction of Gus van Kouwenhouven, president and owner of the Oriental Timber Corporation. Prosecutors accused van Kouwenhouven of practicing a timber-for-weapons trade by trading large concessions of valuable Liberian hardwood, selling them on the international market, and using his companies' ships to deliver machine guns, rocket-propelled grenades, and other war supplies to Charles Taylor. Taylor then allegedly used the weapons to commit war crimes.

45 Bassiouni & Nanda, *supra* note 2 at 35.

offense must be recognized as a crime in both states. Without this dual recognition the state bringing the action has no legal basis to proceed.[46]

The representation principle extends the concept of *comminio juris*; that is, the will of nations to create a semblance of worldwide communal jurisdiction. Hence, the principle is an attempt to promote the idea that offenders have no asylum from punishment.[47] However, with but a few exceptions, application of the representation principle has been minimal.

7. Regulation of Activities Aboard Vessels or Aircraft

Customary international law allows a state to apply its law to activities, persons, or things aboard a vessel or aircraft registered in the state.[48] Additionally, serious offenses committed aboard a foreign vessel or aircraft "in the commerce of the United States" may be within the jurisdiction of the United States under the objective territorial principle.[49]

B. *Limitations on Jurisdiction to Prescribe*

Several limitations restrict a state's jurisdiction to prescribe. Some limitations are imposed by a state's internal laws, whereas others are imposed by international agreements. "Blocking statutes," whereby states prevent their nationals from adhering to foreign extraterritorial jurisdiction in circumstances the blocking state believes are illegal, present a secondary source of limitations.

1. Constitutional Limitations

The U.S. Constitution, the Bill of Rights, and principles of federalism limit the jurisdiction of the U.S. Congress to prescribe and apply law. However, Congress has been held to possess authority, often referred to as its "foreign affairs power," deriving from the implicitly sovereign power of the U.S. government.[50] States are limited in their power to prescribe law not only by the limitations of international law but also by the supremacy clause, U.S. treaties, and federal law.[51] Additionally, states cannot intrude on the exclusive federal authority in federal affairs.[52] Subject to these limitations, exercise of jurisdiction by states is governed by the same jurisdictional principles whether the exercise of jurisdiction has international or solely domestic implications.[53]

46 *Id.* at 36.
47 *Id.* at 37.
48 J. Sweeney, C. Oliver, & N. Leech, THE INTERNATIONAL LEGAL SYSTEM, 146–55, 230–37 (2d ed. 1981).
49 RESTATEMENT (3RD), § 402, Comment (h) and § 502. *See* Treaty on Principles Governing the Activities of States in the Exploration and Use of Outer Space, including the Moon and Other Celestial Bodes, Jan. 27, 1967, 18 U.S.T. 2410, T.I.A.S. No. 6347, 610 U.N.T.S. 205. *See also* S. Gorove, *Criminal Jurisdiction in Outer Space*, in Bassiouni & Nanda, *supra* note 2 at 48–57.
50 *See, e.g., United States v. Curtiss-Wright Export Corp.*, 299 U.S. 204, 318 (1936); *Perez v. Brownwell*, 356 U.S. 253 (1967).
51 *Hines v. Davidowitz*, 312 U.S. 52 (1941).
52 *Zschernig v. Miller*, 309 U.S. 429, 432 (1968).
53 *See generally* B. J. George, Jr., *Extraterritorial Application of Penal Legislation*, 64 MICH. L. REV. 609 (1966); Richard Rotenburg, *Extraterritorial Legislative Jurisdiction and the State Criminal Law*, 38 TEX. L. REV. 763 (1960).

2. Limitations of Reasonableness

Even if one of the bases for jurisdiction is present, both U.S. and international law preclude a state from applying its law to conduct linked to another state or states when such exercise is unreasonable. The determination of whether the exercise of jurisdiction is unreasonable is evaluated in light of several relevant factors, including the following:

(1) the extent to which the activity (a) occurs within the regulating state, or (b) has a substantial, direct, and foreseeable effect upon or in the regulating state;
(2) the links, such as nationality, residence, or economic activity, between the regulating state and the person principally responsible for the activity to be regulated, or between that state and those whom the law or regulation is intended to protect;
(3) the character of the activity to be regulated, the significance of regulation to the regulating state, the extent to which other States regulate such activities, and the extent to which the goals of such regulations are generally accepted;
(4) the existence of justified expectations that might be protected or hurt by the regulation in question;
(5) the significance of regulation to the international political, legal, or economic system;
(6) the extent to which another State may have an interest in regulating the activity; and
(7) the potential of conflict with regulation by other states.[54]

Under established U.S. law and an emerging principle of international law, exercising jurisdiction on one of the bases normally permitted is still unlawful if it is unreasonable. A wide international consensus exists that the links of territoriality or nationality are necessary, but not in all cases sufficient, conditions for the exercise of jurisdiction. As a general proposition, legislatures and administrative agencies in the United States and abroad have not exercised jurisdiction where it would be unreasonable to do so. Courts have usually interpreted general language in a statute as not intended to exercise or authorize the exercise of jurisdiction in circumstances where application of the statute would be unreasonable.[55] How do these factors apply to Hypothetical 2?

According to the Restatement, when regulatory statutes that may result in both civil and criminal liability – such as U.S. antitrust or securities laws – apply, the presence of substantial foreign elements will ordinarily weigh against applying criminal law. In such cases, legislative intent to subject conduct outside the state's territory to its criminal law should be found only on the basis of express statement or clear implication.[56]

A U.S. statute should be construed to apply to a person or activity only if not unreasonable, and to the extent consistent with the extraterritorial jurisdiction principles mentioned earlier,[57] unless such construction is impossible.[58] Similarly, if one construction of a U.S. statute would conflict with the law of another state that has a clearly greater

[54] RESTATEMENT (3RD), § 403.
[55] RESTATEMENT (3RD), § 403, Comment (a).
[56] *Id.*, § 403, Comment (f).
[57] *Id.*, RESTATEMENT (3RD), § 403, Comment (g).
[58] *Id.*, § 403, Comment (g) § 114, and Reporters' Note 2 to that section.

interest,[59] or would subject a person to conflicting commitments,[60] whereas another construction would avoid such a conflict, the latter is preferable. This rule applies to courts, executive branch officials, and regulatory bodies interpreting authority conferred to them by legislation. In addition, the president may rely on this rule while considering a bill submitted for his or her approval. If construction of a statute that fulfills the intent of Congress within the limits of international law is not possible, the statute is nevertheless valid, but its application may cause conflict with the United States' international legal responsibilities.[61]

The application of the principle of reasonableness to the exercise of criminal jurisdiction with respect to acts committed in another state can be viewed as especially intrusive. For example, the House of Lords reacted angrily to U.S. involvement in Westinghouse Corporation's efforts to take the testimony of British witnesses regarding an alleged conspiracy to fix the price of uranium.[62] U.S. enforcement agencies generally try to exercise restraint in applying criminal jurisdiction over activity with substantial foreign elements unless they have strong justification to do so. Examples of U.S. exercise of criminal jurisdiction include, under the special protective principle, efforts to punish immigration fraud and currency counterfeiting.

3. Limitations Imposed by International Agreements

International agreements sometimes limit or try to resolve jurisdictional conflicts. For example, the Draft European Convention on Conflicts of Jurisdiction in Criminal Matters provides for priorities to determine jurisdictional conflicts. It confers upon one state the primary right to exercise jurisdiction while simultaneously recognizing the jurisdiction claimed by other states on the basis of their criminal laws. The convention also provides procedural protection to foreigners tried by courts in the state of primary jurisdiction and introduces the safeguard of *non bis in idem*. A second state is thereby prevented from trying an offender for an offense for which he or she has already been tried in the first state. In general, the state on whose territory the offense is committed has priority.[63] The convention also provides means for collaboration among states that each have jurisdiction.[64]

4. Limitations Imposed by "Blocking Statutes"

By the end of 1980, at least seven foreign states and two Canadian provinces had enacted blocking statutes protecting their citizens against illegal efforts by foreign states, such as the United States, to assert extraterritorial jurisdiction in criminal matters.[65] In 1980, the

59 *Id.*, § 402, Comment (e).

60 *See id.*, § 441.

61 *Id.*, § 403, Comment (g); *see* § *id.*, § 115 and Comments (a) and (b) to that section.

62 *See Rio Tinto Zinc Corp. v. Westinghouse Electric Corp.*, [1979] A.C. 547, esp. at 630 (Viscount Dilhorne) (H.L.E.)), discussed in § 473, Reporters' Note 7.

63 Draft European Conventions on Conflicts of Jurisdiction in Criminal Matters, Art. 2.

64 *Id.*, art. 8. *See also* Council of Europe, Doc. No. 1873, Report on the Settlement of Conflicts of Jurisdiction in Criminal Matters (1965).

65 Note, *Foreign Nondisclosure Law and Domestic Discovery Orders in Antitrust Litigation*, 88 Yale L.J. 612 (1979).

United Kingdom enacted a law specifically targeting U.S. extraterritorial jurisdiction.[66] This law authorizes the Minister of Trade to direct persons in Great Britain to disobey laws or court orders of an "overseas country" insofar as they apply outside the territorial jurisdiction of that country. The law applies where the Minister of Trade determines that compliance with the overseas law or order would damage U.K. trading interests or infringe on the U.K.'s jurisdiction.

Notes and Questions

1. A U.S. statute should be construed to apply to a person or activity only to the extent consistent with the principles of territoriality or nationality and the limitations of reasonableness, unless such construction is not possible. *See* in this regard, RESTATEMENT (3RD), § 402(g) and § 114, and Reporters' Note 2 to that section.

III. Jurisdiction to Adjudicate Criminal Law: General Principles

"Jurisdiction to adjudicate" is the authority of a state to subject persons to the process of its courts, and particularly to enforce the state's laws and regulations. Because the three categories of jurisdiction are implemented by different branches of U.S. federal and state governments, and jurisdictional decisions are implemented by constitutional law, international law, statutory interpretation, foreign policy, and practical considerations, such decisions are not always consistent or rational.[67]

A U.S. court can try a criminal action for violating domestic, but not foreign, criminal law.[68] Even if authorized by statute, the trial of a defendant for violation of a foreign law could be deemed a denial of due process under the Fifth and the Fourteenth Amendments. Courts in the United States can exercise jurisdiction to adjudicate only pursuant to law or the Constitution. Subject to Article II and other constitutional limitations, Congress determines the jurisdiction of federal courts.[69] The jurisdiction of a state court in the United States is determined by the state's constitution and further limited by the U.S. Constitution, in particular the supremacy of treaties and federal law under the supremacy clause.[70]

A state may exercise criminal jurisdiction over a person if the relationship of the person (or thing) to the state makes the exercise of jurisdiction reasonable.[71] A state's exercise of jurisdiction is reasonable if, at the time jurisdiction is asserted, any one of the following applies: (1) the person (or thing) is present in the territory of the state (other than transitorily); (2) the person, if a natural person, is either domiciled, a resident, or a national of the foreign state; (3) the person, if a legal person, is organized pursuant to the law of the state; (4) the person, whether natural or judicial, regularly conducts business in the state; (5) the person, whether natural or judicial, had carried on activity in the state that created liability, but only in respect to such activity; or (6) the person, whether natural or judicial, had conducted outside the state an activity having a substantial, direct,

[66] Protection of British Trading Interests Act, ch. 11 (1980).
[67] RESTATEMENT (3RD), § 421.
[68] RESTATEMENT (3RD), § 422(1); *United States v. Hudson and Goodwin*, 11 U.S. (7 Cranch) 32, 34 (1812).
[69] U.S. CONST. Art. III.
[70] RESTATEMENT (3RD), § 422, comment b.
[71] *Id.*, § 421(1).

or foreseeable effect within the state, which created liability, but only in respect to such activity.[72]

If a person, especially a defendant or third party, appears in a case for a purpose that does not include challenging the exercise of jurisdiction, the appearance generally waives a defense of lack of jurisdiction.[73]

Although U.S. courts will not enforce a foreign criminal law, the United States may and does criminalize committing an act in violation of the law of another state if the United States has jurisdiction to prescribe in the circumstances. Examples include a law making it a crime for a U.S. national to violate the bribery or tax laws of a foreign state, as discussed in the chapters on corruption and tax enforcement. A court cannot exercise jurisdiction over an offense that the United States or a state of the United States could not constitutionally prescribe.[74]

A U.S. court may not try a person unless he or she is before the court when the trial starts.[75] However, the court's jurisdiction is not terminated and the accused will be deemed to have waived the right to be present, if he or she flees after the trial has started or creates a disturbance requiring removal from the courtroom. Although a grand jury may return indictments against a person outside the United States, under existing law a warrant or summons upon the indictment can be served only within the jurisdiction of the United States or in connection with a U.S. extradition request.[76]

Except for crimes committed outside the United States, trials of all crimes under U.S. law must occur in the state where the crime was committed. The requirement is met if any significant element of the crime occurred in the state (e.g., some overt act, some element of a conspiracy, or harm to the victim).[77] Although constitutional, the defendant may waive the venue requirement. Federal statutes provide that crimes committed on the high seas or otherwise not within any state or district may be tried in the district where the offender is arrested or first brought, at his or her last known residence, or in the District of Columbia.[78]

Several constitutional issues, especially those dealing with safeguarding the rights of the accused, may arise when an individual is arrested for an offense in which international elements are present. For instance, under the NATO Status of Forces Agreements[79] and comparable agreements with other countries, the United States has authority to exercise substantial criminal jurisdiction over U.S. military personnel involved in NATO engagements.

U.S. courts have dealt with situations involving contempt convictions and other penalties against persons, including foreign individuals and entities, for failure to respond to

[72] *Id.*, § 421(2).
[73] *Id.*, § 421(3).
[74] Restatement (3rd), § 422, Comment (c).
[75] *Id.*, § 422(2).
[76] *Id.*, § 422, Comment c(iii).
[77] *Id.*, § 422, Comment c(ii), citing *Burton v. United States*, 202 U.S. 344, 26 S.Ct. 688, 50 L.Ed. 1057 (1906); *Hyde v. United States*, 225 U.S. 347 (1912); *United States v. Cores*, 356 U.S. 405, 78 S.Ct. 875, 2 L.Ed.2d 873 (1958).
[78] *See, e.g.*, 18 U.S.C. § 3238; *United States v. Layton*, 519 F.Supp. 942 (N.D.Cal.1981), *affirmed*, 665 F.2d 274 (9th Cir. 1987).
[79] North Atlantic Treaty Status of Forces Agreement, June 19, 1951, 4 U.S.T. 1792, T.I.A.S. No. 246, 199 U.N.T.S. 67. *See also* Christopher Coker, *The Status of Rising Military Forces in Europe: NATO–SOFA, Comparison*, in Bassiouni & Nanda, *supra* note 2 at 115 (1973).

subpoenas issued by U.S. courts.[80] These penalties have been upheld in most cases, despite the fact that many of the defendants have claimed the conflicting law of a foreign nation as a defense.[81] Negotiations between the United States and countries in which such subpoenaed persons reside have resulted in informal agreements. Hence, agreements such as the Memorandum of Understanding on Insider Trading (MOU) between the United States and Switzerland further extend the authority of U.S. courts to enforce discovery orders in criminal and penal administrative enforcement cases.[82]

IV. Jurisdiction to Enforce Criminal Law

"Jurisdiction to enforce" is the exercise by a state of authority to compel or induce compliance. In criminal law it means imposing sanctions for noncompliance with laws and regulations, whether through the use of police, investigative agencies, public prosecutors, courts, or custodial facilities, provided (a) the law enforced is within the state's jurisdiction to prescribe; (b) when enforcement is through the courts, the state has jurisdiction to adjudicate with respect to the person who is the target of enforcement; and (c) the procedures of investigation, arrest, adjudication, and punishment are consistent with the state's obligations under the law of international human rights.[83]

A state's law enforcement officers can exercise their functions in the territory of a second state only with its consent.[84] Although a state may take some measures of nonjudicial enforcement against a person in another state, its law enforcement officers cannot arrest that person in another state and can engage in criminal investigation in that state only with its consent.[85]

Jurisdiction to enforce criminal law is normally exercised by administrative agencies. For example, under the Foreign Corrupt Practices Act,[86] Congress delegated authority to promulgate regulations requiring strict accounting controls and mandatory disclosure to the Securities and Exchange Commission (SEC). Federal agencies have become increasingly aggressive in enforcing criminal law extraterritorially. In the twenty-first century globalization has prompted many states, including the United States, to expand their jurisdiction to enforce criminal law.

A. *Expanded U.S. Assertion of Jurisdiction to Enforce*

Examples of expanded U.S. assertion of jurisdiction to enforce are discussed in the chapters on substantive aspects of criminal law, such as tax, corruption, money laundering,

[80] *Blackmer v. United States*, 284 U.S. 421 (1932); *U.S. v. Toyota Motor Corp.*, 569 F. Supp. 1158 (C.D. Cal. 1983).

[81] *See, e.g., U.S. v. Vetco, Inc.*, 644 F.2d 1324 (9th Cir. 1981); *U.S. v. Field*, 532 F.2d 404, 407 (5th Cir. 1976), *reh'g denied*, 535 F.2d 660 (5th Cir. 1976), *cert. denied*, 45 U.S.L.W. 3341 (1976); *See also* Lenore Browne, *Extraterritorial Discovery: An Analysis Based on Good Faith*, 83 Col. L. Rev. 1320 (1983); Note, *Compelling Production of Documents in Violation of Foreign law: An Examination and Re-evaluation of the American Position*, 50 Fordham L. Rev. 877 (1982).

[82] See, e.g., Bruce Zagaris, *The Netherlands Signs a Treaty with the U.S. for 'Mutual Assistance in Criminal Matters' Which Embraces Tax Matters*, 30 Taxes Int'l 4 (Apr. 1982); Bruce Zagaris, *The Swiss/U.S. Consultations on 'Insider Trading'*, 30 Taxes Int'l 46 (1982).

[83] Restatement (3rd), § 432.

[84] *Id.*, § 432(2).

[85] Restatement (3rd), § 432, Comment (b).

[86] Foreign Corrupt Practices Act of 1977 Pub. L. No. 95–213, 91 Stat. 1494 (1977).

and export control. Immigration law offers another interesting example of the U.S. approach.

On September 21, 1981, in an effort to combat illegal immigration to the United States, President Reagan's Executive Order[87] proclaimed that the entry of undocumented aliens from the high seas would be prevented by the interdiction of vessels carrying such aliens. The order authorizes the Secretary of State to enter into cooperative arrangements with governments of countries from which the illegal immigrations were coming and also authorizes the Coast Guard to stop and board vessels of foreign countries with which the United States has such cooperative agreements. The Coast Guard may only board ships outside the territorial waters of the United States when there is reason to believe that such vessels are engaged in the irregular transportation of persons in violation of U.S. law and of the law of a country with which the United States has an arrangement. The rationale for this assertion of extraterritorial jurisdiction is the protective principle; that is, to protect U.S. sovereignty from a rising tide of undocumented aliens.

The U.S. Coast Guard can also intercept vessels in international waters listed on its weekly publication of suspected narcotics transporters. In *United States v. Keller,*[88] the Coast Guard located such a vessel thirty miles north of Puerto Rico heading toward the United States. The U.S. vessel, which had an American crew, was searched and 300 pounds of marijuana were discovered. Rejecting the defendants' motion to dismiss for lack of subject matter jurisdiction, the court held that, although the acts allegedly occurred outside U.S. territory, jurisdiction existed under the protective principle.[89] In particular, such an invasion violated U.S. customs law controlling the importation of certain controlled substances.[90]

In 1981, Congress extended limited jurisdiction over drug enforcement on the high seas to the U.S. armed forces.[91] Before that, the Coast Guard had exclusive jurisdiction. An amendment to the 1876 Posse Comitatus Act authorizes the armed forces to provide training, advice, and the use of military facilities and equipment to civilian authorities, especially the Coast Guard and U.S. Customs.[92] In 1876, Congress enacted the Posse Comitatus Act to prevent U.S. military personnel from making civil law arrests and, in general, from acting as civil law enforcement agents. The 1981 amendment to the act permits the Armed Forces to work closely with law enforcement agencies engaged in stopping the flow of illegal substances into the United States. However, the amendment leaves intact the basic premise of the Posse Comitatus Act; namely, that U.S. military personnel cannot arrest civilians outside of military bases.

In July 1983, the jurisdictional implications of the amendment applied to a case where the *U.S.S. Kidd*, a Navy destroyer, opened fire on a "suspicious looking" freighter, the *Ranger*, in international waters forty miles north of Puerto Rico.[93] The *Kidd* followed

[87] Exec. Order No. 12,324, 46 Fed. Reg. 48,109 (1981).
[88] *United States v. Keller*, 451 F. Supp. 631 (1978).
[89] *Id.* at 635.
[90] *Id.* However, the court ruled that it lacked jurisdiction over the second count of the indictment, possession of marijuana with intent to distribute, under the protective principle, apparently because the federal statutes proscribing conspiracy to import and attempting to import marijuana could not be applied extraterritorially. The statute that proscribed possession with intent to distribute could only be applied within the boundaries of the United States. *Id.* at 635, n. 8. *See* Note, *Drug Smuggling and the Protective Principle: A Journey into Unchartered Waters*, 39 La. L. Rev. 1189 (1979).
[91] Posse Comitatus Act, Pub. L. No. 97–86 (codified at 18 U.S.C. § 1385 (1982)).
[92] *Id.*
[93] National L.J., Feb. 13, 1984, at A1, col. 4.

the Honduran-registered *Ranger* and eventually hit it. Following the practice of Navy vessels involved in this type of operation, the *Kidd* had lowered its Navy flag and raised a Coast Guard flag before opening fire.[94] Incidents such as this indicate that the U.S. government has and will continue to extend the United States' jurisdiction to enforce its criminal laws.

U.S. government agencies have also expanded their extraterritorial jurisdiction to enforce criminal and administrative penal laws. For instance, the Internal Revenue Service has promulgated regulations expanding income and asset reporting requirements for taxpayers. In 1981 the IRS issued proposed regulations for U.S. citizens who are shareholders of certain foreign corporations to prevent, *inter alia*, tax evasion.[95] Similarly, sections 336 through 342 of the Tax Equity and Fiscal Responsibility Act of 1982 (TEFRA) provide for enforcement of IRS summonses on U.S. citizens residing outside the United States.[96] These regulations restrict taxpayers from using requested documentation to prove their view of the transactions in court.

Another example of an agency expanding its jurisdiction to enforce is the Commodity Futures Trading Commission (CFTC). It published a proposed rule requiring a futures commission merchant (FCM), trader, or foreign broker to provide the CFTC, upon special call, market information concerning his or her accounts.[97] The proposed rule also provided that if the FCM trader or foreign broker fails to respond to the special call, the CFTC may direct the appropriate contract market and all FCMs to prohibit further trades with that person.[98] The proposed rule, as the cases in this section and recent congressional hearings demonstrate,[99] shows that the CTFC has promulgated rules extending its extraterritorial criminal jurisdiction.[100]

B. *Some Results of the Trend toward Expanded Jurisdiction*

The expanded assertion of jurisdiction to enforce criminal laws is increasingly putting individuals and institutions in situations where they must choose between violating U.S. laws or the laws of their home countries. Despite occasional compromises, extraterritorial enforcement efforts often fuel resentment between countries.[101] As discussed earlier, some foreign states have reacted to this situation by enacting blocking legislation. The conflicts require greater restraint in exercising extraterritorial jurisdiction or the use of bilateral and multilateral agreements to resolve conflicts in jurisdiction.

However, if extraterritorial jurisdiction is not expanded, criminals will exploit gaps in jurisdiction to conduct their activities. Under the rule of construction, executive branch officials and regulatory bodies, while interpreting the authority granted to them

94 *Id.*

95 46 C.F.R. 7401 (Prop. Amend. to § 1.600–1 of Income Tax Regulations). *See also* Bruce Zagaris, *The IRS Public Hearing on the Books and Records of Foreign Entities*, 26 TAXES INT'L 6, 7 (Dec. 1981).

96 46 C.F.R. 7401 (Prop. Amend. to § 1.600–1 of Income Tax Regulations).

97 47 C.F.R. § 23,951 (June 2, 1982).

98 *Id.*

99 *See generally* COMM. ON GOVERNMENT OPERATIONS, SILVER PRICES AND THE ADEQUACY OF FEDERAL ACTIONS IN THE MARKET PLACE 1979–80, H.R. Doc. No. 395, 97th Cong., 1st Sess.

100 *See* Michael Greenstone, *The Foreign Commodity Trader: A Regulatory Dilemma*, 30 AD. L. REV. 535–48 (1978).

101 *See* Bruce Zagaris, *Judge Paine Socks it to the Bank of Nova Scotia – The Continuing Saga of the Bank of Nova Scotia Case*, 54 TAXES INT'L 12–20 (Apr. 1984).

in legislation, and the president, while considering a bill submitted for approval, should give the law the construction that would not bring it into conflict with the law of another state that has a clearly greater interest or would subject a person to conflicting commands. A construction that would avoid such a conflict is clearly preferred; *see* RESTATEMENT (3RD), § 403(g).

V. Limitations on the Power to Enforce and Adjudicate

A. *Foreign Government Diplomats*

The United States is party to several important multilateral treaties, as well as a wide network of consular treaties concerning criminal jurisdiction over diplomats.[102] The Vienna Convention on Diplomatic Relations, done in 1961, is the first comprehensive code entered into by the international community concerning diplomatic conduct and relations, and codifies the customary law of diplomatic immunities.[103] The U.S. Congress adopted the Diplomatic Relations Act of 1978, 22 U.S.C. § 254a-e, to implement this convention.

In 1963, the Vienna Convention on Consular Relations was adopted.[104] In many respects it follows the Convention on Diplomatic Relations. However, although Congress has not adopted legislation to implement the Convention on Consular Relations, in general its provisions are self-executing U.S. law. Many provisions reflect customary law and apply between the United States and states not parties to the convention.

A diplomatic agent of a state, accredited to and accepted by another state, is immune from the receiving state's exercise of jurisdiction to prescribe in relation to acts or omissions in the exercise of the agent's official functions, as well as from other regulations that would be incompatible with the agent's diplomatic status, and from arrest, detention, criminal process, and, in general, civil process in the receiving state.[105] Immunity from jurisdiction to adjudicate continues after the person's diplomatic status has ended.[106] To the extent that an agent is not immune from jurisdiction to prescribe, the receiving state may judicially enforce its laws if the sending state waives the agent's immunity from judicial process or if the agent becomes subject to the receiving state's criminal jurisdiction after his or her diplomatic status has ended. In such cases the receiving state can treat any period of limitations under its laws as suspended during the period of immunity.[107]

The immunity from arrest or detention of a diplomatic agent does not exclude measures of self-defense or, in exceptional circumstances, measures to prevent the agent from committing crimes or offenses.[108]

A diplomatic agent's family members – traditionally defined to include the agent's spouse, minor children, and other dependents forming part of the household – are also

[102] *See, e.g.*, Vienna Convention on Diplomatic Relations, Apr. 18, 1961, 23 U.S.T. 3227, T.I.A.S. No. 7502, 500 U.N.T.S. 95 [hereinafter cited as Vienna Convention on Diplomatic Relations]; Vienna Convention on Consular Relations, Apr. 24, 1963, 21 U.S.T. 77, T.I.A.S. No. 6820, 596 U.N.T.S. 261.

[103] Vienna Convention on Diplomatic Relations, *supra*.

[104] 21 U.S.T. 77, T.I.A.S. No. 6820, 596 U.N.T.S. 261. It came into force in 1967 and for the United States in 1969.

[105] RESTATEMENT (3RD), § 464; Vienna Convention on Diplomatic Relations, Art. 31.

[106] Vienna Convention on Diplomatic Relations, Art. 39(2).

[107] *Id.*

[108] [1959] 2 Y.B. INT'L L. COMM. 89, 97.

entitled to the agent's immunities if they are not nationals of the receiving state.[109] Immunity from criminal jurisdiction is also extended to the members of the administrative and technical staffs of the mission and their families.[110] In addition, members of the service staff who are not nationals or permanent residents of the receiving state have immunity from legal process in respect of their official acts or omissions.[111]

A receiving state can declare a person accredited by the sending state to be *persona non grata*, and refuse to accept him or, if he is already serving, ask that he be recalled. If the person is not recalled within a reasonable time, the receiving state may refuse to recognize him as a member of the mission and deny him diplomatic status and immunities.[112] A diplomatic agent declared *persona non grata* may be required to leave the country, but may not be detained or mistreated. A receiving state may declare a diplomatic agent *persona non grata* in circumstances in which the person is believed to have been guilty of serious misconduct but the sending state refuses to waive his immunity from legal process.[113] After a reasonable time has passed for a person declared *non grata* to leave the receiving state, immunity is destroyed, and the receiving state may arrest and prosecute the formerly immune agent.[114]

Immunities are not the personal rights of the individual agent. They are conferred by international law on the sending state and can ordinarily only be waived by that state – and not by the agent without that state's consent.[115]

High officials of a foreign state and their staffs on an official visit or in transit, including those attending international conferences as official representatives of their country, enjoy immunities like those of diplomatic agents when the effect of exercising jurisdiction against the official would be to violate the immunity of the foreign state.[116]

Members of an accredited diplomatic mission and their family members in or transiting the territory of a third state while proceeding to take up or return to a post, or returning to their own country, must be accorded such immunities in the third state as are necessary to ensure the completion of their journey.[117]

Notes and Questions

1. The most important recent case on diplomatic immunities is *Regina v. Bow Street Metropolitan Stipendiary Magistrate and Others, Ex Parte Pinochet Ugarte (No. 3)*, House of Lords [2000] 1 App. Cas. 147, [1999] 2 All E.R. 97. Pinochet, the former president of Chile, was visiting England for medical treatment when Spanish authorities requested his extradition. Spain sought Pinochet for his alleged participation in torture, conspiracy to torture, detention of hostages, and conspiracy to detain hostages, and in a conspiracy to commit murder, which extended to Spain and other countries.

On October 28, 1998, the Queen's Bench Divisional Court quashed both warrants. The first warrant was found not to allege an extraditable offense because it involved

[109] RESTATEMENT (3RD), § 464, Comment (a). Vienna Convention on Diplomatic Relations, Art. 37(1).
[110] Vienna Convention on Diplomatic Relations, Art. 37(2).
[111] Id. Vienna Convention on Diplomatic Relations, Art. 37(2).
[112] Vienna Convention on Diplomatic Relations, Art. 9; RESTATEMENT (3RD), § 464, Comment (b).
[113] RESTATEMENT (3RD), § 464, Comment (b); for waiver, *see* RESTATEMENT (3RD), § 464, Comment j.
[114] Vienna Convention on Diplomatic Relations, Art. 9(2).
[115] RESTATEMENT (3RD), § 464, Comment j; Reporters' Note 15.
[116] RESTATEMENT (3RD), § 464, Comment I. In 1969, the UN General Assembly adopted the Convention on Special Missions (G.A. Res. 2530, 24 U.N. GAOR Supp. No. 30 at 9 (1969)).
[117] Vienna Convention on Diplomatic Relations, art. 40.

Spanish assertion of extraterritorial jurisdiction under circumstances where a U.K. court would not have extraterritorial jurisdiction in an analogous situation. The court found both warrants invalid because Pinochet, as a former head of state, had immunity from arrest and extradition proceedings in the United Kingdom for acts committed when he was head of state. [1998] All E.R. 509.

The Crown Prosecution Service, representing the Spanish government, was granted leave to appeal to the House of Lords on the ground that a point of law of general public importance was involved; namely, "the proper interpretation and scope of the immunity enjoyed by a former head of state from arrest and extradition proceedings in the United Kingdom in respect of acts committed while head of state." On November 25, 1998, by a 3–2 decision, the appeal was allowed and Pinochet was held not to enjoy immunity with respect to international crimes such as torture and hostage-taking committed when he was head of state. [1998] 4 All E.R. 897. On January 15, 1999, the House of Lords set aside the decision and ordered the matter reheard because Lord Hoffman, one of the Law Lords participating in the decision, had undisclosed ties to Amnesty International, an intervenor in the proceedings. [199] 1 All E.R. 577. A new panel heard the appeal and ruled 6–1 in favor of extradition.

2. On January 11, 2000, the Home Secretary announced that he would deny extradition because Pinochet was medically unfit to stand trial. The Home Secretary affirmed his decision on March 2, 2000, despite efforts to challenge the same.

3. The Pinochet proceedings are one example of a trend in international law toward protecting human rights by imposing criminal sanctions on responsible officials and even interfering in the sovereign affairs of the state in which the violations are occurring, based on the theory that preventing egregious human rights violations is a universal imperative. This approach conflicts with and modifies the classical theory of international law, which obligates states to abstain from interfering in the internal affairs of other states. *See*, e.g., Michael Byers, *The Law and Politics of the Pinochet Case*, 10 DUKE J. COMP. & INT'L L. 415, 420 (2000).

Lord Browne-Wilkinson held that if Pinochet organized and authorized torture while he was head of state, Chile nonetheless had agreed to outlaw such conduct. Browne-Wilkinson argued that Chile had agreed with the other parties to the Torture Convention that all signatory states should have jurisdiction to try official torture even if such torture were committed in Chile by the head of state. Hence, Pinochet had no immunity for the torture charges after the Torture Convention took effect in 1988.

Lord Goff of Chieveley, in dissent, found that Pinochet, as a former head of state, was entitled to immunity in relation to criminal acts performed in the course of exercising public functions.

4. What is U.S. law with respect to bringing criminal proceedings against a current or former foreign head of state or head of government? As indicated in *United States v. Noriega*, 117 F.3d 1206 (11th Cir. 1997), the Foreign Sovereign Immunities Act of 1976 does not clearly cover head-of-state immunity.

5. In the *Case Concerning the Arrest Warrant of 11 April 2000 (D.R. Congo v. Belgium)* I.C.J. Rep. 2002, the Democratic Republic of the Congo (DRC) filed in the International Court of Justice (ICJ) an Application instituting proceedings against the King of Belgium in respect of a dispute concerning an "international arrest warrant" issued on April 11, 2000, by a Belgian investigating judge against the Minister for Foreign Affairs in the office of the Democratic Republic of the Congo, Mr. Abdulaye Yerodia Ndombasi.

The Belgian arrest warrant accused Yerodia of making speeches inciting racial hatred and charged him with committing grave breaches of the Geneva Conventions and serious violations of international humanitarian law.

By 13–1, the ICJ found the arrest warrant and its international circulation constituted violations of a legal obligation of Belgium toward the DRC, in that it failed to respect the immunity from criminal jurisdiction and the inviolability that the incumbent Minister for Foreign Affairs of the DRC enjoyed under international law. In a 10–6 ruling, the ICJ found that Belgium had to cancel the arrest warrant.

6. The Nigerian government's detention and surrender of Charles Taylor to the Special Court for Sierra Leone have also raised the issue of former head-of-state immunity. The Special Court held that it was an international court and that, even as a sitting head of state, Taylor had no immunity from its jurisdiction. *Decision on Immunity*, May 31, 2004, Special Court for Sierra Leone, Case No. CSCL-2003–01, found at www.sc-sl.org. For background on Taylor's arrest and surrender, *see* Jason McClurg, *Nigeria Ends Taylor Asylum, Details on Extradition Remain Unanswered*, 22 INT'L ENFORCEMENT L. REP. 174 (May 2006); Jason McClurg, *Appeals Chamber Paves Way for Taylor Trial in The Hague; Pressure Intensifies on Taylor's Inner Circle*, 22 INT'L ENFORCEMENT L. REP. 325 (Aug. 2006).

B. *Immunity of Consular Personnel of Other States*

A consular officer of a state, commissioned to and accepted by another state, is immune from an exercise by the receiving state of jurisdiction to prescribe that which interferes with the officer's official functions, and from other regulation that would be unreasonable to apply to persons of such status. Such a consular officer is immune from arrest, detention, and criminal or civil process in respect of acts or omissions in the exercise of his or her official functions.[118]

In the event a consular official is not protected from criminal process – for example, accusations in respect of acts or omissions outside the exercise of his or her official functions – that official is subject to arrest or detention pending trial only in case of a grave crime and pursuant to a decision of a competent judicial authority, in which case criminal proceedings must be instituted with a minimum of delay.[119] Article 41(3) of the Consular Convention requires that criminal proceedings against a consular officer be conducted "with respect due to him by reason of his official position" and, except where charged with a grave crime, "in a manner which will hamper the exercise of consular functions as little as possible."

Some states in bilateral agreements have extended to consular personnel, on a reciprocal basis, full immunity from criminal jurisdiction, whereas others have consular conventions that afford their officials "most-favored-nation" treatment.[120] Their officials would be entitled to full exemption from criminal jurisdiction, but only on a reciprocal basis, if the treaty partner accords full immunity to the consular personnel of another treaty partner as a result of the "most-favored-nation" provisions.

[118] *Id.*, § 465.
[119] *Id.*, § 465(2); Vienna Consular Convention, Art. 41(1).
[120] U.S.-U.S.S.R. Consular Convention, Reporters' Note 3.

Notes and Questions

1. In *Salazar v. Burresch*, 47 F. Supp. 2d 1105 (C.D.Ca. 1999), plaintiff Rafael Salazar was the Consul General of the Republic of Guatemala in Los Angeles. On April 4, 1997, he was involved in a car accident on a freeway in California. Defendant California Highway Patrol Officer J. Burresch arrived on the scene shortly after the accident. Burresch thought Salazar was intoxicated. Salazar informed Burresch that he was consul general and entitled to immunity. After Salazar allegedly became unruly, Burresch handcuffed Salazar and caused him to be transported to the police station. Salazar submitted to a breath test, which showed a blood alcohol level well above the limit for being presumed intoxicated under California law. Thereafter, he was charged with drunk driving.

Salazar filed a civil rights action against Burresch and another officer who had administered the breath test for violating federal treaty rights, namely the Vienna Convention on Consular Relations (VCCR). In particular, Salazar cited Art. 41 of the VCCR under which "consular officers shall not be liable to arrest or detention pending trial, except in the case of a grave crime and pursuant to a decision by a competent authority."

After reviewing the U.S. Department of State "Guidance for Law Enforcement Officers – Personal Rights and Immunities of Foreign Diplomatic and Consular Personnel," the court found that "the undisputed evidence demonstrates that the conduct of Burresch and Myhre was in compliance with the VCCR, as interpreted by the Department of State Guidelines. Accordingly, this Court grants those Defendants' motion for summary judgment as to Plaintiff's claim under the VCCR." Essentially, the court found that the initial handcuffing of Salazar was permissible because of Burresch's concern for public safety, given Salazar's obvious intoxication and combative behavior. Taking Salazar to the station was reasonable and prudent for Burresch to complete his investigation, protect the safety and welfare of the public, and prevent the commission of a crime, especially where public safety was in imminent danger.

2. *Hypothetical*: Mr. X., a Canadian national, conducts a very successful Asian import-export business from Vancouver. His U.S. subsidiary perpetrated a bribe, which Mr. X. approved. A couple of years later, his family moved to California, partly because they enjoy the climate, the private schools, and the culture. Mr. X. learns he is under investigation by U.S. authorities. His wife is Venezuelan. Mr. X. is friendly with some high-level Venezuelan officials. He secures the position of a Venezuelan diplomat to Panama. Will that help Mr. X. avoid prosecution in the United States if he is indicted? What if his wife participated previously in his business as secretary on the board, but did not participate in the bribe? What happens if Mr. X. is indicted in the United States and then visits his family? What if the visit occurs in transit between Venezuela and Panama?

C. *Immunity of Diplomatic and Consular Premises, Archives, Documents, and Communications*

The premises, archives, documents, and communications of an accredited diplomatic mission or consular post are inviolable and are immune from any exercise of jurisdiction by the receiving state that would interfere with their official use.[121]

[121] Restatement (3rd), § 466, citing Vienna Convention on Diplomatic Relations, Articles 21–24, 27, and 30; Vienna Convention on Consular Relations, Articles 27, 30–33, and 35.

Officials of the receiving state may not enter the premises of a diplomatic or consular mission without consent.[122] Under the Consular Convention the sending state's consent is presumed in case of urgency requiring prompt protective action such as in the event of a fire, hurricane, or a riot.

The private residence of a diplomatic agent or of a member of the administrative and technical staff of a diplomatic mission, who is not a national or permanent resident of the receiving state, has the same status and protection as the premises of the mission.[123] The residences of other mission personnel or consular officials are not inviolable, but persons and papers located therein may enjoy immunities.

The archives of a mission or consulate are inviolable regardless of location.[124] Archives include all papers, documents, correspondence, books, films, tapes, and registers, together with ciphers and codes, card indexes, and the articles of furniture intended for their safekeeping.[125]

The receiving state must permit and protect freedom of communication by the mission or consular post for all official purposes.[126] The mission or post, in communicating with its government or with other missions or posts of its government, may use all appropriate means, including diplomatic or consular couriers, bags, and messages in code or cipher. However, a mission or consular post can install and use a wireless transmitter only with the consent of the receiving state. A diplomatic and consular courier must be protected by the receiving state. The courier enjoys personal inviolability and is not subject to any form of arrest or detention.

A diplomatic or consular bag may not be opened or detained.[127] However, if the competent authorities of the receiving state have "serious reason to believe" that a consular bag contains something other than correspondence, documents, or articles for official use, the authorities may ask that the bag be opened in their presence. If the request is refused, the bag must be returned to its place of origin.[128]

D. *Immunity of Foreign States from Foreign Jurisdiction*

Under the doctrine of sovereign immunity, a state or state instrumentality is immune from the jurisdiction of the courts of another state, except in cases involving the kind of activities that may be conducted by private persons.[129] For instance, a state is not immune in cases arising out of its commercial activity.[130] However, it is immune from the prescriptive jurisdiction of another state with respect to diplomatic and consular

[122] Vienna Convention on Diplomatic Relations, Art. 22; Vienna Convention on Consular Relations, Art. 31.

[123] Vienna Convention on Diplomatic Relations, Arts 30, 37.

[124] Vienna Convention on Diplomatic Relations, Art. 24; Vienna Convention on Consular Relations, Art. 33.

[125] Vienna Convention on Consular Relations, Art. 1(k).

[126] Vienna Convention on Diplomatic Relations, Art. 27(1); Vienna Convention on Consular Relations, Art. 35(1).

[127] Vienna Convention on Diplomatic Relations, Art. 27(3); Vienna Convention on Consular Relations, Art. 35(3).

[128] Vienna Convention on Consular Relations, Art. 35(3).

[129] Restatement (3RD), § 451. "A state instrumentality includes a corporation, association, or other juridical person a majority of whose shares or other ownership interests are owned by the state, even when organized for profit." *Id.* § 452 cmt.a.

[130] *Id.*, § 453.

activities. As a result, nondiplomatic activities that are commercial or private in nature, and in violation of a forum state's criminal laws, are not immune.

Notes and Questions

1. What happens if a foreign state is alleged to have committed a crime? Can it be prosecuted? Is it possible for a state enterprise to be prosecuted? In 2003, the U.S. Attorney in the Central District of California prosecuted Credit Lyonnais, an entity partially owned by the French government, for fraud in connection with its purchase of Executive Life, a California insurance company. *See* Bruce Zagaris, *U.S. Requests Extradition of 4 French Executives in Credit Lyonnais Case and France Refuses Settlement Offer*, 19 INT'L ENFORCEMENT L. REP. 469 (Dec. 2003). Similarly, the U.S. Attorney in Colorado has prosecuted a Nigerian state enterprise for conspiracy and aiding and abetting an advanced fee fraud scheme.

E. *Immunity of an International Organization and Its Diplomats*

International law provides that an international organization generally enjoys such privileges and immunities from the jurisdiction of a member state as are necessary for the fulfillment of the purposes of the organization, including immunity from legal process, financial controls, taxes, and duties.[131]

Immunity may be waived by an appropriate organ of the organization, usually the secretary-general or other chief executive officer, by authority implied in that office or delegated by the general assembly of the organization. Such a waiver must be expressly made.[132]

By international agreement, an official of an international organization is immune from the exercise by a state of jurisdiction to prescribe, adjudicate, or enforce its law in respect of acts or omissions in the exercise of her official functions, and from other exercises of jurisdiction that would interfere with the independent exercise of her official functions or with her status as an international official.[133]

The enactment of the International Organizations Immunities Act[134] extended immunity from suit and legal process to officers and employees of international organizations. In 1946, the U.S. General Assembly adopted the General Convention of Privileges and Immunities by resolution.[135] This convention provides privileges and immunities to three classes of officials; (1) the Secretary-General and all Assistant Secretaries who have full diplomatic immunity, (2) specialized agencies and their staffs, and (3) officials and experts on special assignments.

Although diplomatic personnel are immune from criminal jurisdiction, they are nevertheless required to obey the laws of the receiving state. The method most frequently used to redress a violation of the law of the receiving state by a diplomat is for the receiving state to file a complaint with the person charged with the violation. The most serious action that a host state can enforce against an uncooperative diplomat is expulsion.

[131] RESTATEMENT (3RD), § 467(1).
[132] *Id.*, § 467, Comment (e).
[133] *Id.*, § 469.
[134] 22 U.S.C. § 288 (1976).
[135] *See* text in U.N. Yearbook, 1946–47.

However, such a measure is rarely employed and is usually reserved for political issues such as an agent's participation in the host country's internal affairs.[136]

Notes and Questions

1. On August 8, 2005, the United Nations Independent Inquiry Committee into the UN Oil-for-Food Program issued its third interim report, highlighting the apparent corruption of two high-level UN officials. One of the officials immediately pleaded guilty after the UN waived his immunity. Independent Inquiry Committee into the United Nations Oil-for-Food Program, *Third Interim Report*, Aug. 8, 2005 (www.iic-offp.org).

The committee's report focused on the illicit activities of Benon Sevan in concert with past or present principals of African Middle East Petroleum Co., Ltd. (AMEP), Efraim (Fred) Nadler and Fakhry Abdelnour, and evidence that a UN procurement officer, Alexander Yakovlev, in concert with French businessman Yves Pintore, actively solicited bribes in connection with the Oil-for-Food Program and otherwise presumptively accepted illicit payments from other UN contractors outside the program.

The committee recommended that the UN waive the immunity of Sevan and Yakovlev should law enforcement authorities pursuing active investigations request such waivers. Its report recommended that the UN Secretary-General, on receipt of an appropriate request, make available the necessary information to assist law enforcement authorities in the possible investigation of Messrs. Nadler, Abdelnour, and Pintore. For additional background, *see* Bruce Zagaris, *UN Report on Iraq Oil-for-Food Shows Corruption and UN Official Pleads Guilty*, 21 INT'L ENFORCEMENT L. REP. 394 (Oct. 2005).

F. *Immunity of Premises, Archives, Documents, and Communications of International Organizations*

An international organization enjoys immunity from any exercise of jurisdiction by a member state that would interfere with official use by the organization of its premises, archives, documents, or communications.[137]

VI. *Additional Reading*

A. *Books and Book Chapters*

CHRISTOPHER L. BLAKESLEY, *Extraterritorial Jurisdiction, in* INTERNATIONAL CRIMINAL LAW PROCEDURAL AND ENFORCEMENT MECHANISMS 33–106 (M. Cherif Bassiouni, ed., 2d ed. 1999).

CHRISTOPHER L. BLAKESLEY, TERRORISM, DRUGS, INTERNATIONAL LAW, AND THE PROTECTION OF HUMAN LIBERTY (Transnational Publishers 1992).

REED BRODY & MICHAEL RATNER, THE PINOCHET PAPERS: THE CASE OF AUGUSTO PINOCHET IN SPAIN AND BRITAIN (2000).

PAUL COGGIENS & WILLIAM A. ROBERTS, *Extraterritorial Jurisdiction: An Untamed Adolescent, in* ACTION AGAINST TRANSNATIONAL CRIMINALITY 33–53 (Commonwealth Secretariat and International Bar Association, 1991).

E. DENZA, DIPLOMATIC LAW: COMMENTARY ON THE VIENNA CONVENTION ON DIPLOMATIC RELATIONS (1976).

[136] *See* C. Fenwick, INTERNATIONAL LAW 469–80 (3d ed. 1948).

[137] *Id.*, § 468.

THE EXTRATERRITORIAL APPLICATION OF NATIONAL LAWS (Dieter Lange & Gary Born eds., Kluwer 1987).

B. J. GEORGE, Jr., *Immunities and Exceptions, in* INTERNATIONAL CRIMINAL LAW PROCEDURAL AND ENFORCEMENT MECHANISMS 107–44 (M. Cherif Bassiouni ed., 2d ed. 1999).

L. T. LEE, VIENNA CONVENTION ON CONSULAR RELATIONS (1966).

RESTATEMENT (3RD) of the Foreign Relations Law of the United States (1987 American Law Institute).

E. M. SATOW, GUIDE TO DIPLOMATIC PRACTICE (Gore-Booth ed., 5th ed. 1979).

B. SEN, A DIPLOMAT'S HANDBOOK OF INTERNATIONAL LAW AND PRACTICE (2nd ed. 1979).

B. Periodicals

Christopher L. Blakesley, *United States Jurisdiction over Extraterritorial Crime*, 73 J. CRIM. L. & CRIMINOLOGY (1982).

Christopher L. Blakesley, A *Conceptual Framework for Extradition and Jurisdiction over Extraterritorial Crime*, UTAH L.R. 685 (1984).

Kenneth Dam, *Economic and Political Aspect of Extraterritoriality*, 19 INT'L LAW. 887 (1985).

Georges R. Delaume, *Jurisdiction over Crimes Committed Abroad: French and American Law*, 21 GEO. WASH. L. REV. 173 (1952–53).

William Empson, *The Application of Criminal Law to Acts Committed outside the Jurisdiction*, 6 AM. CRIM. L.Q. 32 (1967).

Andreas Lowenfeld, *Public Law in the International Arena: Conflict of Laws, International Law, and Some Suggestions for Their Interaction*, 163 HAGUE ACADEMY, RECUEIL DES COURS 311 (1979).

H. Maier, *Extraterritorial Jurisdiction at a Crossroad: An Intersection between Public and International Law*, 76 AM. J. INT'L L. 280 (1982).

Bruce Zagaris & Jay Rosenthal, *United States Jurisdictional Considerations in International Criminal Law*, 15 CAL. W. INT'L L.J. 303 (1985).

8 International Evidence Gathering

I. A Hypothetical

Over the last five years, Joseph Borodillo (JB) has developed a successful financial empire, which in recent months has gained "high tech" capabilities. In particular, it has expanded from waste disposal and restaurants and night clubs to counterfeit computer software.[1]

As part of his business enterprises, JB has established a company called SW Ltd. (SW) in Country ABC to import and distribute counterfeit software in the United States. SW buys counterfeit software from CopyIT, a small company in the Commonwealth of Lavadoria. Instead of paying CopyIT for the counterfeit software directly, SW buys computer hardware for the company.

The SW-CopyIT scheme operates as follows:

1. JB sells the counterfeit software and transfers the proceeds to offshore accounts.
2. JB then has SW use its existing account with Grande Verde in Lavadoria to order large quantities of computer equipment.
3. Grande Verde Lavadoria is a wholly owned subsidiary of Grande Verde, a large corporation and major government contractor. Grande Verde actually fills the contract order and receives copies of the purchase order.
4. JB pays Grande Verde for the computer equipment with cashier's checks drawn on several offshore banks. Some, but not all, Grande Verde executives are knowingly involved in these schemes.
5. Grande Verde ships the computer equipment to CopyIT's offices in Lavadoria.

[1] This hypothetical is adopted from "The Baritones" of the Edward Bennett Williams Inn of Court, Washington, D.C., Sept. 20, 2001, in which I participated.

JB pays for counterfeit software imports with the proceeds of the sale of a U.S. company, using money from suspicious sources shipped to a third party in suspicious amounts. In essence, the payments suggest the use of the Black Market Peso Exchange.

Jane Laing, Grande Verde's compliance counsel, reports her concerns about the sales in Lavadoria to Mike Smith, Grande Verde's outside counsel. Mike then decides to make a voluntary disclosure to the U.S. Attorney's Office.

To what extent can Grande Verde cooperate with the government? Can it make anyone available for interviews? Can it turn over records? Can it waive financial privacy rights for its bank accounts?

From the perspective of the U.S. government and the U.S. Attorney's Office, what is the best way to proceed? Can they obtain documents from Grande Verde and CopyIT? Can the U.S. Attorney issue subpoenas to Grande Verde for its records? What if Lavadoria has a blocking statute? What are the effects of bank secrecy? Are there any dual criminality issues?

Assume Lavadoria authorities decide to detain JB for questioning. During the questioning and with the knowledge of the U.S. Attorney, U.S. law enforcement officials, including the FBI, sit in an adjacent room, listening and watching JB's interrogation through a one-way mirror. Lavadorian officials surreptitiously record the interview.

During the questioning, U.S. law enforcement officials periodically suggest questions for JB. The questioning lasts three days, during which JB receives nothing but water and stale bread, is denied access to counsel, and is occasionally hit by the chief Lavadorian interrogator and threatened with indefinite detention. At the end of the third day of interrogation, JB starts to talk and agrees to turn over records, which he obtains from his house shortly thereafter and gives to Lavadorian officials. As a result of the records, Lavadorian officials discover a file cabinet in JB's home, which they seize.

Can the U.S. Attorney use physical evidence seized by Lavadorian authorities without a warrant? What are JB's Fourth Amendment rights in this situation? What if the search is illegal under Lavadorian law?

What about the secret recording made by Lavadorian authorities? Can U.S. prosecutors use it? What if JB confessed after talking to an attorney? What if JB confessed after being told that his detention would continue until he confessed?

Eventually, the U.S. Attorney in Washington, D.C., turns his attention to Grande Verde's involvement in the scheme, both directly and through its Lavadorian subsidiary. He makes a Mutual Legal Assistance Treaty (MLAT) request seeking to depose Grande Verde's executives.

What rights do the complicit and noncomplicit executives have? Can they assert Fifth Amendment rights or ask for immunity from U.S. or Lavadorian prosecution?

Can Grande Verde executives demand to be present at the deposition? Are the "witnesses" entitled to have any attorney present? What are their Sixth Amendment rights?

II. Unilateral Means of Evidence Gathering

The U.S. Code contains special provisions to facilitate the introduction of evidence obtained abroad, regardless of the method used to gather such evidence. According to 18 U.S.C. § 3481, foreign documents and written materials obtained outside the United States can be deemed admissible when appropriately authenticated. Pursuant to 18 U.S.C. §§ 3492 and 3493, in specific situations U.S. consular officers have authority to take testimony abroad and to authenticate foreign documents. 18 U.S.C. § 3505 contains an exception to the hearsay rule. Under § 3505, foreign records of a "regularly conducted activity" will not be excluded as evidence if a foreign certification attests that the record was made at or near the time of the occurrence by or from information given by a person with knowledge of such matters, and that the record was kept in the course of a regularly conducted business activity as a matter of regular practice.

A. *Coercive Means of Obtaining Evidence*

The United States uses at least nine different methods of coercion to obtain evidence located abroad, to obtain testimony from witnesses located abroad, and to secure the transfer of private assets to the United States: (1) compelling testimony of U.S. nationals or residents located abroad through subpoenas issued by federal courts and notwithstanding potential violations of the laws of other countries, especially civil law countries; (2) compelling production of documents located abroad when a U.S. court has personal jurisdiction over the alleged wrongdoer; the documents or other tangible evidence are in the possession, custody, or control of the alleged wrongdoer or a related entity; and the production of the evidence is not protected by an evidentiary privilege[2]; (3) compelling the production of documents located abroad from a third party that is not a target of the investigation or a defendant in the prosecution, including documents of foreign banks or corporations or of foreign branches of U.S. banks or corporations with which the target or defendant conducted business[3]; (4) compelling through a subpoena testimony from a foreign witness in the United States, including persons leaving the United States[4]; (5) compelling the production of documents from foreign entities by a subpoena *duces tecum* of an officer or custodian over whom the United States has personal jurisdiction[5]; (6) compelling "consents" to disclose third-party records as a means to overcome bank secrecy; (7) compelling targets of U.S. criminal investigations and defendants not to seek action abroad to block prosecutors' efforts to obtain evidence[6]; (8) compelling repatriation of assets to pay a fine or taxes or for purposes of forfeiture; and (9) imposing a tax levy on a bank in the United States for funds of a taxpayer located in a foreign branch.[7]

The person whose testimony or assistance is sought often challenges the use of coercive methods to obtain evidence abroad, as do foreign courts. These challenges raise

[2] Most decisions have upheld such coercive measures when used against a U.S. entity and have rejected the argument that ordering a foreign entity to produce the documents would violate the laws of the country in which the documents are located. *In re Marc Rich & Co.*, 707 F.2d 663 (2d Cir.), *cert. denied*, 463 U.S. 1215 (1983); *United States v. Vetco, Inc.*, 691 F.2d 1281 (9th Cir.), *cert. denied*, 454 U.S. 1098, 102 S Ct. 671, 70 L.Ed. 2d 639 (1981).

[3] *See, e.g., In re Sealed Case*, 825 F.2d 494 (D.C. Cir. 1987); *In re Grand Jury Proceedings of Nova Scotia*, 740 F.2d 817 (11th Cir.), *cert. denied*, 469 U.S. 1006 (1984).

[4] *United States v. Field*, 532 F.2d 404 (5th Cir.), *cert. denied*, 429 U.S. 940 (1976); *In re Grand Jury Proceedings (Bowe)*, 694 F2d 1256 (11th Cir. 1982); *see also In re Sealed Case*, 825 F.2d 494 (D.C. Cir. 1987).

[5] *In re Sealed Case*, 832 F.2d 1268 (D.C. Cir. 1987); *In re Grand Jury Proceedings (Bowe)*, 694 F.2d 1256 (11th Cir. 1982).

[6] *United States v. Davis*, 767 F.2d 1025 (2d Cir. 1985); *see also Garpeg, Ltd. V. United States*, 583 F. Supp. 789 (S.D.N.Y. 1984)

[7] *Doe v. United States*, 487 U.S. 201 (1988).

a host of legal issues, including constitutional questions – including the right against self-incrimination, due process, improper search and seizures – and questions of jurisdiction, conflicts of law, and foreign sovereign compulsion. The more difficult coercive techniques often involve third parties abroad and subpoenas directing witness testimony from foreign persons or the production of documents from foreign entities. The coercive techniques often work when federal courts serve them on persons in the United States over whom the court has established jurisdiction, especially if documents or other tangible evidence is believed to be within their possession, custody, or control – even if located abroad.

In re Grand Jury Proceedings v. Bank of Nova Scotia, 691 F. 2d 1384 (11th Cir. 1982)

Morgan, J.

The Bank of Nova Scotia appeals from an order of the United States District Court for the Southern District of Florida holding the Bank of Nova Scotia in civil contempt for failing to comply with an order of the court enforcing a grand jury subpoena *duces tecum*. The Bank of Nova Scotia (the Bank) presents three arguments against enforcing the subpoena. The Bank first contends that there were insufficient grounds to enforce the subpoena. The Bank also contends that enforcing the subpoena would violate due process. Finally, the Bank argues that the subpoena should not be enforced as a matter of comity between nations. We find the Bank's contentions to be without merit, and therefore we affirm the district court....

The Bank of Nova Scotia is a Canadian chartered bank with branches and agencies in forty-five countries, including the United States and the Bahamas. A federal grand jury conducting a tax and narcotics investigation issued a subpoena *duces tecum* to the Bank calling for the production of certain records maintained at the Bank's main branch or any of its branch offices in Nassau, Bahamas, and Antigua, Lesser Antilles, relating to the bank accounts of a customer of the Bank. The subpoena was served on the Bank's Miami, Florida, agency on September 23, 1981. The Bank declined to produce the documents asserting that compliance with the subpoena without the customer's consent or an order of the Bahamian courts would violate Bahamian bank secrecy laws. F24 (omitted).

A hearing was held on the government's motion to compel the Bank to comply with the subpoena on January 13, 1982. At the hearing conflicting evidence was presented as to the degree of control the Miami agency held over documents held at the Nassau branch. The government presented evidence that all bank transactions for accounts in the Bahamian branch could be handled by the Miami agency. The Bank presented evidence that the Miami agency is a one-way conduit for customer communication with the Nassau branch. The Bank also presented an affidavit showing that compliance with the subpoena could expose the Bank to prosecution under the Bahamian bank secrecy law. The affidavit also showed the government could obtain an order of judicial assistance from the Supreme Court of the Bahamas allowing disclosure if the subject of the grand jury investigation is a crime under Bahamian law and not solely criminal under United States tax laws. The government did not make a showing that the documents sought are relevant and necessary to the grand jury's investigation.

After the district court entered an order compelling the Bank to comply with the subpoena, the Bank's Miami agent appeared before the grand jury and formally declined to produce the documents called for by the subpoena. The district court held the Bank in civil contempt and the Bank brings this appeal.

II. Relevance of the Documents

The Bank urges this court to follow the Third Court's holdings in *In re Grand Jury Proceedings*, 486 F.2d 85 (*Schofield I*), (3rd Cir. 1973), and *In re Grand Jury Proceedings*, 507 F.2d 963 (*Schofield II*), (3rd Cir. 1975), *cert. denied*, 421 U.S. 1015 (1975), and require the government to show that the documents sought are relevant to an investigation properly within the grand jury's jurisdiction and not sought primarily for another purpose. The government does not dispute that the district court enforced the subpoena without making a finding that the documents were relevant or necessary for the grand jury's investigation. Rather, the government argues this case is controlled by *In re Grand Jury Proceedings, United States v. McLean*, 565 F.2d 318 (5th Cir. 1977), and *In re Grand Jury Proceedings, United States v. Guerrero*, 567 F.2d 281 (5th Cir. 1978), where the Fifth Circuit declined to follow the Schofield rule absent some showing of harassment or prosecutorial misuse of the system. The bank argues that the Schofield rule, however, should be applied to cases such as this where foreign relations are implicated and where alternative methods are available to obtain the requested information that do not require the Bank to violate foreign law.

The guidelines established by the Third Circuit in *Schofield* are not mandated by the Constitution; the Third Circuit imposed the requirements under the court's inherent supervisory power. *Schofield*, 486 F.2d at 89; *McLean*, 565 F.2d at 320. We decline to impose any undue restrictions upon the grand jury investigative process pursuant to this court's supervisory power.

It is unnecessary to repeat here the vital role the grand jury plays in our system of jurisprudence. See, *In re Grand Jury Proceedings, United States v. Field*, 532 F.2d 404, 407–409 (5th Cir. 1976), *cert. denied*, 429 U.S. 940 (1976). As stated by the court in *McLean*: Any holding that would saddle a grand jury with mini-trials and preliminary showings would assuredly impede its investigation and frustrate the public's interest in the fair and expeditious administration of the criminal laws. *United States v. Dionisio*, 410 U.S. 1, 17 (1973); *In re Grand Jury Proceedings, United States v. McLean*, 565 F.2d at 320.

While it is true courts should not impinge upon the political prerogatives of the government in the sensitive area of foreign relations, *Chicago and Southern Air Lines v. Waterman Steamship Corp.*, 333 U.S. 103 111 (1948), accepting the Bank's position would be a greater interference with foreign relations than the procedures employed here. In essence, the Bank would require the government to choose between impeding the grand jury's investigation and petitioning the Supreme Court of the Bahamas for an order of disclosure.

The court is cognizant that international friction has been provoked by enforcement of subpoenas such as the one in question. See, Restatement (Revised) of Foreign Relations Law of the United States Section 420, Reporter's Note 1. See generally, *Rio Tinto Zinc Corp. v. Westinghouse Electric Corp.*, [1978] A.C. 547, 616, 629–31, 639–40, 650 (H.L.) (Criticizing the United States for claims of "jurisdiction over foreigners in respect to acts done outside the jurisdiction of that country"). But as recognized in *United States v. First National City Bank*, 379 U.S. 378, 384–85 (1965), the various federal courts remain open to the legislative and executive branches of our government if matters such as this prove to have international repercussions. See, e.g., Convention on Double Taxation of Income, September 27, 1951. United States-Switzerland, 2 U.S.T. 1751, T.I.A.S. No. 2316 (Swiss-U.S. Tax Treaty providing for exchange of information for, *inter alia*, the prevention of fraud).

III. Due Process

The Bank contends that compliance with the subpoena would require it to violate the Bahamian bank secrecy law and therefore enforcing the subpoena and imposing contempt sanctions for noncompliance violates due process under *Societe Internationale Pour Participations Industrielles v. Rogers*, 357 U.S. 197 (1958). The Bank argues that once it has shown Bahamian law bars production of the documents and that it is a disinterested custodian of the documents due process prohibits enforcement of the subpoena. We disagree.

The Bank attempts to fashion a due process defense to the contempt proceedings because of its lack of purposeful involvement or responsibility in the subject matter before the court. In essence, the Bank asserts it is fundamentally unfair to require a "mere stakeholder" to incur criminal liability in the Bahamas. The Bank's position does not withstand analysis.

In *Societe Internationale* a Swiss holding company brought an action to recover assets seized under the Trading with the Enemy Act. The district court had ordered production of certain banking records of a Swiss bank pursuant to the government's discovery request. The holding company failed to comply with the court's order, after good faith efforts were made to comply, on the grounds that compliance would violate Swiss penal laws. The district court then dismissed the suit with prejudice due to noncompliance with the production order. In reversing the district court, the Supreme Court did not erect an absolute bar to sanctions being imposed for noncompliance with summons or subpoenas whenever compliance is prohibited by foreign law. *Societe Internationale*, 357 U.S. at 105–106; *United States v. Vetco, Inc.*, 644 F.2d 1324, 1329 (9th Cir. 1981), *cert. denied*, 454 U.S. 1098 (1981). *Societe Internationale* held only that sanction of outright dismissal of that plaintiff's complaint could not be imposed where that plaintiff had acted in good faith, was unable to comply because of foreign law, and was entitled to a hearing on the merits in order for the Trading with the Enemy Act to withstand constitutional challenge. *Societe International*, 352 U.S. at 211–12. Compare, *National Hockey League v. Metropolitan Hockey Club, Inc.*, 427 U.S. 639 (1976), and *Roadway Express, Inc. v. Piper*, 447 U.S. 752, 767 n. 14 (1980) (emphasizing bad faith vs. inability to comply dichotomy). See *United States v. Vetco*, 644 F.2d at 1329–30. The Court left the district court free to impose other sanctions. *Societe International*, 357 U.S. at 213. *Societe Internationale* does not stand for the proposition that a lawfully issued grand jury subpoena may be resisted on constitutional grounds where compliance would violate foreign criminal law. See, e.g., *United States v. Vetco, Inc.*, 644 F.2d at 1329; *Ohio v. Arthur Andersen & Co.*, 570 F.2d 1370 (10th Cir. 1978), *cert. denied*, 439 U.S. 833 (1979); *SEC v. Banca Della Suizzera Italiance*, 92 F.R.D. 111 (S.D.N.Y. 1981).

The Bank has failed to bring itself within the holding of *Societe Internationale*. The district court found the Bank had not made a good faith effort to comply with the subpoena in its order of June 11, 1982. Record at 140. The Bahamian government has not acted to prevent the Bank from complying with the subpoena. Finally, the Bank is not being denied a constitutionally required forum to recover confiscated assets.

IV. Comity

The Bank's final contention is that comity between nations precludes enforcement of the subpoena. The Bank argues that the district court improperly analyzed this case under the balancing test of the Restatement (Second) of Foreign Relations Law of the United States, Section 40 (1965) adopted in *In re Grand Jury Proceedings, United States v. Field*, 532 F.2d 404

(5th Cir. 1976), *cert. denied*, 429 U.S. 940 (1986). The district court concluded that because compliance with the subpoena may cause the Bank to violate Bahamian penal laws, it was appropriate to follow the balancing test adopted in *Field*. Because we conclude this case is controlled by *Field*, we affirm the court below.

In *Field*, contempt penalties were upheld against a nonresident alien who, having been subpoenaed to testify before a grand jury while present in the United States, refused to answer questions before the grand jury, despite the witness's assertion that the very act of testifying would subject him to criminal penalties in his country of residence. *Id.* at 405. The grand jury was investigating the use of foreign banks in evading tax enforcement. Field was an officer of a bank located in the Grand Cayman Islands, British West Indies, and was subpoenaed to testify about matters concerning his bank and its clients. *Id.* at 405–506. After balancing the competing interests of the United States and the Cayman Islands under the Restatement approach, the court affirmed the district court's imposition of contempt sanctions against Field. *Id.* at 407–09.

The situation before us is similar to that in *Field* in all material respects. The Bank has been subpoenaed while subject to the jurisdiction of our courts and has been required to disclose information before a grand jury even though the very fact of disclosure may subject the Bank to criminal sanctions by a foreign sovereign.

The Bank attempts to distinguish *Field* from the case before us on four grounds. The Bank first asserts that the Bank itself is not under investigation by the grand jury, unlike the situation in *Field*. See *United States v. Payner*, 447 U.S. 727 (1980) (Castle Bank and Trust Company of Nassau, Bahamas, under investigation in 1972 as part of narcotics investigation known as "Operation Trade Winds"). A careful reading of *Field* reveals that the fact that Castle Bank and Trust Company was under investigation did not affect the court's analysis. That court was concerned with the proliferation of foreign secret bank accounts utilized by Americans to evade income taxes and conceal crimes. *In re Grand Jury Proceedings, United States v. Field*, 533 F.2d at 407–08. The instant subpoena calls for the production of certain records relating to bank accounts of a United States citizen pursuant to a tax and narcotics investigation.

Second, the Bank argues this case is distinguishable from *Field* because documentary evidence is requested here rather than testimonial evidence as in *Field*. The distinction, while real, is immaterial. The case before us concerns the relations among nations; whether the subpoena will be enforced is a matter of international comity. *Id.* at 407. Comity is "a nation's expression of understanding which demonstrates due regard both to international duty and convenience and to the rights of persons protected by its own laws." *Somportex Limited v. Philadelphia Chewing Gum Corp.*, 453 F.2d 435 (3rd Cir. 1971), *cert. denied*, 405 U.S. 1017 (1972). Whether the requested information is testimonial or documentary, the effect on the competing state interests will be the same. The deference accorded the Bahamian interest is not to be diminished by the form of the requested information.

Third, the bank argues this case is distinguishable from *Field* because the instant subpoena calls for information located in the Bahamas instead of the United States. This argument is without merit for two reasons. First, the disclosure to the grand jury will occur in this country. See *United States v. Vetco, Inc.*, 644 F.2d at 1332. Second, the affront to the Bahamas occurs no matter where the information is originally located; the interest of the Bahamas in preserving the secrecy of these records is impinged by the fact of disclosure itself.

Finally, the Bank contends the government "could avoid rather than provoke disrespect for the sovereignty of a friendly nation" by pursuing the alternative of applying for an order of judicial assistance permitting disclosure from the Supreme Court of the Bahamas. Brief of Appellant at 18. See *United States v. Vetco, Inc.*, 644 F.2d at 1332; *United States v. First National City Bank*, 396 F.2d 897 (2d Cir. 1968); Restatement (Revised) of Foreign Relations Law of the United States Section 420 (Tent. Draft No. 3, 1982). Applying for judicial assistance, however, is not a substantially equivalent means for obtaining production because of the cost in time and money and uncertain likelihood of success in obtaining the order. According to the affidavit from a member of the Honorable Society of Lincoln's Inn, England, and of the Bahamas Bar, the Supreme Court of the Bahamas does not have the power to order disclosure if the subject of the investigation is criminally only under the tax laws of the United States. Therefore, it is not clear to any degree of certainty that the Bahamian court would order disclosure of all the requested documents.

The judicial assistance procedure does not afford due deference to the United States' interests. In essence, the Bank asks the court to require our government to ask the courts of the Bahamas to be allowed to do something lawful under United States law. We conclude such a procedure to be contrary to the interests of our nation and outweigh the interests of the Bahamas.

In *Field* the vital role of a grand jury's investigative function to our system of jurisprudence and the crucial importance of the collection of revenue to the "financial integrity of the republic" outweighed the Cayman Islands' interest in protecting the right of privacy incorporated into its bank secrecy laws. *In re Grand Jury Proceedings, United States v. Field*, 532 F.2d at 407–08. The United Sates' interest in the case before us has not been diminished since *Field* was decided. The Bank asserts the Bahamas' interest in the right of privacy; this interest is similarly outweighed. A Bahamian court would be able to order production of these documents. Banks and Trust Companies Regulation Act, 1965 Bah. Acts No. 64, § 10(1)(a–e). It is incongruous to suggest that a United States court afford greater protection to the customer's right of privacy than would a Bahamian court simply because this is a foreign tribunal. *In re Grand Jury Proceedings, United States v. Field*, 535 F.2d at 408. A statute that is "hardly a blanket guarantee of privacy" does not present a Bahamian interest sufficient to outweigh the United States' interest in collecting revenues and insuring an unimpeded and efficacious grand jury process. See *United States v. Payner*, 447 U.S. 727, 731 (1980) (predecessor statute identical in relevant parts held not to create a reasonable expectation of privacy) . . .

V. Conclusion

Absent direction from the Legislative and Executive branches of our federal government, we are not willing to emasculate the grand jury process whenever a foreign nation attempts to block our criminal justice process. It is unfortunate the Bank of Nova Scotia suffers from differing legal commands of separate sovereigns, but as we stated in *Field*: In a world where commercial transactions are international in scope, conflicts are inevitable. Courts and legislatures should take every reasonable precaution to avoid placing individuals in the situation [the bank] finds [it]self. Yet, this court simply cannot acquiesce in the proposition that United States criminal investigations must be thwarted whenever there is conflict with the interest of other states. *In re Grand Jury Proceedings, United States v. Field*, 535 F.2d at 410.

For the reasons stated above, the judgment entered by the district court is AFFIRMED.

Notes and Questions

1. The United States is the only country that allows discovery not only of relevant material but also of information that cannot be admitted at trial but is reasonably calculated to lead to the discovery of admissible evidence. Not surprisingly, foreign governments, courts, and lawyers criticize such sweeping discovery as unwarranted "fishing expeditions." Foreign practitioners are especially critical of the wide breadth of U.S. discovery combined with compulsory techniques, such as subpoenas and harsh contempt sanctions for noncompliance.

2. In April 1985, the Department of Justice (DOJ) began requiring federal prosecutors planning to seek subpoenas for bank, business, or commercial records reasonably believed to be in a foreign country to first obtain the agreement of the Office of International Affairs (OIA) of the Criminal Division. DOJ also set forth the criteria for authorizing such subpoenas: (a) the availability of alternative methods for obtaining the records in a timely manner, such as mutual assistance treaties, tax treaties, or letters rogatory; (b) the indispensability of the records to the success of the investigation or prosecution; and (c) the need to protect against the destruction of records located abroad and to protect the ability to prosecute for contempt or obstruction of justice for such destruction. In addition, prosecutors must consult with the Office of International Affairs before bringing proceedings relating to the enforcement of subpoenas for records located abroad. They must also obtain OIA's consent before serving a subpoena *ad testificandum* on an officer or attorney of a foreign bank or corporation who is temporarily in or passing through the United States when the testimony sought relates to the officer's or attorney's duties at the bank or corporation.

3. In *United States v. First National Bank of Chicago*, 699 F.2d 341 (7th Cir. 1983), the IRS issued a summons for bank records situated in First National Bank of Chicago's Athens, Greece, branch. The appellate court decided that First Chicago had adequately shown that compliance could subject its employees to substantial criminal penalties under Greek law and that a balancing of relevant competing interests weighed against compelling disclosure. It reversed the judgment of the district court, but remanded for consideration of an order requiring First Chicago to make a good faith effort to secure permission to make the information available. The appellate court upheld First Chicago's refusal to comply with the summons on the basis that the Greek Bank Secrecy Act provided for criminal penalties, including a prison sentence, for violations of the Greek law. The appellate court also applied a balancing test under the Restatement (2d), § 40, finding that the critical act of initially conveying the information would occur in Greece and that it was highly probable that Greek nationals would make the initial disclosure. Additionally, the court found that the extent and nature of the hardship that inconsistent enforcement would impose were important. In this case, although the U.S. interest in collecting taxes was important to U.S. financial integrity, Greece's interest in its bank secrecy laws outweighed the U.S. interest. This contrasts with a different circuit's view of Bahamian law in *In re Grand Jury Proceedings*, 691 F.2d 1384 (11th Cir. 1982).

4. *The First National Bank of Chicago* case is one of the few criminal or administrative cases in which a U.S. court deferred to foreign interests and declined to impose sanctions for noncompliance with a summons. In that regard, Judge Wilkey observed in *Laker Airways v. Sabena, Belgian World Airlines*, 731 F.2d 909 950–51 (D.C. Cir. 1984),

"A pragmatic assessment of those decisions adopting the interest balancing approach indicates none where United States jurisdiction was declined when there was more than a *de minimus* United States interest." *See* also Berta Esperanza Hernandez, *RIP to IRP – Money Laundering and Drug Trafficking Controls Score a Knockout Victory over Bank Secrecy*, 18 N.C. J. INT'L L. & COMM. REG. 235 (1993).

5. Are the holdings of *The First National Bank of Chicago* case and the *Bank of Nova Scotia* case consistent? Are the facts of the cases distinguishable?

6. When a person receives a summons or subpoena that conflicts with foreign law, the recipient can challenge it in two ways. The recipient can refuse to comply and challenge the summons at the enforcement state or can seek a court order to quash or modify the summons or subpoena on the grounds that compliance would be unreasonable or oppressive. *See* FED. R. CRIM. PROCED. 17(c). What is the best way to challenge a summons or subpoena? Does it depend on the facts? What are the pros and cons of the two approaches?

7. In *In re Grand Jury Proceedings* presented earlier, the Bahamian government did not intervene in the case. Do you think that its nonintervention influenced the court in determining that the United States had a greater interest in the case? In contrast, the Swiss government intervened in the lower court proceedings of *United States v. UBS AG*, U.S. District Court for the S.D. Florida, No. 1:09-cv-20423, *Amicus* Brief of Government of Switzerland. In its opposition to enforcement of the John Doe Summons, UBS emphasized that the Bahamian government did not participate in *In re Grand Jury Proceedings* (*United States v. Bank of Nova Scotia*), 691 F.2d 1384 (11th Cir. 1984) ("Nova Scotia I"), *cert. denied*, 462 U.S. 1119 (1983) and its interest in the outcome was not clear. 691 F.2d 1389. In the related decision, *In re Grand Jury Proceedings* (*United States v. Bank of Nova Scotia*), 722 F.2d 657 (11th Cir. 1984) ("Nova Scotia II") *cert. denied*, 469 U.S. 1106 (1985), the Cayman government did not object to providing the information sought and ultimately authorized its release. The nonobjection – even "affirmative cooperation" – of the Cayman Attorney General was also a "significant" factor in *United States v. Davis*, 767 F.2d 1025, 1035 (2d Cir. 1985). In other cases the Swiss government did not oppose the summons. *United States v. Vetco Inc.*, 691 F.2d 1281, 1289 (9th Cir. 1981); *see also SEC v. Banca Della Svizzera Italiana*, 92 F.R.D. 111, 117–18 (S.D.N.Y. 1981). How important in terms of balancing the interests of governments should be either intervention or diplomatic demarche of a foreign government expressing its interest in the case?

B. *Compelled Consent*

Another mechanism whereby prosecutors obtain evidence abroad required for the adjudication of criminal cases is to compel litigants to consent to have foreign banks or holders of such information release it to the U.S. courts or prosecutors making request for the same.

Doe v. United States, 487 U.S. 201 (1988)

JUSTICE BLACKMUN delivered the opinion of the Court.

This case presents the question whether a court order compelling a target of a grand jury investigation to authorize foreign banks to disclose records of his accounts, without identifying those documents or acknowledging their existence, violates the target's Fifth Amendment privilege against self-incrimination.

Petitioner, named here as John Doe, is the target of a federal grand jury investigation into possible federal offenses arising from suspected fraudulent manipulation of oil cargoes and receipt of unreported income. Doe appeared before the grand jury pursuant to a subpoena that directed him to produce records of transactions in accounts at three named banks in the Cayman Islands and Bermuda. Doe produced some bank records and testified that no additional records responsive [487 U.S. 201, 203] to the subpoena were in his possession or control. When questioned about the existence or location of additional records, Doe invoked the Fifth Amendment privilege against self-incrimination.

The United States branches of the three foreign banks also were served with subpoenas commanding them to produce records of accounts over which Doe had signatory authority. Citing their governments' bank-secrecy laws, which prohibit the disclosure of account records without the customer's consent, (1) the banks refused to comply. *See* App. to Pet. for Cert. 17a, n. 2. The Government then filed a motion with the United States District Court for the Southern District of Texas that the court order Doe to sign 12 forms consenting to disclosure of any bank records respectively relating to 12 foreign bank accounts over which the Government knew or suspected that Doe had control. The forms indicated the account numbers and described the documents that the Government wished the banks to produce.

The District Court denied the motion, reasoning that by signing the consent forms, Doe would necessarily be admitting [487 U.S. 201, 204] the existence of the accounts. The District Court believed, moreover, that if the banks delivered records pursuant to the consent forms, those forms would constitute "an admission that [Doe] exercised signatory authority over such accounts." Id., at 20a. The court speculated that the Government in a subsequent proceeding then could argue that Doe must have guilty knowledge of the contents of the accounts. Thus, in the court's view, compelling Doe to sign the forms was compelling him "to perform a testimonial act that would entail admission of knowledge of the contents of potentially incriminating documents," id., at 20a, n. 6, and such compulsion was prohibited by the Fifth Amendment. The District Court also noted that Doe had not been indicted, and that his signing of the forms might provide the Government with the incriminating link necessary to obtain an indictment, the kind of "fishing expedition" that the Fifth Amendment was designed to prevent. Id., at 21a.

The Government sought reconsideration. Along with its motion, it submitted to the court a revised proposed consent directive that was substantially the same as that approved by the Eleventh Circuit in *United States v. Ghidoni*, 732 F.2d 814, *cert. denied*, 469 U.S. 932 (1984). The form purported to apply to any and all accounts over which Doe had a right of withdrawal, without acknowledging the existence of any such account. (2) The District Court denied this motion also, reasoning [487 U.S. 201, 205] that compelling execution of the consent directive might lead to the uncovering and linking of Doe to accounts that the grand jury did not know were in existence. The court concluded that execution of the proposed form would "admit signatory authority over the speculative accounts [and] would implicitly authenticate any records of the speculative accounts provided by the banks pursuant to the consent." App. to Pet. for Cert. 13a, n. 7.

The Court of Appeals for the Fifth Circuit reversed in an unpublished *per curiam* opinion, judgt. order reported at 775 F.2d 300 (1985). Relying on its intervening decision in *In re United States Grand Jury Proceedings* (Cid), 767 F.2d 1131 (1985), the court held that Doe could not assert his Fifth Amendment privilege as a basis for refusing to sign the consent directive, because the form "did not have testimonial significance" and therefore its compelled execution would not violate Doe's Fifth Amendment rights. App. to Pet. for Cert. 7a. (3)

On remand, the District Court ordered petitioner to execute the consent directive. He refused. The District Court accordingly found petitioner in civil contempt and ordered [487 U.S. 201, 206] that he be confined until he complied with the order. Id., at 2a. The court stayed imposition of sanction pending appeal and application for writ of certiorari. Id., at 2a–3a.

The Fifth Circuit affirmed the contempt order, again in an unpublished *per curiam*, concluding that its prior ruling constituted the "law of the case" and was dispositive of Doe's appeal. Id., at 3a; judgt. order reported at 812 F.2d 1404 (1987). We granted certiorari, 484 U.S. 813 (1987), to resolve a conflict among the Courts of Appeals as to whether the compelled execution of a consent form directing the disclosure of foreign bank records is inconsistent with the Fifth Amendment. (4) We conclude that a court order compelling the execution of such a directive as is at issue here does not implicate the Amendment.

It is undisputed that the contents of the foreign bank records sought by the Government are not privileged under the Fifth Amendment. *See Braswell v. United States, ante*, at 108–110; *United States v. Doe*, 465 U.S. 605 (1984); *Fisher v. United States*, 425 U.S. 391 (1976). There also is no question that the foreign banks cannot invoke the Fifth Amendment in declining to produce the documents; the privilege does not extend to such artificial entities. *See Braswell v. United States, ante*, at 102–103; *Bellis v. United States*, 417 U.S. 85, 89–90 (1974). Similarly, petitioner asserts no Fifth Amendment right to prevent the banks from disclosing the account records, for the Constitution "necessarily does not proscribe incriminating statements elicited from another." [487 U.S. 201, 207] *Couch v. United States*, 409 U.S. 322, 328 (1973). Petitioner's sole claim is that his execution of the consent forms directing the banks to release records as to which the banks believe he has the right of withdrawal has independent testimonial significance that will incriminate him, and that the Fifth Amendment prohibits governmental compulsion of that act.

The Self-Incrimination Clause of the Fifth Amendment reads: "No person. shall be compelled in any criminal case to be a witness against himself." This Court has explained that "the privilege protects a person only against being incriminated by his own compelled testimonial communications." *Fisher v. United States*, 425 U.S., at 409, citing *Schmerber v. California*, 384 U.S. 757 (1966); *United States v. Wade*, 388 U.S. 218 (1967); and *Gilbert v. California*, 388 U.S. 263 (1967). The execution of the consent directive at issue in this case obviously would be compelled, and we may assume that its execution would have an incriminating effect. (5) The question on which this case turns is whether the act of executing the form is a "testimonial communication." The parties disagree about both the meaning of "testimonial" and whether the consent directive fits the proposed definitions. . . .

We reject petitioner's argument that this test does not control the determination as to when the privilege applies to oral or written statements. While the Court in Fisher and Doe did not purport to announce a universal test for determining the scope of the privilege, it also did not purport to establish a more narrow boundary applicable to acts alone. To the contrary, the Court applied basic Fifth Amendment principles. An examination of the Court's application of these [487 U.S. 201, 210] principles in other cases indicates the Court's recognition that, in order to be testimonial, an accused's communication must itself, explicitly or implicitly, relate a factual assertion or disclose information. Only then is a person compelled to be a "witness" against himself.

It is consistent with the history of and the policies underlying the Self-Incrimination Clause to hold that the privilege may be asserted only to resist compelled explicit or implicit disclosures of incriminating information. . . .

The consent directive itself is not "testimonial." It is carefully drafted not to make reference to a specific account, but only to speak in the hypothetical. Thus, the form does not acknowledge that an account in a foreign financial institution is in existence or that it is controlled by petitioner. Nor does the form indicate whether documents or any other information relating to petitioner are present at the foreign bank, assuming that such an account does exist. Cf. *United States v. Ghidoni*, 732 F.2d, at 818; *In re Grand Jury Proceedings (Ranauro)*, 814 F.2d 791, 793 (CA1 1987); *In re Grand Jury Subpoena*, 826 F.2d 1166, 1170 (CA2 1987), *cert. pending sub nom. Coe v. United States*, No. 87–517; *In re United States Grand Jury Proceedings (Cid)*, 767 F.2d, at 1132. The form does not even identify the relevant bank. Although the executed form allows the Government access to a potential source of evidence, the directive itself does not point the Government toward hidden accounts or otherwise provide information that will assist the prosecution in uncovering evidence. The Government must locate that evidence "'by the independent labor of its officers,'" *Estelle v. Smith*, 451 U.S. 454, 462 (1981), quoting *Culombe v. Connecticut*, 367 U.S. 568, 582 (1961) (opinion announcing the judgment). As in Fisher, the Government is not relying upon the "'truth-telling'" of Doe's directive to show the existence of, or his control over, foreign bank account records. *See* 425 U.S., at 411, quoting 8 Wigmore 2264, p. 380.

Given the consent directive's phraseology, petitioner's compelled act of executing the form has no testimonial significance either. By signing the form, Doe makes no statement, [487 U.S. 201, 216] explicit or implicit, regarding the existence of a foreign bank account or his control over any such account. Nor would his execution of the form admit the authenticity of any records produced by the bank. Cf., 732 F.2d, at 818–819; *In re Grand Jury Subpoena*, 826 F.2d, at 1170. Not only does the directive express no view on the issue, but because petitioner did not prepare the document, any statement by Doe to the effect that it is authentic would not establish that the records are genuine. Cf. *Fisher*, 425 U.S., at 413. Authentication evidence would have to be provided by bank officials. . . .

Notes and Questions

1. The first prominent case adjudicating the validity of using compelled consent to obtain evidentiary information was *U.S. v. Ghidoni*, 732 F.2d 814 (11th Cir. 1984). *Ghidoni* involved an indictment for tax evasion returned after the Bank of Nova Scotia investigation. Counsel for Ghidoni argued that his Fifth Amendment privilege could be invoked to protect against sanctions resulting from his refusal to sign a consent document that allowed the government to obtain records from the bank's Cayman Islands branch. Before the trial the government served a subpoena for Ghidoni's records on the bank's Miami branch. Ghidoni refused to comply, arguing that signing the consent would be the equivalent of self-incrimination. The court rejected his argument, holding that the act of signing a consent form was not "testimonial" and therefore not incriminating, notwithstanding the fact that the documents released pursuant to the consent might incriminate Ghidoni. The *Doe* case, whose majority opinion is discussed earlier, was the first time the U.S. Supreme Court considered the validity of judicially compelled consents.

2. Though sometimes an effective tool, consent directives have limited application because many foreign courts do not recognize court-ordered consent directives as "voluntary consent" for the purposes of waiving bank secrecy statutes. In this regard, two months after the Eleventh Circuit's decision in *Ghidoni*, the Grand Court of the Cayman Islands ruled that the *Ghidoni* consent did not amount to consent as contemplated by Cayman bank secrecy law. The Grand Court interpreted the consent directive as the foreign court directing the bank to disclose confidential information. *See In re ABC Ltd.*, Cayman Islands Law Reports, July 24, 1984.

3. The efficacy of consent directives depends on the attitude of the government in the country where the desired records are situated. For example, a country's constitutional law may require its courts to ignore compelled consent directives and hence refuse to produce records unless the requesting state has complied with an internal mutual assistance law. *See, e.g., In re Marsoner*, 40 F.3d 959 (9th Cir. 1994) (involving district court efforts to compel a consent directive in a grand jury tax investigation of Austrian bank records. On remand, the lower court determined that the interest of the Austrian government would practically prevent obtaining the records, even if the target consented.).

C. *Constitutional Issues Concerning Admissibility*

When U.S. law enforcement officials conduct cooperative international criminal investigations, defendants and third parties affected by prosecutions and related (e.g., asset forfeiture) proceedings may be able to raise U.S. constitutional or international human rights issues. Such issues may concern whether the protections afforded under the Fourth Amendment or international human rights conventions extend to the search and seizure by U.S. agents of property belonging to nonresident aliens and located in a foreign country. In addition, litigants may be able to raise issues about the validity of the case based on events that may have occurred in the United States and that may thus affect the validity of evidence gathering abroad.

United States v. Verdugo-Urquidez, 494 U.S. 259 (1990)

REHNQUIST, C. J., delivered the opinion of the Court, in which WHITE, O'CONNOR, SCALIA, and KENNEDY, JJ., joined. KENNEDY, J., filed a concurring opinion.... STEVENS, J., filed an opinion concurring.... BRENNAN, J., filed a dissenting opinion, in which MARSHALL, J., joined.... BLACKMUN, J., filed a dissenting opinion....

The question presented by this case is whether the Fourth Amendment applies to the search and seizure by United States agents of property that is owned by a nonresident alien and located in a foreign country. We hold that it does not. [494 U.S. 259, 262]

Respondent Rene Martin Verdugo-Urquidez is a citizen and resident of Mexico. He is believed by the United States Drug Enforcement Agency (DEA) to be one of the leaders of a large and violent organization in Mexico that smuggles narcotics into the United States. Based on a complaint charging respondent with various narcotics-related offenses, the Government obtained a warrant for his arrest on August 3, 1985. In January 1986, Mexican police officers, after discussions with United States marshals, apprehended Verdugo-Urquidez in Mexico and transported him to the United States Border Patrol station in Calexico, California. There, United States marshals arrested respondent and eventually moved him to a correctional center in San Diego, California, where he remains incarcerated pending trial.

Following respondent's arrest, Terry Bowen, a DEA agent assigned to the Calexico DEA office, decided to arrange for searches of Verdugo-Urquidez's Mexican residences located in Mexicali and San Felipe. Bowen believed that the searches would reveal evidence related to respondent's alleged narcotics trafficking activities and his involvement in the kidnapping and torture-murder of DEA Special Agent Enrique Camarena Salazar (for which respondent subsequently has been convicted in a separate prosecution. *See United States v. Verdugo-Urquidez*, No. CR – 87–422 – ER (CD Cal., Nov. 22, 1988)). Bowen telephoned Walter White, the Assistant Special Agent in charge of the DEA office in Mexico City, and asked him to seek authorization for the search from the Director General of the Mexican Federal Judicial Police (MFJP). After several attempts to reach high-ranking Mexican officials, White eventually contacted the Director General, who authorized the searches and promised the cooperation of Mexican authorities. Thereafter, DEA agents working in concert with officers of the MFJP searched respondent's properties in Mexicali and San Felipe and seized certain documents. In particular, the search of the Mexicali residence uncovered a tally sheet, which the Government [494 U.S. 259, 263] believes reflects the quantities of marijuana smuggled by Verdugo-Urquidez into the United States.

The District Court granted respondent's motion to suppress evidence seized during the searches, concluding that the Fourth Amendment applied to the searches and that the DEA agents had failed to justify searching respondent's premises without a warrant. A divided panel of the Court of Appeals for the Ninth Circuit affirmed. 856 F.2d 1214 (1988). It cited this Court's decision in *Reid v. Covert*, 354 U.S. 1 (1957), which held that American citizens tried by United States military authorities in a foreign country were entitled to the protections of the Fifth and Sixth Amendments, and concluded that "[t]he Constitution imposes substantive constraints on the federal government, even when it operates abroad." 856 F.2d, at 1218. Relying on our decision in *INS v. Lopez-Mendoza*, 468 U.S. 1032 (1984), where a majority of Justices assumed that illegal aliens in the United States have Fourth Amendment rights, the Ninth Circuit majority found it "difficult to conclude that Verdugo-Urquidez lacks these same protections." 856 F.2d, at 1223. It also observed that persons in respondent's position enjoy certain trial-related rights, and reasoned that "[i]t would be odd indeed to acknowledge that Verdugo-Urquidez is entitled to due process under the fifth amendment, and to a fair trial under the sixth amendment, and deny him the protection from unreasonable searches and seizures afforded under the fourth amendment." Id., at 1224. Having concluded that the Fourth Amendment applied to the searches of respondent's properties, the court went on to decide that the searches violated the Constitution because the DEA agents failed to procure a search warrant. Although recognizing that "an American search warrant would be of no legal validity in Mexico," the majority deemed it sufficient that a warrant would have "substantial constitutional value in this country," because it would reflect a magistrate's determination [494 U.S. 259, 264] that there existed probable cause to search and would define the scope of the search. Id., at 1230. . . .

The Fourth Amendment provides: [494 U.S. 259, 265]

"The right of the people to be secure in their persons, houses, papers, and effects, against unreasonable searches and seizures, shall not be violated, and no Warrants shall issue, but upon probable cause, supported by Oath or affirmation, and particularly describing the place to be searched, and the persons or things to be seized." . . .

The available historical data show, therefore, that the purpose of the Fourth Amendment was to protect the people of the United States against arbitrary action by their own Government; it was never suggested that the provision was intended to restrain the actions of the Federal Government against aliens outside of the United States territory. [494 U.S. 259, 267]

There is likewise no indication that the Fourth Amendment was understood by contemporaries of the Framers to apply to activities of the United States directed against aliens in foreign territory or in international waters. . . .

We think that the text of the Fourth Amendment, its history, and our cases discussing the application of the Constitution to aliens and extraterritorially require rejection of respondent's claim. At the time of the search, he was a citizen and resident of Mexico with no voluntary attachment to the [494 U.S. 259, 275] United States, and the place searched was located in Mexico. Under these circumstances, the Fourth Amendment has no application . . .

The judgment of the Court of Appeals is accordingly *Reversed*.

Justice STEVENS, concurring in judgment.

In my opinion aliens who are lawfully present in the United States are among those "people" who are entitled to the protection of the Bill of Rights, including the Fourth Amendment. Respondent is surely such a person even though he was brought and held here against his will. I therefore cannot join the Court's sweeping opinion. (*) I do agree, however, with the Government's submission that the search conducted by the United States agents with the approval and cooperation of the Mexican authorities was not "unreasonable" as that term is used in the first clause of the Amendment. I do not believe the Warrant Clause has any application to searches of noncitizens' homes in foreign jurisdictions because American magistrates have no power to authorize such searches. I therefore concur in the Court's judgment.

Justice BRENNAN, with whom Justice MARSHALL joins, dissenting.

The Court today creates an antilogy: the Constitution authorizes our Government to enforce our criminal laws abroad, but when Government agents exercise this authority, the Fourth Amendment does not travel with them. This cannot be. At the very least, the Fourth Amendment is an unavoidable correlative of the Government's power to enforce the criminal law. . . .

What the majority ignores, however, is the most obvious connection between Verdugo-Urquidez and the United States: he was investigated and is being prosecuted for violations of United States law and may well spend the rest of his life in a United States prison. The "sufficient connection" is supplied not by Verdugo-Urquidez, but by the Government. [494 U.S. 259, 284] Respondent is entitled to the protections of the Fourth Amendment because our Government, by investigating him and attempting to hold him accountable under United States criminal laws, has treated him as a member of our community for purposes of enforcing our laws. He has become, quite literally, one of the governed. Fundamental fairness and the ideals underlying our Bill of Rights compel the conclusion that when we impose "societal obligations," *ante*, at 273, such as the obligation to comply with our criminal laws, on foreign nationals, we in turn are obliged to respect certain correlative rights, among them the Fourth Amendment.

By concluding that respondent is not one of "the people" protected by the Fourth Amendment, the majority disregards basic notions of mutuality. If we expect aliens to obey our laws, aliens should be able to expect that we will obey our Constitution when we investigate, prosecute, and punish them. We have recognized this fundamental principle of mutuality since the time of the Framers. James Madison, universally recognized as the primary architect of the Bill of Rights, emphasized the importance of mutuality when he spoke out against the Alien and Sedition Acts less than a decade after the adoption of the Fourth Amendment: . . .

Mutuality also serves to inculcate the values of law and order. By respecting the rights of foreign nationals, we encourage other nations to respect the rights of our citizens. Moreover, as our Nation becomes increasingly concerned about the domestic effects of international crime, we cannot forget that the behavior of our law enforcement agents abroad sends a powerful message about the rule of law to individuals everywhere. As Justice Brandeis warned in *Olmstead v. United States*, 277 U.S. 438 (1928):

"If the Government becomes a lawbreaker, it breeds contempt for law; it invites every man to become a law unto himself; it invites anarchy. To declare that in the administration of the criminal law the end justifies the means . . . would bring terrible retribution. Against that pernicious doctrine, this Court should resolutely set its face." Id., at 485 (dissenting opinion).

Notes and Questions

1. What approach to the definitions of "persons" and "the people" as used in the Constitution seems appropriate? Does it make sense that in an era of globalization the Fourth Amendment protections should be limited to only "the people" of the United States, whereas the due process clause of the Fifth Amendment protects all "persons"?

2. *Self-incrimination and potential foreign prosecutions.* Defendants have occasionally asserted that fear of foreign prosecutions violates protections against self-incrimination. In *United States v. Balsys*, 524 U.S. 666 (1998), the Supreme Court held that a valid Fifth Amendment claim could not be asserted based on this theory. Balsys was a resident alien whom the Department of Justice's Office of Special Investigations (OSI) investigated for misrepresenting his participation in Nazi atrocities in Lithuania during World War II. When OSI pressed to deport Balsys, he refused to respond to its interrogations at a deposition, arguing that his answers could subject him to foreign criminal prosecution by Lithuania, Israel, and Germany. The U.S. Supreme Court held that such concerns were beyond the scope of the Fifth Amendment. Instead, the Court said the clause is limited to fear of prosecution by the same government whose power it limits – U.S. federal and state authorities. However, the Court in dicta said that cooperative conduct between the U.S. and foreign governments might reach a point where fear of foreign prosecution could be "tantamount to a fear of a criminal case brought by the U.S. Government itself." The facts in *Balsys* did not rise to this level.

3. *The "silver platter" doctrine.* When foreign officials obtain evidence for use in criminal proceedings, defendants often argue that the manner in which the evidence was obtained violates arguably applicable constitutional law requirements. U.S. jurisprudence is that "[n]either our Fourth Amendment nor the judicially created exclusionary rule applies to acts of foreign officials." *United States v. Barona*, 56 F.3d 1087, 1091 (9th Cir., 1995). In general, the Fourth Amendment does not apply to actions carried out by foreign officials in their own countries enforcing their own laws, even if U.S. law enforcement officials are present and cooperate to some extent. *United States v. Rosenthal*, 93 F.2d 1214, 1231 (11th Cir. 1986). Hence, if foreign officials obtain evidence through an illegal search in a foreign country, it is admissible in U.S. courts. This "silver platter" doctrine has two exceptions. The defendant or court may invoke the exclusionary rule if (1) the circumstances of the foreign search and seizure are so extreme as to "shock the

conscience" or (2) domestic law enforcement officials have participated in the investigation to such an extent as to convert it into a joint venture between the United States and foreign officials. *See* Note, *The Applicability of the Exclusionary Rule in Federal Court to Evidence Seized and Confessions Obtained in Foreign Countries*, 16 COLUM. J. TRANS. L. 495 (1977); Note, *The New International "Silver Platter" Doctrine: Admissibility in Federal Courts of Evidence Illegally Obtained by Foreign Officers in a Foreign Country*, 2 N.Y.U.J. INT'L L. & POL. 280 (1960).

4. *Joint venture doctrine*. In cases analogous to *U.S. v. Verdugo-Urquidez*, discussed earlier, U.S. courts have held that the exclusionary rule may apply where "American law enforcement officials substantially participated in the search or [where] the foreign officials conducting the search were actually acting as agents for their American counterparts." *United States v. Behety*, 32 F.3d 503, 510 (11th Cir. 1994) (neither DEA agents' communication to Guatemalan authorities regarding arrival of the U.S. vessel in Guatemala to pick up cocaine for export, nor the DEA agents' presence at, and videotaping of, the search of the vessel by Guatemalan officials triggered the exclusionary rule respecting evidence seized during search). *Contra*, *Birdsell v. United States*, 346 F.2d 775, 782 (5th Cir. 1965) (the Fourth Amendment does not apply to an action by a foreign sovereign in its own territory in enforcing its own laws, even though foreign law enforcement officials were present and cooperated to some extent). Some courts scrutinize whether the communication between U.S. and foreign officials leading to the seizure of evidence that is later turned over to U.S. authorities is substantial or adequate to convert the search into a joint venture. *See, e.g.*, *United States v. Hawkins*, 661 F.2d 436 (5th Cir. 1981) (DEA's notification of Panamanian authorities concerning the suspected crash of a plane carrying cocaine was not enough to entitle defendant to Fourth Amendment protections); *United States v. Heller*, 625 F.2d 594, 599–600 (5th Cir. 1980) (tip from U.S. officials to British police concerning defendant was not enough to entitle defendant to Fourth Amendment rights).

5. In *United States v. Usama Bin Laden, et al.*, 132 F. Supp.2d 168 (S.D.N.Y. 2001), Judge Sands denied motions from two defendants charged with participating in the bombings of the U.S. embassies in Kenya and East Africa. The defendants sought to suppress statements made to U.S. authorities while in the custody of Kenyan and South African police. Judge Sands held that statements made to the authorities were subject to the Fifth Amendment right of defendants to not incriminate themselves and that their statements were admissible only upon showing that they were advised of their constitutional rights and knowingly waived them. Judge Sands said Miranda warnings were required, subject to modification to reflect availability of counsel in the foreign country. He found that the advice of rights (AOR) form was defective, for giving the impression that the right to consult with attorney was never available when interrogation occurred in the foreign country. However, Judge Sands found that the defect was cured by oral disclosures that counsel was available. In addition, Judge Sands found that the defendant waived his rights by entering into a document of understanding providing for disclosures in return for trial in the United States. In this connection, the failure to notify the Saudi Arabian consulate that the one defendant was being detained by Kenyan authorities, as required by the Vienna Convention, did not mandate suppression.

6. In *United States v. Neil A. Smith*, 2001 WL 823700 (S.D.N.Y. July 16, 2001), defendant Smith was charged with one count of wire fraud under 218 U.S.C. § 1343; he moved to suppress oral and written statements allegedly made on December 30, 1999, at his

home in Thailand. Smith, age 53, was a U.K. citizen and resident of Thailand who had graduated from high school and received an English-chartered accounting degree after five years of schooling. After filing a complaint against Smith, the U.S. government obtained a provisional arrest warrant from the Thai government. U.S. Secret Service agents accompanied eight Royal Thai Police officers to Smith's residence, where he was orally advised of his Miranda rights by a Secret Service agent and signed a written waiver. Before signing the waiver, Smith asked if he needed a lawyer. Judge Daniels ruled that the requirement to advise a defendant of his Miranda rights "applies with equal force to non-resident aliens interrogated overseas whose only connections to this country are their alleged crimes and subsequent prosecution" (citing *U.S. v. Bin Laden*, 132 F.Supp.2d 168, 185–86 (S.D.N.Y. 2001). However, Judge Daniels explained that a suspect seeking to invoke his Fifth Amendment right to counsel and cause officers to cease their questioning must do so clearly and unambiguously. Judge Daniels observed that Smith was a highly educated and intelligent adult who was advised of his Fifth Amendment rights on three separate occasions. He acknowledged and waived these rights voluntarily even though he was questioned for about nine hours.

7. In *United States v. Bin Laden*, 126 F. Supp.2d 264 (S.D.N.Y. 2000), the court considered a motion to suppress evidence seized during a search of the defendant El-Hage's residence in Nairobi, Kenya, in August 1997, as well as evidence obtained from electronic surveillance of four telephone lines conducted between August 1996 and August 1997. Even though the contested searches occurred in Kenya, the court accepted El-Hage's Fourth Amendment challenge. However, the court found that the searches were proper under the foreign intelligence exception to the warrant requirement for searches targeting foreign powers or their agents conducted abroad. According to the court, the search of El-Hage's residence was proper because the Attorney General's authorization was based on probable cause to suspect that El-Hage was an agent of al Qaeda, a foreign power under the Foreign Intelligence Surveillance Act pursuant to 50 U.S.C. § 1801(a)–(b). The court found that the purpose of the search, "to gather intelligence about al Qaeda, including the status of the Kenyan cell, the points of contact for other al Qaeda cells around the world, as well as any indications of the future terrorist plans of al Qaeda," was proper. It ruled that the incidental interception of El-Hage's conversation during an otherwise lawful surveillance did not violate the Fourth Amendment.

8. *See* Note, *The Extraterritorial Applicability of the Fourth Amendment*, 102 Harv. L. Rev. 162 (1989). The author of the article rejects the *Verdugo-Urquidez* approach and provides an alternative framework for analyzing extraterritorial Fourth Amendment claims. Focusing on who should be entitled to invoke the Fourth Amendment rights defensively in U.S. enforcement proceedings, the note discusses the actual operation of the Fourth Amendment in the foreign context; it proposes a four-part analysis for assessing the constitutionality of foreign searches carried out by U.S. law enforcement officers. By recognizing that standards governing searches abroad necessarily differ from those governing domestic searches, the analysis recommended giving the courts greater flexibility in monitoring international law enforcement. In fact in *United States v. Bin Laden*, 126 F. Supp.2d 264, 276–77, the court observed that acquiring a warrant for overseas searches or surveillance would have been impossible, given the absence of statutory provisions empowering a magistrate to issue a warrant and the unsuitability of traditional warrant procedures for foreign intelligence collection. Additionally, the court noted that the people and agencies upon whom the executive relies for foreign

intelligence collection would be wary of any warrant procedure that did not protect sensitive information.

III. Letters Rogatory

A letter rogatory involves a judicial request to a court in an independent jurisdiction that a witness be examined based on interrogatories sent with the request. Internationally, a letter rogatory is "the medium whereby one country, speaking through one of its courts, requests another country, acting through its own courts and by methods of the requested court procedure and entirely within the latter's control to aid the administration of justice in the former country."[8] Initially based on the comity of courts toward each other, the concept has recently incorporated international conventions and local statutes. A letter rogatory is one of the most frequently used methods of obtaining evidence through compulsory process in the United States 28 U.S.C. § 1782 allows a foreign tribunal to obtain evidence in foreign criminal proceedings. A tribunal can include an investigating magistrate in a civil law country who conducts investigations to determine whether criminal charges should be brought. A foreign tribunal or interested person may initiate a letter rogatory or other request for judicial assistance in a criminal matter. At its discretion a U.S. district court can grant or refuse an order and may impose conditions on such assistance. Usually, if it grants assistance, a U.S. district court will appoint a "commissioner" to supervise the taking of testimony in connection with the request. If the foreign court does not prescribe the procedure to be used in executing the request, § 1782 prescribes the application of the Federal Rules of Civil Procedure. A person who testifies pursuant to a U.S. court order may assert any legally applicable privilege under the laws of the United States or the country in which the relevant proceeding is pending.

U.S. jurisprudence has allowed prosecutors in common law countries to compel the testimony of witnesses in the United States, even when no proceeding is pending before a foreign court, provided that an actual criminal investigation exists in connection with which the testimony is requested, the testimony is requested in order to use it in a proceeding before a court in the requesting state if criminal charges are brought, and criminal proceedings are imminent or very likely.[9]

Recently, the Russian Federation requested the use of letters rogatory to obtain evidence in the United States in a tax case. On November 1, 2000, the U.S. Circuit Court of Appeals for the Ninth Circuit affirmed a district court's dismissal of a motion brought by an anonymous defendant (whose identity is under seal) to dismiss letters rogatory proceedings brought under 28 U.S.C. § 1782 to assist the Russian Federation in connection with an ongoing criminal investigation of alleged tax fraud in the activities of the anonymous defendant.[10] Because the case is under seal and primarily involves an interpretation of § 1782, the court limited the facts to mentioning that the Russian Federation sought U.S. assistance in connection with an ongoing criminal investigation of alleged tax fraud.

[8] *The Signe*, 37 F. Supp. 819, 820 (D.C. La. 1941).

[9] *In Re Request for International Judicial Assistance, Brazil*, 936 F.2d 702, 706 (2d Cir. 1991); *In Re Letter of Request from Crown Prosecution Service*, 870 F.2d 686, 689–92 (D.C. Cir. 1989); *In Re Request for Assistance from Ministry of Legal Affairs of Trinidad and Tobago*, 848 F.2d 1151, 1155–56 (11th Cir. 1988), cert. denied, 488 U.S. 1005 (1989).

[10] *U.S. v. Sealed* 1, 2000 U.S. App. LEXIS 27216 (9th Cir. Nov. 1, 2000).

The appellate court opinion explained that, although the statute was initially enacted in 1948, Congress has continually liberalized its usage by loosening its requirements. For instance, the 1964 amendments substituted the word "tribunal" for "judicial proceedings" to clarify that the law applied to administrative and quasi-judicial proceedings, thereby extending who could request assistance and according district courts broad discretion to act on foreign requests for assistance.[11] In addition, the 1964 statute eliminated a requirement that the foreign proceeding be "pending." Instead, background reports to the legislative history indicate that it was intended only that "the evidence is eventually to be used in such a proceeding."[12]

Notwithstanding the 1964 amendments, other circuit courts have adopted a variety of § 1782 requirements close to the old "pending" requirement. They have concluded that "(t)he determination to grant assistance turns not on whether the proceeding is pending but on whether the requested evidence will likely be of use in a judicial proceeding.... the district judgment should satisfy himself that a proceeding is very likely to occur."[13] Another circuit, denying a Brazilian request, explained, "We think it prudent.... to require that adjudicative proceedings be imminent – very likely to occur and very soon to occur."[14]

In 1996, Congress again amended § 1782, adding "criminal investigations conducted before formal accusation" to the scope of foreign investigations in which the United States is authorized to provide formal assistance. The court said it would not heed the appellant's urging that it read an "imminence" requirement into the current version of § 1782.[15] Instead, the court concluded that neither the plain language of § 1782 nor Ninth Circuit precedent mandated such a requirement.

The appellate court also heard a challenge on the grounds that no ongoing criminal investigation existed to justify a letters rogatory request under § 1782. Here, the appellate court explained that Congress gave the district courts broad discretion in granting judicial assistance to foreign countries, which it could overturn only to avoid an abuse of discretion.[16] The appellate court found no abuse of discretion in the district court's denial of appellant's motion.

The Russian case described earlier indicates the potentially wide-ranging foreign use of letters rogatory, even from countries whose legal and democratic systems are significantly different from those of the United States. In particular, despite limitations of the Russian tax system, which has suffered much public criticism for its due process limitations and susceptibility to corruption, the Ninth Circuit was quite willing to render assistance. In September 2000, the U.S. Senate Foreign Relations Committee recommended, after a hearing, ratification of the proposed U.S.-Russian mutual Assistance in Criminal Matters Treaty, which is now in force (reprinted later in the chapter). As a result, the Russian

[11] *Id.*, at *4, citing, Pub. L. No. 88–619, 78 Stat. 995, 997 § 9 (Oct. 3, 1964); Steven M. Saraisky, *Comment, How to Construe Section 1782: A Textual Prescription to Restore the Judge's Discretion*, 61 U. Chi. L. Rev. 1127, 1131–32 (1994).

[12] Hans Smit, *International Litigation under the United States Code*, 65 Colum. L. Rev. 1015, 1026 (1965).

[13] *In re Request for Assistance from Ministry of Legal Affairs of Trinidad and Tobago*, 848 F.2d 1151, 1155–56 (11th Cir. 1988).

[14] *In re Request for International Judicial Assistance (Letter Rogatory) for the Federative Republic of Brazil*, 936 F.2d 702, 706 (2d Cir. 1991).

[15] *Id.*, at citing *Tang v. Reno*, 77 F.3d 1194, 1996 (9th Cir. 1996).

[16] *U.S. v. Sealed 1*, *supra*, note 10 at 11, citing *In re Request for Assistance from Ministry of Legal Affairs of Trinidad and Tobago*, 848 F.2d 1151, 1154 (11th Cir. 1988).

government and agencies such as its tax authority will be able to easily obtain mutual assistance.[17]

The Ninth Circuit decision in *Sealed 1* is consistent with the U.S. trend toward proactively supporting Russian efforts to improve tax compliance. In this vein, the United States has offered bilateral technical and financial assistance to Russia on tax matters and has participated in multilateral efforts by the International Monetary Fund and World Bank.[18]

28 U.S.C. § 1781 Transmittal of Letter Rogatory or Request

(a) The Department of State has power, directly, or through suitable channels–
  (1) to receive a letter rogatory issued, or request made, by a foreign or international tribunal, to transmit it to the tribunal, officer, or agency in the United States to whom it is addressed, and to receive and return it after execution; and
  (2) to receive a letter rogatory issue, or request made, by a tribunal in the United States, to transmit it to the foreign or international tribunal, officer, or agency to whom it is addressed, and to receive and return it after execution.

28 U.S.C. § 1782 Assistance to Foreign and International Tribunals and to Litigants before Such Tribunals

(a) The district court of the district in which a person resides or is found may order him to give his testimony or statement or to produce a document or other thing for use in a proceeding in a foreign or international tribunal, including criminal investigations conducted before formal accusation. The order may be made pursuant to a letter rogatory issued, or request made, by a foreign or international tribunal or upon the application of any interested person and may direct that the testimony or statement be given, or the document or other thing be produced, before a person appointed by the court. By virtue of his appointment, the person appointed has power to administer any necessary oath and take the testimony or statement. The order may prescribe the practice and procedure, which may be in whole or part the practice and procedure of the foreign country or the international tribunal, for taking the testimony or statement or producing the document or other thing. To the extent that the order does not prescribe otherwise, the testimony or statement shall be taken, and the document or other thing produced, in accordance with the Federal Rules of Civil Procedure.

  A person may not be compelled to give his testimony or statement or to produce a document or other thing in violation of any legally applicable privilege.

(b) This chapter [28 USCS §§ 1781 et seq.] does not preclude a person within the United States from voluntarily giving his testimony or statement, or producing a document or other thing, for use in a proceeding in a foreign or international tribunal before any person and in any manner acceptable to him.

[17] For additional background *see Treaty with Russia on Mutual Legal Assistance in Criminal Matters, Sen. Treaty Doc.* 106–22, 106th Cong., 2d Sess.; Bruce Zagaris, *Senate Foreign Relations Committee Recommends Ratification of Criminal Cooperation Treaties*, 16 Int'l Enforcement L. Rep. 1006 (Nov. 2000).

[18] This discussion of the Ninth Circuit case is from Bruce Zagaris, *U.S. Appellate Court Upholds Letters Rogatory Assistance to Russian Tax Investigation*, 17 Int'l Enforcement L. Rep. 11 (Jan. 2001).

In Re: Letter Rogatory to the Republic of Ireland Misc. No., United States District Court, Eastern District of Michigan Southern Division

International Letter Rogatory

The United States District Court for the Eastern District of Michigan presents its greetings to the judicial authorities in the Republic of Ireland and respectfully requests the assistance of the courts of the Republic of Ireland in connection with a criminal matter. The United States District Court for the Eastern District of Michigan assures the courts of the Republic of Ireland and the appropriate judicial authority designated to execute this request that the courts of the United States are authorized to assist foreign tribunals in the execution of letters rogatory for assistance in criminal matters.

The United States Attorney, who is the federal prosecutor for this District, is investigating charges that Ilene Ruth Moses, a citizen of the United States, Lawrence W. Anderson, a citizen of Canada, and Kenneth Kazerski, a citizen of the United States, violated United States criminal laws by scheming to defraud the Michigan National Bank (MNB) and the Swiss Canto Bank (International) (SCI).

The United States Attorney is informed that evidence relevant to the prosecution of the above-named individuals is located in the Republic of Ireland. He has previously attempted to obtain that evidence through non-judicial diplomatic channels without success. He therefore has requested that this court issue this letter rogatory. The United States Attorney has provided the following factual statement to explain the need for the requested assistance.

U.S. Attorney's Factual Statement

Ilene Ruth Moses was a business woman who ran and owned a company called SMS, Inc. located in Detroit, in the Eastern Judicial District of Michigan. SMS, Inc. purportedly designed and marketed high class women's clothing. In 1983, Ms. Moses also formed and controlled a company called Jolland Company Ltd. (Jolland) of Hong Kong, which was operated primarily in the City of London, United Kingdom. Moses and her colleagues obtained approximately $15 million (US) in business loans from MNB in Michigan between 1983 and 1987 for SMS, Inc. She also obtained another $13.5 million (US) for Jolland, and another company she formed called Ircon AG, from SCI in Zug, Switzerland during June to November, 1987.

Moses and her colleagues were able to obtain the loans because they convinced the lending banks of the validity of alleged business that SMS and Jolland had with an entity called Romtex AG, operated in Zurich, Switzerland but incorporated in Vaduz, Liechtenstein. According to Ms. Moses, Mr. Anderson and Mr. Kazerski, Romtex AG was the conduit into a worldwide textile cartel known as the Romtex Group, which was purportedly made up of European and Asian investors.

Ilene Moses told the banks that she was provided the opportunity to invest with the cartel through the sponsorship of a wealthy benefactor who was a member of the controlling group in the cartel but whose identity had to remain secret. Moses ostensibly supplied the cartel with valuable designs for first class women's fashions via her company, Ircon AG. For this, Ircon AG received from Romtex AG what were purportedly royalty payments amounting to $100,000.00 per month.

Furthermore, Ms. Moses maintained that the Romtex Group included her in profitable business dealings which were carried out through Romtex AG and Jolland. Allegedly, as the Romtex Group marketed Ilene Moses' fashion designs worldwide, it marketed some for Jolland as well. Under the arrangement as described by Ms. Moses, Jolland placed large purchase orders with Romtex AG for the manufacturing and marketing of the designs. Romtex AG, under the control of the Romtex Group, arranged to have the goods manufactured, and then arranged for their sale in Europe and the Orient.

Jolland allegedly realized huge profits on these transactions, which were owed from Romtex AG to Jolland. However, Ms. Moses explained that rather than collect the profits from Romtex AG, she continually reinvested them in new transactions with Romtex. These preferential transactions created very large accounts receivable, owed from Romtex to Jolland. Indeed, nearly all of Jolland's assets consisted of amounts due from Romtex AG. Moses and her associates, Lawrence Anderson and Kenneth Kazerski, created an extensive series of paper transactions to make it appear that this business was real.

Moses was able to obtain her bank loans from SCI and MNB because they were secured by the large amounts allegedly owed from Romtex AG to Jolland, and by the royalty payments owed from Romtex AG to Ircon AG. In addition, Romtex AG pledged promissory notes and its own accounts receivable to secure the Jolland loans. The willingness of MNB and SCI to lend substantial sums to Ms. Moses was the direct result of their belief, induced by her, that Romtex AG was independent of her; conducted real clothing transactions; and had the financial ability to fulfill the obligations that existed on paper between it and Jolland.

However, the United States Attorney has learned that Romtex AG was merely a shell corporation, controlled by Ms. Moses and Lawrence Anderson. The fraud began to unravel when SCI's loans to Jolland became due in the Spring of 1988. Jolland defaulted, and when it did SCI attempted to collect from Romtex AG, inasmuch as Romtex had guaranteed the loans. When Romtex AG failed to live up to its guarantee, SCI began to contact those companies that allegedly owed Romtex AG money for goods that had been delivered, which companies had been identified to SCI by Romtex AG and Jolland. Each of those companies informed SCI that it had no business relationship with Romtex AG or with Jolland, and thus that it owed no money against which SCI could collect.

This revelation caused SCI to contact Swiss law enforcement authorities in the summer of 1988. The Swiss seized all of the records of Romtex AG, and have recently provided those records to the United States Attorney. Those records show that Romtex AG was nominally controlled by one Herman Heller in Switzerland. However, Heller took all of his directions from Lawrence Anderson until April, 1988. Mr. Anderson had been interviewed, and has admitted that he took all of his instruction from Ms. Moses.

The seized records also show that Romtex AG had no contact with any "Romtex Group." The records show that all of the alleged business conducted by Romtex AG was carried on with one of two Hong Kong companies. The first was American Service and Trading Corporation, and the second was Billion Up Enterprises.

The director of Billion Up Enterprises, Kelly Wong, has been interviewed, and has explained that Billion Up was merely a corporate shell that he ran from an office in Hong Kong. Mr. Wong explained that he did so at the request of Kenneth Kazerski, and that he took all of his instructions from Mr. Kazerski or Mr. Anderson. Mr. Wong also explained that he did not manufacture or arrange the manufacture of any clothing, but merely transferred money and messages at the request of Mr. Kazerski or Mr. Anderson. Mr. Wong provided numerous telexes, which demonstrated that he transmitted, under the name of Billion Up, numerous messages that either Mr. Kazerski or Mr. Anderson had instructed him to send to Romtex AG. The majority of these messages purported to concern the manufacture and sale of clothing that was identified in the Jolland purchase orders to Romtex AG.

Mr. Kazerski has been interviewed, and has admitted that he did instruct Mr. Wong in Mr. Wong's contacts with Romtex AG. Mr. Kazerski also admitted that the business described in those messages to Romtex AG did not take place. Finally, Mr. Kazerski admitted that he took all of his directions from Ms. Moses.

In addition, the United States Attorney has obtained various financial records of Romtex AG, Jolland, SMS, Inc., Ms. Moses, and various other Moses companies. Although the analysis of those financial records is not yet complete, the analysis to date shows that all of the money that came into Romtex AG originated with Ms. Moses or one of her companies, usually from one of the loans that Ms. Moses had obtained from one of the banks. Therefore, any money that went from Romtex AG to Jolland or any other Moses company originated with Ms. Moses herself. In short, the investigation of the United States Attorney supports the Swiss conclusion that Romtex was merely a Moses-controlled shell which was used to defraud MNB and SCI.

In early 1988, Lawrence W. Anderson informed Herman Heller and Anthony Surtees, the British agent for Jolland and Ilene Moses, that he was being reassigned by the Romtex Group to Indonesia and that he would be replaced by one A. J. Oldridge with respect to the Moses' business operations. A. J. Oldridge did indeed take on Anderson's apparent role of being the liaison to the Romtex Group from approximately April, 1988 through May of 1989.

In SCI's efforts to collect on the loans, it contacted Herman Heller and Anthony Surtees who, in turn, contacted Lawrence Anderson and subsequently A. J. Oldridge, for assistance and assurances that the Romtex Group would pay the monies owing to SCI. Such assurances from the Group were forthcoming from A. J. Oldridge well into 1988 and into 1989. The communications to and from Oldridge were almost exclusively by means of telefax. A. J. Oldridge maintained an account with the Answering Service Ltd. in London for the time period covering his involvement. Mr. Oldridge sent and received telefaxes through this account. There were also telefaxes to and from MNB during the same time period to this same Answering Service Ltd. under the names of R. Schulz and F. Jeffers, who also purported to be contacts to the Romtex Group. It is suspected that these telefax transmissions were made by A. J. Oldridge or persons known to him. A. J. Oldridge has been identified as Albert Johnson Oldridge, aged 66, a citizen of the United Kingdom, now retired and residing in the Republic of Ireland. To date Mr. Oldridge has refused to discuss the matter with the American prosecutor and the Special Agent of the Federal Bureau of Investigation assigned to this case and has stated that he will not voluntarily appear in the United States to testify. Thus the United States Attorney can only obtain his evidence by deposition.

In the fall of 1989 SMS, Inc. was placed into involuntary bankruptcy. Ilene R. Moses also filed personal bankruptcy. In her schedule of assets signed under penalty of perjury, Ilene Moses reasserted the existence of the accounts receivable purportedly owing from Romtex AG to her company Jolland and SMS.

In the fall of 1992, Ilene Ruth Moses' attorneys voluntarily submitted their client to extensive interviews in Detroit, Michigan, by American and Swiss prosecutors. Ilene Moses admitted no wrongdoing whatever and instead attempted to weave a very complex defense portraying her as the victim of a conspiracy by the Romtex cartel. Moses asserted that the cartel are actually clients of the Union Bank of Switzerland (UBS) with which she had numerous business dealings. During the course of the four days of interviews, Ilene Ruth Moses alleged that a number of Swiss banking officials conspired against her on behalf of the cartel. Two Swiss nationals, Herman Heller and Herbert Wettstein (who was engaged as an auditor of

Romtex AG, are being prosecuted by the Swiss authorities. The Swiss have also issued an arrest warrant for Ilene Moses and their case against her remains open.

The Need for the Evidence Sought

The central issue in this investigation is whether Romtex AG was a fraud perpetrated by Ms. Moses or was a legitimate entity. The United States Attorney seeks evidence from Albert John Oldridge to determine who retained him to succeed Lawrence W. Anderson as the purported liaison to the Romtex Group and who gave him instructions. If Mr. Oldridge identifies Ms. Moses or a person under her control as the person who directed him, this will be very important to convincing a jury that Ms. Moses operated Romtex AG as a fraud. If, on the other hand, Mr. Oldridge identifies somebody else as his contact, that will be important evidence of a defense that should be considered before charges are brought.

The Offenses

There are several violations of United States criminal laws that are being investigated. If Ilene Moses and her associates obtained fraudulent loans from SCI, they committed wire fraud. The pertinent statute provides:

18 U.S.C. § 1343. Fraud by wire, radio, or television.

[Text Omitted]

Also, SCI loan monies were transported to the United States. Therefore, the federal transportation of stolen monies statute was violated. This statute provides in pertinent part:

If Ms. Moses and her colleagues obtained the MNB loans by fraud, they committed bank fraud. The statute provides in pertinent part:

18 U.S.C. § 1344 Bank Fraud

[Text Omitted]

MNB is a bank with deposits insured by the FDC.

It is clear that Ilene Moses obtained these loans premised on the large amount of receivables purportedly owing to Jolland from Romtex AG. If these accounts receivable did not in fact exist, as the Swiss prosecutor has concluded, then Ilene Moses is guilty of bank fraud.

Additionally, since Ilene Moses declared the Romtex accounts receivable as an asset on her involuntary bankruptcy petition, violation of the bankruptcy fraud statute occurred. This statute provides in pertinent part:

18 U.S.C. § 152. Concealment of assets; false oaths and claims; bribery

[Text Omitted]

If the accounts receivable were non-existent then Moses made a false oath and/or declaration on her bankruptcy schedules.

Assistance Required

The United States District Court for the Eastern District of Michigan requests that the appropriate judicial authority designated to execute this international letter rogatory do the following:

1. Order that Albert John Oldridge, who resides in Caheragh, Drimoleague, County Cork, Republic of Ireland, Tel. No. 011–353–28–31158, appear in Dublin at the earliest possible

convenient time in order to be deposed by a Magistrate of the Irish Courts who is to ask the questions on the list attached.

2. Provide at least six weeks advance notice to the United States Attorney of the place and time that the interview is to occur. That notice should be directed to the following:
   George W. Proctor, Esq.
   Director
   Office of International Affairs
   United States Department of Justice
   1400 New York Avenue, N.W.
   Washington, D.C., U.S.A. 20530
   ATTN: BETSY BURKE, SENIOR TRIAL ATTORNEY

With a copy to:
   Saul A. Green
   United States Attorney
   Eastern District of Michigan
   501 Magazine Street
   New Orleans, LA 70130
   ATTN: ROSS I. MACKENZIE, AUSA

3. Require Albert John Oldridge to bring with him to the deposition all records which he possesses or to which he has access pertaining to his relationship with Romtex AG, the Romtex Group, Ilene Ruth Moses, Wayne Carrick, John a/k/a Jack Connor, Paul O'Connor, Lawrence W. Anderson, Jolland Company Ltd., Ircon AG, Metier Service Corporation, Billion-Up Enterprises, Kenneth Kazerski, Douglas Sloan, Anthony C. Surtees, Herman Heller, R. Schulz, F. Jeffers, J. Laker, J. Later, and the law firm of Niklaus & Bruttin in Geneva, Switzerland including, but not limited to:
   a) all correspondence,
   b) telexes or other facsimile transmissions,
   c) notes of meetings and/or telephone conversations,
   d) records of any financial compensation Albert John Oldridge received for any work relating to any of the above named people or entities.

Please accept the assurance of our highest esteem.

Date:______________ ______________________________

THE HONORABLE PAUL V. GADOLA
United States District Judge
Eastern District of Michigan

Questions to Be Asked of Albert John Oldridge

1. Please state your full name.
2. What is the date of your birth?
3. Where were you born?
4. Where do you currently reside?
5. Of what country are you a citizen?
6. Please provide a description of your past and present employment.
7. Have you ever served in the military?
   If so, during what period and in what branch of the military did you serve?

8. Have you ever resided in the United States?
   If so, please describe the dates you resided in the United States; where you resided in the United States; and with whom you were employed during your residency in the United States.
9. Have you ever resided in Canada?
   If so, please describe the dates you resided in Canada; where you resided in Canada; and with whom you were employed during your residency in Canada.
10. Do you know Lawrence W. Anderson?
    If so, how and when did you come to know him?
    When did you last have contact with him?
    Do you possess or have access to any correspondence, notes, or written communications from him or to him?
    Have you discussed with him the Swiss investigation or the United States investigation of Ilene Moses, Lawrence Anderson; SMS, Inc.; Jolland Co., Ltd.; Romtex; Kenneth Kazerski; Ircon AG; Cathay, Ltd.; or Cranship, Ltd.? If so, what did each of you say?
11. Do you know Douglas Sloan?
    If so, how and when did you come to know him?
    When did you last have contact with him?
    Do you possess or have access to any correspondence, notes, or written communications with him?
12. Do you know Jack Connor?
    If so, how and when did you come to know him?
    When did you last have contact with him?
    Do you possess or have access to any correspondence, notes, or written communications with him?
    Have you discussed with him the Swiss investigation or the United States investigation of Ilene Moses, Lawrence Anderson, SMS, Inc.; Jolland Co., Ltd.; Romtex; Kenneth Kazerski; Ircon AG; Cathay, Ltd.; or Cranship, Ltd.? If so, what did each of you say?
13. Do you know Heinz Wengerter?
    If so, how and when did you come to know him?
    When did you last have contact with him?
    Do you possess or have access to any correspondence, notes, or written communications with him?
    Have you discussed with him the Swiss investigation or the United States investigation of Ilene Moses, Lawrence Anderson; SMS, Inc.; Jolland Co., Ltd.; Romtex; Kenneth Kazerski; Ircon AG; Cathay, Ltd.; or Cranship, Ltd.? If so, what did each of you say?
14. Do you know Ilene Ruth Moses?
    If so, how and when did you come to know her?
    When did you last have contact with her?
    Do you possess or have access to any correspondence, notes, or written communications with her?
    Have you discussed with her the Swiss investigation or the United States investigation of Ilene Moses, Lawrence Anderson; SMS, Inc.; Jolland Co., Ltd.; Romtex; Kenneth Kazerski; Ircon AG; Cathay, Ltd.; or Cranship, Ltd.? If so, what did each of you say?

[Remaining Questions and Exhibits Omitted]

Notes and Questions

1. As part of the Comprehensive Crime Control Act of 1984, P.L. 98–473, Congress enacted 18 U.S.C. § 3292. This statute allows the U.S. government, prior to the return of an indictment, to apply to the district court, before which a grand jury is impaneled to investigate the offense, to request the suspension of the running of the statute of limitations for the offense if the court finds by a preponderance of the evidence that an official request has been made for such evidence and it reasonably appears, or reasonably appeared at the time the request was made, that such evidence is, or was, in such foreign country. The statute can be suspended for a maximum of three years. § 3292(c)(2) provides that the period during which the suspension can run must not extend a period within which a criminal case must be initiated for more than six months if all foreign authorities take final action before such period would expire without regard to this statute. In *Bischel v. United States*, 61 F.3d 1429 (9th Cir. 1995), the court construed "final action" of foreign authorities for § 3292(c)(2) purposes as a dispositive response by the foreign government both to the request for records and for a certificate of authenticity of those records, as both were identified in the "official request."

2. *See* discussion of *U.S. v. Kozeny*, 493 F. Supp. 2d 518 (S.D.N.Y.), 2008 US. App. LEXIS 18523 (Aug. 29, 2008), in the chapter on transnational corruption in which two defendants, Messrs. Bourke and Pikerton, moved to dismiss the indictment against them for conspiracy to bribe government officials in Azerbaijan to ensure that the state-owned oil company would be privatized as time barred. Although the DOJ had previously received a court order tolling the statute of limitations and filed the request for assistance with the governments of the Netherlands and Switzerland within the five-year statute of limitations, it did not obtain the § 3292 order until after the five-year period had expired. The court concluded that, although the statutory text was ambiguous, the legislative history of § 3292, the structure of the provisions, the policy rationale behind statutes of limitations, and the doctrine of constitutional avoidance all pointed toward an interpretation of § 3292 that does not allow the government to apply to suspend a statute of limitations after the limitations period has expired. The Second Circuit Court of Appeals affirmed, concluding that the text of § 3292 is not ambiguous.

3. In *In re Letter Rogatory from Justice Court, Dist. of Montreal, Canada*, 523 F.2d 562 (6th Cir. 1975), an appellate court affirmed the district court's decision that a target of a Canadian narcotics prosecution could challenge a subpoena *duces tecum* to a bank issued by the District Court for the Eastern District of Michigan in response to a letter rogatory from a Canadian court. Notwithstanding the government's argument that the defendant lacked standing to challenge the subpoena because the targeted records were the bank's property, the court held that the target had standing to challenge the validity of the subpoena on the theory that it was not authorized by § 1782. However, the court found that the letter rogatory and § 1782 applied to criminal cases, and as a result, Canada could depose the target – thereby rejecting the argument that taking his deposition under § 1782 and later introducing it against him at trial would not contravene his Sixth Amendment right of confrontation.

4. Until the U.S. Supreme Court decision in *Advanced Micro Devices (AMD)*, the circuit courts were split over whether the relevant statutory provisions in U.S. law require that the evidence requested in a letter rogatory be discoverable under the law of the requested state. A core issue is whether there exists a "dual discoverability" requirement (i.e., whether the materials requested be discovered in both jurisdictions). In the *AMD* case, the Supreme Court ruled that AMD could seek judicial access to Intel documents in order to support a

European Commission (EC) antitrust complaint – even if the EC was unwilling to demand production of the Intel documents. *Intel Corp. v. Advanced Micro Devices, Inc.*, 542 U.S. 241 (2004).

5. Under 18 U.S.C. § 3506 any U.S. national or resident who applies to a foreign court or other authority opposing a U.S. government request for evidence must also serve such pleading or other document on the Attorney General or on the appropriate attorney for the government. This requirement applies to letters rogatory, treaty of convention requests, or any other request for evidence made by a court of the United States or an authority of the United States having criminal law enforcement responsibility, to a court or other authority of a foreign country.

6. Some cases have litigated the issue of what constitutes a "proceeding in a foreign or international tribunal" for purposes of 28 U.S.C. § 1782. For instance, in *In re Letter Rogatory from Justice Court, Dist. of Montreal, Canada*, the court held that a criminal investigation not yet reaching the indictment or charging stage qualified. In *In re Request from Ministry of Legal Affairs of Trinidad and Tobago*, 848 F.2d 1151 (11th Cir. 1988), the Eleventh Circuit held that the statute provides the district court discretion to grant judicial assistance in connection with a criminal investigation before a judicial proceeding has started. In the case of *In re Letters Rogatory Issued by Dir. of Insp. of Gov. of India*, 385 F.2d 1017 (2d Cir. 1967), the Second Circuit held that an Indian income tax officer is not a "tribunal" within 28 U.S.C. § 1782.

IV. Requests under Mutual Assistance in Criminal Matters Treaties

Mutual legal assistance treaties (MLATs) are important because they make assistance obligatory as a matter of international law, whereas letters rogatory are executed solely on the basis of comity. A request for MLAT assistance cannot be refused unless specifically allowed by the treaty, and grounds for refusing MLAT assistance are quite limited. An MLAT, either by itself or together with implementing legislation, provides a way for a requesting state to overcome foreign bank secrecy and business confidentiality laws that can otherwise frustrate U.S. investigations. For instance, such provisions are included in the U.S.-Romania treaty. MLATs provide an opportunity to develop procedures to obtain foreign evidence in a form admissible in U.S. courts, especially in the context of complex U.S. evidentiary rules. (Many of the rules that form the foundation of the U.S. adversarial system, such as hearsay rules and the right to confront witnesses, do not have analogues in foreign inquisitorial systems.) MLATs also provide a framework for cooperation in tracing, seizing, and forfeiting criminal assets. Hence, bilateral MLATs offer a predictable and effective regime for obtaining evidence in criminal cases and help federal, state, and local prosecutors pursue international cases in nine treaty countries in Africa, the Middle East, Europe, and the former Soviet Union.

MLATs provide for a variety of assistance: serving of documents, providing records, locating persons, taking the testimony or statements of persons, producing documents, executing requests for search and seizure, forfeiting criminally obtained assets, and transferring persons in custody for testimonial purposes. Most importantly, under MLATs, evidence must be transmitted in a form admissible in the requesting state's courts.

By obligating contracting parties to provide mutual assistance in criminal investigations as well as in "proceedings," MLATs clarify a situation that has created much dispute in the use of letters rogatory. Hence, a contracting party that is merely in the early stages of investigating a case can obtain U.S. assistance. MLATs are self-executing in the United States, amending and supplementing federal law on issues such as the creation of a right of safe conduct, the conferral of authority to detain persons in custody, the creation of a hearsay exception for chain-of-custody evidence, the removal of discretion to refuse to issue subpoenas for testimony and tangible evidence, and the United States' right to disclose confidential information to a requesting country.

Although letters rogatory must be made through the courts in both countries with the involvement of various foreign government agencies – and in some cases embassies – MLATs are much more expeditious, partly because there is a direct link through a "central authority" in each country to process requests.

The Attorney General is the central authority for the United States under all the U.S. MLATs. The Attorney General has delegated these duties as central authority to the Assistant Attorney General in charge of the Criminal Division, who has, in turn, subdelegated authority to the Deputy Assistant Attorneys General and the Director of the Office of International Affairs (OIA) in the Criminal Division of the Department of Justice, pursuant to regulations.

OIA handles all requests under an MLAT, both outgoing and incoming. It is charged with receiving and overseeing execution of incoming requests for investigative or evidence gathering assistance in the United States. OIA consults with appropriate officials in the Justice and State Departments, as well as officials in other agencies as necessary, when required to make discretionary determinations under the treaties in novel, unusual, or sensitive situations.

As of November 1, 2008, the U.S. treaty regime includes MLATs with Anguilla, Antigua and Barbuda, Argentina, Australia, Austria, Barbados, Belgium, Belize, Brazil, Bulgaria, Cyprus, the Czech Republic, Denmark, Dominica, Egypt, Estonia, the European Union, Finland, France, Germany, Greece, Grenada, Hong Kong, Hungary, India, Ireland, Israel, Japan, Latvia, Liechtenstein, Lithuania, Luxembourg, Malaysia, the Netherlands (including the Netherlands Antilles and Aruba), Nigeria, Poland, Portugal, Romania, the Russian Federation, South Africa, South Korea, Spain, St. Kitts and Nevis, St. Lucia, St. Vincent and the Grenadines, Sweden, Trinidad and Tobago, Ukraine, the United Kingdom, and Venezuela.[19]

Treaty Between the United States of America and the Russian Federation on Mutual Legal Assistance in Criminal Matters

Article 1: General Provisions

1. The Parties shall provide to each other, in accordance with this Treaty, comprehensive mutual legal assistance in criminal matters.
2. For the purposes of this Treaty, legal assistance in criminal matters shall mean any assistance provided by the Parties in connection with: prevention, suppression, and investigation of crimes; criminal prosecutions; and other proceedings related to such criminal matters.

[19] For a list of U.S. MLATs Signed, Approved for Ratification and/or Entered into Force as of November 1, 2008, *see U.S. Enforcement Updates*, 25 INT'L ENFORCEMENT L. REP. 89 (January 2009).

3. Legal assistance shall be provided in accordance with the provisions of this Treaty where the conduct that is the subject of the request constitutes a crime under the laws of both Parties. The Requested Party may, in its discretion, also provide legal assistance where the conduct that is the subject of the request would not constitute a crime under the laws of the Requested Party.
4. This Treaty is intended solely for cooperation and legal assistance between the Parties. The provisions of this Treaty shall not give rise to a right on the part of any other persons to obtain evidence, to have evidence excluded, or to impede the execution of a request.
5. For purposes of this Treaty, the term "person" shall mean both individuals and legal entities of the following articles: Article 1(4), Article 2(4), Article 5(3) subparagraphs 1–5, Article 10(1), Article 14, and Article 15(2).

Article 2: Scope of Legal Assistance

Legal assistance under this Treaty shall include:

(1) obtaining testimony and statements;
(2) providing documents, records, and other items;
(3) serving documents;
(4) locating and identifying persons and items;
(5) executing requests for searches and seizures;
(6) transferring persons in custody for testimony or other purposes under this Treaty;
(7) locating and immobilizing assets for purposes of forfeiture, restitution, or collection of fines; and
(8) providing any other legal assistance not prohibited by the laws of the Requested Party.

Article 3: Central Authorities and Procedures for Communications

1. Each Party shall implement the provisions of this Treaty, including the making and receiving of requests, through its Central Authority.
2. For the United States of America, the Central Authority shall be the Attorney General or persons designated by the Attorney General. For the Russian Federation, the Central Authority shall be the Office of the Procurator General of the Russian Federation or persons designated by the Procurator General.
3. The Central Authorities shall communicate directly with one another for the purposes of this Treaty and may agree upon such practical measures as may be necessary to facilitate the implementation of this Treaty.

Article 4: Denial of Legal Assistance

1. The Central Authority of the Requested Party may deny legal assistance if:
   (1) the request relates to a crime under military law that is not a crime under general criminal law
   (2) the execution of the request would prejudice the security or other essential interests of the Requested Party; or
   (3) the request does not conform to the requirements of this Treaty.

2. The Requested Party shall not decline execution of a request on the ground of bank secrecy.
3. Before denying legal assistance pursuant to paragraph 1 of this Article, the Central Authority of the Requested Party shall consult with the Central Authority of the Requesting Party to consider whether legal assistance can be given subject to such conditions as it deems necessary. If the Requesting Party accepts legal assistance subject to these conditions, it shall comply with the conditions.
4. If the Central Authority of the Requested Party denies legal assistance, it shall inform the Central Authority of the Requesting Party of the reasons for the denial.

Article 5: Form and Contents of Requests for Legal Assistance

1. A request for legal assistance shall be in writing, but in urgent situations the Central Authority of the Requested Party may accept a request in another form. If the request is not in writing, the request shall be confirmed in writing within ten days of its receipt by the Requested Party unless the Central Authority of the Requested Party agrees otherwise.
2. The request shall include:
   (1) the identity of the authority on whose behalf the request is made;
   (2) a description of the facts and circumstances of the case;
   (3) the text of the law under which the conduct constitutes a crime;
   (4) a description of the legal assistance sought; and
   (5) a statement of the purpose for which the legal assistance is sought.
3. To the extent necessary and possible, a request shall also include:
   (1) information on the identity and suspected location of a person to be located;
   (2) information on the identity and location of a person to be served, that person's relationship to the proceeding, and the manner in which service is to be made;
   (3) information on the identity and location of a person from whom evidence is sought;
   (4) a list of questions to be asked of a person identified in the request;
   (5) a precise description of the place or person to be searched and of the item to be seized;
   (6) a description of procedures for the execution of the request;
   (7) information as to the allowance and expenses to which a person asked to appear in the territory of the Requesting Party will be entitled; and
   (8) any other information that may be brought to the attention of the Central Authority of the Requested Party to facilitate the execution of the request.
4. The request shall be prepared and signed in accordance with the regulations of the Requesting Party.

Article 6: Language

Except as otherwise agreed by the Central Authorities of the Parties, requests for legal assistance and documents attached thereto shall be accompanied by a translation into the language of the Requested Party.

Article 7: Execution of Requests

1. The Central Authority of the Requested Party shall promptly execute the request or shall transmit it to the authority having jurisdiction to do so. The competent authorities of the Requested Party shall do everything in their power to execute the request in a timely manner.
2. The Central Authority of the Requested Party shall represent the interests of the Requesting Party in executing the request.
3. Requests shall be executed in accordance with the laws of the Requested Party except if this Treaty provides otherwise. The competent authorities of the Requested Party shall have the authority to issue subpoenas, search warrants, or other orders necessary for the execution of requests. Except if prohibited by its laws, the Requested Party shall follow procedures specified in the request.
4. If the Central Authority of the Requested Party considers that execution of a request will interfere with a criminal investigation, criminal prosecution, or proceeding related to a criminal matter ongoing in that State, it may postpone execution, or make execution subject to conditions determined to be necessary after consultations with the Central Authority of the Requesting Party. If the Requesting Party accepts the legal assistance subject to these conditions, it shall comply with the conditions.
5. The Requested Party shall use its best efforts to keep confidential a request and its contents if so requested by the Central Authority of the Requesting Party. If execution of the request would require a breach of this confidentiality, the Central Authority of the Requested Party shall so inform the Central Authority of the Requesting Party, which shall then determine whether the request should be executed under such circumstances.
6. The Central Authority of the Requested Party shall respond to inquiries by the Central Authority of the Requesting Party concerning progress toward execution of the request.
7. Upon request of the Central Authority of the Requesting Party, the Central Authority of the Requested Party shall furnish information in advance about the date and place of the execution of a request. During the execution of a request, the Requested Party shall permit the presence of such persons as are specified therein.
8. The Central Authority of the Requested Party shall promptly inform the Central Authority of the Requesting Party of the outcome of the execution of the request. If the request is not executed, or if execution is delayed or postponed, the Central Authority of the Requested Party shall inform the Central Authority of the Requesting Party of the reasons for non-execution, delay, or postponement.

Article 8: Costs

1. The Requested Party shall pay all costs relating to the execution of the request, except that the Requesting Party shall pay for the fees of experts, the costs of translation, interpretation, and transcription, and the allowances and expenses related to travel of persons pursuant to Articles 11 and 12 of this Treaty.
2. If it becomes apparent that the execution of the request requires expenses of an extraordinary nature, the Central Authorities of the Parties shall consult to determine the terms and conditions under which the requested legal assistance can be provided.

Article 9: Limitations on Use of the Results of Executed Requests

1. The Central Authority of the Requested Party may require that the Requesting Party not use the results of the execution of a request obtained under this Treaty for purposes other than those described in the request without the prior consent of the Central Authority of the Requested Party. In such cases, the Requesting Party shall comply with such limitations on use of the results of the executed request.
2. Nothing in this Article shall preclude the use or disclosure of the results of an executed request to the extent that there is an obligation to do so under the Constitution of the Requesting Party in a criminal prosecution. The Central Authority of the Requesting Party shall notify the Central Authority of the Requested Party in advance of any such possible or proposed use or disclosure.
3. The results of an executed request that have been used for the purpose for which they were provided and, in the course of such use, have been made public in the Requesting Party in accordance with this Treaty may thereafter be used for any purpose.

Article 10: Obtaining Testimony and Evidence in Requested Party

1. A person requested to testify and produce documents, records, or items in the Requested Party shall be summoned, if necessary by subpoena or order, to appear and testify and produce such documents, records, or items, in accordance with the requirements of the law of the Requested Party.
2. In accordance with procedures used in the Requested Party, persons present at the execution of a request shall be permitted to pose questions directly or to formulate questions that shall be posed to the person being questioned, and to make a verbatim transcript of the proceeding using, if necessary, technical means.
3. If the person referred to in paragraph 1 of this Article asserts a claim of immunity, incapacity, or privilege under the laws of the Requesting Party, the evidence shall nonetheless be taken and the claim made known to the Requesting Party for resolution by the authorities of the Requesting Party.

Article 11: Obtaining Testimony in the Requesting Party

1. When the Requesting Party requests the appearance of a person in its territory, the Requested Party shall invite the person to appear before the appropriate authority in the Requesting Party. The Requesting Party shall indicate the extent to which the expenses and allowances will be paid. The Central Authority of the Requested Party shall promptly inform the Central Authority of the Requesting Party of the response of the person. A person who agrees to appear may ask that the Requesting Party advance money to cover these expenses. This advance may be provided through the Embassy or consulate of the Requesting Party.
2. A person appearing in the Requesting Party pursuant to this Article shall not be subject to service of process, or be detained or subjected to any restriction of personal liberty, by reason of any acts or convictions that preceded the person's departure from the Requested Party. If such guarantee cannot be provided for any reason, the Central Authority of the Requesting Party shall indicate this in the request in order to inform

the invited persons and to allow that person to decide whether to appear taking these circumstances into account.

3. The safe conduct provided for by this Article shall cease seven days after the Central Authority of the Requesting Party has notified the Central Authority of the Requested Party that the person's presence is no longer required, or if the person has left the Requesting Party and voluntarily returned to it. The Central Authority of the Requesting Party may, in its discretion, extend this period up to fifteen days if it determines that there is good cause to do so.

Article 12: Transfer of Persons in Custody

1. A person in the custody of either Party whose presence in the other Party is sought for purposes of legal assistance under this Treaty shall be transferred from the sending Party to the receiving party for that purpose if the person consents and if the Central Authorities of both Parties agree.
2. For the purposes of this Article:
   (1) the receiving Party shall have the authority and the obligation to keep the person transferred in custody unless otherwise authorized by the sending Party;
   (2) the receiving Party shall return the person transferred to the custody of the sending Party as soon as circumstances permit or as otherwise agreed by both Central Authorities;
   (3) the receiving Party shall not require the sending Party to initiate extradition proceedings for the return of the person transferred;
   (4) the person transferred shall receive credit for service of the sentence imposed in the sending Party for time served in the custody of the receiving Party; and
   (5) where the sentence imposed expires, or where the sending Party advises the receiving Party that the transferred person is no longer required to be held in custody, that person shall be treated as a person invited pursuant to Article 11 or returned to the sending Party.

Article 13: Production of Official Records

1. Upon request, the Requested Party shall provide the Requesting Party with copies of publicly available records, including documents or information of any nature and in any form in the possession of an executive, legislative, or judicial authority in the Requested Party.
2. The Requested Party may provide copies of any records, including documents or information of any nature and in any form that are in the possession of an executive, legislative, or judicial authority in that Party, but that are not publicly available, but only to the same extent and under the same conditions as such records would be available to the competent authorities of that Party. The Requested Party may in its discretion deny a request pursuant to this paragraph entirely or in part.

Article 14: Location or Identification of Persons and Items

If the Requesting Party seeks the location or identity of persons or information about items in the Requested Party, the Requested Party shall use its best efforts to execute the request.

Article 15: Service of Documents

1. The Requested Party shall make its best efforts to effect service of documents pursuant to a request.
2. The Requesting Party shall transmit any request for the service of a document requiring the appearance of a person before a competent authority in the Requesting Party a reasonable time before the scheduled appearance.
3. The Requested Party shall return to the Requesting Party a proof of service in the manner specified in the request.

Article 16: Search and Seizure

1. The Requested Party shall execute a request for the search, seizure, and transfer of any item to the Requesting Party if the request includes the information justifying such action under the laws of the Requested Party.
2. If requested, every official of the Requested Party who has had custody of a seized item shall certify the identity of the item, the continuity of its custody, and the integrity of its condition.
3. The Requested Party may require that the Requesting Party agree to the terms and conditions deemed necessary to protect third party interests in the item to be transferred.

Article 17: Transfer of Documents, Records, and Other Items

1. When a request for legal assistance concerns the transfer of documents or records, the Requested Party shall transfer true copies thereof, unless the Requested Party expressly requests the originals, in which case the Requested Party shall make every effort to comply with the request.
2. Insofar as not prohibited by its laws, the Requested Party shall transfer documents, records, or other items in such manner or accompanied by such certification as may be requested by the Requesting Party in order to make them admissible according to the law of the Requesting Party. For this purpose, the Central Authorities of the Parties shall exchange information pursuant to Article 3(3) with respect to the requirements for admissibility in their respective legal systems. Documents, records, and other items transferred as requested under this paragraph shall require no further certification to make them available.
3. The Central Authority of the Requested Party may require that the Central Authority of the Requesting Party return, as soon as possible, any documents, records, or other items furnished to it in execution of a request under this Treaty.

Article 18: Proceeds and Instrumentalities of Crime

1. The Parties, in accordance with their laws, shall assist each other in locating, immobilizing, and seizing proceeds, including earnings from, or that are the result of, criminal activities, as well as instrumentalities of crime, for the purpose of: forfeiture; restitution to victims of crime; and collection of fines imposed pursuant to judicial decisions in criminal matters.

2. If the Central Authority of one Party becomes aware that proceeds and instrumentalities of crime that may be subject to forfeiture are located in the territory of the other Party, it may so inform the Central Authority of the other Party so that the other Party may take appropriate measures under paragraph 3 of this Article. The Central Authority receiving the information shall notify the Central Authority providing the information of the action taken.
3. The Party that has immobilized, seized, or forfeited the proceeds and instrumentalities of crime shall dispose of them in accordance with its laws. That Party shall transfer all or part of such assets, or the proceeds of their sale, to the other Party, including for the purpose of forfeiture and restitution (which includes returning them to the rightful owner) insofar as permitted by its laws and to the extent it deems it appropriate and within the time frame and under the conditions it deems acceptable.

Article 19: Consultation

The Central Authorities shall consult, at times mutually agreed to by them, to promote the most effective use of this Treaty.

Article 20: Scope of Application

This Treaty shall apply to any requests presented after its entry into force even if the relevant acts or omissions occurred before that date.

Article 21: Other Legal Bases for Cooperation

The provisions in this Treaty shall not prevent either of the Parties from cooperating and from granting legal assistance in accordance with the provisions of other applicable international treaties and agreements, national laws, and practices.

Article 22: Entry into Force and Termination

1. This Treaty shall be subject to ratification, and shall enter into force upon the exchange of the instruments of ratification, which shall take place as soon as possible.
2. Upon entry into force of this Treaty, the Agreement between the Government of the United States of America and the Government of the Russian Federation on Cooperation in Criminal Matters, signed on June 30, 1995, shall no longer be in force.
3. Either Party may terminate this Treaty by means of written notice to the other Party through the diplomatic channel. Termination shall take effect six months following the date of receipt of such notification.

Done at Moscow, this 17th day of June 1999. . . . letter from Russian Min. of Foreign Affairs omitted.

Notes and Questions

1. Article 1(3) of the U.S.-Russian MLAT requires dual criminality to obligate one of the signatories to give mutual assistance and makes mutual assistance discretionary in the absence of dual criminality. U.S. MLATs with the Bahamas, the Cayman Islands, and

Panama also require dual criminality. However, the majority of U.S. MLATs, especially recent ones, require mutual assistance irrespective of dual criminality. Do you think this may cause a problem when the United States makes an MLAT request for a crime, such as Internet gambling or doing business with Cuba, when such activities are not criminal in the other country, such as England? In fact, English companies have been instrumental in having the European Union threaten to take action in the World Trade Organization against the United States for discriminatory prosecution of Internet gambling operators because U.S. prosecutors allegedly have not prosecuted U.S. operators.

Increasingly international organizations advocate the relaxation or elimination of the dual criminality requirement in mutual legal assistance, especially because mutual legal assistance is less intrusive on the rights of an individual, compared with extradition. Article 46(9)(b) of the UNCAC provides that states may decline to give mutual assistance for corruption offenses on the dual criminality principle. The convention also requires that a "requested state party shall, where consistent with the basic concepts of its legal assistance render assistance that does not involve coercive action." As a result, noncoercive measures, such as taking evidence from voluntary witnesses and providing publicity available documents can be obtained even if the principle of dual criminality is not met. Similarly, FATF recommendation 37 states that countries should, to the greatest extent possible, provide mutual legal assistance, notwithstanding the absence of dual criminality. In the Commonwealth Harare Scheme on mutual legal assistance countries have the discretion to decline requests for assistance on lack of dual criminality, but dual criminality is not a requirement.

2. MLATs include various grounds for a requested state to deny a request. Most treaties specify that assistance is not required if execution of the request would prejudice the security, sovereignty, or other essential interests of the requested state and can be denied if the crime is political. Many treaties hold that assistance may or shall be denied if the crime is exclusively a military offense (e.g., Russian Treaty, Art. 4, 1(1)). Most treaties provide for refusal of assistance if the request relates to the prosecution of a person for acts of which he or she has been acquitted or convicted by a final judgment of a court in the requested state. The U.S.-Switzerland treaty, among others, includes additional grounds for denying assistance – extradition requests, antitrust laws, and violations of tax, customs duty, governmental monopoly, and exchange control regulations. *See* U.S.-Swiss MLAT, Art. 2(1)(c) for the full list.

3. U.S. MLATs, especially those post-1989, generally restrict their use to prosecutors and law enforcement officials. Many specifically exclude defendants and private parties from requesting MLAT assistance.

4. Most MLATs preclude the use of information obtained pursuant to a treaty request for anything other than the purpose stated in the request without the prior consent of the requested state. *See* Art. 9(1) of the U.S.-Russian MLAT.

5. *Regional conventions on mutual assistance*. Regional organizations such as the Council of Europe and the European Union have developed conventions on mutual assistance in criminal matters and a host of other international criminal cooperative arrangements. Interestingly, other countries outside the Council of Europe (CoE) can accede to these instruments. For example, the CoE Convention on Laundering, Forfeiture, etc., includes mutual assistance requirements and is open to non-CoE members.

6. *Inter-American Convention on Mutual Assistance in Criminal Matters*. The United States is also a party to the Inter-American Convention on Mutual Assistance in Criminal

Matters. It extends the U.S. mutual assistance treaty relationships in the hemisphere to countries in which there might not be a sufficient basis to justify the resources needed to conclude separate bilateral treaties. For instance, on ratification, the OAS MLAT would create an immediate treaty relationship between the United States and Peru, with which the United States does not have a bilateral MLAT. Similar MLAT relationships would be created as five additional signatories to the convention finalize the steps required for ratification. Although only three countries have ratified the OAS convention, the United States is urging other countries in the hemisphere to do so.

Unlike the typical modern MLATs that the United States has negotiated, the Inter-American Convention will not serve as the legal basis for asset sharing, which the negotiators determined was best left for bilateral agreements. The OAS convention has certain limitations regarding assistance in cases involving tax offenses. Article 9(f) provides that a party may decline assistance in investigations and proceedings involving certain tax offenses. The United States consistently opposed this provision during the negotiation of the convention. Hence, it proposed an additional protocol to enable assistance in tax matters. The first article of the protocol removes the discretion of protocol signatories to refuse assistance on the grounds that a tax offense is involved. The second article clarifies that the limited dual criminality provision in Article 5 of the convention should be interpreted liberally in cases involving tax offenses. The Optional Protocol was negotiated at the OAS in the early 1990s, adopted and opened for signature by the OAS General Assembly on June 11, 1993, and signed by the United States on January 10, 1995. The United States has ratified with two Understandings in its instrument of ratification for the convention, and one Understanding in its instrument of ratification for the Related Optional Protocol. The proposed texts would clarify the U.S. position regarding certain provisions of the convention and protocol and enable it to obtain greater cooperation on criminal tax cases.[20]

7. *Multilateral conventions with MLAT provisions.* Many multilateral conventions, such as Article 11 of the International Convention against the Taking of Hostages, 1316 U.N.T.S, 205 (1979), and Article 10(1) of the Convention for the Suppression of Unlawful Seizure of Aircraft (Hague Convention), 860 U.N.T.S. 105, 22 U.S.T. (1970), require the signatories to provide one another "the greatest measure of assistance in connection with criminal proceedings" brought in respect of the offense set forth in the conventions. Many of these multilateral enforcement conventions focus on international white collar crime: The UN Conventions Against Transnational Crime and its supplementing protocols 2000 (Palermo Convention): The Council of Europe Convention on Laundering. Search and Seizure and Confiscation of Proceeds from Crime 1990; the OAS Inter-American Convention against Corruption 1999; Council of Europe Civil Law Convention on Corruption 1999; and the CNN Convention against Corruption 2003 (UNCAC). In essence, these conventions and many others create mini-MLATs with respect to the object offense (e.g., terrorist bombings).

In several successful bribery prosecutions, multilateral conventions, such as the OECD Anti-Bribery Convention were important in obtaining evidence of bribery. See, e.g., OECD, MID-TERM STUDY OF PHASE 2 REPORTS: APPLICATION OF THE CONVENTION ON

[20] For additional background on the Senate Foreign Relations Hearing on the proposed MLATs, *see* Bruce Zagaris, *Senate Foreign Relations Committee Recommends Ratification of Criminal Cooperation Treaties*, 16 INT'L ENFORCEMENT L. REP. 1006–9 (NOV. 2000).

Combating Bribery of Foreign Officials in International Business Transactions and the 1997 Recommendation on Combating Bribery an in International Business Transactions 105 Paris: OECD, 2006. A problem is obtaining effective legal assistance from nonparties to the Convention. The unavailability of mutual assistance from a foreign jurisdiction in which a foreign bribe transaction occurs has been listed as the "single most important reason for terminating an investigation" into foreign bribery Id. at 108.

The OECD has stated that the requirement to provide prompt legal assistance to other parties as required by Article 9 of the OECD Anti-Bribery Convention has been used by all the signatures. Importantly mutual assistance is available not only for the purpose of criminal investigations and proceedings, but also for noncriminal proceedings brought against a legal person. Id.

8. *Denial of an MLAT request for abuse of process.* What happens when a requesting state does not obey the requested state's procedural laws? On July 5, 2002, the Supreme Court of British Columbia denied a U.S. request for records under the U.S.-Canadian Mutual Assistance in Criminal Matters treaty. The Court ruled that the United States had abused Canadian law in its efforts to obtain records for an ongoing tax investigation. The decision was directed at perceived abuses by U.S. officials and their refusal to appear before the court and give testimony on their conduct. This case, which is useful for defense counsel and courts facing similar situations, illustrates judicial efforts to balance the need for assistance with respect for the law. For background *see USA v. Schneider*, 2202BCSC1014 (July 5, 2002); Bruce Zagaris, *British Columbia Court Denies US MLAT Request due to Abuse of Process*, 18 Int'l Enforcement L. Rep. 422–24 (Oct. 2002). Finally, on October 3, 2009, the Canadian government extradited Schneider to Germany after a ten-year legal fight to remain in Canada. See Bruce Zagaris, *Canada Extradites Schneider to Germany*, 25 Int'l Enforcement L. Rep. 410–11 (Oct 2009).

9. *Using international human rights provisions to challenge MLAT requests.* Can defendants or third parties invoke international human rights law to block MLAT requests? On May 18, 2001, the Supreme Court of Bermuda denied a U.S. request for an exchange of tax information in a closely watched case because of the taxpayers involved and the conflict between the Tax Information Exchange Agreement (TIEA) and attorney-client privilege. *In the Matter of the Administration of Justice (Prerogative Writs) Act 1978 and in the Matter of the U.S.A.-Bermuda Tax Convention Act, 1986 and In the Matter of an Application by Almon Glen Braswell, Gero Vita International, Inc. and G.B. Data Systems Inc.* (hereafter *Braswell*), in the Supreme Court of Bermuda, Civil Jurisdiction No. 59 of 2000, May 18, 2001. In the case at issue, the court held that the breach of attorney-client privilege required Bermuda to deny the U.S. request for tax information. The U.S. tax investigation began after two former employees of G. B. Data Systems removed privileged correspondence between law firms and U.S. persons involved in the tax controversy. The U.S. Attorney attempted to make use of the privileged correspondence, which the Bermudian Court ruled constituted a breach of the legal professional privilege.

According to the Bermudian Court, the fact that any material used by the United States in requesting information under the act was obtained in breach of confidence and privilege made the U.S. request fatally defective, invalidating the Minister of Finance's decision to render assistance. Explaining its responsibility to "examine the decision to implement the request to see if it was taken in compliance with the relevant laws," the Court reasoned that legal professional privilege is protected under the right to a "fair hearing" in sec. 6(1) of the Bermudian Constitution. In this regard, the European

Convention for the Protection of Human Rights and Fundamental Freedoms (1953), which applies to Bermuda; the UN's Universal Declaration of Human Rights 1968; and the form of Chapter 1 in the Bermudian Constitution require a generous interpretation affording "the full measure of the fundamental rights and freedoms." The Court ruled that "legal professional privilege is a fundamental human right protected by the European Convention for the Protection of Human Rights and Fundamental Freedoms which applies to Bermuda, that it is much more than an ordinary rule of evidence, that it is a fundamental condition on which the administration of justice as a whole rests and that it forms part of the constitutional right to a fair trial and as such cannot be abridged by statute." Further, it ruled that "an incident of a person's constitutional right to a fair trial includes a right to legal professional privilege." Interestingly, the Court's ruling was eventually overturned by the House of Lords.

10. *U.S. constitutional rights and mutual assistance.* The fight against transnational crime has transformed U.S. laws governing international criminal cooperation.[21] An increasing number of prosecutions are bringing the applicability of constitutional rights and provisions of international human rights conventions such as the International Civil and Political Covenant into focus.[22] The tension between the need for cooperation between U.S. and foreign governments and international tribunals and the protection of these rights will likely grow. As mentioned earlier, some OECD countries have insisted that cooperation in criminal tax matters be done only through MLATs. Hence, it becomes important to consider individual rights in the context of MLATs.

11. *Mini-MLATs.* The United States has concluded several mini-MLATs: mutual assistance agreements among governmental agencies. Congress has delegated to federal agencies, such as the Securities and Exchange Commission, and the Commodities Futures Trading Commission, and the U.S. Treasury, the authority to conclude agreements or Memoranda of Understanding with their counterparts in other countries.

12. *Efforts of defendants and third parties to use MLATs.* Defense counsel may attempt to use MLATs to obtain evidence. In at least one case in which the MLAT was silent on the issue of defense access, the U.S. District Court for the Southern District of New York instructed the Department of Justice to make an MLAT request to Switzerland on behalf of the defendant, Michele Sindona.

In a case in which I was involved, defendants persuaded the U.S. court to order the government to allow the defendants to use an MLAT. The court ordered that defense counsel and government agree on a procedure allowing the defense counsel to use the applicable MLAT to gain access to a series of witnesses whose depositions abroad were required and for other forms of evidence gathering. The court sympathized with the defense's need to proactively use the MLAT (*U.S. v. Nanne Hogendoorn,* U.S. District Court for the District of Alaska, Case No. A98–0087-CR (JKS), Transcript of Proceedings, Status Conference, July 15, 1999).

13. In *In Re: Commissioner's Subpoenas*, 325 F.3d 1287 (11th Cir. 2003), the appellate court held that the U.S.-Canada MLAT obligated the United States, at the request of Canada, to issue subpoenas compelling witness testimony in a criminal investigation prior to the filing of formal charges in a Canadian smuggling prosecution. In doing

[21] This discussion of the MLATs is from Bruce Zagaris, *Uncle Sam Extends Reach for Evidence Worldwide*, 15 Crim. Just. 5, 55–56 (2001).

[22] For background *see* Michael Abbell & Mark Andrew Sherman, *The Bill of Rights in Transnational Criminal Litigation*, The Champion 22–29 (1992).

so, the appellate reversed the district court that, on a motion filed by the subpoenaed witnesses, quashed the subpoenas. The appellate court explained that the magistrate judge erred in construing the MLAT to express a clear and unambiguous intent to make requests under the MLAT subject to the limitations of all other substantive law of the United States, including 18 U.S.C. § 1782.

14. *Hypothetical:* You are consulting for a U.S. multinational that has acquired a company in Mexico. The acquisition agreement provides for an earnout whereby the Mexican shareholders of the acquired company have a right to share in the profits of the acquired company for the next two years. However, the acquired company does not meet the level of earnings required to trigger the shareholders' right to obtain the earnout. They nevertheless conduct negotiations in an effort to secure the earnout, but are unsuccessful. As a result they bring a criminal complaint against the U.S. multinational and some of its directors. They hire an aggressive lawyer in Mexico known for planting articles in the Mexican press. This strategy works, and the Mexican press publishes articles discussing the criminal investigation and reporting that the Mexican government is requesting the help of the U.S. government. What if any action can you take as U.S. counsel in support of the U.S. multinational?

15. *Mutual assistance in the Commonwealth.* The Commonwealth is an association of fifty-three independent states that provides a forum for consultation and cooperation in, among other things, criminal and enforcement matters. In 1986, the Commonwealth Law Ministers agreed to the Harare Scheme on Mutual Assistance in Criminal Matters (available at http://www.thecommonwealth.org). It requires the participating member countries to enact national laws consistent with the provisions of the scheme that allow the relevant authorities of the requested country to respond to requests from other Commonwealth countries. The scheme is intended to eliminate any requirement for an MLAT between Commonwealth members. One of its advantages over a traditional MLAT is that it provides more detail on the domestic process that should be utilized to fulfill requests. Another benefit is that it resolves differences as to when a criminal proceeding has started. *See* Kimberly Prost, *Cooperation in Penal Matters in the Commonwealth, in* II INTERNATIONAL CRIMINAL LAW 413–53. (M. Cherif Bassiouni ed., 3d ed. 2008).

16. International Best Practices. A UNODC-sponsored report of an informal expert working group on mutual legal assistance has made a useful reside of the following best practice recommendations:

(a) strengthening the effectiveness of central authorities for mutual legal assistance and related central authorities, such as financial intelligence units;
(b) ensuring awareness of national legal requirements and best practice for domestic and foreign officials involved in the mutual legal assistance process;
(c) expediting mutual assistance through the use of alternatives to formal mutual legal assistance reports, such as the use of joint investigation teams;
(d) maximizing personal direct contact between officers in different countries, together with abolishing or reducing technical obstacles to execution of arguments in the requested state.[23] How can international organizations, governments, and civil society provide international best practices in mutual legal assistance?

[23] UNITED NATIONS OFFICE ON DRUGS AND CRIME, REPORT OF THE INFORMAL EXPERT WORKING GROUP ON MUTUAL LEGAL ASSISTANCE CASEWORK BEST PRACTICE, Vienna: UNODC, 2001.

17. Case-Specific Agreements. Occasionally the United States and other governments conclude agreements on specific high-level cases. For instance, between 1976 and 1982, the U.S. Department of Justice concluded a series of executive agreements with twenty-eight countries to facilitate the unblossing and transfer of investigative information and evidence between law enforcement agencies of the respective countries in specific investigations and prosecutions. The majority of the investigations concerned alleged bribes paid to high-ranking foreign officials by large U.S. aircrafts manufacturers, especially Lockheed, McDonnell Douglas and Boeing. They are limited to one or more specified investigations see, e.g., B.A. Ristau, *International Cooperation in Penal Matters: The "Lockheed Agreements,"* 1983 MICH. YEARBOOK OF INT'L LEGAL STUDIES, 85, 85-90 (C. Boardman 1983); M. ABBELL, OBTAINING EVIDENCE ABROAD IN CRIMINAL CASES, *supra*, § 3–4.

V. *Additional Reading Material and References*

A. *Books*

MICHAEL ABBELL, OBTAINING EVIDENCE ABROAD IN CRIMINAL CASES (Dec. 2004 updated in 2009).

STRATEGIES OF THE EU AND THE US IN COMBATING TRANSNATIONAL ORGANISED CRIME (Brice De Ruyver, Gert Vermeulen, & Tom Vander Beken eds., 2002) (especially Workshop 1, Integrity of and Control on Information Exchange; Workshop 2, Transborder Operational Activities; Workshop 3, International/Regional Legal Framework for Combating Organized Crime; and Workshop 4, Intelligence Gathering in the Context of Peacekeeping Activities).

CHRISTOPHER MURRAY & LORNA HARRIS, MUTUAL ASSISTANCE IN CRIMINAL MATTERS (2000).

ETHAN A. NADELMANN, COPS ACROSS BORDERS: THE INTERNATIONALIZATION OF U.S. CRIMINAL LAW ENFORCEMENT, Chapter 6, "International Evidence Gathering" (1993).

POLICING ACROSS NATIONAL BOUNDARIES (Malcolm Anderson & Monica Den Boer eds.) (1994).

UNITED NATIONS OFFICE ON DRUGS AND CRIME, REPORT OF THE INFORMAL EXPERT WORKING GROUP ON MUTUAL ASSISTANCE CASEWORK BEST PRACTICE, VIENNA: UNODC, 2001.

B. *Periodicals and Book Chapters*

Demostenes Chryssikos, *Commentary on the United Nations Draft Model Law on Mutual Assistance in Criminal Matters, in* II INTERNATIONAL CRIMINAL LAW 403–11 (M. Cherif Bassiouni ed., 3d ed. 2008).

Alan Ellis, Robert L. Pisani & David S. Gualtieri, *United States Treaties on Mutual Assistance in Criminal Matters, in* INTERNATIONAL CRIMINAL LAW PROCEDURAL AND ENFORCEMENT MECHANISMS 403–56 M. Cherif Bassiouni ed., 2d ed. 1999).

Lionel Frei & Stefan Trechsel, *Origins and Applications of the United States-Switzerland Treaty on Mutual Assistance in Criminal Matters*, 31 HARV. INT'L L.J. 77–98 (1990).

Coen Mulder & Bert Swart, *Sub-Regional Arrangements: The Benelux and Nordic Countries, in* INTERNATIONAL CRIMINAL LAW PROCEDURAL AND ENFORCEMENT MECHANISMS 393–402 (M. Cherif Bassiouni ed., 2d ed. 1999).

Michael Plachta, *Cooperation in Criminal Matters in Europe: Different Models and Approaches, in* II INTERNATIONAL CRIMINAL LAW 455–89 (M. Cherif Bassiouni ed., 3d ed. 2008).

Kimberly Prost, *Cooperation in Penal Matters in the Commonwealth, in* II INTERNATIONAL CRIMINAL LAW 413–53 (M. Cherif Bassiouni ed., 3d ed. 2008).

Dionysios D. Spinellis, *Securing Evidence Abroad: A European Perspective, in* INTERNATIONAL CRIMINAL LAW PROCEDURAL AND ENFORCEMENT MECHANISMS 351–88 (M. Cherif Bassiouni ed., 2d ed. 1999).

Bruce Zagaris, *Gathering Evidence from and for the United States, in* INTERNATIONAL CRIMINAL LAW PROCEDURAL AND ENFORCEMENT MECHANISMS 457–88 (M. Cherif Bassiouni ed., 2d ed. 1999).

Bruce Zagaris, *Obtaining Evidence of Foreign Crimes from United States Businesses, in* INTERNATIONAL TRADE AVOIDING CRIMINAL RISKS Chapter 20 (William M. Hannay ed., 1991).

Bruce Zagaris, *United States Treaties on Mutual Assistance in Criminal Matters, in* II International Criminal Law Procedural and Enforcement Mechanisms 385–402 (M. Cherif Bassiouni ed., 3d ed. 2008).

Bruce Zagaris & Constantine G. Papavizas, *Recent Decisions by United States Courts on the Exercise of Subpoena Powers to Secure Evidence Abroad in Criminal Matters, in* International Criminal Law: A Guide to U.S. Practice and Procedure 301–32 (Ved P. Nanda & M. Cherif Bassiouni eds. 1987).

9 Extradition and Alternatives

I. Introduction

When suspects flee a country to avoid prosecution, that country's authorities must gain custody of them before they can be tried and convicted. The most common way to gain custody is through extradition, whereby one state – the requested state – transfers custody of a fugitive or accused person, known as the relator, to another state – the requesting state – for criminal prosecution. During the process the relator can choose to return voluntarily, waiving extradition. States can also gain custody over a relator through legal tools like exclusion and deportation or through abduction by fraud ("luring") or by force.

The number of extradition cases has risen dramatically over the past fifty years, both in the United States and abroad. According to the Department of State, U.S. courts certified 137 extradition requests between 1945 and 1960 – an average of only 9 per year.[1] In 1995, in contrast, the United States extradited 79 people to other countries and received custody of 131.[2]

Several factors discussed throughout this book have contributed to this enormous increase, including globalization, the expansion of free trade, and broadened access to international communication and travel. Many states, including the United States, have concluded extradition treaties and related enforcement mechanisms and devoted increasing resources to investigating and prosecuting transnational crime.

II. A Hypothetical

You represent Anne Celtic, a dual national of Belize and the Netherlands. Celtic is a well-known entrepreneur in Belize, with extensive connections to the country's business elite and government. The former minority owner of a bank, she now spends most of her time running a hotel and an Internet gaming business that she owns. In responding to this hypothetical, you should review the U.S.-Belize extradition treaty and the list of extraditable offenses in the U.S.-Netherlands extradition treaty, both of which are included in this chapter.

A prosecutor in Louisiana has brought criminal charges against Celtic for violating Louisiana criminal laws prohibiting Internet gaming and for tax crimes arising from her failure to declare and pay taxes on the gains from the profits earned from the business.

Internet gaming is legal in Belize, and the country is host to a number of gaming businesses. In fact, the Belizean government has attempted to encourage the growth of this sector, which has generated skilled employment opportunities in the country. Although Belize has criminal laws against tax violations, the government rarely prosecutes tax offenses. Belize has a robust international financial services sector and makes active efforts to attract financial services.

The U.S. government has formally requested Celtic's extradition from Belize to face U.S. criminal charges. How should Celtic handle the U.S. extradition request? What are her potential defenses?

What if the United States requested Celtic's extradition from the Netherlands? The U.S.-Netherlands extradition treaty uses the list method to determine extraditable offenses. Furthermore, Netherlands law precludes extradition of Dutch nationals unless the requesting country agrees to allow an offender, if extradited, tried, and convicted, to return to the Netherlands to serve the sentence if desired.

[1] *See* Note, *Executive Discretion in Extradition*, 62 COLUM. L. REV. 1313 n. 1 (1962).

[2] *See* S. EXEC. REP. NO. 104–27, Extradition Treaty with Hungary, 10th Cong., 2d Sess., 1 (1996).

III. The Extradition Process

When a requesting state makes an extradition request, counsel must carefully consider the legal process and domestic law in both the requested and requesting states. Domestic law normally delimits the officials authorized to demand and agree to extradition, the necessary procedures, and the circumstances in which extradition is or is not appropriate.

Domestic law often requires a treaty as the basis for extradition and in turn governs the recognition, interpretation, and application of such treaties. In most states, international human rights laws and domestic statutes establish procedural safeguards to ensure that a relator is only surrendered if the requested state's courts and executive find that the requesting state has met the requirements of the extradition treaty and law. Although the U.S. extradition process is summarized in this chapter, each state has its own procedure. It is important to remember that important differences exist in each legal system, especially, for instance, between common law and civil law states. Hence, extradition involves an application of comparative law.

A. *When the United States Is the Requested State*

In the United States, the Constitution, the applicable extradition treaty, 18 U.S.C § 3181–91, and the jurisprudence of U.S. courts applying the provisions of the applicable treaty and U.S. statutory law govern extradition proceedings. With respect to dual criminality requirements, federal criminal laws and the criminal laws of the state wherein the federal proceedings are conducted on the basis of the extradition warrant will apply.[3]

The procedural and evidentiary rules of the requested state apply in extradition proceedings. In some cases international human rights conventions may determine the procedural and evidentiary rules. In the United States the Constitution controls, followed by the applicable federal statute, and applicable provisions of the Federal Rules of Criminal Procedure and the Federal Rules of Criminal Evidence. However, the United States regards extradition as *sui generis* and hence subject to the procedural and evidentiary rules applicable to civil proceedings. For instance, federal courts docket extradition cases as "miscellaneous" and habeas corpus review of extradition orders as "civil." As a result, courts have held that the Federal Rules of Criminal Procedure and the Federal Rules of Criminal Evidence do not apply to extradition hearings, with some exceptions, because they are not for the purpose of determining guilt or innocence.

When the U.S. government is the requested state and acts on behalf of the requesting state, it must only prove "probable cause." It can meet this standard using evidence that would not otherwise be admissible in criminal matters, including hearsay evidence. The relator cannot introduce evidence to prove innocence or even rebut government evidence. However, he or she can introduce evidence to "clarify" or "explain" the government's evidence. The relator cannot subpoena evidence or witnesses from the requesting state. Discovery for both sides is limited. The relator's rights of confrontation and cross-examination are limited to cases where the government presents the testimony of a

[3] For additional background *see* M. Cherif Bassiouni (ed.), 2 International Criminal Law 417–422 (1986) on whose account this discussion is based. See also Michael Abbell, Extradition to and from the United States, chapters 2 to 4 (2007).

person present in the United States. The court determines the adequacy of the evidence pursuant to the analogous "probable cause" hearings.

The United States receives extradition requests from the diplomatic agents of the requesting state and transmits them through the U.S. Attorney in the federal district where the target of the request is believed to be located. The U.S. Attorney's Office in that district then initiates proceedings to obtain an arrest warrant for the relator.

The first stage in U.S. extradition proceedings is a hearing before a U.S. magistrate or judge shortly after arrest of the relator to determine whether the person arrested is the one named in the arrest warrant and to permit arguments by the relator for admission to bail. U.S. jurisprudence authorizes the court to release the relator on bail pending the determination of his or her extraditability if that person can show "special circumstances" justifying bail. The seriousness of the charges against the relator and the relator's connections with the community both factor into bail decisions. The U.S. government can argue that the risk of flight may prevent the United States from meeting its treaty obligations. At subsequent proceedings, the relator or government can try to reargue the issue of bail. If the relator has no means to hire counsel, the court will appoint a counsel under the Criminal Justice Act.

During the extradition hearing the court tries to determine whether the U.S. government, acting on behalf of the requesting state, has established (1) that "probable cause" evidence establishes the relator's identity, (2) that the criminal charges against the relator are extraditable offenses within the relevant treaty, and (3) that the charges fulfill the requirements of "double criminality," as well as any other treaty and statutory requirements. The probable cause requirement is met when evidence presented by the government constitutes probable cause that the relator has committed the offenses for which extradition is requested and that no grounds exist with the treaty or the applicable statute for denial of extradition.

Although the government cannot appeal an order denying extradition, it can reintroduce a request even when the request is based on the same, or substantially the same facts, that a court has already adjudicated.

If a relator is found extraditable, he or she can have the order reviewed by petitioning for a writ of habeas corpus. Alternatively, a relator can file suit requesting a declaratory judgment or mandamus (the latter if there is a clear abuse of discretion by the court or the government). A habeas review is limited to the following issues: the proper identity of the relator, the existence of a treaty, the extraditability of the crime charged, the existence of probable cause, the existence of double criminality, and the absence of any grounds for denial of extradition. The district court adjudicating the habeas petition will rule on the questions of law concerning those issues, reviewing the facts only insofar as they relate to these legal issues. The court cannot substitute its judgment for the U.S. magistrate or judge who heard the case unless on the face of the record it appears that the magistrate or judge abused judicial discretion, failed to apply proper legal standards, erred with respect to the sufficiency of the evidence supporting the existence of probable cause, or failed to recognize grounds for denying extradition.

If a judge reviewing the habeas petition upholds the order of extradition, the relator can appeal to the U.S. Court of Appeals, which will then only review the decision of the judge in the habeas proceedings or the legal grounds stated earlier. In some cases the U.S. government has taken the position that the relator has a right to only one appeal – the habeas petition. Unless the relator files for and obtains a stay of the surrender, the

U.S. government may decide to extradite while a habeas petition appeal is still pending. If the relator does not obtain a favorable decision on appeal, he or she may file a motion for a rehearing en banc before the same circuit court and petition the U.S. Supreme Court for a writ of certiorari.

If the court in a habeas order finds the relator nonextraditable, which is tantamount to a reversal of the order of extradition, the government may appeal that order to a U.S. circuit court. If that circuit court's decision is negative, the government can file a motion for a rehearing en banc before the same circuit court. If that decision is also negative, the government can file a petition for a writ of certiorari before the U.S. Supreme Court.

B. *When the United States Is the Requesting State*

When the United States is the requesting state, the process is greatly influenced by the domestic laws, procedures, institutions, and policies of the requested state. Treaties with other countries largely control the process. The United States participates in the extradition through diplomatic contacts with counterpart officials in the requested state. The U.S. Department of Justice and its counterparts in the Ministry of Justice abroad will cooperate to ascertain that the United States provides all the information and evidence these officials require.[4]

Sometimes, as the discussion of the case involving the U.S. government request for the extradition of Jacob "Kobi" Alexander from Namibia shows, politics can play an important part, especially if the relator develops strong contacts with the requested state.

U.K. Court Denies U.S. Extradition Request for Former Hotel Owner, Citing Prosecutors' Delays

REPRINTED FROM 23 INT'L ENFORCEMENT L. REP. 358 (SEPT. 2007)

by Bruce Zagaris

On June 28, 2007, a U.K. court denied a U.S. extradition request for 77-year-old Stanley Tollman, a wealthy hotelier accused of bank fraud and tax evasion. Tim Workman, Senior District Judge of the City of Westminster Magistrates' Court, ruled that while the alleged revenue offenses were extraditable, the excessive delays in seeking Tollman's extradition made it "unjust and oppressive" for him to stand trial.[5]

Judge Workman applied section 82 of the Extradition Act 2003, which reads, "a person's extradition to a category two territory is barred by reason of passage of time if (and only if) it appears that it would be unjust or oppressive to extradite the defendant by reason of the passage of time since he is alleged to have committed the extradition offence."[6] Judge Workman calculated the passage of time in this case as a range of 11 to 16 years for the fraud offenses and a range of 8 to 13 years for the tax evasion charges.

In response to the U.S. government's contentions that the delay in prosecuting Tollman should have redounded against Tollman and was caused by his fugitive status, Workman observed that Tollman left the U.S. unimpeded and before he was indicted by the grand jury.

[4] *See* M. Abbell, *supra* note 3 at, § 5–1.
[5] *United States of America v. Stanley Tollman*, In the City of Westminister Magistrates' Court, June 28, 2007 (available at http://services/services.taxanalysts.com).
[6] Available at http://www.opsi.gov.uk/acts/acts2003/20030041.htm.

Although conceding that the U.S. considers Tollman a fugitive, Judge Workman did not consider the "evidence that the accused fled the country or that he is therefore responsible for the delay," and ruled that Tollman was allowed to apply for a dismissal of the extradition charges due to the passage of time.

Evidence given in support of Tollman's application showed that a number of witnesses have died since the case was initiated, and that others have trouble remembering important details. A key witness, Arnold Tollman, Stanley Tollman's brother, died in 2004. Another witness, Derek Evans, died in 2002. Judge Workman also noted that Stanley Tollman's wife, Beatrice Tollman, whose case was already discharged by the court on the basis of her physical and mental health, could not give "cogent evidence of the facts that would have been within her knowledge" for the same health reasons.

Judge Workman also harshly criticized the behavior of Assistant United States Attorney Stanley Okula. Judge Workman found that Okula "displayed personal animosity towards Stanley Tollman and his family [by declaring] that he intends to make Tollman's 'life as miserable as possible'... and was looking forward to having a 'perp walk' with Beatrice Tollman." In addition, a Canadian court found in 2006 that an "unequivocal abuse of process of the court" occurred when Okula tried to bring Gavin Tollman to the U.S. from Canada outside of any formal extradition proceedings. However, Judge Workman concluded that Okula's actions did not by themselves "constitute sufficient evidence to make a finding of 'oppression' which would bar extradition."

Judge Workman ruled for Tollman largely based on his wife's failing health. Doctors testified that Tollman's extradition to the U.S. would have "an inevitable and disastrous effect upon her health" and also that "her health has already shown a considerable deterioration in recent months." As a result, Judge Workman decided that "extradition would inevitably cause oppression to Mrs. Tollman and through her to Mr. Tollman who is caring for her at the present time" and therefore ruled that "by virtue of the passage of time, it would now be unjust and oppressive for the defendant to be extradited."[7]

U.K. National Wins Partial Victory in Resisting U.S. Extradition Request

REPRINTED FROM 24 INT'L ENFORCEMENT L. REP. 175 (MAY 2008)

by Bruce Zagaris

On March 12, 2008, the Appellate Committee of the House of Lords gave a partial victory to U.K. national Ian Norris in his effort to resist extradition to the United States.[8] The U.S. government seeks his extradition to stand trial in the Eastern District of Pennsylvania on a four-count indictment. On June 1, 2005, the court sent the case to the Home Secretary for his decision on whether Norris should be extradited.[9] On September 29, 2005, the Home Secretary ordered that he should. The Queen's Bench Divisional Court upheld the district judge's decision.[10]

[7] *U.K. Will Not Extradite U.S. Man Wanted on Days Inn Tax Charges*, DAILY REP. FOR EXEC., July 6, 2007, at K-1.

[8] *Norris v. Government of the United States of America and others*, [2008] UKHL 16 (House of Lords Session 2007–8), Mar. 12, 2008, on appeal from [2007] EWHC 71 (Admin), http://business.timesonline.co.uk/tol/business/law/article3537275.ec. For more information *see* Bruce Zagaris, *U.S. Extradition from the U.K. Engenders Controversies*, 21 INT'L ENFORCEMENT LAW REP. 312 (18 Jan. 2007).

[9] [2005] UKCLR 1205.

[10] [2007] EWHC 71 9Admin), [2007] 1 WLR 1730.

In 2002, Norris retired as chief executive officer of the Morgan Crucible group after having worked in the carbon division of the group for 29 years. The parent company was based in England; subsidiary companies of the group were based in North Carolina and Pennsylvania. In 1999, the U.S. government started to investigate allegations of price-fixing in the carbon industry in the U.S. As a result of the investigations, two U.S. Morgan subsidiaries paid substantial fines. Most of Morgan's directors and officers received immunity from prosecution as part of a plea bargain arrangement. However, Norris and some others were not. In September 2004, a grand jury in the Eastern District of Pennsylvania returned the indictment.

1. Conspiracy to Price-Fix

The first count alleges that Norris conspired with certain other European producers of carbon products used in the transport, industrial, and consumer product markets to operate a price-fixing agreement or cartel in a number of countries, including the U.S. The charge is a statutory offense of strict liability. It does not require proof of fraud, deception, or dishonesty, and count 1 of the indictment does not contain such allegation. Counts 2, 3, and 4 of the indictment allege conspiracy to obstruct justice, witness tampering, and causing a person to alter, destroy, mutilate, or conceal an object with the intent to impair the object's availability for use in an official proceeding.

On Count 1 the court concluded the common law recognized that an agreement in restraint of trade might be unreasonable in the public interest, and in such cases the agreement would be held to be void and unenforceable. Unless there exist aggravating features such as fraud, misrepresentation, violence, intimidation, or inducement of a breach of contract, such agreements were not actionable or indictable; in the course of the authorities a number of different reasons were provided for the conclusion.

The court explained that statutory criminalization of cartels was first introduced by the Enterprise Act of 2002. At the time of its enactment the legislative history indicated that engaging in a cartel at the time constituted only a civil law infringement in the U.K. When the Bill came before the Parliament, ministers in both Houses stated that no criminal prosecutions in relation to such conduct were possible before the 2002 Act came into force. As a result, on April 23, 2002, the Minister responsible for extradition told the U.S. that it would not be possible to extradite Sir Anthony Tennant, whom U.S. authorities accuse of price-fixing.

The 2002 Act determines that an individual is guilty of an offense if he dishonestly agrees with one or more other persons to make or implement, or to cause to be made or implemented, arrangements for price-fixing. The enactment of the 2002 Act indicated that there was not a common offense of price-fixing.

The committee concluded that mere price-fixing (that is, the making and implementation of a price-fixing agreement without aggravating features) was not, at any time relevant to count 1, a criminal offense in the U.K. Norris's appeal in relation to this court must therefore be allowed and the lower court's order was quashed.

The committee concluded that the mere undeclared participation in a cartel was not at the material time, in the absence of aggravating features, a criminal offense in the U.K. either at common law or under statute. Hence, Norris's conduct cannot have been characterized as a conspiracy to defraud although it would have been otherwise had the allegation been, for example, that he and his co-conspirators, having entered into a price-fixing agreement, agreed in addition to deceive their customers by making false representations to the contrary. While such conduct would have been an aggravating feature, no such conduct is alleged in the extradition. Hence, the committee found that the absence of dishonesty as an essential ingredient of conspiracy to defraud precludes its fulfillment of the requirement of double criminality for purposes of U.K. extradition.

2. Obstruction of Justice

The Committee considered whether Norris could be extradited on Counts 2 to 4 of the indictment, alleging various forms of obstruction of justice, all relating to the criminal investigation into price-fixing in the carbon products industry which was being conducted by the grand jury in the Eastern District of Pennsylvania. While the Committee found obstruction of justice extraditable, it observed that Section 87(1) of the 2003 Extradition Act requires the extradition judge to decide whether a person's extradition would be incompatible with his Convention rights scheduled to the Human Rights Act 1998. This requires a judgment on the proportionality of an order of extradition in all the circumstances, having regard to the defendant's rights under article 8 and any other relevant article. The district judge considered that question and resolved it adversely to Norris. However, the judge exercised his judgment on the basis that Norris was to be extradited on the main price-fixing count, and not merely the subsidiary counts. The Committee remanded the case for the judge to decide this issue, observing that the determination may require evidence of witnesses.

3. Analysis

Norris is free to remain in the U.K. until a magistrate's court hears his case; no hearing has yet been set. Other businessmen and the Serious Fraud Office are scrutinizing the case. The business and legal communities have supported Norris.[11]

A FINANCIAL TIMES editorial underscored that the decision does not redress the continuing imbalance in Britain's legal relationship with the U.S. The editorial observed that the decision highlights the second-class status of Britain in terms of its extradition arrangement with the U.S. Normally, such arrangements are reciprocal and require the same standards of evidence from both countries. The large scope of U.S. extraterritorial jurisdiction and the length and cost of complex white collar cases make it extremely difficult for foreigners, and have energized some of the mainstream British media to demand changes in the U.K.-U.S. extradition relationship.[12]

Alexander Requests Dismissal of Presiding Officer of Namibian Extradition Proceeding

REPRINTED FROM 23 INT'L ENFORCEMENT L. REP. 378 (OCT. 2007)

by Bruce Zagaris

On August 10, 2007, Jacob "Kobi" Alexander, the former chief executive of Comverse Technology, filed an application to declare as unconstitutional the appointment of Petrus Unengu, the chief of Namibia's lower courts, as presiding officer at his extradition hearing. The U.S. government has requested that Namibia extradite Alexander to face an indictment in

[11] Michael Herman, *Partial Victory for Businessman in US Extradition Fight*, TIMESONLINE, Mar. 12, 2008. For more on this subject see Bruce Zagaris, *Australia Issues Warrants for Arrest in Anticipation of Extradition of U.S. Doctor on Medical Work* 23 INT'L ENFORCEMENT LAW REP. 18 (Jan. 2007).

[12] Editorial, *Extraditing Britons*, FIN. TIMES, Mar. 14, 2008.

U.S. District Court in Brooklyn on 35 counts of conspiracy, securities fraud, wire fraud, and money laundering in connection with backdating of Comverse stock options.[13] After his indictment Alexander did not return from a family holiday in Israel and the U.S. government declared him a fugitive.[14]

Alexander's application contends that Unengu's appointment violated Namibian legal principles of the separation of powers because Unengu is an administrative official. In his place Alexander has requested that the Ministry of Justice reinstate Magistrate Uuatja Uuanivi, who ordered Alexander released on a $1.4 million bail in October 2006. In December 2006, Alexander had his local bank accounts unfrozen.[15]

Meanwhile, the Namibian Ministry of Home Affairs is investigating Alexander's immigration application for a two-year work visa. The Namibian government alleges that Alexander's application might have contained "some misrepresentation" because it failed to mention the 10 years he had lived in New York. Namibian law requires applicants for work visas to produce police certificates from any country where they have lived in the last 10 years, showing a clean criminal record.[16]

The Alexander extradition case is a classic case of the use of wealth to set a favorable environment by a relator. Alexander has used his considerable wealth to invest in low-rent housing and other economic development activities that have a significant macroeconomic impact on a relatively poor country. Alexander's counsel has made creative legal maneuvers that have achieved success. For instance, he immediately obtained bail and has been able to delay the extradition proceedings on a number of occasions. These maneuvers would not have been available to relators without monetary resources. However, the challenge of Unengu's appointment is risky because it could have a significantly adverse impact not only on Alexander's case, but on all the other cases over which Unengu presides.

Notes and Questions

1. The decision by Judge Workman in the Tollman case indicates the sensitivities of requested states to fairness in the requesting state, notwithstanding the rule of noninquiry. As a result of media exposure of U.S. abuses of terrorist suspects in the period after September 11, 2001, increasingly the judiciary and executive branch in requested states do not give the United States the benefit of the doubt on cases as they previously did.

2. Does Judge Workman's decision also reflect a concern with humanitarian considerations, given the relatively harsh sentence for the charges and Tollman's age (77 years old)? Interestingly and somewhat unusually Judge Workman took into consideration the adverse impact of extradition on Stanley Tollman's wife Beatrice for whom Stanley was caring.

3. The Ian Norris case illustrates the difficulty the United States has, as the requesting state, when the extraditable crimes are complex offenses. The complexity of white collar crimes sometimes causes double criminality problems.

[13] John Grobler, *Ex-Comverse Chief Keeps Maneuvering to Avoid Return in Options Case*, N.Y. TIMES, Aug. 11, 2006.

[14] *Id.* For additional background on the ruling, *see* Bruce Zagaris, *Namibia Court Grants Comverse CEO Bail on U.S. Extradition Request*, 22 INT'L ENFORCEMENT L. REP. 472 (Dec. 2006).

[15] Grobler, *supra note* 13.

[16] *Id.*

4. One of the most controversial white collar cases between the United States and the United Kingdom is that of the Nat West 3. They are three British businessmen – Giles Darby, David Bermingham, and Gary Mulgrew – who in 2002 were indicted in Houston on seven counts of wire fraud against their former employer, Greenwich NatWest, at the time a division of National Westminster Bank. After a high-profile battle in the British courts they were extradited from the United Kingdom to the United States in 2006. On November 28, 2007, they each pleaded guilty to one count of wire fraud in exchange for the other charges being dropped. On February 22, 2008, they were each sentenced to thirty-seven months in prison. In November, 2008, it was announced they will spend the rest of their sentences in the United Kingdom.

The extradition raised several issues. First, the relators' counsel contended that the crime was committed by British citizens living in Britain against a British company based in London. Hence, any resulting criminal case fell under British legal and territorial jurisdiction and should be tried by a British court. However, British authorities decided not to prosecute because of lack of evidence. Second, the counsel argued that it would be very difficult to obtain a fair trial in Texas. The case could have taken years to come to trial (the trial was scheduled to begin in September 2006, but was repeatedly postponed to January 2008). The three would be forced to remain in the United States far away from their families. In addition, while on bail they would be not be able to find gainful employment needed to fund a legal defense against the charges brought against them. In fact the court allowed them to seek employment in the United States provided they remained in Houston. In addition, the relators' counsel argued that they would have difficulty presenting a defense because most of the evidence and witnesses were overseas, in the United Kingdom, and the witnesses would be reluctant to come to Texas. Finally, counsel for the Nat West and the British media alleged that the extradition arrangements between the United States and the United Kingdom are highly unequal. Although it is comparatively easy to extradite British citizens to the United States, it is difficult to extradite Americans to Britain. The media focused on the fact that the United States does not have to produce a prima facie case – or even any "reasonable case" to extradite U.K. citizens, whereas there is no comparable facility to extradite U.S. citizens to the United Kingdom. *See, e.g.*, Catherine Heard, *Fair Trials International's Policy Paper: A Brief Review of U.S.-U.K. Extradition under the Extradition Act of 2003 from a Human Rights Perspective*, 25 INT'L ENFORCEMENT L. REP. 2 (Jan. 2008). What do you think about the alleged inequality between the U.S. and U.K. extradition procedures? Does this violate the idea of reciprocity?

5. The case of Jacob "Kobi" Alexander has been pending since mid-June 2006. In almost three years the U.S. government as the requesting state has not succeeded in even having Mr. Alexander kept in custody or his accounts frozen, even though he is basically charged with fraud offenses, which are normally a traditional extraditable crime. What would stop any wealthy fugitive from trying to buy influence with the requested state by making donations to badly needed development projects, such as low-income housing? How can the requesting state successfully counteract such political strategies?

6. Normally the Ministry of Justice in the requested state represents the requesting state. As a result, the requesting state can rely on government officials for strategic advice and day-to-day handling of the case. However, in several jurisdictions, such as in the Caribbean, governments lack counsel with specialized extradition training. As a result, a requesting state must hire private practitioners qualified to litigate extradition requests.

Defendants must also find private counsel – usually at least one attorney in both the requested and requesting states.

The short supply of specialized extradition attorneys and the fact that effective representation often requires a lawyer who is familiar with both extradition and substantive white collar criminal defense complicate a defendant's efforts to obtain effective counsel. In light of the limited number of expert extradition counsel, the political sensitivity of many extradition matters, and the length of some extradition proceedings, the selection of proper counsel is a critical element in every case.

7. Because of the complexities of choosing extradition counsel, many defendants rely on recommendations from other attorneys. Bar associations, especially international bar associations or international branches of national bar associations, are good sources of referrals. Law directories also increasingly provide information on potential counsel.

C. *Extradition Treaties*

As an example, the full text of the U.S.-Belize extradition treaty follows.

Extradition Treaty between the Government of the United States of America and the Government of Belize[17]

Article 1 – Obligation to Extradite

The Contracting States agree to extradite to each other, pursuant to the provisions of this Treaty, persons sought for prosecution or convicted of an extraditable offense by the authorities in the Requesting State.

Article 2 – Extraditable Offenses

1. An offense shall be an extraditable offense if it falls within any of the descriptions listed in the Schedule annexed to this Treaty, which is an integral part of the Treaty, or any other offense, provided that in either case the offense is punishable under the laws in both Contracting States by deprivation of liberty for a period of more than one year or by a more severe penalty.
2. An offense shall also be an extraditable offense if it consists of an attempt or a conspiracy to commit, aiding or abetting, counseling or procuring the commission of, or being an accessory before or after the fact to, any offense described in paragraph 1.
3. For the purposes of this Article, an offense shall be an extraditable offense:
   (a) whether or not the laws in the Contracting States place the offense within the same category of offenses or describe the offense by the same terminology; or
   (b) whether or not the offense is one for which United States federal law requires the showing of such matters as interstate transportation, or use of the mails or of other facilities affecting interstate or foreign commerce, such matters being merely for the purpose of establishing jurisdiction in a United States federal court.
4. If the offense was committed outside of the territory of the Requesting State, extradition shall be granted in accordance with this treaty if the laws in the Requested State provide

[17] *See* TREATY DOC. No. 106–38, Extradition Treaty with Belize, 106th Cong., 2d Sess. (2000).

for punishment of an offense committed outside of its territory in similar circumstances.

5. If extradition has been granted for an extraditable offense, it shall also be granted for any other offense specified in the request even if the latter offense is punishable by one year's deprivation of liberty or less, provided that all other requirements for extradition are met.

Article 3 – Nationality

Extradition shall not be refused on the ground that the person sought is a national of the Requested State.

Article 4 – Political and Military Offenses

1. Extradition shall not be granted if the offense for which extradition is requested is a political offense.
2. For the purposes of this Treaty, the following offenses shall not be considered to be political offenses:
   (a) a murder or other willful crime against the person of a Head of State of one of the Contracting States, or of a member of the Head of State's family;
   (b) an offense for which both Contracting States have the obligation pursuant to a multilateral international agreement to extradite the person sought or to submit the case to their competent authorities for decision as to prosecution; and
   (c) a conspiracy or attempt to commit any of the foregoing offenses, or aiding or abetting a person who commits or attempts to commit such offenses.
3. Notwithstanding the terms of paragraph 2 of this Article, extradition shall not be granted if the executive authority of the Requested State determines that the request was politically motivated.
4. The executive authority of the Requested State may refuse extradition for offenses under military law which are not offenses under ordinary criminal law.

Article 5 – Prior Prosecution

1. Extradition shall not be granted when the person sought has been convicted or acquitted in the Requested State for the offense for which extradition is requested.
2. Extradition shall not be precluded by the fact that the authorities in the Requested State have decided not to prosecute the person sought for the acts for which extradition is requested, or to discontinue any criminal proceedings which have been instituted against the person sought for those acts.

Article 6 – Extradition Procedures and Required Documents

1. All requests for extradition shall be submitted through the diplomatic channel.
2. All requests shall be supported by:
   (a) documents, statements, or other types of evidence which describe the identity, and probable location of the person sought;

(b) evidence describing the facts of the offense and the procedural history of the case;
(c) evidence as to:
(i) the provisions of the laws describing the essential elements of the offense for which extradition is requested;
(ii) the provisions of the law describing the punishment for the offense; and
(iii) the provisions of law describing any time limit on the prosecution; and
(d) the documents, statements, or other types of evidence specified in paragraph 3 or paragraph 4 of this Article, as applicable.

3. A request for extradition of a person who is sought for prosecution shall also be supported by:
(a) a copy of the warrant or order of arrest, if any, issued by a judge or other competent authority of the Requesting State;
(b) a document setting forth the charges; and
(c) such evidence as would be found sufficient, according to the law of the Requested State, to justify the committal for trial of the person sought if the offense of which the person has been accused had been committed in the Requested State.

4. A request for extradition relating to a person who has been convicted of the offense for which extradition is sought shall, in addition to the materials listed in paragraph 2 of this Article, be supported by:
(a) a copy of the judgment of conviction or, if such copy is not available, a statement by a judicial authority that the person has been convicted;
(b) evidence establishing that the person sought is the person to whom the conviction refers;
(c) a copy of the sentence imposed, if the person sought has been sentenced, and a statement establishing to what extent the sentence has been carried out; and
(d) in the case of a person who has been convicted in absentia, the documents required by paragraph 3 of this Article.

Article 7 – Admissibility of Documents

The documents which accompany an extradition request shall be received and admitted as evidence in extradition proceedings if:

(a) in the case of a request from the United States, they are authenticated by an officer of the United States Department of State and are certified by the principal diplomatic or consular officer of Belize resident in the United States;
(b) in the case of a request from Belize, they are certified by the principal diplomatic or consular officer of the United States resident in Belize, as provided by the extradition laws of the United States; or
(c) they are certified or authenticated in any other manner accepted by the law of the Requested State.

Article 8 – Lapse of Time

Extradition shall not be denied because of the prescriptive laws of either the Requesting State or the Requested State.

Article 9 – Provisional Arrest

1. In case of urgency, a Contracting State may request the provisional arrest of the person sought pending presentation of the request for extradition. A request for provisional arrest may be transmitted through the diplomatic channel or directly between the United States Department of Justice and the Attorney General in Belize. Such a request may also be transmitted through the facilities of the International Criminal Police Organization (INTERPOL), or through such other means as may be settled by arrangement between the Contracting States.
2. The application for provisional arrest shall contain:
   (a) a description of the person sought;
   (b) the location of the person sought, if known;
   (c) a brief statement of the facts of the case, including, if possible, the time and location of the offense;
   (d) a description of the laws violated;
   (e) a statement of the existence of a warrant of arrest or a finding of guilt or judgment of conviction against the person sought; and
   (f) a statement that a request for extradition for the person sought will follow.
3. The Requesting State shall be notified without delay of the disposition of its application and the reasons for any denial.
4. A person who is provisionally arrested may be discharged from custody upon the expiration of sixty (60) days from the date of provisional arrest pursuant to this Treaty if the executive authority of the Requested State has not received the formal request for extradition and the supporting documents required in Article 6. The person arrested pursuant to this Article shall have the right of access to the courts for such remedies and recourses as are provided by the law of the Requested State.
5. The fact that the person sought has been discharged from custody pursuant to paragraph 4 of this Article shall not prejudice the subsequent re-arrest and extradition of that person if the extradition request and supporting documents are delivered at a later date.

Article 10 – Decision and Surrender

1. Extradition shall be granted only if the evidence is found sufficient according to the law of the Requested State either to justify the committal for trial of the person sought if the offense of which the person is accused had been committed in the territory of the Requested State or to prove that the person is the identical person convicted by the courts of the Requesting State.
2. The Requested State shall promptly notify the Requesting State through the diplomatic channel of its decision on the request for extradition.
3. If the request is denied in whole or in part, the Requested State shall provide an explanation of the reasons for the denial. The Requested State shall provide copies of pertinent judicial decisions upon request.
4. If the request for extradition is granted, the authorities of the Contracting States shall agree on the time and place for the surrender of the person sought.
5. If the person sought is not removed from the territory of the Requested State within the time prescribed by the law of that State, that person may be discharged from custody, and the Requested State may subsequently refuse extradition for the same offense.

Article 11 – Temporary and Deferred Surrender

1. If the extradition request is granted in the case of a person who is being proceeded against or is serving a sentence in the Requested State, the Requested State may temporarily surrender the person sought to the Requesting State for the purpose of prosecution. The person so surrendered shall be kept in custody in the Requesting State and shall be returned to the Requested State after the conclusion of the proceedings against that person, in accordance with conditions to be determined by mutual agreement of the Contracting States.
2. The Requested State may postpone the extradition proceedings against a person who is being prosecuted or who is serving a sentence in that State. The postponement may continue until the prosecution of the person sought has been concluded or until such person has served any sentence imposed.

Article 12 – Requests for Extradition Made by Several States

If the Requested State receives requests from the other Contracting State and from any other State or States for the extradition of the same person, either for the same offense or for different offenses, the executive authority of the Requested State shall determine to which State it will surrender the person. In making its decision, the Requested State shall consider all relevant factors, including but not limited to:

(a) whether the requests were made pursuant to treaty;
(b) the place where each offense was committed;
(c) the respective interests of the Requesting States;
(d) the gravity of the offenses;
(e) the nationality of the victim;
(f) the possibility of further extradition between the Requesting States; and
(g) the chronological order in which the requests were received from the Requesting States.

Article 13 – Seizure and Surrender of Property

1. To the extent permitted under its law, the Requested State may seize and surrender to the Requesting State all articles, documents, and evidence connected with the offense in respect of which extradition is granted. The items mentioned in this Article may be surrendered even when the extradition cannot be effected due to the death, disappearance, or escape of the person sought.
2. The Requested State may condition the surrender of the property upon satisfactory assurances from the Requesting State that the property will be returned to the Requested State as soon as practicable. The Requested State may also defer the surrender of such property if it is needed as evidence in the Requested State.
3. The rights of third parties in such property shall be duly respected.

Article 14 – Rule of Speciality

1. A person extradited under this Treaty may not be detained, tried, or punished in the Requesting State except for:

(a) the offense for which extradition has been granted or a differently denominated offense based on the same facts on which extradition was granted, provided such offense is extraditable, or is a lesser included offense;
(b) an offense committed after the extradition of the person; or
(c) an offense for which the executive authority of the Requested State consents to the person's detention, trial, or punishment. For the purpose of this subparagraph:
(i) the Requested State may require the submission of the documents called for in Article 6; and
(ii) the person extradited may be detained by the Requesting State for 90 days, or for such longer period of time as the Requested State may authorize, while the request is being processed.

2. A person extradited under this Treaty may not be extradited to a third State for an offense committed prior to his surrender unless the surrendering State consents.
3. Paragraphs 1 and 2 of this Article shall not prevent the detention, trial, or punishment of an extradited person, or the extradition of that person to a third State, if:
(a) that person leaves the territory of the Requesting State after extradition and voluntarily returns to it; or
(b) that person does not leave the territory of the Requesting State within 10 days of the day on which that person is free to leave.

Article 15 – Waiver of Extradition

If the person sought consents to surrender to the Requesting State, the Requested State may surrender the person as expeditiously as possible without further proceedings.

Article 16 – Transit

1. Either Contracting State may authorize transportation through its territory of a person surrendered to the other State by a third State. A request for transit shall be transmitted through the diplomatic channel or directly between the Department of Justice in the United States and the Attorney General in Belize. Such a request may also be transmitted through the facilities of the International Criminal Police Organization (INTERPOL), or through such other means as may be settled by arrangement between the Contracting States. It shall contain a description of the person being transported and a brief statement of the facts of the case. A person in transit may be detained in custody during the period of transit.
2. No authorization is required where air transportation is used and no landing is scheduled on the territory of the Contracting State. If an unscheduled landing occurs on the territory of the other Contracting State, the other Contracting State may require the request for transit as provided in paragraph 1. That Contracting State may detain the person to be transported until the request for transit is received and the transit is effected, so long as the request is received within 96 hours of the unscheduled landing.

Article 17 – Representation and Expenses

1. The Requested State shall advise, assist, appear in court on behalf of the Requesting State, and represent the interests of the Requesting State, in any proceedings arising out of a request for extradition.

2. The Requesting State shall bear the expenses related to the translation of documents and the transportation of the person surrendered. The Requested State shall pay all other expenses incurred in that State by reason of the extradition proceedings.
3. Neither State shall make any pecuniary claim against the other State arising out of the arrest, detention, examination, or surrender of persons sought under this Treaty.

Article 18 – Consultation

The Department of Justice of the United States and the Attorney General of Belize may consult with each other directly in connection with the processing of individual cases and in furtherance of maintaining and improving procedures for the implementation of this Treaty.

Article 19 – Application

This Treaty shall apply to offenses committed before as well as after the date it enters into force, provided that extradition shall not be granted for an offense committed before this Treaty enters into force which was not an offense under the laws of both Contracting States at the time of its commission. Nothing in this Treaty shall be construed to criminalize any conduct that was not subject to criminal sanctions at the time the offense was committed.

Article 20 – Ratification and Entry into Force

1. This Treaty shall be subject to ratification; the instruments of ratification shall be exchanged as soon as possible.
2. This Treaty shall enter into force upon the exchange of the instruments of ratification.
3. Upon the entry into force of this Treaty, the Extradition Treaty between the Government of the United Kingdom of Great Britain and Northern Ireland and the Government of the United States of America, signed at London June 8, 1972, shall cease to have any effect between the United States and Belize. Nevertheless, the prior Treaty shall apply to any extradition proceedings in which the extradition documents have already been submitted to the courts of the Requested State at the time this Treaty enters into force, except that Article 15 of this Treaty shall be applicable to such proceedings. Article 14 of this Treaty shall apply to persons found extraditable under the prior Treaty.

Article 21 – Termination

Either Contracting State may terminate this Treaty at any time by giving written notice to the other Contracting State, and the termination shall be effective six months after the date of receipt of such notice.

D. *Extradition Treaties Using the List of Offenses*

Many older extradition treaties include a defined list of extraditable offenses. For example, Article 2(1) of the U.S.-Netherlands extradition treaty (TIAS 10733), which entered into force on September 15, 1983, lists the following extraditable offenses:

> (a) offenses referred to in the Appendix to the treaty, which are punishable under the laws of both Contracting Party; (b) offenses, which listed in the Appendix to the

treaty or not, provided they are punishable under the Federal laws of the U.S. and the Netherlands. The Appendix lists the following 36 offenses: (1) murder, assault with intent to commit murder; (2) manslaughter; (3) malicious wounding; inflicting grievous bodily harm; (4) arson; (5) rape, indecent assault, incest, bigamy; (6) unlawful sexual acts with or upon children under the age specified by the laws of both the Requesting and Requested State; (7) willful abandonment of a minor or other dependent person when the life of that minor or that dependent person is or is likely to be injured or endangered; (8) kidnapping, abduction, false imprisonment; (9) robbery, burglary, larceny, embezzlement; (10) fraud, including obtaining property, money, or valuable securities by false pretenses, deceit, falsehood, or other fraudulent means; (11) bribery, including soliciting, offering, and accepting; (12) extortion; (13) receiving, possessing, or transporting anything of value knowing it to have been unlawfully obtained; (14) offenses relating to criminal breach of trust; (15) an offense against the laws relating to counterfeiting and forgery, including the forging of seals, trademarks, documents, or use of such forgeries; (16) an offense against the laws relating to international transfers of funds; (17) an offense against the laws relating to importation, exportation or transit of goods, articles, or merchandise, including violations of customs laws; (18) offenses relating to slavery or the illegal transporting of persons; (19) offenses against the laws relating to bankruptcy; (20) offenses against the laws relating to prohibition of private monopoly or unfair trade practices; (21) perjury, subornation of perjury, making a false statement to a government agency or official; (22) offenses relating to willful evasion of taxes and duties; (23) any act or omission intended or likely to: (a) endanger the safety of an aircraft in flight or of any person on board such aircraft; or (b) destroy or render any aircraft incapable of flight; (24) any unlawful seizure or exercise of control of an aircraft in flight by force or violence, or by threat of force or violence, or by any other form of intimidation; (25) any unlawful act or omission intended or that is likely to endanger the safety of any person in a railway train or in any vessel or other means of transportation; (26) piracy, mutiny, or any mutinous act committed on board a vessel; (27) malicious damage to property; (28) offenses against the laws relating to the traffic in, or the possession, production, or manufacture of narcotic drugs, cannabis, psychotropic drugs, cocaine and its derivatives, and other dangerous drugs and chemicals; (29) offenses against laws relating to poisonous chemicals or substances injurious to health; (30) offenses against the laws relating to firearms, ammunition, explosives, incendiary devices, or nuclear materials; (31) offenses against the laws relating to the abuse of official authority; (32) offenses against the laws relating to obstruction of justice; (33) offenses relating to securities and commodities; (34) facilitating or permitting the escape of a person from custody; (35) incitements to violence; and (36) any other act for which extradition may be granted in accordance with the laws of both Contracting Parties.

E. *U.S. Statutes*

In the United States, Title 18 of the United States Code, Sections 3181 through 3195, governs extradition. The relevant sections are excerpted in the following:

§ 3181. Scope and Limitation of Chapter

(a) The provisions of this chapter relating to the surrender of persons who have committed crimes in foreign countries shall continue in force only during the existence of any treaty of extradition with such foreign government.

(b) The provisions of this chapter shall be construed to permit, in the exercise of comity, the surrender of persons, other than citizens, nationals, or permanent residents of the United States, who have committed crimes of violence against nationals of the United States in foreign countries without regard to the existence of any treaty of extradition with such foreign government if the Attorney General certifies, in writing, that
  (1) evidence has been presented by the foreign government that indicates that had the offenses been committed in the United States, they would constitute crimes of violence as defined under section 16 of this title; and
  (2) the offenses charged are not of a political nature.

(c) As used in this section, the term "national of the United States" has the meaning given such term in section 101(a)(22) of the Immigration and Nationality Act (8 U.S.C. 1101 (a)(22)).

§ 3182. Fugitives from State or Territory to State, District, or Territory

Whenever the executive authority of any State or Territory demands any person as a fugitive from justice, of the executive authority of any State, District, or Territory to which such person has fled, and produces a copy of an indictment found or an affidavit made before a magistrate of any State or Territory, charging the person demanded with having committed treason, felony, or other crime, certified as authentic by the governor or chief magistrate of the State or Territory from whence the person so charged has fled, the executive authority of the State, District, or Territory to which such person has fled shall cause him to be arrested and secured, and notify the executive authority making such demand, or the agent of such authority appointed to receive the fugitive, and shall cause the fugitive to be delivered to such agent when he shall appear. If no such agent appears within thirty days from the time of the arrest, the prisoner may be discharged.

§ 3183. Fugitives from State, Territory, or Possession into Extraterritorial Jurisdiction of United States

Whenever the executive authority of any State, Territory, District, or possession of the United States demands any American citizen or national as a fugitive from justice who has fled to a country in which the United States exercises extraterritorial jurisdiction, and produces a copy of an indictment found or an affidavit made before a magistrate of the demanding jurisdiction, charging the fugitive so demanded with having committed treason, felony, or other offense, certified as authentic by the Governor or chief magistrate of such demanding jurisdiction, or other person authorized to act, the officer or representative of the United States vested with judicial authority to whom the demand has been made shall cause such fugitive to be arrested and secured, and notify the executive authorities making such demand, or the agent of such authority appointed to receive the fugitive, and shall cause the fugitive to be delivered to such agent when he shall appear.

If no such agent shall appear within three months from the time of the arrest, the prisoner may be discharged.

The agent who receives the fugitive into his custody shall be empowered to transport him to the jurisdiction from which he has fled.

§ 3184. Fugitives from Foreign Country to United States

Whenever there is a treaty or convention for extradition between the United States and any foreign government, or in cases arising under section 3181 (b), any justice or judge of the United States, or any magistrate judge authorized to do so by a court of the United States, or any judge of a court of record of general jurisdiction of any State, may, upon complaint made under oath, charging any person found within his jurisdiction, with having committed within the jurisdiction of any such foreign government any of the crimes provided for by such treaty or convention, or provided for under section 3181 (b), issue his warrant for the apprehension of the person so charged, that he may be brought before such justice, judge, or magistrate judge, to the end that the evidence of criminality may be heard and considered. Such complaint may be filed before and such warrant may be issued by a judge or magistrate judge of the United States District Court for the District of Columbia if the whereabouts within the United States of the person charged are not known or, if there is reason to believe the person will shortly enter the United States. If, on such hearing, he deems the evidence sufficient to sustain the charge under the provisions of the proper treaty or convention, or under section 3181 (b), he shall certify the same, together with a copy of all the testimony taken before him, to the Secretary of State, that a warrant may issue upon the requisition of the proper authorities of such foreign government, for the surrender of such person, according to the stipulations of the treaty or convention; and he shall issue his warrant for the commitment of the person so charged to the proper jail, there to remain until such surrender shall be made.

§ 3185. Fugitives from Country under Control of United States into the United States

Whenever any foreign country or territory, or any part thereof, is occupied by or under the control of the United States, any person who, having violated the criminal laws in force therein by the commission of any of the offenses enumerated in the following, departs or flees from justice therein to the United States, shall, when found therein, be liable to arrest and detention by the authorities of the United States, and on the written request or requisition of the military governor or other chief executive officer in control of such foreign country or territory shall be returned and surrendered as hereinafter provided to such authorities for trial under the laws in force in the place where such offense was committed.

(1) Murder and assault with intent to commit murder;
(2) Counterfeiting or altering money, or uttering or bringing into circulation counterfeit or altered money;
(3) Counterfeiting certificates or coupons of public indebtedness, bank notes, or other instruments of public credit, and the utterance or circulation of the same;
(4) Forgery or altering and uttering what is forged or altered;
(5) Embezzlement or criminal malversation of the public funds, committed by public officers, employees, or depositaries;
(6) Larceny or embezzlement of an amount not less than $100 in value;
(7) Robbery;
(8) Burglary, defined to be the breaking and entering by nighttime into the house of another person with intent to commit a felony therein;
(9) Breaking and entering the house or building of another, whether in the day or nighttime, with the intent to commit a felony therein;

(10) Entering, or breaking and entering the offices of the Government and public authorities, or the offices of banks, banking houses, savings banks, trust companies, insurance or other companies, with the intent to commit a felony therein;
(11) Perjury or the subornation of perjury;
(12) A felony under chapter 109A of this title;
(13) Arson;
(14) Piracy by the law of nations;
(15) Murder, assault with intent to kill, and manslaughter, committed on the high seas, on board a ship owned by or in control of citizens or residents of such foreign country or territory and not under the flag of the United States, or of some other government;
(16) Malicious destruction of or attempt to destroy railways, trams, vessels, bridges, dwellings, public edifices, or other buildings, when the act endangers human life.

This chapter, so far as applicable, shall govern proceedings authorized by this section. Such proceedings shall be had before a judge of the courts of the United States only, who shall hold such person on evidence establishing probable cause that he is guilty of the offense charged.

No return or surrender shall be made of any person charged with the commission of any offense of a political nature.

If so held, such person shall be returned and surrendered to the authorities in control of such foreign country or territory on the order of the Secretary of State of the United States, and such authorities shall secure to such a person a fair and impartial trial.

§ 3186. Secretary of State to Surrender Fugitive

The Secretary of State may order the person committed under sections 3184 or 3185 of this title to be delivered to any authorized agent of such foreign government, to be tried for the offense of which charged.

Such agent may hold such person in custody, and take him to the territory of such foreign government, pursuant to such treaty.

A person so accused who escapes may be retaken in the same manner as any person accused of any offense.

§ 3187. Provisional Arrest and Detention within Extraterritorial Jurisdiction

The provisional arrest and detention of a fugitive, under sections 3042 and 3183 of this title, in advance of the presentation of formal proofs, may be obtained by telegraph upon the request of the authority competent to request the surrender of such fugitive addressed to the authority competent to grant such surrender. Such request shall be accompanied by an express statement that a warrant for the fugitive's arrest has been issued within the jurisdiction of the authority making such request charging the fugitive with the commission of the crime for which his extradition is sought to be obtained.

No person shall be held in custody under telegraphic request by virtue of this section for more than ninety days.

§ 3188. Time of Commitment Pending Extradition

Whenever any person who is committed for rendition to a foreign government to remain until delivered up in pursuance of a requisition, is not so delivered up and conveyed out of the United States within two calendar months after such commitment, over and above the time actually required to convey the prisoner from the jail to which he was committed, by the readiest way, out of the United States, any judge of the United States, or of any State, upon application made to him by or on behalf of the person so committed, and upon proof made to him that reasonable notice of the intention to make such application has been given to the Secretary of State, may order the person so committed to be discharged out of custody, unless sufficient cause is shown to such judge why such discharge ought not to be ordered.

§ 3189. Place and Character of Hearing

Hearings in cases of extradition under treaty stipulation or convention shall be held on land, publicly, and in a room or office easily accessible to the public.

§ 3190. Evidence on Hearing

Depositions, warrants, or other papers or copies thereof offered in evidence upon the hearing of any extradition case shall be received and admitted as evidence on such hearing for all the purposes of such hearing if they shall be properly and legally authenticated so as to entitle them to be received for similar purposes by the tribunals of the foreign country from which the accused party shall have escaped, and the certificate of the principal diplomatic or consular officer of the United States resident in such foreign country shall be proof that the same, so offered, are authenticated in the manner required.

§ 3195. Payment of Fees and Costs

All costs or expenses incurred in any extradition proceeding in apprehending, securing, and transmitting a fugitive shall be paid by the demanding authority.

All witness fees and costs of every nature in cases of international extradition, including the fees of the magistrate judge, shall be certified by the judge or magistrate judge before whom the hearing shall take place to the Secretary of State of the United States, and the same shall be paid out of appropriations to defray the expenses of the judiciary or the Department of Justice as the case may be.

The Attorney General shall certify to the Secretary of State the amounts to be paid to the United States on account of said fees and costs in extradition cases by the foreign government requesting the extradition, and the Secretary of State shall cause said amounts to be collected and transmitted to the Attorney General for deposit in the Treasury of the United States.

Notes and Questions

1. *Need for treaty.* As set forth in U.S. statutes, the United States can extradite only pursuant to an extradition treaty. *See Valentine v. Untied States ex rel. Neidecker*, 299 U.S. 5 (1936); RESTATEMENT (3D) of Foreign Relations, § 475, Comment 5 and Reporters' Note 3.

2. *Executive Agreement if authorized by statute may comply with treaty requirement.* In *Ntakirutimana v. Reno*, 184 F.3d 419, 427 (5th Cir. 1999), the appellate court affirmed denial of a relator's habeas corpus petition alleging that the district court erred because the U.S. Constitution requires an Article II treaty for the surrender of a person to the

International Criminal Tribunal for Rwanda. The court found the argument does not apply where there is an executive-congressional agreement.

F. *Standing*

United States v. Puentes, 50 F.3d 1567 (11th Cir. 1995)

The appellate court heard arguments about whether the accused, Ramon Puentes, had standing to raise the "specialty doctrine" so he could limit his prosecution in the United States to the specific charges for which he was extradited from Uruguay.

The government pointed out that the circuit had not specifically addressed whether a defendant has standing to assert a violation of an extradition treaty. The court observed that under the doctrine of specialty, a nation that receives a criminal defendant under an extradition treaty may try the defendant only for those offenses for which the other nation granted extradition.

The opinion observed that all of the circuit courts of appeals have not embraced the holding the court would announce. Other courts have held that an extradited individual lacks standing to assert the doctrine of specialty in the absence of an express objection on the part of the requested nation. These courts consider the principle of specialty to be a matter of international law that inures solely to the benefit of the requested nation, conferring no rights on the accused. Cf. *Shapiro v. Ferrandina*, 478 F.2d 894, 906 (2d Cir.), *cert. dismissed*, 414 U.S. 884 (1973). Such courts have relied on the international law rule of construction that only nations may enforce treaty obligations, and inferred that an individual cannot assert rights under a treaty in U.S. courts. However, the opinion found the analysis flawed because it ignored both the history of the concept of extradition and U.S. jurisprudence [i.e., *U.S. v. Rauscher*, 119 U.S. 407 (1886)].

The opinion reasoned that the individual's rights are derivative of the rights of the requested nation. According to *Rauscher*, even in the absence of a protest from the requested state, an individual extradited pursuant to a treaty has standing to challenge the court's personal jurisdiction under the rule of specialty. The opinion held that an individual extradited pursuant to an extradition treaty has standing under the doctrine of specialty to raise any objections which the requested nation might have asserted. However, the extradited individual enjoys the right at the sufferance of the requested nation. The requested state, as a sovereign, can waive its right to object to a treaty violation and hence deny the defendant standing to object to such an action.

Notes and Questions

1. Which position do you find more compelling – the international law rule of construction that only nations may enforce treaty obligations or the Eleventh Circuit in *Puentes*?

2. How should a court react to silence or failure to object to a defendant raising the specialty doctrine or another argument?

3. How does the requirement of dual criminality interact with the right of specialty?

4. How rigidly do prosecutors adhere to the rule of specialty? *See, e.g.*, Hugh Chadwick Thatcher, Note, *The Doctrine of Specialty: An Argument for a More Restrictive Rauscher Interpretation after* State v. Pang, 31 VAND. J. TRANSNAT'L L. 1321 (1998).

5. Some courts do not allow relators to raise claims of procedural violations in the extradition process. In *United States v. Antonakeas*, 255 F.3d 714 (9th Cir, 2001), the court held that "unlike the substantive right of specialty, procedural violations do not give rise to individually enforceable rights."

G. *Grounds to Deny Extradition*

1. Extradition of Nationals

A number of countries do not extradite their nationals or only extradite them in certain cases. Despite calls from other countries to reexamine this position, nonextraditing countries have maintained these policies with an eye toward domestic political considerations and concerns about sovereignty. They seem to feel that their national interests outweigh international concerns. *See* Michael Plachta, *(Non-)Extradition of Nationals: A Neverending Story?*, 13 EMORY INT'L L. REV. 77, 79 (1999). Some countries have agreed to extradite nationals who have committed especially heinous crimes, and some have reserved extradition as an option in such cases. Other countries, particularly the Netherlands, will only extradite nationals on the condition that, if tried and convicted, they be returned to their home country to serve their sentence.

Under one approach, some countries have agreed to extradite nationals except in certain cases. For example, the 1996 extradition treaty between the United States and Hong Kong provides in Article 1 that the treaty applies to "any person." Agreement for the Surrender of Fugitive Offenders, Dec. 20, 1996, U.S.-H.K., 36 I.L.M. 842 (Treaty Doc. 105–3). Article 3 states that "surrender shall not be refused on grounds relating to the nationality of the person sought." The article also provides two exceptions. The United States "reserves the right to refuse the surrender of [its] nationals . . . in cases in which the requested surrender relates to the defense, foreign affairs or essential public interest or policy of the United States." The government of Hong Kong reserved a similar right.

The controversial case of Samuel Sheinbein, who was born in the United States, has received significant media attention. As a teenager, Sheinbein fled to Israel after he committed a grisly murder and invoked Israeli nationality law to frustrate U.S. extradition requests. After several years of successfully resisting U.S. extradition, he pled guilty to homicide charges, receiving a sentence that was comparatively lenient by U.S. guidelines. *See* Abraham Abramovsky & Jonathan I. Edelstein, *The Sheinbein Case and the Israeli-American Extradition Experience: A Need for Compromise*, 32 VAND. J. TRANST'L L. 305 (1999).

The U.S. government has prioritized the ability to extradite nationals in extradition treaty negotiations.

2. Jurisdictional Issues

Some post-1960 U.S. extradition treaties give the requested state discretion to deny extradition when the requested offense is committed, at least in part, within its territorial jurisdiction. If such a provision does not exist, a requested state has the authority to prosecute the offense itself, thereby precluding subsequent extradition to the requesting state. Additionally, some countries' domestic laws impose an obligation to prosecute any offense committed within their territory. Hence, if extradition documents show that a requested offense was committed in whole or in part in the territory of a requested country, that country may have a duty to prosecute the case itself.

When a requesting state brings charges on a jurisdictional assertion not recognized by the requested state, the latter may decline extradition. *See* Art. 4(c) and (f) of the UN Model Extradition Treaty. U.S. extradition treaties assert that interstate transportation or the use of U.S. wires or mail – essentially, wire or mail fraud – may form the basis for jurisdiction.

3. Exclusions

Some extradition treaties exclude offenses of a fiscal or economic nature. *See, e.g.*, Bruce Zagaris, *U.S. Efforts to Extradite Persons for Tax Offenses*, 25 Loy. L.A. Int'l Comp. L.Rev. 653–96 (2003). However, modern U.S. extradition treaties include offenses such as tax evasion, organized crime, drug trafficking, and money laundering. *See* the discussion of the *Tollman* case previously for treatment by the U.K. courts of a United States government's extradition request on tax matters.

4. Statute of Limitations Issues

The majority of the U.S. extradition treaties in force address the role of statutes of limitations in extradition proceedings. A significant number bar extradition if prosecution for the offense would be barred by the relevant statute of limitations in the requested state had the offense been committed there. Some U.S. extradition treaties prohibit extradition if prosecution is barred only by the applicable statute of limitations in the country requesting extradition. Other U.S. extradition treaties prohibit extradition if prosecution or service of sentence is barred by the applicable statute of limitations of either the requesting or the requested state. The U.S.-Irish extradition treaty offers a fourth approach, leaving the issue of whether prosecution is barred by reason of lapse of time to be raised as a defense at trial in the requesting country. *See* Michael Abbell, Extradition to and from the United States, § 3–2(18).

5. Double Jeopardy or *Non bis in Idem*

Sometimes a requesting state requests the extradition of a person who has been convicted or acquitted, or who is being tried, in the requested state for the same acts or offense for which the requesting state seeks extradition. Extraditing a person would not violate the double jeopardy clause of the Fifth Amendment to the U.S. Constitution, but it would violate the principles and policies on which the clause is based. *See Petite v. United States*, 361 U.S. 529 (1960).

With two exceptions, all U.S. extradition treaties concluded since World War II prohibit extradition of persons convicted, acquitted, or being tried in the requested state for the same acts or offenses for which their extradition is requested. The great majority of these treaties preclude extradition only if the requested person had been convicted or acquitted, or was being tried, in the requested state for the same "offense" *See, e.g.*, 1980 U.S.-Mexico Extradition Treaty, Art. 6. However, a few preclude extradition in such circumstances if the requested person had been convicted or acquitted, or was being tried, for the same "acts" in the requested state. *See, e.g.*, Supplementary U.S.-France Extradition Treaty, 1971, Art. VI.

The U.S. government has interpreted very narrowly the use of the term "offense" in this context. Unless the requested person has been convicted or acquitted in that country "of exactly the same crime with which he is charged in" the requesting country, it "would not be enough that the same facts were involved." Hence, it contends that by using the term "offense" rather than the term "acts," an offender accused in one country of illegally importing narcotics and in the other country of unlawfully exporting the same drugs would not be "insulate[d]" against extradition. S. Exec. Rep. No. 104–2, EXTRADITION TREATY WITH JORDAN, 104th Cong., 1st Sess. 8–9 (1995). U.S. courts have also interpreted the provision narrowly.[18]

6. Lack of Identity

Relators may argue that they are not the person whose extradition is requested, even if they look like the person who allegedly committed the requested offense and have the same or a similar name. *See, e.g., In re Extradition of Cervantes Valles*, 268 F. Supp. 2d 758 (S.D. Tex. 2003) (litigating the allegation of mistaken identity). Normally, relators are allowed to introduce evidence that they could not have been at or near the scene of the requested offense even though requested persons are not normally allowed to introduce evidence to contradict the evidence submitted by the requesting state. *See Charlton v. Kelly*, 229 U.S. 447, 461–62 (1913); *Collins v. Loisel*, 259 U.S. 309, 316–17 (1922); *c.f.*, *In re Sindona*, 450 F.Supp. 672, 685 (S.D.N.Y. 1978) (the court ruled that mere alibi testimony of defense witnesses contradicting evidence submitted by a requesting state is not admissible).

7. Lack of Dual Criminality

Lack of dual criminality is sometimes an effective defense in extradition for complex white collar crimes. Dual criminality is a longstanding requirement in extradition law and practice of almost all countries. If the requirement of dual criminality is not fulfilled, extradition is denied. The dual criminality principle requires that for an act to be extraditable, it must constitute a crime under the laws of both the state requesting extradition and the state from which extradition is requested.

A wide variety of practice exists among states applying the dual criminality principle. In extradition cases some states adhere to a technical approach to dual criminality. They require some correspondence or conceptual similarity between the crime in the requesting and requested states. For instance, if a requested state does not recognize the crime of possession of proceeds of crime, as distinct from money laundering, extradition may be denied because the foreign crime is not known to its law. DAVID CHAIKIN AND J.C. SHARMAN, CORRUPTION AND MONEY LAUNDERING: A SYMBIOTIC RELATIONSHIP 130 (Palgrave Macmillan 2009). Most states do not require the corresponding offense in the requested state be described by the same name as the alleged crime in the requesting state. These states hold that it is not necessary that the crime be conceptually similar in both countries. In practice, a trend is to relax the dual criminality requirement by

[18] *Elcock v. United States*, 80 F. Supp. 2d 70 (E.D.N.Y. 2000).

adoption of the "conduct test" in international treaties, national legislatures, and courts, Id. at 130–31.

In most recent U.S. extradition treaties that allow extradition for virtually all felonies under the laws of the requesting state that are also felonies under the U.S. laws the main limitation placed on extradition from the United States by the dual criminality requirement has been in cases of exporting currency from foreign countries for which no counterpart offense exists under U.S. law. Many other circumstances exist in which other foreign offenses, especially new white collar crimes (e.g., money laundering, cybercrime, securities crimes, and export control crimes) and especially crimes that may have political sensitvity (i.e., export contral crimes), would not be extraditable. MICHAEL ABBELL, EXTRADITION TO AND FROM THE LIMITED STATES § 143(4) (Transnational Publishers, June 21, 2007).

8. Capital Punishment

What happens if a requesting state requests extradition of a person who may be subject to the death penalty? Significant international precedents require courts in some jurisdictions to deny extradition where capital punishment is a possibility unless the requesting state explicitly agrees not to impose the death penalty if the relator is extradited, prosecuted, and convicted. *See, e.g., Soering v. United Kingdom*, European Court of Human Rights, 163 Eur. Ct. H.R. (Ser. A) (1989), in which the European Human Rights Court held that Britain's prospective extradition of a young German national detainee would violate his fundamental rights. The Court cited the "death row phenomenon," whereby the young detainee would face on average between six and eight years on death row in conditions that would be "inhumane" or "degrading" in violation of Article 3 of the European Convention on Human Rights. That convention provides, "No one shall be subjected to torture or to inhuman or degrading treatment or punishment." Eventually, the United Kingdom extradited Soering following U.S. assurances that he would not be tried for capital crimes by the Commonwealth of Virginia. Soering was convicted of two counts of first-degree murder and sentenced to two terms of life imprisonment on June 22, 1990. *See* INTERNATIONAL HUMAN RIGHTS: PROBLEMS OF LAW, POLICY, & PRACTICE 768 (Richard B. Lillich & Hurst Hannum eds., 3d ed. 1995); *Soering v. Deeds*, 255 Va. 457, 499 S.E.2d 514 (1998) (denial of habeas corpus).

Although paragraph 103 of the *Soering* decision states that capital punishment per se does not violate the European Convention on Human Rights (even though Protocol No. 6 to that Convention prohibits it for states parties to the Protocol), the South African Constitutional Court has concluded that the death penalty violates the South African constitutional prohibition of cruel, inhuman, or degrading punishment. *State v. Makwanyane*, 1995 (3) SALR 391 (CC).

In *The Netherlands v. Short*, 29 I.L.M. 1375 (1990), U.S. military authorities asked the Netherlands to surrender a U.S. soldier accused of murdering his wife and trying to dispose of her body using a large blender. The United States refused to give assurances that it would not seek the death penalty. The Dutch Supreme Court did not find that Protocol No. 6 necessarily superseded the obligation to surrender the accused. However, after balancing the competing interests, it held that Short's interest in not being surrendered was entitled to priority. At one point the United States tried to take Short by force, an attempt that Dutch authorities thwarted. Eventually, the Dutch surrendered Short after U.S. authorities reversed course and agreed not to charge a capital offense.

In 1996, the Italian Constitutional Court held that giving Italian officials in extradition cases the authority to rule on the sufficiency of the assurances given by the United States that capital punishment would not be imposed violated the Italian Constitution. The court explained that the constitutional prohibition of the death penalty was absolute and forbade extradition based on the evaluation of such assurances. The U.S.-Italian extradition treaty provided that extradition "shall" be refused in the absence of such assurances. Other extradition treaties state that the requested state "may" deny extradition in the absence of assurances. *See* Andrea Bianchi, *International Decision: Venezia v. Ministero de Grazia e Giustizia*, 91 AM. J. INT'L L. 727 (1997).

H. *Limitations on the Requested State: The Specialty Doctrine*

U.S. Court in Tampa Upholds Magistrate in Partial Victory to Colombian Defendant

REPRINTED FROM 21 INT'L ENFORCEMENT L. REP. 441 (NOV. 2005)

by Bruce Zagaris

On September 12, 2005, U.S. District Judge Elizabeth Kovachevich issued an opinion affirming the Report and Recommendation entered on June 23, 2005, by Magistrate Judge Elizabeth Jenkins in the case of *United States v. Joaquin Mario Valencia-Trujillo*.[19]

The case concerned the application of a condition in the extradition warrant in the case and in the Colombian constitution. In particular, the extradition warrant specified that, insofar as the indictment charged offenses committed before 1997, the warrant conditioned extradition on not trying the defendant for actions committed prior to the effective date of Legislative Act No. 1, 1997, which amended article 35 of the Political Constitution, and which authorized extradition of Colombians by birth. Article 35 of the Colombian Constitution allows the extradition of Colombian born nationals, but states that extradition will not occur when it concerns crimes committed before the promulgation of the law (December 17, 1997).

On August 22, 2002, a federal grand jury charged Mr. Valencia-Trujillo with membership in the Cali Cartel, a Colombian drug trafficking organization, and four counts of criminal conduct, including: (1) conspiring to import cocaine into the U.S.; (2) conspiring to possess cocaine with the intent to distribute it in the U.S.; (3) conducting a continuing criminal enterprise; and (4) conspiring to commit money laundering offenses.

On January 28, 2003, the U.S. requested Valencia-Trujillo's extradition. The U.S. request claimed that each of the charges included, and was independently supported by, manifest acts that occurred after December 17, 1997.

Magistrate Jenkins' report recommended that Judge Kovachevich strike the parts of the indictment that concern the crimes committed before December 17, 1997, thereby eliminating 26 alleged actions in the conspiracy and leaving 10. However, Magistrate Jenkins did not grant the defendant's motions to bar prosecutors from presenting evidence pertaining to allegations that drug trafficking was a pattern starting as early as 1988. Judge Jenkins said that the defendants could still make motions at the appropriate time and the court would adjudicate the same when they arose. Jenkins' order did not address the allegations filed in the withdrawn prosecution filing, leaving open the issue of bribery and Article 35.

[19] *United States v. Joaquin Mario Velancia-Trujillo*, U.S. Dist. Ct., M.D.Fla., Tampa Div., Case No. 8:02 CR-329-T-17EAJ.

Judge Kovachevich's order discusses the objections to the Report and Recommendation of Magistrate Judge Jenkins filed by both the defendant and the U.S. government.

The defendant objected to the portion of the Report and Recommendation in which the court denied defendant's argument that the rule of dual criminality prohibits prosecution under 18 U.S.C. § 2, the Federal aiding and abetting statute. Judge Kovachevich disagreed with the defendant's assertion of insufficient authority to deny its claim, citing ample precedent from the U.S. Court of Appeals for the Eighth Circuit and the U.S. Supreme Court.

Judge Kovachevich rejected defendant's arguments that the rule of speciality "did not require redaction of the conspiracy counts . . . to reflect an alleged starting date of December 17, 1997, as opposed to [f]rom an unknown date which was later than 1988, and continuing to the present." Defendant asserted that, because extraditions for pre-December 17, 1997 conduct were not allowed under any circumstances under Colombian law, the U.S. cannot prosecute Colombia citizens for such conduct under any theory. Hence, the magistrate judge's recommendations concerning special jury instructions and an accompanying jury form do not go far enough. Judge Kovachevich explained that the defendant seemed to misunderstand the distinction between the prosecution of charges pursuant to an extradition order and evidence of prior acts which may or may not appropriately be considered under the Federal Rules of Evidence, 403, 404(b). For instance, F.R.E. 404(b) allows several permissible uses of evidence of "other crimes, wrongs, or acts" including prior bad acts. Hence, while the magistrate-judge decided to redact predicate acts 1–26 in Count III of the indictment to uphold the doctrine of speciality, such redaction does not preclude further consideration by the court as to whether evidence of pre-December 17, 1997, acts is relevant and admissible in support of defendant's prosecution for post-December 17, 1997 acts.

The U.S. government objected to the recommendation that predicate acts 1–26 be redacted from Count III of the indictment. Judge Kovachevich explained that the doctrine of speciality required such redaction though evidence of predicate acts 1–26 may yet be found admissible at trial.

IV. The Political Offense Exception and the Rule against Noninquiry

A. *The Political Offense Exception*

In most traditional treatments of extradition a large component is the political offense exception. Because the political offense exception applies only to cases of political violence and most often terrorist charges, crimes against humanity, and war crimes, it does not arise in white collar cases, unless the white collar charge(s) are added to the political violence charges. Hence, the treatment here is cursory.

U.S. jurisprudence has especially used the incidence test, where the court looks to see if (1) the alleged extraditable crimes were committed during the occurrence of an uprising or other violent political disturbance at the time of the charged offense and if (2) it is a charged offense that is "incidental to," "in the course," or "in furtherance of" the uprising. *Quinn v. Robinson*, 783 F.2d 776, 797 (9th Cir. 1986); *Eain v. Wilkes*, 641 F.2d 504, 518 (7th Cir.), *cert. denied*, 454 U.S. 894, 102 S. Ct. 390, 70 L.Ed.2d 208 (1982); *Garcia-Guillern v. United States*, 450 F.2d 1189, 1192 (5th Cir. 1971), *cert. denied*, 405 U.S. 989, 92 S. Ct. 1251, 13 L.Ed.2d 455 (1972).

The international community has recently excluded from the political offense exception criminal acts that are "inconsistent with international standards of civilized conduct," including violent acts directed against civilians. *In re Doherty*, 599 F. Supp. 270,

275 (S.D.N.Y. 1984). For instance, the International Convention for the Suppression of Terrorist Bombings forbids the use of the political offense exception for conduct condemned under Article 2. Other counterterrorism conventions also limit the use of the political offense exception.

B. *The Rule of Noninquiry*

The "rule of noninquiry" is a customary international law principle that requires an extradition court to limit its inquiries into the fairness or sufficiency of foreign justice systems, including the procedures and treatment that the relator may endure after surrender. *See Ahmad v. Wigen*, 910 F.2d 1063 (2d Cir. 1990). Unless statutes provide otherwise, the ultimate decision to extradite resides within the exclusive prerogative of the executive in the exercise of its power to conduct foreign affairs.

As a result of this rule, extradition occurs in cases where relators have allegedly faced impending torture or death, prosecution for offenses outside the scope of the extradition request, unfair trials, double jeopardy, in absentia convictions, and the absence of a statute of limitations. *Kamrin v. United States*, 725 F.2d 1225, 1227–28 (9th Cir. 1984); *Arnbjornsdottir-Mendler v. United States*, 721 F.2d 679, 683 (9th Cir. 1983) (affirming a district court's refusal to decide whether the fugitive would be subject to brutal and unfair treatment upon return to the requesting state based on the rule of noninquiry).

In dicta some courts have reserved a possible exception to the rule of noninquiry where the procedures or punishments that a relator may experience on surrender are "antipathetic to a federal court's sense of decency." *Gallina v. Fraser*, 278 F.2d 77, 78 (2d Cir. 1960). Despite the fact that a number of cases refer to the *Gallina* language, no authority exists for successfully invoking it as a mechanism to bar extradition. *See Cornejo-Barreto v. Siefer*, 389 F.3d 1307, 1088 (9th Cir.), *vacated as moot*, 389 F.3d 1307 (9th Cir. 2004); *Arnbjornsdottir-Mendler v. United States*, 721 F.2d 679, 683 (9th Cir. 1983).

The *Cornejo-Barreto* cases – *see, e.g., Cornejo-Barreto I*, 218 F.3d 1004 (9th Cir.), reversed in relevant part, 389 F.3d 1307, 1080 (9th Cir.) (*Cornejo-Barreto II*), *vacated as moot*, 389 F.3d 1307 (9th Cir. 2004) – illustrate efforts of the judiciary to adjudicate the rule of noninquiry involving Cornejo-Barreto, a Mexican citizen. He resisted U.S. efforts to extradite him to Mexico on the basis that Article 3 of the Convention against Torture and Other Cruel, Inhuman or Degrading Treatment or Punishment (CAT), as implemented by the Foreign Affairs Reform and Restructuring (FARR) Act of 1998, 8 U.S.C. § 1231 precluded his extradition. Article 3 of the CAT forbids a contracting party from extraditing, expelling, or returning a person to another state where there exists "substantial grounds for believing that he would be in danger of being subject to torture." The decisions of the circuit court panels were not consistent. Eventually, the case was terminated when the U.S. government filed an unopposed motion to dismiss the case as moot due to the expiration in Mexico of the applicable statute of limitations and Mexico's diplomatic note withdrawing the request. Although the Ninth Circuit vacated the panel decision in *Carnejo-Barreto II*, it denied the government's request to vacate other published opinions in the case. 389 F.3d 1307 (9th Cir. 2004).

Notes and Questions

1. Do you think the rule of noninquiry is appropriate and good policy? Why? The allegations of the U.S. government's violation of torture and related laws in the detention of persons designated as noncombatants in the war on terrorism may give rise to the

interposition of torture defenses on U.S. extradition requests and implicate the doctrine of noninquiry.

V. Alternatives to Extradition

A. *Rendition*

Rendition can involve either acceptable conduct outside an extradition process or conduct that violates legal precepts or is highly suspect. For example, deportation of an accused alien can be considered permissible or impermissible depending on various legal policies at stake and circumstances involved. *See generally* RESTATEMENT § 475, Reporters' Note 6; 74 PROC., AM. SOC. INT'L L. 274–89 (1980) (remarks of Evans, Kenney, Gordon, and editors Bassiouni, Williams, and Zagaris).

The surrender of fugitives to and from Commonwealth countries is called rendition and is governed by the Fugitive Offenders Act.[20] Under this legislation there is no list of extraditable offenses, no provisions on double criminality or specialty, and no exemptions for political offenders.

Notes and Questions

1. The Commonwealth Scheme for Rendition, adopted in 1990 at a Commonwealth Conference, forms the basis for domestic rendition legislation and provides for a range of safeguards as comprehensive or more so than most extradition arrangements. *See* Kimberly Prost, *Cooperation in Penal Matters in the Commonwealth, in* II INTERNATIONAL CRIMINAL LAW: MULTILATERAL AND BILATERAL ENFORCEMENT MECHANISMS 413, 414–23 (M. Cherif Bassiouni ed. 2008).

Ruiz Massieu v. Reno, 915 F. Supp. 681 (D. N.J. 1996)

BARRY, District Judge

Plaintiff, Mario Ruiz Massieu, seeks a permanent injunction enjoining the deportation proceeding instituted against him pursuant to 8 U.S.C. § 1251(a)(4)(C)(i) and a declaration that the statute, which has not previously been construed in any reported judicial opinion, is unconstitutional. That statute, by its express terms, confers upon a single individual, the Secretary of State, the unfettered and unreviewable discretion to deport any alien lawfully within the United States, not for identified reasons relating to his conduct in the United States or elsewhere but, rather, because that person's mere presence here would impact in some unexplained way on the foreign policy interests of the United States. Thus, the statute represents a breathtaking departure both from well established legislative precedent which commands deportation based on adjudications of defined impermissible conduct by the alien in the United States, and from well established precedent with respect to extradition which commands extradition based on adjudications of probable cause to believe that the alien has engaged in defined impermissible conduct elsewhere.

Make no mistake about it. This case is about the Constitution of the United States and the panoply of protections that document provides to the citizens of this country and those

[20] R.S.C. 1985, c. F-32. *See* P. O'Higgins, *Extradition within the Commonwealth*, 9 INT'L & COMP. L.Q. 486 (1960).

non-citizens who are here legally and, thus, here as our guests. And make no mistake about this: Mr. Ruiz Massieu entered this country legally and is not alleged to have committed any act within this country which requires his deportation. Nor, on the state of this record, can it be said that there exists probable cause to believe that Mr. Ruiz Massieu has committed any act outside of this country which warrants his extradition, for the government has failed in four separate proceedings before two Magistrate Judges to establish probable cause. Deportation of Mr. Ruiz Massieu is sought merely because he is here and the Secretary of State and Mexico have decided that he should go back.

The issue before the court is not whether plaintiff has the right to remain in this country beyond the period for which he was lawfully admitted; indeed, as a "non-immigrant visitor" he had only a limited right to remain here but the right to then go on his way to wherever he wished to go. The issue, rather, is whether an alien who is in this country legally can, merely because he is here, have his liberty restrained and be forcibly removed to a specific country in the unfettered discretion of the Secretary of State and without any meaningful opportunity to be heard. The answer is a ringing "no." . . .

[From March through December of 1995, the Government tried four times, each unsuccessfully, to extradite Ruiz Massieu]

With that, the government seemingly accepted defeat as to Mr. Ruiz Massieu's extraditability. It was then, however, that this case took a turn toward the truly Kafkaesque. On December 22, 1995, immediately after Magistrate Judge Chesler issued his opinion, Mr. Ruiz Massieu was taken into custody by the Immigration and Naturalization Service ("the INS") pursuant to a previously unserved and unannounced detainer dated September 29, 1995. In addition, he was served with an INS Order to Show Cause and Notice of Hearing. The notice advised Mr. Ruiz Massieu that he was ordered to show cause as to why he should not be deported because, the Secretary of State has made a determination that, pursuant to Section 241(a)(4)(C) of the Immigration and Nationality [sic] Act, 8 U.S.C. § 1251(a)(4)(C), there is reasonable ground to believe your presence or activities in the United States would have potentially serious adverse foreign policy consequences for the United States. . . . No further explanation of the ground for Mr. Ruiz Massieu's alleged deportability was tendered.

Sometime after notice was served on Mr. Ruiz Massieu, the INS produced an October 2, 1995 letter addressed to Attorney General Janet Reno from Secretary of State Warren Christopher. [see attachment at end of case]. The letter urged the Attorney General to effect Mr. Ruiz Massieu's "expeditious deportation" "to Mexico" based on the Secretary's conclusion that Mr. Ruiz Massieu's presence in the United States will have potentially serious adverse foreign policy consequences for the United States. *Id.* The letter referenced the "serious allegations" that are pending in Mexico against Mr. Ruiz Massieu and the recent strides that both governments have taken in "our ability to cooperate and confront criminality on both sides of the border." *Id.* At bottom, the Secretary's request was premised on the proposition that "our inability to return to Mexico Mr. Ruiz Massieu – a case the Mexican Presidency has told us is of the highest importance – would jeopardize our ability to work with Mexico on law enforcement matters. It might also cast a potentially chilling effect on other issues our two governments are addressing." *Id.*

The relevant deportation statute, § 241(a)(4)(C)(i) of the Immigration and Naturalization Act ("INA"), provides simply that "an alien whose presence or activities in the United States the Secretary of State has reasonable ground to believe would have potentially serious adverse foreign policy consequences for the United States is deportable." 8 U.S.C. § 1251(a)(4)(C)(i).

Because an indication of the Secretary of State's belief is all that the statute by its terms requires, the October 2, 1995 letter, alone, comprised (and remains) the universe of evidence that the INS has offered to support its charge of Mr. Ruiz Massieu's deportability. A master calendar proceeding, the first stage of deportation hearings held pursuant to section 242 of the INA, was scheduled to begin on January 19, 1996. On January 17, 1996, however, Mr. Ruiz Massieu filed a complaint in this court requesting that the deportation proceedings be preliminarily and permanently enjoined, and that section 241(a)(4)(C) of the INA be declared unconstitutional.

The complaint contains three core constitutional claims: (1) the deportation proceeding evidences selective enforcement in retaliation for Mr. Ruiz Massieu's exercise of his First Amendment right to criticize the Mexican political system; (2) the deportation proceeding represents a "de facto" extradition and is an attempt to overrule, albeit indirectly, four federal court decisions, in violation of the separation of powers; and (3) section 241(a)(4)(C)(i) of the INA is unconstitutionally vague, in violation of the due process clause of the Fifth Amendment. The United States Department of Justice, on behalf of all defendants, has responded that section 241(a)(4)(C)(i) withstands constitutional attack both facially and as applied to Mr. Ruiz Massieu. In addition, it has taken the position that this court lacks jurisdiction to hear the case on the grounds that (1) what is at issue is a nonjusticiable political question; (2) Mr. Ruiz Massieu has failed to exhaust his administrative remedies under the INA; and (3) the doctrine of constitutional avoidance counsels against this court reaching the ultimate issues presented in Mr. Ruiz Massieu's complaint....

[The court determined that the district court has jurisdiction to hear plaintiff's due process claims, administrative exhaustion is not required, and the claims are ripe. Next, it addressed the political question claim of the government.]

The government contends that the dispute at issue is one over the foreign policy of the United States and, therefore, presents a nonjusticiable political question. According to the government, the wisdom of the Secretary's and the Attorney General's policy determinations cannot be reviewed by this or any other court. With the "wisdom" assertion, this court could not agree more. Neither the legislature's vast power over deportation issues, nor the executive department's exclusive control over matters of foreign policy, however, are enough to transform this dispute into a nonjusticiable political question.

Given the overtones of international diplomacy that infuse this case, it would not be unreasonable to think of this controversy in political terms. As the Supreme Court has emphatically stated, however, the presence of constitutional issues with significant political overtones does not automatically invoke the political question doctrine. Resolution of litigation challenging the constitutional authority of one of the three branches cannot be evaded by courts because the issues have political implications in the sense urged by [the government]. *INS v. Chadha*, 462 U.S. 919, 942–43 . . . (1983). What is at issue in this case is not review of a foreign policy determination but, rather, the constitutionality of an act of Congress and the decision of the executive to enforce that act against an individual within this nation's borders, thus declaring that individual expendable. "No policy underlying the political question doctrine suggests that Congress or the Executive, or both acting in concert and in compliance with Art. I, can decide the constitutionality of a statute; that is a decision for the courts." *Id.* at 941–42. *See also Shahla v. INS*, 749 F.2d 561, 563 n.2 (9th Cir. 1984) (recognizing that while "the judicial branch must show deference to the political branches of government in foreign policy matters[,] nevertheless, we believe that the judicial branch may examine whether the political branches have used a foreign policy crisis as an excuse for treating aliens arbitrarily"). In short, this court finds the resolution of this constitutional controversy to be well within the role traditionally reserved for the judiciary. . . .

This court now turns its attention to the substance of the challenge before it. In terms of due process, plaintiff attacks § 241(a)(4)(C)(i) of the INA on two distinct, though related, grounds. The first contention is that the statute is void for vagueness. The second is that, by its terms, the statute denies plaintiff, and any alien deported thereunder, a meaningful opportunity to be heard before being subjected to the severe deprivation of liberty that is deportation. Additionally, the court has sua sponte raised the issue of whether the statute is so devoid of standards that it represents an unconstitutional delegation of legislative power to the executive. . . .

[The court determined that governmental power over aliens "is circumscribed by the constitutional constraints imposed on the exercise of all governmental authority." Next, it found the statute void for vagueness while noting the following.]

"Foreign policy" cannot serve as the talisman behind which Congress may abdicate its responsibility to pass only sufficiently clear and definite laws when those laws may be enforced against the individual. See *Shahla v. INS*, 749 F.2d 561, 563 n.2 (9th Cir. 1984) ("the judicial branch may examine whether the political branches have used a foreign policy crisis as an excuse for treating aliens arbitrarily"). Although the executive's discretionary authority over foreign affairs is well established, Congress cannot empower the executive to employ that authority against the individual except through constitutional means. See *Valentine v. United States ex rel. Neidecker*, 299 U.S. 5, 9 . . . ("the Constitution creates no executive prerogative to dispose of the liberty of the individual. Proceedings against him must be authorized by law. There is no executive discretion to surrender him to a foreign government, unless that discretion is governed by law"). If the Constitution was adopted to protect individuals against anything, it was the abuses made possible through just this type of unbounded executive authority.

There can be no more graphic illustration of the exercise of unbounded executive authority than that seen in this case. In this case, the Secretary has determined that plaintiff is expendable – for "foreign policy" reasons which the Secretary need neither explicate nor defend – merely because Mexico wants plaintiff back. Had plaintiff overstayed his welcome, had he entered this country illegally, or had he committed a crime while here – all clearly defined grounds for deportation – he would be entitled to a host of protections, not the least of which would be notice of the prohibited conduct and a meaningful opportunity to be heard. Similarly, if it were believed that plaintiff had committed a crime in Mexico, his extradition would, presumably, have again been sought and, again, there would be no problem of vagueness and he would be entitled to substantial protections. Extradition, after all, is the time-tested mechanism used by this country and other civilized countries to send a criminal back, a mechanism that the government has unsuccessfully utilized vis-a-vis plaintiff in four separate court proceedings. § 241(a)(4) (C)(i) does an end run around and, indeed, subverts the extradition framework, which would never permit the return of an alien merely because he is considered undesirable by his government. . . .

[Next, the court found that there was a denial of an opportunity to be heard.]

In the final analysis, this court is convinced that a balancing of the appropriate factors tips well in plaintiff's favor. Absent a meaningful opportunity to be heard, the Secretary of State's unreviewable and concededly "unfettered discretion" to deprive an alien, who lawfully entered this country, of his or her liberty to the extent exemplified by this case is, in this court's view, unconstitutional. Accordingly, this court now holds that § 241(a)(4)(C)(i) of the INA, 8 U.S.C. § 1251(a)(4)(C)(i) is unconstitutional both on its face and as applied....

[The court also found that there was an unconstitutional delegation of legislative power to the executive, and concluded as follows.]

For the reasons stated above, this court now finds that § 241(a)(4)(C)(i) of the INA is unconstitutional. Accordingly, the deportation proceedings instituted against plaintiff, pursuant thereto, will be permanently enjoined.

ATTACHMENT

THE SECRETARY OF STATE

WASHINGTON

October 2, 1995

Dear Madam Attorney General:

I am writing to inform you that, pursuant to Section 241(a)(4)(C) of the Immigration and Nationality Act, 8 U.S.C. section 1251(a)(4)(C), I have concluded that the presence of Mario Ruiz Massieu in the United States would have potentially serious foreign policy consequences for the United States. Accordingly, I request that you take all steps possible, consistent with the Immigration and Nationality Act and other relevant law, to effect his deportation to Mexico.

My decision to invoke INA section 241(a)(4)(C) with respect to Mr. Ruiz Massieu is based on the following considerations: As you are well aware, the United States and Mexico have made tremendous progress in the past five years in strengthening one of our most important and vital bilateral relationships. The range of issues that unite our two nations – from combatting international drug trafficking, to addressing vexing problems of legal and illegal migration, to fortifying trade and investment in one of the world's largest and fastest growing markets – is complex and varied.

One aspect of our relationship that has received the utmost attention from both governments is our ability to cooperate to confront criminality on both sides of the border. We have seen successes on this front, but we continue to seek enhanced cooperation. With easy transit between the United States and Mexico and extensive and ever-increasing ties, this is an area of vital importance to the United States. Our inability to return to Mexico Mr. Ruiz Massieu – a case the Mexican presidency has told us is of the highest importance – would jeopardize our ability to work with Mexico on law enforcement matters. It might also cast a potentially chilling effect on other issues our two governments are addressing.

Furthermore, the case in question involves charges against the former second ranking law enforcement authority in Mexico and a man connected through his circle of family and friends to the center of power in Mexican politics. Serious allegations against such a high former official are unprecedented in modern Mexico. The case against Mr. Ruiz Massieu and the arrest and trial for related crimes of Mr. Raul Salinas, brother of the former President, were the dramatic and unequivocal signs of the determination of President Zedillo and his Attorney General to break the so-called "culture of impunity" that long protected corrupt politicians, officials and other powerful elite from being held accountable for their actions and crimes. President Zedillo's anti-corruption drive has resonated throughout Mexico and continues to receive strong support from the Mexican people.

The U.S. Government has consistently urged Mexico to take the steps towards reform in its justice system that President Zedillo is so forcefully pursuing. The ability to prosecute Mr. Ruiz Massieu and other powerful individuals in Mexico for the crimes of which they are accused is key to the success of Zedillo's pledge to transform totally the judicial and law enforcement system and to rid Mexico of corruption and abuse of power. Should the U.S. Government not return Mr. Ruiz Massieu to Mexico, our support of such reforms would be seen as hollow and self-serving and would be a major setback for President Zedillo and our combined efforts to chart a new and effective course of U.S.-Mexican relations.

Our efforts to remove Mr. Ruiz Massieu from the United States should be directed at achieving his direct return to Mexico. When apprehended in New Jersey, Mr. Ruiz Massieu was attempting to depart the United States just days after being called for questioning in Mexico with regard to the crimes with which he was subsequently charged. If our efforts to remove him from the United States result in his ability to depart to a destination other than Mexico, the U.S. Government will almost certainly be viewed by Mexican officials and the Mexican public as not only permitting, but also aiding his successful escape from justice.

Accordingly, I have concluded that Mr. Ruiz Massieu's presence in the United States would have potentially serious adverse foreign policy consequences for the United States, as provided for in INA Section 241(a)(4)(C). I request that you take all reasonable efforts to ensure Mr. Ruiz Massieu's expeditious deportation from the United States. Further, in light of the Mexican Government's interest in having Mr. Ruiz Massieu returned to Mexico, I also request that you do everything possible, consistent with the Immigration and Nationality Act, to effect his deportation to Mexico.

Sincerely,
Warren Christopher

Notes and Questions

1. An appellate court reversed the district court's decision in *Ruiz Massieu* because the plaintiff did not exhaust his administrative remedies. *See Massieu v. Reno*, 91 F.3d 416 (3d Cir. 1996), *cert. denied*, 527 U.S. 1023 (1999). On May 30, 1997, an immigration court ruled that Ruiz Massieu could not be deported because the U.S. government did not show sufficient evidence to establish that his presence in the United States would have potentially adverse foreign policy results. After the Immigration and Nationality Service appealed to the Board of Appeals, the Board, in a 12–2 decision, found that the Secretary of State's determination was conclusory and vacated the immigration judge's ruling. *See In re Ruiz-Massieu*, Interim Decision No. 3400 (B.I.A., June 10, 1999).

In August 1999, a federal grand jury in Houston indicted Ruiz-Massieu for money laundering, charging that the $9 million he had deposited in Texas banks constituted proceeds of crime from narcotics traffickers. For a discussion of how federal prosecutors and police commanders allegedly paid Ruiz-Massieu as much as $1 million to be assigned to profitable posts along the border and in other major drug areas, *see* PETER ANDREAS, BORDER GAMES: POLICING THE U.S.-MEXICO DIVIDE 63 (2000).

On September 15, 1999, two days before his arraignment, Ruiz-Massieu committed suicide by taking an overdose of antidepressants at his New Jersey apartment. Ruiz-Massieu had been under house arrest for approximately four years when he committed suicide. His suicide was controversial in Mexico, where Ruiz-Massieu had been the Assistant Attorney General in charge of narcotics during the Salinas administration. Mexican authorities were investigating Ruiz-Massieu's role heading the investigation of the assassination of his brother José Francisco Ruiz-Massieu, which was done to allegedly cover up the role of Carlos Salinas's brother Raul Salinas. The assassination occurred on September 28, 1994, just six months after the assassination of Luis Colosio, the leading candidate for the Mexican presidency.

The Mexican government was frustrated that it could not obtain custody of and prosecute Ruiz-Massieu, a suspect in the most celebrated investigation at the time in Mexico. On November 23, 1994, a week before Zedillo's inauguration, Ruiz-Massieu called a press conference, announcing his resignation and accusing top PRI leaders of blocking his probe of his brother's killing. The next day he left Mexico and was arrested at Newark airport en route to Spain. *See, e.g.*, Tim Golden, *Mexico's Ex-Drug Chief, Indicted, Is Found Dead in U.S.*, N.Y. TIMES, Sept. 16, 1999, at A1; JULIA PRESTON & SAMUEL DILLON, OPENING MEXICO: THE MAKING OF A DEMOCRACY 238–39, 312–314 (2004).

2. In the deportation case Ruiz-Massieu argued that it is not lawful to use deportation to circumvent the safeguards provided for relators by the law of extradition. The district court did not adjudicate this argument because it ruled that the statutory basis for deportation was unconstitutional. However, in dicta the court observed that other aliens have been deported after extradition requests were denied by the courts. The court cited *Matter of McMullen*, 17 I. & N. Dec. 542.

3. The *Doherty* case illustrated alternative efforts to use extradition and deportation to surrender an alleged Irish terrorist to Ireland. *See, e.g., In Matter of Doherty*, 599 F.Supp. 20 (S.D.N.Y. 1984); *Doherty v. United States Dep't of Justice*, 908 F.2d 1108 (2d Cir. 1990), *rev'd on other grounds, INS v. Doherty*, 502 U.S. 314 (1992). Is it fair for a government to alternatively use extradition and deportation to surrender a relator, reverting to the latter if efforts to extradite fail?

B. *Luring (Trickery)*

Regular rendition of a person, usually by extradition, occurs when an individual is surrendered by a requested country to a requesting state. Rendition is irregular when individuals are taken from one country to another against their free will, without the consent of the nation from which they were taken. At times, governments use deceit, fraud, and tricks to lure individuals from the country of their residence to a location where there is jurisdiction to arrest them. Unlike in an abduction by force, weapons are not used to get the suspect to the location where the arrest will occur. Whether a trick can be just as coercive as a gun remains controversial. The United States has consistently upheld the legitimacy of the practice of luring, contrary to the policies of many other nations.

1. The U.S. Position on Luring

It is longstanding policy of the U.S. government to use "luring" as an alternative to extradition, and U.S. courts have upheld the constitutionality of the practice. The United States has authorized law enforcement authorities to lure defendants from their home countries, even when the United States has an extradition treaty with those countries.

United States v. Yunis, 681 F. Supp. 909 (D.D.C. 1988), *rev'd on other gds.*, 859 F.2d 953 (D.C. Cir. 1988)

Defendant, Fawaz Yunis, a citizen of Lebanon, was lured out of his homeland, arrested in international waters off the coast of Cyprus, and forcibly brought to the United States to face charges of hostage taking and aircraft piracy. His counsel argues that the arresting officers failed to respect the defendant's constitutional rights when he was arrested and that they unlawfully secured inculpatory statements from him while he was being brought back to the United States. He has moved to dismiss the indictment on grounds that the circumstances surrounding the arrest were outrageous and violated defendant's due process rights. Counsel has also moved to suppress his client's inculpatory statements and written confession claiming that his rights were not voluntarily or knowingly waived. . . .

Defendant's counsel has moved to dismiss the entire multi-count indictment on two grounds: first, the government's actions contravened its extradition treaty obligations with Lebanon and Cyprus, and second, the government used excessive and outrageous force when arresting defendant in violation of Fifth Amendment rights to due process. Both grounds present threshold questions of standing and jurisdiction: whether Yunis can assert violations of an extradition treaty absent objections or protests by either Lebanon or Cyprus, and whether the defendant, a nonresident alien, can invoke the protective cloak of our Constitution for actions committed beyond the territorial borders of the United States.

For the reasons set forth . . . the Court concludes that individuals, alone, are not empowered to enforce extradition treaties. Therefore, it need not reach the issue whether the United States breached its treaty obligations. As to the Fifth Amendment claims, the Court determines that the Constitution applies abroad to aliens but that the government's actions did not rise to the level of "outrageousness" that "shocks the conscience" and warrants dismissal of the indictment. . . .

Before the Court can determine whether the government's actions were so outrageous as to "shock the conscience" and violate defendant's due process rights, it must resolve the threshold inquiry: whether the constitutional restraints apply to governmental activity overseas. The Constitution is silent regarding its application overseas and the Supreme Court has never definitively resolved whether aliens are protected by the Constitution.[21]

Although the Supreme Court has never explicitly addressed whether the Constitution applies to aliens overseas, it has consistently reaffirmed the principle that our government is one of enumerated powers without authority to act beyond the limitations of the Constitution.

[21] The most relevant Supreme Court decisions concerning the application of rights to overseas aliens are *Johnson v. Eisentrager*, 339 U.S. 763 (1950) and *Reid v. Covert*, 354 U.S. 1 (1957). In *Eisentrager*, American military authorities were involved in the arrest of criminals in China and their conviction and incarceration in Germany after World War II. Later, writs of habeas corpus were sought in American courts. About their application for relief, the Supreme Court wrote, "The Constitution does not confer a right of personal security or an immunity from military trial and punishment upon an alien enemy engaged in the hostile service of a government at war with the United States." *Id.* 339 U.S. at 785.

Some courts have interpreted *Eisentrager* broadly to prohibit any application of the Constitution overseas. Others have read the case more narrowly as denying constitutional rights to enemy aliens in occupied territories during a declared war.

Several years later, the Court ruled in a plurality opinion that citizens overseas enjoyed full constitutional protections from acts of their government. *Reid v. Covert*, 354 U.S. 1 (1957) involved two women stationed with their husbands on overseas military bases. Each killed her husband and was tried without a jury. The Court overturned the convictions, holding that "the United States is entirely a creature of the Constitution. Its powers and authority have no other source. It can only act in accordance with all the limitations imposed by the Constitution." *Id.* at 5–6. Lower courts have interpreted *Reid* as holding that the reach of the Constitution does not stop at the border. Whenever the United States exercises its sovereignty outside the country, it must act in accordance with the limitations imposed by the Constitution. However, *Reid* involved U.S. citizens residing overseas. Since *Reid*, the Court has had no occasion to rule on the extraterritorial application of the Constitution to nonresident aliens. *See* Stephan, *Constitutional Limits on the Struggle against International Terrorism: Revisiting the Rights of Overseas Aliens*, 19 CONN. L. REV. 831, 831–842 (1987).

This fundamental principle was heralded more than a century ago in *Ex parte Milligan*, 71 U.S. (4 Wall) 2 (1886). "The Constitution of the United States is a law for rulers and people, equally in war and in peace, and covers with the shield of its protection all classes of [persons], at all times, and under all circumstances." In other cases, the Supreme Court has held that the Constitution regulates and restricts the conduct of the federal government "whenever and wherever the sovereign power of that government is exerted." *Balzac v. Porto Rico*, 258 U.S. 298 (1922). Indeed, even in *United States v. Curtiss-Wright Export Corp.*, 299 U.S. 304 (1936), a case routinely cited for the proposition that executive powers are strongest in the realm of foreign affairs, the Court's opinion reads, "every . . . government power, must be exercised in subordination to the applicable provisions of the Constitution." 299 U.S. at 320. Granting the United States unfettered powers to secure the arrest of a nonresident alien overseas runs directly contrary to the Court's theory of constituted powers. As Justice Louis Brandeis eloquently stated in *Olmstead v. United States*, 277 U.S. 438, 485 (1928), "To declare that in the administration of the criminal law the ends justify the means—to declare that the government may commit crimes in order to secure the conviction of a private criminal – would bring terrible retribution."

The majority of circuits have applied the Constitution extraterritorially and required the United States government to conform to constitutional proscriptions when acting overseas.[22] Similarly, *The Restatement (revised) of Foreign Relations Law* supports extending constitutional rights to aliens in certain cases.[23] Although our Court of Appeals has never explicitly embraced this trend,[24] this Court finds the majority view compelling and persuasive and concludes that the Constitution applies to circumscribe the activity of federal officials overseas.

Method of Arrest as a Violation of Defendant's Fifth Amendment Rights

Concluding that the Constitution extends to governmental activities overseas is only the starting point of the inquiry. The Court now turns to the fundamental question raised by

22 *See, e.g.*, *United States v. Pinto-Mejia*, 720 F.2d 248, 259, 261 (2d Cir. 1983); *United States v. Marino-Garcia*, 679 F.2d 1373, 1384 (11th Cir. 1982), *cert. denied*, 459 U.S. 1114, (1983); *United States v. Green*, 671 F.2d 46, 53 (1st Cir. 1982); *United States v. Williams*, 617 F.2d 1063, 1078 (5th Cir. 1980).

23 Notes to the RESTATEMENT provide that "although the matter has not been authoritatively adjudicated, at least some actions by the United States in respect of foreign nations outside the country are also subject to constitutional limitations." § 721, Comment m & Reporters' Note 16.

24 Indeed, the case law in this circuit is quite murky. In a relatively early case, the court explicitly refused to permit foreign aliens to raise constitutional objections. *Pauling v. McElroy*, 278 F.2d 252, 254 n. 3 (D.C. Cir.), *cert. denied*, 264 U.S. 835 (1960) (in dismissing a suit brought by overseas aliens to enjoin nuclear testing, the court held that overseas aliens have no standing to assert constitutional claims). In later cases, the court appeared more receptive to granting aliens rights under the Constitution. *Dostal v. Haig*, 652 F.2d 173, 176 (D.C. Cir. 1981) (in rejecting challenge by Berlin citizens that the Army violated their due process rights, the court "accepted *arguendo* that the Bill of Rights is fully applicable to govern the conduct of U.S. officials in Berlin," but found no substantive violation); *Cardenas v. Smith*, 733 F.2d 909, 913 (D.C. Cir. 1984) (in conferring standing on a Colombian citizen objecting to the U.S. government's seizure of her Swiss bank account without any notice, court stated that "an injury endured abroad is not less of an injury for Article III standing purposes because it happened on foreign soil").

However, in the circuit's most recent treatment of the subject, it explicitly refused to rule on the application of the Bill of Rights to aliens overseas. In *Sanchez-Espinoza v. Reagan*, 770 F.2d 202, 208 (D.C. Cir. 1985), a case involving Nicaraguan citizens seeking compensation for injuries suffered at the hands of the U.S.-supported Contradoros, the court wrote, "[w]e do not reach the question whether the protections of the Constitution extend to noncitizens abroad." However, it ultimately refrained from exercising jurisdiction over the action under the political question doctrine. Neither aliens nor U.S. citizens were conferred standing to proceed with the case. Therefore, *Sanchez* can be interpreted as holding that an alien cannot assert any greater rights under the Constitution than a U.S. citizen.

defendant's motion: does the Constitution impose any restraints on the methods used to arrest a defendant and bring him within the jurisdiction of this Court?

The Supreme Court in two decisions has developed well reasoned precedents that forcible abduction neither offends due process nor requires dismissal of an indictment. *Ker v. Illinois*, 119 U.S. 436 (1886) and *Frisbie v. Collins*, 342 U.S. 519 (1952). *Ker* involved a defendant who while residing in Peru was indicted for larceny in Illinois. He was forcibly abducted from Peru by a Pinkerton agent, brought to Illinois, tried and convicted. *Frisbie* involved the forcible abduction – seizure, handcuffing, and blackjacking – of a defendant from his home in Illinois to Michigan to stand trial for murder. The Court reasoned that "due process of law is satisfied when one present in court is convicted of a crime after having been fairly apprized of the charges against him and after trial in accordance with constitutional procedural safeguards. There is nothing in the Constitution that requires a court to permit a guilty person rightfully convicted to escape justice because he was brought to trial against his will." *Frisbie*, 342 U.S. at 522.

Despite intense criticism of the doctrine,[25] the Supreme Court has continued to reaffirm the *Ker-Frisbie* doctrine. *See Immigration & Naturalization Service v. Lopez-Mendoza*, 468 U.S. 1032 (1984); *United States v. Crews*, 445 U.S. 463, 474 (1980); *Stone v. Powell*, 428 U.S. 465 (1976); *Gerstein v. Pugh*, 420 U.S. 103, 119 (1975) ("Nor do we retreat from the established rule that illegal arrest or detention does not void a subsequent conviction.").

While defendant's counsel concedes that as a general rule, our jurisprudence has relied upon the safeguards of the system itself and has, on most occasions, turned a blind eye to the methods used to bring a person to Court, he nonetheless contends that this action falls into what is commonly referred to as the *Toscanino* exception, *United States v. Toscanino*, 500 F.2d 267 (2d Cir. 1974). There, the defendant also alleged that he was subjected to torture and abuse by United States officials. Reasoning that the government should not be given a *carte blanche* to bring defendants to the jurisdiction of the United States by torture and brutal force and then permitted to utilize the fruits of its own lawlessness, the Second Circuit ruled that a court in the name of due process is required to divest itself of jurisdiction "where it has been acquired as the result of the government's deliberate, unnecessary and unreasonable invasion of the accused's constitutional rights." *Toscanino*, 500 F.2d at 275.

The extensive torture suffered by the defendant in *Toscanino* is worthy of recitation to illustrate the benchmark for the type of outrageous conduct necessary to invoke the exception to *Ker-Frisbie* and warrant the radical remedy of dismissal. The government abducted defendant from Uruguay and subjected him to a series of tortures: denial of sleep and nourishment for days at a time, forced walks for excessive hours accompanied by kicking and beating him when he could no longer stand, pinching his fingers with metal pliers, flushing alcohol into his eyes and nose and forcing other fluids up his anal passage, and finally, attaching electrodes to his extremities and genitals. 500 F.2d at 270. Even in face of that record, the trial court refused to dismiss the indictment, concluding that United States officials were not involved in that conduct. *United States v. Toscanino*, 398 F. Supp. 916 (E.D.N.Y. 1975).

Shortly after *Toscanino*, the Second Circuit stressed the narrowness of its holding and reaffirmed the vitality of the *Ker-Frisbee* doctrine. *United States v. ex rel. Lujan v. Gengler*, 510 F.2d 62 (2d Cir. 1975), *cert. denied*, 421 U.S. 1001 (1975). Although *Gengler* did not involve any allegations of torture – the defendant argued that federal officials lured him to neutral territory

[25] For an extensive list of articles criticizing the doctrine *see* M. Bassiouni, II International Criminal Law, Chapter 5, note 17 (1986 ed.).

under fraudulent business pretenses – it stands for the proposition that absent "government conduct of a most shocking and outrageous character," dismissal is not warranted. *Id.* at 65. "Not every violation by prosecution or policy... requires nullification of the indictment." *Id.* at 66.

Although most circuits have acknowledged the exception carved out by *Toscanino*, it is highly significant that *no* court has ever applied it to dismiss an indictment. They have uniformly treated *Toscanino* as a very narrow exception to *Ker-Frisbie*. See Shafer, *District Court Jurisdiction over Criminal Suspects Who Were Abducted in Foreign Countries*, 64 A.L.R. Fed. 292.

Two distinct grounds have been relied upon in refusing to dismiss an indictment under the *Toscanino* exception: either courts conclude that the torturous activity did not rise to the level of outrageousness warranting dismissal, or conclude that United States officials were not directly involved in the torturous activity. In the first, the courts have used the allegations of torture in *Toscanino* as a threshold standard for outrageousness, and uniformly concluded that the government's conduct did not rise to that level of outrageousness, shocking the conscience and warranting dismissal. *See, U.S. v. Rosenthal*, 793 F.2d 1214, 1232 (11th Cir. 1986), *cert. denied*, 480 U.S. 919, 107 S.Ct. 1377 (1987) (defendant abducted from Bahamas on narcotic charges, the court declined to adopt the *Toscanino* exception but even if applicable, found no evidence of conduct which shocked the conscience); *U.S. v. Darby*, 744 F.2d 1508 (11th Cir. 1986), *cert. denied*, 471 U.S. 1004 (1985) (Honduran citizen abducted from Honduras, driven at gunpoint to airport, and forced on plane for trial in United States; court held that defendant had not "alleged the sort of cruel, inhuman and outrageous treatment" to warrant dismissal); *U.S. v. Reed*, 639 F.2d 896 (2d Cir. 1981) (Bahamian defendant, residing in the Bahamas, deceitfully enticed by CIA agents to board a plane bound for Bimini; agents placed a cocked gun at his head and forced him to lie on aircraft floor for the duration of the flight and then twisted his arm as he exited the plane; court found that use of revolver and threatening language not "gross mistreatment" warranting dismissal); *U.S. v. Cordero*, 668 F.2d 32 (1st Cir. 1981) (defendants arrested, abducted in Venezuela to face drug charges in Puerto Rico. In refusing to dismiss the indictment, the court concluded that although defendants were subjected to poor treatment, insulted, and slapped when abducted and while in jail were poorly fed and forced to sleep on the floor, those conditions "are a far cry from deliberate torture warranting dismissal."). Several of the previous cases involved serious allegations of torture and abuse. The fact that not *one* of the courts relied on *Toscanino* to dismiss the indictment highlights the extreme narrowness of that exception and underscores the force of the *Ker-Frisbie* doctrine.

In cases where defendants have urged the court to dismiss the indictment solely on the grounds that they were fraudulently lured to the United States, courts have uniformly upheld jurisdiction. *United States v. Wilson*, 732 F.2d 404, 411 (5th Cir.), *cert. denied*, 469 U.S. 1099 (1984). In *Wilson*, undercover agent persuaded defendant to leave his refuge in Libya. The court refused to dismiss the indictment concluding that "Wilson has simply been the victim of a nonviolent government trick; any irregularity in a criminal defendant's apprehension will not vitiate proceedings against him." 721 F.2d. at 972.

In the second line of cases, where it was determined that the United States officials were not involved in the alleged brutality or torture, the courts saw no purpose in dismissing the indictment. *See United States v. Lopez*, 542 F.2d 283 (5th Cir. 1876) (United States agents played no role in alleged torture of defendant in Dominican Republic); *United States v. Lira*, 515 F.2d 68 (2nd Cir. 1975) (defendant charged with distribution of narcotics beaten and tortured with electrodes by Chilean police, no involvement by United States police). The purpose underlying the *Toscanino* rule is to deter police misconduct by barring the government from using the fruits of its deliberate lawlessness. When the United States is not involved in the torturous activity, no purpose would be served by dismissing the indictment.

In this action, there is no dispute that United States law enforcement officers were fully involved in the planning and execution of defendant's arrest. However, defendant has failed either to allege or to show any actions committed by these officers that meet the standard of outrageousness established by *Toscanino* and its progeny requiring this Court to divest itself of jurisdiction.

The record in this proceeding has been reviewed with care and the Court fails to find the type of cruel, inhumane and outrageous conduct that would warrant dismissal under *Toscanino*. That is not to say that the Court accepts the government's representations in its December 1, 1987, response to defendant's pretrial motion that Yunis "was treated with the greatest care and with due deference to whatever personal requests he made during the voyage from the Mediterranean to the United States." Even the government has admitted that "there may well have been in hindsight too much force brought upon Mr. Yunis' wrists" when he was forced down and thrown to the deck during the course of his arrest. Trans. of Motions Hearing, Dec. 23, 1987, at 38. Indeed, the two agents immediately involved believed that the amount of force and method used in effectuating the arrest were necessary to ensure that the defendant did not attempt to jump overboard.

Similarly, although the defendant may not have been given the best or even adequate medical care, the treatment provided was not so poor as to be "cruel and inhumane." The testimony of the three treating physicians, Drs. Braddock, Gore and Gabriel, refuted the government's representations that the doctors remained at Yunis' "beckon call. [sic]" Trans. at 45 (Dec. 23, 1987). Indeed, despite the defendant's constant complaints concerning the condition of and the pain emitting from his fractured wrists, the orthopedist, Dr. Gore, did not examine Yunis until September 15, the third day into the naval voyage. When he conducted his initial examination of the defendant's wrists, he recommended ice treatment and elevation and at the motions hearing testified that in his judgment placing casts on the defendant's wrists without the use of x-ray would be "excessive and overkill." Tran. of Jan. 20, 1988 at 187.[26] Dr. Keith Gabriel, the physician who treated Yunis after he entered the United States, offered alternative advice. Given the defendant's symptoms and in the absence of x-ray facilities, he would have "at least offer[ed] the patient some type of immobilization, whether that might be a splint or a cast, or simply an adhesive wrapping, like an ace wrap." Trans. of test., Jan. 25, 1988, at 39. However, merely because the two doctors prescribed contrary treatment, does not transform Dr. Gore's at worst negligent diagnosis and prescription into malicious, inhumane conduct. Moreover, the defendant's nausea and sea sickness were certainly not the result of any deliberate actions by the government. Indeed, several of the FBI agents involved in the operation appeared to suffer from motion sickness.

Finally, even if the procedure employed in transporting the defendant by airplane from the Saratoga to the United States was extremely confining, it did not rise to the level of outrageousness that shocks the conscience. S. A. David Johnson, who was primarily responsible for the hostage rescue team, testified that it was necessary to tranquilize the defendant and place him in the Stokes later due to the size of the plane and the need to protect the aircraft and the personnel on board. Trans. of Johnson at 53.

[26] It is undisputed that there were no x-ray facilities on board the *Butte*.

Even if the Court were to accept each and every allegation of excessiveness made by the defendant, taken together, they simply do not rise to the deliberate torture and abuse alleged in *Toscanino*. However, the defendant is not left without any relief from the government's allegedly illegal law enforcement practices. He is afforded all the procedural and substantive constitutional safeguards provided every criminal defendant facing trial.

Indeed, the discussion and resolution of defendant's motion to suppress, which follows, demonstrate the premise and significance of the *Ker-Frisbie* doctrine – that a defendant's rights to due process of law are satisfied by the protections afforded a defendant at trial.

Notes and Questions

1. On applicability of the U.S. Constitution abroad, *see also United States v. Tiede*, Crim. Case No. 78–001A (U.S. Ct. for Berlin Mar. 14, 1979), 85. F.R.D. 227 (1979), reprinted in 19 I.L.M. 179 (1980); *United States v. Yunis*, 681 F. Supp. 896, 906 (D.D.C. 1986); *United States v. Verdugo-Urquidez*, 110 S.Ct. 1056, 1066 (1990) (Rehnquist, C.J., dictum concerning the U.S. use of armed force abroad and that "restrictions on searches and seizures which occur incident to such action . . . [can] be imposed by . . . treaty . . . ").

2. Courts have consistently upheld jurisdiction in cases where defendants move to dismiss based solely on the fact that they were lured to the United States. *See United States v. Reed*, 639 F.2d 896 (2d Cir. 1981) (upholding the constitutionality of Reed's arrest). Central Intelligence Agency agents lured Reed to leave Bimini Island in the Bahamas by telling him that the private plane he boarded was bound for Nassau, not Florida. The court held that Reed's Fourth Amendment rights were not violated because his detention resulted from a valid arrest warrant. The court ruled that there was no due process violation or *Toscanino* exception on the basis of the absence of brutal torture. *Reed*, 639 F.2d at 901.

In *United States v. Wilson*, 732 F.2d 404, 411 (5th Cir.), *cert. denied*, 469 U.S. 1099 (1984), an agent enticed the former U.S. intelligence operative to leave Libya through deceit. The court denied the defendant's motion to dismiss the indictment because Wilson was simply "the victim of a nonviolent government trick . . . any irregularity in a criminal defendant's apprehension will not vitiate proceedings against him." *Yunis*, 681 F. Supp. at 919 (quoting *Wilson*, 721 F.2d at 972). Hence, U.S. agents planned and executed Yunis's and Wilson's arrest, but did not employ extreme torture or abuse. Therefore, the arrest and their conduct were not deemed outrageous by the *Toscanino* exception.

3. The United States employs luring and deception by law enforcement officials to coerce a suspect to enter a locality where a valid arrest can occur. Under the *Ker-Frisbie* doctrine, such a practice is held constitutional because it achieves the same goal as forcible abduction, but by using tricks and not force. However, some governments do not use or endorse as easily as does the United States the practice of luring.

2. International Consensus against the Practice of Luring

Many countries strongly disagree with the U.S. position that irregular rendition is an acceptable law enforcement tool. They have often disapproved of or opposed luring as a means to bring a person into a jurisdiction, regarding it as unacceptable as forcible abduction.

In the case of Kenneth Walker, a Canadian citizen, U.S. Customs officials employed Barry Brokaw, a former business associate of Walker's, to arrange a weapons deal with him. After many solicitations, Walker agreed to try to procure for Brokaw the requested arms. Walker was hesitant until he confirmed with "Prince," also a U.S. undercover agent, that Ecuador was a legal destination for arms sales. Walker did not learn that the weapons were really destined for Chile until he was indicted.

Later, Prince asked Walker to meet with him in New York, but Walker declined and suggested a meeting in Toronto. Finally, Prince convinced Walker to meet with him in the Bahamas with the promise of an all-expenses-paid trip. The U.S. agents arranged for Walker to receive his airline ticket at the last possible moment before departure. Walker learned that the flight had been routed through New York only after he had boarded the plane. The U.S. agents appeared to lure Walker into the United States because they did not have enough evidence to extradite him from Canada. Walker was subsequently arrested upon disembarking in New York to change planes.

After spending approximately six months in pretrial detention in many different cells, Walker pled guilty and was released on bond prior to sentencing. Walker decided not to return for sentencing and hence became a fugitive. The U.S. government requested his extradition. In an unprecedented response, after several exchanges of diplomatic correspondence, Canada refused even to convene a hearing on the extradition request. It cited violations of Canadian law and sovereignty, especially the fact that the United States had initiated a sting procedure and lured one of its nationals without any notice to the Canadian government.

Walker filed a civil suit against the U.S. government and the persons who participated in the operation. The United States claimed immunity. The Canadian trial court rejected the United States' assertion and ruled that an improper restraint on a person does not always have to be physical. The court reasoned that if a person's will is overcome by force or fraud, the person has been "abducted." In this case, a false imprisonment happened when Mr. Walker boarded the airplane in Toronto acting on the misrepresentations of the United States.[27] Such a practice was an abduction and therefore a violation of the Criminal Code of Canada, R.S.C. 1985, C-46, s. 279 (1)(b). However, the Canadian appellate courts reversed and held that the United States and other defendants were immune.

The Canadian response to the Walker incident illustrates the reactions of a minority of nations to the use of luring in the practice of transnational law enforcement. In addition to filing a diplomatic note formally protesting the actions of U.S. Customs officials, the Canadian government supported Walker during subsequent litigation.

Cyprus and the Bahamas are two other nations that have objected to U.S. use of luring as an alternative to extradition. The United States indicted Hossein Alikhani for allegedly violating a U.S. statute prohibiting the export of natural gas equipment to Libya.[28] Alikhani, a Cypriot citizen, learned of the U.S. embargo against Libya from Mr. Al Baumler, sales manager of Turbo Power and Marine Systems (TPMS), and as a result did not pursue any sales to Libya. However, a year after the incident, Baumler offered to supply parts to Alikhani while concealing his true identity as an informant of the U.S. Customs Service. Baumler and other agents sent letters through a front company advising Alikhani how to perform the business deal while conforming to American law. Alikhani relied on this information in deciding to complete the business transaction with Baumler.

[27] *Walker v. Bank of New York, Inc.*, (1993) 16 O.R. (3d) 596 (Gen. Div).
[28] *See* Libyan Sanctions Regulations, 31 C.F.R § 550 (1994).

In October 1992, Baumler persuaded Alikhani to attend a business meeting in the Bahamas. On his arrival Alikhani was met by undercover agents at the Bahamian airport. At that time, the agents told Alikhani that he would travel to another Bahamian island, and he agreed to board the plane under that presumption. However, after takeoff when the plane departed Bahamian airspace, the U.S. agents revealed their true identities and arrested Alikhani.

The government of the Bahamas and the government of Cyprus formally sent diplomatic notes protesting his abduction. After six months in pretrial detention, during which he was without his eyeglasses and hence unable to review documents pertaining to his case, Mr. Alikhani pled guilty.[29] The plea bargain agreement forbade any complaints by the defendant concerning the circumstances of his arrest. However, on his return to Cyprus, Alikhani brought a lawsuit to overturn the part of the plea bargain agreement where he agreed not to challenge his arrest and conviction.[30]

Both Alikhani and Walker filed petitions to adjudicate U.S. conduct during their arrests.[31] However, because the U.S. government has not ratified the Inter-American Convention on Human Rights, but is bound by the OAS Charter as supplemented by the American Declaration, the plaintiffs can only bring their petition in the Inter-American Commission on Human Rights (IACHR), which cannot directly compel enforcement or provide monetary relief. *Cf. Velasquez Rodriguez Case*, Inter-Am. Ct. H.R. (29 July 1988). *See* in regard to the use of the IACHR, the discussion of the European and Inter-American human rights systems in Chapter 14.

Recent court decisions in several countries have held that the mere physical presence of a person before the court is not sufficient to confer jurisdiction. Common and civil law countries such as New Zealand, Britain, Zimbabwe, South Africa, and Switzerland have condemned the practice of abduction by giving their courts discretion not to exercise jurisdiction.[32] This trend could lead to an absolute bar on the exercise of jurisdiction where an abduction by force or deceit has occurred.

Some in the international law community view the practice of abduction by fraud as a violation of territorial sovereignty and international law, violations that do pertain if forcible abduction without foreign state consent occurs.[33] The Restatement codifies the

[29] Alikhani has since protested his acceptance of the plea agreement because of his psychological coercion, his wrongful denial of bail, the inability to participate in his defense due to wrongful deprivation of his eyeglasses, and the inability to have access to counsel, partly due to problems in the prison facilities in the aftermath of a hurricane in the Miami area, where he was incarcerated.

[30] *See Hossein Alikhani, et al. v. United States, et al.*, S.D. Fla. (Case No. 93–8513 CIV-ZLOCH).

[31] *Kenneth Walker, et al. v. United States*, Inter-American H.R. Commission, filed July, 1995. Eventually the commission dismissed the case for failure to exhaust domestic remedies in the United States.

[32] *See, e.g., R. v. Hartley* [1978] 2 NZLR 199; *S. v. Reahan* 1992 (1) South African Criminal Law Reports 307 (ZS) at 317 (Zimbabwe); *S. v. Ebrahim*, in 31 I.L.M. 890 (Feb. 26, 1991); *Bennett v. Horseferry Road Magistrates Court*, 2 All E.R. 318 (1993). For an example of civil law country jurisprudence on this matter, see the decision of the Swiss Federal Supreme Court of July 25, 1982, Eur. Grundr Zeitschrift (1983) 435; and 39 Swiss Yearbook of International Law (1983); *Resolutions Proposed by International Committees*, International Law Association, Buenos Aires Conference 17 (1994).

[33] The international community is also very much opposed to the U.S. practice of abduction by force. After the U.S. Supreme Court's *Alvarez-Machain* decision, which upheld jurisdiction of a defendant brought to the United States through the use of force, *United States v. Alvarez-Machain*, 112 S.Ct. 2188 (1992), there was strong opposition by many foreign nations to the decision itself and, in general, to the use of abduction by force. Paul Hoffman, *Kidnapping Foreign Criminal Suspects*, 15 Whittier L. Rev. 419, 421 (1994). In addition, the Inter-American Juridical Committee issued a strong ruling condemning the practice in the context of the *Alvarez-Machain* case.

customary international law principle that a nation's agents may not use police powers and seize an individual from another nation without obtaining consent from the other nation's government, and even foreign state consent would not obviate human rights violations.[34]

C. *Abduction*

In general, the judiciary in the United States, Canada, and the United Kingdom has taken the position that a fugitive should not succeed in escaping trial merely because he or she was brought illegally into the jurisdiction of the prosecuting state. This practice is known by the Roman maxim, *mala captus bene detentus*, which means that the court once in possession of the accused has jurisdiction over the person and all that is required is a fair trial. Some states employ force in several ways either to obtain custody or even assassinate suspects. These measures include, *inter alia*: diversion of aircraft and vessels in order to arrest some of the passengers who are suspects, capture during war or in self-defense, and assassination; they are beyond the scope of this chapter. For a discussion of such measures, *see* International Criminal Law Cases and Materials 497–505 (Jordan J. Paust et al. eds., 2000).

An exception in U.S. cases has involved violations of treaty law. *See, e.g., Cook v. United States*, 288 U.S. 102 (1933); *United States v. Ferris*, 19 F.2d 925, 926 (N.D. Cal. 1927); *see also* (all re: customary international law) *The Apollon*, 22 U.S. (9 Wheat.) 362, 370–71, 376–79 (1824); *Motherwell v. United States ex rel. Alexandroff*, 107 F. 437, 446 (3d Cir. 1901)(Gray, J., concurring), *rev'd*, 183 U.S. 424 (1902). Although the U.S. Second Circuit Court of Appeals in *United States v. Toscanino* also declared that there exists an exception in cases in which the manner in which the fugitive is apprehended "shocks the conscience of the Court," this exception has not since been applied to exclude jurisdiction.

United States v. Toscanino, 500 F.2d 267 (2d Cir. 1974)

Mansfield, Circuit Judge

Francisco Toscanino appeals from a narcotics conviction entered against him in the Eastern District of New York by Chief Judge Jacob Mishler after a jury trial. Toscanino was sentenced to 20 years in prison and fined $20,000. He contends that the court acquired jurisdiction over him unlawfully through the conduct of American agents who kidnapped him in Uruguay, used illegal electronic surveillance, tortured him and abducted him to the United States for the purpose of prosecuting him here. We remand the case to the district court for further proceedings in which the government will be required to respond to his allegations concerning the methods by which he was brought into the Eastern District and the use of electronic surveillance to gather evidence against him.

Toscanino, who is a citizen of Italy, and four others were charged with conspiracy to import narcotics into the United States in violation of 21 U.S.C. §§ 173 and 174 in a one count indictment returned by a grand jury sitting in the Eastern District on February 22, 1973. The

[34] *See* Restatement, §§ 432–433; Kristin Berdan Weissman, *Extraterritorial Abduction: The Endangerment of Future Peace*, 27 U.C. Davis L. Rev. 459, 474 (1994); also see Paust, *After* Alvarez-Machain*; Abduction, Standing, Denials of Justice, and Unaddressed Human Rights Claims*, 67 St. John's L. Rev. 551 (1993).

other defendants were S. Nicolay, Segundo Coronel, Roberto Arenas and Umberto Coronel. Also named as a conspirator but not as a defendant was one Hosvep Caramian. At a joint trial of all the defendants (except for Nicolay who had fled to Argentina), which began on May 22, 1973, the only government witness against Toscanino was Caramian who testified that he met with Toscanino in Montevideo, Uruguay, during the summer of 1970 and agreed to find buyers for a shipment of heroin into the United States, which would be delivered by Nicolay. Caramian testified further that in November, 1970, he left Uruguay and came to the United States where he met with Arenas and the Coronel brothers who agreed to buy the heroin. On November 30, 1970, Caramian received part of Toscanino's shipment delivered by Nicolay in Miami, Florida, but ultimate distribution of the narcotics was intercepted by government agents who posed as buyers from Arenas and the Coronel brothers. Toscanino, testifying in his own behalf, denied any knowledge of these transactions. On June 5, 1973, the jury returned a verdict of guilty against him and all the other defendants.

Toscanino does not question the sufficiency of the evidence or claim any error with respect to the conduct of the trial itself. His principal argument, which he voiced prior to trial and again after the jury verdict was returned, is that the entire proceedings in the district court against him were void because his presence within the territorial jurisdiction of the court had been illegally obtained. He alleged that he had been kidnapped from his home in Montevideo, Uruguay, and brought into the Eastern District only after he had been detained for three weeks of interrogation accompanied by physical torture in Brazil. . . .

The government prosecutor neither affirmed nor denied these allegations but claimed they were immaterial to the district court's power to proceed.

Toscanino alleged further that, prior to his forcible abduction from Montevideo, American officials bribed an employee of the public telephone company to conduct electronic surveillance of him and that the results of the surveillance were given to American agents and forwarded to government prosecutors in New York. According to Toscanino the telephone company employee was eventually arrested in Uruguay for illegal eavesdropping and was indicted and imprisoned. In connection with these later allegations Toscanino moved, pursuant to 18 U.S.C. § 3594, to compel the government to affirm or deny whether in fact there had been any electronic surveillance of him in Uruguay.

Toscanino's motion for an order vacating the verdict, dismissing the indictment and ordering his return to Uruguay was denied by the district court on November 2, 1973, without a hearing. Relying principally on the decisions of the Supreme Court in *Ker* v. *Illinois*, 119 U.S. 436, 7 S.Ct. 225, 30 L.Ed. 421 (1886), and *Frisbie* v. *Collins*, 342 U.S. 519, 72 S.Ct. 509, 96 L.Ed. 541 (1952), the court held that the manner in which Toscanino was brought into the territory of the United States was immaterial to the court's power to proceed, provided he was physically present at the time of trial. . . .

In an era marked by a sharp increase in kidnapping activities, both here and abroad, *see, e.g.*, NEW YORK TIMES, Jan. 5, 1974, at 25, col. 6, Dec. 13, 1973, at 2, col. 5, Oct. 17, 1973, at 14, col. 5, we face the question, as we must in the state of the pleadings, of whether a federal court must assume jurisdiction over the person of a defendant who is illegally apprehended abroad and forcibly abducted by government agents to the United States for the purpose of facing criminal charges here. The answer necessitates a review and appraisal of two Supreme Court decisions, heavily relied upon by the government and by the district court, *Ker* v. *Illinois*, 119 U.S. 436, 7 S.Ct. 225, 30 L.Ed. 421 (1888), and *Frisbie* v. *Collins*, 342 U.S. 519, 72 S.Ct. 509, 96 L.Ed. 541 (1952). For years these two cases have been the mainstay of a doctrine to the effect that the government's power to prosecute a defendant is not impaired by the illegality of the method by which it acquires control over him. This teaching originated almost 90 years ago in *Ker*. While residing in Peru, Ker was indicted by an Illinois grand jury for larceny and embezzlement. At the request of the Governor of Illinois, the President, invoking the current treaty of extradition between the United States and Peru, issued a warrant authorizing a Pinkerton agent to take custody of Ker from the authorities of Peru. The warrant, however was never served, probably for the reason that by the time the agent arrived there, armed forces of Chile, then at war with Peru, were in control of Lima. See *Ker v. Illinois* Revisited, 47 AM. J. INT'L L. 678 (1953). Instead Ker was forcibly abducted by the agent, placed aboard an American vessel and eventually taken to the United States, where he was tried and convicted in Illinois. The Supreme Court rejected Ker's argument that he was entitled by virtue of the treaty with Peru to a right of asylum there and held that the abduction of Ker did not violate the Due Process Clause of the Fourteenth Amendment (then less than 20 years old), which was construed as merely requiring that the party be regularly indicted and brought to trial "according to the forms and modes prescribed for such trials." The Court accordingly held that Ker might be tried by Illinois, regardless of the method by which it acquired control over him.

Sixty-six years later the Supreme Court again faced the question in *Frisbie* v. *Collins*, *supra*, in a slightly different context. There a Michigan state prisoner, petitioning for habeas corpus, alleged that he had been brought from Chicago, Illinois, to Michigan for trial only after he had been kidnapped, handcuffed and blackjacked in Chicago by Michigan police officers who had gone there to retrieve him. The prisoner claimed that his conviction in Michigan violated the Due Process Clause of the Fourteenth Amendment as well as the federal Kidnapping Act, 18 U.S.C. § 1201, and was therefore a nullity. Rejecting the due process claim the Supreme Court explained,

> "This court has never departed from the rule announced in *Ker* v. *Illinois*, 119 U.S. 436, 444, [7 S.Ct. 225, 229, 30 L.Ed. 421], that the power of a court to try a person for crime is not impaired by the fact that he had been brought within the court's jurisdiction by reason of a 'forcible abduction.' No persuasive reasons are now presented to justify overruling this line of cases. They rest on the sound basis that due process of law is satisfied when one present in court is convicted of crime after being fairly apprized of the charges against him and after a fair trial in accordance with constitutional procedural safeguards."

Thus, under the so-called "Ker-Frisbie" rule, due process was limited to the guarantee of a constitutionally fair trial, regardless of the method by which jurisdiction was obtained over the defendant. Jurisdiction gained through an indisputably illegal act might still be exercised, even though the effect could be to reward police brutality and lawlessness in some cases.

Since *Frisbie* the Supreme Court, in what one distinguished legal luminary describes as a "constitutional revolution," see Griswold, *The Due Process Revolution and Confrontation*, 119 U. PA. L. REV. 711 (1971), has expanded the interpretation of "due process." No longer is it limited to the guarantee of "fair" procedure at trial. In an effort to deter police misconduct, the term has been extended to bar the government from realizing directly the fruits of its own deliberate and unnecessary lawlessness in bringing the accused to trial....

In light of these developments we are satisfied that the "Ker-Frisbie" rule cannot be reconciled with the Supreme Court's expansion of the concept of due process, which now protects the accused against pretrial illegality by denying to the government the fruits of its exploitation of any deliberate and unnecessary lawlessness on its part. Although the issue in most of the cases forming part of this evolutionary process was whether evidence should have been excluded (*e.g.*, *Mapp*, *Miranda*, *Wong Sun*, *Silverman*), it was unnecessary in those cases to invoke any other sanction to insure that an ultimate conviction would not rest on governmental illegality. Where suppression of evidence will not suffice, however, we must be guided by the underlying principle that the government should be denied the right to exploit its own illegal conduct, *Wong Sun* v. *United States*, 371 U.S. 471, 488, 83 S.Ct. 407, 9 L.Ed.2d 441 (1963), and when an accused is kidnapped and forcibly brought within the jurisdiction, the court's acquisition of power over his person represents the fruits of the government's exploitation of its own misconduct. Having unlawfully seized the defendant in violation of the Fourth Amendment, which guarantees "the right of the people to be secure in their persons . . . against unreasonable . . . seizures," the government should as a matter of fundamental fairness be obligated to return him to his *status quo ante*.

Faced with a conflict between the two concepts of due process, the one being the restricted version found in *Ker-Frisbie* and the other the expanded and enlightened interpretation expressed in more recent decisions of the Supreme Court, we are persuaded that to the extent that the two are in conflict, the *Ker-Frisbie* version must yield. Accordingly we view due process as now requiring a court to divest itself of jurisdiction over the person of a defendant where it has been acquired as the result of the government's deliberate, unnecessary and unreasonable invasion of the accused's constitutional rights. This conclusion represents but an extension of the well-recognized power of federal courts in the civil context to decline to exercise jurisdiction over a defendant whose presence has been secured by force or fraud. See *In re Johnson*, 167 U.S. 120, 126, 17 S.Ct. 735, 42 L.Ed. 103 (1896); *Fitzgerald Construction Co.* v. *Fitzgerald*, 137 U.S. 98, 11 S.Ct. 36, 34 L.Ed. 608 (1890).

If the charges of government misconduct in kidnapping Toscanino and forcibly bringing him to the United States should be sustained, the foregoing principles would, as a matter of due process, entitle him to some relief. The allegations include corruption and bribery of a foreign official as well as kidnapping, accompanied by violence and brutality to the person. Deliberate misconduct on the part of United States agents, in violation not only of constitutional prohibitions but also of the federal Kidnapping Act, *supra*, and of two international treaties obligating the United States Government to respect the territorial sovereignty of Uruguay, is charged. See U.N. Charter, art. 2; O.A.S. Charter, art. 17. The conduct alleged here satisfies those tests articulated by the Supreme Court in its most recent "entrapment" decision, *United States* v. *Russell*, 411 U.S. 432, 93 S.Ct. 1637, 36 L.Ed.2d 366 (1973), where, in holding that due process did not bar prosecution for the manufacture and sale of an illegal drug, even though a government undercover agent had supplied a scarce chemical required for its synthesis, it noted that the government agent had violated no constitutional prohibition or federal law and had committed no crime in infiltrating the defendant's drug enterprise. It furthermore appeared that the type of undercover activity engaged in there by the agent was necessary in order to gather essential evidence. Here, in contrast, not only were several laws allegedly broken and crimes committed at the behest of government agents but the conduct was apparently unnecessary, as the extradition treaty between the United States and Uruguay, see 35 Stat. 2028, does not specifically exclude narcotics violations so that a representative of our government might have been able to conclude with Uruguay a special arrangement for Toscanino's extradition. *Cf. Fiocconi* v. *Attorney General of United States*, 339 F. Supp. 1242, 1244 (S.D.N.Y. 1972).

In any event, since *Ker* and *Frisbie* involved state court convictions only, the views expressed in those cases would not necessarily apply to the present case, which is an appeal from a judgment entered by a federal district court. Here we possess powers not available to a federal court reviewing a state tribunal's resolution of constitutional issues. In this case we may rely simply upon our supervisory power over the administration of criminal justice in the district courts within our jurisdiction.... Clearly this power may legitimately be used to prevent district courts from themselves becoming "accomplices in willful disobedience of law." See *McNabb, supra* at 345. Moreover the supervisory power is not limited to the admission or exclusion of evidence, but may be exercised in any manner necessary to remedy abuses of a district court's process. *Cf. Rea* v. *United States*, 350 U.S. 214, 76 S.Ct. 292, 100 L.Ed. 233 (1955). Drawing again from the field of civil procedure, we think a federal court's criminal process is abused or degraded where it is executed against a defendant who has been brought into the territory of the United States by the methods alleged here. *Cf. Commercial Mutual Accident Co.* v. *Davis*, 213 U.S. 245, 29 S.Ct. 445, 53 L.Ed. 782 (1909); *Fitzgerald Construction Co.* v. *Fitzgerald, supra*. We could not tolerate such an abuse without debasing "the processes of justice."

If distinctions are necessary, *Ker* and *Frisbie* are clearly distinguishable on other legally significant grounds which render neither of them controlling here. Neither case, unlike that here, involved the abduction of a defendant in violation of international treaties of the United States. *Frisbie* presented an alleged interstate abduction in which the appellant was clearly extraditable and an order returning him to his asylum state, Illinois, would have been an exercise in futility since Illinois would have been obligated to return him to Michigan for trial. U.S. Const. Art. IV, § 2, cl. 2; 18 U.S.C. § 3182. Although the appellant in *Ker* argued that his forcible abduction by the Pinkerton agent violated the extradition treaty between the United States and Peru, the Supreme Court disagreed, holding that the extradition treaty did not apply and that it would have been violated by the demanding state only if, after receiving a fugitive, it tried him for a crime other than that for which he was surrendered. See *United States v. Rauscher*, 119 U.S. 407, 7 S.Ct. 234, 30 L.Ed. 425 (1888). Here, in contrast, Toscanino alleges that he was forcibly abducted from Uruguay, whose territorial sovereignty this country has agreed in two international treaties to respect. The Charter of the United Nations, the members of which include the United States and Uruguay, see Department of State, Treaties in Force 402–03 (1973), obligates "All Members" to "refrain ... from the threat or use of force against the territorial integrity of political independence of any state...." See U.N. Charter, art. 2 para. 4. Additionally, the Charter of the Organization of American States, whose members also include the United States and Uruguay, see Department of State, Treaties in Force 359 (1973), provides that the "territory of a state is inviolable; it may not be the object, even temporarily ... of ... measures of force taken by another state, directly or indirectly, on any grounds whatever...." *See* O.A.S. Charter, art. 17.

That international kidnappings such as the one alleged here violate the U.N. Charter was settled as a result of the Security Council debates following the illegal kidnapping in 1960 of Adolf Eichmann from Argentina by Israeli "volunteer groups." In response to a formal complaint filed by the U.N. representative from Argentina pursuant to article 35 of the U.N. Charter[35] the Security Council, by eight votes to none (with two abstentions and one member – Argentina – not participating in the vote), adopted a resolution condemning the kidnapping and requesting "the Government of Israel to make appropriate reparation in accordance with the Charter of the United Nations and rules of international law...." U.N. Doc. S/4349 (June 23, 1960), quoted in W. Friedmann, O. Lissitzyn & R. Pugh,

[35] Article 35 of the UN Charter permits member nations to bring "any dispute ... to the attention of the Security Council or of the General Assembly."

International Law: Cases and Materials 497 (1969). The resolution merely recognized a long standing principle of international law that abductions by one state of persons located within the territory of another violate the territorial sovereignty of the second state and are redressable usually by the return of the person kidnapped. See *The Vincenti Affair*, 1 Hackworth, *Digest of International Law* 624 (1920); *The Cantu Case*, 2 Hackworth 310 (1914); *The Case of Blatt and Converse*, 2 Hackworth 309 (1911).

Since the United States thus agreed not to seize persons residing within the territorial limits of Uruguay, appellant's allegations in this case are governed not by *Ker* but by the Supreme Court's later decision in *Cook* v. *United States*, 288 U.S. 102, 53 S.Ct. 305, 77 L.Ed. 641 (1933). In *Cook* officers of the United States Coast Guard boarded and seized a British vessel, the Mazel Tov, in violation of territorial limits fixed by a treaty then in force between the United States and Great Britain. The Supreme Court held that the government's subsequent libel for forfeiture of the vessel in the federal district court was properly dismissed, since under the treaty the forcible seizure was incapable of giving the district court power to adjudicate title to the vessel regardless of the vessel's physical presence within the court's jurisdiction.... Thus *Ker* does not apply where a defendant has been brought into the district court's jurisdiction by forcible abduction in violation of a treaty.... It derives directly from the Court's earlier decision in *United States* v. *Rauscher*, 119 U.S. 407, 7 S.Ct. 234, 30 L.Ed. 425 (1888), decided the same day as *Ker* and written by the same Justice. In *Rauscher*, the Court held that United States courts were barred from trying a fugitive, surrendered by Great Britain pursuant to a treaty of extradition, for a crime other than that for which he had been extradited, at least until he had been afforded an opportunity to return to the country from which he had been brought. In reaching this result the Court rejected the argument that even where a trial might be in violation of a treaty obligation, the defendant's exclusive remedy was an "appeal to the executive branches of the treaty governments for redress." See 119 U.S. at 430–432. See also *Johnson* v. *Browne*, 205 U.S. 309, 27 S.Ct. 639, 51 L.Ed. 816 (1907)....

The case is remanded to the district court for further proceedings not inconsistent with this opinion. Our remand should be construed as requiring an evidentiary hearing with respect to Toscanino's allegations of forcible abduction only if, in response to the government's denial, he offers some credible supporting evidence including specifically evidence that the action was taken by or at the direction of United States officials. Upon his failure to make such an offer the district court may, in its discretion, decline to hold an evidentiary hearing.

Notes and Questions

1. The Restatement has adopted the *Toscanino* exception. *See* Restatement § 433 (2), Comm. c and Reporters' Note 3. The majority of text writers are also opposed to *mala captus* practices. *See, e.g.*, M. C. Bassiouni, International Extradition in United States Law and Practice § 2–9 (1983). In later cases such as *United States v. Herrera*, 504 F.2d 859 (5th Cir. 1974); *United States ex rel. Lujan* v. *Gengler*, 510 F. 2d 62 (2d Cir. 1975); *United States* v. *Lira*, 515 F.2d 68 (2d Cir 1975); and *United States* v. *Marschener*, 470 F. Supp. 201 (D. Conn. 1979), the *Toscanino* decision was distinguished and explained. For instance, the court in *Gengler* distinguished it because government agents do not have a carte blanche to arrest and return defendants from abroad to the United States by the use of torture, brutality, and similar outrageous conduct. However, not every violation of law by the government or irregularity in the circumstances of a defendant's arrival in the jurisdiction is enough to deprive a criminal court of jurisdiction. In that case the court found the conduct of the U.S. government agents was not outrageous, and additionally the offended state did not object to that conduct. In fact, the "*Toscanino* exception" has

failed to require the court to divest itself of jurisdiction in every case but *United States* v. *Caro-Quintero,* 745 F. Supp. 599 (C.D. Cal. 1990). That decision was later reversed by the U.S. Supreme Court in *United States* v. *Alvarez-Machain,* 112 S.Ct. 2188 (1992), presented later in the chapter. How important are the responses or lack thereof of the government of the country from which the defendant is taken? Or of the government of which he is a citizen?

2. In 1985, the UN Security Council recognized that "abductions are offenses of grave concern to the international community, having severe adverse consequences for the rights of the victims and for the promotion of friendly relations and co-operation among States." The resolution condemned "unequivocally all acts of . . . abduction" and recognized the "obligation of all States in whose territory hostages or abducted persons are held urgently to take all appropriate measures to secure their safe release and to prevent the commission of acts of hostage-taking and abduction in the future" UNSC Res. 579 (1985), reprinted in 25 ILM 243 (1986). What value do you think the resolution can have legally?

3. The UN Human Rights Committee has found that forcible abductions can violate the human rights of the abductee. Views of the Human Rights Committee on the Complaint of Lopez, 36 U.N. GAOR, Supp. No. 40, at 176–84, U.N. Doc. A/36/40 (1981); *see also id.* at 185–89; RESTATEMENT § 432, Reporters' Note 1; *id.* § 702 (c). The Human Rights Committee, in *Canon Garcia v. Ecuador* (Decision of May 11, 1991, U.N. Doc. CCPR/C/43/319/1988), has also found that Ecuador violated Article 9 of the Covenant by participating in an abduction to the United States of a person accused of drug trafficking. In Europe, abductions are also considered to violate human rights that protect the individual from the arbitrary deprivation of liberty. *See, e.g., Bozano v. France,* Ser. A, No. 111 (18 Dec. 1986), 9 EHRR 297 (1987), (2 Dec. 1991), 13 EHRR 428 (1991). In *Bozano,* the European Court found a violation of Article 5(1) of the European Convention on Human Rights in a context where the individual had been found to be not extraditable from France (to Italy, the requesting state). Nonetheless, the French government issued a deportation order, and French police took him against his will to Switzerland where he was extradited to Italy to serve his sentence after conviction in Italy *in absentia.* The European Court explained that "'lawfulness' implies absence of any arbitrariness," that the deportation was a disguised form of extradition contrary to French judicial rulings, and that the individual's "deprivation of liberty . . . was neither 'lawful' . . . , nor compatible with the 'right to security of person'" within the meaning of the Convention. *Id.* at paras. 58–60. In *Bennett v. Horseferry Road Magistrate's Court,* [1993] All ER 138 (House of Lords), jurisdiction was refused where a person had been deported from South Africa. The English courts regarded it as disguised extradition. *See also* International Law Association, REPORT OF THE SIXTY-SIXTH CONFERENCE – BUENOS AIRES, ARGENTINA 142, 162–65 (1994) (noting several of those cases just cited as well as cases in New Zealand, Zimbabwe, South Africa, and Switzerland).

United States v. Alvarez-Machain, 504 U.S. 655 (1992)

Rehnquist, Chief Justice

The issue in this case is whether a criminal defendant, abducted to the United States from a nation with which it has an extradition treaty, thereby acquires a defense to the jurisdiction of this country's courts. We hold that he does not, and that he may be tried in federal district court for violations of the criminal law of the United States.

Respondent, Humberto Alvarez-Machain, is a citizen and resident of Mexico. He was indicted for participating in the kidnap and murder of United States Drug Enforcement Administration (DEA) special agent Enrique Camarena-Salazar and a Mexican pilot working with Camarena, Alfredo Zavala-Avelar. The DEA believes that respondent, a medical doctor, participated in the murder by prolonging agent Camarena's life so that others could further torture and interrogate him. On April 2, 1990, respondent was forcibly kidnapped from his medical office in Guadalajara, Mexico, to be flown by private plane to El Paso, Texas, where he was arrested by DEA officials. The District Court concluded that DEA agents were responsible for respondent's abduction, although they were not personally involved in it. *United States* v. *Caro-Quintero*, 745 F. Supp. 599, 602–604, 609 (C.D. Cal. 1990).

Respondent moved to dismiss the indictment, claiming that his abduction constituted outrageous governmental conduct, and that the District Court lacked jurisdiction to try him because he was abducted in violation of the extradition treaty between the United States and Mexico. *Extradition Treaty, May 4, 1978, [1979] United States-United Mexican States*, 31 U.S.T. 5059, T.I.A.S. No. 9656 (Extradition Treaty or Treaty). The District Court rejected the outrageous governmental conduct claim, but held that it lacked jurisdiction to try respondent because his abduction violated the Extradition Treaty. The district court discharged respondent and ordered that he be repatriated to Mexico. *Caro-Quintero, supra*, at 614.

The Court of Appeals affirmed the dismissal of the indictment and the repatriation of respondent, relying on its decision in *United States* v. *Verdugo-Urquidez*, 939 F.2d 1341 (9th Cir. 1991), cert. pending, No. 91–670. 946 F.2d 1466 (1991). In *Verdugo*, the Court of Appeals held that the forcible abduction of a Mexican national with the authorization or participation of the United States violated the Extradition Treaty between the United States and Mexico. Although the Treaty does not expressly prohibit such abductions, the Court of Appeals held that the "purpose" of the Treaty was violated by a forcible abduction, 939 F.2d, at 1350, which, along with a formal protest by the offended nation, would give a defendant the right to invoke the Treaty violation to defeat jurisdiction of the district court to try him. The Court of Appeals further held that the proper remedy for such a violation would be dismissal of the indictment and repatriation of the defendant to Mexico.

In the instant case, the Court of Appeals affirmed the district court's finding that the United States had authorized the abduction of respondent, and that letters from the Mexican government to the United States government served as an official protest of the Treaty violation. Therefore, the Court of Appeals ordered that the indictment against respondent be dismissed and that respondent be repatriated to Mexico. 946 F.2d, at 1467. We granted *certiorari* . . . and now reverse. . . .

In construing a treaty, as in construing a statute, we first look to its terms to determine its meaning. . . . The Treaty says nothing about the obligations of the United States and Mexico to refrain from forcible abductions of people from the territory of the other nation, or the consequences under the Treaty if such an abduction occurs. Respondent submits that Article 22(1) of the Treaty which states that it "shall apply to offenses specified in Article 2 [including murder] committed before and after this Treaty enters into force," 31 U.S.T., at 5073–5074, evidences an intent to make application of the Treaty mandatory for those offenses. However, the more natural conclusion is that Article 22 was included to ensure that the Treaty was applied to extraditions requested after the Treaty went into force, regardless of when the crime of extradition occurred.

More critical to respondent's argument is Article 9 of the Treaty which provides:

1. Neither Contracting Party shall be bound to deliver up its own nationals, but the executive authority of the requested Party shall, if not prevented by the laws of that Party, have the power to deliver them up if, in its discretion, it be deemed proper to do so.
2. If extradition is not granted pursuant to paragraph 1 of this Article, the requested Party shall submit the case to its competent authorities for the purpose of prosecution, provided that Party has jurisdiction over the offense." *Id.*, at 5065.

According to respondent, Article 9 embodies the terms of the bargain which the United States struck: if the United States wishes to prosecute a Mexican national, it may request that individual's extradition. Upon a request from the United States, Mexico may either extradite the individual, or submit the case to the proper authorities for prosecution in Mexico. In this way, respondent reasons, each nation preserved its right to choose whether its nationals would be tried in its own courts or by the courts of the other nation. This preservation of rights would be frustrated if either nation were free to abduct nationals of the other nation for the purposes of prosecution. More broadly, respondent reasons, as did the Court of Appeals, that all the processes and restrictions on the obligation to extradite established by the Treaty would make no sense if either nation were free to resort to forcible kidnapping to gain the presence of an individual for prosecution in a manner not contemplated by the Treaty. *Verdugo, supra,* at 1350.

We do not read the Treaty in such a fashion. Article 9 does not purport to specify the only way in which one country may gain custody of a national of the other country for the purposes of prosecution. In the absence of an extradition treaty, nations are under no obligation to surrender those in their country to foreign authorities for prosecution.... (United States may not extradite a citizen in the absence of a statute or treaty obligation). Extradition treaties exist so as to impose mutual obligations to surrender individuals in certain defined sets of circumstances, following established procedures. See 1 J. Moore, *A Treatise on Extradition and Interstate Rendition,* § 72 (1891). The Treaty thus provides a mechanism which would not otherwise exist, requiring, under certain circumstances, the United States and Mexico to extradite individuals to the other country, and establishing the procedures to be followed when the Treaty is invoked.

The history of negotiation and practice under the Treaty also fails to show that abductions outside of the Treaty constitute a violation of the Treaty. As the Solicitor General notes, the Mexican government was made aware, as early as 1906, of the *Ker* doctrine, and the United States' position that it applied to forcible abductions made outside of the terms of the United States-Mexico extradition treaty. Nonetheless, the current version of the Treaty, signed in 1978, does not attempt to establish a rule that would in any way curtail the effect of *Ker*. Moreover, although language which would grant individuals exactly the right sought by respondent had been considered and drafted as early as 1935 by a prominent group of legal scholars sponsored by the faculty of Harvard Law School, no such clause appears in the current treaty.

Thus, the language of the Treaty, in the context of its history, does not support the proposition that the Treaty prohibits abductions outside of its terms. The remaining question, therefore, is whether the Treaty should be interpreted so as to include an implied term prohibiting prosecution where the defendant's presence is obtained by means other than those established by the Treaty. See *Valentine*, 299 U.S., at 17, 57 S.Ct., at 106 ("Strictly the question is not whether there had been a uniform practical construction denying the power, but whether the power had been so clearly recognized that the grant should be implied.").

Respondent contends that the Treaty must be interpreted against the backdrop of customary international law, and that international abductions are "so clearly prohibited in international law" that there was no reason to include such a clause in the Treaty itself. Brief for Respondent 11. The international censure of international abductions is further evidenced, according to respondent, by the United Nations Charter and the Charter of the Organization of American States. *Id.*, at 17, 57 S.Ct., at 106. Respondent does not argue that these sources of international law provide an independent basis for the right respondent asserts not to be tried in the United States, but rather that they should inform the interpretation of the Treaty terms.

The Court of Appeals deemed it essential, in order for the individual defendant to assert a right under the Treaty, that the affected foreign government had registered a protest. *Verdugo*, 939 F.2d, at 1357 ("in the kidnapping case there must be a formal protest from the offended government after the kidnapping"). Respondent agrees that the right exercised by the individual is derivative of the nation's right under the Treaty, since nations are authorized, notwithstanding the terms of an extradition treaty, to voluntarily render an individual to the other country on terms completely outside of those provided in the Treaty. The formal protest, therefore, ensures that the "offended" nation actually objects to the abduction and has not in some way voluntarily rendered the individual for prosecution. Thus the Extradition Treaty only prohibits gaining the defendant's presence by means other than those set forth in the Treaty when the nation from which the defendant was abducted objects.

This argument seems to us inconsistent with the remainder of respondent's argument. The Extradition Treaty has the force of law, and if, as respondent asserts, it is self-executing, it would appear that a court must enforce it on behalf of an individual regardless of the offensiveness of the practice of one nation to the other nation....

More fundamentally, the difficulty with the support respondent garners from international law is that none of it relates to the practice of nations in relation to extradition treaties. In Rauscher, we implied a term in the Webster-Ashburton Treaty because of the practice of nations with regard to extradition treaties. In the instant case, respondent would imply terms in the extradition treaty from the practice of nations with regards to international law more generally. Respondent would have us find that the Treaty acts as a prohibition against a violation of the general principle of international law that one government may not "exercise its police power in the territory of another state." Brief for Respondent 16. There are many actions which could be taken by a nation that would violate this principle, including waging war, but it cannot seriously be contended that an invasion of the United States by Mexico would violate the terms of the extradition treaty between the two nations.

In sum, to infer from this Treaty and its terms that it prohibits all means of gaining the presence of an individual outside of its terms goes beyond established precedent and practice. In Rauscher, the implication of a doctrine of specialty into the terms of the Webster-Ashburton Treaty which, by its terms, required the presentation of evidence establishing probable cause of the crime of extradition before extradition was required, was a small step to take. By contrast, to imply from the terms of this Treaty that it prohibits obtaining the presence of an individual by means outside of the procedures the Treaty establishes requires a much larger inferential leap, with only the most general of international law principles to support it. The general principles cited by respondent simply fail to persuade us that we should imply in the United States-Mexico Extradition Treaty a term prohibiting international abductions.

Respondent and his amici may be correct that respondent's abduction was "shocking," Tr. of Oral Arg. 40, and that it may be in violation of general international law principles. Mexico has protested the abduction of respondent through diplomatic notes, App. 33–38, and the decision of whether respondent should be returned to Mexico, as a matter outside of the Treaty, is a matter for the Executive Branch. We conclude, however, that respondent's abduction was not in violation of the Extradition Treaty between the United States and Mexico, and therefore the rule of *Ker* v. *Illinois* is fully applicable to this case. The fact of respondent's forcible abduction does not therefore prohibit his trial in a court in the United States for violations of the criminal laws of the United States.

The judgment of the Court of Appeals is therefore reversed, and the case is remanded for further proceedings consistent with this opinion. So ordered.

Stevens, J. (dissenting)

The Court correctly observes that this case raises a question of first impression.... The case is unique for several reasons. It does not involve an ordinary abduction by a private kidnapper, or bounty hunter, as in *Ker* v. *Illinois*, 119 U.S. 436, 7 S.Ct. 225, 30 L.Ed. 421 (1886); nor does it involve the apprehension of an American fugitive who committed a crime in one State and sought asylum in another, as in *Frisbie* v. *Collins*, 342 U.S. 519, 72 S.Ct. 509, 96 L.Ed. 541 (1952). Rather, it involves this country's abduction of another country's citizen; it also involves a violation of the territorial integrity of that other country, with which this country has signed an extradition treaty....

The extradition treaty with Mexico is a comprehensive document containing 23 articles and an appendix listing the extraditable offenses covered by the agreement. The parties announced their purpose in the preamble: the two Governments desire "to cooperate more closely in the fight against crime and, to this end, to mutually render better assistance in matters of extradition." From the preamble, through the description of the parties' obligations with respect to offenses committed within as well as beyond the territory of a requesting party, the delineation of the procedures and evidentiary requirements for extradition, the special provisions for political offenses and capital punishment, and other details, the Treaty appears to have been designed to cover the entire subject of extradition. Thus, Article 22, entitled "Scope of Application" states that the "Treaty shall apply to offenses specified in Article 2 committed before and after this Treaty enters into force," and Article 2 directs that "[e]xtradition shall take place, subject to this Treaty, for willful acts which fall within any of [the extraditable offenses listed in] the clauses of the Appendix." Moreover, as noted by the Court,... Article 9 expressly provides that neither Contracting Party is bound to deliver up its own nationals, although it may do so in its discretion, but if it does not do so, it "shall submit the case to its competent authorities for purposes of prosecution."

The Government's claim that the Treaty is not exclusive, but permits forcible governmental kidnaping, would transform these, and other, provisions into little more than verbiage. For example, provisions requiring "sufficient" evidence to grant extradition (Art. 3), withholding extradition for political or military offenses (Art. 5), withholding extradition when the person sought has already been tried (Art. 6), withholding extradition when the statute of limitations for the crime has lapsed (Art. 7), and granting the requested State discretion to refuse to extradite an individual who would face the death penalty in the requesting country (Art. 8), would serve little purpose if the requesting country could simply kidnap the person. As the Court of Appeals for the Ninth Circuit recognized in a related case, "[e]ach of these provisions would be utterly frustrated if a kidnapping were held to be a permissible course of governmental conduct." *United States* v. *Verdugo-Urquidez*, 939 F.2d 1341, 1349 (1991). In addition, all of these provisions "only make sense if they are understood as requiring each treaty signatory to comply with those procedures whenever it wishes to obtain jurisdiction over an individual who is located in another treaty nation." *Id.*, at 1351.

It is true, as the Court notes, that there is no express promise by either party to refrain from forcible abductions in the territory of the other Nation.... Relying on that omission, the Court, in effect, concludes that the Treaty merely creates an optional method of obtaining jurisdiction over alleged offenders, and that the parties silently reserved the right to resort to self-help whenever they deem force more expeditious than legal process. If the United States, for example, thought it more expedient to torture or simply to execute a person rather than to attempt extradition, these options would be equally available because they, too, were not explicitly prohibited by the Treaty. That, however, is a highly improbable interpretation of a consensual agreement, which on its face appears to have been intended to set forth comprehensive and exclusive rules concerning the subject of extradition. In my opinion, "the manifest scope and object of the treaty itself," *Rauscher*, 119 U.S. at 422...., plainly imply a mutual undertaking to respect the territorial integrity of the other contracting party....

It is shocking that a party to an extradition treaty might believe that it has secretly reserved the right to make seizures of citizens in the other party's territory. Justice Story found it shocking enough that the United States would attempt to justify an American seizure of a foreign vessel in a Spanish port:

> "But, even supposing, for a moment, that our laws had required an entry of The Apollon, in her transit, does it follow, that the power to arrest her was meant to be given, after she had passed into the exclusive territory of a foreign nation? We think not. It would be monstrous to suppose that our revenue officers were authorized to enter into foreign ports and territories, for the purpose of seizing vessels which had offended against our laws. It cannot be presumed that Congress would voluntarily justify such a clear violation of the laws of nations." *The Apollon*, 9 Wheat. 362, 370–371, 6 L.Ed. 111 (1824) (emphasis added).

The law of nations, as understood by Justice Story in 1824, has not changed. Thus, a leading treatise explains: "A State must not perform acts of sovereignty in the territory of another State....

> "It is ... a breach of International Law for a State to send its agents to the territory of another State to apprehend persons accused of having committed a crime. Apart from other satisfaction, the first duty of the offending State is to hand over the person in question to the State in whose territory he was apprehended." 1 *Oppenheim's International Law* 295, and n. 1 (H. Lauterpacht 8th ed. 1955).

Commenting on the precise issue raised by this case, the chief reporter for the American Law Institute's Restatement of Foreign Relations used language reminiscent of Justice Story's characterization of an official seizure in a foreign jurisdiction as "monstrous:"

> "When done without consent of the foreign government, abducting a person from a foreign country is a gross violation of international law and gross disrespect for a norm high in the opinion of mankind. It is a blatant violation of the territorial integrity of another state; it eviscerates the extradition system (established by a comprehensive network of treaties involving virtually all states)."

...A critical flaw pervades the Court's entire opinion. It fails to differentiate between the conduct of private citizens, which does not violate any treaty obligation, and conduct expressly authorized by the Executive Branch of the Government, which unquestionably constitutes a flagrant violation of international law, and in my opinion, also constitutes a breach of our treaty obligations. Thus, at the outset of its opinion, the Court states the issue as "whether a criminal defendant, abducted to the United States from a nation with which it has an extradition treaty, thereby acquires a defense to the jurisdiction of this country's courts." *Ante*, at 2190. That, of course, is the question decided in *Ker* v. *Illinois*, 119 U.S. 436, 7 S.Ct. 225, 30 L.Ed. 421 (1886); it is not, however, the question presented for decision today.

The importance of the distinction between a court's exercise of jurisdiction over either a person or property that has been wrongfully seized by a private citizen, or even by a state law enforcement agent, on the one hand, and the attempted exercise of jurisdiction predicated on a seizure by federal officers acting beyond the authority conferred by treaty, on the other hand, is explained by Justice Brandeis in his opinion for the Court in *Cook* v. *United States*, 288 U.S. 102, 53 S.Ct. 305, 77 L.Ed. 641 (1933). That case involved a construction of a Prohibition Era treaty with Great Britain that authorized American agents to board certain British vessels to ascertain whether they were engaged in importing alcoholic beverages. A British vessel was boarded 11 miles off the coast of Massachusetts, found to be carrying unmanifested alcoholic beverages, and taken into port. The Collector of Customs assessed a penalty which he attempted to collect by means of libels against both the cargo and the seized vessel.

The Court held that the seizure was not authorized by the treaty because it occurred more than 10 miles off shore. The Government argued that the illegality of the seizure was immaterial because, as in *Ker*, the Court's jurisdiction was supported by possession even if the seizure was wrongful. Justice Brandeis acknowledged that the argument would succeed if the seizure had been made by a private party without authority to act for the Government, but that a different rule prevails when the Government itself lacks the power to seize....

The same reasoning was employed by Justice Miller to explain why the holding in *Rauscher* did not apply to the *Ker* case. The arresting officer in *Ker* did not pretend to be acting in any official capacity when he kidnapped Ker. As Justice Miller noted, "the facts show that it was a clear case of kidnapping within the dominions of Peru, without any pretence of authority under the treaty or from the government of the United States." *Ker* v. *Illinois*, 119 U.S., at 443, 7 S.Ct., at 229 (emphasis added). The exact opposite is true in this case, as it was in *Cook*.

The Court's failure to differentiate between private abductions and official invasions of another sovereign's territory also accounts for its misplaced reliance on the 1935 proposal made by the Advisory Committee on Research in International Law. See *ante*, at 2194–2195, and n.13. As the text of that proposal plainly states, it would have rejected the rule of the *Ker* case. The failure to adopt that recommendation does not speak to the issue the Court decides today. The Court's admittedly "shocking" disdain for customary and conventional international law principles, see *ante*, at 2195, is thus entirely unsupported by case law and commentary....

As the Court observes at the outset of its opinion, there is reason to believe that respondent participated in an especially brutal murder of an American law enforcement agent. That fact, if true, may explain the Executive's intense interest in punishing respondent in our courts. Such an explanation, however, provides no justification for disregarding the Rule of Law that this Court has a duty to uphold. That the Executive may wish to reinterpret the Treaty to allow for an action that the Treaty in no way authorizes should not influence this Court's interpretation. Indeed, the desire for revenge exerts "a kind of hydraulic pressure... before which even well settled principles of law will bend,"... but it is precisely at such moments that we should remember and be guided by our duty "to render judgment evenly and dispassionately according to law, as each is given understanding to ascertain and apply it." The way that we perform that duty in a case of this kind sets an example that other tribunals in other countries are sure to emulate.

The significance of this Court's precedents is illustrated by a recent decision of the Court of Appeal of the Republic of South Africa. Based largely on its understanding of the import of this Court's cases – including our decision in *Ker* v. *Illinois* – that court held that the prosecution of a defendant kidnapped by agents of South Africa in another country must be dismissed. *S* v. *Ebrahim*, S. Afr. L. Rep. (Apr.-June 1991). The Court of Appeal of South Africa – indeed, I suspect most courts throughout the civilized world – will be deeply disturbed by the "monstrous" decision the Court announces today. For every Nation that has an interest in preserving the Rule of Law is affected, directly or indirectly, by a decision of this character. As Thomas Paine warned, an "avidity to punish is always dangerous to liberty" because it leads a Nation "to stretch, to misinterpret, and to misapply even the best of laws." To counter that tendency, he reminds us:

> "He that would make his own liberty secure must guard even his enemy from oppression; for if he violates this duty he establishes a precedent that will reach to himself."

Notes and Questions

1. Discuss whether the majority or dissenting opinion is more persuasive and why.

2. Upon remand, the defendant argued that, notwithstanding the extradition treaty, the abduction nevertheless violated other international laws and that *Ker*, therefore, did not control. *See United States v. Alvarez-Machain*, 971 F.2d 310 (9th Cir. 1992). The Court of Appeals ruled that the Supreme Court's decision precluded it from considering the issue. The District Court ultimately dismissed the charges against Alvarez-Machain because of insufficient evidence. The judge lectured the prosecution about the woeful lack of evidence to sustain its case despite the significant government and judicial resources spent. See Seth Mydons, *Judge Clears Mexican in Agent's Killing*, N.Y. TIMES, Dec. 15, 1992, at A20.

3. For differing views on the Supreme Court's holding in this case or related issues, *see, e.g.*, SECRETARIA DE RELACIONES EXTERIORES, LIMITS TO NATIONAL JURISDICTION vols. 1 and 2 (Mexico 1992 and 1993); Abraham Abramovsky, *Extraterritorial Abductions: America's Catch and Snatch Policy Run Amok*, 31 VA. J. INT'L L. 151 (1991); Valerie Epps, *Forcible Abduction, Jurisdiction and Treaty Interpretation*, INT'L PRACT. NOTEBOOK NO. 55, at 6 (1992); Michael Glennon, *State-Sponsored Abduction: A Comment on* United States v. Alvarez-Machain, 86 AM. J. INT'L L. 746 (1992); Jimmy Gurulé, *Terrorism, Territorial Sovereignty, and the Forcible Apprehension of International Criminals Abroad*, 17 HAST. INT'L & COMP. L. REV. 457 (1994); John Quigley, *Government Vigilantes at Large: The Danger to Human Rights from Kidnapping of Suspected Terrorists*, 10 HUM. RTS. Q. 193 (1988); Hernan Ruiz-Bravo, *Monstrous Decision: Kidnapping Is Legal*, 24 HAST. CONST. L.Q. 833 (1993)).

4. Does *Alvarez-Machain* recognize a broad general right to abduct abroad, or was the matter framed more narrowly? Refer to the specific jurisdictional issue outlined by the Chief Justice and his conclusion. Importantly, the Court stated that the abduction might be "shocking" but that, as a matter outside the treaty, it was for the executive branch to decide whether the respondent should be returned to Mexico. How do subsequent cases, such as *Noriega* presented later, implement the precedent?

5. Is the holding in *Alvarez-Machain* that the abduction of the defendant was legal as a matter of domestic and international law, or is it merely a limit on the remedies available to abducted relators?

6. Do you think the nature of the alleged crime – the assassination of DEA agent Kiki Camarena and his pilot – was determinative? Did the abduction meet the requirements of necessity and proportionality?

7. On June 29, 2004, the U.S. Supreme Court ruled in the case of Humberto Alvarez-Machain, the Guadalajara, Mexico, physician whom the U.S. Drug Enforcement Administration (DEA) abducted from his home.[36] The Court held he was not entitled to a remedy under either the Federal Tort Claims Act (FTCA)[37] or the Alien Tort Statute (ATS).[38] However, the Court did uphold the validity of the ATS although it cautioned the federal judiciary to use it sparingly. Do you think the 2004 and prior decisions were influenced by U.S. politics? Would the Supreme Court have curtailed the application of the ATS if the case had not concerned the prosecution of persons allegedly involved in the kidnapping and torture of a U.S. DEA official?

United States v. Noriega, 117 F.3d 1206 (11th Cir. 1997)

Manuel Antonio Noriega appeals: (1) his multiple convictions stemming from his involvement in cocaine trafficking; (FN 1 omitted) and (2) the district court's denial of his motion for a new trial based on newly discovered evidence. In attacking his convictions, Noriega asserts that the district court should have dismissed the indictment against him due to his status as a head of state and the manner in which the United States brought him to justice. Noriega also contends that the district court committed two reversible evidentiary errors. Alternatively, he seeks a new trial based on his discovery of: (1) the government's suppression of its pact with a non-witness; and/or (2) certain allegations, lodged after his conviction, that a group associated with the undisclosed, cooperating non-witness bribed a prosecution witness. We affirm Noriega's convictions and the district court's order denying his trial motions.

On February 4, 1988, a federal grand jury for the Southern District of Florida indicted Manuel Antonio Noriega on drug-related charges. At that time, Noriega served as commander of the Panamanian Defense Forces in the Republic of Panama. Shortly thereafter, Panama's president, Eric Arturo Delvalle, formally discharged Noriega from his military post but Noriega refused to accept the dismissal. Panama's legislature then ousted Delvalle from power. The United States, however, continued to acknowledge Delvalle as the constitutional leader of Panama. Later, after a disputed presidential election in Panama, the United States recognized Guillermo Endara as Panama's legitimate head of state.

On December 15, 1989, Noriega publicly declared that a state of war existed between Panama and the United States. Within days of this announcement by Noriega, President George Bush directed United States armed forces into combat in Panama for the stated purposes of "safeguarding American lives, restoring democracy, preserving the Panama Canal treaties, and seizing Noriega to face federal drug charges in the United States." *United States v. Noriega*, 746 F. Supp. 1506, 1511 (S.D. Fla 1990). The ensuing military conflagration resulted in significant casualties and property loss among Panamanian civilians. (FN 2 omitted).

[36] *Sosa v. Alvarez-Machain et al.*, 542 U.S. 692 (2004) (U.S. Supreme Court Nos. 03–339 and 03–485 June 29, 2004).
[37] 28 U.S.C. § 1346(b)(1), §§ 2671–2680.
[38] 28 U.S.C. § 1350.

Noriega lost his effective control over Panama during this armed conflict, and he surrendered to United States military officials on January 3, 1990. Noriega then was brought to Miami to face the pending federal charges.

Following extensive pre-trial proceedings and a lengthy trial, a jury found Noriega guilty of eight counts in the indictment and not guilty of the remaining two counts. The district court entered judgments of conviction against Noriega upon the jury's verdict and sentenced him to consecutive imprisonment terms of 20, 15 and five years, respectively....

Noriega next contends his conviction should be reversed because he alleges he was brought to the United States in violation of the Treaty Providing for the Extradition of Criminals, May 25, 1904, United States of America-Republic of Panama, 34 Stat. 2581 ("U.S.-Panama Extradition Treaty"). The Supreme Court's decision in *United States v. Alvarez-Machain*, 504 U.S, 655, 119 L. Ed. 2d 441, 112 S. Ct. 2188 (1992), forecloses this argument. (FN4 omitted) In Alvarez-Machain, the Court considered the issue of "whether a criminal defendant, abducted to the United States from a nation with which it has an extradition treaty, thereby acquires a defense to the jurisdiction of this country's courts." Id. at 657. In answer, the Court stated: "We hold that he does not, and that he may be tried in federal district court for violations of the criminal law of the United States." Id.

In reaching this decision, the Court considered whether the treaty at issue expressly barred abductions. It determined that the treaty's provision that "neither Contracting Party shall be bound to deliver up its own nationals ...' [fails] to specify the only way in which one country may gain custody of a national of the other country for purposes of prosecution." Id. at 663–64 (quoting Extradition Treaty, May 4, 1978, United States of America-United Mexican States, *31 U.S.T.* 5059 ("U.S.-Mexico Extradition Treaty:). The Court also rejected the argument that, by entering into an extradition treaty with Mexico, the United States impliedly agreed to seek custody of persons in Mexico only via extradition. Id. at 668–69 ("To infer from this Treaty and its terms that it prohibits all means of gaining the presence of an individual outside of its terms goes beyond established precedent and practice.").

The article of the U.S.-Panama Extradition Treaty upon which Noriega relies for his extradition treaty claim contains almost the same language as the provision of the U.S.-Mexico Extradition Treaty at issue in Alvarez-Machain. See U.S.-Panama Extradition Treaty, art. 5 (Neither of the contracting parties shall be bound to deliver up its own citizen or subject..."). Noriega contends that Alvarez-Machain is distinguishable despite the near identity of the relevant clauses because, at the time the United States entered into the U.S.-Panama Extradition Treaty, it knew or should have known that Panama's constitution prohibited the extradition of its nationals. This bald assertion, even if accepted, does not save Noriega's claim. A clause in Panama's constitution regarding the extradition of Panamanians, at most, informs the United States of the hurdles it will face when pursuing such extraditions in Panama; such a provision says nothing about the treaty signatories' rights to opt for self-help (i.e., abduction) over legal process (i.e., extradition).

Under Alvarez-Machain, to prevail on an extradition treaty claim, a defendant must demonstrate, by reference to the express language of a treaty and/or the established practice thereunder, that the United States affirmatively agreed not to seize foreign nationals from the territory of its treaty partner. Noriega has not carried this burden, and therefore, his claim fails.

Notes and Questions

1. Do you agree with the appellate court's minimal consideration of the motion to dismiss, on due process grounds, Noriega's argument that his arrest by military invasion was so unconscionable as to constitute a violation of substantive due process? Should it

matter that the invasion and arrest resulted in the deaths of thousands of people and the destruction of neighborhoods in Panama?

2. Do you think U.S. politics, especially historical deference to the executive branch, played a major role in the Court's decision?

3. Does the dicta that under *Alvarez-Machain* a defendant must show by reference to the express language of a treaty and/or the established practice thereunder that the United States affirmatively agreed not to seize foreign nationals contribute to the rule of law? To U.S. foreign policy?

4. In the aftermath of the September 11 terrorist attacks, the U.S. government engaged in a number of extraordinary renditions, whereby alleged terrorists were abducted from foreign countries, brought to detention centers abroad, and interrogated. The practices precipitated a series of protests, inquiries by both the Council of Europe and the European Union, protests by other governments, and detainee lawsuits. *See, e.g.*, Joan Fitzpatrick, *Rendition and Transfer in the War against Terrorism: Guantánamo and Beyond*, 25 Loy. L.A. Int'l Comp. L. Rev. 457 (2003); Bruce Zagaris, *International Organizations, Foreign Prosecutors and Victims Target U.S. Extraordinary Rendition Program*, 23 Int'l Enforcement L. Rep. 55 (Feb. 2007); Bruce Zagaris, *Inquiry Shows Canadian, U.S. Officials Violated Arar's Human Rights*, 22 Int'l Enforcement L. Rep. 435 (2006). Can the fact that intelligence agencies are primarily responsible for extraordinary renditions and limit them to interrogating high-profile terrorists in the war on terror distinguish them from abductions in criminal cases and justify their use?

Dragan Nikolic (ICTY "Decision on Interlocutory Appeal Concerning Legality of Arrest")

5 June 2003

Appeals Chamber (Judges Meron [Presiding], Pocar, Shahabuddeen, Güney and El Madhi)

The Decision

The Appeals Chamber dismissed the Appeal.

The Reasoning (footnotes omitted)

The question before the Appeals Chamber was whether the International Tribunal can exercise jurisdiction over the Appellant notwithstanding the alleged violations of Serbia and Montenegro's sovereignty (FN omitted) and of the Accused's human rights committed by SFOR and, by extension, the Office of the Prosecutor ("OTP"), acting in collusion with the unknown individuals who abducted the Accused from Serbia and Montenegro.

The Impact of a Breach of a State's Sovereignty in the Exercise of Jurisdiction

As noted by the Appeals Chamber, this is a novel issue for the International Tribunal. There is no case-law on the point and the Statute and the Rules do not offer much guidance. The Appeals Chamber had therefore to rely on national case-law. (FN omitted) After a review of the relevant cases, it admitted that it is "difficult to identify a clear pattern in this case-law" and noted that "caution is needed when generalising." Nevertheless it identified two principles that seem to have support in State Practice as evidenced by the practice of their courts:

> "First, in cases of crimes such as genocide, crimes against humanity and war crimes which are universally recognised and condemned as such ("Universally Condemned Offences"), courts seem to find in the special character of these offences and, arguably,

in their seriousness, a good reason for not setting aside jurisdiction. Second, absent a complaint by the State whose sovereignty has been breached or in the event of a diplomatic resolution of the breach, it is easier for courts to assert their jurisdiction." (FN omitted)

The Appeals Chamber observed that Universally Condemned Offences are a matter of concern to the international community as a whole. It found that there is "a legitimate expectation that those accused of these crimes will be brought to justice swiftly" and that "[a]ccountability for these crimes is a necessary condition for the achievement of international justice, which plays a critical role in the reconciliation and rebuilding based on the rule of law of countries and societies torn apart by international and internecine conflicts." (FN omitted) The Appeals Chamber considered that "the damage caused to international justice by not apprehending fugitives accused of serious violations of international humanitarian law is comparatively higher than the injury, if any, caused to the sovereignty of a State by a limited intrusion in its territory, particularly when the intrusion occurs in default of the State's cooperation." (FN omitted) It held that "in cases of Universally Condemned Offences, jurisdiction should [not] be set aside on the ground that there was a violation of the sovereignty of a State, when the violation is brought about by the apprehension of fugitives from international justice, whatever the consequences for the international responsibility of the State or organisation involved." (FN omitted)

The Appeals Chamber found that this is all the more so in cases where the State has not lodged any complaint, thus accepting de facto the Tribunal's jurisdiction. It held that a fortiori this holds all the more so when such abductions do not violate State sovereignty. It therefore held that even if the conduct of the Accused's captors is to be attributed to SFOR in violation of Serbia and Montenegro's sovereignty, there will still be a basis for jurisdiction.

The Impact of a Violation of an Accused's Human Rights in the Exercise of Jurisdiction

The Trial Chamber had found in the Impugned Decision that the treatment of the Appellant was not of such an "egregious" nature as to impede the exercise of jurisdiction without excluding that jurisdiction could be excluded in cases where an accused is very seriously mistreated. The Appeals Chamber upheld the approach of the Trial Chamber. It stated that "certain human rights violations are of such a serious nature that they require that the exercise of jurisdiction be declined." (FN omitted)

However it held that "[a]part from such exceptional cases [...] the remedy of setting aside jurisdiction will [...] usually be disproportionate" and that "[t]he correct balance must therefore be maintained between the fundamental rights of the accused and the essential interests of the international community in the prosecution of persons charged with serious violations of international humanitarian law." (FN omitted)

In the present case, the Appeals Chamber did not find that the rights of the Accused had been "egregiously" violated and therefore did not find that the Tribunal should be impeded from exercising jurisdiction even if the conduct of the Accused's captors was to be attributed to SFOR.

Notes and Questions

1. Do you think the decision is making a special exception for universally condemned offenses? If so, is this an appropriate line to draw in determining when abduction is a proper measure to gain custody?

2. Compare the jurisprudence of this decision with that of the majority opinion of the U.S. Supreme Court in *Alvarez-Machain*.

VI. *Additional Reading*

A. *Books*

MICHAEL ABBELL, EXTRADITION TO AND FROM THE UNITED STATES (Transnational Publishers)(2004 loose-leaf).
M. CHERIF BASSIOUNI, INTERNATIONAL EXTRADITION: UNITED STATES LAW AND PRACTICE (4th ed. 2002).
CARLOS Cezón GONZÁLEZ, DERECHO EXTRADITICIONAL (Madrid: Dykinson 2003).
EXTRADITION LAWS AND TREATIES, UNITED STATES (loose-leaf, I.I. Kavass & A. Sprudzs comp. 1980–).
GEOFF GILBERT, TRANSNATIONAL FUGITIVE OFFENDERS IN INTERNATIONAL LAW (1998).
ELAINE F. KRIVEL, THOMAS BEVERIDGE, & JOHN W. HAYWARD, A PRACTICAL GUIDE TO CANADIAN EXTRADITION (2002).
ANNE WARNER LA FOREST, LA' FOREST'S EXTRADITION TO AND FROM CANADA (3rd ed. 1991).
IVAN A. SHEARER, EXTRADITION IN INTERNATIONAL LAW (1971).
CHRISTINE VAN DEN WIJNGAERT, THE POLITICAL OFFENSE EXCEPTION TO EXTRADITION (1980).

B. *Articles*

25 LOY. L.A. INT'L & COMP. L.REV. NO. 3 (2003) (issue has nine articles devoted to extradition).
Abraham Abramovsky, *Extraterritorial Abductions: America's "Catch and Snatch" Policy Run Amok*, 31 VA. J. INT'L L. 151 (1991).
Abraham Abramovsky & Jonathan I. Edelstein, *The Sheinbein Case and the Israeli-American Extradition Experience: A Need for Compromise*, 32 VAND. J. TRANSNAT'L L. 305 (1999).
Christopher L. Blakesley, *A Conceptual Framework for Extradition and Jurisdiction over Extraterritorial Crimes*, 1984 UTAH L. REV. 685.
Ethan A. Nadelmann, *The Evolution of United States Involvement in the International Rendition of Fugitive Criminals*, 25 N.Y.U. J. INT'L L. POL. 813 (1993).
Paul O'HIGGINS, *The History of Extradition in British Practice*, 13 INDIAN Y.B. INT'L AFF. 78 (1964).
John T. Parry, *The Lost History of International Extradition Litigation*, 43 VA. J. INT'L L. 93 (2002).
Michael PLACHTA, *(Non-)Extradition of Nationals: A Neverending Story?* 13 EMORY INT'L L REV. 77 (1999).
Bert Swart, *Extradition, in* INTERNATIONAL CRIMINAL LAW IN THE NETHERLANDS 107 (Bert Swart & A. Klip eds.), (1997).

C. *Source Material*

Commonwealth Scheme for Rendition of Fugitive Offenders (as amended 1990) LMM (90) 32.
European Convention on Extradition (http://conventions.coe.int).
OAS, Inter-American Extradition Convention (www.oas.org).
UN Model Treaty on Extradition, General Assembly Resolution 45/116, 45 U.N. GAOR, Supp. No. 49A, at 211, U.N. Doc. A/45/59A (1991), as amended by General Assembly Resolution 52/88, 52 U.N. GAOR, Supp. No. 49, at 213, U.N. Doc. A/52/49 (Vol. 1).
United States Department of Justice, UNITED STATES ATTORNEYS MANUAL, Title 9-Criminal Division, Chapter 15 (International Extradition and Related Matters), and CRIMINAL RESOURCE MANUAL.

10 International Prisoner Transfer

I. Hypotheticals

A. Your law firm is asked to represent Mr. X. In 1988, the U.S. Attorney charged him with tax crimes, wire and mail fraud, and embezzlement from a privately held firm where he was a principal. A few months after the indictment, a publicly held firm was acquired. However, in the previous year, Mr. X. had become a national of the Netherlands and began living in that country. In 1998, the United States commenced extradition proceedings, and finally, in 2004, a Netherlands court ruled that Mr. X. was extraditable. His counsel appealed, but Mr. X. fled the country.

In 2006, Mr. X., now approximately fifty years old, is arrested in Spain and accused of using a false identity. Spanish authorities are also investigating Mr. X. on potential money laundering charges. When his family consults you, Spanish authorities are not yet aware of Mr. X.'s identity. However, they have seized his briefcase, which contains a diary and phone book, and customs officials have noted his American accent.

Mr. X. has two former wives, one of whom resides in the United States with a child they had together. Mr. X's second wife resides in the Netherlands, with two children she had with him. Over the last three years, Mr. X. has had a relationship with a Dutch national, and they want to marry.

Mr. X. says that his goals are to avoid extradition to the United States. If that proves impossible, he wants to ensure that he can serve out any sentence, if convicted, in the Netherlands. How can he accomplish this goal? In particular, what are the pros and cons of (1) returning to the Netherlands to face the false identity charges or (2) returning to the United States from Spain? What about resisting extradition to the United States or vigorously contesting the U.S. charges? Please advise Mr. X.

Would it make any difference if Mr. X. was an opposition party leader, the charges occurred three months before a presidential election, and instead of embezzlement he was accused of fraud in his political commercials? What if he was charged with immigration violations?

Mr. X.'s counsel decides to disclose his identity and advise the U.S. prosecutor that he is willing to surrender voluntarily. However, the U.S. prosecutor advises defense counsel that he is in no hurry to bring Mr. X. back to the United States. Mr. X. wants to know if he will receive credit in the United States, after he is returned, for his time on remand in the United Kingdom, especially if he is not allowed to transfer. Please advise.

B. You represent Mr. A. The United States has requested A.'s extradition on FCPA-related charges. Under sentencing guidelines Mr. A. would serve about fifteen months if he pleads guilty. The Netherlands does not extradite its nationals unless the requesting state agrees to allow them to serve their sentences in the Netherlands. A problem is that Mr. A. cannot apply to transfer until one to two weeks after he arrives at his final prison institution. The entire process may take eighteen to twenty-four months because the Justice Department needs to process his application, give the prosecutor and law enforcement officials an opportunity to comment, and then hold a waiver hearing before a U.S. magistrate or judge. By then, his sentence would be practically completed.

How should the requesting state and its court treat the extradition application? What, if anything, can the United States do to resolve this potential obstacle to extradition?

C. You represent a Latin American state, Brazuela. The new Attorney General wants to have the ability to allow Brazuelans who are incarcerated abroad to return to serve their sentences and to allow foreigners in Brazuela to enter into prisoner transfers. Half of the prisoners in Brazuela are from neighboring countries. What are the best ways to achieve the objective?

II. Introduction

The precursors of modern prisoner transfer treaties are nineteenth-century legal instruments. Members of the German Federation then concluded special jurisdictional treaties mutually committing to enforce penal judgments enacted in other contracting states. In 1865, the Convention on Customs and Neighbor Relations between France and Monaco, still in force, provided for the transfer of prisoners. The Colonial Prisoners Removal Acts of 1869 and 1884 authorized the parole and repatriation to the United Kingdom of a foreign national.[1]

[1] Michal Plachta, Transfer of Prisoners under International Instruments and Domestic Legislation 197–202 (1993).

In the late 1960s, the increased global mobility resulting from broader access to travel, the growth in transnational crime, and humanitarian concerns led governments to change penal codes to expressly preclude enforcement of foreign penal judgments.[2] Governments and criminal justice professionals observed that the social reintegration of the offender, one of the main purposes of criminal sentencing, was jeopardized by the disabilities endured by foreign prisoners: language barriers; differences in climate, food, social backgrounds, and cultural norms; the lack of communication with the outside world; and the lack of information and vocational training. These barriers led to discrimination against foreign prisoners in a host of situations, including obtaining furloughs, receiving visitors, and communicating with family members. Foreign prisoners were often denied access to furloughs or early release programs because they were perceived as greater flight risks.

Prison authorities also face difficulties dealing with foreign prisoners, especially in countries with large populations of foreign inmates.[3] The increased administrative burden of foreign prisoners has created an incentive for sentencing states to transfer prisoners, thereby reducing the toll on their limited resources and serving the humanitarian goal of socially reintegrating an offender.[4]

Modern transfer of prisoner agreements and arrangements have arisen out of the instruments of cooperation among the Nordic countries,[5] a convention among Benelux countries,[6] and agreements between France and francophone African countries.[7] For instance, in 1948 the Nordic countries concluded an agreement on the recognition and enforcement of criminal judgments, restricted only to the enforcement of fines. In 1963, uniform legislation was enacted covering the enforcement of custodial sentences.[8] Such enforcement is not restricted to nationals of the requested state, but extends to cases where the sentenced person is a domiciliary of the requested state. In the mid-1970s, the International Law Association promulgated a model convention, which the UN began to discuss.[9]

The U.S. government was also pressured to begin negotiating prisoner transfer treaties by publicity surrounding the horrific conditions encountered by U.S. citizens imprisoned abroad, especially those convicted of drug offenses in Turkey and Mexico. In 1983, the Council of Europe's Convention on Transfer of Sentenced Persons was opened for signature to also include governments outside of the Council of Europe.

[2] Helmutt Epp, *The European Convention, in* INTERNATIONAL CRIMINAL LAW 563 (M. C. Bassiouni ed., 1999).

[3] *Id.*

[4] *Id.*

[5] Plachta, *supra* note 1 at 197–202.

[6] The 1968 Benelux Convention (among Belgium, the Netherlands, and Luxembourg) never came into force partly because the Benelux countries ratified the European Convention of 1983. For the text of the Benelux Convention and Explanatory Report, *see Bulletin Benelux* 1968 (4).

[7] For background *see* Plachta, *supra* note 1 at 243–47.

[8] Act on Cooperation between Finland and Other Scandinavian Countries in the Enforcement of Sentences given in Criminal Cases, June 20, 1963.

[9] For the UN Model Agreement on the Transfer of Foreign Prisoners, which was not adopted until 1985, *see* U.N. Doc. A/CONF.121/22, para. 57.

III. Transfer of Prisoner Instruments

European Convention on the Transfer of Sentenced Prisoners[10]

***

Article 1 – Definitions

For the purposes of this Convention:

(a) "sentence" means any punishment or measures involving deprivation of liberty ordered by a court for a limited or unlimited period of time on account of a criminal offense;
(b) "judgment" means a decision or order of a court imposing a sentence;
(c) "sentencing State" means the State to which the sentenced person may be, or has been, transferred in order to serve his sentence.

Article 2 – General Principles

1. The Parties undertake to afford each other the widest measure of co-operation in respect of sentenced persons in accordance with the provisions of this Convention.
2. A person sentenced in the territory of a Party may be transferred to the territory of another Party, in accordance with the provisions of this Convention, in order to serve the sentence imposed on him. To that end, he may express his interest to the sentencing State or to the administering State in being transferred under this Convention.
3. Transfer may be requested by either the sentencing State or the administering State.

Article 3 – Conditions for Transfer

1. A sentenced person may be transferred under this Convention only on the following conditions:
   (a) If that person is a national of the administrating state;
   (b) If the judgement is final;
   (c) If, at the time of receipt of the request for transfer, the sentenced person still has at least six months of the sentence to serve or if the sentence is indeterminate;
   (d) If the transfer is consented to by the sentenced person or, where in view of his age or his physical or mental condition one of the two States considers it necessary, by the sentenced person's legal representative;
   (e) If the acts or omissions on account of which the sentence has been imposed constitute a criminal offense according to the law of the administering State or would constitute a criminal offense if committed on its territory; and
   (f) If the sentencing and administering States agree to the transfer.
2. In exceptional cases, Parties may agree to a transfer even if the time to be served by the sentenced person is less than that specified in paragraph 1.c.

[10] The convention is open to states that are nonmembers in the Council of Europe. Many countries outside the Council of Europe, including the United States, have ratified the convention. The participation of common law countries was significant because the convention took into account the experiences of those countries. In particular, the participation of Canada and the United States led to the adoption of special final clauses, giving these states the option to sign the convention from the start, without a formal invitation to accede to it.

3. Any State may, at the time of signature or when depositing its instrument of ratification, acceptance, approval or accession, by a declaration addressed to the Secretary General of the Council of Europe, indicate that it intends to exclude the application of one of the procedures provided in Article 9.1.a and b in its relations with other Parties.
4. Any State, may at any time, by a declaration addressed to the Secretary General of the Council of Europe, define, as far as it is concerned, the term "national" for the purposes of this Convention.

Article 4 – Obligation to Furnish Information

1. Any sentenced person to whom this Convention may apply shall be informed by the sentencing State of the substance of this Convention.
2. If the sentenced person has expressed an interest in the sentencing State in being transferred under this Convention, that State shall so inform the administering State as soon as practicable after the judgment becomes final.
3. The information shall include
   (a) the name, date and place of birth of the sentenced person;
   (b) his address, if any, in the administering State;
   (c) a statement of the facts upon which the sentence was based;
   (d) the nature, duration and date of commencement of the sentence.
4. If the sentenced person has expressed his interest to the administering State, the sentencing State shall, on request, communicate to that State the information referred to in paragraph 3 above.
5. The sentenced person shall be informed, in writing, of any action taken by the sentencing State or the administering State under the preceding paragraphs, as well as of any decision taken by either State on a request for transfer.

Article 5 – Requests and Replies

1. Requests for transfer and replies shall be made in writing.
2. Requests shall be addressed by the Ministry of Justice of the requesting State to the Ministry of Justice of the requested State. Replies shall be communicated through the same channels.
3. Any Party may, by a declaration addressed to the Secretary General of the Council of Europe indicate that it will use other channels of communication.
4. The requested State shall promptly inform the requesting State of its decision whether or not to agree to the requested transfer.

Article 6 – Supporting Documents

1. The administering State, if requested by the sentencing State, shall furnish it with:
   (a) a document or statement indicating that the sentenced person is a national of that State;
   (b) a copy of the relevant law of the administering State which provides that the acts or omissions on account of which the sentence has been imposed in the sentencing State constitute a criminal offense according to the law of the administering State, or would constitute a criminal offense if committed on its territory;
   (c) a statement containing the information mentioned in Article 9.2.

2. If a transfer is requested, the sentencing State shall provide the following documents to the administering State, unless either State has already indicated that it will not agree to the transfer:
   (a) a certified copy of the judgement and the law on which it is based;
   (b) a statement indicating how much of the sentence has already been served including information on any pre-trial detention, remission, and any other factor relevant to the enforcement of the sentence;
   (c) a declaration containing the consent to the transfer as referred to in article 3.1.d; and
   (d) whenever appropriate, any medical or social reports on the sentenced person, information about his treatment in the sentencing State, and any recommendation for his further treatment in the administering State.
3. Either State may ask to be provided with any of the documents or statements referred to in paragraphs 1 or 2 above before making a request for transfer or taking a decision on whether or not to agree to the transfer.

Article 7 – Consent and Its Verification

1. The sentencing State shall ensure that the person required to give consent to the transfer in accordance with Article 3.1.d does so voluntarily and with full knowledge of the legal consequences thereof. The procedure for giving such consent shall be governed by the law of the sentencing State.
2. The sentencing State shall afford an opportunity to the administering State to verify through a consul or other official agreed upon with the administering State, that the consent is given in accordance with the conditions set out in paragraph 1 above.

Article 8 – Effect of Transfer for Sentencing State

1. The taking into charge of the sentenced person by the authorities of the administering State shall have the effect of suspending the enforcement of the sentence in the sentencing State.
2. The sentencing State may no longer enforce the sentence if the administering State considers enforcement of the sentence to have been completed.

Article 9 – Effect of Transfer for Administering State

1. The competent authorities of the administering State shall:
   1. continue the enforcement of the sentence immediately or through a court or administrative order, under the conditions set out in Article 10, or
   2. convert the sentence, through a judicial or administrative procedure, into a decision of that State, thereby substituting for the sanction imposed in the sentencing State a sanction prescribed by the law of the administering State for the same offence, under the conditions set out in Article 11.
2. The administering State, if requested, shall inform the sentencing State before the transfer of the sentenced person as to which of these procedures it will follow.
3. The enforcement of the sentence shall be governed by the law of the administering State and that State alone shall be competent to take all appropriate decisions.

4. Any State which, according to its national law, cannot avail itself of one of the procedures referred to in paragraph 1 to enforce measures imposed in the territory of another Party on persons who for reasons of mental condition have been held not criminally responsible for the commission of the offence, and which is prepared to receive such persons for further treatment may, by way of a declaration addressed to the Secretary General of the Council of Europe, indicate the procedures it will follow in such cases.

Article 10 – Continued Enforcement

1. In the case of continued enforcement, the administering State shall be bound by the legal nature and duration of the sentence as determined by the sentencing State.
2. If, however, this sentence is by its nature or duration incompatible with the law of the administering State, or its law so requires, that State may, by a court or administrative order, adapt the sanction to the punishment or measure prescribed by its own law for a similar offence. As to its nature, the punishment or measure shall, as far as possible, correspond with that imposed by the sentence to be enforced. It shall not aggravate, by its nature or duration, the sanction imposed in the sentencing State, nor exceed the maximum prescribed by the law of the administering State.

Article 11 – Conversion of Sentence

1. In the case of conversion of sentence, the procedures provided for by the law of the administering State apply. When converting the sentence, the competent authority:
    1. shall be bound by the findings as to the facts insofar as they appear explicitly or implicitly from the judgment imposed in the sentencing State;
    2. may not convert a sanction involving deprivation of liberty to a pecuniary sanction;
    3. shall deduct the full period of deprivation of liberty served by the sentenced person; and
    4. shall not aggravate the penal position of the sentenced person, and shall not be bound by any minimum which the law of the administering State may provide for the offence or offences committed.
2. If the conversion procedure takes place after the transfer of the sentenced person, the administering State shall keep that person in custody or otherwise ensure his presence in the administering State pending the outcome of that procedure.

Article 12 – Pardon, Amnesty, Commutation

Each Party may grant pardon, amnesty or commutation of the sentence in accordance with its Constitution or other laws.

Article 13 – Review of Judgment

The sentencing State alone shall have the right to decide on any application for review of the judgment.

Article 14 – Termination of Enforcement

The administering State shall terminate enforcement of the sentence as soon as it is informed by the sentencing State of any decision or measure as a result of which the sentence ceases to be enforceable.

Article 15 – Information on Enforcement

The administering State shall provide information to the sentencing State concerning the enforcement of the sentence:

1. when it considers enforcement of the sentence to have been completed;
2. if the sentenced person has escaped from custody before enforcement of the sentence has been completed; or
3. if the sentencing State requests a special report.

Article 16 – Transit

1. A Party shall, in accordance with its law, grant a request for transit of a sentenced person through its territory if such a request is made by another Party and that State has agreed with another Party or with a third State to the transfer of that person to or from its territory.
2. A Party may refuse to grant transit:
   1. if the sentenced person is one of its nationals, or
   2. if the offence for which the sentence was imposed is not an offence under its own law.
3. Requests for transit and replies shall be communicated through the channels referred to in the provisions of Article 5.2 and 3.
4. A Party may grant a request for transit of a sentenced person through its territory made by a third State if that State has agreed with another Party to the transfer to or from its territory.
5. The Party requested to grant transit may hold the sentenced person in custody only for such time as transit through its territory requires.
6. The Party requested to grant transit may be asked to give an assurance that the sentenced person will not be prosecuted, or, except as provided in the preceding paragraph, detained, or otherwise subjected to any restriction on his liberty in the territory of the transit State for any offence committed or sentence imposed prior to his departure from the territory of the sentencing State.
7. No request for transit shall be required if transport is by air over the territory of a Party and no landing there is scheduled. However, each State may, by a declaration addressed to the Secretary General of the Council of Europe at the time of signature or of deposit of its instrument of ratification, acceptance, approval or accession, require that it be notified of any such transit over its territory.

Article 17 – Language and Costs

* * *

Article 18 – Signature and Entry into Force

1. This Convention shall be open for signature by the member States of the Council of Europe and non-member States which have participated in its elaboration. It is subject to ratification, acceptance or approval. Instruments of ratification, acceptance or approval shall be deposited with the Secretary General of the Council of Europe.
2. This Convention shall enter into force on the first day of the month following the expiration of a period of three months after the date on which three member States of the Council of Europe have expressed their consent to be bound by the Convention in accordance with the provisions of paragraph 1.
3. In respect of any signatory State which subsequently expresses its consent to be bound by it, the Convention shall enter into force on the first day of the month following the expiration of a period of three months after the date of the deposit of the instrument of ratification, acceptance or approval.

Article 19 – Accession by Nonmember States

1. After the entry into force of this Convention, the Committee of Ministers of the Council of Europe, after consulting the Contracting States, may invite any State not a member of the Council and not mentioned in Article 18.1 to accede to this Convention, by a decision taken by the majority provided for in Article 20.d of the Statute of the Council of Europe and by the unanimous vote of the representatives of the Contracting States entitled to sit on the Committee.
2. In respect of any acceding State, the Convention shall enter into force on the first day of the month following the expiration of a period of three months after the date of deposit of the instrument of accession with the Secretary General of the Council of Europe.

Article 20 – Territorial Application

1. Any State may at the time of signature or when depositing its instrument of ratification, acceptance, approval or accession, specify the territory or territories to which this Convention shall apply.
2. Any State may at any later date, by a declaration addressed to the Secretary General of the Council of Europe, extend the application of this Convention to any other territory specified in the declaration. In respect of such territory the Convention shall enter into force on the first day of the month following the expiration of a period of three months after the date of receipt of such declaration by the Secretary General.
3. Any declaration made under the two preceding paragraphs may, in respect of any territory specified in such declaration, be withdrawn by a notification addressed to the Secretary General. The withdrawal shall become effective on the first day of the month following the expiration of a period of three months after the date of receipt of such notification by the Secretary General.

Article 21 – Temporal Application

This Convention shall be applicable to the enforcement of sentences imposed either before or after its entry into force.

Article 22 – Relationship to other Conventions and Agreements

1. This Convention does not affect the rights and undertakings derived from extradition treaties and other treaties on international co-operation in criminal matters providing for the transfer of detained persons for purposes of confrontation or testimony.
2. If two or more Parties have already concluded an agreement or treaty on the transfer of sentenced persons or otherwise have established their relations in this matter, or should they in future do so, they shall be entitled to apply that agreement or treaty or to regulate those relations accordingly, in lieu of the present Convention.
3. The present Convention does not affect the right of States party to the European Convention on the International Validity of Criminal Judgments to conclude bilateral or multilateral agreements with one another on matters dealt with in that Convention in order to supplement its provisions or facilitate the application of the principles embodied in it.
4. If a request for transfer falls within the scope of both the present Convention and the European Convention on the International Validity of Criminal Judgments or another agreement or treaty on the transfer of sentenced persons, the requesting State shall, when making the request, indicate on the basis of which instrument it is made.

Article 23 – Friendly settlement

* * *

Article 24 – Denunciation

* * *

Notes and Questions

1. *Participating countries.* The following countries participate in the Council of Europe Convention: Austria, Ireland, Bahamas, Italy, Belgium, Luxembourg, Bulgaria, Malta, Canada, Netherlands, Croatia, Norway, Cyprus, Poland, Czech Republic, Portugal, Denmark, Republic of Slovakia, Finland, Slovenia, France, Spain, Federal Republic of Germany, Sweden, Greece, Switzerland, Hungary, Trinidad/Tobago, Iceland, Turkey, Hong Kong, and the United Kingdom. In addition, the convention applies to the following UK territories: Anguilla, Gibraltar, Cayman Islands, Henderson Island, British Indian Ocean Territory, British Virgin Islands, Isle of Man, Ducie and Oena Islands, Montserrat, Falkland Islands, Pitcairn, Sovereign Base areas of Akrotiri and Dhekelia in the Island of Cyprus, and St. Helena and St. Helena Dependencies.

2. Due to the lack of ratifications of the European Convention on the International Validity of Criminal Judgements, a committee of member state experts and representatives of Canada, the United States, and the Commonwealth Secretariat were convened to prepare the convention.

3. *CoE Convention and the requirement that the applicant be a national of the administering state.* Official commentaries on the convention explain that it is not necessary for a transfer applicant to be a national of only the administering state. Contracting states can decide to apply the convention, when appropriate, in cases of dual or multiple nationality, even when the other nationality (or one of the other nationalities) is that of

the sentencing state. However, even where all conditions for transfer are fulfilled, the requested state retains discretion to deny a transfer. As a result, a sentencing state is free to refuse a requested transfer if it concerns one of its own nationals.

Art. 3.1(a) should be read in conjunction with Art. 3(4), which grants contracting states the possibility to define, by means of a declaration, the term "national." This possibility, corresponding with Article 61b of the European Convention on Extradition, is designed to enable contracting states to extend application of the convention to nonnationals within the strict meaning of domestic nationality legislation. For example, it could be read to cover stateless persons or citizens of other states who have established roots in the country through permanent residence.

4. *CoE Convention and the requirement that length of sentence be of a duration of at least six months.* The requirement that a transfer applicant have at least six months remaining in his or her sentence reflects both the belief that social rehabilitation requires ample time and the pragmatic concern of cost effectiveness. Regarding the latter, transferring a prisoner is costly; the considerable expenses incurred by the states involved must be proportionate to the benefits realized by completing the transfer.

In exceptional cases contracting states may agree to a transfer when less than six months of a sentence remain. This allows states to cover cases where the prospects of rehabilitation are favorable despite a sentence of less than six months or where the transfer can be executed quickly and inexpensively.

5. *CoE Convention and the requirement that the offender must consent to the transfer.* This requirement, one of the basic elements of the transfer mechanism established by the convention, is not contained in the European Convention on the International Validity of Criminal Judgments. The requirement is based on the CoE Convention's goal of facilitating rehabilitation: transferring a prisoner without his or her consent would work against this goal.

The requirement of the offender's consent should be read together with the Article 7 requirements on giving and verifying consent.

The sentenced person's legal representative decides whether to consent in cases in which one of the two states considers it necessary in view of the age or the physical or mental condition of the sentenced person. The reference to the sentenced person's "legal representative" does not imply that the representative must be legally qualified. It includes any person duly authorized by law to represent the sentenced person, such as a parent or someone specially authorized by the competent authority.

6. *OAS Convention.* In addition to the European legal instruments, there is a multilateral Organization of American States (OAS) Convention on the Transfer of Prisoners. The United States signed the OAS treaty on January 10, 1995. It was submitted to the Senate on September 30, 1996; approved by the Senate Foreign Relations Committee on September 27, 2000; approved by the full Senate on October 18, 2000; and then signed by the president. On May 25, 2001, the United States deposited instruments of accession with the OAS, and the convention entered into force for the United States on June 24, 2001.

In addition to the United States, the convention applies to Canada, Costa Rica, Panama, Venezuela, and Mexico.

7. *Berlin Convention.* Several former Soviet republics have concluded the Convention on the Transfer of Persons Sentenced to Imprisonment for Enforcement on the Sanction in the State of their Nationality of 1978. Based on the principle of nationality, it precludes

transfer to the country of ordinary residence or domicile; however, like the U.S.-Mexico treaty, it is not applicable when the offender is a resident of the sentencing state. The authority to request enforcement is primarily within the competence of the sentencing state, although it does not exclude initiatives by the prisoner's country of nationality, the prisoner, or close relatives. Like the European Convention on the International Validity of Criminal Judgements, the Convention does not require the prisoner to consent.

8. *UN Model Agreement on the Transfer of Prisoners.* In 1975, the Fifth UN Congress on the Prevention of Crime and the Treatment of Offenders discussed the problem of foreign prisoners and their repatriation. In 1980, at the Sixth UN Congress in Caracas, Resolution 13 urged member states to "consider the establishment of procedures whereby such transfers of offenders may be effected, recognizing that any such procedures can only be undertaken with the consent of both the sending and receiving countries and either with the consent of the prisoners or in his interest." The UN Committee on Crime Prevention and Control prepared a draft model agreement on the transfer of prisoners that was considerably influenced by regulations in the Council of Europe draft convention on the transfer of sentenced persons. In 1985, the model, intended to serve as a basis for bilateral and multilateral agreements, was endorsed by the Seventh UN Congress on the Prevention of Crime and the Treatment of Offenders.[11]

9. *Bilateral prisoner transfer conventions.* The United States has bilateral treaties on prisoner transfers with Mexico, Canada, Bolivia, the Federated States of Micronesia, the Marshall Islands, Palau, Panama, Turkey, Peru, Thailand, and France. Because the European Convention on the Transfer of Sentenced Prisoners and the Inter-American Convention are open for accession by other countries, the U.S. government has told states wanting a prisoner transfer relationship that they should accede to one of the multilateral conventions on prisoner transfer. As of June 9, 2009, fourteen countries have ratified the Inter-American Convention on Serving Criminal Sentences Abroad.

10. *U.S. policy on prisoner transfer treaties.* What if a client is incarcerated abroad and would like to transfer to the United States, but the country of incarceration does not have a treaty with the United States? What is the best way to persuade the country to conclude a treaty? In recent years, it has been the posture of the United States to encourage countries to consider acceding to a multilateral convention (i.e., the Council of Europe or OAS Conventions) rather than initiating the lengthy and costly process of negotiating, signing, and ratifying new bilateral treaties. This is an area where a multilateral approach has proven effective in offering an existing mechanism that new states can join, as well as standardizing transfer procedures for current members.

11. *Status of forces agreements.* These are treaties that the United States has entered into with other governments to govern the terms and conditions under which their military personnel will be present in that other country. The North Atlantic Treaty, Status of Forces, 4 U.S.T. 1992, June 19, 1951, (NATO SOFA) is one of the principal agreements. Art. VII(3) of the NATO SOFA provides that

> (a) The military authorities of the sending State shall have the primary right to exercise jurisdiction over a member of a force or of a civilian component in relation to
>
> (i) offenses solely against the property or security of that State, or offenses solely against the person or property of another member of the force of civilian component of that State or of a dependent;

[11] Epp, *supra* note 1 at 568–69.

(ii) offenses arising out of any act or omission done in the performance of official duty.

(b) In the case of any other offense the authorities of the receiving state shall have the primary right to exercise jurisdiction.

(c) If the State having the primary right decides not to exercise jurisdiction, it shall notify the authorities of the other State as soon as practicable. The authorities of the State having the primary right shall give sympathetic consideration to a request from the authorities of the other State for a waiver of its right in cases where that other State considers such waiver to be of particular importance.

Art. VII(7)(b) states, "The authorities of the receiving State shall give sympathetic consideration to a request from the authorities of the sending State for assistance in carrying out a sentence of imprisonment pronounced by the authorities of the sending State under the provisions of this Article within the territory of the receiving State."

Art. VII(8) of the treaty provides protection against double jeopardy for the military prisoner, exempting violations of rules of discipline. Art. VII(9) lists the procedural protections that must be observed by the receiving state.

The transfer of prisoners treaties prohibit transfer in the case of military offenses. However, such transfer is not necessarily inconsistent with the provisions of the NATO SOFA because under this treaty the military authorities of the sending state would have primary authority to prosecute these types of offenses, and in other cases the ordinary criminal offenses would be under the jurisdiction of the receiving state. M. Cherif Bassiouni & Grace M. W. Gallagher, *Policies and Practices of the United States, in* INTERNATIONAL CRIMINAL LAW 505, 512 (M. C. Bassiouni ed.), citing Major James R. Coker, *The Status of Visiting Military Forces in Europe: NATO-SOFA, A Comparison*, in 2 A TREATISE ON INTERNATIONAL CRIMINAL LAW 115 (M. Cherif Bassiouni & Ved P. Nanda, eds. 1973).

12. *Transfer on the basis of reciprocity*. Austria,[12] Switzerland,[13] and Germany[14] have enacted legislation implementing international transfer instruments that also provide for a repatriation of prisoners on the basis of reciprocity. These laws do not just regulate the transfer of prisoners; rather, they are comprehensive instruments addressing extradition, mutual assistance, transfer of proceedings, and transfer of the enforcement of sentences (referred to as acts on international mutual assistance in criminal matters). Under the above-mentioned prisoner transfer laws of these three countries the international agreements are self-executing and hence have priority over the provisions of the statutes. If the provisions are not self-executing, national law must be applied to interpret such provisions, or additional implementation legislation must be enacted.

13. *Implementation legislation*. Some countries that transfer only on the basis of international agreements have enacted legislation for the implementation of such treaties (e.g., U.S. legislation implementing the U.S.-Mexico Treaty, Act of Oct. 28, 1977, Pub. L. No. 95–144, 91 Stat. 1212; or the Canadian Transfer of Offenders Act, Bill C-21 of Mar. 17, 1978).

[12] Austria ARHG, Act on Extradition and Mutual Assistance, Federal Law Gazette No. 529/1979, enacted Jan. 1, 1980.

[13] Swiss IRSG, Act on International Mutual Assistance in Criminal Matters, S.R. 353.1, enacted Jan. 1, 1983.

[14] German IRG, Act on International Mutual Assistance in Criminal Matters, Federal Law Gazette 1982 I.S. 2071, enacted July 1, 1983.

IV. U.S. Prisoner Transfer Law

A. *U.S. Statutory Framework*

18 U.S.C. § 4100 Scope and Limitation of Chapter

(a) The provisions of this chapter relating to the transfer of offenders shall be applicable only when a treaty providing for such a transfer is in force, and shall only be applicable to transfers of offenders to and from a foreign country pursuant to such a treaty. A sentence imposed by a foreign country upon an offender who is subsequently transferred to the United States pursuant to a treaty shall be subject to being fully executed in the United States even though the treaty under which the offender was transferred is no longer in force.

(b) An offender may be transferred from the United States pursuant to this chapter only to a country of which the offender is a citizen or national. Only an offender who is a citizen or national of the United States may be transferred to the United States. An offender may be transferred to or from the United States only with the offender's consent, and only if the offense for which the offender was sentenced satisfies the requirement of double criminality as defined in this chapter. Once an offender's consent to transfer has been verified by a verifying officer, that consent shall be irrevocable. If at the time of transfer the offender is under eighteen years of age, or is deemed by the verifying officer to be mentally incompetent or otherwise incapable of knowingly and voluntarily consenting to the transfer, the transfer shall not be accomplished unless consent to the transfer be given by a parent or guardian, guardian ad litem, or by an appropriate court of the sentencing country. The appointment of a guardian ad litem shall be independent of the appointment of counsel under section 4109 of this title.

(c) An offender shall not be transferred to or from the United States if a proceeding by way of appeal or of collateral attack upon conviction or sentence be pending.

(d) The United States upon receiving notice from the country which imposed the sentence that the offender has been granted a pardon, commutation, or amnesty, or that there has been ameliorating modification or a revocation of the sentence shall give the offender the benefit of the action taken by the sentencing country.

18 U.S.C. § 4103 Applicability of United States Laws

All laws of the United States, as appropriate, pertaining to prisoners, probationers, parolees, and juvenile offenders shall be applicable to offenders transferred to the United States, unless a treaty or this chapter provides otherwise.

18 U.S.C. 4108 Verification of Consent of Offender to Transfer to the United States

(a) Prior to the transfer of an offender to the United States, the fact that the offender consents to such transfer and that such consent is voluntary and with full knowledge of the consequences thereof, a United States magistrate, or by a citizen specifically designated by a judge of the United States as defined in section 451 of title 28, United States Code. The designation of a citizen who is an employee or officer of a department or agency of the United States shall be with the approval of the head of that department or agency.

(b) The verifying officer shall inquire of the offender whether he understands and agrees that the transfer will be subject to the following conditions:

(1) only the country in which he was convicted and sentenced can modify or set aside the conviction or sentence, and any proceedings seeking such action may only be brought in that country;
(2) the sentence shall be carried out according to the laws of the United States and that those laws are subject to change;
(3) if a United States court should determine upon a proceeding initiated by him or on his behalf that his transfer was not accomplished in accordance with the treaty or laws of the United States, he may be returned to the country which imposed the sentence for the purpose of completing the sentence if that country requests his return; and
(4) his consent to transfer, once verified by the verifying officer, is irrevocable.

(c) The verifying officer, before determining that an offender's consent is voluntary and given with full knowledge of the consequences, shall advise the offender of his right to consult with counsel as provided by this chapter. If the offender wishes to consult with counsel before giving his consent, he shall be advised that the proceedings will be continued until he has had an opportunity to consult with counsel.

(d) The verifying officer shall make the necessary inquiries to determine that the offender's consent is voluntary and not the result of any promises, threats, or other improper inducements, and that the offender accepts the transfer subject to the conditions set forth in subsection (b). The consent and acceptance shall be on an appropriate form prescribed by the Attorney General.

(e) The proceedings shall be taken down by a reporter or recorded by suitable sound recording equipment. The Attorney General shall maintain custody of the records.

18 U.S.C. § 4112 Loss of Rights, Disqualification

An offender transferred to the United States to serve a sentence imposed by a foreign court shall not incur any loss of civil, political, or civic rights nor incur any disqualification other than those which under the laws of the United States or of the State in which the issue arises would result from the fact of the conviction in the foreign country.

Notes and Questions

1. *Transfer of offenders on probation.* 18 U.S.C. § 4104 provides for transfer to the United States of an offender on probation, although the Attorney General must determine that the appropriate U.S. district court is willing to supervise the offender before approving the transfer. Once the offender is transferred to U.S. custody, the Attorney General brings him or her before a U.S. district court. The court then places the offender under the supervision of its probation officers. Probation may be revoked in accordance with 18 U.S.C. § 3653 and Rule 32(f), Fed. Rules of Crim. Procedure.

2. *Transfer of offenders serving sentence of imprisonment.* 18 U.S.C. § 4105(a) provides that an offender imprisoned in a foreign country transferred to the custody of the Attorney General must remain in the custody of the Attorney General under the same conditions and for the same period of time as an offender who had been committed to the custody of the Attorney General by a U.S. court for the period of time imposed by the sentencing court.

Under § 4105(b) the Attorney General must give the transferred offender credit toward service of the sentence for any days, prior to the date of commencement of the sentence, spent in custody in connection with the offense or acts for which the sentence was imposed.

Under § 4105(c)(1) the transferred offender is entitled to all credits for good time, for labor, or any other credit toward the service of the sentence that had been given by the transferring country for time served as of the time of the transfer. After the transfer, the offender must in addition be entitled to credits toward service of sentence for satisfactory behavior, computed on the basis of the time remaining to be served at the time of the transfer and at the rate provided in section 18 U.S.C. § 3624(b) for a sentence of the length of the total sentence imposed and certified by the foreign authorities. The credits must be combined to provide a release date for the offender pursuant to 18 U.S.C. § 3624(a).

§ 4105(2) provides that, if the country from which the offender is transferred does not give credit for good time, the basis of computing the deduction from the sentence must be the sentence imposed by the sentencing court and certified to be served upon transfer, at the rate provided in 18 U.S.C. § 3624(b).

3. *Verification of consent of offender from the United States.* § 4107 provides that, before transfer of an offender from the United States, a U.S. magistrate or a judge must verify the fact that the offender consents to such transfer and that such consent is voluntary and with full knowledge of the consequences. The procedures are similar to the provisions in § 4108 described earlier.

4. *Transfer after verification of consent from the United States.* The time between the approval of a transfer request by the United States and by the other nation and the actual transfer varies widely. A wait of at least three months is typical.

5. *Documents required for transfer.* Documents required for prisoner transfer applications vary depending on the treaty and the laws or procedures of the country in which a prisoner is incarcerated. U.S. citizens or nationals incarcerated abroad should contact U.S. consular authorities at the U.S. embassy or consulate, who will assist inmates in obtaining the necessary documents and completing any required forms.

Foreign nationals incarcerated in the United States should consult prison authorities about their interest in the transfer. In the case of foreign nationals in federal prisons, prison authorities will arrange for submission of the necessary documents to the U.S. Department of Justice, which serves as the central authority for international prisoner transfer. Documentation provided to the Department of Justice generally includes the following:

- Form or letter signed by prisoner indicating an interest in transfer
- Birth certificate or passport
- Judgment or sentence
- Presentence report
- Fingerprints and photograph
- Sentence calculation
- Prison progress report (security level, disciplinary reports, prison jobs, program participation, psychological evaluation, current medical condition)
- Immigration status
- Family and residence information

6. *Transfer of military persons.* Are U.S. military persons governed by prisoner transfer treaties? Yes. 10 U.S.C. § 955 provides that prisoner transfer treaties do apply to U.S. military personnel.

7. *Transferred prisoners' civil rights.* The applicable U.S. statute provides that a person may suffer only such losses and disqualification as "would result from the fact of the conviction in the foreign law." The goal of this provision is to eliminate disabilities, although neither the treaties nor the statute provides for expungement of records of transferred offenders. In the United States such persons would have a U.S. detention record based on a foreign conviction without the right of expungement. The offender might have had the potential of expunging such conviction had the conviction been rendered by a U.S. court. Whether a country will impose disabilities based on foreign criminal sentences depends on the extent to which it recognizes and enforces foreign penal judgments. *See, e.g.*, M. Cherif Bassiouni, *Introduction to Recognition of Foreign Penal Judgments, in* II International Criminal Law: Multilateral and Bilateral Enforcement Mechanisms 507 (M. Cherif Bassiouni, 3d ed. 2009).

B. *State Participation*

A U.S. state can transfer prisoners to their countries of citizenship if it has enacted appropriate legislation. As of March 27, 2006, all fifty states had enacted such laws. The Bureau of Prisons Web site (http://www.bop.gov) maintains a list of contacts for each state.

There is a distinction between prisoners serving sentences in state or local facilities and prisoners convicted in federal courts serving sentences in federal facilities in the United States. The Department of Justice's International Prisoner Transfer Program Web site (http://www.usdoj.gov/criminal/oeo/index.htm) lists participating states.

It is difficult in some states to transfer because they lack enthusiasm for the program and hence do not grant requests and when they do it takes much more time to obtain a transfer.

However, most states in the United States lack enthusiasm for prisoner transfer treaties, and some have indicated an unwillingness to participate in such transfers. Even though every state and the Commonwealth of the Northern Mariana Islands have enacted implementing legislation, only a handful (Arizona, Florida, Illinois, Massachusetts, New Mexico, New York, Minnesota, Washington, Alabama, and Idaho) are currently participating in prison transfers. (Vermont participates only with respect to prisoners seeking transfer to Canada.) Prisoner transfer treaties require the consent of three parties – (1) the transferring state, (2) the receiving state, and (3) the prisoner – before a transfer can take place. In addition, a prisoner incarcerated in a state institution must obtain the consent of the state's authorities as well in order to transfer pursuant to a treaty (18 U.S.C. § 4102 (6)). Bilateral U.S. prisoner transfer treaties, such as the U.S.-Canada treaty, provide that the approval of the state or provincial authority, as well as that of the federal authority, must be obtained in cases involving prisoners sentenced by state or provincial courts.

C. *Transferring to the United States*

Although prisoners can be transferred to foreign countries from both state and federal prisons, only the federal prison system may receive and assume responsibility for American prisoners transferred to the United States from other countries. Thus, even if a U.S. national imprisoned abroad has committed the type of offense that would ordinarily be tried in a state court, he or she will be placed in a federal prison facility (and have a release date determined by the U.S. Parole Commission) upon transfer to the United States.

U.S. Department of Justice, International Prisoner Transfer Unit: Prisoner Transfer Information for Americans Incarcerated Abroad

The International Prisoner Transfer program, which is authorized by federal law and international treaties, is administered by the United States Department of Justice. An American prisoner is not eligible for transfer to the United States until he has been sentenced by the foreign country. Once sentencing occurs the application process can be initiated. Whether the prisoner or the American Embassy makes the formal transfer request to the foreign country will depend upon the terms of the particular treaty governing the transfer.

In addition to the requirement that the prisoner be sentenced, there are other general requirements that must be satisfied before a transfer can occur. The judgment and sentence must be final, which means that there can be no pending appeals or collateral attacks. There also must be sufficient time remaining on the sentence for an application to be processed. Normally this period is six months but sometimes it is a year. Some foreign governments require the prisoner to pay any fines or restitution that are imposed as part of the sentence before transfer can occur and sometimes even before the approval decision is made. Other treaties prohibit the transfer of certain types of offenses such as immigration, military, and political offenses.

A prisoner who is interested in transferring should contact the Defender Services Division of the Administrative Office of the U.S. Courts to obtain advice as to whether a transfer would be an appropriate option for the prisoner. Some prisoners decide not to apply for transfer after consulting with a federal public defender ("FPD") and learning that they will spend less time in custody if they remain in the foreign country than if they transfer to the United States and have their sentence administered according to United States sentencing provisions. If the prisoner has questions concerning how his sentence will be administered in the United States, he should write to:

Chief, Defender Services Division

Administrative Office of the United States Courts

Washington, D.C. 20544

Attn: Prisoner Transfer Treaty Matters

In this letter, the prisoner should clearly state that he is seeking advice about international prisoner transfer and should provide the following information to allow the FPD to give the best advice possible:

1. Full name and any aliases;
2. Date and place of birth;
3. Date of the offense and date of arrest;
4. Precise offense of conviction including any known statutory cites;
5. Sentence imposed including any fines or restitution;
6. Any projected release dates through parole or other form of early release;
7. Any labor credits or other prison work credits that may be earned;
8. A detailed description of the offense, that includes the foreign government's version of the offense. This description should include whether a weapon was used or present

when the offense was committed. If a drug offense is involved, the offense description should include the type of drugs involved and the quantity;

9. A description of the prisoner's role in the offense in relation to others who may have participated in the offense;
10. Whether the prisoner cooperated, provided any confession or took any other action showing that he accepted responsibility for his unlawful conduct;
11. An accurate description of his prior misdemeanor or felony record in the United States including prior sentences, whether he was under criminal justice supervision (probation, parole, or supervised) at the time of the offense, and whether any outstanding warrants exist against him; and
12. An accurate mailing address where the prisoner can be reached.

Upon receiving this information, the Defender Service Division will assign the matter to an FPD for review and response. If the prisoner has provided all of the information listed above, the FPD should be able to give the prisoner a reasonably informed estimate of how the foreign sentence will be administered in the United States should the prisoner be transferred there. Once the case is assigned, it usually takes four to eight weeks for the FPD to respond to the prisoner with advice about the likely manner in which the sentence will be administered.

If, after receiving the information from the FPD, the prisoner still wishes to transfer, either he or the American Embassy (depending on the requirements of the applicable treaty) should apply for transfer to the foreign government. Thereafter, the foreign government or the American Embassy will assemble the necessary documents for the application package. This package will include the foreign sentencing documents, a summary and translation of the offense behavior and prisoner information, a copy of the travel document (proof of citizenship) and information regarding the prisoner classification and conduct. Once these documents are assembled they will be forwarded to the International Prisoner Transfer Unit ("IPTU") of the Criminal Division of the Department of Justice. The IPTU will review the application and decide whether to approve the request. If both the IPTU and the foreign government approve the request, the IPTU will make arrangements for a consent verification hearing. At the consent verification hearing, which is presided over by a federal magistrate and where the prisoner is represented by an FPD, a determination is made whether the prisoner understands the outcome of the transfer and whether he consents to the transfer. If the prisoner consents to the transfer, arrangements are made with the Federal Bureau of Prisons and the foreign government to transport him back to the United States where he will be incarcerated in a federal prison. When the day for the transfer arrives, the prisoner should be prepared. He should have disposed of all of his belongings except for a small amount of personal property, for example, glasses, medications, bibles, cash (preferably in a money order denominated in dollars), family photos, etc. Other than a wedding band, no jewelry is permitted including watches, earrings and necklaces. Hair bands, clasps, and braids will also be prohibited. Prohibited property and additional personal property like clothing, books, and appliances should be mailed to the prisoner's home before the transfer. Because the prisoner will likely wear leg irons for the transfer, a pair of socks for the day of the transfer is advisable. The prisoner will be subject to a full body search before transfer.

Once the prisoner is returned to the United States, the foreign sentencing documents will be copied and given to a United States Probation Officer. The probation officer will review these documents and then visit the prisoner to collect background information. After a brief investigation, the probation officer will prepare a "post sentence investigation report." This report, which takes about thirty to sixty days to prepare, will include a recommendation as to the period of confinement and period of supervised release that would apply after considering the relevant United States Sentencing Guidelines. Thereafter, the United States Parole Commission will review the case and decide the length of time the prisoner should remain in prison and the period of supervised release that will apply when the prisoner is released from prison.

Family members and representatives can obtain additional information from two useful Web sites: the Department of State (http://travel.state.gov/transfer.html) and the Department of Justice (http://www.usdoj.gov/criminal/oeo/). Prisoners who are applying for transfer may be represented by an attorney but need not be. The overwhelming majority of applicants to the prisoner transfer program are not represented by an attorney. Because of limitations imposed by the Privacy Act, 5 U.S.C. § 552a, the Department of Justice cannot provide information about individual prisoner transfer cases without a signed waiver of confidentiality from the prisoner. This law applies whether the inquiring party is the prisoner's congressman or family member.

Notes and Questions

1. *Physical transfer to the United States after the verification hearing.* Officials of the Federal Bureau of Prisons travel to the foreign country to escort the prisoner to the United States. The transferee returns to the United States in the custody of these officials and is placed in a federal prison. As a matter of security policy of the Federal Bureau of Prisons, information about specific dates and timing of a transfer is not provided to the prisoner, family, or other persons until the actual transfer has occurred.

2. *Posttransfer processing.* A federal probation officer interviews the prisoner shortly after the transfer to obtain personal history information. The officer forwards the interview report to the appropriate federal probation office, which conducts a background investigation of the transferee equivalent to a presentence investigation report. Upon completion, normally within thirty days, the investigation report is transmitted to the federal institution housing the transferee.

After the institution receives the background report, a transferree convicted of an offense committed before November 1, 1987, will receive a parole hearing at the next regularly scheduled parole hearing date for that institution. Pursuant to the Parole Commission regulations the hearing should occur "within 120 days of a prisoner's arrival at a Federal institution or as soon thereafter as practicable."[15] The Parole Commission applies the criteria in determining a transferee's presumptive parole release date pursuant to 18 U.S.C. § 4106 and the jurisprudence implementing the law.

Transferees convicted of foreign offenses committed after October 31, 1987, are processed in essentially the same fashion, except that in lieu of a parole hearing, the U.S. Parole Commission, after completion of the posttransfer background investigation by the U.S. Probation Service,[16] determines the offender's release date and period and conditions of supervised release "as though the offender were convicted in a United States district court of a similar offense," such as by applying the federal sentencing guidelines.[17]

3. *Inquiries about transfer of persons incarcerated abroad to the United States and related matters.* Questions about individual arrest cases of U.S. citizens abroad should

[15] 28 C.F.R. § 2.12(a).

[16] 18 U.S.C. § 4106A(b)(1)(D).

[17] 18 U.S.C. § 4106A(b)(1). For a more comprehensive and useful discussion see MICHAEL ABBELL, INTERNATIONAL PRISONER TRANSFERS § 4–7 (Dec. 2004).

be addressed to the Office Of American Citizens Services and Crisis Management, Overseas Citizens Services, Room 4817 N.S., Department Of State, 2201 C Street N.W., Washington, D.C. 20520–4818; Tel: (202) 647–5225 or (202) 647–5226.

4. *Requirement that offense not be a political offense.* Art. II(4) of the Mexican Treaty prohibits the transfer of offenders who have been convicted of political offenses. The French and Thai treaties include similar provisions that appear to preclude such transfers.[18] The Turkish treaty allows the country that would administer the sentence discretion to refuse to accept transfer of an offender convicted of a political offense.[19] Generally speaking, a sentencing country will not approve transfer of an American offender who committed an offense against its security or government, except as part of a negotiated diplomatic resolution of a particular case. As a result, prisoners convicted of political offenses are normally precluded from transferring under treaties.

5. *Requirement that the sentence not be a capital sentence.* The Inter-American Convention and three U.S. bilateral transfer treaties specifically make offenders who are subject to death sentences ineligible for transfer.[20] Three other treaties practically preclude transfers for offenders subject to death sentences by specifying the types of sentences that may be transferred.[21] Persons subject to the death sentences will not be able to take advantage of one of the key purposes of the treaty – the improvement of the chances of the offender's reintegration into his or her own society.

6. *Requirement that the offense not be an immigration offense.* The U.S.-Mexico and U.S.-Canada treaties preclude transfer of persons convicted of immigration offenses.[22] Nevertheless, Mexico has allowed the transfer of American nationals convicted of immigration offenses when the offenses were merely unlawful entry and the offenders were also convicted of more serious transferable offenses.

7. *Requirement that the offense not be a military offense.* Most prisoner transfer treaties in which the United States participates do not allow the transfer of persons convicted of purely military offenses, such as desertion. The Bolivian treaty forbids transfer of anyone convicted under military law. Other treaties permit transfer of offenders convicted of ordinary criminal offenses in courts-martial.

The Council of Europe Convention, the Inter-American Convention, and the U.S.-Thailand Treaty, which do not include military offense provisions, provide ample discretion for countries to refuse transfer of military offenders.

8. *Requirement that the offender not be a domiciliary of the sentencing country.* Two U.S. prisoner transfer treaties, with Mexico and Turkey, preclude transfer of country nationals who are domiciliaries of the sentencing country.[23] "Domiciliary" is defined as a person who has resided in the sentencing country for at least five years with the intent to remain in that country.[24] The United States has denied transfer applications for a number of offenders pursuant to the provisions in the Mexican treaty. It is likely to exercise its broad general discretionary authority under other treaties for the same purpose.

18 French Treaty, Art. 5(a); Thai Treaty, Art. II(3).
19 Art. V(b).
20 Inter-American Convention, Art. III(5); Bolivian Treaty, Art. III(3); Panamanian Treaty, Art. III(3); Peruvian Treaty, Art. III(3).
21 Canadian Treaty, Art. III(7); Mexican Treaty, Art. IV(6); Thai Treaty, Art. III(4).
22 Art. IV(6).
23 Mexican Treaty, Art. II(3); Turkish Treaty, Art. IV(c).
24 Mexican Treaty, Art. IX(4); Turkish Treaty, Art. I(f).

D. *Transferring from the United States*

Pursuant to 28 C.F.R. §§ 527.43 and 527.44, the U.S. Bureau of Prisons has established formal procedures governing the notification of foreign nationals in Bureau of Prisons custody of their possible eligibility for transfer and prescribing the manner in which their requests for transfer are to be processed. In practice, federal prisoners initiate requests to transfer by completing and signing a Federal Prison System Transfer Inquiry Form (BP-297). After signing the form, the offender will continue to be able to withdraw his or her request until the transfer has been formally verified.

The prospective transferee's inquiry form and other relevant information regarding the offender's personal history and role in the commission of the offense of which he or she was convicted, including the Pre-Sentence Investigation Report, are sent by the institution in which the offender is incarcerated to the U.S. Bureau of Prisons in Washington, D.C., which in turn sends them to the International Prisoner Transfer Unit (IPTU), Office of Enforcement Operations, Criminal Division, U.S. Department of Justice. The IPTU reviews the request to determine whether the prisoner is eligible to transfer. If the prisoner appears to be eligible, the IPTU asks the U.S. Attorney's office that prosecuted the applicant for its views on whether there exists any reason why the United States should refuse the transfer. The IPTU also asks the views of the federal agency that investigated the offense that led to the applicant's conviction.

In recent years, the Department of Justice has denied a much higher percentage of transfer applications of federal prisoners wanting to serve their federal sentences in their countries of nationality than in the late 1970s and early 1980s. One of the reasons is the trend in U.S. criminal justice policy to be increasingly "tough" on crime. Another reason is that, since November 1, 1987, offenders have to serve 87 percent of their sentences before being released on supervised release, as compared to only one-third or less of their sentences before that. Most, if not all, of the U.S. treaty partners require offenders convicted in their countries to serve a smaller portion of their sentences before becoming eligible for conditional arrest. Hence, in many circumstances, the transfer of offenders is likely to substantially decrease the effective length of their sentences.

An increasing number of federal transfer applicants have been sentenced under the Sentencing Reform Act of 1984. The Department of Justice is not anxious to grant early transfer because such transfers undermine the sentencing philosophy upon which that act is based. For instance, when dealing with requests by federal offenders to transfer to countries with which the United States has only infrequent transfers, especially where the administering country may convert the U.S. sentence, pursuant to Articles 8 and 11 of the Council of Europe Convention, to a sentence of the prospective administering country, the IPTU requests the prospective administering country to advise it as to the manner in which the transferred sentence would be executed in that country (including the probable periods of incarceration and supervised release of the transfer applicant). Only if the IPTU believes that the transfer would not unduly diminish the punishment of the offender in relation to the severity of the offense for which he or she was convicted will it give its final approval to the transfer. The IPTU's increasing reluctance to approve transfers to countries with a more progressive penal regime has led to more frequent denials of initial transfer requests. As a result, federal prisoner transfer applicants are increasingly likely to make more than one transfer request before their transfers will be approved.[25]

E. *U.S. Administrative Procedure*

The Department of Justice has issued regulations concerning the implementation of transfers to the United States. In C.F.R. Sec. 0.64–2, the Attorney General delegated to the Assistant Attorney General, Criminal Division, general responsibility for the implementation of prisoner transfer treaties:

> The Assistant Attorney General in charge of the Criminal Division is authorized to exercise all of the power and authority vested in the Attorney General under Section 4102 of Title 18, U.S. Code, which has not been delegated to the Direct of the Bureau of Prisons under 28 CFR 0.96b, including specifically the authority to find the transfer of offenders to or from a foreign country under a treaty as referred to in Pub.L. 95–44 [sic] appropriate or inappropriate. The Assistant Attorney General in charge of the Criminal Division is authorized to redelegate this authority to his Deputy Assistant Attorneys General, the Senior Associate Director of the Office of Enforcement Operations and, in the Senior Associate Director's absence, the Director, Office of Enforcement Operations.

The Assistant Attorney General of the Criminal Division has redelegated his authority under 28 C.F.R. Sec. 0.64–2 to the Deputy Assistant Attorneys General and to the Senior Associate Director of the Criminal Division's Office of Enforcement Operation as follows:

> By virtue of the authority vested in me by Sec. 0.64–2 of Title 28 of the code of Federal Regulations, the authority delegated to me by that section to exercise all of the power and authority vested in the Attorney General under Section 4102 of Title 18, U.S. Code, which has not been delegated to the Director of the Bureau of Prisons, including specifically the authority to find the transfer of offenders to or from a foreign country under a treaty as referred to in Pub. L. 95–44 [sic] appropriate or inappropriate, is hereby redelegated to each of the Deputy Assistant Attorneys General and the Senior Associate Director's Absence, the Director of the Office of Enforcement Operators at the Criminal Division.

In 28 C.F.R. Sec. 0.96b, the Attorney General delegated all authority concerning the custody and physical movement of transferring prisoners and certain administration functions to the Director, Bureau of Prisons as follows:

> The Director of the Bureau of Prisons and officers of the Bureau of Prisons designated by him are authorized to receive custody of offenders and to transfer offenders to and from the United States of America under a treaty as referred to in Pub.L. 95–144; to make arrangements with the States and to receive offenders from the States for transfer to a foreign country; to act as an agent of the United States to receive the delivery from a foreign government of any person being transferred to the United States under such a treaty; to render to foreign countries and to receive from them certifications and report required under a treaty; and to receive custody and carry out the sentence of

[25] Michael Abbell, International Prisoner Transfer, *supra* note 17 at § 7–3.

imprisonment of such a transferred offender as required by that statute and any such treaty. [order No. 758–77, 42 FR 63139, December 15, 1977]

28 C.F.R. Sec. 0.97 permits the Director of the Bureau of Prisons to redelegate to any of its subordinates any of the authority, functions, or duties rested in the Director in Sec. 0.96b. In 28 C.F.R. Sec. 527.46, the U.S. Bureau of Prisons has also promulgated regulations regarding (1) receiving custody of a U.S. citizen from foreign authorities, (2) the designation of staff to receive and transport the inmate to the United States, and (3) the processing of the inmate after transfer to the United States. 28 C.F.R. Sec. 527.45 governs transfer of state prisoners to other countries. 28 C.F.R. Sec. 527.44 provides for transfer of Bureau of Prison inmates to other countries.

After a prisoner indicates the desire to participate in a prisoner transfer process, the signatory country has discretion to assist or to refuse the request. Considerations include to what extent a government has unfettered discretion in its processing of and deciding the request and whether the prisoner requesting transfer has any right to expect a minimal level of care from a governmental agency in reviewing his or her request to transfer.

The U.S. Department of Justice has issued its own internal guidelines to evaluate prisoner applications for transfer.

Guidelines for Evaluating Prisoner Applications for Transfer

(1) Likelihood of Social Rehabilitation

Beyond the practical concerns of alleviating prison crowding and dealing administratively with foreign national prisoners, many of whom have very limited English language ability, the central rationale behind transferring foreign prisoners to their home countries is to facilitate the prisoner's social rehabilitation. Rehabilitation is, of course, one of the principal purposes of incarceration in civilized societies. This goal is expressly stated in the Preambles to most of the prisoner transfer treaties ("to provide better administration of justice by adopting methods furthering the offender's social rehabilitation," [Mexican treaty]; "facilitating [the prisoner's] successful reintegration into society," [Canadian treaty]; "further the ends of justice and social rehabilitation of sentenced persons," [COE Convention]). Prisoner transfer assumes that such social rehabilitation is more likely to occur in the prisoner's home country, closer to his family and within his own culture. In addition, since many foreign national prisoners will be deported when their sentences have been served, it may not make sense to further their adjustment to a society in which they will not be allowed to remain after release.

In evaluating whether social rehabilitation really will be furthered by transferring a prisoner, a number of factors are considered:

(a) Acceptance of responsibility. The acceptance of responsibility is a condition precedent for rehabilitation. Acceptance of responsibility is a positive factor for transfer, and is demonstrated by cooperation with the authorities, providing complete and candid information as to involvement in the offense, and/or the timely entry of a guilty plea.

(b) Criminal history. For purposes of evaluating rehabilitative potential, there is a difference between a low-level, minor, first-time or infrequent offender, and a career criminal. Contrast, for example, the rehabilitative potential of an offender who was paid a few hundred dollars to drive drugs into the United States, with that of a drug kingpin.

(c) Seriousness of the offense. The seriousness of the offense, the critical factor in any sentencing decision, is equally important in evaluating whether serving out all or most of his sentence in the United States will do more for the prisoner's rehabilitation than transferring him to what may be a less punitive and possibly less lengthy incarceration.
(d) Criminal ties to the sending and receiving countries. If a prisoner has criminal ties to the receiving country, transferring him could well be more likely to facilitate reintegration into his criminal milieu than to facilitate rehabilitation into civil society.
(e) Family and other social ties to the sending and receiving countries. This is a critical factor for two reasons. First, it is an important assumption of the prisoner transfer program that social rehabilitation is most likely near the prisoner's family, and least likely far away. Second, the most likely prediction about the prisoner's behavior upon release is that he will reunite with his family. If the prisoner's family is in the receiving country, it is far more likely that he will stay there. If, however, that family is in the sending country, one must assume that the released prisoner will try to return to the sending country, not only negating any social rehabilitation benefits from transfer but also negating the prisoner's deportation as well.

There are obviously any number of family situations, and no one rule can control every case. Set out below is the general approach of the International Prisoner Transfer Unit when the prisoner has family members residing in the United States:

(i) Prisoner is single and childless. Where his parents and siblings live will be controlling for this category (except in the unusual case where the prisoner was raised by others in the receiving country);
(ii) Prisoner is ceremonially married. The location of the spouse is controlling. The presumption is that the prisoner should be in the same country as his spouse;
(iii) Prisoner has a common law spouse. The location of the common law spouse can be very important, depending on the apparent longevity and stability of the common law relationship (that is, how close in practice the common law spouse is to a legal spouse) and whether any children, particularly still minor children, have issued from it (that is, how close the common law situation is to a traditional family);
(iv) Prisoner is either single or separated and has children. The prisoner's relation to the children is critical. For example, adult children living on their own in the United States would normally be less of a factor against transfer than minor children in the United States. Minor children in the United States who have always lived with the other parent and never, or almost never, with the prisoner would be less of a factor against transfer than minor children for whom the prisoner had been the custodial parent or to whom the prisoner had otherwise been very close; in these cases, it is generally assumed that transferring the prisoner away from the children would not accomplish the social goals of transfer, and that the prisoner would attempt to return to the children upon release.

(a) Transfers to third countries. Occasionally, we are asked to transfer a prisoner whose most significant ties are neither to the receiving country nor to the sending country, but are to a third country with which the United States does not have a treaty. Such cases need to be carefully evaluated. If the receiving country will accept the prisoner, if the prisoner is not a major violator, and if incarceration there seems to be in the prisoner's best interest, we will sometimes permit the transfer to take place.

(b) Humanitarian concerns. By this, we usually mean the terminal illness of the prisoner or a member of his immediate family. Occasionally, humanitarian concerns justify a transfer which would otherwise not be approved, so long as the transfer would not violate the treaty; an example of this would be the terminal illness of the prisoner himself. Other times, humanitarian concerns are simply treated as another factor supporting transfer; an example of this would be the grave illness of a parent or child. Illnesses for which the prisoner is being or could be treated in the United States, or the advanced age of parents, do not justify a transfer on humanitarian grounds.
(c) Length of time in the United States. Beyond the legal requirements in the treaties with a domiciliary clause (see above), length of time in the sending country is an important social factor. If the prisoner has been in the United States for such a long time that he has in fact become a member of this society, his social rehabilitation will not be facilitated by sending him to a different one.

(2) Law Enforcement Concerns

Social rehabilitation is not the only purpose of incarceration, and therefore cannot be the sole consideration in evaluating prisoner transfer requests or take precedence over all other objectives. Law enforcement and justice concerns must also be considered, regardless of the possible consequences for the prisoner's social rehabilitation. These considerations are the normal ones in any sentencing or parole decision:

(a) Seriousness of the offense. The more serious the offense, the more important the certainty of incarceration in the place it was committed becomes.
(b) Public sensibilities. Would the return of the prisoner to a foreign country so outrage public sensibilities because of the extremely serious nature of the prisoner's crimes or the circumstances surrounding the prisoner's crimes as to outweigh the rehabilitation considerations?
(c) Public policy. Would the return of the prisoner to a foreign country be contrary to the public policy of the United States?
(d) Reintegration and renewed criminal activity in receiving country. Are the prisoner's ties to criminal elements in his home country such that his return there would simply facilitate a resumption of his criminal activity? Would transfer enhance the possibility of reprisal or intimidation?
(e) Possible sentencing disparity. When a prisoner is transferred, responsibility for administering his sentence belongs exclusively to the receiving country. Under most of the bilateral treaties, the receiving country takes over the transferred sentence, but that sentence is then carried out under the laws and regulations of the receiving country, including any provisions for reduction of the term of confinement by parole, conditional release, good time release, or otherwise. Under the French and Turkish bilateral treaties and the COE Convention, the receiving country has the additional option of converting the sending country's sentence, through either a judicial or administrative procedure, into its own sentence; that is, the receiving country may substitute the penalty under its own laws for a similar offense. (There are certain limitations on converting the sentence. The receiving country is bound by the findings of facts insofar as they appear from the judgment, cannot convert a prison term into a fine, and cannot lengthen the prison term.) However, regardless of whether the sentence is

continued or converted, responsibility for administering it rests solely with the receiving state.

(f) Law enforcement and prosecutorial needs in the sending country. These must be considered before transfer, since once the prisoner is transferred, the sending country no longer has any authority or control over him. Before approving transfer, the sending country must therefore consider factors such as:
   (i) Is the prisoner's testimony needed against codefendants?
   (ii) Are there fugitives in the prisoner's case whose apprehension would require the prisoner's presence to help make the case against them?
   (iii) Are there other open cases or investigations involving the prisoner?
   (iv) Is there a need for further debriefing by law enforcement agents in the sending country?

(g) Unpaid court-ordered assessments, fines, or restitution. Because all supervisory authority over the prisoner is terminated when the prisoner transfers, financial obligations of the prisoner need to be settled prior to transfer.

(3) Likelihood of Return to the United States

Allowing a foreign national prisoner to serve out the remainder of his United States sentence in his own country only makes sense if the prisoner will remain in his own country after his release. Therefore, a critical consideration in evaluating a transfer request is whether in fact the prisoner will stay in the receiving country, or will return to the sending country. We look at a number of factors in making this determination:

(a) Existing ties to the United States. This has been discussed in detail under Family and other social ties to the sending and receiving countries, above. The location of the prisoner's family, his residence and domiciliary status in the United States and the receiving country (for example, does he still own a residence in the United States, does he have any obvious residence in the receiving country), whether he had a non-criminal occupation or professional career in the sending or receiving country, the relative proximity of the receiving country's borders to the United States and how easy or difficult it would be as a practical matter to return to the United States, and his immigration status, are all factors to take into account in determining whether the prisoner would likely remain in the receiving country.

(b) Previous prisoner transfer. If a prisoner has previously been the beneficiary of a treaty transfer, he is ineligible for transfer. Reapplications after a previous transfer are always denied.

(c) Previous deportations and illegal reentries. Recent deportation(s) or numerous illegal entries into the United States will generally bar a treaty transfer.

Special Considerations for State Prisoners

(1) State approval required: Where a sentenced person has been convicted by a state of the United States of crimes under the laws of that state and is in the custody of authorities of that state (as opposed to having been convicted in the federal courts of a crime under the United States Code), the United States will not approve a transfer unless the state first gives it consent.

(2) Deference to state requests: Generally, the Department of Justice defers to a state's judgment, and approves the transfer of state prisoners approved by the state.

(3) Exceptions: A compelling federal interest will cause the Department to disapprove a state request for the transfer of one of its prisoners. The most frequently invoked federal interest is the protection of our borders from illegal reentries by transferred prisoners. Therefore, the Department will always consider the likelihood that the prisoner will illegally return to the United States before giving final approval to a state request for transfer.

Scalise v. Edwin Meese III, Attorney General of the United States, et al., 687 F. Supp. 1239 (N.D. Ill. 1988)

Plaintiffs Joseph Scalise and Arthur Rachel are in a jail in a land far away. They want to come home. The Attorney General of the United States has the power to grant their wish, but he refuses to exercise it. Plaintiffs seek a writ of mandamus ordering the Attorney General to establish regulations which would govern the grant or denial of their request, as well as an order finding the Attorney General's refusal a violation of their due process rights. They have moved for summary judgment of their complaint.... For the reasons set forth below, plaintiff's motion will be granted and the writ of mandamus will issue.

Five years ago, plaintiffs, citizens of the United States, went to London, England, for a trip. While they were there, they armed themselves with a firearm and robbed a jewelry store. They escaped with around $3.6 million dollars in jewels, including the famous Marlborough Diamond.

They did not remain free for long. The British authorities soon caught up with them, though not with the stolen jewels. Plaintiffs were tried and convicted in the Old Bailey for violations of the Theft Act of 1968. The British judge sentenced them to fifteen years in prison, with their terms of imprisonment commencing August 6, 1984.

Under British law, plaintiffs will be eligible for release in July, 1993, although they will apparently be eligible for "parole license," a term with which this court is not familiar, in July of this year.

In any case, plaintiffs do not wish to remain in England. Beginning shortly after their incarceration, they began inquiring into the possibility of their being transferred to the United States to serve out their sentences. On July 1, 1985, the United States and the United Kingdom, in conjunction with a number of other countries, ratified the Convention on the Transfer of Sentenced Persons ("the Convention").

This court has determined that the Attorney General has violated its duty under the Act to promulgate regulations setting both standards and guidelines to govern the requests of Americans incarcerated abroad to be transferred to an American prison. This court has also found that the Attorney General acted arbitrarily and capriciously, and abused his discretion, in denying the request of the plaintiffs in this case. Finally this court has concluded that the Attorney General deprived plaintiffs of due process of law in denying their requests under the Act without a sufficient explanation and elaboration of his decision and without affording them an opportunity to rebut....

In the United States, authority for the implementation of the Convention is vested with the Attorney General under the Transfer of Offenders to and From Foreign Countries Act ("the Act"), P.L. No. 95–144, 91 Stat. 1212, 18 U.S.C. § 4100 *et seq*. The Act provides, in pertinent part:

Section 4102. Authority of the Attorney General
The Attorney General is authorized –

(1) to act on behalf of the United States as the authority referred to in the treaty;
(2) to receive custody of offenders under a sentence of imprisonment, on parole, or on probation who are citizens or nationals of the United States correctional institutions, or assign them to the parole or probation authorities for supervision;
(3) to make regulations for the proper implementation of such treaties in accordance with this chapter and to make regulations to implement this chapter . . .

After the Convention went into effect, plaintiffs wrote letters to both the British and American authorities requesting transfer to American prisons. The British authorities told them that England would agree to their transfer, provided that the United States did likewise. The Justice Department, acting on behalf of the Attorney General, however, declined their request. In a letter from Phillip T. White, Director of the Criminal Division of the Office of International Affairs of the Justice Department, to Anne M. Burke, attorney for Plaintiff Joseph Scalise, the Justice Department explained its decision:

This is in reply to your letter of August 29, 1986. The principal factors we took into consideration in making the decision not to request Mr. Scalise's transfer were: the relative seriousness of his offense; his extensive criminal record; the manner of his return to the United Kingdom; his "A" security classification in the United Kingdom, the highest security category; and the likelihood that a transfer would not further his rehabilitation.

Plaintiffs contend that the Attorney General has violated the Act and the Due Process Clause by failing to promulgate regulations and guidelines governing requests for transfer under the Convention, and by refusing to give them a hearing on their requests.

The Attorney General, in turn contends that the Act does not require him to promulgate regulations or guidelines, and that this decision in this case was well within the permissible discretion granted to him by the Act. The Attorney General also argues that the Convention and the Act create no legitimate expectations for American prisoners incarcerated abroad and, accordingly, that his refusal to provide plaintiffs a hearing on their request cannot violate the Due Process Clause.

What the Attorney General does not do, however, is to provide this court with any evidentiary material to oppose plaintiffs' summary judgment motion. The Attorney General states: that plaintiff mailed the stolen jewels to America before they were caught and that they would be a threat to their communities. Yet, he presents not a single shred of evidence to support these factual assertions. Such unsupported assertions are inadequate in a motion for summary judgment, and therefore will not be considered by this court in its resolution of the motion. . . .

Although the Attorney General asserts that plaintiff is not entitled to mandamus because the Act does not impose a duty on the Attorney General to promulgate regulations, the Attorney General does not argue that if such a duty exists, plaintiff lacks the right to enforce it. This court agrees with the Attorney General's implied concession that the Act gives plaintiff a private right to enforce the terms of both the Act and the Convention. . . .

In determining whether the Act imposes on the Attorney General "a plainly defined and peremptory duty" to promulgate regulations and guidelines for the transfer of prisoners, this court's only function is to give effect to Congress' intent.

Under existing treaties and this legislation, the Attorney General must agree to the receipt or transfer of an offender. The committee was concerned that the Attorney General exercise his discretion on this concern with care. In most cases and possibly almost all cases, he should agree to any receipt or transfer, if the offender requests or voluntarily consents to such transfer. However they [sic] may be an unusual situation, involving possibly a dangerous offender, where the Attorney General should not agree to the return of the offender, and his immediate eligibility for parole, to the United States. Similarly, there may be an unusual situation, involving an individual in American persons [sic], who for matters of future law enforcement, continuing investigation, or other national interests, should not be sent to his home country. The committee therefore expects the Attorney General to promptly establish regulations and to provide standards and guidelines which will govern the exercise of his consent to receive or transfer offenders. H. Rep. No. 95–720, 95th Cong., 1st Sess., reprinted in 1977 U.S. Code Cong. & Admin. News 3146, 3155.

The Attorney General's position – his interpretation of the statute he is "charged with enforcing" – that the Act permits him to deal with transfer requests on an ad hoc basis is thus totally unfounded. Congress clearly intended that the Attorney General would grant such requests in almost all cases, and would promulgate regulations and guidelines to deal with those "unusual situations" in which denial of such requests might be warranted. Furthermore, the Attorney General reproduced for this court a portion of the very position of the Act's legislative history which clarifies that, although he retains discretion as to the content of such regulations, he does not with respect to his duty to promulgate them. Thus, there can be no doubt that the Attorney General is aware of his duty and has consciously chosen not to fulfill it.

Accordingly, this court finds a plain and peremptory duty on the part of the Attorney General to promulgate regulations, a duty sufficiently clear to invoke this court's mandamus jurisdiction. . . .

Because the Attorney General acted without the guidance of regulations specifically required by the Act, his denial of plaintiffs' requests constitutes an abuse of discretion, and requires reversal, as a matter of law. . . .

At a minimum, however, the Attorney General should provide a prisoner whose request has been denied with both a specific explanation and elaboration of the grounds for his decision, and an opportunity to rebut them. . . .

In this case, the Attorney General responded to plaintiffs' requests with a single-paragraph letter. . . . This response leaves this court without a meaningful basis for reviewing his decision. . . .

Accordingly, this court orders the Attorney General to promulgate regulations pursuant to its authority under the Act within a reasonable time. This court further orders the Attorney General, after the establishment of these regulations, to determine the eligibility of plaintiffs for transfer to America, to inform the plaintiffs of his decision, and, if negative, to afford the plaintiffs an opportunity to respond to this decision either in writing or, if plaintiffs choose, through personal representatives in this country.

Notes and Questions

1. *Policy implications.* What is your take on the policy dimensions of the *Scalise* case? Is it proper for the United States, as a signatory country, to deny transfer in an effort to pressure offenders to bargain with authorities or surrender proceeds of crime or to punish them? For example, the government could persuade U.S. citizens imprisoned abroad to cooperate with local authorities by forcing them to choose between being

transferred back to the United States and forfeiting their appeal rights or remaining in a "substandard" foreign prison.[26]

2. *Families of offenders.* What, if any, role can the family of the offender play in trying to facilitate the transfer? Because of limitations imposed by the Privacy Act, 5 U.S.C. § 552a, the Department of Justice cannot provide information about individual prisoner transfer cases without a signed waiver of confidentiality from the prisoner. This law applies whether the inquiring party is the prisoner's member of Congress or family member. Occasionally, families can assist prisoners by assembling documents, such as birth certificates, passports, and medical records.

Prisoners who are applying for transfer may be represented by an attorney, but need not be. The overwhelming majority of applicants to the prisoner transfer program are not represented by an attorney.

Families may bring pertinent matters to the attention of the Department of Justice by writing to the International Prisoner Transfer Unit. Telephone calls should be limited to confirming that the letter has been received.

Letters may be addressed to

United States Department of Justice

10th & Constitution Avenue, N.W.

Criminal Division

Office of Enforcement Operations

International Prisoner Transfer Unit

John C. Keeney Building

Washington, D.C. 20530

To authorize the Department of Justice to discuss a case with an attorney, with family members, or with others, the prisoner needs to send the International Prisoner Transfer Unit a waiver. No particular form need be followed, though it should include the following information:

I (name of prisoner) do hereby authorize the United States Department of Justice to discuss my application for an international prisoner transfer with (name(s) of any authorized persons, along with telephone numbers and/or addresses for the authorized persons).

________ Signature

________ Date

F. *Challenges to Prisoner Transfers*

Pedro Rosado et al. v. Benjamin Civiletti, 621 F.2d 1179 (2d Cir. 1980)

Respondent U.S. sought review of the judgment entered in the U.S. District Court for the District of Connecticut which granted petitioner prisoners' petitions for writs of habeas corpus pursuant to 28 U.S.C. § 2231(b)(3) and 18 U.S.C. § 3244(4).

26 Abraham Abramovsky & Steven J. Engles, A *Critical Evaluation of the Mexican-American Transfer of Penal Sanctions Treaty*, 64 Iowa L. Rev. 275, 284 (1979).

In the case before us, petitioners are held in custody under federal authority. They have urged the district court to discharge its constitutional obligation to hear their claims and release them from custody. They have demonstrated that their convictions, under the laws of the sovereign state of Mexico, manifested a shocking insensitivity to their dignity as human beings and were obtained under a criminal process devoid of even a scintilla of rudimentary fairness and decency. Accordingly, we reaffirm the authority of the federal courts to hear due process claims raised, as they are here, by citizens held prisoner within the territorial jurisdiction of the United States. Nevertheless, we also recognize the laudable efforts of the executive and legislative branches, by both treaty and statute, to ameliorate, to their utmost power, the immense suffering of United States citizens held in Mexican jails. Indeed, because the statutory procedures governing transfers of these prisoners to United States custody are carefully structured to ensure that each of them voluntarily and intelligently agreed to forgo his right to challenge the validity of his Mexican conviction, and because we must not ignore the interests of those citizens still imprisoned abroad, we hold that the present petitioners are estopped from receiving the relief they now seek.

In 1978, Efran Caban, Raymond Velez, Pedro Rosado, and Felix Melendez filed petitions in the District of Connecticut seeking release from federal incarceration in the Danbury Correctional Facility. The petitioners, all United States citizens, had been arrested in Mexico in November 1975 for narcotics offenses. They were subsequently convicted and sentenced to nine years' imprisonment by the Mexican courts. (FN 1 omitted). In December 1977, the petitioners were transferred to United States custody pursuant to a treaty between the United States and Mexico providing for the execution of penal sentences imposed by the courts of one nation in the prisons of the other. (FN 2 omitted) Under the terms of the treaty, each transferring prisoner is required to consent to his transfer, and is permitted to contest the legality of any change of custody in the courts of the receiving nation. (FN 3 omitted). Thus, the petitioners in this case argued that their consents to transfer had been unlawfully coerced and that their continued detention by United States authorities based upon the convictions in Mexico violated their right to due process of law guaranteed by the Fifth Amendment. In support of federal jurisdiction, petitioners relied upon 18 U.S.C. § 3244, (FN 4 omitted) as well as various sections of Title 28, including 28 U.S.C. § 2241. (FN 5 omitted). To the extent that 18 U.S.C. § 3244(1) (FN 6 omitted) purports to reserve to Mexican courts exclusive jurisdiction over challenges to the petitioners' convictions or sentences, they claimed that the limitation suspends the privilege of the writ of habeas corpus in violation of Art. I, § 9, cl. 2 of the Constitution....

In substance, the petitioners' testimony establishes that Caban and Freddie DePalm, also a United States citizen, departed New York's Kennedy Airport on November 18, 1975, for a vacation in Acapulco, Mexico. At the airport, the two men had become acquainted with Velez and the three sat together and conversed during the flight to Mexico. When their Aero Mexico airliner made its first scheduled landing in Mexico City, the passengers were informed there would be a one hour delay before proceeding to Acapulco. During the layover, Caban, DePalm, and Velez decided to leave the airport terminal and go to a Holiday Inn nearby. While browsing in the hotel's gift shop, the Americans were approached by six Mexicans in civilian dress, guns drawn, who stated that the Americans were under arrest. No arrest warrants were produced, nor did the Mexicans identify themselves as police officials. Nonetheless, Caban, DePalm, and Velez were each handcuffed and taken to an isolated area of the airport terminal.

In the terminal, Caban watched his captors drag Velez into a room, then heard Velez cry out in pain for close to an hour. Caban himself was taken into a separate room where he was searched, stripped and his legs bound. A watch, jewelry, and $400 in cash were taken from his person, but no drugs or contraband were found in his possession. Caban was then shown a photograph of a man represented to be Ramon Rodriguez and asked whether he knew him. When he denied any knowledge of Rodriguez, water was poured over his naked body and an electric cattle prod applied, first to his mouth, then to his testicles and buttocks. His persistent denial of any acquaintance with the man in the photograph led to repeated torture with the electric prod. Thereafter, Caban's interrogators suspended him from the ceiling by clamping a handcuff to his wrist and attaching it to a hook, causing him to lose consciousness from time to time. He remained in this position throughout the day while his captors continued to beat him, threatening to kill him if he refused to admit an acquaintance with Rodriguez. By the end of the day, the weight of Caban's suspended body against the handcuff caused a bone in his arm to break and tear through his wrist.

That night, Caban, DePalm, and Velez were taken to Los Separos detention center in Mexico City. Caban noticed that Velez was swollen and bruised, and that he was unable to walk unassisted. At Los Separos, the men were placed in small separate cells containing cement slabs for beds and no plumbing. They were held incommunicado for eight days. The food was inedible and the entire cellblock reeked of human excrement. Throughout their stay at Los Separos, interrogators continued to beat and torture the men with an electric prod in any attempt to elicit confessions (FN 11 omitted).

Two days after Caban's arrest in Mexico City, Rosado was arrested in Acapulco upon his arrival on a flight from New York. Though unemployed, Rosado had planned to take a two-day vacation in Acapulco. After passing through customs at the airport, he was confronted by five plainclothes Mexicans bearing pistols and a submachine gun, who asked him to accompany them to a room in the airport. In the room Rosado saw Melendez, who also had been detained upon his arrival in Acapulco. Rosado was held in the room for two hours while his luggage and personal effects were searched. His ticket, visa, jewelry, and $900 in cash were seized, and he was then driven to a nearby police station along with Melendez.

The following morning, the two Americans were flown to Mexico City along with several other prisoners arrested that day and, like Caban, DePalm, and Velez, ended their journeys at Los Separos. When they arrived, Rosado saw the badly beaten body of a man he later learned to be Caban. Melendez was taken into an interrogation room, and Rosado listened from an adjacent holding area as Melendez screamed in apparent agony. After Melendez was returned to the holding area, Rosado was asked by one Mexican officer whether he was ready to tell the truth. When Rosado's responses failed to satisfy his inquistor, his hands were handcuffed behind his back, his pants lowered, and an electric prod was applied for several minutes at a time to his testicles and penis. Rosado then watched as Melendez was similarly questioned, with the interrogators alternating between beatings and electric torture.

After seven or eight days of unceasing brutality, each of the prisoners was finally taken to the prosecutor's office at Los Separos. Caban was told to sign a statement acknowledging his acquaintance with Rodriguez, but refused. Instead, he signed a paper disclaiming any knowledge of Rodriguez or his activities. Rosado was given a statement confessing participation in a gang seeking to import cocaine into Mexico, but he too refused to sign, stating that his sole purpose in coming to Mexico was for a vacation. At no time during the prisoners' initial detention and interrogation were they apprised of the charges against them, or permitted to consult with counsel.

Following their visits to the prosecutor, Caban, DePalm, Velez, Rosado, and Melendez were all transferred to Lecumberri Prison, the so-called "Black Castle," where they were crowded into tiny, unheated cells with only two or three beds for ten or twelve prisoners. . . .

Shortly after their transfer to Lecumberri, the prisoners were brought to los hugados, a courtroom within the prison. There, they were crowded into a small pen separated from the courtroom by a chain link fence. A judge's law secretary briefly informed the men they had been charged with illegal importation of cocaine, and then sent them back to their cells. Approximately one month later, the prisoners returned to los hugados and were formally advised by the law secretary that they had been indicted for illegal importation of cocaine. The men were shown copies of the statements that had previously been read to them by the prosecutor at Los Separos, and asked whether they were true. Both Caban and Rosado disclaimed the reports, insisting that they were false. The law secretary offered to help the prisoners for a fee but was told that they did not have enough money. The entire proceeding lasted no longer than ten minutes.

Two weeks after this "arraignment," the prisoners were brought back to los hugados, ostensibly for a correo constitutional, that is, an opportunity to confront the witnesses against them. Inside the courtroom, Caban saw the officers who had detained and questioned him at the Mexico City Airport, but none of the officers who had arrested Rosado in Acapulco was present. Once again, the law secretary presided over the proceeding, asking each officer whether he ratified his earlier statement against the defendants. At no time were the prisoners permitted to cross-examine the arresting officers, to read the officers' statements, or to speak to the charges against them. The entire proceeding was over in less than fifteen minutes.

Seven months later, on August 10, 1976, the men returned to los hugados and were informed by the law secretary that a judge had considered their cases and had sentenced each man to nine years' imprisonment. At no time did they see the judge who sentenced them, obtain the assistance of counsel, or confront the witnesses against them. . . .

After the prisoners expressed an interest in transferring to United States custody, an attorney from the Federal Public Defender's Office in Texas met with each individually and explained in detail the consequences of a transfer under the Treaty. On December 5, 1977, the men appeared separately before a United States magistrate at the prison to verify their consents to transfer. (FN 29 omitted). The magistrate questioned each petitioner about his knowledge of the Treaty's provisions, specifically asking each man whether he understood and agreed to abide by the condition requiring challenges to his conviction or sentence to be brought by proceedings instituted in Mexican courts. Each was advised that if a United States court subsequently determined his consent to transfer had not been given in accordance with the Treaty or United States law, he could be returned to Mexico to serve the remainder of his sentence. In each case, once the magistrate satisfied himself that the applicant's consent to transfer was given knowingly and voluntarily, without threat or coercion, he permitted the petitioner to sign a standard form of consent. . . .

Of paramount importance, however, is the interest of those Americans currently incarcerated in Mexico. Whatever hope the Treaty extends of escaping the harsh realities of confinement abroad will be dashed for Americans (FN 45 omitted) if we permit these three petitioners to rescind their agreement to limit their attacks upon their convictions to Mexico's courts. We refused to scuttle the one certain opportunity open to Americans incarcerated abroad to return home, an opportunity, we note, the benefit of which Caban, Velez, and Rosado have already received. In holding these petitioners to their bargain, we by no means condone the shockingly brutal treatment to which they fell prey. Rather, we hold open the door for others similarly victimized to escape their torment.

The judgment of the district court is reversed.

Notes and Questions

1. Another case similar to *Rosado* is *Pfeifer v. U.S. Bureau of Prisoners*, 615 F.2d 873 (9th Cir. 1980) (affirming the district court's holding that the U.S. Constitution has no relation to the validity of Pfeifer's foreign conviction for a foreign crime; that U.S. petitioner's consent to transfer constituted a waiver of, or at least an agreement not to assert, any constitutional right the offender might have regarding his or her conviction; and that the consent was obtained in a manner that met the constitutional tests for a valid waiver). *See also in accord, Mitchell v. United States*, 483 F. Supp. 291 (E.D. Wis. 1980).

G. *Posttransfer Issues*

Litigation on behalf of U.S. citizens is generally filed posttransfer, because U.S. courts will not have jurisdiction to consider an individual case before the defendant has returned to U.S. soil. 18 U.S.C. § 4104(a) provides that "an offender serving a sentence of imprisonment in a foreign country transferred to the custody of the Attorney General shall remain in the custody of the Attorney General under the same conditions and for the same period of time as an offender who had been committed to the custody of the Attorney General by a court of the U.S. for the period of time imposed by the sentencing court."

The transferred prisoners must be given credit for all the time served in the sentencing state,[27] including credit for good time, labor, or any other credit.[28] The implementing law makes all issues concerning probation and parole subject to U.S. jurisdiction pursuant to 18 U.S.C. § 4203.[29] Although offenders may have been ineligible for parole in the foreign country, their arrival in the United States makes them immediately eligible for parole under section 4106(c). This affords transferees greater benefits than persons convicted under U.S. law. 18 U.S.C. §§ 4104(c) and 4106(b) provides that transferred probationers and parolees will be treated as if their conviction had been rendered by a U.S. court, but presumably without the benefit of collateral attacks upon the conviction.[30]

V. Future Trends

The adoption and implementation of multilateral prisoner transfer conventions such as the Council of Europe and OAS Conventions and the UN Model Agreement on the Transfer of Prisoners demonstrate an increasing awareness that the social rehabilitation of offenders who have committed a crime in a foreign country is best served by early repatriation to their home country. Because proceedings in the sentencing state often delay repatriation of offenders, states and international organizations have discussed the

27 18 U.S.C. § 4105(b).

28 18 U.S.C. § 4105(c)(1).

29 18 U.S.C. § 4106.

30 M.C. Bassiouni & Grace M.W. Gallagher, *Transfer of Prisoners: Policies and Practices of the United States, in*, II International Criminal Law: Procedural and Enforcement Mechanisms 535–36 (M.C. Bassiouni ed., 1999).

possibility of transferring the criminal proceedings together with the alleged offender being held in pretrial custody. Council of Europe members have already developed such rules.[31] However, concerns over the competence of foreign courts to try domestic criminal offenses and over appropriate evidentiary requirements remain.

Transfer of prisoners principles are not unified in much of the world in which economic integration is not far advanced. Nevertheless, globalization, increasing transborder criminalization, and growing international criminal cooperation all place pressure on the unification of transfer of prisoners principles.

The appropriate and increasing use of prisoner transfer treaties will also depend on their interaction with other related international enforcement mechanisms, especially, in addition to mutual assistance in criminal matters and extradition treaties, in recognition and execution of foreign and international penal sanctions and transfer of proceedings.[32]

VI. *Additional Reading*

A. *Books*

Michael Abbell, International Prisoner Transfer (Dec. 2004).

Michal Plachta, Transfer of Prisoners under International Instruments and Domestic Legislation (1993).

B. *Articles and Book Chapters*

Abraham Abramovsky, *A Critical Evaluation of the American Transfer of Penal Sanctions Policy*, 61 Wis. L. Rev. 25 (1980).

Abraham Abramovsky & Stephen Engels, *A Critical Evaluation of the Mexican-American Transfer of Penal Sanctions Treaty*, 64 Iowa L. Rev. 275 (1979).

Mohamed Abdul-Aziz, *International Perspective on Transfer of Prisoners and Execution of Foreign Penal Judgements*, *in* II International Criminal Law: Multilateral and Bilateral Enforcement Mechanisms 529 (M. C. Bassiouni ed., 2009).

Hans-Jürgen Bartsch, *Council of Europe-Legal Cooperation in 1982, Repatriation of Foreign Prisoners*, Y.B. Eur. L. 306 (1982).

M. C. Bassiouni, *Perspectives on the Transfer of Prisoners between the United States and Mexico and the United States and Canada*, 11 Vand. J. Transnat'l L. 249 (1978).

M. Cherif Bassiouni & Grace M. W. Gallagher, *Transfer of Prisoners: Policies and Practices of the United States*, *in* II International Criminal Law: Procedural and Enforcement Mechanisms 505 (M. C. Bassiouni ed., 1999).

William V. Dunlap, *Dual Criminality in Penal Transfer Treaties*, 29 Va. J. Int'l L. 813 (1989).

Ronald M. Emanuel, *Intervention of Constitutional Powers: The Prisoner Transfer Treaties*, 1 Fla. J. Int'l L. 203–225 (1986).

Helmutt Epp, *The European Convention*, *in* II International Criminal Law: Procedural and Enforcement Mechanisms 563 (M. C. Bassiouni ed., 2d ed. 1999).

Note, *American Prisoners in Foreign Prisons: The Prisoner Transfer Treaties*, 2 Dick. J. Int'l L. 331, 337 (1984).

Note, *Constitutional Problems in the Execution of Foreign Penal Sentences: The Mexican-American Prisoner Transfer Treaties*, 90 Harv. L. Rev. 1500 (1977).

[31] *See, e.g.*, the European Convention on the Transfer of Criminal Proceedings of 1970, Europe. T.S. No. 70, by which a request to prosecute establishes a jurisdiction of the requested state.

[32] For a discussion of materials concerning transfer of prisoners together with mutual assistance in criminal matters, transfer of proceedings, and recognition and execution of foreign and international penal sanctions, *see* International Criminal Law Cases and Materials (Jordan J. Paust et al. eds., Chapter 6, 2d ed. 2000).

Note, *Prisoner Transfer Treaties: Need for the Elimination or Modification of the Retention Provision*, 13 CAL. W. INT'L. L.J. 321 (1983).

Note, *Rosado V. Civiletti*, 8 SYRACUSE J. INT'L L. & COM. 186 (1980).

Note, *Voluntary and Intelligent Consent to Transfer under Prisoner Exchange Treaty Estops Habeas Corpus Relief*, 54 TEMP. L.Q. 357 (1981).

Jordan Paust, *The Unconstitutional Detention of Prisoners by the United States under the Exchange of Prisoners Treaty, in* INTERNATIONAL ASPECTS OF CRIMINAL LAW: ENFORCING UNITED STATES LAW IN THE WORLD COMMUNITY 204 (Richard B. Lillich ed. 1981).

Robert L. Pisani & Theodore Simon, *The United States Treaties on Transfer of Prisoners: A Survey* 17 PAC. L.J. 823–862 (1986).

Ira P. Robbins, A *Constitutional Analysis of the Prohibition against Collateral Attack in the Mexican–American Prisoner Exchange Treaty*, 26 UCLA L. REV. 1 (1978).

T. M. Schaffer, *Justice with Mercy: The Treaties with Canada and Mexico for the Execution of Penal Judgments*, 4 BROOK. J. INT'L L. 246 (1978).

Irwin P. Stotzky & Alan C. Swan, *Due Process Methodology and Prisoner Exchange Treaties: Confronting an Uncertain Calculus*, 62 MINN. L. REV. 732 (1978).

Detlev Vagts, A *Reply to "A Critical Evaluation of the Mexican-American Transfer of Penal Sanctions Treaty,"* 64 IOWA L. REV. 325 (1979).

Sharon Williams, *Consular Access to Detained Persons*, 29 INT'L & COMP. L.Q. 239, 249 (1980).

Bruce Zagaris & Maureen T. Walsh, *The United States-Mexico Treaty on the Execution of Penal Sanctions: The Case for Reevaluating the Treaty and Its Policies in View of NAFTA and Other Developments*, 2 SW J. L. & TRADE AM. 385–450 1995).

C. Source Material

U.S. Dept. of Justice, office of Enforcement Operating, Guidelines for Evaluating Applications for Transfer (http://www.usdoj.gov/criminal/oeo/links/intlprisoner/guidelines.html).

U.S. Dept. of Justice, office of Enforcement Operating, Prisoner Transfer Information for Americans Incarcerated Abroad (http:www.usdoj.gov/criminal/oeo/docs/americans.arrested.pdf).

U.S. Dept. of Justice, Transfer of State Prisoners (has the state statute and state contact person for prisoner transfers) (www.usdoj.gov/criminal/oeo/links/intlprisoner/transfer/html).

U.S. Dept. of Justice, List of Participating Countries in U.S. International Prisoner Transfer Program (http://www.doj.gov/criminal/oeo/links/intlprisoner/lists.html).

11 The United Nations

I. The United Nations

A. *Making and Implementing Treaties*

The United Nations has fundamentally changed the classic mode of international law-making by reshaping the negotiation and conclusion of treaties. International conventions no longer limit membership to state parties; they have grown to include international organizations such as the European Union. In the context of international white collar crime, the UN's changes to modern, multilateral treaty making encompass many aspects of transnational crime.[1] In a given year, the UN holds approximately 3,500 meetings and to date has participated in the conclusion of hundreds of multilateral agreements.[2]

Specific provisions of the UN Charter, as well as those governing the work of its specialized agencies, address the conclusion and approval of multilateral legal instruments. For example, Article 92(3) of the UN Charter provides that United Nations Economic and Social Council (ECOSOC) may "prepare draft conventions for submission to the General Assembly, with respect to matters falling within its competence."[3] Today, the UN

[1] José E. Alvarez, International Organizations as Law-makers 273 (2005).

[2] *Id.*, citing Roy Lee, "Multilateral Treaty-making and Negotiation Techniques: An Appraisal," *in* Contemporary Problems of International Law: Essays in Honour of Georg Schwarzenberger on his 80th Birthday 157 (Bin Cheng & Edward D. Brown eds., Stevens & Sons, 1998).

[3] Alvarez, *supra* note 1 at 275.

addresses a diverse range of subjects based on the needs of a variety of sponsoring international organizations.[4] It has helped facilitate the negotiation and implementation of significant multilateral treaties dealing with the prevention, investigation, and prosecution of transnational white collar crime.

During the past century the scope of treaties has grown to include conflict prevention and peacekeeping and to codify a broad array of transnational criminal issues. Increasingly, as we see in later chapters, the number of participants has also increased. The UN provides an appropriate forum and host for the discussion of strategies to prevent and combat transnational crime, including treaty making. In addition, the work has spawned the establishment of specialized UN agencies, such as the UN Crime Prevention and Criminal Justice Program and the UN Office on Drugs and Crime, both based in Vienna.[5]

The UN increasingly serves as a forum for the negotiation of treaties against illicit trade. As mentioned in the chapter on transnational organized crime, the 1998 UN Convention against Illicit Traffic in Narcotic Drugs and Psychotropic Substances, which took effect in 2000, provided precedents for a number of actions and concepts that subsequent treaties against transnational crime would emulate. In particular, the convention requires signatory countries to criminalize various drug trafficking crimes, including money laundering, and to adopt detailed laws with respect to the instrumentalities and proceeds of crime, including tracing, freezing, confiscating, and forfeiting such instrumentalities and proceeds. It also includes value forfeiture, so that, if the instrumentalities and proceeds are no longer available, the signatory country can forfeit substitute assets of the same value. The convention requires signatory countries to consider negotiating regional and bilateral conventions so they can cooperate even more closely. It has a number of articles devoted to signatory countries' obligations to offer mutual assistance to other signatories, including in criminal matters, extradition, and exchange of information.

The UN Vienna Counterdrug Convention of 1988 served as a model for both the UN Convention against Transnational Organized Crime (TOC) elaborated in Palermo, Sicily, in December 2000, and the UN Convention against Transnational Corruption. The UN Convention against TOC emulates the UN Vienna Counterdrug Convention in that it establishes definitions of organized criminal groups and requires signatories to criminalize the conduct proscribed by it, including participation in an organized crime group, corruption, money laundering, and obstruction of justice. It has three separate protocols: one on the smuggling of migrants, a second on trafficking in persons, and a third on small arms trafficking. By 2004, ninety-four countries had ratified the Palermo Convention, whereas sixty-four and seventy-six had ratified the migrant smuggling and human trafficking protocols, respectively. Seventy-nine countries are members of the small areas trafficking protocol.

As mentioned in Chapter 4 on transnational corruption, the UN Convention against Transnational Corruption (UNCAC), elaborated in October 2003, emulates and builds on both the UN Vienna Counterdrug Convention and the Palermo Conventions. It requires signatory countries to criminalize conduct proscribed by it, namely transnational corruption and related offenses. Like the two other UN conventions, it makes money

[4] *Id.* at 277.

[5] Moisés Naím, Illicit: How Smugglers, Traffickers, and Copycats Are Hijacking the Global Economy 186 (2005).

laundering a crime and requires forfeiture. It also requires a wide array of private sector due diligence measures.

These UN conventions establish norms and definitions and hence the basis for moral authority, diplomatic pressure, advocacy, and public awareness.[6] They also codify international criminal law. For example, by the time the third UN convention – UNCAC – required the overriding of financial secrecy in order to engage in international cooperation, to criminalize money laundering, and to provide for asset forfeiture, these standards had become codified.

How can the UN ensure effective implementation of its conventions, given the large number of signatories, their diverse legal and cultural composition, and their varying degrees of resources and political commitment? The resource differential among states and between states and other actors, including criminals, means that without technical and financial assistance small states may struggle to compete with the very criminals – especially transnational organized crime syndicates – that the conventions are designed to control. In small, weak, and failed states, illicit trading networks and other criminals can influence key government agencies – customs, courts, banks, and ports. They can recruit or influence journalists, politicians, and business leaders. They can infiltrate and start legitimate businesses, such as radio and television stations and newspapers.[7] They can afford to contribute significantly to all political parties, so that the winners will be indebted to them. Therefore, the UN tries to foster effective implementation through facilitating technical and financial assistance to the small, developing states and designing and constructing effective regimes. The conventions create bodies to monitor implementation and consider periodic revisions in the treaties. The UN conventions also provide increasingly for implementation by regional organizations and civil society.

UN treaty efforts to address the trade in small arms have faced particular controversy. When international and domestic conflicts threaten peace and security, as in the former Yugoslavia, Rwanda, and Sierra Leone, the UN has resorted to Security Council resolutions and economic sanctions. In July 2001, it held a Conference on the Illicit Trade in Small Arms and Light Weapons in All Its Aspects, hoping to establish a minimal regulatory framework for the small arms trade. Although nongovernmental organizations and some governments spent months preparing for the meeting, the conference failed. Undersecretary of State John Bolton (later the U.S. ambassador to the UN) railed against documents that he said would violate the United States' "constitutional right to keep and bear arms." The U.S. government categorically rejected proposals concerning sales to nonstate actors, again citing violations of the U.S. Constitution. Wayne La Pierre, the president of the U.S. National Rifle Association, accused the conference of trying to override a sovereign country's freedom by imposing a global standard.[8] The U.S. opposition to addressing illicit trade in small arms reflects the effective lobbying of the U.S. gun industry. The continuing U.S. government opposition exemplifies that business sectors can be stakeholders in transnational criminal regimes. As a result, they can play important roles in blocking or helping implement international enforcement regimes.

As discussed in Chapters 8 and 9 on evidence gathering and extradition, the UN, through the UN Crime Prevention and Criminal Justice Program (CPCJP), has

[6] *Id.* at 186–87.
[7] *Id.* at 27.
[8] *Id.* at 64.

developed model conventions on mutual assistance in criminal matters and extradition. The CPCJP also regularly provides technical and financial assistance to countries interested in strengthening their criminal justice and international criminal cooperation systems. In this way it helps promote the main principles of international criminal cooperation and criminal justice, just as the Security Council does when it wields its power.[9] Because of the importance of mutual assistance, the CPCJP has ensured that comprehensive mutual assistance provisions are included in the UN conventions on transnational crime, including the UN Vienna Counterdrug Convention, the Palermo Convention, and the UN Convention against Transnational Corruption. In addition, the CPCJP compiles data on mutual assistance, trying to determine the inefficiencies in applying mutual assistance provisions and ways to overcome the same.

B. *The Security Council as a Source of Authority on Transnational White Collar Crime*

Since 1989, the UN Security Council has adopted fifty to ninety resolutions each year.[10] These resolutions sometimes amend, de facto, the UN Charter and provide general legislative guidance.[11] In particular, in the aftermath of the Cold War and the subsequent decline in the use of the veto by the five permanent Security Council members, the Council's lawmaking potential has become stronger.[12] Recourse to Security Council practice also provides guidance on the law,[13] especially with respect to the rules governing the use of force and threats to peace and security such as conflict diamonds, transnational organized crime, and transnational white collar crime.

The Security Council generally addresses threats and breaches of the peace that do not require that a targeted state has violated either Article 2(4), customary rules concerning the use of force, or even international law.[14] The Council's normative authority is based on its coercive powers and its legitimacy, at least compared to more self-interested actors such as the states using force or reacting to it. Much of the Council's lawmaking is based on the perception in the international community that it is authorized to act and is "the principal institution for building, consolidating, and using the authority of the international community . . . the linch-pin of order and stability, the framework within which members of the international system negotiate agreements on the rules of behavior and the legal norms of proper conduct to preserve the society of states."[15]

When it adopts resolutions, the Security Council uses its legitimating authority in several different ways.[16] Some resolutions declare that certain conduct, such as human trafficking or the use of conflict diamonds to purchase weapons, is illegal. In this context,

[9] Alvarez, *supra* note 1 at 189, citing Steve B. Ratner, *The Security Council and International Law*, *in* THE UN SECURITY COUNCIL 593 (David Malone ed., 2004).

[10] Alvarez, *supra* note 1 at 184, fn. 2, citing Peter Wallensteen & Patrik Johansson, *Security Council Decisions in Perspective*, *in* THE UN SECURITY COUNCIL 17, 18 (David M. Malone ed., 2004).

[11] Alvarez, *supra* note 1 at 185.

[12] *Id.* at 186.

[13] *Id.* at 186–87.

[14] *Id.* citing Roslyn Higgins, THE DEVELOPMENT OF INTERNATIONAL LAW THROUGH THE POLITICAL ORGANS OF THE UNITED NATIONS 204 (1963).

[15] Gareth Evans and Mahomed Shanoun, "The Responsibility to Protect," 81 FOREIGN AFFAIRS 99, at 106 (Nov/Dec 2002).

[16] Alvarez, *supra* note 1 at 189, citing Steve B. Ratner, *The Security Council and International Law*, in David Malone, *supra* note 9 at 593.

a resolution may provide legal guidance, especially with respect to measures to prevent criminal conduct – economic sanctions, embargoes, and even the use of force. A resolution may promote positive action to prevent transnational crime, calling for the adoption of laws, asset freezing, and international technical assistance to weak and small states. A resolution may enforce compliance by calling for economic sanctions, the use of force, negotiation among warring actors, the establishment of inquiries and formal criminal investigations, and ultimately the establishment of criminal ad hoc courts such as the tribunals for the former Yugoslavia and Cambodia. Although these measures generally focus on a ceasefire or peace agreement, they often compel authorities to investigate and prosecute the crimes that facilitate conflicts, such as arms, human, and drug trafficking or the use of child soldiers. In many cases, the crimes are intertwined with the conflict and cannot be easily separated.

The Security Council's adoption of two counterterrorism resolutions, Resolutions 1373 and 1267, presents a good example of de facto legislating that Professor José Alvarez calls global hegemonic international law. As a result of these resolutions, UN members must take broad action to bring their private sectors into compliance with expansive due diligence requirements. The resolutions also establish an oversight body, the Counterterrorism Committee (CTC), to ensure proper implementation of the counterterrorism enforcement requirements.[17] According to critics of the UN, the CTC and 1267 sanctions committee staff are not selected on the basis of diversity or expertise in international law. Instead, critics argue that the committees serve to export – and impose – U.S. counterterrorism laws around the world.[18]

Because states must report directly to the Security Council, it retains executive control over implementation of the resolutions. This situation facilitates adoption of incentives and punishments for states that fail to comply with the resolutions and gives the Council significant enforcement power. Similarly, the reporting schemes and the supervision enable the Council to directly control implementation.[19] In effect, according to critics, the Council imposes obligations on UN member states that cannot withdraw from the underlying treaty regime that serves as the basis for the Council's power.

As a result of the lack of transparency in the work of the 1267 committee and the absence of appeal rights, its work has had the appearance of hegemonic patron–client action. No one knows how the committee makes its determinations, including the relevant standard of proof. Further, the fact that the work of the 1267 committee and the Security Council is not subject to relevant human rights standards allows the Council to refute arguments that its functions violate international human rights law.[20]

Sir Jeremy Greenstock, the U.K. permanent representative at the UN and the first chairman of the CTC, underscored the importance of implementing counterterrorism measures. Resolution 1373 built on provisions found in the twelve UN conventions against terrorism and also contained strong operational messages for UN members to

[17] Alvarez, *supra* note 1 at 200–02.

[18] *Id. See also* Serge Schmemann, *United Nations to Get a U.S. Anti-terror Guide*, N.Y. TIMES, Dec. 19, 2001 available at http://www.globalpolicy.org/unitedstates/unpolicy/gen2001/1219guide.htm (discussing that the report by the United States under 1373 to the Security Council and describing the broad range of action taken under the USA PATRIOT ACT was intended as a model for other countries. Through the American Bar Association, the U.S. government recruited lawyers to provide technical assistance to other countries in the adoption of counterterrorism enforcement laws.

[19] *Id.* at 203–4.

[20] *Id.* at 205–6.

quickly develop effective measures.[21] In this regard, Nicholas Rostow, General Counsel to the U.S. Mission to the UN and an active participant in the CTC, confirmed that the committee used independent experts to assess member state reports.[22]

Professor John Murphy has suggested that the CTC should request more detailed information concerning the apprehension, rendition, prosecution, and punishment of persons who commit crimes covered by the twelve UN counterterrorism conventions. Alternatively, the UN Terrorism Prevention Branch, which is part of the Centre for International Crime Prevention in Vienna, could be assigned the job of collecting such information with respect to some of the counterterrorism conventions.[23] Ambassador Greenstock has suggested that the Centre for International Crime Prevention might also provide "model law and guidance on implementation" for the other eleven counterterrorism conventions.[24] Both the counterterrorism resolutions and the UN Convention on Terrorist Financing have many prevention policy provisions, requiring state signatories to impose due diligence obligations on the private sector. Violations of such due diligence obligations often constitute crimes or at least administrative penal infractions.

C. *The UN General Assembly as a Source of International Law*

As the only universal organization with very broad authority, the General Assembly, when it adopts resolutions, can be a source of customary international law. Such law arises when there exists (1) consistent practice by various states with regard to a situation within the domain of international relations, (2) continuation of that practice over a considerable period of time, (3) that practice is required by or is consistent with law, and (4) general acquiescence in the practice by other states.[25] General Assembly (GA) resolutions can help facilitate the development of customary international law: a custom may be thought unintentional, unconscious, disorderly, uncertain, or uneven.[26]

The General Assembly offers states a transparent, accessible forum in which to debate, and scholars a reference source of customary international law.[27]

D. *The UN as a Proponent of International Criminal Cooperation and Criminal Justice Solutions*

The UN helps the international community conceptualize emerging threats to global security and develop appropriate responses. For example, the UN Secretary-General's

[21] John F. Murphy, The United States and the Rule of Law in International Affairs 308 (2004), citing the presentation by Ambassador Greenstock at the Symposium: Combating International Terrorism: The Contribution of the United Nations, held in Vienna on 3–4 June 2002, at http://www.un./orgs/docs/sc/committees/1373/viennanotes.htm.

[22] *Id.* at 308, citing Nicholas Rostow, *Before and After: The Changed UN Response to Terrorism since September 11*, 35 Cornell Int'l L.J. 475, 483 (2002).

[23] Murphy, *supra* note 20 at 309.

[24] *Id.* at 322, fn. 73, citing Ambassador Greenstock's presentation at the Symposium: Combating International Terrorism: The Contribution of the United Nations, held in Vienna on 3–4 June 2002.

[25] Alvarez, *supra* note 1 at 259, citing Frederic C. Kirgis, *Custom on a Sliding Scale*, 81 Am. J. Int'l L. 146, 1t 146 (1987).

[26] *Id.*, citing *Comments by E. Jimenez de Arechaga, in* Change and Stability in International Law-Making 1 (Antonio Cassese & Joseph H.H. Weiler, eds., Walter de Gruyter, 1988).

[27] *Id.* at 260.

High-Level Report on Threats, Challenges, and Change addresses emerging criminal threats in the context of globalization.

UN Secretary-General's High-Level Report on Threats, Challenges, and Change

UNITED NATIONS (2004) (UNITED NATIONS FOUNDATION PRESS) (www.un.org/secureworld)

A More Secure World – Synopsis

Toward a New Security Consensus

The United Nations was created in 1945 above all else "to save succeeding generations from the scourge of war" – to ensure that the horrors of the World Wars were never repeated. Sixty years later, we know all too well that the biggest security threats we face now, and in the decades ahead, go far beyond States waging aggressive war. They extend to poverty, infectious disease and environmental degradation; war and violence within States; the spread and possible use of nuclear, radiological, chemical and biological weapons; terrorism; and transnational organized crime. The threats are from non-State actors as well as States, and to human security as well as State security.

The preoccupation of the United Nations founders was with State security. When they spoke of creating a new system of collective security they meant it in the traditional military sense: a system in which States join together and pledge that aggression against one is aggression against all, and commit themselves in that event to react collectively. But they also understood well, long before the idea of human security gained currency, the indivisibility of security, economic development and human freedom. In the opening words of the Charter, the United Nations was created "to reaffirm faith in fundamental human rights" and "to promote social progress and better standards of life in larger freedom."

The central challenge for the twenty-first century is to fashion a new and broader understanding, bringing together all these strands, of what collective security means – and of all the responsibilities, commitments, strategies and institutions that come with it if a collective security system is to be effective, efficient and equitable.

If there is to be a new security consensus, it must start with the understanding that the front-line actors in dealing with all the threats we face, new and old, continue to be individual sovereign States, whose role and responsibilities, and right to be respected, are fully recognized in the Charter of the United Nations. But in the twenty-first century, more than ever before, no State can stand wholly alone. Collective strategies, collective institutions and a sense of collective responsibility are indispensable.

The case for collective security today rests on three basic pillars. Today's threats recognize no national boundaries, are connected, and must be addressed at the global and regional as well as the national levels. No State, no matter how powerful, can by its own efforts alone make itself invulnerable in today's threats. And it cannot be assumed that every State will always be able, or willing, to meet its responsibility to protect its own peoples and not to harm its neighbors.

We must not underestimate the difficulty of teaching a new consensus about the meaning and responsibilities of collective security. Many will regard one or more of the threats we identify as not really being a threat to international peace and security. Some believe that HIV/AIDS is a horrible disease, but not a security threat. Or that terrorism is a threat to some States, but not all. Or that civil wars in Africa are a humanitarian tragedy, but surely not a problem for international security. Or that poverty is a problem of development, not security.

Differences of power, wealth and geography do determine what we perceive as the gravest threats to our survival and well-being. Differences of focus lead us to dismiss what others perceive as the gravest of all threats to their survival. Inequitable responses to threats further fuel division. Many people believe that what passes for collective security today is simply a system for protecting the rich and powerful. Such perceptions pose a fundamental challenge to building collective security today. Stated baldly, without mutual recognition of threats there can be no collective security. Self-help will rule, mistrust will predominate and cooperation for long-term mutual gain will elude us.

What is needed today is nothing less than a new consensus between alliances that are frayed, between wealthy nations and poor, and among peoples mired in mistrust across an apparently widening cultural abyss. The essence of that consensus is simple: we all share responsibility for each other's security. And the test of that consensus will be action.

Collective Security and the Challenge of Prevention

Any event or process that leads to large-scale death or lessening of life chances and undermines State as the basic unit of the international system is a threat to international security. So defined, there are six clusters of threats with which the world must be concerned now and in the decades ahead:

- Economic and social threats, including poverty, infectious disease and environmental degradation
- Inter-State conflict
- Internal conflict, including civil war, genocide and other large-scale atrocities
- Nuclear, radiological, chemical and biological weapons
- Terrorism
- Transnational organized crime

In its first 60 years, the United Nations has made crucial contributions to reducing or mitigating these threats to international security. While there have been major failures and shortcomings, the record of successes and contributions is underappreciated. This gives hope that the Organization can adapt to successfully confront the new challenges of the twenty-first century.

The primary challenge for the United Nations and its members is to ensure that, of all the threats in the categories listed, those that are distinct do not become imminent and those that are imminent do not actually become destructive. This requires a framework for preventive action which addresses all these threats in all the ways they resonate most in different parts of the world. Most of all, it will require leadership at the domestic and international levels to act early, decisively and collectively against all these threats – from HIV/AIDS to nuclear terrorism – before they have their most devastating effect.

In describing how to meet the challenge of prevention, we begin with development because it is the indispensable foundation for a collective security system that takes prevention seriously. It serves multiple functions. It helps combat the poverty, infectious disease and environmental degradation that kill millions and threaten human security. It is vital in helping States prevent or reverse the erosion of State capacity, which is crucial for meeting almost every class of threat. And it is part of a long-term strategy for preventing civil war and for addressing the environments in which both terrorism and organized crime flourish.

Collective Security and the Use of Force

What happens if peaceful prevention fails? If none of the preventive measures so far described stop the descent into war and chaos? If distant threats do become imminent? Or if imminent threats become actual? Or if a non-imminent threat nonetheless becomes very real and measures short of the use of military force seem powerless to stop it?

We address here the circumstances in which effective collective security may require the backing of military force, starting with the rules of international law that must govern any decision to go to war if anarchy is not to prevail. It is necessary to distinguish between situations in which a State claims to act in self-defence; situations in which a State is posing a threat to others outside its borders; and situations in which the threat is primarily internal and the issue is the responsibility to protect a State's own people. In all cases, we believe that the Charter of the United Nations, properly understood and applied, is equal to the tasks. Article 51 needs neither extension nor restriction of its long-understood scope, and Chapter VII fully empowers the Security Council to deal with every kind of threat that States may confront. The task is not to find alternatives to the Security Council as a source of authority but to make it work better than it has.

That force *can* legally be used does not always mean that, as a matter of good conscience and good sense, it *should* be used. We identify a set of guidelines – give criteria of legitimacy – which we believe that the Security Council (and anyone else involved in these decisions) should always address in considering whether to authorize or apply military force. The adoption of these guidelines (seriousness of threat, proper purpose, last resort, proportional means and balance of consequences) will not produce agreed conclusions with push-button predictability, but should significantly improve the chances of teaching international consensus on what have been in recent years deeply divisive issues.

We also address here the other major issues that arise during and after violent conflict, including the needed capacities for peace enforcement, peacekeeping and peacebuilding, and the protection of civilians. A central recurring theme is the necessity for all members of the international community, Developed and developing States, to be much more forthcoming in providing and supporting deployable military resources. Empty gestures are all too easy to make; an effective, efficient and equitable collective security system demands real commitment.

A More Effective United Nations for the Twenty-First Century

The United Nations was never intended to be a utopian exercise. It was meant to be a collective security system that worked. The Charter of the United Nations provided the most powerful States with permanent membership on the Security Council and the veto. In exchange, they were expected to use their power for the common good and promote and obey international law. As Harry Truman, then President of the United States, noted in his speech to the final plenary session of the founding conference of the United Nations Organization, "we all have to recognize – no matter how great our strength – that we must deny ourselves the license to do always as we please."

In approaching the issue of United Nations reform, it is as important today as it was in 1945 to combine power with principle. Recommendations that ignore underlying power realities will be doomed to failure or irrelevance, but recommendations that simply reflect raw distributions of power and make no effort to bolster international principles are unlikely to gain the widespread adherence required to shift international behaviour.

Proposed changes should be driven by real-world need. Change for its own sake is likely to run the well-worn course of the endless reform debates of the past decade. The litmus test is this: does a proposed change help meet the challenge posed by a virulent threat?

Throughout the work of the High-Level Panel on Threats, Challenges and Change, we have looked for institutional weaknesses in current responses to threats. The following stand as the most urgently in need of remedy:

- The General Assembly has lost vitality and often fails to focus effectively on the most compelling issues of the day.
- The Security Council will need to be more proactive in the future. For this to happen, those who contribute most to the Organization financially, militarily and diplomatically should participate more in Council decision-making, and those who participate in Council decision-making should contribute more to the Organization. The Security Council needs greater credibility, legitimacy and representation to do all that we demand of it.
- There is a major institutional gap in addressing countries under stress and countries emerging from conflict. Such countries often suffer from attention, policy guidance and resource deficits.
- The Security Council has not made the most of the potential advantages of working with regional and subregional organizations.
- There must be new institutional arrangements to address the economic and social threats to international security.
- The Commission on Human Rights suffers from a legitimacy deficit that causes doubts on the overall reputation of the United Nations.
- There is a need for a more professional and better organized Secretariat that is much more capable of concerted action.

The reforms we propose will not by themselves make the Untied Nations more effective. In the absence of Member States reaching agreement on the security consensus contained in the present report, the United Nations will underachieve. Its institutions will still only be as strong as the energy, resources and attention devoted to them by Member States and their leaders.

Notes and Questions

1. Since 1988, the UN has increasingly elaborated comprehensive treaties that have provided bases for widespread international criminal cooperation. Many of the cooperative mechanisms in the treaties also have served as models to be duplicated on regional and bilateral bases.

2. The UN conventions have had an important impact through their establishment of norms, definitions, and a basis for moral authority. For instance, the provisions on anti-money laundering and asset forfeiture, as contained in the UN Counterdrug Convention, have been emulated in national legislation and many regional and bilateral treaties.

3. The UN conventions also help develop international enforcement regimes that have dynamic momentum.

4. The UN Security Council has served as a de facto source of legislation on international criminal law in areas such as counterterrorism and war crimes.

5. What are some examples of how the UN General Assembly serves as a source of international criminal law?

6. You are counsel to the Secretary-General of the UN. The Secretary-General asks you to advise on how the UN can persuade some signatories of the 1988 UN Convention against Illicit Traffic in Narcotic Drugs and Psychotropic Substances to implement the provisions of 5b.i that require them to contribute "the value of such proceeds and property, or funds derived from the sale of such proceeds or property, or a substantial part thereof, to intergovernmental bodies specialising in the fight against illicit traffic in and abuse of narcotic drugs and psychotropic substances." In particular, the Secretary-General wants to help fund the programs of the UN Office of Drugs and Crime (UNODC). Its limited resources preclude it from providing technical and financial assistance to signatories and thereby fulfilling the goals of the convention.

II. Specialized UN Criminal Justice Work

A. *General Assembly Resolutions 46/152*

General Assembly Resolution 46/152 (1991) 18 December 1991, 77th plenary meeting 46/152

CREATION OF AN EFFECTIVE UNITED NATIONS CRIME PREVENTION AND CRIMINAL JUSTICE PROGRAM

The General Assembly,

Alarmed by the scope of criminality and by the dangers posed to the welfare of all nations by the rising incidence of crime generally and by the many forms of criminal activity that have international dimensions,

Alarmed also by the high cost of crime in both human and material terms, especially in its new and transnational forms, and aware of the effects of crime both on States and on individual victims,

Recalling that, in its resolution 45/108 of 14 December 1990, it decided to establish an intergovernmental working group to produce a report elaborating proposals for an effective crime prevention and criminal justice programme and suggesting how that programme could most appropriately be implemented,

Acknowledging with appreciation the work of the Intergovernmental Working Group on the Creation of an Effective International Crime and Justice Programme, which met at Vienna from 5 to 9 August 1991,

Acknowledging with appreciation also the work of the Ministerial Meeting on the Creation of an Effective United Nations Crime Prevention and Criminal Justice Programme, held in Paris from 21 to 23 November 1991,

Recognizing that criminality is a major concern of all nations and that it calls for a concerted response from the international community aimed at preventing crime and recidivism, improving the functioning of criminal justice and law enforcement, and increasing respect for individual rights,

Acknowledging that a United Nations programme devoted to crime prevention and criminal justice can only be effective with the direct involvement of Member States,

Convinced that the principal purpose of such a programme should be to provide practical assistance to States in combating both national and transnational crime,

Noting the principles contained in the Milan Plan of Action and the Guiding Principles for Crime Prevention and Criminal Justice in the Context of Development and a New International Economic Order, as well as other pertinent instruments formulated by United Nations congresses on the prevention of crime and the treatment of offenders and approved by the General Assembly,

Recalling its relevant resolutions in which it stressed the importance of the Commission on Human Rights and the Centre for Human Rights of the Secretariat with regard to respect for human rights in the administration of justice,

Recognizing the urgent need to promote and intensify international cooperation in crime prevention and criminal justice, and the fact that this cooperation can be effective only if it is executed with the direct participation of the receiving States, with due respect for their needs and priorities,

1. Takes note with appreciation of the report of the Ministerial Meeting on the Creation of an Effective United Nations Crime Prevention and Criminal Justice Programme;
2. Approves the statement of principles and programme of action, annexed to the present resolution, recommending the establishment of a United Nations crime prevention and criminal justice programme;
3. Supports a clearer definition of the mandate of the programme with regard to crime prevention and criminal justice, under the aegis and guidance of the United Nations, whose aim will be to respond to the most pressing priorities and needs of the international community in the face of both national and transnational criminality;
4. Requests the Secretary-General to give a high level of priority within the United Nations framework, and within the overall existing United Nations resources, to the activities of the United Nations crime prevention and criminal justice programme;
5. Decides that the United Nations crime prevention and criminal justice programme shall be devoted to providing States with practical assistance, such as data collection, information and experience sharing, and training, in order to achieve the goals of preventing crime within and among States and of improving the response to crime;
6. Invites Member States to give their political and financial support and to take measures that will ensure the implementation of the provisions of the statement of principles and programme of action as they relate to the strengthening of the United Nations crime prevention and criminal justice programme in terms of its structure, content and priorities;
7. Requests the Secretary-General to take the necessary action within the overall existing United Nations resources in accordance with the financial rules and regulations of the United Nations and to provide appropriate resources for the effective functioning of the United Nations crime prevention and criminal justice programme in accordance with the principles outlined in the statement of principles and programme of action;
8. Urges all entities of the United Nations system, including the regional commissions, the United Nations congresses on the prevention of crime and the treatment of offenders, the United Nations institutes for the prevention of crime and the treatment of offenders, the specialized agencies and the relevant intergovernmental and non-governmental

organizations, to assist the United Nations crime prevention and criminal justice programme in fulfilling its tasks;

9. Encourages all developed countries to review their aid programmes in order to ensure that there is a full and proper contribution in the field of criminal justice within the overall context of development priorities;
10. Decides to recommend that a commission on crime prevention and criminal justice be established as a functional commission of the Economic and Social Council, which would hold its inaugural meeting during 1992, and recommends that the meeting of the Committee on Crime Prevention and Control scheduled for February 1992 be cancelled and that the funds necessary for the work of the new commission be made available within the programme budget for the biennium 1992–1993;
11. Requests the Economic and Social Council at its organizational session for 1992:
    (a) To dissolve the Committee on Crime Prevention and Control;
    (b) To establish the commission on crime prevention and criminal justice as a new functional commission of the Economic and Social Council, in accordance with the recommendations contained in the statement of principles and programme of action;
    (c) To endorse the role and functions of the United Nations congresses on the prevention of crime and the treatment of offenders, in accordance with the recommendations contained in the statement of principles and programme of action;
12. Decides that the present members of the Committee on Crime Prevention and Control should be invited to participate during the first two days of the inaugural session of the new commission, at the expense of their respective Governments, except in the case of Committee members from least developed countries, in order to facilitate an orderly transition;
13. Also decides to retain for the United Nations crime prevention and criminal justice programme, without prejudice to additional funds that may be made available by the Secretary-General, all funds currently allocated to the programme, as well as any savings realized by restructuring;
14. Requests the Secretary-General to report to the General Assembly at its forty-seventh session on measures taken to implement the statement of principles and programme of action.

ANNEX

Statement of Principles and Programme of Action of the United Nations Crime Prevention and Criminal Justice Programme

We, Member States of the United Nations,

Assembled in Paris to consider ways and means of promoting international cooperation in crime prevention and criminal justice and of strengthening the United Nations crime prevention and criminal justice programme in order to make it fully effective and responsive to the needs and priorities of Member States,

Considering that one of the purposes of the United Nations, as stated in the Charter of the United Nations, is to achieve international cooperation in solving international problems of an economic, social, cultural or humanitarian character, and in promoting and encouraging respect for human rights and for fundamental freedoms for all without distinction as to race, sex, language, or religion,

Convinced of the urgent need for more efficient international mechanisms to assist States and to facilitate joint strategies in the field of crime prevention and criminal justice, thus consolidating the role of the United Nations as the focal point in that field,

Noting the importance of the principles contained in the Milan Plan of Action and the Guiding Principles for Crime Prevention and Criminal Justice in the Context of Development and a New International Economic Order, as well as other pertinent instruments formulated by United Nations congresses on the prevention of crime and the treatment of offenders and approved by the General Assembly,

Reaffirming the responsibility assumed by the United Nations in crime prevention and criminal justice,

Bearing in mind the goals of the United Nations in the field of crime prevention and criminal justice, specifically the reduction of criminality, more efficient and effective law enforcement and administration of justice, the observance of human rights and the promotion of the highest standards of fairness, humanity and professional conduct,

Recognizing that it is essential to elicit active support for, and to provide the means of assistance for the development of, an effective United Nations crime prevention and criminal justice programme and to devise appropriate implementation mechanisms,

Deeply concerned about the extent and growth of crime, with its financial, economic and social consequences,

Alarmed at the high cost of crime in both human and material terms, as well as in its new national and transnational forms, and aware of the effects of crime both on States and on individual victims,

Recognizing that the primary responsibility for crime prevention and criminal justice rests with Member States,

Emphasizing the need for strengthened regional and international cooperation to combat crime and recidivism, to effect the improved functioning of criminal justice systems, to promote respect for individual rights and to safeguard the rights of victims of crime and the general security of the public,

Aware that there is unanimity about the need to create a new, vigorous United Nations crime prevention and criminal justice programme, as well as agreement on the need to establish an intergovernmental body for policy-making and priority-setting, to strengthen the effectiveness of the Secretariat unit within the Centre for Social Development and Humanitarian Affairs of the United Nations Office at Vienna, and to increase technical cooperation to help countries, particularly developing countries, translate United Nations policy-guidelines into practice, including training,

Determined to translate our political will into concrete action:

(a) By creating the essential mechanisms for practical collaboration against common problems;
(b) By providing a framework for inter-State cooperation and coordination to respond to the serious new forms and transnational aspects and dimensions of crime;
(c) By establishing information exchanges concerning the implementation and effectiveness of the United Nations norms and standards in crime prevention and criminal justice;

(d) By providing means of assistance, particularly to developing countries, for more effective crime prevention and more human justice;
(e) By establishing an adequate resource base for a truly effective United Nations crime prevention and criminal justice programme,
(f) Proclaim our strong commitment to the above-mentioned goals and agree on the following:

I. Statement of Principles

1. We recognize that the world is experiencing very important changes resulting in a political climate conducive to democracy, to international cooperation, to more widespread enjoyment of basic human rights and fundamental freedoms, and to the realization of the aspirations of all nations to economic development and social welfare. Notwithstanding these developments, the world today is still beset by violence and other forms of serious crime. These phenomena, wherever they occur, constitute a threat to the maintenance of the rule of law.
2. We believe that justice based on the rule of law is the pillar on which civilized society rests. We seek to improve its quality. A humane and efficient criminal justice system can be an instrument of equity, constructive social change and social justice, protecting basic values and peoples' inalienable rights. Every right of the individual should enjoy the protection of the law against violation, a process in which the criminal justice system plays an essential role.
3. We have in mind the fact that the lowering of the world crime rate is related to, among other factors, the improvement of the social conditions of the population. The developed countries and the developing countries are experiencing difficult situations in this respect. Nevertheless, the specific problems encountered by the developing countries justify priority being given to dealing with the situation confronting these countries.
4. We believe that rising crime is impairing the process of development and the general well-being of humanity and is causing general disquiet within our societies. If this situation continues, progress and development will be the ultimate victims of crime.
5. We also believe that the growing internationalization of crime must generate new and commensurate responses. Organized crime is exploiting the relaxation of border controls designed to foster legitimate trade and, hence, development. The incidence and scope of such crimes may increase further in the coming years unless sound preventive measures are taken. It is thus particularly important to anticipate events and to assist Member States in mounting suitable preventive and control strategies.
6. We recognize that many criminal offences have international dimensions. In this context, there is an urgent need for States to address, while respecting the sovereignty of States, problems arising in collecting evidence, extraditing offenders and promoting mutual legal assistance, for example, when such offences are committed across frontiers or when frontiers are used to escape detection or prosecution. Despite differences in legal systems, experience has shown that mutual assistance and cooperation can be effective countermeasures and can help to prevent conflicts of jurisdiction.
7. We also recognize that democracy and a better quality of life can flourish only in a context of peace and security for all. Crime poses a threat to stability and to a safe

environment. Crime prevention and criminal justice, with due regard to the observance of human rights, is thus a direct contribution to the maintenance of peace and security.

8. We must ensure that any increases in the capacity and capabilities of perpetrators of crime are matched by similar increases in the capacity and capabilities of law enforcement and criminal justice authorities. By pooling our knowledge and developing suitable countermeasures, success in the prevention of crime and the reduction of victimization can be maximized. We recognize in particular the need to improve and strengthen the means of the crime prevention and control authorities in the developing countries, whose critical economic and social situation is further increasing the difficulties in this area.
9. We call on the international community to increase its support of technical cooperation and assistance activities for the benefit of all countries, including developing and smaller countries, and for the purpose of expanding and strengthening the infrastructure needed for effective crime prevention and viable, fair and humane criminal justice systems.
10. We acknowledge the contribution of the United Nations crime prevention and criminal justice programme to the international community. We note that it is a long-recognized fact that inadequate resources have been devoted to the implementation of the programme, which has in the past been inhibited from achieving its potential. We also note that a strengthening of the resources devoted to the implementation of the programme was called for by the Sixth United Nations Congress for the Prevention of Crime and the Treatment of Offenders, the Seventh United Nations Congress for the Prevention of Crime and the Treatment of Offenders and the Eighth United Nations Congress for the Prevention of Crime and the Treatment of Offenders. We further note that the Committee on Crime Prevention and Control, at its eleventh session, gave priority attention to the conclusions and recommendations of a subcommittee established to provide an overview of the problem of crime and to assess the most efficient means of stimulating practical international action in support of Member States, in pursuance of General Assembly resolution 44/72 of 8 December 1989. The Committee, in its resolution 11/3 of 16 February 1990, unanimously approved a report of the subcommittee on the need for the creation of an effective international crime and justice programme. That report, which was endorsed by the Eighth Congress, was used as an important tool for the establishment of the United Nations crime prevention and criminal justice programme, in line with the provisions of General Assembly resolution 45/108.
11. We accordingly recommend intensified international cooperation in crime prevention and criminal justice, including the creation of an effective United Nations crime prevention and criminal justice programme.
12. We are convinced that there is a need for Governments to define more clearly the role and functions of the United Nations crime prevention and criminal justice programme and the secretariat of the programme and to determine priorities within that programme.
13. We strongly believe that the review of the programme should aim at strengthening its effectiveness, improving its efficiency and establishing an adequate Secretariat support structure.

II. Programme of Action

A. Definition

14. The United Nations crime prevention and criminal justice programme shall bring together the work of the commission on crime prevention and criminal justice, the United Nations institutes for the prevention of crime and the treatment of offenders, the network of government-appointed national correspondents in the field of crime prevention and criminal justice, the Global Crime and Criminal Justice Information Network and the United Nations congresses on the prevention of crime and the treatment of offenders in providing assistance to Member States in their efforts to reduce the incidence and costs of crime and in developing the proper functioning of their criminal justice systems. The establishment of this programme will be effected in accordance with the procedures defined below and within the framework of the total available resources of the United Nations.

B. Goals

15. The programme shall be designed to assist the international community in meeting its pressing needs in the field of crime prevention and criminal justice and to provide countries with timely and practical assistance in dealing with problems of both national and transnational crime.
16. The general goals of the programme shall be to contribute to the following:
    (a) The prevention of crime within and among States;
    (b) The control of crime both nationally and internationally;
    (c) The strengthening of regional and international cooperation in crime prevention, criminal justice and the combating of transnational crime;
    (d) The integration and consolidation of the efforts of Member States in preventing and combating transnational crime;
    (e) More efficient and effective administration of justice, with due respect for the human rights of all those affected by crime and all those involved in the criminal justice system;
    (f) The promotion of the highest standards of fairness, humanity, justice and professional conduct.

C. Scope of the United Nations Crime Prevention and Criminal Justice Programme

17. The programme shall include appropriate forms of cooperation for the purpose of assisting States in dealing with problems of both national and transnational crime. In particular, it may include:
    (a) Research and studies at the national, regional and global levels on specific prevention issues and criminal justice measures;
    (b) Regular international surveys to assess trends in crime and developments in the operation of criminal justice systems and in crime prevention strategies;
    (c) Exchange and dissemination of information among States on crime prevention and criminal justice, particularly with regard to innovative measures and the results achieved in their application;

(d) Training and upgrading of the skills of personnel working in the various areas of crime prevention and criminal justice;

(e) Technical assistance, including advisory services, particularly in respect of the planning, implementation and evaluation of crime prevention and criminal justice programmes, training and the use of modern communication and information techniques; such assistance may be implemented by means of, for example, fellowships, study tours, consultancies, secondments, courses, seminars and demonstration and pilot projects.

18. Within the framework of the programme, the United Nations should directly carry out the above-mentioned forms of cooperation or should act as a coordinating or facilitating agent. Special attention should be paid to the creation of mechanisms to provide flexible and appropriate assistance and to respond to the needs of Member States at their request, without duplicating the activities of other existing mechanisms.

19. For the purpose of those forms of cooperation, Member States should establish and maintain reliable and effective channels of communication among themselves and with the United Nations.

20. The programme may also include, as appropriate, while respecting the sovereignty of States, a review of the effectiveness and application of and, where necessary, further development and promotion of international instruments on crime prevention and criminal justice.

D. Programme Priorities

21. In developing the programme, areas of priority shall be determined in response to the needs and concerns of Member States, with particular consideration being given to the following:

(a) Empirical evidence, including research findings and other information on the nature and extent of crime and on trends in crime;

(b) The social, financial and other costs of various forms of crimes and/or crime control to the individual, the local, national and international community, and to the development process;

(c) The need of developing or developed countries, which are confronting specific difficulties related to national or international circumstances, to have recourse to experts and other resources necessary for establishing and developing programmes for crime prevention and criminal justice that are appropriate at the national and local levels;

(d) The need for a balance within the programme of work between programme development and practical action;

(e) The protection of human rights in the administration of justice and the prevention and control of crime;

(f) The assessment of areas in which concerted action at the international level and within the framework of the programme would be most effective;

(g) Avoidance of overlapping with the activities of other entities of the United Nations system or of other organizations.

22. The commission on crime prevention and criminal justice shall not be bound by mandates conferred prior to its formation, but shall assess them on their merits by applying the principles mentioned in paragraph 21 above.

E. Structure and Management

1. *Commission on Crime Prevention and Criminal Justice*

23. A commission on crime prevention and criminal justice shall be established as a functional commission of the Economic and Social Council. The commission shall have the power to create ad hoc working groups and to appoint special rapporteurs, as it deems necessary.
24. Membership: The commission shall consist of forty Member States of the United Nations, elected by the Economic and Social Council on the basis of the principle of equitable geographical distribution. Its members shall serve for a term of three years, except that the terms of one half of the first elected members, whose names shall be chosen by lot, shall expire after two years. Each Member State shall make every effort to ensure that its delegation includes experts and senior officials with special training and practical experience in crime prevention and criminal justice, preferably with policy responsibility in the field. Provisions should be made in the regular budget of the United Nations to defray the travel costs of the representatives of the least developed countries that are members of the Commission.
25. Sessions: The commission shall hold annual sessions of not more than ten working days.
26. Functions: The commission shall have the following functions:
    (a) To provide policy guidance to the United Nations in the field of crime prevention and criminal justice;
    (b) To develop, monitor and review the implementation of the programme on the basis of a system of medium-term planning in accordance with the priority principles provided in paragraph 21 above;
    (c) To facilitate and help to coordinate the activities of the United Nations institutes for the prevention of crime and the treatment of offenders;
    (d) To mobilize the support of Member States for the programme;
    (e) To prepare for the United Nations congresses on the prevention of crime and the treatment of offenders and to consider suggestions regarding possible subjects for the programme of work as submitted by the congresses.

2. *Committee on Crime Prevention and Control*

27. The Committee on Crime Prevention and Control should be dissolved by the Economic and Social Council upon the establishment by the Council of the commission on crime prevention and criminal justice. There will be a basic need for involving independent experts in the area of crime prevention and control.
28. The commission shall, when necessary, use the services of a limited number of qualified and experienced experts, either as individual consultants or in working groups, in order to assist in the preparations for and follow-up work of the commission. Their advice shall be transmitted to the commission for consideration. The commission shall be encouraged to seek such advice whenever it is needed. One of the major tasks of the experts shall be to assist in the preparations for the United Nations congresses on the prevention of crime and the treatment of offenders.

3. *United Nations Congresses on the Prevention of Crime and the Treatment of Offenders*

29. The United Nations congresses on the prevention of crime and the treatment of offenders, as a consultative body of the programme, shall provide a forum for:
    (a) The exchange of views between States, intergovernmental organizations, non-governmental organizations and individual experts representing various professions and disciplines;
    (b) The exchange of experiences in research, law and policy development;
    (c) The identification of emerging trends and issues in crime prevention and criminal justice;
    (d) The provision of advice and comments to the commission on crime prevention and criminal justice on selected matters submitted to it by the commission;
    (e) The submission of suggestions, for the consideration of the commission, regarding possible subjects for the programme of work.
30. In order to enhance the effectiveness of the programme and to achieve optimal results, the following arrangements should be implemented:
    (a) The congresses should be held every five years, for a period of between five and ten working days;
    (b) The commission shall select precisely defined topics for the congresses in order to ensure a focused and productive discussion;
    (c) Quinquennial regional meetings should be held under the guidance of the commission on issues related to the agenda of the commission or of the congresses, or on any other matters, except when a region does not consider it necessary to hold such a meeting. The United Nations institutes for the prevention of crime and the treatment of offenders should be fully involved, as appropriate, in the organization of those meetings. The commission shall give due consideration to the need to finance such meetings, in particular in developing regions, through the regular budget of the United Nations;
    (d) Action-oriented research workshops on topics selected by the commission, as part of the programme of a congress, and ancillary meetings associated with the congresses should be encouraged.

4. *Organizational Structure of the Secretariat and of the Programme*

31. The secretariat of the programme shall be the permanent body responsible for facilitating the implementation of the programme, the priorities of which shall be established by the commission on crime prevention and criminal justice and for assisting the commission in conducting evaluations of the progress made and analyses of the difficulties encountered. For that purpose, the secretariat shall:
    (a) Mobilize existing resources, including institutes, intergovernmental organizations, non-governmental organizations and other competent authorities for the implementation of the programme;
    (b) Coordinate research, training and the collection of data on crime and justice, and provide technical assistance and practical information for Member States, particularly through the Global Crime and Criminal Justice Information Network;

(c) Assist the commission in the organization of its work and in the preparations, in accordance with the directions of the commission, for the congresses and any other events relating to the programme;
(d) Ensure that the potential donors of criminal justice assistance are put in touch with countries needing the help in question;
(e) Make the case for assistance in the field of criminal justice to the appropriate funding agencies.

32. It is recommended to the Secretary-General that, in recognition of the high priority that should be accorded to the programme, an upgrading of the Crime Prevention and Criminal Justice Branch of the Centre for Social Development and Humanitarian Affairs of the Secretariat into a division should be effected as soon as possible, under the conditions set out in paragraph 14 above, bearing in mind the structure of the United Nations Office at Vienna.
33. The Professional staff of the secretariat of the programme shall be called "Crime Prevention and Criminal Justice Officers."
34. The secretariat of the programme shall be directed by a senior official responsible for the overall day-to-day management and supervision of the programme, communicating with the relevant government officials, the specialized agencies and intergovernmental organizations whose activities are relevant to the programme.

F. Programme Support

1. *United Nations Institutes for the Prevention of Crime and the Treatment of Offenders*

35. The activities of the United Nations institutes for the prevention of crime and the treatment of offenders should be supported by Member States and the United Nations, with particular attention being given to the needs of such institutes located in developing countries. Given the important role of such institutes, their contributions to policy development and implementation, and their resource requirements, especially those of the United Nations African Institute for the Prevention of Crime and the Treatment of Offenders, [they] should be fully integrated into the overall programme.

2. *Coordination among the United Nations Institutes for the Prevention of Crime and the Treatment of Offenders*

36. The institutes should keep one another and the commission on crime prevention and criminal justice informed on a regular basis about their programme of work and its implementation.
37. The commission may request the institutes, subject to the availability of resources, to implement select elements of the programme. The commission may also suggest areas for inter-institute activities.
38. The commission shall seek to mobilize extrabudgetary support for the activities of the institutes.

3. *Network of Government-Appointed National Correspondents in the Field of Crime Prevention and Criminal Justice*

39. Member States should designate one or more national correspondents in the field of crime prevention and criminal justice as focal points for the purpose of maintaining

direct communication with the secretariat of the programme and other elements of the programme.

40. The national correspondents shall facilitate contact with the secretariat on matters of legal, scientific and technical cooperation, training, information on national laws and regulations, legal policy, the organization of the criminal justice system, crime prevention measures and penitentiary matters.

4. *Global Crime and Criminal Justice Information Network*

41. Member States shall support the United Nations in the development and maintenance of the Global Crime and Criminal Justice Information Network in order to facilitate the collection, analysis, exchange and dissemination, as appropriate, of information and the centralization of inputs from non-governmental organizations and scientific institutions in the field of crime prevention and criminal justice.

42. Member States shall undertake to provide the Secretary-General on a regular basis and upon request with data on the dynamics, structure and extent of crime and on the operation of crime prevention and criminal justice strategies in their respective countries.

5. *Intergovernmental and Non-Governmental Organizations*

43. Intergovernmental and non-governmental organizations and the scientific community are a valuable source of professional expertise, advocacy and assistance. Their contributions should be fully utilized in programme development and implementation.

G. Funding of the Programme

44. The programme shall be funded from the regular budget of the United Nations. Funds allocated for technical assistance may be supplemented by direct voluntary contributions from Member States and interested funding agencies. Member States are encouraged to make contributions to the United Nations Trust Fund for Social Defence, to be renamed the United Nations Crime Prevention and Criminal Justice Fund. They are also encouraged to contribute in kind for the operational activities of the programme, particularly by seconding staff, organizing training courses and seminars, and providing the requisite equipment and services.

Notes and Questions

1. In 1991, the UN Crime Prevention and Criminal Justice Program was reorganized. At the time, UN officials debated whether the resources devoted to the program – a very modest 0.15 percent of its annual operating budget – were sufficient. (The final paragraph of the Annex to the resolution, para. 44, provides for funding of the program from the regular UN budget).

Funds allocated for technical assistance may be supplemented by direct voluntary contributions from member states and interested funding agencies. Member states are also encouraged to contribute to the United Nations Crime Prevention and Criminal Justice Fund and to contribute in kind for the operational activities of the program, especially by seconding staff, organizing training courses and seminars, and providing equipment and services.

2. The UN has also rethought the priorities of the UN Crime Prevention and Criminal Justice Program. Until 1991, the program had primarily focused on holding congresses to exchange ideas, network, prepare legal instruments, and encourage international cooperation. What are the program's new priorities? *See* paragraph 21 of Resolution 46/152.

3. Paragraph 28 of Resolution 46/152 includes provisions to enlist the services of independent experts. This is a partial effort to compensate for the dissolution of the Committee on Crime Prevention and Control, which previously served as an in-house repository of experts.[28]

4. One of the key jobs of the UN Crime Prevention and Criminal Justice Program has been to set standards on the delivery of criminal justice through the preparation of reports and the adoption of standards during congresses. Critics argue, however, that in the 1970s and 1980s the CPCJP adopted too many instruments, many of which had insufficient support and could not be implemented. The disputed instruments include the Standard Minimum Rules for the Treatment of Prisoners, the Torture Declaration, the Code of Conduct for Law Enforcement Officials, the Caracas Declaration, and the capital punishment safeguards.[29] Are these standards binding on domestic courts? If not, can they be cited as the standard of care that courts or administrative tribunals can apply to persons? If they can neither bind nor influence the standard of care, then what, if any, value do they have? Are they worth the time and resources that go into their elaboration?

5. The UN Crime Prevention and Criminal Justice Program prepared and approved model treaties for international cooperation in the criminal process at the UN Congresses on the Prevention of Crime and the Treatment of Offenders in 1985 and 1990. These treaties included a Model Treaty on Extradition,[30] a Model Treaty on Mutual Assistance in Criminal Matters,[31] a Model Treaty on the Transfer of Proceedings in Criminal Matters,[32] a Model Treaty on the Transfer of Supervision of Offenders Conditionally Sentenced or Conditionally Released,[33] and a Model Treaty for the Prevention of Crimes That Infringe on the Cultural Heritage of Peoples in the Form of Movable Property.[34] Are these model treaties binding? If not, what are the value and purpose of such model treaties? Given that other international organizations, such as the Council of Europe and the Commonwealth Secretariat and Legal Ministers, have their own model treaties, what is the purpose of the UN model treaties? In light of resource constraints, does it make sense to have multiple model treaties for international criminal cooperation? If not, what should be done to minimize the duplication?[35]

6. You are an attorney at the Ministry of Justice in the Latin American principality of Paramonga. The Minister of Justice has asked why Paramonga only has a few old

[28] For a discussion of the priorities in the 1991 resolution and background generally regarding the program, *see* Roger S. Clark, The United Nations Crime Prevention and Criminal Justice Program 35–52 (1994).

[29] *Id.* at 98–108.

[30] G.A. Res. 45/116, 45 U.N. GAOR, Supp. No. 49A, at 211, U.N. Doc. A/45/49 (1991).

[31] G.A. Res. 45/117, at 215.

[32] G.A. Res. 45/118, at 219.

[33] G.A. Res. 45/119, at 221.

[34] *Eighth United Congress on the Prevention of Crime and the Treatment of Offenders, Havana, Cuba, 27 August–7 September* 1990, Report prepared by the Secretariat, at 110, U.N. Doc. A/CONF. 144/28 (1990). Unlike the other model treaties, this model was not adopted as a General Assembly resolution.

[35] *Clark, supra* note 27 at 199–228.

extradition treaties and no other criminal cooperation agreements. He asks you to prepare a memorandum on the main UN instruments and analyze whether any of them are suitable for Paramonga. How can you apply UN instruments in this situation?

B. *Regional United Nations Institutes*

The United Nations institutes, also known as the Crime Prevention and Criminal Justice Program Network, are a varied collection of entities, each with a relationship with the Secretariat. Some of these entities do not use the word "Institute" in their names. These entities include the following:

1) The UN Interregional Crime and Justice Research Institute (UNICRI), a UN entity that operates on an interregional basis;
2) Four affiliated regional institutes: the UN Asia and Far East Institute for the Prevention of Crime and the Treatment of Offenders (UNAFEI), at Fuchu, Japan (whose geographical scope includes Asia and the Pacific); the European Institute for Crime Prevention and Control, affiliated with the United Nations (HEUNI), at Helsinki, Finland (covering Europe); the United Nations Latin American Institute for the Prevention of Crime and the Treatment of Offenders (ILANUD), at San Jose, Costa Rica; and the United Nations African Regional Institute for the Prevention of Crime and the Treatment of Offenders (UNAFRI), at Kampala, Uganda (which covers Africa);
3) Three associate entities that cooperate closely with the United Nations: the Arab Security Studies and Training Centre (ASSTC), at Riyadh, Saudi Arabia (a regional center covering the Arab world); the Australian Institute of Criminology (AIC), at Woden, Australia (a subregional institute, covering the Pacific); and the International Centre for Criminal Law Reform and Criminal Justice Policy, at Vancouver, Canada (whose scope is international).

E.S.C. Res. 1992/22 pt. IV, para. 3(h), foresees the affiliation of more entities because it encourages the Secretary-General to develop "criteria and procedures for the creation and affiliation of new United Nations institutes or centres that would join those referred to in paragraph 35 of General Assembly resolution 46/152 for consideration by the Commission at its second session, and the favorable review of requests by groups of States to establish United Nations subregional institutes."

A fourth associate entity, the International Institute of Higher Studies in Criminal Sciences, which is a subsidiary of the International Association of Penal Law, has formally joined the network after a long informal relationship. Established at Siracusa, Italy, in Sicily in 1972, this institute is devoted to studies, research, and the advancement of criminal sciences, with particular emphasis on the development of human rights.[36] Professor M. Cherif Bassiouni is president of this institute.

The UN Interregional Crime and Justice Research Institute (UNICRI), which was originally established as the United Nations Social Defense Research Institute in 1968, is the most important of the institutes and was designed to be the research arm of the

[36] *Id.*, at 84–85, citing *Activities of the United Nations Interregional Crime and Justice Research Institute and Other Institutes, Progress Report of the Secretary-General*, U.N. Doc. E/CN.15/1993/8 (1993).

UN crime program. Its work has expanded from research to training and field activities, particularly to assist developing countries.

The UN regional institutes have been engaged in active programs of research, training courses, technical assistance, seminars, and publications.[37]

Notes and Questions

1. A civil society organization in your country approaches you and expresses interest in developing a UN regional institute. What would be some of the considerations in deciding to establish such an institute? How broad or narrow could you make its activities?

2. The UN regional institutes have played critical roles in helping implement UN conventions and model rules. In addition, some of them, especially the International Institute of Higher Studies in Criminal Sciences, have been instrumental in developing new institutions, such as the International Criminal Court.

III. Additional Reading

A. *Books*

José E. Alvarez, International Organizations as Law-makers (2005).
Roger S. Clark, The United Nations Crime Prevention and Criminal Justice Program (1994).
Rosalyn Higgins, The Development of International Law through the Political Organs of the United Nations (1963).
M. López-Rey, A Guide to United Nations Criminal Policy (1985).
Stanley Meissler, The U.N.: The First Fifty Years (1997).
B. Sloan, United Nations General Assembly Resolutions in Our Changing World (1991).
James Taub, Kofi Annan and the United Nations in an Era of American Power (2006).
The UN Security Council (David M. Malone ed., 2004).
United Nations, Compendium of United Nations Standards and Norms in Crime Prevention and Criminal Justice (1992).

B. *Articles*

W. Clifford, *The Standard Minimum Rules for the Treatment of Prisoners*, 66 Proc. Am. Soc. Int'l L. 232 (1972).
W. Clifford, *The Committee on Crime Prevention and Control*, 34 Int'l Rev. Crim. Pol'y 11 (1978).
P. Cornil, *International Standards for the Treatment of Prisoners*, 26 Int'l Rev. Crim. Pol'y 3 (1968).
E. Galway, *United Nations Technical Assistance in Crime Prevention and Control*, 34 Int'l Rev. Crim. Pol'y 22 (1978).
J. Hartman, *"Unusual" Punishment: The Domestic Effects of International Norms Restricting the Application of the Death Penalty*, 52 U. Cin. L. Rev. 655 (1983).
L.L. Lamborn, *The United Nations Declaration on Victims: Incorporating "Abuse of Power,"* 19 Rutgers L.J. 59 (1987).
M. López-Rey, *Aspects and Problems of the Role of United Nations Assistance to Developing Countries in the Field of Social Defence*, 39 Rev. Int'l Droit Penale 21 (1968).
M. López-Rey, *The First U.N. Congress on the Prevention of Crime and the Treatment of Offenders*, 47 J. Crim. L. Criminol. & Police Sci. 526 (1957).
K. Neudek, *United Nations Crime Prevention and Criminal Justice Programme*, 1 Europ. J. Crim. Pol'y & Res. 185 (1993).
T. Treves, *The UN Body of Principles for the Protection of Detained or Imprisoned Persons*, 84 Am. J. Int'l L. 578 (1990).

[37] *Id.* at 84–9.

E. Vetere, *The Role of the United Nations: Working for a More Effective International Co-operation*, in PRINCIPLES AND PROCEDURES FOR A NEW TRANSNATIONAL CRIMINAL LAW, PROCEEDINGS OF AN INTERNATIONAL WORKSHOP ORGANIZED BY THE SOCIETY FOR THE REFORM OF CRIMINAL LAW AND THE MAX PLANCK INSTITUTE FOR FOREIGN AND INTERNATIONAL CRIMINAL LAW (A. Easer & O Lagodny eds. 1992), Freiburg-im-Breisgau, Germany, May 21–25, 1991.

12 The World Bank Group

I. Overview and History

The World Bank Group (WBG) is an umbrella group of international financial institutions charged with promoting free market development to combat poverty. Established in 1944 during the famed Bretton Woods conference, the WBG includes two institutions – the International Bank for Reconstruction and Development (IBRD) and the International Development Association (IDA) – and three affiliated institutions: the International Finance Corporation (IFC), the Multilateral Investment Guarantee Agency, and the International Centre for Settlement of Investment Disputes (ICSID). Based in Washington, D.C., the WBG is run by a board of directors representing 185 stakeholder countries.

The World Bank Group (WBG) includes the International Monetary Fund (IMF), the World Bank (WB), and the other constituent entities. To fulfill its overall mission of fighting poverty, it helps countries strengthen development efforts by providing loans and technical assistance for institutional capacity building, as well as loans for infrastructure and environmental improvements. It provides resources, shares knowledge, and facilitates the development of partnerships in the public and private sectors.

The IMF's overall mission is macroeconomic and involves financial surveillance throughout the world. Through its activities, the IMF works to promote international monetary cooperation; facilitate the expansion and balanced growth of international trade; promote foreign currency exchange stability; and assist in the establishment of multilateral systems of payment. The IMF promotes international monetary stability by making loans to countries to allow them to correct maladjustments in their balance of payments without resorting to measures that may negatively affect national or international prosperity.[1]

The IMF sets standards through its operational policies. For example, since the 1950s, it has attached conditions to loans made to states in need of economic assistance.[2] These conditions allow recipients to obtain fund financing beyond the IMF member's Article IV commitment to meet their declared exchange rate parity with gold or the United States dollar referred to as the (automatic the "gold tranche") if they implement economic and financial adjustment programs that the IMF considers satisfactory.[3] In 1997, the IMF followed the World Bank and broadened these conditions to include general good governance. The IMF and World Bank have conditioned loans and projects on whether public policies are in place to avoid bribery, corruption, and fraudulent activity in the management of public resources.[4]

The International Finance Corporation (IFC), a member of the World Bank Group, describes itself as the "private sector arm of the World Bank Group." The IFC shares

[1] For more information about the IMF, *see* http://www.imf.org.

[2] *See generally* Edith Brown Weiss et al., eds., The World Bank, International Financial Institutions, and the Development of International Law (ASIL 1999).

[3] José E. Alvarez, International Organizations as Lawmakers 242 (2005), citing Andre Newburg, *The Changing Roles of the Bretton Woods Institutions: Evolving Concepts of Conditionality, in* International Monetary Law: Issues for the New Millennium 81, at 84 (Mario Giovanoli, ed., 2000). For a discussion of the IMF members Article IV commitment to meet their declared exchange rate parity with gold or the United States dollar, see Jan Kregel, IMF Contingency Financing for Middle Income Countries with Access to Private Capital Markets: An Assessment of the Proposal to Create a Resource Augmentation Line, UN Conference on Trade and Development, G-24 Discussion Paper Series, No. 47, Oct 2007, at 3.

[4] *id.*

the World Bank's long-term goal of alleviating poverty and works toward that goal by providing financial investment and advisory services to the developing world. According to its literature, the IFC has five current strategic priorities: strengthening its focus on frontier markets, particularly the small and medium enterprise (SME) sector; building long-term partnerships with emerging global players in developing countries; differentiating the IFC from competitors through sustainability; addressing constraints to private sector investment in infrastructure, health, and education; and developing domestic financial markets through institution building and the use of innovative financial products.

II. A Hypothetical

Rubonga, one of the world's most impoverished countries, has been plagued by governance and corruption problems since its founding. Recently, Rubongan government engineers have discovered oil, gold, and diamonds. The Rubongan government has asked the World Bank Group for help developing its infrastructure and building its natural resources sector.

One year ago, as part of a World Bank aid project, Rubonga promised to use 50 percent of its budgetary resources for poverty reduction programs. Now, however, the dynamically increasing prices of its natural resources give Rubonga an unanticipated windfall. Rubonga's president, who assumed power in a violent coup four years ago, has just informed the WBG that Rubonga will no longer meet the 50 percent allocation requirement. What should the WBG do? Should it terminate aid? What are the alternatives?

In Rubonga there are a number of civil society groups whose purposes include governance and anticorruption activities. What, if anything, can those groups do? Can they participate in the WBG's activities with respect to governance and anticorruption?

XYZ Engineering has helped construct an oil pipeline in Rubonga. It obtained the contract to develop the pipeline through a longstanding agent. XYZ's new CEO has heard rumors that, during pricing negotiations with Rubonga's procurement company, XYZ's representative received an email from someone in the procurement company about the prices that would be acceptable. What, if anything, should the CEO do in response? What should the CEO do if he learns that the agent was sharing some of his fees with a friend at the procurement company?

ABC Engineering, which bid unsuccessfully on the oil pipeline contract, has heard the same rumors about the close relationship between XYZ's agent and the procurement company. What, if anything, can ABC do to ascertain if the decision to award the contract to XYZ was improper? In its investigation of the awarding the contract to XYZ, ABC Engineering has discovered that a few years ago its agent in Rubonga also made some suspicious payments in connection with resolving the nonconforming evaluation of the performance of ABC's contract and thereafter the proposed penalty for ABC was removed. Should ABC do anything about this?

III. The World Bank's Initial Forays into Criminal Justice

Until the mid-1980s, the International Monetary Fund (IMF) resisted proactive involvement in enforcement cooperation and criminal law or criminal justice issues, such as anti-money laundering (AML) and counterterrorist financial enforcement (CTFE), anticorruption, and improving the overall criminal justice system of a country. It perceived its role as helping with financial regulation, not enforcement and criminal law.

World Bank officials gradually perceived the importance of building the rule of law, although that effort did not lend itself to a single strategy or reform measure. Development agencies have devised a number of reform programs to advance elements of the rule of law.

Criminal and related enforcement law projects arise out of the World Bank's public sector governance goals and its fundamental mission to help governments work better in client countries. The Public Sector Group, which is part of the Poverty Reduction and Economic Management (PREM) Network, holds that the World Bank must focus more of its efforts on building efficient and accountable public sector institutions, rather than simply providing discrete policy advice. The World Bank's experience in East Asia and to some extent Russia suggests that good policies are not enough – it cannot afford to look the other way when a country is plagued by deeply dysfunctional public institutions that limit accountability, set perverse rules of the game, and are incapable of sustaining development.[5]

Within its Public Sector Governance group is the Law and Justice Institutions department. The work of this department is based on the belief that fair and efficient courts; clearly written, coherent laws; and other attributes of a well-functioning legal system are integral to sustainable development and poverty reduction. Hence, the World Bank is involved in various law and justice reforms in developing and transitioning countries.[6]

The World Bank has gradually come to realize that courts and other components of a public legal system directly affect the public safety, commerce, and overall quality of life of citizens. Public confidence in and public respect for the rule of law and administration of justice are integrally linked with the operation of a community's law enforcement system and the delivery of justice to ordinary citizens. Delay, inefficiency, bias, and corruption on the part of the police, the prosecutor, the judge, or other justice sector officials diminish public respect and public confidence in government and in the justice system especially.[7]

World Bank, Justice Reform

(WORLD BANK WEB SITE, ACCESSED FEB. 24, 2007)

"Well-functioning justice systems are a key component of the Rule of Law. That is why reforms of justice systems have become an important area of development cooperation. Though early legal reform efforts focused on changes to the substantive laws, it is now widely recognized that drafting new laws is by itself insufficient. Reform of the institutions that create, apply and enforce the law is also necessary.

Justice reform entails reform of a staggering array of institutions. Courts are obviously key, but the justice sector is also made up of ministries of justice, the legal profession, the

[5] World Bank, *Public Sector Governance*, World Bank Web site http://web.worldbank.org/WBSITE/EXTERNAL/TOPICS/EXTPUBLICSECTORANDGOVERNANCE (accessed Feb. 24, 2007).

[6] *See Law and Justice Institutions*, World Bank Web site (accessed Feb. 24, 2007).

[7] Walleed H. Malik (World Bank attorney), "Challenges of Forging Civil Society Partnership for Judicial Reform," (undated) www1.worldbank.org/publicsector/legal/venezuelapaper.doc (accessed Feb. 24, 2007).

police, prosecutors, public defenders, ombudsmen and others. The scope of justice reform also comprises all kinds of dispute resolution mechanisms. It includes those provided by the courts, but also alternative dispute resolution mechanisms.

The justice sector also relies on a number of legal professionals with various profiles. Judges, court staff, bailiffs, lawyers and notaries are all actors in the system. Consequently, justice reform deals with each of them, including the way they are educated and trained.

The Law and Justice Institutions department works to reform justice institutions, including the Ministries of Justice, Office of the Attorney General, the police, the prosecution, the public defense, ombudsman, and bar associations.

World Bank, Law Reform

Sound legal frameworks are prerequisites for economic growth and social development. The process through which laws and regulations are conceptualized, drafted, enacted, publicized and enforced is the foundation of a society governed by the rule of law. Legal reform is an ongoing and incremental process that involves the executive and legislative branches, law reform commissions, non-governmental organizations, and the public. For most countries, legal reform addresses new international standards, responds to social and economic issues, expands access to justice or improves court operations. Effective and coherent legal reform requires a comprehensive and sustainable approach that avoids importing "models" inconsistent with national legal and socioeconomic norms. Effective legal reform also promotes opportunity, security, and empowerment for the world's poor.

Although legal reform efforts often involve institutional restructuring, rewriting old laws and drafting new ones remain a necessary component of most legal reform projects. Moreover, many development projects that do not constitute legal reform per se, such as administrative reforms, infrastructure projects, environmental initiatives, nonetheless require changes in the substantive law. Yet even in stable, democratic countries, creating sound laws and regulations is a challenge. In developing and transitioning countries, political interference, a lack of experience and resources, and the constraints imposed by weak enforcement agencies often make the job of law drafting even harder.

Reformers sometimes also fall into the trap of believing that new laws can solve problems simply by virtue of the fact that the laws exist. Yet laws and regulations that are overly complex or that fail to take into account weaknesses in the agencies that will enforce them or the greater social context can create more problems than they solve. Governments struggling to create a minimal political consensus may find that their laws, often filled with last minute additions and deletions, conflict with one another or fail to serve the purposes intended. A tendency to over-regulate can lead to regulations that are ignored, harming the reputation of the legal system as a whole.

Law reform involves a number of elements: lawmaking, such as code reform, law commissions, and drafting law; the legal framework and the judicial sector, including the international law (especially international human rights law) and the constitutional law components; and sector-specific laws, such as corporate governance, tax laws, and bankruptcy laws.

The decision of the World Bank Group to become involved in criminal justice has multiplier effects because all of the international financial institutions (e.g., regional development banks) have emulated their priorities and supplemented their work. *See, e.g.*, the work of the Asian Development Bank in section IV.C.2.

Notes and Questions

1. The idea that the WBG can and should help developing countries' criminal justice and legal systems arises in part out of the U.S. government's experience supporting development of the rule of law, including criminal law programs, to help achieve democracy. A recurrent theme in U.S. foreign policy since the last four decades of the twentieth century, this approach became by the 1990s a virtually unchallenged U.S. foreign policy doctrine. *See, e.g.*, EXPORTING DEMOCRACY: THE UNITED STATES AND LATIN AMERICA (Abraham F. Lowenthal ed., 2 volumes, 1991). What are the arguments for not including criminal justice and criminal law in development work?

2. One aspect of supporting the rule of law as part of a governance, democracy, and anticorruption program is supporting the judiciary. In most democracies, an independent judiciary with well-trained jurists provides a critical check on the power of the legislative and executive branches. *See, e.g.*, TRANSITION TO DEMOCRACY IN LATIN AMERICA: THE ROLE OF THE JUDICIARY (Irwin P. Stotszky ed., 1993).

3. Does the traditional reluctance of the World Bank Group and other development organizations to participate in the criminal justice and criminal law elements of development arise out of the traditional separation of criminal and civil law? In the legal world, this separation has been reflected in the way law firms have traditionally avoided combining civil and criminal law practices in the same firm. Common law firms, especially in the United States, were the first to break from the tradition of separating civil and criminal law work.

4. The recent inclusion of criminal justice and legal reform components on the agendas of the WBG and other development organizations shows how the issue of separating criminal law from other legal areas has evolved. For example, the WBG initially decided to include criminal justice in some of its law modernization and reform projects. Subsequently, the WBG included anticorruption policies, as discussed later. Even the inclusion of anticorruption policies has undergone a dynamic, albeit controversial, evolution in 2007–2008.

5. Governability, a major goal of World Bank Group projects, refers to the ability of a government to impose values on its society and to exercise ultimate authority in the context of generally accepted rules and procedures. Democratic governability includes the notion of procedures, guarantees, and freely contested, periodic elections with maximum participation of a citizenry that enjoys basic rights, including freedom of speech and assembly. It also includes institutions that ensure the accountability of chief executives to courts and legislatures and that provide the administrative capacity for governments to carry out basic tasks, such as collecting taxes and enforcing the law. *See* John Bailey & Roy Godson, ORGANIZED CRIME & DEMOCRATIC GOVERNABILITY: MEXICO AND THE U.S.-MEXICAN BORDERLANDS 217 (2000).

IV. Money Laundering

The World Bank and the International Monetary Fund share identical goals with respect to anti-money laundering (AML) and combating the financing of terrorism (CFT). They work together on achieving these goals.

After the September 11, 2001, terrorist attacks, the World Bank and IMF Boards of Executive Directors adopted action plans to strengthen anti-money laundering (AML) and combating the financing of terrorism (CFT) programs. In July and August 2002, they recognized the FATF Forty Recommendations on Money Laundering and the Nine Special Recommendations on Terrorist Financing as the relevant international standards for AML/CFT. The boards added AML and CFT to the list of areas of WBG operational work and began a twelve-month pilot program using a universal, comprehensive AML/CFT assessment in November 2002.[8]

A. *Awareness Building*

1. The Global Dialogue Series

The IMF/World Bank have worked to raise awareness within country leadership about AML/CFT issues, their implications, and the available resources and assistance. To do so, they have established a series of Regional Policy Global Dialogues on AML/CFT. These interactive video conferences for member countries within a given geographic region enable government officials from those countries, staff of the IMF/World Bank, FATF-Style Regional Bodies (FSRBs), regional development banks, and other international organizations to discuss and exchange information.

The Dialogues discuss the challenges countries face in combating illicit money flows, and they enable participants to share the lessons of success, identify specific problems for countries in that region, and gain an understanding of the types of assistance countries need to combat money laundering and terrorist financing.

The Global Dialogue Series focuses on a number of key questions, including the following:

- How can the IMF/World Bank help countries improve their responses to money laundering and terrorist financing?
- How do money laundering and terrorist financing fit into the broader framework of corruption and poor governance?
- What has been the response of governments to the new international standards of anti-money laundering and counter-terrorist financing? What are the current challenges for regulators? What is the appropriate institutional structure for each country in implementing an effective program to combat money laundering and terrorist financing?
- What are the future challenges in combating money laundering and terrorist financing in participating countries?

The Dialogues enable senior policymakers in participating countries to offer their views on the economic costs of criminal abuse of financial systems, especially money laundering and the financing of terrorism. The Dialogues also air practical means of sustaining economic development and financial market integrity in the face of illicit money movements and financial crime. Policymakers learn from each other by drawing on the experiences of their peers and the broader experience of international experts.

[8] Paul Allan Schott, Reference Guide to Anti-Money Laundering and Combating the Financing of Terrorism X-1–X-3 (IMF/World Bank 2003).

2. Country Assistance Strategy (CAS)

The World Bank is integrating the results of the Financial Sector Assistance Program (FSAP), which includes AML, into the broader range of development measures in the Country Assistance Strategy (CAS), which establishes the priorities for the World Bank's program for a given country on a three-year basis in consultation with the government of that country. Since March 2002, AML/CFT assistance follows systematic reviews of FSAP findings and is included in the CASs. The World Bank prioritizes giving technical assistance to countries where weaknesses in the integrity of the AML/CFT regime may pose significant governance and development risks. CASs also discuss and make recommendations on AML/CFT issues in countries that have been deficient in meeting international standards and best practices.

B. *Developing a Universal AML/CFT Assessment Methodology*

Since 2002, the IMF/World Bank have cooperated with the FATF and international organizations and networks, such as the Basel Committee on Banking Supervision, International Association of Securities Commissioners, the International Association of Insurance Supervisors, and the Egmont Group to produce a single, comprehensive AML/CFT assessment methodology. At its October 2002 plenary meeting, FATF endorsed this methodology, which has 120 criteria covering each of the FATF Forty and Special Recommendations, including implementation of criminal law enforcement. It includes the legal and institutional AML/CFT framework for a country and the establishment of financial intelligence units (FIUs). The methodology also covers relevant UN Security Council resolutions, international conventions, and other international standard setters, and gives an in-depth assessment of preventive measures for financial institutions.

1. Twelve-Month Pilot Program

On November 15, 2002, the World Bank approved the assessment program for a twelve-month pilot period. The IMF/World Bank have focused on pairing the assessment with appropriate technical assistance to help countries fight money laundering and terrorist financing and bring their AML/CFT regime into compliance with the FATF's Forty Recommendations and Special Recommendations. The pilot program has been relatively well received.

2. Reports on the Observance of Standards and Codes

The IMF/World Bank have developed an AML/CFT assessment program designed to produce Reports on the Observance of Standards and Codes (ROSCs). The assessments leading to a ROSC are conducted following two methods, one using reports made in the context of mutual evaluations by the FATF and by participating FSRBs, the other (applicable to countries that are not members of the FATF or an FSRB) using a report made by a IMF/World Bank-led mission. The ROSC process is a voluntary, cooperative, and uniform process. Hence, the AML/CFT assessments conducted by the IMF/World Bank are done only at the request of a country.[9]

[9] *Id.* at X-5–6.

C. *Building Institutional Capacity*

1. Training Conferences

The IMF/World Bank organize targeted training conferences on specific AM/CFT issues, utilizing public officials involved in AML/CFT from a particular region. For example, in 2002 they organized technical assistance conferences in Montevideo, Uruguay, and in Moscow. The FIRST Initiative[10] sponsored the conferences with the organizational support of the IMF/World Bank.

The Moscow conference focused on establishing operational financial intelligence units (FIUs), and it targeted countries that did not have operational FIUs or had newly operational FIUs. Experts from Eastern European countries that recently met AML/CFT compliance standards presented their experience and best practices. Conference participants met counterpart officials from other member countries and representatives from organizations that provide technical assistance.[11]

Argentina Regional Summit on Counterterrorism Financial Enforcement Creates New Working Group

EXCERPTED FROM 22 INTERNATIONAL ENFORCEMENT L. REP. 222 (JUNE 2006)

by Bruce Zagaris

On March 10, 2006, at the conclusion of a regional summit of counterterrorism financial enforcement, the Central Bank of Argentina announced the creation of a working group to promote hemispheric measures to prevent terrorist financing. The Central Bank of Argentina, along with the IMF, had organized the summit.[12]

Martín Redrado, the President of the Central Bank, said that [the] Argentine government would form a committee to coordinate the counterterrorism activities of various Argentina agencies. Argentine President Néstor Kirchner will analyze a legislative project to improve the operability of the Argentine Financial Intelligence Unit.

High level officials from the Federal Reserve and the U.S. Department of Treasury, the Federation of the Banks of Florida, the Latin American Federation of Banks, the central banks of Brazil, Uruguay, Paraguay, and Chile, distinct associations of banks of Argentina, and international financial institutions, such as the Inter-American Development Bank and the World Bank participated in the meeting.

The Central Bank will produce a work document to be debated by the rest of the entities represented and will coordinate the next activities, documents, and meetings. Such analysis will have the following goals: (1) realize a description of the problem of the informality of the region apart from the relevant evidence in Argentina; (2) propose recommendations and proceedings to apply in countries with high informality, which permit differentiating this phenomenon from criminal activities of narcotics trafficking and terrorism; (3) promote joint

[10] http://www.firstinitiative.org.
[11] Paul Allan Schott, *supra* note 8 at X-6 (World Bank/IMF 2003).
[12] Banco Central el la República Argentina Central Bank of Argentina), *Creación de un Grupo de Trabajo para la Prevención del Financiamiento del Terrorismo (Creation of a Work Group for the Prevention of Terrorism Financing)*, Communication No. 48488 (Mar. 10, 2006).

actions among central banks of the region, with the aim of favoring communication and serving the bounds to request initiatives from the private sector; (4) seek the participation of central banks of the region as auditors of first instance, with the object of reducing the uncertainty and mitigation of discrimination against local financial entities; and (5) incorporate mechanisms of relation among financial institutions, which serve as references of reputations among its participants.

The document will be presented in Washington, D.C. to the authorities and others responsible for international recommendations on this material.

In the regional summit – which focused on the implementation of policies in force in the battle against terrorism financing – public and private sector parties agreed to cooperate.

The summit emphasized recent regulations including the obligation to disclose the existence of financial assets of subjects identified by authorities, and the establishment of special precautions in terms of conservation of transactions and guides that identify suspicious operations. The summit discussed the requirement that financial entities must report the existence of persons that appear on lists of suspected terrorists, not only of the UN but also of the U.S., the EU, and Canada.

At the summit, speakers reiterated the importance of the cooperative exchange of information and of tools designed to control international terrorist financial flows, and the effort to develop hemispheric norms on the subject.

A number of high-level officials and experts on counter terrorist financial enforcement (CTFE) participated in the regional summit.

2. Delivery of Technical Assistance to Individual Countries

The goals of the IMF technical assistance, as described in its Articles of Agreement, are "to contribute to the development of the productive resources of member countries by enhancing the effectiveness of economic policy and financial management." In practice, the IMF fulfills this objective by helping countries develop their human and institutional capacity to design and implement effective macroeconomic and structural policies, put in place reforms that strengthen their financial sectors, and reduce their vulnerability to crises.[13]

The receipt of technical assistance is one of the benefits of IMF membership. The IMF normally provides such assistance free of charge to any requesting member country, within its resource constraints. About three-quarters of IMF technical assistance goes to low and lower middle income countries, particularly in sub-Saharan Africa and Asia. Postconflict countries are also major beneficiaries. A wide range of other countries seek technical assistance to strengthen their capacities. Through assisting countries to reduce their weaknesses and vulnerabilities, technical assistance also contributes to a more robust and stable global economy.

The IMF's efforts to strengthen the international financial system have led to demands for technical assistance. For example, countries have asked for help to address financial sector weaknesses identified within the framework of the joint IMF/World Bank Financial Sector Assessment Program; to adopt and adhere to international standards and codes for financial, fiscal, and statistical management; to implement recommendations from

[13] IMF, *Technical Assistance*, IMF Factsheet (Sept. 2004).

offshore financial centers assessments; and to strengthen measures to combat money laundering and the financing of terrorism. At the same time, there is a continuing demand for technical assistance to help low-income countries build their capacity to design and implement poverty-reducing and growth programs and for the more traditional areas of economic development and regulation.

The IMF attaches great importance to country ownership of the assistance process. The recipient country is fully involved in the entire process of technical assistance, from identification of need, to implementation, monitoring, and evaluation.

The IMF provides technical assistance in various ways. Support is often provided through short staff missions of limited duration sent from headquarters and the placement of experts and/or resident advisors for periods ranging from a few weeks to a few years (if the intention is to field a long-term advisor, countries may be asked to make a financial or in-kind contribution). Assistance might also be provided in the form of technical and diagnostic reports, training courses, seminars, workshops, and online advice and support.

The IMF has increasingly adopted a regional approach to the delivery of technical assistance and training for government officials.

IMF technical assistance is financed from both internal and external sources. The IMF directly finances technical assistance delivery, supervision, and administrative and other overhead costs; this accounts for about one-fifth of its total net administrative budget. The IMF also administers funding provided by bilateral and multilateral donors. Such cooperation and resource sharing has two benefits: it leverages the resources available for technical assistance, and it helps avoid duplication of efforts.

Bilateral donors include Australia, Austria, Brazil, Canada, China, Denmark, Finland, France, Germany, India, Ireland, Italy, Japan, Luxembourg, the Netherlands, New Zealand, Norway, Portugal, Russia, Singapore, Sweden, Switzerland, the United Kingdom, and the United States. Multilateral donors include the African Development Bank, the Arab Monetary Fund, the Asian Development Bank, the European Commission, the Inter-American Development Bank, the United Nations, the United Nations Development Program (UNDP), and the World Bank. In FY 2004, external financing accounted for more than one-quarter of the IMF's total technical assistance and training activities, with Japan being the most generous donor.[14]

Since 1999, measures have been undertaken to strengthen the effectiveness of IMF technical assistance, in the following ways: integrating it more closely with surveillance and lending programs; reinforcing coordination with other providers, especially the World Bank; improving modalities of delivery, especially through the establishment of regional centers; strengthening the monitoring and evaluation of assistance programs; and promoting the dissemination of information on those programs more widely. The IMF's Independent Evaluation Office is also undertaking a review of this technical assistance to derive operational recommendations that can enhance its contribution to the overall IMF mandate.[15]

In reality, the IMF's ROSCs and FSAPs can generate an unlimited amount of incentives or compulsion, depending on one's perspective, for technical assistance in implementing an AML and CFT regulatory and enforcement regime. In effect, most major and even mid-level countries were not in full compliance with the first generation of AML

[14] *Id.*
[15] *Id.*

standards at the time that FATF issued its Forty Recommendations and added CTF regulatory requirements. As a result, depending on the stringency of the ROSC and FSAP evaluations, the IMF has the capacity to generate an endless amount of technical assistance.

Asian Development Bank Approves New Anti-Money Laundering Policy, 19 Int'l Enforcement L. Rep. 247 (July 2003)

by Bruce Zagaris

On April 1, 2003, the Asian Development Bank (ADB) approved a policy to increase anti-money laundering (AML) and counter terrorism financial (CTF) enforcement efforts in the Asian and Pacific region through increased assistance to its developing member countries (DMCs), improved cooperation and cooperation with other organizations, and an enhanced internal system to protect its own funds from misuse.[16]

The decision to adopt this policy cements the prioritization of AML and CTF enforcement within the broad context of its work in poverty reduction, strengthening financial systems, and promoting good governance and anticorruption.

The ADB has pledged to complement rather than duplicate programs of other international organizations and groups, such as the Financial Action Task Force on Money Laundering (FATF), the United Nations, the International Monetary Fund, the World Bank, and FATF-style regional bodies, especially the Asia Pacific Group on Money Laundering (APG).

The ADB will customize its work to take into account the region's special problems and circumstances, such as weak institutional capacity, inadequate laws, and lack of specialized training for government officials to implement relevant laws.

According to Motoo Noguchi, an ADB counsel who has worked on AML projects, many ADB member countries are in the process of establishing or improving their legal and regulatory frameworks necessary for effective AML and CTF enforcement based on internationally accepted standards. Nevertheless, the international standards continue to change and hence requests for ADB technical assistance (TA) from its DMCs continue to increase rapidly.

The main elements of the ADB policy are:

1. ADB will include AML and CTF enforcement in policy dialogue with DMCs, especially when the latter request ADB assistance.
2. TA grants as well as project, program, and TA loans, and funds from other sources administered by ADB, will be provided to raise awareness of the risks that these issues pose; establish or strengthen legal, regulatory, and institutional frameworks; and build capacity. ADB will also help with research and holding regional conferences and workshops.
3. The ADB will strengthen collaboration with other international organizations to ensure consistency in strategy, ensure better coordination, and avoid duplication. The ADB will have increased presence at international and regional meetings on AML and CTF enforcement.
4. The ADB will continue to monitor and strengthen its procedures to ensure that its funds are not misused through fraudulent procurement, contracting, and accounting.

[16] Asian Development Bank, *New Policy in Fight Against Money Laundering and Terrorist Financing*, April 1, 2003.

5. The ADB will provide additional staff and training to strengthen capacity and expertise to handle the issues and respond quickly to DMCs' requests for assistance.[17]

The ADB will develop a formal network among its various departments and offices to put the policy into operation and provide coordination and monitoring.

After four years the ADB will review the policy's progress. It has already provided a number of loans and TA projects to strengthen its DMCs' financial sectors, as well as several TA projects and loan components focusing on fighting money laundering.[18]

The new policy of the ADB mirrors the growing involvement by international financial institutions (IFIs), such as the IMF and World Bank Group, and regional IFIs, such as the Inter-American Development Bank in prioritizing their work on AML and CTF enforcement. For many years, IFIs shunned rule of law and administration of justice projects, preferring physical projects and infrastructure building. As IFIs have prioritized governance and transparency, they have given greater prominence to AML and CTF enforcement and anticorruption issues.

3. Coordination of Technical Assistance

Working with donor organizations and international organizations, the IMF/World Bank developed an initiative to coordinate AML/CFT technical assistance (TA) requests. The AML/CFT TA coordination initiative identifies high-priority TA needs and fills gaps in the delivery of TA, strengthens the roles of the FSRBs in TA coordination at the regional level, and increases information flow on TA needs.

The IMF/World Bank have organized a network of contacts among participating organizations to facilitate coordination and communication of TA activities and to identify TA providers and potential sources of funding. Past experience suggests that TA coordination should be handled on a regional basis by FSRBs. Donors and providers should identify and respond to immediate country needs for AML/CFT TA and consider additional ways for the FSRB secretariats to play a strengthened role in coordinating TA within their regions.

The IMF/World Bank have taken primary responsibility in maintaining the TA database and working individually with the FSRBs secretariats. As the TA priorities are collected by the FSRBs, the IMF/World Bank transmit these requests to, and coordinate with, the various donors and TA providers.[19]

4. Surveillance

This process of monitoring and consultation, normally referred to as "surveillance," has rapidly evolved as the world economy has changed. IMF surveillance has also become increasingly open and transparent in recent years.[20]

The contagion effect of recent financial crises has underscored the importance of effective surveillance. In response, the IMF has undertaken many initiatives to strengthen its capacity to detect vulnerabilities and risks at an early stage, to help member countries

[17] *Id.*

[18] *Id.*

[19] Schott, *supra* note 8 at X-8.

[20] IMF, *IMF Surveillance, IMF Factsheet* (Sept. 2004).

strengthen their policy frameworks and institutions, and to improve transparency and accountability of its member countries.[21]

The IMF has a mandate under Article IV of its Articles of Agreement to exercise surveillance over the exchange rate policies of its members to ensure the effective operation of the international monetary system. In 1977, an Executive Board decision recognized that the IMF's appraisal of exchange rate policy requires a comprehensive analysis of the general economic situation and policy strategy of each member country.

The goals of surveillance are the same today as in 1977. However, the framework for surveillance has evolved significantly both to promote the benefits and to respond to the challenges of an increasingly open world economy, including the dramatic expansion of international capital flows and, hence, the potential danger of the contagion effect of financial crises in a country, group of countries, and a region.

Exchange rate, monetary, and fiscal policies remain at the center of IMF surveillance. The IMF provides advice on issues ranging from the choice of exchange rate regime to how to ensure consistency between the exchange rate regime and the stance of fiscal and monetary policies.

Structural policies – such as those governing a country's international trade, labor markets, and energy sectors – became more important to IMF surveillance in the 1980s as economic growth slowed in many industrial countries in the wake of a major oil price shock. Debt crises in the developing world and the breakup of the Soviet Union further underlined the need for structural change in many countries. Today, structural issues are included in the IMF's policy dialogue with its member countries whenever they have an important impact on macroeconomic performance.

Financial sector issues have received increasing emphasis in IMF surveillance following a series of banking crises in industrial and developing countries in the 1990s. In 1999, the IMF and the World Bank created a joint Financial Sector Assessment Program (FSAP) to assess the strengths and weaknesses of countries' financial sectors. In those countries that have participated, FSAP findings provide important inputs into IMF surveillance.

Institutional issues – such as central bank independence, financial sector regulation, corporate governance, and policy transparency and accountability – have also become increasingly important to IMF surveillance in the wake of financial crises and in the context of some member countries' transitions from planned to market economies. In recent years, the IMF and the World Bank have taken a central role in developing, implementing, and assessing internationally recognized standards and codes that are crucial for the efficient functioning of a modern economy.[22]

One example of the contribution of IMF surveillance to AML/CFT policy is the IMF's study of financial intelligence units.[23] This book, which analyzes more than ten years of FIU operation, notes that more than eighty FIUs have gained admission

[21] For instance, as a result of the contagion effect of financial crises, the Financial Stability Forum was formed outside of the IMF and issued its report on offshore financial centers (OFCs), classifying them into three levels of compliance with international standards. *See* Financial Stability Forum, *Report of the Working Group on Offshore Financial Centres* (April 2000), available at http://www.fsforum.org/publications/publication_23_31.html.

[22] IMF, *IMF Surveillance, supra.*

[23] International Monetary Fund/World Bank, Financial Intelligence Units: An Overview (133 pp., 2004, ISBN 1–58906–349-X).

into the Egmont Group, the informal international association of FIUs established in 1995.[24] The book summarizes the wide variety of FIU arrangements: administrative, law-enforcement, judicial- or prosecutorial, and "mixed" or "hybrid" FIU models. It reviews the international conventions that encourage countries to establish FIUs and notes the core principles of financial sector supervision and model laws. The book also discusses the institutional autonomy and accountability of FIUs, organizational and staffing issues, and security considerations. Today, as many countries plan to establish or reorganize FIUs, *Financial Intelligence Units: An Overview* is a useful guide.

Chapter 2 of the handbook discusses the key issues involved in establishing FIUs, including consultations with the private sector, financing, and the various forms an FIU can take in a government structure. The third chapter considers the core functions of an FIU – receiving and analyzing suspicious transaction reports and disseminating the resulting intelligence – and provides examples from different countries. Chapter 4 discusses some of the most important additional functions assigned to certain FIUs, such as monitoring the reporting institutions' compliance with AML/CFT. Chapter 5 discusses the enhancement of the effectiveness of FIUs. The final chapter describes the international assessment process for FIUs in the context of overall AML/CFT framework assessments.[25]

Assessing the risks and vulnerabilities of large, volatile capital flows has become a central focus of IMF surveillance in recent years. Although surveillance has always focused on crisis prevention, the growth and development of global capital markets have required an expansion of the scope of surveillance beyond the traditional, more narrow focus on current account positions and external debt sustainability.[26]

"Article IV consultations," as IMF surveillance discussions are known, usually take place once a year. IMF economists visit a member country to gather information and hold discussions with its government and central bank officials, and often with private investors, labor representatives, members of parliament, and civil society organizations as well. The IMF mission then submits a report to the IMF's Executive Board for discussion. The Board's views are subsequently summarized and transmitted to the country's authorities.

In recent years, the IMF has worked to make surveillance more transparent. Before 1997, the IMF's assessments of member countries' policies were treated as confidential documents. Now, nine out of ten member countries agree to the publication of a Public Information Notice, which summarizes the staff's and the Board's views, and four out of five countries agree to publication of the staff report itself (FY2004 data).[27] Transparency means that countries whose AML and CFT regulatory and enforcement regimes fall below the FATF standards are likely to be exposed and embarrassed. Nevertheless, because countries undergoing a review have the option of keeping the FSAP review confidential, the pressure on noncomplying countries is more subtle than the FATF noncooperative countries and territories (NCCT) process.

The IMF continuously reviews global economic trends and developments in a process known as multilateral surveillance. The IMF also regularly examines economic

[24] The Egmont Group Financial Intelligence Unit (FIUs), at www.egmontgroup.org/about_egmont.pdf.

[25] For additional background, see Bruce Zagaris, *IMF/World Bank Publish Handbook on Financial Intelligence Units*, 21 INT'L ENFORCEMENT L. REP. 49 (Feb. 2005).

[26] IMF, *IMF Surveillance, supra* note 20.

[27] *Id.*

developments and policies pursued under regional arrangements such as the European Union and the West African Economic and Monetary Union. IMF surveillance of its member countries provides important input to the multilateral and regional surveillance processes and vice versa.

The IMF also publishes a biannual World Economic Outlook, which discusses the state of the world economy and provides in-depth analysis of specific issues and challenges. In addition, the biannual Global Financial Stability Report assesses the stability of global financial markets and identifies potential systemic weaknesses.

Notes and Questions

1. The ability of countries to maintain the confidentiality of Article IV consultations has made them more willing to undergo such reviews than to submit to an FATF mutual evaluation, which is published and can result in FATF blacklisting. Does the fact that Article IV reviews are performed by the IMF, an international organization with a universal membership, whereas FATF is an informal network composed of a small number of countries, give the Article IV reviews more legitimacy?

2. To what extent does the long tradition of Article IV consultations influence their acceptance by IMF members?

3. One of the continuing problems in the application of Article IV consultations is that not all countries are subject to them. For instance, the United States does not undergo Article IV consultations. A number of small offshore financial centers (SOFCs) have argued that the United States' exemption from such consultations, coupled with its status as the chief source of financing for AML and CFT initiatives, has created an unfair playing field in the international market for financial services. Since the late 1990s, the U.S. Government Accountability Office (GAO) has repeatedly reported that the lack of appropriate United States corporate vehicle transparency standards has allowed Eastern European organized crime groups to use U.S. shell corporations to open bank accounts and receive proceeds of crime. According to these same GAO reports, the United States has received many requests for mutual assistance in criminal matters concerning such corporations, but the gaps in transparency of corporate vehicles have prevented the United States from cooperating effectively.

4. The IMF conference in Argentina, described earlier, and the decision to create a working group to promote hemispheric measures to prevent terrorist financing illustrate how the educational and institutional aspects of the WBG's AML and CFTE programs often interact.

5. Some commentators have urged the IMF to impose robust counterterrorism conditionalities in its loans. For instance, they urge that the requirements of UN Security Resolution 1371 should be imposed. What are the pros and cons of imposing such conditionalities? *See, e.g.*, Olivera Medenica, *The World Bank, the IMF and the Global Prevention of Terrorism, A Role for Conditionalities*, 29 BROOK J. L. 664, 704–7 (2004).

6. Although the World Bank Group has a universal membership and hence enhanced legitimacy in developing and enforcing standards compared, for instance, to the FATF or OECD, commentators point out that the WBG and IMF are nevertheless controlled by the large states. Hence, they argue that devising and then imposing standards on the developing countries that necessarily will need WBG capital and not on the large states causes legitimacy problems. *See*, e.g., Robert P. Delonis, *International Financial Standards and Codes: Mandatory Regulation without Representation*, 36 N.Y.U. J. INT'L

Law & Pol. 563, 563–64 (2004 (despite the IMF's statements to the contrary, the methods used by the IMF to promote universal implementation of standards and codes make their adoption essentially mandatory for developing states that seek, or may seek, access to IMF or private capital. Additionally, the control and policymaking structures of these institutions overly exclude developing states and their citizens. This exclusion violates the norm of democratic governance and risks diminished policy compliance because of that violation).

D. *Research and Analysis*

The WBG periodically conducts research and publishes guides on AML, CFT, and related issues such as financial intelligence units and regulatory frameworks for hawalas and other remittance systems.

1. Analysis of the Hawala System

Book Review: *Regulatory Frameworks for Hawala and Other Remittance Systems, Monetary and Financial Systems Department, International Monetary Fund* (2005)

REPRINTED FROM INT'L ENFORCEMENT L. REP. 22 423 (NOVEMBER 2006)

Reviewed by Bruce Zagaris

In the last five years the international community and especially the organizations responsible for anti-money laundering and counter-terrorism financial enforcement have focused attention on the problems of hawala and other remittance systems. *Regulatory Frameworks for Hawala and Other Remittance Systems* is a collection of essays arising out of the First International Conference on Hawala, organized in May 2002 by the United Arab Emirates. The book includes a collection of essays on regulatory frameworks in remitting and receiving countries and some general articles on the problems that can arise when regulating remittance systems.

R. Barry Johnston, Assistant Director in the Monetary and Financial Systems Department of the IMF, discusses "Work of the IMF in Informal Funds Transfer Systems." Johnston's chapter explains that in countries where financial capacity is limited, informal funds transfer (IFT) systems play a critical role. IFT systems can have economic implications, such as macroeconomic consequences, especially in countries in which large volumes of transactions are channeled through such systems. Certain characteristics of IFT systems, including anonymity and lack of official scrutiny, may make them vulnerable to use by criminals for money laundering and terrorist financing.

The IMF sets forth various factors the international community should consider when designing regulatory and supervisory systems: (1) the regulatory structure should be appropriate and commensurate to the risks, especially in view of the limited knowledge of IFT systems and the extent to which those systems are exploited by criminals; (2) remittances are very important to migrant workers who send money home and IFT systems represent an important source of income for some countries; (3) informal systems are very difficult to regulate without sending the systems further underground and hence the international community must show the IFT operators and participants that the benefits of regulation will outweigh the costs; (4) the international community must design supervisory and regulatory guidelines that take local circumstances into account; (5) the international community will need to use multiple approaches, including promoting the formal sector in fund transfers, as several countries have done successfully; and (6) the international community needs to specifically acknowledge the difficulties of implementing effective regulation in conflict-afflicted countries.

Even in the aftermath of the Abu Dhabi Declaration of the First International Conference on Hawala and the best practices paper on FATF Special Recommendation VI, the international community needs to study the following issues: (1) licensing or registration requirements and the rationale for choosing one over another; (2) the need for a fit-and-proper or due diligence test by a competent authority of owners and managers of an IFT; (3) implementation of anti-money laundering regulations for customer identification, record keeping, and reporting of suspicious transactions and counterterrorist finance regulations; (4) the merits and costs of having compliance monitoring and sanctions with IFT regulatory systems and the experience with self-regulatory compliance systems; (5) the public sector's obligations to consumers once IFT systems are regulated and the best ways to discharge such obligations; and (6) building acceptance of regulatory frameworks for IFT systems and in creating the capacity to implement the regulation.

Nikos Passas, Professor at Northeastern University, College of Criminal Justice, Boston, discusses "Formalizing the Informal? Problems in the National and International Regulation of Hawala." The chapter has the themes that (1) hawala serves honest people as well as serious criminals; (2) financial controls of terrorism are critical but no panacea; (3) a counterproductive overemphasis has targeted hawala as uniquely vulnerable to abuse; (4) current regulatory arrangements fail to meet stated objectives; and (5) careful consideration of sound empirical evidence and genuine dialogue with the sector are indispensable.

The most promising approach to hawala regulation is through outreach to all stakeholders. Ascertaining the views of hawaladars and building a consensus will likely result in future compliance and transparency or traceability of transactions. Encouraging further cost reductions and more convenient and accessible formal remittance avenues would ensure the continuation of these services to needy communities.

At the domestic level, countries like the U.S. would be wise to harmonize their federal, state, and local rules and responses on the basis of evidence, appreciation, and understanding of the networks they seek to supervise and control. Internationally, consideration should be given to the establishment of specific policy goals and urging countries to meet them in their own way, consistent with local traditions, culture, and socioeconomic conditions, so that the international community promotes legal harmonization while permitting the necessary diversity and flexibility.

The author observes that a demand-side approach to counterterrorism must supplement supply-side, law enforcement, and military approaches. Terrorism is also a socioeconomic and political issue reflecting both local and global problems. Long-term success must have policies that address the fundamental problems underlying extremism of all kinds.

Raúl Hernández-Coss, a financial sector specialist in the World Bank's Financial Market Integrity (FSEFI) unit, discusses "Comparing Mature and Nascent Remittance Corridors: U.S.-Mexico and Canada-Vietnam." The chapter considers the U.S.-Mexico corridor as a mature market for formal remittance as compared to the Canada-Vietnam corridor as a nascent stage in the shift to formal systems. The distinction suggests that researchers and policymakers should acknowledge that different remittance corridors face different priorities based on their stage of development and other factors and hence should focus on different policies when shifting to formal systems. The lessons for the nascent market is that it must focus on setting the conditions for efficient formal remittance mechanisms. These conditions include providing market players, both in the sending and recipient economy, with more information on the magnitude of the corridor, the potential networks available for origination and distribution, a better understanding of the informal channels used in the corridor, their possible links with illicit proceeds, and most important, a deeper analysis of the demand for financial services by senders. The final condition could facilitate the creation of new products that support the use of multiplatform schemes to conduct remittance transactions.

Saeed Al-Hamiz, the Executive Director of the Banking Supervision and Examination Department of the Central Bank of the U.A.E., discusses "Hawala: A U.A.E. Perspective." The chapter observes that the U.A.E. considers that hawala is popular because it is often faster and more reliable in reaching the beneficiary, transmission charges are cheaper compared to banks and money exchanges, the hawala rate is better than the official banking exchange rate, and it can be used in rural areas, which in some countries lack formal banking facilities.

In November 2002, the Central Bank of the U.A.E. issued a public notice inviting hawaladars to register with the following conditions: (1) a simple certificate will be issued, free of charge, to registering hawaladars with assurance that their names and details will be kept safe at the bank; (2) a hawaladar must maintain a record of each transaction, including the details of the remitter and full particulars of the hawaladar's bank account; (3) details of reverse transactions (inward remittances) should be registered; (4) hawaladars must report transfers they suspect may be related to money laundering; and (5) hawaladars must submit returns to the Central Bank. All hawaladars (124) applying have obtained certificates. The system is in the infant stage.

Maud J. Bökkerink, a financial sector expert in the Monetary and Financial Systems Department of the IMF, discusses "The Netherlands–Supervision of Money Remittance Offices." Informal money remittance services are prohibited in the Netherlands unless the service providers are registered with the central bank. Since August 1998, money remittance providers have been obliged to report unusual transactions.

Applicants for a money remittance must furnish, *inter alia,* information on the identity and criminal records of the directors, owners, and managers, as well as the operational management. The central bank can refuse applications if it believes the integrity of the financial system would be impaired or if the management or administrative organization is not adequate to ensure the proper conduct of business or compliance with other statutory obligations to which the office is subject.

A money remittance office must also provide a bank guarantee to assure consumer protection. Money remittance providers must pay a fee to register and an annual fee to cover the cost of supervision. Both cost U.S. $3,000. Money transaction offices also pay an annual fee as a percentage of their annual fees to fully recover the costs of supervision.

Since the Money Transaction Offices Act came into force in July 2002, approximately half of the applications for registration have been refused. As of September 15, 2004, 31 money transaction offices had been registered. In several cases where the registration was refused, the central bank followed up to see if the offices had stopped their money remittance business. Some investigations led to a cease and desist order while other cases were referred to the public prosecutor.

An inspection team of the central bank performs onsite inspections of registered money remittance offices two to four times annually. Money remittances must send a monthly financial report, submit annual accounts and an annual report. The enforcement unit of the central bank, to see if money remittance offices are operating without a registration, visits certain locations, checks the Internet with dedicated software, and checks national and regional publications and newspapers. The Financial Expertise Center (FEC), an interagency coordinating body for the exchange of information on financial crime established in 1998, has two consultative bodies for information sharing and cooperation: a research group and an investigation group. The FEC also collects information not only on registered offices, but also on illegal offices and has proposed additional investigations. In 2004, the public prosecutor investigated six cases proposed by the project team.

David Faulkner, senior policy adviser for Financial Systems and International Standards, H.M. Treasury, discusses "U.K. Regulation of Money Service Businesses." The chapter describes how the U.K. regulates its money service businesses (MSBs. The U.K. has taken a two pronged approach to regulating MSBs, depending on whether they operate in the formal or informal realms. Businesses in the informal sector are stand-alone and independent. H.M. Customs regulates and supervises them.

The U.K. has over 2,500 registered money service operators conducting their business in over 32,000 premises, half of which are post offices. More than 40 significant traders, such as Western Union, exist. The rest are largely self-standing, independent, and individual businesses. 90 percent of them have fewer than five employees. They offer check cashing, currency exchange, and money transmission facilities, including some 800 specifically registered as providing informal money transmission services. All services are subject to the regulatory regime.

MSBs must register with Customs and pay a fee of $60 for each premises from which they operate. Businesses failing to register are subject to financial penalties of up to $5,000. Once a business is registered, a customs officer visits. MSBs must meet CATCH: confirm the identity of their customs; appoint a money laundering reporting officer; train their staff; control their business by having anti-money laundering systems in place; and hold all records for at least five years.

Samuel Muzele Maimbo, a financial sector specialist in the South Asia Region of the World Bank, discusses "Challenges of Regulating and Supervising the Hawaladars of Kabul." In September 2004, the Central Bank introduced legislation to regulate and supervise the activities of money service providers in Afghanistan. Reforming the informal sector is complicated because of the increasing opium production in Afghanistan and an emerging nexus of drug trafficking with terrorist and militant groups. Implementing the new regulations will be challenging for the central bank because (1) the informal financial system has a long history of independence and self-regulation; (2) incentives for compliance are undermined by the weakness of the legal and judicial framework for the prosecution of financial crimes; and (3) investigating money laundering and terrorist financing is complex, especially in the context of the large size of the Afghan drug economy and the emerging risk of a nexus of drug trafficking with terrorist or militant groups.

The chapter discusses the rationale for regulating informal financial services and outlines the special challenges of the central bank in Afghanistan. It concludes with two modest recommendations: the need to continue strengthening the legal and judicial system; and the need to continue cooperating with the association of hawaladars.

Paulo Roberto Gonçalves, head of the Foreign Exchange Surveillance Division of the Department of Surveillance of Illegal Activities in the Central Bank of Brazil, discusses "Banco Central do Brasil's Foreign Exchange System." It comments on the Brazilian foreign exchange system and why informal money transfers are not allowed. The Brazilian surveillance procedure aims to maintain the regular operation of the system. It describes how only authorized banks can conduct financial transfers from and to foreign countries.

Andres Arboleda Uribe, formerly the Director of Regulation in Superintendencia Bancaria de Colombia, discusses "Regulatory and Supervisory Framework of Funds Transfers in Colombia." The chapter describes Colombia's experience implementing a regulatory framework for money transfers capable of attracting money remitters to cross the line to a formal system. It describes the supervisory practices and procedures that Colombia has applied since 1991. The author describes the characteristics of funds transfers in Colombia, the requirements for obtaining a license, the challenges and results of the supervision model that was adopted, and the consequences for providers who opt to work illegally. According to Uribe, countries that apply extreme controls, so that residents cannot remove their funds, are extremely susceptible to the development of black markets. A better system is liberalized markets combined with good prudential regulation and supervision of funds transfer providers. A regulatory scheme requiring applicants to have minimum qualifications to be licensed as money remitters, combined with full-disclosure standards, permanent onsite and offsite supervision, zero tolerance to illegality, and cooperation among authorities, both national and overseas, facilitates confidence, and helps promote a business of enormous importance to a country's economy.

Charles Lengalenga, the executive secretary of the Eastern and Southern African Anti-Money Laundering Group discusses "Some Critical Issues on Informal Value Transfer Systems in Eastern and Southern African Anti-Money Laundering Group (ESAAMLG) Member Countries." The chapter describes the overall historical development of informal value transfer systems (IVTSs) in the ESAAMLG region and considers how the lack of formal banking facilities has affected the evolution of the IVTS. The article considers a number of possible interventions by ESAAMLG member countries that could minimize the possibility of an IVTS being used as a vehicle for financing of illegal activities, including terrorist financing. The chapter examines the possible challenges that may be inherent in the available interventions.

The chapter concludes that it will take a lot of persuasion by all concerned international stakeholders to persuade some member countries to realize the need to focus on IVTSs as possible terror financing routes. The very nature and economic composition of most member countries will necessitate a "softly-softly" approach, recognizing the cash-based feature of our economies. Taking a prescriptive approach without properly unraveling the key issues related to the use of IVTSs could worsen the situation by causing the involved players to drive their activities underground. Although all 14 ESAAMLG members have agreed to adopt and implement the 8 FATF special recommendations on terrorist financing, most of them are still in the process of implementing the first stages of the FATF 40 recommendations on anti-money practices. Hence, it will take time before they make any meaningful progress in putting IVTSs into the scope for appropriate regulation.

Mohamed Djirdeh Houseein, Chairman of the Somali Financial Services Association since August 2004, discusses "Somalia: The Experience of Hawala Receiving Countries." Since January 26, 1991, Somalia has disintegrated into several parts. It has no central government and no organs of government, such as central or commercial banks or police or law enforcement forces. Twenty-six percent of Somalians depend totally on hawala transfers, and up to 66 percent depend on it for 50 percent of their basic needs. Hawala is the only mechanism businesses have to transfer funds out of Somalia to purchase imports. In Somaliland, the Bank of Somaliland registers hawala companies. The bank issues a Certificate of Authorized

Exchange Dealer for a fee and a deposit of US$3,000. With this, the municipality issues a license to operate. No other regulation exists. The Somali hawala companies have established the Somali Financial Services Association (SFSA), their first attempt at self-regulation. The UNDP Somalia and EU Somalia offices are assisting. The SFSA needs professional management, training, and capacity building. Somalia and the international community should work toward setting affordable, transparent, and reasonable regulations of Somalia and other hawala networks. Continuous outreach and active dialogue are essential.

The book also contains the Abu Dhabi Declaration on Hawala, made at the conclusion of the First International Conference on Hawala, on May 16, 2002; the Second International Conference on hawala, Conference Statement, Abu Dhabi, April 5, 2004, the Interpretative Note to Special Recommendation VI: Alternative Remittance; and Combating the Abuse of Alternative Remittance Systems; International Best Practices, June 20, 2003.

The book is an excellent source of concise policy discussions on alternatives for regulating alternative remittance systems.

2. Reference Guides

The WBG has produced various reference guides, including a general guide on AML/CFT[28] and the comprehensive FIU reference discussed earlier.

On May 5, 2009, the World Bank published Stolen Asset Recovery: A Good Practices Guide for Non-Conviction Based Asset Forfeiture by Theodore S. Greenberg, Linda Samuel, Wingate Grant, and Larissa Gray. The book discusses how an increasing number of jurisdictions have embarked on non-convicted-based (NCB) recovery of assets as a tool for asset recovery at regional and multilateral levels. The book discusses thirty-six key concepts – legal, operational, and practical – that an NCB asset forfeiture system should encompass to be effective in recovering stolen assets. These concepts are explored through practical experiences, examples from cases, and excerpts from NCB asset forfeiture legislation.

Notes and Questions

1. The IMF has done an excellent job discussing the critical role of hawala and hawaladars, showing that, even though there are serious AML/CFT problems with money remittance systems, they also perform important legitimate roles in developing countries. One of the reasons the IMF is able to provide a balanced analysis of hawalas and money remittance systems is that, instead of focusing only on AML regulatory and enforcement matters as does FATF, the WBG has primary responsibility for fostering economic development.

2. The WBG's publication of reference guides is an important activity that flows naturally from its AML/CFT activities.

V. Financial Stability Board

On October 30, 1998, the G7 ministers and governors reinforced their commitment to reforms to the international financial system and financial stability in a declaration

[28] Schott, *supra* note 8.

that recommended the creation of a Financial Stability Forum (FSF). At a meeting in Bonn, Germany, on February 20, 1999, they endorsed the creation of a FSF that would bring together: national authorities responsible for financial stability in significant international financial centers, namely treasuries, central banks, and supervisory agencies; sector-specific international groupings of regulators and supervisors engaged in developing standards and codes of good practice; international financial institutions charged with surveillance of domestic and international financial systems and monitoring and fostering implementation of standards; and committees of central bank experts concerned with market infrastructure and functioning. Its purpose is to promote international financial stability through information exchange and international cooperation in financial supervision and surveillance.[29] It seeks to coordinate the efforts of these various financial bodies to promote international financial stability, improve the functioning of markets, and reduce systemic risk.[30]

On April 14, 1999, the FSF first met in Washington, D.C. Andrew Crockett, General Manager of the Bank for International Settlements, was appointed chairman of the FSF in a personal capacity.

On April 2, 2009, the Communique of the G20 meeting contained undertakings to strengthen international financial regulation and enforcement, including the strengthening of the FSF, now renamed the Financial Stability Board (FSB), and to act against noncooperative jurisdictions, including tax havens.

To strengthen the financial system, the leaders agreed to establish a new Financial Stability Board as a successor to the FSF with a strengthened mandate, and that the FSB should collaborate with the IMF to give early warnings of macroeconomic and financial risks and the actions required to address them; to reshape regulatory systems so that the authorities can identify and take account of macro prudential risks; to extend regulation and oversight to all systemically important financial institutions, instruments, and markets, including systemically important hedge funds; to improve the quality, quantity, and international consistency of capital in the banking system; to act against noncooperative jurisdictions, including tax havens, and to impose sanctions to protect public finances and financial systems, end bank secrecy, and promote the international exchange of tax information; to require the accounting standard setters to work urgently with supervisors and regulators to improve standards on valuation and provisioning and achieve a single set of high-quality global accounting standards; and to extend regulatory oversight and registration to credit rating agencies to ensure they meet the international code of good practice, especially to prevent unacceptable conflicts of interest.[31]

Notes and Questions

1. Although the WBG did not host and manage the FSF, it played a key role in identifying the need for a mechanism to respond to the gap in international financial architecture. In addition, the work of the FSF has influenced the Article IV consultations.

[29] Financial Stability Forum, Genesis of the FSF, http://www.fsforum.org/about/genesis_of_the_fsf.html, accessed Mar. 10, 2007.

[30] Financial Stability Forum, *Financial Stability Forum*, Feb 12, 2007, http://www.fsforum.org/home/home.html, accessed Mar. 9, 2007.

[31] G20 London Summit – Leaders' Statement (2 April 2009).

2. Other mechanisms and groups with which the WBG interacts closely in the context of AML/CTFE and international financial architecture include the FATF, OECD, Basel Group of Central Bankers, International Organization of Security Commissioners, and International Association of Insurance Supervisors.

VI. Transnational Corruption

The WBG agenda has incorporated governance and anticorruption (GAC) measures since former bank president James Wolfensohn's "cancer of curruption" speech at the 1996 WBG annual meeting. Several WBG documents reflect the emergence of this emphasis, including *Helping Countries Combat Corruption: The Role of the World Bank* (1997); the 1997 World Development Report, *The State in a Changing World*; and the 2000 World Bank strategy paper, *Reforming Public Institutions and Strengthening Governance*.[32]

In 1998, the WB established its Oversight Committee on Fraud and Corruption. In January 2000, an independent review led by former U.S. Attorney General Richard Thornburgh recommended that the committee be upgraded to "a true policy-making body . . . for addressing fraud and corruption." In response, Wolfensohn established the Department of Institutional Integrity.[33]

In 2006, the World Bank Group began a number of anticorruption initiatives that, together with the coming into effect of the Council of Europe Anti-Corruption Convention; and UN Convention against Corruption (UNCAC), should have an important impact on the procurement processes of international financial institutions (IFIs).[34]

The Department of Institutional Integrity (INT) is the internal unit designated by the World Bank Group to investigate allegations of fraud and corruption in its operations and of staff misconduct. In addition to conducting investigations, the INT helps improve compliance with World Bank policies and prevent corruption through a variety of means, including training WB staff to detect and deter fraud and corruption in WBG projects and improve control and compliance systems. The World Bank publishes an annual integrity report with aggregate data, outcomes, and generic descriptions of significant cases. To ensure the independence of its activities, the director of the Integrity Department reports directly to the president of the World Bank Group.

The IMF's Approach to Promoting Good Governance and Combating Corruption – A Guide[35]

The IMF places great emphasis on good governance when providing policy advice, financial support, and technical assistance to its 184 member countries. It promotes good governance

[32] *Id.* at ii.

[33] For background on the World Bank's anticorruption program see Independent Panel Review of the World Bank Group Department of Institutional Integrity, Sept 13, 2007/http://siteresources.worldbank.org/News/resources/volker_report_sept 12, for_we.

[34] These initiatives came as part of World Bank President Paul Wolfowitz's focus on anticorruption efforts. *See* Bruce Zagaris, *Wolfowitz Outlines World Bank's Anti-corruption Plan*, 22 Int'l Enforcement L. Rep. 229 (June 2006).

[35] IMF, *The IMF's Approach to Promoting Good Governance and Combating Corruption – A Guide*, Last Updated: June 20, 2005 (http://www.imf.org).

by helping countries ensure the rule of law, improve the efficiency and accountability of their public sectors, and tackle corruption. In so doing, the IMF limits itself to economic aspects of governance that could have a significant macroeconomic impact. The IMF also has strong measures in place to ensure the integrity of its own organization.

How Are Governance and Corruption Related?

The term governance, as generally used, encompasses all aspects of the way a country, corporation, or other entity is governed. It includes the economic-policy interactions that fall within the mandate and expertise of the IMF. Relevant questions with regard to those policies are: their effectiveness; their transparency, and thus the accountability of policy makers; and the extent to which they meet internationally accepted standards and good practices. Corruption is a narrower concept than governance. It is often defined as the abuse of public authority or trust for private benefit. The two concepts are closely linked. Where there is poor governance, there are greater incentives and more scope for corruption. Thus, the promotion of good governance helps combat corruption. It complements efforts that target corruption more directly, such as raising public awareness and strengthening the enforcement of anticorruption legislation. There is also a reverse link: corruption undermines governance to the extent that it distorts policy decisions and their implementation.

Why Does the IMF Care So Much about Good Governance?

The IMF's operations and its relations with member states have always been concerned with good governance. But in 1996, the policymaking committee of its Board of Governors added an explicit mandate. In its Declaration on Partnership for Sustainable Global Growth, the Interim Committee stressed, among other things, the importance of "promoting good governance in all its aspects, including by ensuring the rule of law, improving the efficiency and accountability of the public sector, and tackling corruption, as essential elements of a framework within which economies can prosper."

An overview of corruption around the world shows that many of its most commonly cited causes and consequences are economic in nature. It is natural that these are covered by the IMF in its relations with its member countries. As for causes, corruption thrives in the presence of: excessive government regulation and intervention in the economy; substantial exchange and trade restrictions; and complex tax laws requiring frequent contacts between taxpayers and inspectors. Corruption is further favored by lax spending controls, and when the government provides goods, services, and resources at below-market prices (e.g., foreign exchange, credit, public utilities and housing, access to education and health facilities, and access to public land). There is potential for corruption when officials take decisions that are potentially costly to private individuals or companies (for instance, tax incentives, zoning laws, timber rights and rights to extract mineral resources, investment permits, privatizations, and monopoly rights over exports and imports or domestic activities). Factors that contribute indirectly to corruption include: the quality and remuneration of the civil service, the effectiveness of deterrents, and the example set by the country's leadership.

There is no doubt that corruption can have a major negative impact on economic performance. Corruption can reduce investment and economic growth. It diverts public resources to private gains, and away from needed public spending on education and health. It tends to compress operation and maintenance expenditures, while boosting beyond levels that are socially desirable public investment and defense spending, both highly amenable to corruption. Finally, by reducing tax revenue, corruption can complicate macroeconomic management, and because it tends to do so in a regressive way, it can accentuate income inequality.

Where Is the IMF's Policy on Good Governance Described?

In 1997, the IMF's Executive Board adopted a guidance note that sought to promote greater attention to governance issues, by the IMF staff, management and Executive Board alike (Good Governance – The IMF's Role). In February 2001, the IMF Executive Board evaluated the experience with the guidance note (Executive Board Reviews IMF's Experience in Governance Issues – Public Information Notice) on the basis of a staff paper (Review of the Fund's Experience in Governance Issues) that described the evolution of the Fund's role in governance since 1997. At the conclusion of its discussion, the Executive Board supported this evolution, stressing that prevention should be the centerpiece of the IMF's governance strategy.

What Are the Limitations to the IMF's Role in Promoting Good Governance?

The 1997 Guidance Note, Good Governance – The IMF's Role, describes how the IMF, given its mandate and expertise, is best placed to contribute to good governance (including the avoidance of corrupt practices) through its policy advice and technical assistance in two spheres, namely:

- improving the management of public resources through reforms covering public sector institutions (e.g., the treasury, central bank, public enterprises, civil service, and the official statistics function), including administrative procedures (e.g., expenditure control, budget management, and revenue collection), and
- supporting the development and maintenance of a transparent and stable economic and regulatory environment conducive to efficient private sector activities (e.g., price systems, exchange and trade regimes, and banking systems and their related regulations).

The 1997 Guidance Note describes the broad role for the IMF in governance, but also indicates the boundaries to that role. The most important one is that the IMF should get involved in governance issues only when they have a significant current or potential impact on macroeconomic performance. The IMF must also limit itself to the economic aspects of those issues, since those are within its mandate and expertise.

Finally, IMF staff are encouraged to collaborate closely with other multilateral institutions with complementary areas of expertise, in particular the World Bank. World Bank staff has accumulated much practical experience with good governance and anticorruption measures and compiled databases for measuring governance performance. This work is presented on the World Bank's public Web site, by both the governance and public sector reform network and the World Bank Institute.

In What Directions Is the IMF's Role in Governance Expanding?

Since 1997, the IMF's role in promoting good governance has expanded considerably. The main initiative has been to encourage transparency and accountability in economic policies through the development and promotion of internationally recognized standards, and codes of good practices in data dissemination; fiscal, monetary, and financial policy transparency; and banking, insurance, and securities regulation and supervision, and payment system oversight. The Fund also introduced minimum standards for the control, accounting, reporting, and auditing systems of the central banks of countries to which it lends, this in order to safeguard the use of Fund resources. In its work, the IMF increasingly emphasizes the need for adequate systems for tracking public expenditure on poverty reduction; although important for all poor countries, this is particularly so for the group of heavily indebted poor countries (HIPCs) receiving debt relief. Finally, the IMF is intensifying its involvement in international anti-money laundering and combating the financing of terrorism. These efforts are aimed at ensuring the integrity of countries' financial systems. In addition, countering money laundering supports the international anticorruption drive. It makes it more difficult to hide bribes in bank accounts abroad thereby reducing the rewards, which in turn should discourage the soliciting or accepting of bribes.

The Bank has also worked to ensure that aid for natural resource projects results in sustainable development, especially in less developed countries. The Bank's involvement in Chad's oil projects exemplifies this work.

On July 14, 2006, the World Bank and Chad reached an agreement on the use of Chad's oil revenue, resolving a growing dispute over Chad's oil industry.[36] The agreement requires Chad to use 70 percent of its 2007 budgetary resources for poverty-reduction purposes, which include health, education, infrastructure, demining, and rural development.[37] The agreement became possible partly because the dynamically increasing price of oil gives Chad an unanticipated windfall.

The agreement involves a 650-mile pipeline that the bank helped finance in 1999 so landlocked Chad could export its oil.[38] The World Bank approved a $4 billion pipeline to carry oil from fields in the south of Chad to Cameroon. In mid-2004, the oil began flowing, bringing more than $400 million to Chad.[39]

Until the end of 2005, most oil royalties were paid into a special fund in London, where they were earmarked for poverty reduction projects such as schools and health clinics. In October 2005, Chad President Idriss Deby unilaterally ended that arrangement, explaining that he needed more money for security forces as fighting by rebels increased and refugees continued to come across the border from Sudan. On January 6, 2006, World Bank President Paul Wolfowitz effectively blocked the government's access to the London fund after he was unable to persuade Deby to suspend his action ending the arrangement. In April 2006, an interim agreement of three months freed some of the money.[40]

Chad, one of Africa's most impoverished countries, was ranked last, alongside Bangladesh, on Transparency International's 2005 index of corruption perceptions.

The new agreement, which only covers 2007, brings a greater portion of Chad's oil revenue under the control of an independent oversight committee and simultaneously gives the Chad government more flexibility to spend the money on electricity and telecommunications

[36] The following section is reprinted from Bruce Zagaris, *World Bank and Chad Reach Agreement on Use of Oil Profits*, 22 INT'L ENFORCEMENT L. REP. 371 (September 2006). Lydia Polgreen, *World Bank Reaches Pact with Chad over Use of Oil Profits*, N.Y. TIMES, July 15, 2006, at A5, col. 1.

[37] Paul Blustein, *Chad, World Bank Settle Dispute over Oil Money*, WASH. POST, July 15, 2006, at D1, col. 4.

[38] *Id.*

[39] Polgreen, *supra* note 36.

[40] Blustein, *supra* note 37.

infrastructure instead of traditional poverty reduction programs. Next year a final agreement to deal with Chad's oil revenue will be discussed.[41]

According to the World Bank, the Bank and the Chadian authorities have also agreed to strengthen the College de Controle et Surveillance des Revenues Petrolieres – an independent body with oversight on the use of the oil revenues for poverty reduction – by making sure it has adequate resources.[42]

The agreement allows the World Bank to continue its anticorruption program while affording Chad more discretion to spend its oil revenue. Development and corruption specialists will closely monitor implementation of the agreement to see if it actually results in more development, reducing corruption and poverty in Chad.

A. *Programs to Ensure Proper Procurement Regulations to Minimize Corruption*

World Bank, Public Expenditure Institutional Assessment[43]

This assessment of budgetary institutions includes models for assessing formal public expenditure institutional arrangements and for assessing the capability of cabinet arrangements for social and sectoral policymaking. The toolkit has been piloted extensively in Thailand, Indonesia, Uganda, Malawi, Ghana, Australia, New Zealand, Colombia, and Benin, but is now being extended to assess the fit between budgetary institutions and the particular executive/legislature configurations. There is a short and long version of the diagnostic – both versions are prefaced by a short description of the diagnostic, and an outline of the diagnostic framework (accessed from the World Bank Web site).

B. *Enforcement and Sanctions: Suspension, Debarment, Blacklisting*

1. Actions to Report Fraud and Corruption and Blacklisting Ineligible Persons

The Department of Institutional Integrity (INT) investigates allegations of fraud or corruption in WBG-financed operations, as well as allegations of staff misconduct within the WBG. Persons doing business with the WBG are asked to report fraud and corruption to the INT.

Examples of issues that should be reported to INT for further review include suspected contract irregularities and violations of the World Bank's procurement guidelines; bid manipulation or collusion; coercive practices; fraudulent bids; fraud in contract performance or in an audit inquiry; product substitution; price manipulation; substandard or inferior parts or materials; cost or labor mischarges; kickbacks, bribery, or acceptance of gratuities; abuse of authority; misuse of WBG funds or funds entrusted to it; travel-related fraud; theft and embezzlement; benefits and allowance fraud; conflict of interest; misrepresentation; forgery; and involvement of WBG staff in any of the aforementioned.[44]

[41] Polgreen, *supra* note 36.

[42] Diana I. Gregg, *World Bank, Chad Reach Deal on Channeling Oil Revenue for Poor,* Daily Rep. For Exec. July 17, 2006, at A11.

[43] World Bank Group, *Public Expenditure Institutional Assessment* http://web.worldbank.org/WBSITE/EXTERNAL/TOPICS/EXTPUBLICSECTORANDGOVERNANCE/EXTANTICORRUPTION, accessed Mar. 11, 2007.

[44] World Bank Group, Department of Institutional Integrity, Reporting Fraud and Corruption, World Bank Web site, accessed Aug. 8, 2006.

When contacting INT, complainants are asked to make their complaint as specific as possible, providing specific details of the alleged wrongdoing such as where and when (dates and times if available), the identity of the perpetrators, how the individual or firm committed the alleged wrongdoing, and why they believe the activity was improper. Complainants are asked to furnish any available documentation or witnesses to corroborate their allegations.

Complainants who prefer to remain anonymous are encouraged to use WBG's anonymous phone line or a free email service such as Hotmail or Yahoo. By so doing, the complainant can correspond with INT as necessary to seek clarification or additional information. The WBG investigates complaints made anonymously to the best of its ability, but complainants are asked to bear in mind that anonymous allegations are often more difficult to pursue.

2. Blacklisting and Disclosing Ineligible and Sanctioned Persons

If a sanction is imposed on a respondent to a World Bank Sanctions Committee proceeding, as provided in Section 13(d) of the Sanctions Committee Procedures, information concerning the identity of each sanctioned party and the sanctions imposed are publicly disclosed. Persons found to have committed fraud or corruption are subject to various types of penalties, including letters of reprimand and debarment for a period of time or permanently.

Each investment project financed by the World Bank is governed by a legal agreement between the World Bank and the government agency receiving the funds. One of the key obligations in the "loan agreement" is that governments abide by the World Bank's procurement policies as detailed in the *Guidelines: Procurement under IBRD Loans and IDA Credits*.

The Bank's Web site includes a list of ineligible firms and individuals who are ineligible for WB-financed contracts for the periods indicated because they were found to have violated the fraud and corruption provisions of the procurement guidelines or the consultants guidelines, clauses 1.14 and 1.22, respectively. These findings were made through an administrative process in which accused firms and individuals were allowed to respond to allegations.

In the case of a debarred firm, ineligibility extends to any firm or individual who directly or indirectly controls the debarred firm or any firm that the debarred firm directly or indirectly controls. In the case of a debarred individual, ineligibility extends to any firm that the debarred individual directly or indirectly controls.[45]

Investigations of fraud and corruption are confidential, and the WBG does not normally comment publicly on them. However, under special circumstances, it may confirm that an investigation is occurring or has been closed or that a WB report conveying the results of the investigation has been sent to the appropriate counterpart in the government. In matters pending before the Sanctions Committee, a designated WB representative will make such confirmation with the approval of the chair of the Sanctions Committee, with the concurrence of the general counsel; in all other matters, it will make such confirmation with the approval of the chair of the Investigation Policy Committee, with

[45] *Id.*

the concurrence of the general counsel. In the case of IFC or Multilateral Investment Guarantee Agency (MIGA) matters, "general counsel" refers to their general counsel.

C. *Voluntary Compliance*

On August 1, 2006, the World Bank's Board of Directors formally approved a Voluntary Disclosure Program designed to strengthen its anticorruption programs.[46] The Voluntary Disclosure Program (VDP) is an initiative to uncover corruption in WB-financed projects through the voluntary cooperation of participating firms and individuals.[47] The program, managed by the Department of Institutional Integrity, permits entities that have engaged in past fraud and corruption to avoid administrative sanctions if they disclose all prior wrongdoing and satisfy standardized, nonnegotiable terms and conditions.[48] Private sector participants are required to commit to stop paying bribes or engaging in fraud, corruption, collusion, or coercion. They must disclose all misconduct in WB projects or contracts during the five years prior to their entry into the VDP, implement a monitored compliance program for three years, and pay the costs associated with participation in the VDP.

Private sector firms, NGOs, and individuals can participate, although entities under active investigation by the World Bank are not eligible. In exchange for full cooperation, participants avoid public debarment for disclosed past misconduct and benefit from the WB's assurances of confidentiality. To date, the World Bank has publicly debarred more than 330 firms and individuals, whose names and terms of sanction are posted on its Web site.[49] World Bank officials believe that information provided by participating companies will expose patterns of corruption in bank projects, reveal the identity of other corrupt participants, and help the bank modify the design and implementation of projects to minimize corruption.[50]

Although the VDP does not impose monetary "penalties," participants must pay for most costs associated with the process. These costs can be significant, especially for large firms with international operations and a history of involvement in WB projects. The VDP adjusts to the size of the participant, and the World Bank has offered to provide technical assistance with VDP obligations to firms with fewer than fifty employees. Such assistance could include performing internal investigations, drafting investigation reports, developing compliance programs, and monitoring implementation.[51]

The WB will keep a VDP participant's identity confidential permanently, unless the participant violates the material terms and conditions of the VDP and is publicly debarred.[52] However, the WB will share nonconfidential information resulting from a participant's disclosures in a redacted format that protects the identity of the participant

46 The following section is reprinted from Bruce Zagaris, *World Bank Initiates Anti-Corruption Voluntary Disclosure Program*, 22 INT'L ENFORCEMENT L. REP. 393 (October 2006).

47 Pascale Dubois & Bart Stevens, *World Bank Launches Voluntary Disclosure Program, World Bank Press Release* No. 2007/35/INT, Aug. 1, 2006.

48 *Id.*

49 *Id.*

50 Krishna Guha, *World Bank in Broad Anti-Corruption Drive*, FIN. TIMES, Aug. 6, 2006.

51 World Bank, *Frequently Asked Questions about the VDP*, http://web.worldbank.org, accessed Aug. 7, 2006.

52 *Id.*

and in aggregate form in annual reports. A country provided with VDP disclosures in a redacted report can use those disclosures to guide its own independent investigations – the program does not preclude a country from taking action against any entity it discovers and finds liable under its laws.[53]

The World Bank has initiated the VDP pursuant to Article 37 of the UN Convention against Corruption (UNCAC). The provisions of Article 37 urge countries to encourage persons who participate or have participated in the commission of an offense to furnish information useful to competent authorities for investigative and evidentiary purposes, in exchange for mitigated punishment.

Because both the UNCAC and the OECD Anti Corruption Conventions (discussed in more detail in Chapter 4 on Transnational Corruption) have come into force, firms have greater law enforcement risks. Additionally, in many countries the cost of paying bribes is becoming prohibitive for many firms. Companies also do not know which other companies are disclosing information under the VDP and may want to avoid being named by a VDP participant.[54]

The VDP program has detailed provisions for the operation of a compliance monitor (CM). The CM monitors the participant's compliance with the VDP terms and conditions. The CM must have access to the participant's files, books, records, materials, sites, and employees. The participant exclusively bears all reasonable costs, including compensation and properly incurred expenses, associated with the retention of the CM. The VDP ensures the independence of the CM. For instance, the participant cannot terminate the CM without the prior written consent of the WB. The participant must terminate the CM promptly on written request by the WB and choose a successor CM within sixty days after such termination. The participant cannot hire any CM with whom it has had a prior relationship. It cannot invoke any doctrine or privilege to prevent the CM from transmitting any information, reports, or documents to the WB. The CM must send written reports on the first, second, and third anniversaries of the date when the participant received written notification from the WB that verification was complete. As part of its annual comprehensive review, the CM must make scheduled visits to the participant. In addition, the WB may direct the CM to make unannounced visits and inspections if the WB has a reasonable basis to believe that the participant has engaged in misconduct. The WB may itself make such unannounced visits. The CM must make written reports on the adequacy of the policies, procedures, and compliance measures that the participant is required to devise and implement under the VDP terms and conditions; the status of the participant's implementation of the policies, procedures, and compliance measures; any finding by the CM of any continued misconduct by the participant; and reasonable recommendations where appropriate.[55]

Other international financial institutions will likely emulate the World Bank's Voluntary Disclosure Program. In conjunction with new anticorruption conventions, the VDP may help reduce bribery in international procurement by bringing new prosecutions and civil lawsuits by a host of victims, including governments, companies who lost procurements because of corruption, and nongovernmental organizations suing on behalf

[53] *Id.*

[54] *Id.*

[55] World Bank, Department of Institutional Integrity, VDP, *VDP Protocol 8, Participant Hires a Compliance Monitor*, July 20, 2006.

of citizens and consumers. In short, if widely adopted, the VDP may significantly reduce future corruption in World Bank projects and procurement.

D. *Technical Assistance*

One of the principal activities of the WBG's governance and anticorruption (GAC) program is to render technical assistance to strengthen the capacity of governments to carry out GAC policies and activities.

World Bank, Anticorruption Laws

http://www1.worldbank.org/publicsector/legal/reforminglaws.htm#3 (ACCESSED FEB. 24, 2007)

Enforcing Income and Asset Declaration Laws

Although many nations have enacted laws requiring public servants to disclose their income and assets, effective enforcement has often been a challenge. Detecting when a public servant's lifestyle is inconsistent with his or her disclosure statement is time-consuming and difficult, and public prosecutors may not have either the resources or skills to conduct such investigations. This gap can sometimes be filled by civil society groups. . . .

Using Noncriminal Laws to Combat Corruption

Although criminal law is most commonly invoked to attack corruption, often prosecution is not the only, or even the most effective way, of deterring or punishing those who take or pay bribes or otherwise corrupt the governmental process. Prevailing in a criminal case can be very difficult. To protect the rights of the accused, the laws of most nations set a very high standard of proof in criminal cases. In corruption cases, this burden can be particularly difficult to meet because the acts are clandestine and there is no obvious victim ready to present evidence. Moreover, even a successful prosecution does not guarantee that the beneficiaries of corruption will have to disgorge their profits. One alternative are the remedies found in the civil (noncriminal) laws of many nations. The standard of proof is often lower than in criminal cases, and the remedy almost always includes recovery of the proceeds of the crime. In the United States, the False Claims Act provides that any citizen may bring a lawsuit against those alleged to have defrauded the federal government, and if the plaintiff succeeds, he or she is entitled to keep a percentage of the amount recovered. In South Africa, a Special Investigating Unit has been established to use the civil laws to combat corruption.

IMF/Netherland Program Legal and Judicial Reform in Indonesia 2000–2004

EXTERNAL EVALUATION FINAL REPORT: JAN. 16, 2005, AT 6–7

Program: Anticorruption

Pervasive corruption in Indonesia affects every institution in the country. No reform effort can avoid the problem. Precisely because of the extent and depth of it, however, neither is there an obvious approach to the matter. Corruption in the courts, which soon infected the commercial courts, inevitably compelled the Program's attention.

Several innovations in the commercial courts – for example, ad hoc judges, legitimation of dissenting opinions, oversight of court session, public access to decisions – were intended to check the problem. The Program's engagement on corruption issues, however, was limited and uncertain. It supported a newly formed Joint Investigating Team (JIT), led originally by a respected and recently retired Supreme Court justice, focused on judicial corruption. It also provided assistance to the Office of Public Prosecution in developing capacity to deal with public interest bankruptcy issues. And it prepared a policy paper on judicial corruption. Little came of this initial Phase I program, however. The JIT met much opposition, and by the time it requested Program assistance, it may have been too late. In early 2001 it was challenged in the Supreme Court and dissolved by a much disputed but unsurprising decision. Assistance to the Office of Public Prosecution was ended when it became clear that it had done nothing by way of investigating bankruptcy related issues and was unlikely to do so.

Thereafter the Program's concern with corruption narrowed and became rather more focused. It provided limited assistance to a new Commission for the Audit of the Wealth of State Officials (KPKPN), largely by way of a study tour to Thailand with the Asia Foundation. A request to the Program for assistance in merging the KPKPN into the Anticorruption Commission was pending at the time of the evaluation. The Program's main focus, however, was to support preparations for development of an Anticorruption Court. The Program's intentions were by and large implemented. It helped to fashion parliamentary and other strategies behind creation of the new court and supported development of a blueprint for the court and plans for its programs. The Anticorruption Court was finally created by Parliament in mid-2004.

Our evaluation of the Program's anticorruption work was hampered by having had too little access to persons with knowledge of it. Staunching corruption was not the Program's primary focus, however, although its effect on the commercial courts was of great concern. Once the Program turned its attention to supporting the Blueprints process, its anticorruption work was grounded in that approach, which emphasized a foundation for comprehensive institutional development constructed entirely by Indonesians. Through the Anticorruption Commission, the Anticorruption Court, the Judicial Commission and the Blueprints, a framework is being structured and mechanisms developed to institutionalize means of addressing abuse and regulating professionalism. The evaluation team thinks it fair to say that the Program has served to catalyze this process and helped to steer it in the right direction.

The Program's work on anticorruption has been useful but limited. Even more than the other projects, there is not yet enough evidence to evaluate. The new Anticorruption court is barely off the ground. Its successful evolution, however, depends substantially on support from within the administration and Parliament, which remains uncertain. As in the case of judicial reform, anticorruption has substantial pressure behind it from society, committed NGOs, and much of the press. Similar public clamor was lacking for the commercial courts as a stand alone entity. Dealing with corruption in the commercial courts was hardly possible in isolation given their wider context

Notes and Questions:

1. Why did anticorruption policy work lag behind the inclusion of criminal justice and law modernization and reform? For instance, from the early 1980s through 1996, WB Counsel Ibrahim Shiharta used to warn World Bank lawyers not to use the "c" (shorthand for corruption) word. The refusal of the World Bank to include

anticorruption programs led to Peter Eigen's resignation from the World Bank and his subsequent creation of Transparency International, an international NGO whose purpose is to sensitize countries to the importance of anticorruption programs and help them develop them.

2. Some of the reasons why the WBG was reluctant to include anticorruption efforts in its programs and work continue in force. Some board members have expressed concern that a focus on governance and anticorruption (GAC) policies will result in a loss of faith and trust in the WBG. Because corruption is so entrenched in many developing countries and because their governments have alternative sources of assistance, the WBG's emphasis on GAG will lead to fewer projects and deteriorating relations between the WBG and the developing world. GAG proponents counter that any loss of projects and deterioration would be short term, and they assert that sustainable poverty alleviation and development projects require GAC components.

3. On May 17, 2007, Paul Wolfowitz announced his resignation as president of the World Bank, four days after a special bank investigative committee concluded that he had violated his contract by breaking ethical and governance rules in arranging a generous pay and promotion package for Shaha Ali Riza, his companion, in 2005. His resignation followed weeks of rancor between Wolfowitz and the bank board.

Soon after Wolfowitz became president of the WB, on March 31, 2005, he clashed with various sectors at the bank over issues including his campaign against corruption, in which he suspended aid to several countries without consulting board members.[56] In response to Wolfowitz's decision to unilaterally suspend loan projects, the World Bank's Executive Board ordered him to create a coherent anticorruption policy; when Wolfowitz attempted to do so, the Board rejected his proposals.[57]

Wolfowitz's resignation called into question the future of the WB's anticorruption and governance policy. Interestingly, his focus on GAC shed light on the WB's need to improve its own governance. The tradition is to have the U.S. president choose a U.S. citizen to head the World Bank. Indeed, President Bush appointed Wolfowitz without prior consultation with WB shareholders. In the wake of Wolfowitz's departure, many commentators are calling for international, merit-based selection criteria for future WB leaders.[58]

A second example of flawed WB internal controls involves Wolfowitz's appointment in 2006 of Suzanne Folsom, a Republican Party activist, to head the Department of Institutional Integrity. The World Bank's staff association, which lobbied for Wolfowitz's removal, claims that Wolfowitz misled staff about Folsom's appointment, saying it was the result of a competitive international search. In fact, Wolfowitz later admitted he had chosen her in preference to an international short list of candidates.[59]

In the end, the WBG accused Wolfowitz of violating the organization's own transparency and governance policies. This breakdown seems to have occurred because of three interrelated aspects:

1. An increasing lack of transparency in the application of its development policies; for example, in population, climate change, governance, and anticorruption.

[56] Steven Weisman, *Wolfowitz Resigns, Ending Long Fight at World Bank*, N.Y. Times, May 18, 2007, at A1, col. 1.
[57] Peter S. Goodman, *Ending Battle, Wolfowitz Resigns from World Bank*, Wash. Post, May 18, 2007, at A1.
[58] Editorial, *Picking a World Bank President*, N.Y. Times, May 19, 2007, at A24, col. 1.
[59] Eoin Callan & Krishna Guha, *Wolfowitz Loyalists Back under Spotlight*, Fin. Times, Apr. 20, 2007.

2. Serious breaches of internal human resources policies in certain instances, which create double standards and also impair its ability to engage with clients on governance issues.
3. Parallel lines of authority and bypassing of lines, leaving clients and staff confused and demoralized.[60]
4. Do you think the WB should terminate its aid programs to countries such as Chad that refuse to implement anticorruption and governance procedures? Should the WB try to engage civil society in developing and implementing GAC programs?
5. Can the WBG coordinate any of its white collar crime and criminal justice initiatives (e.g., AML/CFTE, governance, and anticorruption)? Give some examples of the linkages in the context of the WBG's work.
6. What are the potential interactions, if any, between WBG anticorruption enforcement and national criminal prosecutions?

VII. Regime and Institution Building

The relative youth of international enforcement institutions and regimes limits the work of the WBG. In the areas of AML and anticorruption, the lack of international institutions and their informality (e.g., FATF) have required the WBG to play important roles in formulating AML/CTF standards and helping develop harmonized national and international (e.g., the Egmont Group) institutions.

A. *Serving as a Forum for Developing Commitments and Adopting Obligations*

How to Curb Crime and Its Impact on Private Sector Growth

http://rru.worldbank.org/discussions/discussion.aspx?id=32;
ACCESSED APR. 29, 2007

Countries with high crime rates often find it difficult to attract, retain, and expand private investment. Firms must divert resources away from productive uses, which translates into reduced competitiveness and lower investment (or even disinvestments). Crime is a multi dimensional phenomenon, but crime-tackling strategies often focus on partial dimensions, primarily seeking to increase penalties. Experience shows that a more effective strategy combines this approach with a positive strategy to tackle the underlying causes of crime, such as undertaking broader institutional reforms and reducing poverty. Some of the institutional reforms could include maintaining efficient data collection systems, law enforcement capacity, and social programs for at-risk groups.

This approach to fighting crime raises the following questions: Do developing countries have the resources and institutional strengths to replicate this holistic approach to curbing crime? What are appropriate policy responses to reducing crime? Do negative (tougher penalties) or positive approaches work better? Do successful policies depend on the type of crime and firm characteristics – that is, size, sector, location – and target specific groups? Are high crime rates really a deterrent to private investment? Can

[60] Text of IEG statement April 22, 2007, Memo Current Events and the World Bank Group's Development Effectiveness, Statement of the Director-General, Evaluation to the Board of Executive Directors, April 20, 2007.

businesses continue to grow and to tackle crime through private channels? Are there countries with high crime rates that nevertheless manage to show sustained growth?

B. *Providing Information*

One of the current World Bank Group's projects focuses on the economics of crime and violence. The research arises out of its work on civil wars and their impact on the economics of crime and violence.

Crime and Violence

http://www.worldbank.org/research/conflict/crime.htm

The second core part of our research project focuses on "The Economics of Crime and Violence." Here we try to uncover the economic causes of crime and violence using the same analytical approach that we outlined in previous sections. We are interested in identifying the similarities and differences between crime and violence at the micro level and the macro level (civil wars). We also aim to develop a host of policy recommendations on how the incidence of violent crime might be reduced and its social impact mitigated.

There are several components to the "Crime and Violence" part of our project. We summarize these components below by presenting a list of research proposals submitted by analysts from within the Bank and from academic institutions, examining the whole array of issues in connection with the Economics of Crime and Violence (each topic summarizes a cluster of research proposals and corresponds to several individual papers):

1. The Causes of Violent Crime
2. The Analysis of Victimization Surveys
3. The Costs of Violent Crime
4. Monitoring the Incidence of Crime around the World
5. Analysis of Intra-household Violence
6. Comparative Assessment of Judicial Systems
7. The Political Economy of Police Behavior and Deterrence
8. Violent Crime in the Aftermath of Civil War

The civil war and crime components are related both methodologically and conceptually. There is a core set of determinants (especially poverty) that drive both phenomena; and at the microeconomic level, members of same target groups are the key agents whose participation decisions determine whether an insurgency or a violent crime happens.

To emphasize the relationship between political and criminal violence, we propose to apply similar models from economic theory to both components of our research. We will essentially model an agent's decision to participate in criminal activity or civil war as the product of a rational cost-benefit analysis. We will consider how a number of variables may affect that calculus and we expect to find that many of these variables are important for both crime and rebellion. Our theories follow the economics literature in modeling the economic opportunity cost of illegal or subversive activity and comparing it to the expected utility of such activity to determine the rational reasons for participation in crime and violence. Political factors are also relevant in that respect and our research will try to merge them with economic determinants for the first time in the literature on crime and civil war.

Thus, the methods used in the papers on civil war (game-theoretic modeling, cross-sectional quantitative studies, qualitative analytical narratives and case studies) will also be used in the component of the research project that analyzes crime. The crime component will also focus on both predictive and corrective aspects of crime management. The research papers that focus on predictive aspects will uncover the underlying causes of violent crime and identify differences in crime patterns spatially and temporarily. They will also analyze the permissive causes of crime, such as the political economy of policing, or the dynamics of organized crime, as well as the effects of broad political instability and economic poverty on criminal behavior.

Research papers on crime will also focus on corrective aspects of crime management. These papers will analyze survey data to identify who are the victims of violent crime in developing countries and in different localities within countries; as well as to identify the types of crime that are more prevalent and more violent (e.g., crime against property; crime against persons; intra-household; intra-poor crime). Further, these studies will identify the segments of the population that are more prone to crime and will then examine policies that have been successful in reducing violent crime. Based on these analyses, the project will try to assess the tradeoff between expending resources on predictive and preventive activities to reduce the incidence of crime as opposed to corrective activities.

Policy Dimensions

Our research is directly policy-relevant and will produce several important policy insights and prescriptions. Specifically, our research will be geared by a concern to identify the best possible strategy for the Bank's resource-allocation decision with respect to conflict: in other words, should the Bank dedicate the bulk of its resources to (1) conflict prediction and prevention; (2) conflict management; or (3) postconflict reconstruction and peace building? With respect to crime, should resources be allocated to (1) prevention or (2) remedial intervention?

Conflict-Affected Countries

http://rru.worldbank.org/themes/conflictaffectedcountries/

Private sector development is an integral part of the rehabilitation process in conflict-affected countries and territories. Research on conflict and poverty has proven that long-term economic growth is essential for lasting peace and stability. Private sector activity, if conducted in a responsible manner, can stimulate growth, create jobs, foster good governance and sound institutions, and ultimately promote peace.

Governments recovering from conflict must do their part to create an enabling environment that attracts both domestic and foreign investment. Companies must adopt conflict-sensitive business practices to ensure that their activities contribute to peace and stability, not work against them. Determining the capacity and limitations of private sector development in conflict environments is a key challenge for policymakers.

The WBG discusses and has programs on, *inter alia*, attracting investment infrastructure after conflict, aid and investment flows after conflict, managing postconflict resource rents, and international companies and conflict reconstruction. The WBG itself has various resources, such as a Conflict Prevention and Reconstruction Group, Low-Income Countries under Stress, MIGA in Conflict-Affected Countries, and Economics of Civil

War, Crime and Violence. In addition, the WBG has partnered with several other organizations, such as the Department of Peace and Conflict Research, Uppsala University, Conflict-Prevention and Post-Conflict Reconstruction Network, Business and Human Rights Resource Center, International Crisis Group, and Development Gateway: Microfinance in Post Conflict.

C. *Strengthening Compliance and Enforcement*

The World Bank Institute Web Portal on Partnerships to Combat Corruption provides an introduction to the Business, Competitiveness and Development (BCD) Team's Learning Program on Business Ethics and Anti-Corruption. The Learning Program consists of a series of activities leading up to and following the plenary session, "Partnerships to Combat Corruption: Rising to the Challenge," that took place at the 2006 IMF/World Bank Board of Governors Annual Meetings in Singapore. It also serves as a resource center for business and NGO leaders, policymakers, and future leaders interested in business-led partnerships, perspectives, and solutions on fighting corruption (see http://info.worldbank.org/etools/bcdwebportal; accessed on April 29, 2007).

The Humanitarian Accountability Partnership (HAP) is the humanitarian sector's first international self-regulatory body, striving to make humanitarian action accountable to its intended beneficiaries: those people whose lives are at risk due to armed conflict or other calamitous events. It shares a commitment to making humanitarian action accountable to disaster survivors. At the heart of this endeavor lies HAP´s Principles of Accountability (www.hapinternational.org; accessed on April 29, 2007).

D. *Harmonization*

Because the World Bank Group assesses compliance and provides technical and financial assistance on topics such as governance, anticorruption, AML/CTF, and specifically on the preparation of laws to implement obligations under international conventions and international standards, it helps foster harmonization. Given that many international standards are only "soft law" obligations and inconsistently implemented, the WBG's status as a universal organization provides significant legitimacy to the standards. Its provision of manuals for instituting, guiding, and providing technical and financial assistance on drafting laws contributes significantly to harmonizing selective international white collar crime.

E. *Technical Assistance*

As already mentioned, the WBG Group provides technical assistance on topics such as governance, anticorruption, anti-money laundering, and counterterrorism financing and specifically on the preparation of laws to implement obligations under international conventions and international standards. The need of WBG members to respond to systemic defects in their financial system and governance motivates them to accept technical assistance in remedying the defects the WBG finds in the FSAPs and ROSCs.

The World Bank Institute provides training through conferences and seminars and links governments and ministries to Web sites of NGOs and international organizations.

Notes and Questions

1. Do you think the WBG should engage in regime and institution building to combat or control crime? Which macroeconomic arguments support allocating resources and programs for crime control and criminal justice?

2. WBG work on the economics of crime and violence, arising out of its work on the economic ramifications of civil wars, underscores the nexus between the breakdown of civil order and failing economic development. Early in his tenure, former WB president Paul Wolfowitz faced a related dispute when Christiaan Poortman, WB vice president for the Middle East, disagreed with Wolfowitz's demand that the World Bank establish a greater presence in Iraq; shortly thereafter, in response to an order transferring him to Kazakhstan, Poortman resigned. Steven R. Weisman, *How Battles at Bank Ended 'Second Chance' at a Career*, N.Y. TIMES, May 18, 2007, at A12, col. 3.

3. Because the WBG's work on criminal justice regime and institution building is relatively recent, it is likely to undergo substantial and dynamic development.

4. The WBG often serves as a model for multilateral – especially regional – development banks (MDBs). How has the WBG's participation in international white collar crime and criminal justice activities affected the policies and programs of MDBs?

VIII. *Additional Reading*

A. *Books*

PAUL BLUSTEIN, THE CHASTENING: INSIDE THE CRISIS THAT ROCKED THE GLOBAL FINANCIAL SYSTEM AND HUMBLED THE IMF (PublicAffairs 2001).

THOMAS CAROTHERS, AIDING DEMOCRACY ABROAD: THE LEARNING CURVE (Brookings Institute 2003).

WILLIAM DELPHOS, INSIDE THE WORLD BANK GROUP: PRACTICAL GUIDE FOR INTERNATIONAL BUSINESS EXECUTIVES (Oxford Univ. Press 1998).

EXPORTING DEMOCRACY: THE UNITED STATES AND LATIN AMERICA (Abraham F. Lowenthal ed., 1991, 2 volumes).

THEODORE S. GREENBERG, LINDA M. SAMUEL, WINGATE GRANT, & LARISSA GRAY, STOLEN ASSET RECOVERY: A GOOD PRACTICES GUIDE FOR NON-CONVICTION BASED FORFEITURE (World Bank Group 2009).

INTERNATIONAL MONETARY FUND, LEGAL DEPARTMENT, SUPPRESSING THE FINANCING OF TERRORISM: A HANDBOOK OF LEGISLATIVE DRAFTING (2003).

INTERNATIONAL MONETARY FUND/WORLD BANK GROUP, FINANCIAL INTELLIGENCE UNITS: AN OVERVIEW (2004).

INTERNATIONAL MONETARY FUND, REGULATORY FRAMEWORKS FOR HAWALA AND OTHER REMITTANCE SYSTEMS (2005).

SEBASTIAN MALLABY, THE WORLD'S BANKER: A STORY OF FAILED STATES, FINANCIAL CRISES, AND THE WEALTH AND POVERTY OF NATIONS (Council on Foreign Relations Books, Penguin Press 2006).

THE MANY FACES OF CORRUPTION: TRACKING VULNERABILITIES AT THE SECTOR LEVEL (J. Edgardo Campos & Sanjay Pradham eds., World Bank Group 2007).

PAUL S. MCCLURE, A GUIDE TO THE WORLD BANK (World Bank Publications 2003).

LAWRENCE J. MCQUILLAN & PETER C. MONTGOMERY, THE INTERNATIONAL MONETARY FUND (Hoover Institution Press 1999).

W. PAATII OFOSU-AMAAH, COMBATING CORRUPTION: A COMPARATIVE REVIEW OF SELECTED LEGAL ASPECTS OF STATE PRACTICE AND MAJOR INTERNATIONAL INITIATIVES (International Bank for Reconstruction and Development 1999).

RICHARD PEET, THE UNHOLY TRINITY: THE IMF, WORLD BANK, AND THE WTO (Zed Books, 2003).

Paul Allan Schott, Reference Guide to Anti-Money Laundering and Combating the Financing of terrorism (World Bank/IMF 2003).

Stolen Asset Recovery: A Good Practices Guide for Non-Conviction Based Asset Forfeiture (Theodore S. Greenberg, Linda Samuel, Wingate Grant, & Larissa Gray eds. (World Bank 2009).

B. *Articles*

Herbert R. Morais, *Fighting International Crime and its Financing: The Importance of Following a Coherent Global Strategy Based on the Rule of Law*, 50 Vill. L.Rev. 583 (2005).

Joy Smallwood, *Combating the Financing of Terrorism: The Roles of the IMF*, 50 Vill. L.Rev. 645 (2005).

C. *Source Material*

The World Bank Group Web site has a treasure trove of useful material, including *Anticorruption in Transition: A Contribution to the Policy Debate*, September 2000.

Anticorruption in Transition 2 – Corruption in Enterprise-State Interactions in Europe and Central Asia 1999–2002 (ACT2), March 2004, World Bank Press Release.

Helping Countries Combat Corruption: Progress at the World Bank Since 1997 (September 2000 OCS/PREM).

Simon Johnson & Daniel Kaufmann, "Institutions and the Underground Economy," *in* A Decade of Transition: Achievements and Challenges (O. Havrylyshyn & S. M. Nsouli eds., 2009).

13 INTERPOL

I. Introduction

In September 1923, police chiefs from twenty countries met in Vienna, Austria, without diplomatic authority or instructions from their government, and formed the organization now known as the International Criminal Police Organization, or INTERPOL. The organization was established without the normal formality of a treaty ratified by member states. Although the absence of a treaty may make INTERPOL unconventional, police organizations and governments throughout the world have broadly participated in INTERPOL since its inception. As of May 1, 2009, 187 countries participate in INTERPOL, making it a truly universal organization in terms of its membership.

INTERPOL's mandate includes the investigation and suppression of drug trafficking, money laundering, bank fraud, smuggling, trafficking in illicit arms and stolen works of art, financial fraud, illicit electronic fund transfers, piracy of cassettes and videotapes, hijacking of planes and ships, theft, arson, and terrorism, as well as the tracking of fugitives from such offenses. INTERPOL assists in transmitting information about individual cases and fugitives as well as trends in crimes, but it does not actually conduct arrests. On white collar crime issues INTERPOL helps in the investigation and prosecution of cases, and it collects and disseminates data on crime trends and new police techniques. It also provides technical assistance, especially to developing countries, both on general police techniques and on responding to specific crimes.

II. Hypotheticals

1. Country X and Country Y do not have diplomatic relations. Country X has evidence that Mr. A, one of its nationals, in cooperation with Z entity, which has close relations with the government of Country Y, has been counterfeiting its currency and also trafficking drugs into Country X. Both Country X and Y are members of INTERPOL. Please advise Country X on what, if anything, INTERPOL may do to assist in preventing further criminal activities and helping arrest and prosecute Mr. A. and the Z entity. Would your advice differ if Country X had evidence that nationals of Country Y's navy crossed into its territorial waters to perform a security operation? In that situation, Country X has arrested them and is considering prosecuting them, but Country Y vigorously disputes that the action occurred in the territorial waters of Country X. Country X wants to prosecute agents, both governmental and nongovernmental, of Country Y that organized and assisted in the naval operation. Country Y has already issued criminal warrants against the law enforcement officials and the superiors of Country X for the illegal seizure of their naval officers. Can Country Y obtain assistance from INTERPOL?

2. Mr. P. is the main opposition leader in Country A, which has been a dictatorship for the last fifty years. Mr. P. has become a very popular politician, and the polls predict he has a real chance of winning the election. Two weeks before the election he is accused of defaming the president against whom he is running and of crimes against national security because of his close ties with foreign agents of Country B with which Country A has not had diplomatic relations in two decades; the two countries were also engaged in a war lasting five years that ended about ten years ago. At the request of Country A's public prosecutor, INTERPOL National Central Bureau has requested the issuance of a Red Notice. What should INTERPOL do? Does the INTERPOL Secretary-General have a role? What Mr. P. gave reports about massive bribes in the media and shared documents showing that the president had deposited $50 million during the last two years into his own bank accounts in offshore jurisdictions?

III. The Constitution of INTERPOL

General Provisions

Article 1

The Organization called the 'INTERNATIONAL CRIMINAL POLICE COMMISSION' shall henceforth be entitled: 'THE INTERNATIONAL CRIMINAL POLICE ORGANIZATION – INTERPOL'. Its seat shall be in France.

Article 2

Its aims are:

(1) To ensure and promote the widest possible mutual assistance between all criminal police authorities within the limits of the laws existing in the different countries and in the spirit of the 'Universal Declaration of Human Rights';
(2) To establish and develop all institutions likely to contribute effectively to the prevention and suppression of ordinary law crimes.

Article 3

It is strictly forbidden for the Organization to undertake any intervention or activities of a political, military, religious or racial character.

Article 4

Any country may delegate as a Member to the Organization any official police body whose functions come within the framework of activities of the Organization.

The request for membership shall be submitted to the Secretary General by the appropriate governmental authority.

Membership shall be subject to approval by a two-thirds majority of the General Assembly.

Structure and Organization

Article 5

The International Criminal Police Organization – INTERPOL shall comprise:

* The General Assembly
* The Executive Committee
* The General Secretariat
* The National Central Bureaus
* The Advisers

The General Assembly

Article 6

The General Assembly shall be the body of supreme authority in the Organization. It is composed of delegates appointed by the Members of the Organization.

Article 7

Each Member may be represented by one or several delegates; however, for each country there shall be only one delegation head, appointed by the competent governmental authority of that country.

Because of the technical nature of the Organization, Members should attempt to include the following in their delegations:

(a) High officials of departments dealing with police affairs,
(b) Officials whose normal duties are connected with the activities of the Organization,
(c) Specialists in the subjects on the agenda.

Article 8

The functions of the General Assembly shall be the following:

(a) To carry out the duties laid down in the Constitution;
(b) To determine principles and lay down the general measures suitable for attaining the objectives of the Organization as given in Article 2 of the Constitution;
(c) To examine and approve the general programme of activities prepared by the Secretary General for the coming year;
(d) To determine any other regulations deemed necessary;
(e) To elect persons to perform the functions mentioned in the Constitution;
(f) To adopt resolutions and make recommendations to Members on matters with which the Organization is competent to deal;
(g) To determine the financial policy of the Organization;
(h) To examine and approve any agreements to be made with other organizations.

Article 9

Members shall do all within their power, in so far as is compatible with their own obligations, to carry out the decisions of the General Assembly.

Article 10

The General Assembly of the Organization shall meet in ordinary session every year. It may meet in extraordinary session at the request of the Executive Committee or of the majority of Members.

Article 11

11.1 The General Assembly may, when in session, set up special committees for dealing with particular matters.

11.2 It may also decide to hold regional conferences between two General Assembly sessions.

Article 12

12.1 At the end of each session, the General Assembly shall choose the place where it will meet for its next session.

12.2 The General Assembly may also decide where it will meet for its session in two years time, if one or more countries have issued invitations to host that session.

12.3 If circumstances make it impossible or inadvisable for a session to be held in the chosen meeting place, the General Assembly may decide to choose another meeting place for the following year.

Article 13

Only one delegate from each country shall have the right to vote in the General Assembly.

Article 14

Decisions shall be made by a simple majority except in those cases where a two-thirds majority is required by the Constitution.

The Executive Committee

Article 15

The Executive Committee shall be composed of the President of the Organization, the three Vice-Presidents and nine Delegates.

The thirteen members of the Executive Committee shall belong to different countries, due weight having been given to geographical distribution.

Article 16

The General Assembly shall elect, from among the delegates, the President and three Vice-Presidents of the Organization.

A two-thirds majority shall be required for the election of the President; should this majority not be obtained after the second ballot, a simple majority shall suffice.

The President and Vice-Presidents shall be from different continents.

Article 17

The President shall be elected for four years. The Vice-Presidents shall be elected for three years. They shall not be immediately eligible for re-election either to the same posts or as Delegates on the Executive Committee.

* * *

Article 18

The President of the Organization shall:

(a) Preside at meetings of the Assembly and the Executive Committee and direct the discussions;
(b) Ensure that the activities of the Organization are in conformity with the decisions of the General Assembly and the Executive Committee;
(c) Maintain as far as is possible direct and constant contact with the Secretary General of the Organization.

Article 19

The nine Delegates on the Executive Committee shall be elected by the General Assembly for a period of three years. They shall not be immediately eligible for re-election to the same posts.

Article 20

The Executive Committee shall meet at least once each year on being convened by the President of the Organization.

Article 21

In the exercise of their duties, all members of the Executive Committee shall conduct themselves as representatives of the Organization and not as representatives of their respective countries.

Article 22

The Executive Committee shall:

(a) Supervise the execution of the decisions of the General Assembly;
(b) Prepare the agenda for sessions of the General Assembly;
(c) Submit to the General Assembly any programme of work or project which it considers useful;
(d) Supervise the administration and work of the Secretary General;
(e) Exercise all the powers delegated to it by the Assembly.

* * *

The General Secretariat

Article 25

The permanent departments of the Organization shall constitute the General Secretariat.

Article 26

The General Secretariat shall:

(a) Put into application the decisions of the General Assembly and the Executive Committee;
(b) Serve as an international centre in the fight against ordinary crime;
(c) Serve as a technical and information centre;
(d) Ensure the efficient administration of the Organization;
(e) Maintain contact with national and international authorities, whereas questions relative to the search for criminals shall be dealt with through the National Central Bureaus;

(f) Produce any publications which may be considered useful;
(g) Organize and perform secretariat work at the sessions of the General Assembly, the Executive Committee and any other body of the Organization;
(h) Draw up a draft programme of work for the coming year for the consideration and approval of the General Assembly and the Executive Committee;
(i) Maintain as far as is possible direct and constant contact with the President of the Organization.

Article 27

The General Secretariat shall consist of the Secretary General and a technical and administrative staff entrusted with the work of the Organization.

Article 28

The appointment of the Secretary General shall be proposed by the Executive Committee and approved by the General Assembly for a period of five years. He may be re-appointed for other terms but must lay down office on reaching the age of sixty-five, although he may be allowed to complete his term of office on reaching this age.

He must be chosen from among persons highly competent in police matters.

In exceptional circumstances, the Executive Committee may propose at a meeting of the General Assembly that the Secretary General be removed from office.

Article 29

The Secretary General shall engage and direct the staff, administer the budget, and organize and direct the permanent departments, according to the directives decided upon by the General Assembly or Executive Committee.

He shall submit to the Executive Committee or the General Assembly any propositions or projects concerning the work of the Organization.

He shall be responsible to the Executive Committee and the General Assembly.

He shall have the right to take part in the discussions of the General Assembly, the Executive Committee and all other dependent bodies.

In the exercise of his duties, he shall represent the Organization and not any particular country.

Article 30

In the exercise of their duties, the Secretary General and the staff shall neither solicit nor accept instructions from any government or authority outside the Organization. They shall abstain from any action which might be prejudicial to their international task.

Each Member of the Organization shall undertake to respect the exclusively international character of the duties of the Secretary General and the staff, and abstain from influencing them in the discharge of their duties.

All Members of the Organization shall do their best to assist the Secretary General and the staff in the discharge of their functions.

National Central Bureaus

Article 31

In order to further its aims, the Organization needs the constant and active co-operation of its Members, who should do all within their power which is compatible with the legislations of their countries to participate diligently in its activities.

Article 32

In order to ensure the above co-operation, each country shall appoint a body which will serve as the National Central Bureau. It shall ensure liaison with:

(a) The various departments in the country;
(b) Those bodies in other countries serving as National Central Bureaus;
(c) The Organization's General Secretariat.

Article 33

In the case of those countries where the provisions of Article 32 are inapplicable or do not permit effective centralized co-operation, the General Secretariat shall decide, with these countries, the most suitable alternative means of co-operation.

* * *

Budget and Resources

Article 38

The Organization's resources shall be provided by:

(a) The financial contributions from Members;
(b) Gifts, bequests, subsidies, grants and other resources after these have been accepted or approved by the Executive Committee.

Article 39

The General Assembly shall establish the basis of Members' subscriptions and the maximum annual expenditure according to the estimate provided by the Secretary General.

Article 40

The draft budget of the Organization shall be prepared by the Secretary General and submitted for approval to the Executive Committee.

It shall come into force after acceptance by the General Assembly.

Should the General Assembly not have had the possibility of approving the budget, the Executive Committee shall take all necessary steps according to the general outlines of the preceding budget.

Relations with other Organizations

Article 41

Whenever it deems fit, having regard to the aims and objects provided in the Constitution, the Organization shall establish relations and collaborate with other intergovernmental or non-governmental international organizations.

The general provisions concerning the relations with international, intergovernmental or non-governmental organizations will only be valid after their approval by the General Assembly.

The Organization may, in connection with all matters in which it is competent, take the advice of non-governmental international, governmental national or non-governmental national organizations.

With the approval of the General Assembly, the Executive Committee or, in urgent cases, the Secretary General may accept duties within the scope of its activities and competence either from other international institutions or organizations or in application of international conventions.

* * *

Article 50

This Constitution shall come into force on 13th June 1956.

Notes and Questions

1. Would you characterize INTERPOL as a standard international organization (IO) or a network? Although INTERPOL coordinates efforts among national police forces to combat crimes when either the crimes or the criminals cross international boundaries, its IO structure is standard. It has a General Assembly in which all member states (approximately 187 as of May 11, 2009) have representation, an Executive Committee of thirteen members elected from among its members, and a Secretariat, which a Secretary-General manages with a staff of more than 400 and an annual budget of approximately $30 million. Member dues are its chief source of funding and are based on the national GDPs of member countries. INTERPOL has its headquarters in Lyon, France. J. SAMUEL BARKIN, INTERNATIONAL ORGANIZATIONS: THEORIES AND INSTITUTIONS 124 (Palgrave MacMillan 2006).

2. Interestingly INTERPOL did not start as an IO, but rather as an NGO called the International Police Commission (IPC). In 1923, the police chief of Vienna and police officials from twenty countries attending an international police conference created the IPC and its constitution, which a number of police organizations in various countries accepted. However, the constitution was not submitted to the governments for ratification. Although initially the IPC consisted only of police departments, it gradually evolved into an IO. In 1948, it was granted UN consultative status and in 1956 was upgraded from a commission to an organization. In 1971, it obtained full IO status by Special Arrangement with the Economic and Social Council (ECOSOC). *See*, e.g., MICHAEL FOONER, A GUIDE TO INTERPOL: THE INTERNATIONAL CRIMINAL POLICE ORGANIZATION IN THE UNITED STATES (National Institute of Justice 1985). As required by Art. 7 of its constitution, each representative is "appointed by the competent governmental authority of that country." Nevertheless, Art. 2 specifies that involvement is restricted to criminal

police authorities. Hence, INTERPOL is characterized as a traditional functional IO, in which country representatives are functional experts selected from the relevant national bureaucracy. Barkin, *supra*, at 124.

3. A key element of INTERPOL's success is its requirement of mutual assistance among all police authorities without distinction on political, social, or economic bases. In practice, its membership includes police authorities from democracies, limited monarchies, and dictatorships; ideologies of member countries are based on capitalist, socialist, and mixed philosophies. Its constitution's reference to providing the "widest possible mutual assistance" does not restrict such assistance to members only. Periodically, INTERPOL cooperates with nonmembers on specific cases. Fooner, *supra*, at 39.

4. Note that the General Assembly serves as a forum for international discussion of policing issues and adopts resolutions on these issues.

5. One of the important functions of the Secretariat, both on its own and in cooperation with police forces in member countries, is to study and collect data on various key and emerging forms of international criminal activity and to coordinate activities among these forces. For instance, as shown later, the Secretariat collects data and coordinates activities on a variety of transnational white collar crimes. Its activities enable national police agencies and other interested persons, such as victims, interested IGOs, and NGOs, to benefit from its work.

6. Art. 3 of its constitution provides that "it is strictly forbidden for the Organization to undertake any intervention or activities of a political, military, religious or racial character." In 1950, FBI Director J. Edgar Hoover withdrew the United States from INTERPOL because he believed it had grossly violated its constitutional prohibition against political activity. Mr. Hoover protested INTERPOL's issuance of a Red Notice at the request of the Czechoslovak government for its nationals who had commandeered two aircraft and forced them to land in U.S.-occupied Germany even though the State Department agreed to their request for political asylum.

7. How does the prohibition in Article 3 of the INTERPOL constitution that forbids INTERPOL from undertaking "any intervention or activities of a political, military, religious or racial character" square with the need for police cooperation against international terrorism?

From the 1950s through the 1970s, INTERPOL in effect acquiesced to the idea that acts by international terrorists should be presumed to be political in nature. Article 3 was interpreted as precluding its involvement in combating terrorism, even though terrorist acts might include murder, kidnapping, extortion, robbery, arson, drug trafficking, and other forms of serious crimes that are unquestionably within its mandate. Over time, a consensus developed among INTERPOL members that it should deal with terrorism.[1]

IV. Legislative Authority for U.S. Membership and the National Central Bureau (NCB)

22 U.S.C. § 263A International Criminal Police Organization

The Attorney General is authorized to accept and maintain, on behalf of the United States, membership in the International Criminal Police Organization, and to designate any

[1] Fooner, *id.* at 9–10.

departments and agencies which may participate in the United States representation with that organization. Each participating department and agency is authorized to pay its pro rata share, as determined by the Attorney General, of the expenses of such membership. The total dues to be paid for the membership of the United States shall not exceed $120,000 per annum.

Executive Order 12425 of June 16, 1983, Designating INTERPOL an International Organization

By virtue of the authority vested in me as President by the Constitution and statutes of the United States, including Section 1 of the International Organizations Immunities Act (59 Stat. 669, 22 U.S.C. 288), it is hereby ordered that the International Criminal Police Organization (INTERPOL), in which the United States participates pursuant to 22 U.S.C. 263a, is hereby designated as a public international organization entitled to enjoy the privileges, exemptions and immunities conferred by the International Organizations Immunities Act; except those provided by Section 2(c), the portions of Section 2(d) and Section 3 relating to customs duties and federal internal-revenue importation taxes, Section 4, Section 5, and Section 6 of that Act. This designation is not intended to abridge in any respect the privileges, exemptions or immunities which such organization may have acquired or may acquire by international agreement or by Congressional action.

Ronald Reagan
The White House
June 16, 1983

INTERPOL Rules on INTERPOL Police Cooperation and Control of its Archives

15.1 Subject

15.1.1 This chapter deals with the Rules on the processing of information for the purposes of international police co-operation.

15.2 References

15.2.1 Rules adopted by the General Assembly at its 72nd session (Benidorm, Spain, 2003) in Resolution AG-2003-RES-04. Entered into force on 1 January 2004.

15.2.2. . . .

15.2.3 Rules amended by Resolution AG-20054-RES-15 adopted by the General Assembly at its 74th session (Berlin, Germany, 2005). Entered into force on 1 January 2006.

The Secretary General

Preamble

Considering Article 2 of the Organization's Constitution, which provides that its aims are to ensure and promote the widest possible mutual assistance between all criminal police authorities within the limits of the laws existing in the different countries and in the spirit of the 'Universal Declaration of Human Rights,' and to establish and develop all institutions likely to contribute effectively to the prevention as well as the suppression of ordinary law crimes,

Considering Article 3 of the Organization's Constitution, which forbids it to undertake any intervention or activities of a political, military, religious or racial character,

Deeming that the processing of information constitutes an essential tool for co-operation between all the Member States, thereby allowing the Organization to fulfill its mission,

Bearing in mind Article 26 (b) of the Organization's Constitution as well as Article 26 (c), which provides that the General Secretariat shall serve as a technical and information centre, and thus be responsible for processing police information,

Also bearing in mind that the processing of information by the General Secretariat within the Organization's buildings and premises is not subject to any national laws,

Considering Articles 31 and 32 of the Constitution and, in particular, the central liaison role of the NCBs, in supervising and co-ordinating all forms of participation by the various departments of their countries in the Organization's activities.

Considering that under the terms of Articles 8(b) and 8(d) of the Constitution, the General Assembly is empowered to determine principles and lay down the general measures suitable for attaining the objectives of the Organization as given in Article 2 of the Constitution, and to determine any other regulations deemed necessary,

The General Assembly adopted the following Rules at its 72nd session held in Benidorm, Spain, in 2003. They were modified at its 74th session, held in Berlin, Germany, in 2005.

Article 1: Definitions

1. Ordinary-law crimes means crimes as referred to in Article 2 (b) of the Constitution but not those excluded by Article 3 of the said Constitution.
2. Information means any item of information or set of items of information (personal or otherwise, and irrespective of the sources) pertaining to constituent elements of ordinary-law crimes, in compliance with Article 1(a) above, the investigation and prevention of such crimes, the prosecution and punishment of offences, and any information pertaining to missing persons and unidentified dead bodies.
3. Personal information means any information relating to an identified or identifiable natural person: an identifiable natural person is one who can be identified, directly or indirectly, in particular by reference to an identification number or to one or more factors specific to his [1] identity, or to his physiological, psychic, economic, or social characteristics.
4. Particularly sensitive information means any personal information revealing racial or ethnic origin; political opinions; philosophical, religious or other convictions; or concerning health or sexuality.
5. National Central Bureau means anybody provided for in Articles 32 and 33 of the Organization's Constitution.
6. Authorized national institution means any official public national institution or any entity legally authorized to fulfill the role of a public institution in enforcing the criminal law and which has received the express authorization of its country's NCB to consult or provide information via the Organization's channels within the limits set by the said NCB.
7. Authorized international entity means any entity, as referred to in Article 41 of the Constitution, which has concluded an agreement with the Organization authorizing it to process information directly through the Organization's channels.
8. Source of the information means the entity providing the information through the Organization's channels.

9. Police information system means all the Organization's databases and networks which can be used for processing information, through its channels, for the purposes of international police co-operation.
10. Processing of information includes any operation or set of operations (automated or manual) applied to information in any form or on any medium, from the moment it is accessed to the moment it is destroyed, and any exchange in between.
11. Specific international interest to the police means any information, as defined in Article 1 (b) above, which may be of interest to the police or law enforcement authorities because of its direct link with the Organization's aims as defined in Article 3.1 below.
12. Notices mean international INTERPOL notifications containing sets of information recorded in the police information system and circulated by the General Secretariat, for purposes referred to in Article 3.1 (a) below.
13. A crime analysis means the identification of and the provision of insight into the relationship between crime data or between crime data and other potentially relevant crime data with a view to prosecutorial, police and judicial practice.

Article 2: Purpose and Scope

1. The present Rules set out the conditions and basic procedures according to which information is processed by the Organization or through its channels for the purposes of international police co-operation (Article 3.1 below), or for any other legitimate purpose (Article 3.2 below), with due respect for the basic rights of individuals in conformity with Article 2 of the Organization's Constitution and the Universal Declaration of Human Rights to which the said Article refers.
2. The present Rules apply to any operation to process information, by automated or other means, on any medium or in any form.
3. The General Secretariat, the National Central Bureaus, the authorized national institutions, and the authorized international entities using the police information system and the information transmitted thereon shall be required to observe the provisions of the present Rules and the texts to which they refer.

Article 3: Purposes for Which Information Is Processed

3.1 Processing for international police co-operation purposes

1. Information shall be processed by the Organization or through its channels in order to prevent, investigate and prosecute ordinary-law crimes, as referred to in Article 1 (a) above, to assist with such investigations and for the following reasons:
   1. A search for a person with a view to his arrest;
   2. To obtain information about a person who has committed or is likely to commit, or has participated or is likely to have participated (directly or indirectly) in an ordinary-law crime;
   3. To warn police authorities about a person's criminal activities;
   4. To locate a missing person;
   5. To locate a witness or victim;
   6. To identify a person or a dead body;
   7. To locate or identify objects;

8. To describe or identify *modus operandi*, offenses committed by unidentified persons, the characteristics of counterfeits or forgeries, and seizures of items connected with trafficking operations.

2. Information may also be processed, as provided for in (a) above, for the purpose of identifying threats and criminal networks.
3. The purpose for which information is processed must be stated explicitly for each database.

3.2 Processing for any other legitimate purpose

1. The General Secretariat may also process information, outside of the police information system, for any other legitimate purpose, i.e. for administrative reasons, scientific research and publications (historical, statistical, or journalistic) or to defend the interests of the Organization, its members or staff in the context of a trial, a settlement, pre-litigation procedures, post-trial or appellate proceedings, in conformity with Article 10.4 below.
2. Such processing shall be the subject of implementing rules as described in Article 23 (c,3) below. The rules shall specify the storage conditions and retention period for information thus processed.

Role of the General Secretariat

Article 4

4.1 General provisions

1. Under Article 26 (b) of the Constitution, the General Secretariat shall serve as an international center in the fight against international ordinary-law crime. To this effect, within the limits and under the conditions set in the present Rules, the General Secretariat is responsible for:
   1. Processing information it receives or collects, in accordance with the rules the Organization has adopted on such matters;
   2. Ensuring that the provisions of the present Rules and the texts to which they refer are observed during any operation to process information through the Organization's channels;
   3. Deciding on the type and structure of the Organization's telecommunications network(s) and databases without prejudice to the provisions of Article 22 (d) or Article 29 (1) of the Organization's Constitution;
   4. Developing and maintaining those telecommunications network(s) and databases, as well as the means necessary for National Central Bureaus, authorized national institutions and authorized international entities to have access to them;
   5. Developing and verifying the security of those telecommunications network(s) and databases;
   6. Housing the Organization's databases on its premises.
2. The General Secretariat is also empowered to take any appropriate steps which may contribute effectively to combating international ordinary-law crime, within the limits of the tasks set for it and the provisions of the present Rules. For that purpose, it may,

inter alia, request information (Article 4.2 below) or conclude co-operation agreements involving the exchange of information (Article 4.3 below).

4.2 Request for information

1. In conformity with the provisions of Article 4.1 (b) above and subject to the provisions of Article 4.3 below, the General Secretariat may request information, particularly in the following cases:
   1. It has reasons to believe that it is necessary to achieve the objectives of the Organization and in keeping with the aims pursued;
   2. The request is made in the context of a case or specific project;
   3. Its request is motivated by a desire to ensure that an item of information is processed in conformity with the present Rules, or to ensure the quality of that information;
2. The General Secretariat may not request information from an authorized national institution without having obtained prior authorization from the National Central Bureau of the member country concerned, unless the said National Central Bureau has not replied to the General Secretariat within 45 days of being so informed, it being understood that the National Central Bureau retains the right to oppose this communication with an authorized national institution in its country at any moment.

4.3 Conclusion of co-operation agreements

1. Before an international entity may provide information, or be requested to do so, on a regular basis, the General Secretariat shall conclude a co-operation agreement for that purpose with the said entity, under the conditions below.
2. The General Secretariat shall request the opinion of the Commission for the Control of Interpol's Files about any co-operation agreement involving operations to process personal information, in conformity with the Rules relating to the Control of Information and Access to Interpol's Files. This will in particular be the case in situations referred to in Articles 20.2 (a) and 21 (a,4) below.
3. The General Secretariat shall forward the opinion of the Commission for the Control of Interpol's Files to the Executive Committee, which may require that the co-operation begun in the context of a project be modified, or may oppose such co-operation if it has not yet been established. This will in particular be the case in situations referred to in Articles 20.2 (b) and 21 (a,5) below.
4. For any regular co-operation with an international organization, as referred to in Article 41 of the Constitution, the General Secretariat shall obtain authorization to engage in such co-operation from the General Assembly, and shall comply with the provisions of the Rules governing access by an intergovernmental organization to the INTERPOL telecommunications network and databases.
5. Every year, the General Secretariat shall prepare a list of the entities with which co-operation agreements involving information processing have been concluded, and shall provide the list to the General Assembly and the Commission for the Control of Interpol's Files for their information.
6. The provisions of any co-operation agreement dealing with a processing of information shall be in conformity with the provisions of the present Rules and the text to which they refer.

Article 5: Role of Entities in the Processing of Information

5.1 General provision

Whenever necessary, and at least once a year, the General Secretariat shall remind the National Central Bureaus and the entities with which it has concluded a co-operation agreement of their role and responsibilities connected with the information they process through the Organization's channels, particularly with regard to the accuracy of that information and its relevance in relation to the purpose for which it is provided.

5.2 Role of the National Central Bureaus in their relations with the authorized national institutions

1. In carrying out their liaison function – as defined in Article 32 (a) of the Organization's Constitution – between the General Secretariat and the authorized national institutions, the National Central Bureaus shall be responsible vis-à-vis the General Secretariat for the entities and persons they have authorized to consult, or supply information for, the police information system.
2. With regard to their responsibility vis-à-vis the authorized national institutions, prior to authorizing them to consult, or to provide information through, the Organization police information system, the National Central Bureaus shall first establish that procedures conforming to their national laws have been put in place to ensure and to continue to ensure that the said entities respect the present Rules (in particular Article 10.1 (a,5) below) and the texts to which they refer.

5.3 Provision of information

1. The National Central Bureaus, authorized national institutions and authorized international entities shall continue to be responsible for the information which they provide through the police information system and which may be recorded in the Organization's files.
2. The information sources shall be required to take any appropriate steps to:
   1. Ensure that the information continues to fulfill the conditions for being processed by the Organization, as required by the present Rules and the texts to which they refer;
   2. Ensure the accuracy and relevance of the information and inform the General Secretariat of any change or deletion which needs to be carried out regarding that information (via the National Central Bureau, in the case of authorized national institutions), or carry out such changes or deletions if they themselves have recorded the information directly in one of the Organization's databases.

5.5 Use of information

1. Prior to the use of any information obtained through the Organization's police information system, the National Central Bureaus, authorized national institutions and authorized international entities must check with the General Secretariat and the source of that information to ensure that the information is still accurate and relevant.
2. It is understood that:
   1. Authorized national institutions shall conduct the necessary checks and additional investigations via their NCBs;

2. Authorized international entities shall conduct the necessary checks and additional information requests in consultation with the source of the information via the General Secretariat.

The Organization's Databases

Article 6

6.1 Different categories of databases

The police information system is composed of the following databases, in which information sent and received over the Organization's network can be recorded:

1. The central database: this is the Organization's main database used *a priori* for processing information received or obtained by the General Secretariat, and items of information which make it possible to manage it, in compliance with the present Rules and the texts to which they refer.
2. The specialized databases:
   1. The subsidiary databases to the central database are those linked to the central database by an indexing system in conformity with Article 6.1 (d) below and contain information which, because of its specific nature, cannot be recorded directly in the central database;
   2. Extractions are databases which may be linked to the indexing system in conformity with Article 6.1 (d) below, and contain information processed in another of the Organization's databases and then copied into the said databases.
   3. The autonomous databases are not linked to the central database by an indexing system for security reasons but are also subject to the provisions of the present Rules and the texts to which they refer.
3. Analysis files are working files created for the purpose of crime analysis as defined in Article 1 (m) above.
4. The indexing system is an automated system allowing the General Secretariat to link the information and databases in the police information system, to facilitate the information management and searches and also to inform the user where an item of information may be recorded, notably for co-ordinating analysis work relating to that information, with due respect for the processing restrictions the source of the information has imposed, in conformity with Article 5.4 (b.ii) above.

6.2 Conditions for setting up and deleting databases

1. When any new database is set up or whenever a database is deleted, the General Secretariat:
   1. shall inform the Commission for the Control of Interpol's Files, if the database contains or is linked to personal information, and shall request its opinion, and
   2. shall inform the Executive Committee, to which the General Secretariat shall forward the opinion of the Commission for the Control of Interpol's Files if necessary; the Executive Committee shall retain the possibility of requiring the deletion or amendment of any database
2. Every year the General Secretariat shall forward to the General Assembly and to the Commission for the Control of Interpol's Files, a list of all the new databases

developed, indicating in particular their position in the overall police information system, the purpose of each, the nature of the information they may be used to store, and the processing rights attaching to each database.

3. Specialized databases, in the sense of Article 6.1 (b) above, may only be set up in the following cases:
   1. When it is necessary and relevant for reasons of a technical, legal or security nature, or to facilitate the processing of information, or secure the management of rights of access to that information, or for information to be studied in the context of a project concerning working information or a crime analysis operation;
   2. When it is not likely to prejudice the integrity, security, topicality or relevance of the information processed in those databases.
4. Such a database could be set up, in particular, to process particularly sensitive information or because of the particularly sensitive nature of the subject being dealt with.
5. The additional conditions under which databases may be set up and deleted shall be laid down in implementing rules as referred to in Article 23 below.

Article 7: The Right to Process Information

1. All information transmitted through the Organization's channels or obtained by the General Secretariat may be processed in the Organization's files if, and only if the conditions on processing laid down in the present Rules, and in the texts to which they refer, are met, and subject to the restrictions attached to its processing.
2. The present Rules shall not apply to requests from individuals for access to the Organization's files, which must be forwarded to the Commission for the Control of Interpol's Files, in accordance with the Rules relating to the Control of Information and Access to Interpol's files, as referred to in Article 25 below.
3. Notwithstanding the Rules relating to the Control of Information and Access to Interpol's Files, referred to in Article 25 below, requests from individuals for access to the Organization's files cannot be processed in the police information system except under the conditions provided for in those Rules.

Article 8: Confidentiality of Information

1. The source of an item of information, whether it be a National Central Bureau, authorized national institution, or authorized international entity shall determine its level of confidentiality, thereby classifying the information.
2. The General Secretariat may attribute a confidentiality level to the information which is higher than that attributed by the source, in the light of the risks to international police co-operation, or to the Organization, its staff, and its member countries of processing, and more particularly of disclosing, the information.
3. The General Secretariat shall determine the level of confidentiality of the value it adds to an item of information, notably when it carries out analysis work or issues a notice, it being understood that, on retransmission, it must respect the restrictions the source referred to in the analysis has imposed on the said item of information.
4. The General Secretariat may also classify a database in the same conditions as those mentioned above.

5. The General Secretariat, in co-ordination with the entities concerned, may draw up equivalence tables for its levels of classification and those used by the National Central Bureaus, the authorized national institutions, and authorized international entities whenever that is deemed necessary.
6. The different levels of confidentiality of information shall be determined and the conditions attached to each level shall be indicated in the implementing rules.

Article 9: Processing Security

1. The General Secretariat shall take all necessary measures to protect the security, i.e. integrity, and confidentiality of information provided and processed through the police information system.
2. To this effect, the General Secretariat shall *inter alia* develop the appropriate technical, legal and procedural means to ensure that only duly authorized persons are able to process an item of information.

* * *

Article 10: General Conditions for Processing Information

10.1 General provisions

1. Processing of information through the Organization's channels may only be carried out if all the following conditions are met:
    1. It complies with the Constitution and relevant provisions in the Organization's rules;
    2. It is in accordance with one of the purposes referred to in Article 3 of the present Rules and the requirements of Article 2 of those Rules;
    3. It is relevant and connected with cases of specific international interest to the police;
    4. It is not such that it might prejudice the Organization's aims, image or interests, or the confidentiality (see Article 8 above) or security (see Article 9 above) of the information;
    5. It is carried out by its source in the context of the laws existing in its country, in conformity with the international conventions to which it is a party, and with the Organization's Constitution.
2. The information is considered, *a priori*, to be accurate and relevant, if it has been provided by a National Central Bureau, an authorized national institution, or authorized international entity.
3. In conformity with Article 12 (a) below, if there is any doubt about whether the criteria for processing an item of information are being met, the General Secretariat shall consult the source of that information, or the National Central Bureau concerned, if the source of the information is an authorized national institution. It shall take all other appropriate steps to ensure that the criteria have indeed been met. The information may then be recorded with a view to obtaining supplementary information to permit its retention in the police information system.
4. The General Secretariat shall take all appropriate steps to prevent any direct or indirect prejudice the information may cause to the member countries, the Organization or its

staff, and with due respect for the basic rights of individuals the information concerns, in conformity with Article 2 of the Organization's Constitution and the Universal Declaration of Human Rights.

5. The processing of information in the central database and the specialized databases, particularly for the crime analysis files, shall be the subject of implementing rules intended to define the purpose of the database concerned, the nature of information which may be recorded therein, and the methods of processing information in the said database, in conformity with Article 23 (c,2) below.

10.2 Provisions relating to particularly sensitive information

a. Particularly sensitive information in any form or on any medium may only be processed if:
   1. It is relevant and of particularly important criminalistic value for achieving the aims of the Organization and the purposes of the processing as described in Article 3.1 of the present Rules;
   2. It is linked to one or more items of information processed by the Organization;
   3. It is described objectively and contains no judgment or discriminatory comments.
b. The processing of such information shall be subject to implementing rules, in conformity with Article 23 (c,4) below.

* * *

10.5 Provisions relating to the processing of notices

1. Notices shall be published by the General Secretariat either at its own initiative or at the request of a National Central Bureau, authorized national institution or authorized international entity in conformity with Article 1 (l) above.
2. Before publishing and circulating a notice, in particular to entities other than the National Central Bureaus, the General Secretariat shall assess whether it is necessary and advisable to do so, in the light of Articles 2 and 3 of the present Rules and the required security measures, bearing in mind the risks run to international police co-operation, the Organization, its staff, and its member countries.
3. The conditions and methods of processing notices shall be laid down in implementing rules, in conformity with Article 23 (c,5) below.

Article 11: General Procedure for Processing Information

1. Irrespective of the processing form or medium, the General Secretariat shall process information:
   1. So that the original information shall be distinguishable from deductions and conclusions drawn from that information, particularly in the context of working information and crime-analysis work;
   2. Without distorting its contents;
   3. Specifying:
      1. the source(s) of the information;
      2. the level of confidentiality of the information, giving details of the scope of processing rights and, any restrictions imposed;

   3. the status of the person who is the subject of the information, in conformity with provisions yet to be determined of the implementing rules;
   4. the deadline for examining the need to retain the information, calculated in conformity with the provisions of Article 13 below.
2. When the General Secretariat processes one or more items of information concerning the one or more persons involved or likely to be involved in one or more linked criminal cases being processed by the Organization, it shall link those items of information, unless the source of the information expressly opposes such linking, in conformity with Article 5.4 above.

Article 12: Cases When the General Secretariat Must Consult the Source of an Item of Information

The General Secretariat must consult the source of an item of information in the following cases:

1. When the General Secretariat has reason to believe that the conditions for processing information referred to in the present Rules and the texts to which they refer are no longer being met, in conformity with Article 10.1 (c) above;
2. At the latest, six months prior to the deadline for examining the need to retain an item of information concerning a person who is the subject of a notice or is wanted, to ask the source of the information whether it considers it is still necessary and relevant to retain the item in the Organization's files, and
3. If, three months before the deadline for assessing the need to retain an item of information concerning a person who is the subject of a notice or is wanted, the source of that information has not replied to the General Secretariat's request, the General Secretariat shall send it a further request.

* * *

15.3 Provisions specifically concerning notices

1. When the information on which a notice is based is modified, the General Secretariat assesses the need to retain the notice. If necessary, it shall modify the notice.
2. When the information on which a notice was based is destroyed, the General Secretariat must also destroy the notice.
3. When the General Secretariat cancels a notice it may retain the information on which the notice or diffusion was based for a maximum of five years, in conformity with the provisions of Article 14 (c,3) above.

Article 16: Consequences of Modification, Blocking or Destruction of an Item of Information

16.1 Action taken by the General Secretariat

1. When the General Secretariat modifies, blocks access to, or destroys, in application of Article 15.2 (b), an item of information which has been provided by a National Central Bureau, an authorized national institution or an authorized international entity and concerns a wanted person or a person who is the subject of a request for information:

1. It shall inform the source of the information, and shall explain the reasons for its action, unless:
   i. the source was notified of the modification, blocking or destruction of the information during the three months prior to the date on which it was actually destroyed;
   ii. the information destroyed was not personal in nature;
2. It shall indicate the reasons why it modified, blocked access to, or destroyed the information;
3. It shall modify, block access to or destroy in the same way all copies of the information in any other database in the Organization's police information system, subject to Article 16.2 below;
4. It shall assess the consequences of that action on all operations relating to the processing of the information concerned and any related information. If necessary, it shall take any steps considered to be essential.

16.2 Retention of elements of an item of information

1. When the General Secretariat destroys an item of information, it may nevertheless retain:
   1. Those elements strictly necessary for identifying the criminal or suspected criminal concerned, the name of the source, and the type of crime concerned, with a view to directing a requesting entity to the source of the information, unless that source has expressly opposed the retention of such items of information;
   2. The elements of an item of information which make it possible to avoid unauthorized or erroneous processing of the said item of information;
   3. The information necessary for the pursuit of any other legitimate purpose (in the sense of Article 3.2 above).

* * *

Article 17: Methods of Providing Information

17.1 General remarks

1. The General Secretariat may provide an item of information, subject to the provisions of the present Rules and the texts to which they refer, and if all the following conditions are met:
   1. To further the purposes of international police co-operation as referred to in Article 3 of the present Rules and within the limits of Article 2 of those Rules,
   2. Either in response to a reasoned request, or on its own initiative, to a National Central Bureau, an authorized national institution or an authorized international entity, it being understood that:
      1. in the case of a reasoned request, the General Secretariat may nevertheless require the requesting entity to provide a descriptive summary of the facts justifying the request,
      2. in the case of direct access, reasons are reputed to have been given,
      3. to provide information on its own initiative to the entities referred to above, the General Secretariat must consider their interventions to be necessary in the light of the Organization's aims, in which case the Secretariat shall specify the purposes for which it is communicating the information;

   3. Subject to any restrictions imposed in application of Article 5.4 above;
   4. With the express prior authorization of the National Central Bureau or the authorized international entity which is the source of the information, before it is forwarded to an entity other than a National Central Bureau, an authorized national institution or an authorized international entity.
2. The General Secretariat may only provide an item of particularly sensitive information when it is relevant and of a particular criminalistic value for the pursuit of the Organization's aims and for the purposes for which the said information is being processed (see Article 3.1 (a) of the present Rules), subject to any restrictions imposed by the source of the information, as provided for in Article 5.4 above.
3. Nothing in the present Rules shall prevent the General Secretariat from providing an item of information, even without having obtained prior authorization from the authorized entity which originally supplied it, in the following cases:
   1. When the information has come into the public domain;
   2. It is a matter of urgency, as defined in Article 17.2 below;
   3. Its provision is necessary to defend the interests of the Organization, its Members or its agents, as understood in Article 3.2 below.
4. No provision of the present Rules shall hinder the possibility, when justified by exceptional circumstances, of providing police information from one of the Organization's member countries to institutions or authorities of the same country to which the services of that State, involved in the enforcement of the criminal law, must account for their actions by virtue of the law.
5. When the General Secretariat is not empowered to provide an item of information to a requesting entity by virtue of restriction imposed by the source of that information, as provided for in Article 5.4 above, it may transmit the request to the source of the information which may be able to answer the request.
6. The provision of information through the Organization's channels must be carried out:

   - in the context of the relevant national and regional laws,
   - in conformity with the international conventions to which the sources of the information are party,
   - in conformity with the Organization's Constitution and its appendices

Article 18: Methods of Communication

1. When the General Secretariat provides an item of information, if it considers it necessary, or if the source of the information so requests, it shall send a copy of the request and a copy of the communication to the source of the information concerned.
2. When the General Secretariat provides an item of information, it shall indicate:
   1. The source;
   2. Any restrictions on processing of the information;
   3. Any conditions regarding retention of the information;
   4. The date of receipt;
   5. The latest date after which the need to retain the information should be assessed;
   6. The main corrigenda and updates to the information;
   7. The status of the person concerned, where personal information is concerned.

* * *

Article 20: Direct Access, Downloading and Interconnection

20.1 General provisions

1. The General Secretariat may authorize a National Central Bureau, an authorized national institution or an authorized international entity to access the police information system directly, to download an item of information from one of the Organization's databases, or to make interconnections between the network and the Organization's databases, if all the following conditions have been fulfilled:
    1. The Organization has adopted implementing rules (in conformity with Article 23 (c,6) below) governing such operations and specifying the conditions and procedures for carrying them out, or in the interim, sufficient conditions have been established to ensure respect for the principles set forth in the present Rules and the spirit of those Rules;
    2. Such an operation shall be carried out in conformity with the provisions of the present Rules and the texts to which they refer, and in particular shall be relevant and of specific interest in relation to the Organization's aims and the purposes for which the information is processed, as defined by Articles 2 and 3 of the present Rules;
    3. The proposed processing is not subject to any restrictions, as provided for in Article 5.4 above.
    4. The authorized international entities have expressly undertaken to:
        i. observe and enforce the rules on use of the police information system and the processing of information referred to in the present Rules and the texts to which they refer,
        ii. allow only expressly authorized persons to benefit from the possibilities of direct access, downloading and interconnection,
        iii. modify, block or delete an item of information if the Organization so requests, on the basis of the provisions of the present Rules.
    5. Subject to the provisions of Article 20.2 below, relating to, downloading and interconnection
2. The General Secretariat shall keep a log of consultations of direct access databases, of downloading operations and interconnections, management of which shall be defined in the implementing rules in conformity with Article 23 below.

20.2 Provisions relating to direct access

Direct access to the police information system by an intergovernmental organization which has concluded a co-operation agreement with the Organization shall be the subject of an agreement or of special provisions, in conformity with the Rules governing access by an intergovernmental organization to the INTERPOL telecommunications network and databases.

* * *

Article 22: Requesting and Providing Information in Urgent Situations

1. An urgent situation, as defined in Article 17.1 (c,2), shall be deemed to exist when the Secretary General considers there to be a real, imminent threat to the Organization

or to its staff, to a member country, or its citizens or residents, and when that threat is likely to endanger the physical safety of the persons concerned.

2. When an urgent situation exists, the General Secretariat shall be empowered to communicate any item of information relating to a threat to any National Central Bureau, after having notified the source of the information and unless express opposition to that communication has been received from the source of the information within the time limit stipulated by the General Secretariat in the light of the said threat.
3. Furthermore, the General Secretariat shall inform the Executive Committee and the Commission for the Control of Interpol's Files as soon as possible that it has applied the urgency procedure.
4. The procedure for applying the urgency procedure may be described in implementing rules.

* * *

Article 24: Settlement of Disputes

Disputes that arise between National Central Bureaus, authorized national institutions, authorized international entities, or between one of these entities and the General Secretariat in connection with the application of the present Rules and the implementing rules to which they refer, should be solved by concerted consultation. If this fails, the matter may be submitted to the Executive Committee and, if necessary, to the General Assembly in conformity with the procedure to be established.

Article 25: Monitoring the Processing of Information in INTERPOL's Files and Access to Such Information

The procedure for verifying conformity with the present Rules on the processing of information by the Organization, and access by persons and legal entities to the Organization's files, shall be laid down in a set of rules relating to the Control of Information and Access to Interpol's Files.

Article 26: Entry into Force of the Present Rules

The present Rules shall enter into force on 1 January 2006.

Notes and Questions:

1. A key concept underlying the operation of police cooperation under INTERPOL is the important role of the National Central Bureau of ICPO-INTERPOL. What exactly is a National Central Bureau? The NCB is the body in each country that has been appointed to be its representative for international police cooperation within the framework of the ICPO-INTERPOL. The INTERPOL NCB is at the national level the correspondent, the representative, and the competent responsible authority of INTERPOL.

2. Why should there be an NCB? Would it not be more efficient to just provide that the Commissioner of Police or the equivalent be the competent authority with which to deal with Interpol? Several reasons militate in favor of establishing the NCB as the competent authority.

The structures of police forces and especially law enforcement agencies vary greatly among countries. For instance, the United States has no national police force. Instead, it has various law enforcement agencies. In fact, the United States traditionally has rotated the agencies that serve as the head of its NCB. The multiplicity of police forces in a particular country raises problems of competence that an outside party cannot resolve.

Maintaining international relations between police internationally requires language skills and assembling in a central office the necessary language and other specialists. Cooperation with foreign authorities requires coordination and cohesion among police and law enforcement agencies that are achieved more easily by a department at the national level. The rules, traditions, ways, and means of police cooperation require a precise discipline that is best fulfilled and implemented by specialists. The proper and precise transmission both of incoming and outgoing communications on crime requires centralization by a competent authority. Because police cooperation within the framework of the ICPO-INTERPOL requires varied forms of action by the police services of a country, the NCB must draw on and facilitate cooperation from diverse agencies.

3. How should a government proceed to establish its NCB? The answer will depend on the organization of the police force within each country. In a country where the police have no central authority, the country will set up an entirely new department with the sole function of international police cooperation. For instance, the NCBs of Belgium, the Netherlands, the United States, and several other countries were established in this way. In a country where the police force is wholly or partially centralized, a controlling body will exist.

In most such countries the national police department is appointed as the NCB. Usually, a particularly well-placed department within the national police force is chosen to handle cooperation within the framework of the ICPO-INTERPOL. The choice of department should be made according to the following general principles:

a. A "department" and not a "person" must be appointed because of the official, permanent, and impersonal character of international cooperation.
b. A department with broad powers and considerable moral authority should be selected. The head of this department should be in a position to give orders, to have them respected, or at least to make suggestions that carry weight.
c. Preferably, a police department should be appointed as the NCB and should be especially well situated to start immediate police action in a criminal investigation at any time. Because the main goal of ICPO-INTERPOL is the fight against international crime, departments working within the framework of the NCB should be able to order police action.

In practice, high-level departments in the police force have been appointed as NCBs. The heads of these departments, who automatically become the heads of the NCBs, have positions enabling them to assume significant responsibilities. However, these department heads are not always physically able to take on the actual daily work themselves. Therefore, they must surround themselves with a team of colleagues who discharge these concrete, specific duties under their responsibility and supervision. Typically, under the orders of these heads, this team is known as the "group handling cases" involving international police cooperation. Some NCBs may show variants because of how their countries' police agencies are structured, but this organizational pattern is a basic one.[2]

4. What are the legal and practical implications of the manner in which an NCB is appointed? Does it matter whether the U.S. Congress enacted a law to provide for U.S. membership and participation in ICPO-INTERPOL? Compare the procedure and legislative framework of Germany (Law of 8.41957, art. 7), Argentina (Decree no. 684, art. 2 of January 22, 1962), Belgium (Decree of the Minister of Justice of September 14, 1925), Brazil (Decree no. 1380 of September 11, 1962), France (Ministerial order of Dec. 18, 1928), and Lebanon (Presidential decree no. 3844 of March 11, 1960).

5. What are the legal aspects, if any, of the designation of INTERPOL as an organization that is eligible for the International Organizations Immunities Act? What would happen if INTERPOL mistakenly transmits information that causes harm to the person whose identify is confused?

6. What are the goals and jurisdiction of the NCB and the means to implement the goals?

Article 32 of the Constitution of the Organization explains the liaison goals of an NCB.

> The fundamental aim of the NCBs is to contribute to the fight against domestic law crimes on an international level; exchange of information, the opening of international investigations, the transmission of requests, identifications, and the start of police cooperation (e.g., arrests).
>
> Over the years, as the ICPO-INTERPOL has expanded the scope of its activities, the NCBs have participated in various technical and theoretical studies, activities that are expected to continue expanding. The NCB should implement or cause the implementation of the decisions made by the Organization. It should ensure the active participation of the country in international cooperation. The NCB has the responsibility of informing and educating police and other law enforcement officials in its country of the possibilities and requirements of international police cooperation so that the police and law enforcement agencies outside the NCB may be aware of its operations and the potential for solving crimes. The NCB will normally represent its country at the General Assemblies of the Organization. It is advisable for the NCB to be associated with other important police agencies concerned with combating and preventing crime in the country.

7. What are the main components of an NCB's work? As set forth in Article 32 of the INTERPOL constitution, the NCB should work with the different departments in its own country, with NCBs in other countries, and with the General Secretariat of INTERPOL.

Its responsibility to work with "different departments" covers not only departments under the authority of the same administrative service but also all other departments in the country liable to be involved in international police cooperation: local police branches in decentralized areas (states, provinces, towns, Customs and Immigration offices, the Department of Treasury, and so forth). Various law enforcement authorities, and not just police, may be involved. A major function of the NCBs is communication and relations with other NCBs. These relations should be fast and efficient, but also courteous.

[2] For additional background on the operation of NCBs, *see* Michael Fooner, INTERPOL: ISSUES IN WORLD CRIME AND INTERNATIONAL CRIMINAL JUSTICE 209–16 (1989).

The General Secretariat can only carry out its constitutional role if it receives full cooperation from the NCBs. Cooperation between the NCBs and the General Secretariat is vital to the success of police cooperation and should be complete, precise, and rapid.[3]

8. What working methods are used by NCBs in implementing the purposes of INTERPOL work? Should the NCB constitute merely a liaison service or should it be an agency for police operations? In other words, should the NCB undertake, for the purposes of international cooperation, police action such as arrests, seizures, and investigations? Although everything depends on the internal organization of the national police, a line of action can be selected more easily by referring to the distinction between the body appointed as the NCB and the group handling the routine work of cooperation. Some argue that the body appointed as the NCB should be authorized to order or at least to start important police operations. Success depends on the NCB's ability to take real action. Others maintain that, in normal circumstances, all branches of a country's police and law enforcement should contribute their support to international police action, working with the NCB either because they are ordered to do so by superiors or because they are motivated to do so in the spirit of cooperation.

In the majority of countries and cases, the NCB only needs to set the apparatus in motion. The group handling INTERPOL cases must undertake urgent operations but have a minimum amount of scope in this area for purposes of cooperation. If the INTERPOL group limits "direct" action to these cases and if the group turns the case over to the service that could normally handle it, practically no risk of rivalry or conflict will exist. If the police branches normally concerned are notoriously inadequate and fail to provide an NCB with constant, diligent cooperation, it is conceivable that the group in charge of INTERPOL cases may exercise "operational" powers of a more extensive nature than those foreseen in the preceding paragraph. In such cases, the definition and allocation of roles are left to the country in question.

The INTERPOL NCB must be able to supervise to some extent the handling of cases involving international cooperation through other police branches. It is essentially a liaison service. However, a difference exists between working as a liaison service and operating as a mere letter-box. The official with the responsibility for outside cooperation should also be able to supervise the handling of cases that originate with other branches of the force.

Article 33 of the INTERPOL constitution provides that where it is impossible or impractical to appoint a single NCB in a specific country, several "INTERPOL centers" may be designated, by virtue of their geographical position or their special facilities. For example, the United Kingdom appointed the Hong Kong police force, an annex of the British NCB, as responsible for that territory. In addition, in Mexico and in Guatemala, alongside the NCB there exists a permanent correspondent that handles only counterfeiting cases.[4]

9. How does INTERPOL disseminate information to facilitate cooperation? INTERPOL prepares several forms of information: individual notices, stolen property notices, *modus operandi* sheets, circular letters, summary reports, and technical brochures. The General Secretariat has sole authority over their distribution, with the individual notices regarded as the most important. These notices are single sheets summarizing

[3] Fooner, *id.* at 212–14.

[4] Fooner, *id.* at 214–17.

the biography and identity of international fugitives and suspects and are color coded in five ways. Except for the "green" warning, individual notices are issued on the request of a member country.

A Red Notice is given to request either detention, arrest, or extradition. The General Secretariat will issue it only if an NCB member makes a specific request and only if certain criteria are fulfilled. The offender must be described by sufficient means to allow positive identification, with such information as name, aliases, place and date of birth, physical description, fingerprints, and a photograph. The authorities of the requesting country must issue a judicially issued warrant for the offender's arrest, with the reasons for it, a statement on the crime, or the investigation relating it to the warrant. A commitment must be made that, as soon as the wanted individual is detained, the requesting country will take legal action for extradition. A statement must specify who in the requesting country has responsibility for acting in the matter.

The Secretariat must ascertain that all the criteria are fulfilled, including conformity to the rule that only common crimes are considered and those with political, military, religious, or racial involvement are excluded. If a disagreement occurs on this point, the Secretary-General must take steps to resolve the problem. Ultimately, member countries are not obligated to detain, arrest, or extradite anyone unless they want to. Taking action on a wanted notice is totally within the discretion of each member country. However, reciprocity does provide an incentive to respect each other's request.

The Blue Notice circulates a description to obtain additional police information about a person, such as to check his identity, obtain a more complete list of his convictions, or to discover his recent location or destination. The General Secretariat issues these inquiries without seeking arrest or any other action.

INTERPOL circulates Green Notices – descriptions of recidivists who may be on the move and may be dangerous or who may be part of an organized criminal activity that is mobile. Police agencies receiving such notices may be prepared to prevent the suspects from committing offenses or may be alerted so as to arrest them promptly.

The Black Notice is published and disseminated concerning corpses that are discovered without any indication of identity or with a false identity. Descriptions, fingerprints if possible, and the circumstances of the discovery are reported to help in solving both criminal and noncriminal cases.

Yellow Notices are circulated containing descriptions of persons who are missing or who are amnesia victims when circumstances provide reasons for taking action on such persons.

INTERPOL members and their NCBs can also distribute information about international suspects or fugitives or request cooperation of various types by issuing their own information sheets. These notices can be distributed to as many countries as the issuing country wishes, and the criteria of the General Secretariat need not be fulfilled. A member NCB may issue such a notice as an interim step to expeditiously distribute information while the General Secretariat follows its more deliberate procedure, completing all the necessary steps. The NCB may also issue such a notice if it cannot compile all the information that is officially required.

10. Does public international law properly regulate police cooperation? Stéphane Doumbé-Billé, director of the International Law Center at the University of Lyon, spoke at a colloquium on January 31 and February 1, 2008, sponsored by the ICPO-INTERPOL General Secretariat, on international police cooperation in the context of public international law. Notes 10 through 14 are based on presentations at this

colloquium.[5] Although it is not common to combine international police cooperation with public international law (PIL), international police cooperation is thought of as being on the margin of public international law. PIL has not been able to give enough of a context to international criminal law. Another issue is whether PIL properly regulates police cooperation. International law does not deal perfectly with police cooperation.

10. Increasingly international law is interacting with international police cooperation. Dr. Rutsel Silvestre Martha, LL.M., the then general counsel of INTERPOL, discussed the *Savarkar* case in his presentation, "International Law and the Specificity of International Police Cooperation." The case of the arrest and repatriation of Sarvakar between France and Great Britain, decided by the Permanent Court of International Arbitration on February 24, 1911,[6] is probably the only one in which a tribunal established under international law settled a dispute over police cooperation. Martha said that the award in the *Savarkar* case, the arguments made by the parties, and the commentators' comments and interpretation of the meaning of the ruling reveal the uncertainties on how to appreciate police cooperation from the perspective of international law. These uncertainties include (1) the legal qualification and imputability of the state of arrangements for enforcement cooperation established by the police with their foreign colleagues; (2) the permissibility of police enforcement cooperation without the formalities of extradition or any other existing formal arrangements for mutual assistance having been complied with; (3) the admissibility in the court of information obtained by police through the international police cooperation network; and (4) the need for the police to assure international mutual assistance at a pace and with a reach that cannot be provided by the established treaty network for mutual assistance in criminal matters.

The following principles apply to these uncertainties: (1) the police enforcement jurisdiction is inherently territorial, which makes international police enforcement cooperation a logical and practical necessity; (2) due to the presumptive freedom of action of states, subject to customary international law rules, conventional undertakings, and general principles of law, countries are free to determine whether, how, and with whom they cooperate in police enforcement matters; (3) the presumptive freedom of action of states also bears with it an indifference to international law with regard to its forms and formalities, which provides the legal backdrop for the informal and operationally oriented forms of extrajudicial international police enforcement cooperation; (4) no evidence exists that, in matters of international mutual assistance in criminal matters, general international law has abandoned the doctrine of *electa una via*, which implies a presumption against the exclusivity of mutual assistance arrangements; (5) a general duty to seek and provide each other the widest possible mutual assistance in criminal matters has evolved, arising from the principle of due diligence on the one hand and the various multilateral conventions on international and transnational crimes on the other; and (6) the permissibility of police cooperation without the formalities of extradition or mutual assistance treaties – including the establishment of international police enforcement organizations, the extrajudicial surrender of suspects and fugitives and the extrajudicial gathering of evidence abroad – is qualified by the requirement to balance enforcement needs and the fundamental rights of natural persons recognized by international law.

[5] *See* Bruce Zagaris, *Interpol Holds Meeting on International Police Cooperation in the Context of Public International Law*, 21 Int'l Enforcement L. Rep. 169 (May 2008).

[6] *Arrest and Repatriation of Savarkar*, award of 25 October 1925, 11 NRIAA, p. 243; also at http://www.pac-cpa.org/upload/files/Savakar%20Award%20PCA.pdf.

The inherently territorial nature of police enforcement jurisdiction under international law and the need to manage the transnational elements of crime that the police confront almost daily give rise to various options for the police, ranging from unilateral actions in foreign territory, arranging "informal" consensual operations with the local police authorities, and using the so-called formal channels for mutual assistance in criminal matters. Police are aware that because finally their work must be presented to a competent court, the question of whether the extraterritorial operation will stand up in court is of great importance in the decision-making process. Hence, the legal and the simultaneously very practical questions police must answer when considering extraterritorial enforcement operations concern what would be the consequences of an international wrong in the court that would deal with the criminal case. The answer differs in each country, depending on how domestic courts are authorized to treat international law in their proceedings.

11. What happens when an NCB member, such as a large country, does not implement the requirements of a Red Notice? According to Dr. Martha in one case INTERPOL received a Red Notice involving a North African country's request for arrest of a person from a Northern European country concerning a theft charge. The North African country did not receive action on its request. As a result, INTERPOL pressed the Northern European country for an answer. The two governments engaged in consultation and eventually entered into a special extradition arrangement whereby the person was extradited, prosecuted, and incarcerated.

12. How are the powers of international organizations involved in police cooperation exercised? Mr. Olivier Fourès, a staff member of the Legal Department of ICPO-INTERPOL, said that initially police cooperation and the international responsibility of international organizations may not seem to have much in common. However, in view of the increasing need for cooperation at the international level, the institutional model and the legal framework of international organizations may appear to be an appropriate way to structure the exercise of certain functions linked to police cooperation, even if exercise of police powers fundamentally remains the exclusive prerogative of states, which alone enjoy the right to exercise sovereignty on their own territories.

As the role of international organizations in police cooperation continues to expand, the number of internationally illicit acts that could be committed by these organizations also increases: an increase in obligations at the international level is synonymous with an increase in the potential for an organization to be held responsible for its acts. Initially, the goal is to highlight the greater role that the law of responsibility must play in the context of police cooperation because of the growing number of international organizations involved in this area, their functions, and those subjects who may become "creditors" of such responsibility. The second stage will involve linking the realities of police cooperation with the theory of responsibility of international organizations, especially in the light of the remarks made by INTERPOL to the international law commission on this subject.

13. How does international police cooperation interact with the responsibility of international organizations? Ms. Frédérique Lozanorios, who in 2008 was reading for a doctorate at the University of Lyon, discussed that INTERPOL must oversee and cooperate with an increasing number of organizations. For instance, the General Secretariat of INTERPOL must process information in conformity with its constitution and with international law. In the *Yerodia* case, INTERPOL issued a notice that it should not have issued: it

relayed an international arrest warrant request by Belgium for which the defendant had immunity.[7] We must think of to whom international organizations owe responsibility and may be liable. International organizations enter into agreements not only with INTERPOL but with other international organizations and governments.

A question arises regarding private individuals and the potential for their suffering prejudice due to police cooperation. INTERPOL processes information that has an influence on the rights of individuals, and it allows officials to have access to that information. The control over INTERPOL files has been criticized due to the lack of remedies both within INTERPOL and within national countries. Currently, INTERPOL rules allow persons suffering prejudice to obtain redress from the INTERPOL member country. The question is how will new and increased cooperation enable INTERPOL to meet these new responsibilities of redressing injuries suffered by persons from INTERPOL's implementations of erroneous Red Notice and other law enforcement initiative of INTERPOL members. Another issue concerns persons seconded to work for INTERPOL and international organizations. Of the 542 persons employed at the INTERPOL General Secretariat and its regional organizations, one-third are seconded by governments.

Lozanorios explained that INTERPOL's constitution has been criticized for the way in which international law relates to it. There are also issues about how the National Central Bureaus (NCBs) and INTERPOL relate to each other. For instance, the *Steinberg*, *Church of Scientology*,[8] and other cases held that NCBs are neither agents nor subsidiaries and their acts are not attributable to the organization.

14. How can practice comply with the theory of responsibilities of international organizations (IOs)? According to Lozanorios, NCB actions are limited by national legislation; if an IO only acts through national legislation, it is not independent. INTERPOL has submitted some of these problems and questions to the International Law Commission. Although sovereignty is an issue with respect to IOs and INTERPOL, responsibility must give rise to some liability.

V. Substantive White Collar Crime Areas

A. *Theft of Stolen Cultural Property*

4th Meeting of the INTERPOL Expert Group (IEG) on Stolen Cultural Property

LYON, 14 FEBRUARY 2007

Recommendations

The participants at the 4th Meeting of the INTERPOL Expert Group (IEG) on Stolen Cultural Property, held in Lyon on 14 February 2007:

[7] *Case Concerning the Arrest Warrant of 11 April 2000 (Democratic Republic of the Congo v. Belgium)*, International Court of Justice, General List, No. 121, Feb. 14, 2002.

[8] *Church of Scientology in the Netherlands Foundation et al. v. Herold (1) AND (2) Heinrich Bauer Verlag*, Judgement of 4 June 1980, NJ (1981) No. 501, 65 International Law Reports (the Chief of the German Federal Office of Criminal Investigation cannot be held personally responsible in the Netherlands for acts of international police cooperation he authorized in Germany because those acts are essentially the performance of state functions and hence those acts can only be regarded as acts performed by him in his official capacity and not as a private person. Hence, the state is responsible for acts of the state).

ACKNOWLEDGING the on-going disastrous looting of world archaeological sites,

AWARE of the lack of precise information on the pillaging and subsequent trafficking of Afghan cultural property,

CONSIDERING the lack of public awareness of the need for the protection of cultural heritage,

NOTING the need of national law enforcement agencies for acknowledged experts stating the origin and the authenticity of suspicious cultural property thought to come from Iraq,

RECALLING the recommendation adopted at the first meeting of the INTERPOL Expert Group held at the General Secretariat on 17 February 2004 that UNESCO, with the assistance of staff from Iraqi museums and other scientific institutions concerned, draw up a list of experts and organizations which may be consulted, via the INTERPOL National Central Bureaus, about the origins of archaeological objects seized by law-enforcement services,

RECOGNIZING that the internet is being increasingly used to sell cultural property,

Recommend:

- Interpol member countries:
  - to raise public awareness of the need for the protection of cultural property and use the media to disseminate appropriate preventive measures;
- The INTERPOL General Secretariat:
  - to publish as soon as possible on its secure web site the list of experts for Iraqi cultural property established by UNESCO in order to make this tool available without further delay and to inform its member countries;
  - to include the list of experts in its future Global INTERPOL Experts Database;
  - to sensitize INTERPOL member countries to decentralize access to this database through the I-24/7 to enable law enforcement officers to use this list of experts;
- UNESCO:
  - to continue to collect and make rapidly available information on the actual situation of pillaging and trafficking of Afghan cultural property as a basis for targeted countermeasures;
  - The INTERPOL General Secretariat, UNESCO and ICOM:
  - to publish simultaneously a press release following the dispatch of the joint letter concerning the sale of cultural property using the Internet;
  - to continue to support training initiatives in the fight against the illicit traffic in cultural property.

B. *Corruption*

INTERPOL first became actively involved in initiatives to curb corruption in April 1998, when its General Secretariat hosted the First International Conference on Corruption-Related Crimes in Lyon, France.

During this conference it was recommended that the INTERPOL Group of Experts on Corruption (IGEC), be established and mandated to develop and implement an anticorruption strategy. This strategy's objective was not only to raise awareness of the major issues but also to improve law enforcement's ability and effectiveness in the fight against corruption. This proposal was unanimously endorsed and adopted by the participants of this conference.

1. Structure of the IGEC

The IGEC is made up in equal numbers of law enforcement representatives from the INTERPOL regions: Africa, the Americas, Asia, the Middle East, and Europe. This structure facilitates coordination and harmonization of the different national and regional approaches to combating corruption. In addition, the work of the IGEC is complemented by a variety of other international players in the anticorruption campaign because of the general belief that law enforcement should combat corruption (as a phenomenon) holistically, in cooperation with all the major players and the community at large. The "The Terms of Reference" for IGEC were endorsed in January 2003 in Hong Kong.

2. IGEC's Current Membership

Currently, IGEC is comprised of experts representing Austria, Australia, Canada, Egypt, Hong Kong (China), Malaysia, Mexico, Thailand, the United Kingdom, and the United States, plus the European Commission, the Inter-American Development Bank, Transparency International, University of Ottawa, and the INTERPOL General Secretariat.

3. IGEC's Activities

As of this writing, the IGEC had met 24 times and has completed the following projects:

- It has drafted a mission statement, as well as a "working" definition of corruption.
- It drafted a Declaration of Intent for law enforcement, encompassing a Code of Ethics, and a Code of Conduct, which was subsequently adopted by the INTERPOL General Assembly in Seoul 1999.
- It conducted a two "Police Integrity Survey" of its 187 member countries; the objective of which was to benchmark members' current ability to effectively combat corruption.
- It formulated a draft set of "Global Standards to Combat Corruption in Police Forces/Services," which were institutionalized by the INTERPOL General Assembly held in Cameroon in October 2002. They are currently available in five languages.
- It published in 2003 a "Library of Best Practice" designed to aid investigators of corruption cases (see the later description).

IGEC is now focusing its efforts on the following:

- Refining and implementing an international network of "national contact points," to serve as a point of first contact for operational cooperation;
- Revising and updating the Library of Best Practice;
- Developing a model for ethics-based training;
- Developing a model to monitor within member countries the implementation and the efficacy of the Global Standards.

The Library of Best Practices

The Library is available on a CD-ROM, as well as on the restricted access part of Interpol's Web site.

It should serve first and foremost as a reference or pointer system to those organizations that actively lead the fight against corruption. For this reason, each contribution clearly states the source of the article. The reader will also find (attached as an appendix) a comprehensive list of agencies with an anticorruption mandate, including contact particulars for each of those agencies.

The library also serves to provide law enforcement officers with sufficient information on an array of important topics, which should improve their ability and effectiveness in combating corruption. The objective of this tool is to facilitate the implementation and realization of the "Global Standards to Combat Corruption in Police Forces/Services" (www.interpol.int).

4. INTERPOL Global Standards to Combat Corruption in Police Forces/Services

These "Global Standards" have been prepared by the INTERPOL Group of Experts on Corruption (IGEC), convened by INTERPOL as one of its initiatives to implement the General Assembly's Declaration to Combat Corruption, taken in Seoul, Korea in 1999, and mandated at the 69th Meeting of the General Assembly (Rhodes, 2000).

These Global Standards were presented to the 70th General Assembly (Budapest, 2001) which, in resolution AG-2001-RES-04 (adopted by 108 votes for, 1 against, 5 abstentions), commended the work of the IGEC, requested comments from the members by 30 June 2002, and directed the General Secretariat to make a final report to the 71st General Assembly to be held in Yaounde, Cameroon. During the General Assembly in Yaounde, the INTERPOL membership voted overwhelmingly in favor of adopting the Global Standards, and tasked the IGEC with facilitating the implementation of these Standards.

These Standards consist of several principles and numerous measures designed to improve the resistance to succumbing to corruption, as well as the efficacy in combating it, and to represent an ideal to which we are confident that our member countries will strive towards. These Standards have been well received by the international law enforcement community and mark the beginning of a pro-active approach for law enforcement to combating Corruption.

C. *Recovery and Return of Stolen Vehicles*

1. Overview of the Problem

Illicit trafficking of vehicles is a form of organized crime that generates both large profits for the perpetrators (estimated at USD 19 billion, which disappears into a parallel economy) and a feeling of insecurity that affects the general public, particularly because of the increased use of violence to steal the vehicles. A key aspect of this crime is the need to legalize the stolen vehicles for the criminals to achieve a monetary gain.

Vehicle crime is a highly organized criminal activity and affects all parts of the globe. It is often linked to organized crime and terrorism. The vehicles are not only stolen for the cars themselves; sometimes, their trafficking finances other crimes. They can also be used as bomb carriers or in the perpetration of other crimes.

The INTERPOL General Secretariat developed the Automated Search Facility-Stolen Motor Vehicle (ASF-SMV) database to support police in member countries in the fight against international vehicle theft and trafficking.

As of December 2008, the database held more than 4.6 million records of reported stolen motor vehicles. Close to 151 countries use the database regularly. Of these, more than 122 countries have shared their national stolen vehicle database records with INTERPOL. More than 31,000 motor vehicles were discovered worldwide in 2008 through the ASF-SMV database.

2. Working Groups within INTERPOL

At the international level, several working groups organized and chaired by the General Secretariat meet on a regular basis and have developed several projects to address the issue, including Project FORMATRAIN and Project Mar Adriatico.

Project FORMATRAIN

Project FORMATRAIN – an acronym from FORMAtion and TRAINing – assists investigators with information on vehicle and document identification, investigative strategies, techniques and tools, databases, legal preconditions, etc. The aim of the project is to create a standardized training program to facilitate investigations of international vehicle crime with basic, intermediate and advanced courses; teach trainers; and take advantage of the worldwide INTERPOL network for the sharing of expertise. Representatives from Australia, Belgium, Finland, Japan, Germany, the United Kingdom, the United States, and Zimbabwe have attended working group meetings (www.interpol.int).

The first training, hosted by the Finnish National Police School, took place in 2003. Participants of the working group come from the National Bureau of Investigation of Finland (NCB Helsinki), SOCA London (UFD Organized Vehicle Crime) and the INTERPOL General Secretariat. The most recent working group meeting was held in Vienna in June 2009.

Project Mar Adriatico

Project Mar Adriatico – was initiated by the Italian NCB. The General Secretariat has assumed the international coordination of this operation. Vehicle crime experts from Portugal, Greece, and Turkey joined the Working Group at its last meeting and took part in discussions along experts from Spain, Italy, Germany, and Bulgaria.

Furthermore, INTERPOL vehicle crime representatives regularly attend meetings of the Baltic Sea Task Force Expert Group, which focuses on co-operation and common operations in the region (www.interpol.int).

D. *Financial and High-Tech Crimes*

Financial and high-tech crimes – currency counterfeiting, money laundering, intellectual property crime, payment card fraud, computer virus attacks, and cyberterrorism, for example – can affect all levels of society.

Currency counterfeiting and money laundering have the potential to destabilize national economies and threaten global security, as these activities are sometimes used by terrorists and other dangerous criminals to finance their activities or conceal their profits.

Intellectual property crime is a serious financial concern for car manufacturers, luxury goods makers, media firms, and drug companies. Most alarmingly, counterfeiting endangers public health, especially in developing countries, where the World Health Organization estimates that more than 60 percent of pharmaceuticals are fake.

"Spam" is becoming more than just a nuisance for Internet users, as criminals are using it in increasingly sophisticated ways to defraud consumers, cripple computer systems, and release viruses. In 2000, the so-called Love Bug virus, which affected millions of computers around the world within hours, exposed the vulnerability of corporate and government networks to such attacks.

New technologies open up many possibilities for criminals to carry out traditional financial crimes in new ways. One notable example is "phishing," whereby a criminal attempts to acquire through email or instant messaging sensitive information such as passwords or credit card details by pretending to be a legitimate business representative. With this information, the criminal can commit fraud and even money laundering.

INTERPOL has stepped up its efforts in this area, working with stakeholders such as pharmaceutical makers, Internet service providers, software companies, central banks, and other relevant bodies to devise solutions to thwart criminals and protect consumers.

INTERPOL's chief initiatives in the area of financial and high-tech crime focus on:

- Payment cards
- Money laundering
- Intellectual property crime
- Currency counterfeiting
- New technologies

1. Currency Counterfeiting

Globalization has made possible myriad transnational criminal schemes designed to exploit financial payment systems. Fraud schemes involving credit cards, identity theft, bank fraud, or the most fundamental financial crime – the production of counterfeit currency – prosper across national boundaries.

Although counterfeiting has diminished substantially since the establishment of special law enforcement units assigned to fight it, it remains a danger to national economies and to consumers. Recent developments in photographic and computer technology, as well as printing devices, have made the production of counterfeit money relatively easy, thereby increasing the threat.

The effective protection of currencies from counterfeiters increasingly depends on partnerships among law enforcement agencies, financial institutions, and other expert organizations. These partnerships bridge geographic, jurisdictional, cultural, and organizational divisions, which were once impediments toward providing comprehensive and coordinated solutions for combating modern financial crimes.

Communication through INTERPOL's I-24/7 global police communications system and the efforts of its Counterfeit and Security Documents Branch (CSDB) are geared to assist in strengthening these partnerships.

The General Secretariat has brought together members of the law enforcement community, paper manufacturing industry, and printing community by organizing and hosting international counterfeiting conferences throughout the world to specifically address counterfeiting concerns. Ten such conferences have been held since 1929.

The INTERPOL Web site lists the currencies of all 187 INTERPOL member countries and provides links to individual central banks' Web sites.

2. Intellectual Property Crime

Intellectual property (IP) crime includes a wide range of counterfeiting and piracy offenses including trademark, patent, and copyright infringement. The last decade has seen a steady global increase in these types of criminal offenses because of the ready availability of modern technology to counterfeiters, who systematically use it to facilitate IP crime. Counterfeiting is so widespread that few legitimately manufactured goods are not copied in one form or another and the rights of their owners infringed.

In 2008, the Organization for Economic Cooperation and Development (OECD) published a report entitled "The Economic Impact of Counterfeiting." It estimated that the global trade in counterfeit goods was U.S.$200 billion, not including domestically produced and consumed counterfeit/pirated goods, and pirated digital products distributed via the Internet, representing between 5 to 7 percent of the value of global trade. In addition to hurting legitimate businesses and trade, counterfeiting leads to the loss of government tax revenue. More worryingly, as in the case with counterfeit medicines, it threatens public safety and health. More recent surveys indicate that the volume of counterfeiting and piracy activities has increased significantly since the publication of the OECD report.

The industrialized scale of counterfeiting is itself an indicator of the involvement of organized crime. Moving the large amount of counterfeit goods in the global marketplace requires an efficient and effective distribution network, and this provides opportunities for organized criminals to manipulate counterfeit products to generate significant profits.

INTERPOL offers national police forces in member countries and industries affected by counterfeiting a central point of reference on IP crime. It also facilitates and coordinates international enforcement action against transnational and organized criminals involved in IP crime.

INTERPOL member countries have recognized the involvement of organized crime in IP crime. The 69th General Assembly in Rhodes, Greece, in 2000, adopted a resolution on IP crime (AGN/69/RES/6). It directed the General Secretariat to raise awareness of the problem and develop a strategic plan to combat IP crime in close cooperation with affected industries.

INTERPOL convened the first Expert Group on July 23, 2002, which adopted the name INTERPOL Intellectual Property Crime Action Group (IIPCAG). It is now an integral part of the INTERPOL IP Crime Unit and meets twice a year. Its mission is to assist the General Secretariat in providing a collective response to the threat posed by organized criminal involvement in IP crime.

Membership in the IIPCAG varies depending on the location of meetings. However, the core members are as follows:

1. International organizations: International Criminal Police Organization-INTERPOL, World Customs Organization (WCO), World Intellectual Property Organization (WIPO), and the European Commission
2. Law enforcement: An Garda Siochana, Ireland, Criminal Police Directorate, Croatia, Department of Public Security, People's Republic of China, Europol, Guardia di Finanza, Italy, Metropolitan Police, United Kingdom, National Board of Customs, Finland, Policia Federal, Brazil, Police Service of Northern Ireland, Royal Canadian Mounted Police, Canada, U.S. Federal Bureau of Investigation, U.S. Food and Drug Administration, U.S. Immigration and Customs Enforcement); and
3. Cross-industry representative bodies and private sector: Alliance against Counterfeiting (AAC), Coalition for Intellectual Property Rights (CIPR), Global Anti-Counterfeiting Network, Global Business Leaders Alliance against Counterfeiting (GBLAAC), International Anti-Counterfeiting Group (IACG), International Anti-Counterfeiting Coalition (IACC), International Federation for the Phonographic Industries (IFPI), Microsoft Corporation, Motion Picture Association (MPA), Pharmaceutical Security Institute (PSI), Procter & Gamble, REACT UK, and Union des Fabricants, France.

The General Secretariat invites other experts to participate in meetings or provide specialist support when the need arises. When an IIPCAG meeting is hosted by another country, interested parties in that country and region are invited to participate.

IIPCAG has six subcommittees that focus on developing initiatives and delivering solutions to stakeholders, member countries, and industries affected by IP crime.

a. *Public Awareness Subcommittee*

This subcommittee ensures that the law enforcement community in member countries and affected industries are aware of the services available from the INTERPOL IP Crime Unit and the IIPCAG. It also ensures that policymakers in government and law enforcement are aware of the nature of IP crime and the extent of organized criminal involvement in counterfeiting and piracy.

b. *Training and Best Practice Subcommittee*

An urgent need exists to give support and training in IP crime for national police forces in member countries. Traditionally, customs officials, by the very nature of their role, intercept counterfeit goods when they cross international borders. However, police forces have typically focused on other priorities such as burglary, homicide, robbery, and other violent crimes. This subcommittee therefore performs a useful function, complementing the work of the Public Awareness Subcommittee by designing and delivering training materials that can be used to train police in member countries.

c. *Exchange of Information/Databases Subcommittee*

The transnational nature of counterfeiting and piracy requires a coordinated response from the public authorities and industries affected by IP crime. In this connection, the IIPCAG is trying to develop mechanisms for the efficient and timely exchange of information that can be used to maximize opportunities for intervention by police and other law enforcement agencies. This is a demanding and difficult task. The subcommittee is working to identify the type of information available and how it can be stored in a way that meets the needs of all stakeholders.

d. *Resources Subcommittee*

Because neither the public nor the private sector can solve the problem of transnational counterfeiting and piracy alone, the IIPCAG is seeking a public-private partnership to focus scarce resources where they will be most effective. This subcommittee examines resource availability and seeks to encourage other stakeholders to invest in collective efforts to reduce the impact of counterfeiting and piracy.

e. *Operations Subcommittee*

The Operations Subcommittee helps the INTERPOL IP Crime Unit identify opportunities for deploying Operation Jupiter where it will be most effective. The purpose of Operation Jupiter is to facilitate and coordinate enforcement action against transnational IP crime. Cross-industry representative bodies and other stakeholders know the nature and extent of the losses caused by counterfeiting and piracy. They can also identify counterfeiting "hotspots" where intervention by national police forces and other law enforcement agencies has the best chance of success. This subcommittee considers all available sources of information, and this evaluation is part of the ongoing selection process used by the INTERPOL IP Crime Unit to prioritize Operation Jupiter deployments.

3. Links between IP Crime and the Financing of Terrorist Activities

Many terrorist groups participate in a variety of organized crimes to fund their activities. As terrorist groups tend to act in similar ways to transnational organized crime groups, law enforcement must carefully monitor how their activities evolve. IP crime is a high-profit, low-risk crime, which inevitably motivates criminals to engage in it. As a result, INTERPOL remains concerned about the possibility that some terrorist groups will seize the opportunity to finance their activities through IP crime. It is therefore monitoring the extent to which terrorist groups actually engage in IP crime.

4. Money Laundering

In recent years, the INTERPOL General Assembly has passed several resolutions that have called on member countries to concentrate their investigative resources in identifying, tracing, and seizing the assets of criminal enterprises. These resolutions have also called on member countries to increase the exchange of information in this field and encourage governments to adopt laws and regulations that would allow access, by police, to the financial records of criminal organizations and to enable the confiscation of proceeds gained by criminal activity (Resolutions AGN/55/RES/18, 1986; AGN/56/RES/11, 1987; AGN/60/RES/4, 1991; AGN/66/RES/15, 17, and 18, 1997). The INTERPOL General Assembly meeting in New Delhi in 1997 called on member countries that had not yet done so to ratify the 1988 United Nations Convention against Illicit Traffic in Narcotic Drugs and Psychotropic Substances and to urge their governments to implement the convention and the powers it gives their law enforcement institutions (Resolution AGN/66/RES/15, 1997).

The INTERPOL General Assembly in 1995 adopted this working definition of money laundering: "any act or attempted act to conceal or disguise the identity of illegally obtained proceeds so that they appear to have originated from legitimate sources."

a. *Working Group on Money Laundering and Terrorism Financing*

The fifth meeting of the INTERPOL Working Group on Money Laundering and Terrorism Financing was held at the INTERPOL General Secretariat in Lyon, France, on November 21, 2007; representatives from the United Nations Office of Drug Control, U.S. Department of Treasury, Europol, and special investigators from various countries attended.

At an earlier workshop concerning information-sharing between select NCBs and financial intelligence units (FIUs), recommendations were made to: (1) identify "demonstration cases" involving NCBs that are already receiving money laundering information from FIUs; (2) submit a resolution encouraging this type of cooperation to INTERPOL's General Assembly session in Berlin in September 2005; and (3) seek formal recognition of the FIU/NCB relationships through incorporation into the Egmont Group's "Principles of Information Exchange between Financial Intelligence Units."

At the 2005 meeting of the Working Group, participants unanimously agreed to expand the subgroup on cash couriers and alternative remittance systems, both in terms of membership and by soliciting views from other policy-setting organizations.

The United Nations Office on Drugs and Crime (UNODC), agreed to organize training courses on money laundering in cooperation with INTERPOL.

b. *IMoLIN Database*

The Internet-based information network IMoLIN serves as a clearinghouse for money laundering information for the benefit of all national and international anti-money laundering agencies. It was developed and is administered by the Global Program against Money Laundering of UNODC on behalf of the United Nations and other international organizations, including INTERPOL. There are five main features of IMoLIN, and all but one are accessible to the public:

1. AMLID (Anti Money Laundering International Database): Compendium and analysis of national anti-money laundering laws and regulations, as well as information on national contacts and authorities. The database is password-restricted.
2. Reference data: research and analysis, bibliography, conventions, legal instruments, and model laws.
3. Country page: includes full text of anti-money laundering legislation where available and links to national FIUs.
4. Calendar of events: chronological listing of training events, conferences, seminars, workshops, and other meetings in the anti-money laundering field.
5. Current events: current news of recent anti-money laundering initiatives.

c. *International Meetings and Cooperation*

The INTERPOL General Secretariat works closely with other international organizations to foster international awareness of the importance of using financial investigative techniques against organized criminal activities. Most importantly, this cooperation is aimed at supporting each international organization's efforts in these areas and avoiding duplication. The following international organizations have provided mutual cooperation and assistance in the development of international programs related to the assets of criminal organizations: Asia Pacific Group on Money Laundering (APG), Caribbean Financial Action Task Force (CFATF), Egmont Group, European Banking Federation Fraud Working Group, European Bank for Reconstruction and Development (EBRD), Financial Action Task Force (FATF), International Monetary Fund (IMF), International Organization of Securities Commissions (IOSCO), International Banking Security Association (IBSA), International Air Transport Association (IATA), Institut de Formation Interbancaire (INSIG), World Customs Organization (WCO), Inter-American Development Bank (IADB), Organization of American States/Comision Interamericana para el Control del Abuso de Drogas (OAS/CICAD), Offshore Group of Banking Supervisors (OGBS), and the Select Committee of Experts on the Evaluation of Anti-Money Laundering Measures (PC-R-EV Committee – Council of Europe).

5. Payment Cards

The General Secretariat has played an instrumental role in helping law enforcement and industry partners around the world address the growing problem of payment card fraud. As the use of payment cards continues to increase, the frequency and extent of fraud will also continue to expand. The payment card industry and law enforcement community are working to develop enhanced production and security measures to deter payment card fraud, but criminals continue to devise more sophisticated methods to override such features. As a result, the need for communication and information sharing remains very important, and this is where INTERPOL can provide valuable assistance.

In the mid-1990s, the General Secretariat brought together various experts in the field for the First International Conference on Payment Card Fraud. The Payment Card Working Group was established after the conference. Experts from the Hong Kong Police, Royal Canadian Mounted Police, U.S. Secret Service, U.K. National Criminal Intelligence Service, Netherlands National Police Agency, and the payment card industry attended the group's first meeting. The representatives shared their expertise and established a classification system for payment cards.

In 1997, in New Delhi, the 66th General Assembly approved a proposal for a central database to be housed at the General Secretariat. By 2000, the database was established at the General Secretariat; it allowed for the classification of altered or counterfeit cards submitted by certified law enforcement and industry experts through forensic analysis. The database is currently accessible to member countries and has proved to be a useful tool for the law enforcement community. INTERPOL is committed to keeping the database up to date.

6. Information Technology Crime

INTERPOL has actively engaged in combating information technology crime (ITC) by convening the following regional working parties made up of the heads or experienced members of national computer crime units: the European Working Party on Information Technology Crime, African Regional Working Party on Information Technology Crime, Asia-South Pacific Working Party on Information Technology Crime, and the Latin America Working Party on Information Technology Crime.

The Steering Committee coordinates and harmonizes the various regional working party initiatives. The chairperson, vice-chairperson, a third member from each regional working party sits on the Steering Committee, whose work is co-ordinated by the representative coordinated by the General Secretariat. Organizations outside of INTERPOL – most notably, the High Tech Crime Subgroup of the G8, the International Chamber of Commerce, the United Nations Asia Institute for the Prevention of Crime and the Treatment of Offenders, and several academic institutions – have been involved with the Steering Committee's initiatives as well.

7. Information Security and Crime Prevention

INTERPOL has initiatives that review, monitor, and update the interaction of technology, information, and crime prevention. In particular, it is active in discussing wireless technology, 3G mobile phones, multimedia messaging, and virtual money. INTERPOL provides a checklist for crime prevention on information security and new technologies. It also discusses the best means to effectively implement the provisions of the Council of Europe Convention on Cyber Crime.

VI. NCB Regional Activities

For several years regionalization has been an important element of INTERPOL's strategy to deliver focused services to its member countries. Regionalization is a dynamic process that offers new opportunities and challenges. Its central theme is the delivery of INTERPOL's key services on a regional basis, recognizing both the diversity of regional needs and today's political realities.

There are five regions of INTERPOL: Africa, Americas, Asia, Europe, and Middle East, and North Africa. Each holds a policy-level conference every other year (except Europe, which holds one every year). Delegates to INTERPOL's Executive Committee are elected from each of the regions.

Europe has its own INTERPOL secretariat and committee (European Liaison Bureau and INTERPOL European Committee). In Africa three subregions have established equivalent structures. Whereas the INTERPOL European Committee is representative of the entire region – it has eight members only – the African subregional committees have full representation by the chiefs of police of all countries in the respective subregions.

Regions are identified on a geopolitical basis, not simply on geography. Some countries do not form part of a regional group but their interests must meet, and many key services need to continue to be delivered on an international level.

Regional geopolitical groupings that have been identified include:

South America	Southern Africa	Near and Middle East	EU
Central America	East Africa	SE Asia (ASEAN)	CIS
Caribbean	Central Africa	SAARC group	Baltic Sea
North America	West Africa	Australia and South Pacific	North Africa

Interpol delivers the following services regionally:

- identify law enforcement needs (nation or group) for central coordination and tailored solutions;

- technical support through personnel working with General Secretariat oversight to a global standard;
- training and development (coordination, standard setting, and monitoring);
- facilitating access to training;
- coordination of operational activities within context of local priorities and action plans (locally controlled and owned);
- regional crime analyses and reports;
- proposal of or contributing to plans and strategies arising from regional analyses and reports;
- assist implementation of those plans and strategies;
- liaison/problem-solving/facilitating solutions (e.g., information blockages and communication difficulties);
- secretariat function (including for local/regional organization);
- identify technical needs of member countries with a view to finding solutions;
- enhancing two-way flow of information (general or for specific crime issues);
- promoting and facilitating INTERPOL solutions to identified needs;
- marketing and public relations;
- implementing and monitoring central policy on security and confidentiality;
- performance evaluation;
- identifying linked initiatives and taking steps to avoid overlap and duplication;
- positioning the organization in the regional political arena;
- meetings, conferences, and committees (run, assist, identify need for new, attend);
- supporting organizations with linked or complementary objectives;

Rules and Responsibilities for Regional Sub-Bureaus

Where they exist or may be created, the Sub-Regional Bureaus are frequently the unit through which these services will be delivered.

The overall objective of the Sub-Regional Bureaus is to support member states (especially National Central Bureaus) in both their national and international efforts to deal with crime. The Sub-Regional Bureaus form an integral part of Interpol's General Secretariat whereas National Central Bureaus are national structures that operate under the authority of national administrations.

The role of the Sub-Regional Bureau has a particular importance when it operates within a regional structure comprising a committee of chiefs of police, subcommittees (e.g., legislation, training, and operational activities) and the Sub-Regional Bureau as secretariat to that regional structure. This model has proved particularly successful in Southern Africa.

The responsibilities of the National Central Bureaus will not be diluted through regionalization but will be encouraged and assisted by the Sub-Regional Bureaus to reach the level of performance expected of them and to provide an effective service to all law enforcement partners in their respective countries. INTERPOL does not intend to mandate the creation of regional structures and so it is not inevitable that all National Central Bureaus will be members of an identified region. Equally there may be different models for Sub-Regional Bureaus according to their needs and the resources available to them.

Where there is no Sub-Regional Bureau in any given region the services listed above will nevertheless be provided by Interpol. Where other regional structures exist or are created, the potential for delivery of these INTERPOL services in partnership with those structures will always be an important consideration.

VII. Staff

Approximately 450 staff members from more than eighty countries are employed at the INTERPOL General Secretariat, regional bureaus, and the liaison office at the United Nations, working in any of the organization's four official languages: Arabic, English, French, and Spanish. A third of these employees are either seconded or detached by the national law enforcement administrations in INTERPOL's 187 member countries; the remaining are international civil servants hired under contract directly by the organization. INTERPOL accepts applications from nationals of all member countries to ensure that it remains truly representative.

VIII. International Liaison

INTERPOL seeks to forge ties with all international bodies, governmental authorities, and NGOs whose mission is to fight crime and protect the public's safety. These collaborations occur formally, through the signing of cooperation agreements and adoption of international conventions, and more informally, through INTERPOL's participation in international symposia, conferences, and working groups. The aims are to ensure that expertise and information are shared, that resources are not wasted or efforts duplicated, and that all organizations with a stake in the fight against international crime are able to exploit their comparative advantages most effectively.

A. *International Agreements and Procedure*

Interpol has signed cooperation agreements with the United Nations, including related bodies such as UNESCO; with the International Criminal Court; and with regional authorities such as the European Central Bank, Organization of African Unity, and Arab Interior Ministers' Council. It has also established strong relationships with a wide variety of international organizations and NGO, acting in different fields of interest to the organization. To provide a clear legal basis for working together, INTERPOL has concluded a number of cooperation agreements with these day-to-day partners.

In conformity with Article 41 of INTERPOL's constitution, agreements concerning relations with other international organizations may be concluded by the ICPO-INTERPOL. The General Assembly must approve such agreements. Once approved, the president of the organization (or the Secretary-General by delegation) is authorized to sign them.

However, in accordance with Article 22 of its constitution, the General Assembly at its 67th session (Cairo, 1998) and 69th session (Rhodes, 2000) delegated to the Executive Committee the power (conferred on it by Article 41 of the constitution) to approve cooperation agreements with other international organizations (AGN/67/RES/4, AGN/69/RES/8). In fact, the General Assembly simplified the procedure and accelerated the process of negotiating cooperation agreements initiated by AGN/64/RES/11.

Many draft agreements have therefore been negotiated on the basis of a model cooperation agreement (AGN/67/RAP/7, Appendix 1) and have been submitted to the Executive

Committee for approval. The INTERPOL Secretary General was authorized to sign them once approved.

Yet, some agreements do not need to be approved by the General Assembly or the Executive Committee. For instance, agreements concluded with UN subsidiary bodies are not subject to the formal procedure established by Article 41 of the Constitution.

With effect from January 3, 2001, INTERPOL is a party to the 1986 Vienna Convention on the Law of Treaties between States and International Organizations or between International Organizations (see Instrument of accession). Agreements concluded by the organization respect the essential conditions of this convention.

B. *Police Cooperation Agreements*

The development of a model police cooperation agreement is a concept that has quite naturally gained ground within INTERPOL. Indeed, it seems obvious that the organization should provide its member countries with the legal tools they need to facilitate cooperation that they initiate bilaterally. A model agreement has therefore been compiled on the basis of numerous studies, which reflects a wealth of experience in international police cooperation.

In creating this instrument, in particular for those member states that have not yet developed this form of cooperation to a large extent, INTERPOL is fulfilling its role as set out in its constitution, namely "to ensure and promote the widest possible mutual assistance between all criminal police authorities, and to establish and develop all institutions likely to contribute effectively to the prevention and suppression of ordinary law crimes."

IX. Additional Reading

A. *Books*

MALCOLM, Anderson, POLICING THE WORLD: INTERPOL AND THE POLITICS OF INTERNATIONAL POLICE COOPERATION. (Oxford University Press 1989).

FENTON S. BRESLER, INTERPOL. (Sinclair-Stevenson 1992).

MICHAEL FOONER, INTERPOL: THE INSIDE STORY OF THE INTERNATIONAL CRIME-FIGHTING ORGANIZATION. (Henry Regnery 1973).

MICHAEL FOONER, INTERPOL (Plenum Press 1983).

MICHAEL FOONER, INTERPOL: ISSUES IN WORLD CRIME AND INTERNATIONAL JUSTICE (Springer-Verlag 1989).

MICHAEL FOONER, INTERPOL, ISSUES IN WORLD CRIME AND INTERNATIONAL CRIMINAL JUSTICE (CRIMINAL JUSTICE AND PUBLIC SAFETY) (Springer 2002).

OMAR GARRISON, THE SECRET WORLD OF INTERPOL. (Ralston-Pilot 1976).

MARY Jo Grotenrat, THE INTERPOL IMBROGLIO (Authorhouse 2004).

INTERPOL, INTERPOL: 75 YEARS OF INTERNATIONAL POLICE COOPERATION (Kensington Publications 1998).

J. D. McLean, INTERNATIONAL COOPERATION IN CIVIL AND CRIMINAL MATTERS (Oxford University Press 2005).

B. *Articles*

Michael Barnett & Liv Coleman, *Delegation or Arrogation? The Sociological Significance of the Curious Case of INTERPOL*. Program on International Organizations and Change Conference, Budapest, June 26–28, 2003. http://www.internationalorganizations.org/budapest_coleman_and_barnett.pdf

Mathieu Deflem & Lindsay C. Maybin, *INTERPOL and the Policing of International Terrorism: Developments and Dynamics since September 11*, *in* TERRORISM: RESEARCH, READINGS, & REALITIES, 175–91 (Lynne L. Snowden & Brad Whitsel eds., Pearson Prentice Hall 2005).

C. *Electronic*

The INTERPOL Web site is a very fruitful source of materials on INTERPOL.

14 Economic Integration and Business Crimes

I. Introduction

Economic integration plays an important role with respect to transnational white collar crimes, although for the most part, governments concluding free trade agreements (FTAs) and economic integration agreements have seen that element as an afterthought. Persuading legislatures to overcome nationalist sentiments and limit sovereignty in order to support the negotiation and ratification of FTAs or single markets consumes significant political capital. The decision to include regulatory – let alone criminal and quasi-criminal measures – within an FTA or single market arrangement is not taken lightly.

As a result of political decisions to minimize criminal and enforcement institutions and mechanisms when sovereign states enter into an FTA, common market, or an economic integration arrangement, criminals are often quick to identify and exploit opportunities to enlarge their illicit operations. The lowered barriers allow them to conduct crime transnationally.

In some cases signatories include criminal and enforcement provisions and mechanisms relating to one or two economic sectors in FTAs and single market arrangements. For instance, as noted later, due to intense and successful lobbying by U.S. intellectual property interests, NAFTA provisions cover intellectual property and customs enforcement.

The relationship among economic integration, international criminal and enforcement cooperation, and criminal justice integration is thus ambiguous and complex. Yet, all involve state responses to increases in transnational interactions among nonstate actors and try to mitigate the tensions and frictions that hamper efficient cross-border interactions.

Successful criminal justice systems require three elements: information, evidence, and the accused or convicted person. The more dispersed these elements are and the less they exist within the physical jurisdiction of the investigating government, the greater the obstacles for law enforcement. The main barrier impeding international law enforcement efforts is the sovereignty that some countries assert, because normally a national government without the agreement of another government cannot perform criminal justice activities in the other government's territory. To do so would violate the territorial sovereignty of the other government. Additionally, sovereign states have distinctive political, social, economic, and legal systems and cultures. Criminals can and do take advantage of the distinctions that prevent effective international enforcement cooperation (e.g., requirements of dual criminality in order to extradite or provide mutual assistance in criminal matters). National and subnational law enforcement officials try to nullify the advantages criminals derive from operating across borders and reduce, circumvent, or transcend the frictions that impede international law enforcement.[1]

By reducing controls on transnational commerce through common market arrangements and FTAs, states can reduce the administrative burdens of transnational cooperation between customs and criminal justice officials. Economic integration reduces border control and expands the ability to move goods, services, capital, and people. Hence, it requires law enforcement officials to compensate for the loss of border controls and the subsequent increase in economic and other crimes.[2]

The evolutionary processes of law enforcement cooperation involve harmonization, in which three processes are implicated: regularization of relations among law enforcement officials of different states, accommodation among systems that retain their essential differences, and homogenization of systems toward a common norm.[3] The more rudimentary and asymmetrical nature of international criminal cooperation and criminal justice harmonization in the Americas contrasts sharply with the closer cooperation and criminal justice harmonization in Western Europe.[4]

II. Western Europe and Regional Integration

Western Europe is the principal laboratory for incubating new approaches to international criminal and enforcement cooperation. As early as 1958, the establishment of the

[1] Ethan Nadelmann, *Harmonization of Criminal Justice Systems*, in The Challenge of Integration: Europe and the Americas 247, 247–51 (Peter H. Smith ed., North-South Center 1993).
[2] *Id.* at 272.
[3] *Id.*, at 254–55.
[4] *Id.* at 270.

European Crime Committee provided an early platform for working on a daily basis with substantial international criminal and enforcement issues.

A. *The Council of Europe*

Established in 1949, the Council of Europe (French: Conseil de l'Europe) is the oldest international organization working toward European integration. It seeks to develop common democratic principles throughout Europe based on the European Convention on Human Rights and other sources of international law, democratic development, the rule of law, and cultural cooperation. It has forty-seven member states.

Its statutory institutions are the Committee of Ministers, comprising the foreign ministers of each member state; the Parliamentary Assembly, composed of members from the parliaments of each member state; and the Secretary General, who heads the secretariat of the Council of Europe.

The Council of Europe (CoE) has been an important source of international criminal and enforcement cooperation.

1. The European Committee on Crime Problems

The Committee of Ministers of the Council of Europe, established in 1958, entrusted the European Committee on Crime Problems (CDPC) with overseeing and coordinating the CoE's activities in the field of crime prevention and crime control. The CDPC meets at CoE headquarters in Strasbourg, France. It identifies priorities for intergovernmental legal cooperation; makes proposals to the Committee of Ministers on activities in the fields of criminal law and procedure, criminology, and penology; and implements these activities.

The CDPC holds a plenary session every year, in which the following participate: national delegations from member states; representatives of the Parliamentary Assembly and of the Congress of Local and Regional Authorities of Europe; representatives of both the European Commission and the Secretariat General of the Council of the European Union; observers from Canada, the Holy See, Japan, Mexico, and the United States; and observers from intergovernmental and nongovernmental organizations.

The CDPC elects its Bureau, composed of the chair and eight other members, as well as the members of its three advisory bodies: the Criminological Scientific Council, the Council for Penological Cooperation, and the Council for Police Matters. The Department of Crime Problems provides the Secretariat. The Bureau and three advisory bodies provide much of the CDPC's strategy and planning efforts.

The CDPC has many committees, including the following: Council for Penological Cooperation; Council for Police Matters; Committee of Experts on the Operation of European Conventions in the Penal Field; Committee of Experts on new ways of dealing with juvenile delinquency and the role of juvenile justice; Committee of Experts on the management of life-sentenced and other long-term prisoners; Committee of Experts on remand in custody and its implications of the management of penal institutions; Committee on Transnational Criminal Justice; Committee of Experts on the protection of witnesses and *pentiti* in relation to acts of terrorism; Committee of Experts on the treatment of sex offenders in penal institutions and in the community; Committee of Experts on the revision of the Convention on Laundering, Search, Seizure and Confiscation of the Proceeds from Crime; Select Committee of Experts on the Evaluation of Anti-Money-Laundering Measures (MONEYVAL); and the Group of Specialists on Criminal Law and Criminological Aspects of Organized Crime.

One of the most important contributions of the CDPC is its elaboration of a host of conventions on international criminal and enforcement cooperation. Some of them are open to nonmembers of the CDPC. They include the European Convention on the Punishment of Road Traffic Offences; European Convention on the Protection of the Archaeological Heritage; European Convention on the International Validity of Criminal Judgments; European Convention on the Transfer of Proceedings in Criminal Matters; European Convention on the Non-Applicability of Statutory Limitation to Crimes against Humanity and War Crimes; European Convention on Extradition and the Additional Protocols thereto; European Convention on the Suppression of Terrorism; European Convention on Mutual Assistance in Criminal Matters and the Additional Protocols thereto; European Convention on the Obtaining Abroad of Information and Evidence in Administrative Matters; European Convention on the Control of the Acquisition and Possession of Firearms by Individuals; Convention on the Transfer of Sentenced Persons and the Additional Protocol thereto; Protocol No. 6 to the Convention for the Protection of Human Rights and Fundamental Freedoms concerning the Abolition of the Death Penalty; European Convention on Offences relating to Cultural Property; European Convention on Spectator Violence and Misbehavior at Sports Events and in particular at Football Matches; European Convention for the Prevention of Torture and Inhuman or Degrading Treatment or Punishment and the Protocols thereto; Convention on Mutual Administrative Assistance in Tax Matters; Agreement on illicit traffic by sea, implementing Article 17 of the United Nations Convention against Illicit Traffic in Narcotic Drugs and Psychotropic Substances; Convention on the Protection of Environment through Criminal Law; Criminal Law Convention on Corruption and the Additional Protocol thereto; Civil Law Convention on Corruption; Convention on Cybercrime; Protocol No. 13 to the Convention for the Protection of Human Rights and Fundamental Freedoms, concerning the abolition of the death penalty in all circumstances; Council of Europe Convention on the Prevention of Terrorism; Council of Europe Convention on Action against Trafficking in Human Beings; and Council of Europe Convention on Laundering, Search, Seizure and Confiscation of the Proceeds from Crime and on the Financing of Terrorism.

An important contribution of the Council of Europe conventions is that many countries outside the Council of Europe are members. For instance, eighteen nonmember countries of the Council of Europe are signatories to the Convention on the Transfer of Sentenced Persons.

2. The European Court of Human Rights

In 1950, the Council of Europe adopted the European Convention for the Protection of Human Rights and Fundamental Freedoms (ECHR), which as of May 23, 2009, has forty-seven states parties. The ECHR established the European Commission and the European Court of Human Rights. The European Commission and Court can hear and adjudicate cases both between states and between legal persons (e.g., private individuals, and corporations) application and states.

Typically individuals can file a case, known as an "application," claiming some violation of the ECHR. The Court will first make a finding as to whether the application is admissible, determining issues such as whether the applicant exhausted domestic remedies, whether the application was filed within six months of exhaustion, and whether the case is pending before another international tribunal. If the application is admissible, the Court will endeavor to settle the dispute. If it cannot reach a settlement, the European Court will decide the case on the merits. If the Court finds a violation of the ECHR, the state party has the obligation to obey the decision. The decisions can include compensation and attorney's fees and costs awards.[5]

The European Court adjudicates state liability for failure to investigate, prosecute, and punish gross human rights violations and other crimes. For instance in *X. & Y. v. The Netherlands*, 91 Eur. Ct. H.R. (Ser. A) (1985), 8 E.H.R.R. 235 (1986), the court reviewed a state's response to a claim of sexual violence concerning a sixteen-year-old Dutch girl with mental disabilities who was allegedly raped by an acquaintance. The Court has declared that state parties have affirmative duties in criminal law contexts. *See, e.g., Assenov. v. Bulgaria*. Eur. Ct.HJ.R. (ser. A) (1998) (state duty to investigate police brutality); Ergi v. Turkey, Eur. Ct.H.R. (Ser. A 1998) (duty to investigate the circumstances of the applicant's death during a security force operation); *Güleç v. Turkey*, Eur.Ct.H.R. (Ser.A) (1998) (duty to investigate the applicant's death during a clash with police during a demonstration). *See* discussion in Francisco Forest Martin & Richard J. Wilson, THE RIGHTS INTERNATIONAL COMPANION TO CRIMINAL LAW AND PROCEDURE (Kluwer Law 1999) at 53. The Court has ruled on a variety of police practices, such as eavesdropping, search and seizure, the exclusionary rule, arrest, pretrial publicity, and the presumption of innocence. In addition, it has adjudicated a variety of cases on trial due process, including the examination of witnesses and documents, the right against self-incrimination, ex post facto or retrospective criminal laws, and double jeopardy or *non bis in idem*. *Id.* at 164–312. The Court has also made extradition contingent on the requested state assuring it would not apply the death penalty. *Soering v. United Kingdom*, E.C.H.R., 161 Eur. Ct. H.R. (Ser.A)(1989), 11 E.H.R.R. 439 (1989).

B. *The European Communities and the European Union*

As the European Communities moved close to developing a single market, some of its members took action to ensure that the single market would not unduly jeopardize criminal and enforcement cooperation. In one of the early mechanisms some EU members with common borders concluded the Schengen Agreement.

CONVENTION

from 19 June 1990

APPLYING THE SCHENGEN AGREEMENT OF 14 JUNE 1985 BETWEEN THE GOVERNMENTS OF THE STATES OF THE BENELUX ECONOMIC UNION, THE FEDERAL REPUBLIC OF GERMANY AND THE FRENCH REPUBLIC, ON THE GRADUAL ABOLITION OF CHECKS AT THEIR COMMON BORDERS

The Kingdom of Belgium, the Federal Republic of Germany, the French Republic, the Grand Duchy of Luxembourg and the Kingdom of the Netherlands, hereinafter called the Contracting Parties,

[5] FRANCISCO FOREST MARTIN & RICHARD J. WILSON, THE RIGHTS INTERNATIONAL COMPANION TO CRIMINAL LAW & PROCEDURE: AN INTERNATIONAL HUMAN RIGHTS & HUMANITARIAN LAW SUPPLEMENT 22–23 (1999).

Taking as their basis the Schengen Agreement of 14 June 1985 on the gradual abolition of checks at their common borders,

Having decided to implement the intention expressed in that agreement of bringing about the abolition of checks at their common borders on the movement of persons and facilitating the transport and movement of goods,

Whereas the Treaty establishing the European Communities, supplemented by the Single European Act, provides that the internal market shall comprise an area without internal frontiers.

Whereas the aim pursued by the Contracting parties coincides with that objective, without prejudice to the measures to be taken to implement the provisions of the Treaty,

Whereas the implementation of that intention requires a series of appropriate measures and close co-operation between the Contracting Parties,

Have agreed as follows:

TITLE II ABOLITION OF CHECKS AT INTERNAL BORDERS AND MOVEMENT OF PERSONS

CHAPTER 1 CROSSING INTERNAL FRONTIERS

1. Internal borders may be crossed at any point without any checks on persons being carried out.
2. Where public policy or national security so require, however, a Contracting Party may, after consulting the other Contracting Parties, decide that for a limited period national border checks appropriate to the situation will be carried out at internal borders. If public policy or national security require immediate action, the Contracting Party concerned shall take the necessary measures and shall inform the other Contracting Parties thereof at the earliest opportunity.
3. The abolition of checks on persons at internal borders shall not affect either Article 22 below or the exercise of police powers by the competent authorities under each Contracting Party's legislation throughout its territory, or the obligations to hold, carry and produce permits and documents provided for in its legislation.
4. Checks on goods shall be carried out in accordance with the relevant provisions of this Convention.

CHAPTER 2 CROSSING EXTERNAL BORDERS

Article 3

1. External borders may in principle be crossed only at border crossing points during the fixed opening hours. More detailed provisions, and exceptions and arrangements for minor border traffic, as well as the rules applicable to special categories of maritime traffic such as yachting and coastal fishing, shall be adopted by the Executive Committee.
2. The Contracting Parties undertake to introduce penalties for the unauthorized crossing of external borders at places other than crossing points or at times other than the fixed opening hours.

Article 4

1. The Contracting Parties guarantee that as from 1993 passengers on flights from Third States who board internal flights will first be subject, upon arrival, to personal and hand

baggage checks in the airport of arrival of their external flight. Passengers on internal flights who board flights bound for Third States, will first be subject, on departure, to personal and hand baggage checks in the airport of departure of their external flight.

***.

Article 5

1. For visits not exceeding three months entry into the territories of the Contracting Parties may be granted to an alien who fulfills the following conditions:
   (a) in possession of a valid document or documents permitting them to cross the border, as determined by the Executive Committee;
   (b) in possession of a valid visa if required;
   (c) if applicable, submits documents substantiating the purpose and the conditions of the planned visit and has sufficient means of support, both for the period of the planned visit and to return to their country of origin or to travel in transit in a Third State, into which their admission is guaranteed, or is in a position to acquire such means legally;
   (d) has not been reported as a person not to be permitted entry;
   (e) is not considered to be a threat to public policy, national security or the international relations of any of the Contracting Parties.
2. Entry to the territories of the Contracting Parties must be refused to any alien who does not fulfill all the above conditions unless a Contracting Party considers it necessary to derogate from that principle on humanitarian grounds or in the national interest or because of international obligations. In such cases permission to enter will be restricted to the territory of the Contracting Party concerned, which must inform the other Contracting Parties accordingly.
3. These rules shall not preclude the application of special provisions concerning the right of asylum or of the provisions of Article 18.
4. An alien who holds a residence permit or a return visa issued by one of the Contracting Parties or, if required, both documents, shall be permitted to enter in transit, unless their name is on the national list of persons reported as not to be refused entry which is held by the Contracting Party at the external borders of which they arrive.

Article 6

1. Cross-border movement at external borders shall be subject to checks by the competent authorities. Checks shall be made in accordance with uniform principles, within the scope of national powers and national legislation, account being taken of the interests of all Contracting Parties throughout the Contracting Parties' territories.

***

2. The competent authorities shall use mobile units to exercise surveillance on external borders between crossing points; the same shall apply to border crossing points outside normal opening hours. This surveillance shall be carried out in such a way as not to encourage people to circumvent the checks at crossing points. The surveillance procedures shall, where appropriate, be fixed by the Executive Committee.

3. The Contracting Parties undertake to deploy enough appropriate officers to conduct checks and maintain surveillance along external borders.
4. An equivalent level of control shall be exercised at external frontiers.

Article 7
The Contracting Parties shall assist each other and shall maintain constant, close co-operation with a view to the effective exercise of checks and surveillance. They shall in particular exchange all relevant, important information, with the exception of data relating to named individuals, unless otherwise provided in this Convention, shall as far as possible harmonize the instructions given to the authorities responsible for checks and shall promote the uniform training and retraining of officers manning checkpoints. Such co-operation may take the form of the exchange of liaison officers.

Article 8
The Executive Committee shall take the necessary decisions relating to the practical procedures for implementing border checks and surveillance.

CHAPTER 3 VISAS

* * *

Article 9.1. The Contracting Parties undertake to adopt a common policy on the movement of persons and in particular on the arrangements for visas. They shall give each other assistance to that end. The Contracting Parties undertake to pursue by common agreement the harmonization of their policies on visas.

TITLE III – Police and Security

CHAPTER 1 POLICE CO-OPERATION

Article 39

1. The Contracting Parties undertake to ensure that their police authorities shall, in compliance with national legislation and within the limits of their responsibilities, assist each other for the purposes of preventing and detecting criminal offences, insofar as national law does not stipulate that the request is to be made to the legal authorities and provided the request or the implementation thereof does not involve the application of coercive measures by the requested Contracting Party. Where the requested police authorities do not have jurisdiction to implement a request, they shall forward it to the competent authorities.
2. The written information provided by the requested Contracting Party under paragraph 1 may not be used by the requesting Contracting Party as evidence of the criminal offence other than with the agreement of the relevant legal authorities of the requested Contracting Party.
3. Requests for assistance referred to in paragraph 1 and the replies to such requests may be exchanged between the central bodies responsible in each Contracting Party for international police co-operation. Where the request cannot be made in good time by the above procedure, it may be addressed by the police authorities of the requesting Contracting Party directly to the competent authorities of the requested Party, which

may reply directly. In such cases, the requesting police authority shall as soon as possible inform the central body responsible in the requested Contracting Party for international police co-operation of its direct application.

4. In border regions, co-operation may be covered by arrangements between the responsible Ministers of the Contracting Parties.
5. The provisions of this Article shall not preclude more detailed present or future bilateral agreements between Contracting Parties with a common border. The Contracting Parties shall inform each other of such agreements.

Article 40

1. Police officers of one of the Contracting Parties who, within the framework of a criminal investigation, are keeping under observation in their country, a person who is presumed to have taken part in a criminal offence to which extradition may apply, shall be authorized to continue their observation in the territory of another Contracting Party where the latter has authorized cross-border observation in response to a request for assistance which has previously been submitted. Conditions may be attached to the authorization.

On request, the observation will be entrusted to officers of the Contracting Party in whose territory it is carried out.

The request, for assistance referred to in the first subparagraph must be sent to an authority designated by each of the Contracting Parties and having jurisdiction to grant or to forward the requested authorization.

2. Where, for particularly urgent reasons, prior authorization of the other Contracting Party cannot be requested, the officers conducting the observation shall be authorized to continue beyond the border the observation of a person presumed to have committed offences listed in paragraph 7, provided that the following conditions are met:
   (a) the authorities of the Contracting Party designated under paragraph 5, in whose territory the observation is to be continued, must be notified immediately, during the observation, that the border has been crossed;
   (b) a request for assistance submitted in accordance with paragraph 1 and outlining the grounds for crossing the border without prior authorization shall be submitted without delay.

Observation shall cease as soon as the Contracting Party in whose territory it is taking place so requests, following the notification referred to in (a) or the request referred to in (b) or where authorization has not been obtained five hours after the border was crossed.

3. The observation referred to in paragraphs 1 and 2 shall be carried out only under the following general conditions:
   (a) The officers conducting the observation must comply with the provisions of this Article and with the law of the Contracting Party in whose territory they are operating; they must obey the instructions of the local responsible authorities.
   (b) Except in the situations provided for in paragraph 2, the officers shall, during the observation, carry a document certifying that authorization has been granted.
   (c) The officers conducting the observation must be able at all times to provide proof that they are acting in an official capacity.

(d) The officers conducting the observation may carry their service weapons during the observation save where specifically otherwise decided by the requested party; their use shall be prohibited save in cases of legitimate self-defence.
(e) Entry into private homes and places not accessible to the public shall be prohibited.
(f) The officers conducting the observation may neither challenge nor arrest the person under observation.
(g) All operations shall be the subject of a report to the authorities of the Contracting Party in whose territory they took place; the officers conducting the observation may be required to appear in person.
(h) The authorities of the Contracting Party from which the observing officers have come shall, when requested by the authorities of the Contracting Party in whose territory the observation took place, assist the enquiry subsequent to the operation in which they took part, including legal proceedings.

* * *

6. The Contracting Parties may, at bilateral level, extend the scope of this Article and adopt additional measures in implementation thereof.
7. The observation referred to in paragraph 2 may take place only for one of the following criminal offences:
    - assassination,
    - murder,
    - rape,
    - arson,
    - counterfeiting,
    - armed robbery and receiving of stolen goods,
    - extortion,
    - kidnapping and hostage taking,
    - traffic in human beings,
    - illicit traffic in narcotic drugs and psychotropic substances,
    - breach of the laws on arms and explosives,
    - use of explosives,
    - illicit carriage of toxic and dangerous waste.

Article 41

1. Officers of one of the Contracting Parties following, in their country, an individual apprehended in the act of committing one of the offences referred to in paragraph 4 or participating in one of those offences, shall be authorized to continue pursuit in the territory of another Contracting Party without prior authorization where given the particular urgency of the situation it was not possible to notify the competent authorities of the other Contracting Party by one of the means provided for in Article 44 prior to entry into that territory or where these authorities have been unable to reach the scene in time to take over the pursuit.

The same shall apply where the person pursued has escaped from provisional custody or while serving a custodial sentence.

The pursuing officers shall, not later than when they cross the border, contact the competent authorities of the Contracting Party in whose territory the pursuit is to take place. The pursuit will cease as soon as the Contracting Party on the territory of which the pursuit is taking place so requests. At the request of the pursuing officers, the competent local authorities shall challenge the pursued person so as to establish his identity or to arrest him.

* * *

5. Pursuit shall be subject to the following general conditions:

(a) The pursuing officers must comply with the provisions of this Article and with the law of the Contracting Party in whose territory they are operating; they must obey the instructions of the competent local authorities.
(b) Pursuit shall be solely over land borders.
(c) Entry into private homes and places not accessible to the public shall be prohibited.
(d) The pursuing officers shall be easily identifiable, either by their uniform or by means of an armband or by accessories fitted to their vehicle; the use of civilian clothes combined with the use of unmarked vehicles without the aforementioned identification is prohibited; the pursuing officers must at all times be able to prove that they are acting in an official capacity.
(e) The pursuing officers may carry their service weapons; their use shall be prohibited save in cases of legitimate self-defence.
(f) Once the pursued person has been apprehended as provided for in paragraph 2fb1, for the purpose of bringing him before the competent local authorities he may be subjected only to a security search; handcuffs may be used during his transfer; objects carried by the pursued person may be seized.
(g) After each operation mentioned in paragraphs 1, 2 and 3, the pursuing officers shall present themselves before the local competent authorities of the Contracting Party in whose territory they were operating and shall give an account of their mission; at the request of those authorities, they must remain at their disposal until the circumstances of their action have been adequately elucidated; this condition shall apply even where the pursuit has not resulted in the arrest of the pursued person.
(h) The authorities of the Contracting Party from which the pursuing officers have come shall, when requested by the authorities of the Contracting Party in whose territory the pursuit took place, assist the enquiry subsequent to the operation in which they took part, including legal proceedings.

6. A person who, following the action provided for in paragraph 2, has been arrested by the competent local authorities may, whatever his nationality, be held for questioning. The relevant rules of national law shall apply by analogy.

If the person is not a national of the Contracting Party in the territory of which he was arrested, he shall be released no later than six hours after his arrest, not including the hours between midnight and 9:00 in the morning, unless the competent local authorities have previously received a request for his provisional arrest for the purposes of extradition in any form whatever.

* * *

8. This Article shall be without prejudice, where the Contracting Parties are concerned, to Article 27 of the Benelux Treaty of 27 June 1962 on Extradition and Mutual Assistance in Criminal Matters as amended by the Protocol of 11 May 1974;

9. On signing this Convention, each Contracting Party shall make a declaration in which it shall define, on the basis of paragraphs 2, 3 and 4 above, the procedures for implementing pursuit in its territory for each of the Contracting Parties with which it has a common border.

A Contracting Party may at any moment replace its declaration by another declaration, provided the latter does not, restrict the scope of the former.

Each declaration shall be made after consultations with each of the Contracting Parties concerned and with a view to obtaining equivalent arrangements on both sides of internal borders.

10. The Contracting Parties may, on a bilateral basis, extend the scope of paragraph 1 and adopt additional provisions in implementation of this Article.

Article 42

During the operations referred to in Articles 40 and 41, officers operating on the territory of another Contracting Party shall be regarded as officers of that Party with respect to offences committed against them or by them.

Article 44

1. In accordance with the relevant international agreements and accounts being taken of local circumstances and the technical possibilities, the Contracting Parties shall set up, in particular in border areas, telephone, radio, and telex lines and other direct links to facilitate police and customs co-operation, in particular for the transmission of information in good time for the purposes of cross-border observation and pursuit.
2. In addition to these short-term measures, they will in particular examine the following possibilities:
   (a) the exchange of equipment or the assignment of liaison officials provided with appropriate radio equipment;
   (b) the widening of the frequency bands used in border areas;
   (c) the establishment of a common link for police and customs services operating in these same areas;
   (d) co-ordination of their programmes for the procurement of communications equipment, with a view to achieving the introduction of standardized compatible communications systems.

Article 47

1. The Contracting Parties may conclude bilateral agreements providing for the secondment, for a specified or unspecified period, of liaison officers from one Contracting Party to the police authorities of the other Contracting Party.
2. The secondment of liaison officers for a specified or unspecified period is intended to promote and to accelerate co-operation between the Contracting Parties, particularly by providing assistance:
   (a) in the form of the exchange of information for the purposes of fighting crime by means both of prevention and of punishment,
   (b) in complying with requests for mutual police assistance and legal assistance in criminal matters;
   (c) for the purposes of missions carried out by the authorities responsible for the surveillance of external borders.

3. Liaison officers shall have the task of giving advice and assistance. They shall not be competent to take independent police action. They shall supply information and perform their duties in accordance with the instructions given to them by the Contracting Party of origin and by the Contracting Party to which they are seconded. They shall make reports regularly to the head of the police service to which they are seconded.
4. The Contracting Parties may agree within a bilateral or multilateral framework that liaison officers from a Contracting Party seconded to third States shall also represent the interests of one or more other Contracting Parties. Under such agreements, liaison officers seconded to third States shall supply information to other Contracting Parties when requested to do so or on their own initiative and shall, within the limits of their powers, perform duties on behalf of such Parties. The Contracting Parties shall inform one another of their intentions as regards the secondment of liaison officers to third States.

CHAPTER 2 MUTUAL ASSISTANCE IN CRIMINAL MATTERS

Article 48

1. The provisions of this Chapter are intended to supplement the European Convention of 20 April, 1959, on Mutual Assistance in Criminal Matters as well as, in relations between the Contracting Parties which are members of the Benelux Economic Union, Chapter II of the Benelux Treaty on Extradition and Mutual Assistance in Criminal Matters of 27 June 1962, as amended by the Protocol of 11 May 1974, and to facilitate the implementation of these agreements.
2. Paragraph 1 shall not affect the application of the broader provisions of the bilateral agreements in force between the Contracting Parties.

Article 50

1. The Contracting Parties undertake to afford each other, in accordance with the Convention and the Treaty referred to in Article 48, mutual assistance as regards infringements of their rules of law with respect to excise duty, value added tax and customs duties . . .
2. Requests based on evasion of excise duties may not be rejected on the grounds that the country requested does not levy excise duties on the goods referred to in the request.

* * *

Article 51
The Contracting Parties may not make the admissibility of letters rogatory for search or seizure dependent on conditions other than the following:

(a) the offence giving rise to the letters rogatory is punishable under the law of both Contracting Parties by a custodial sentence or a security measure restricting liberty of a maximum of at least six months or is punishable under the law of one of the two Contracting Parties by an equivalent penalty and under the law of the other Contracting Party as an infringement of the regulations which is prosecuted by the administrative authorities where the decision may give rise to proceedings before a criminal court.

(b) execution of the letters rogatory is consistent with the law of the requested Contracting Party.

Article 53

1. Requests for assistance may be made directly between legal authorities and returned through the same channels.
2. Paragraph 1 shall not prejudice the possibility of requests being sent and returned between Ministries of Justice or through the intermediary of national central offices of the International Criminal Police Organization.
3. Requests for the temporary transfer or transit of persons provisionally under arrest or detained or who are the subject of a measure depriving them of their liberty, and the periodic or occasional exchange of data from the judicial records must be effected through the Ministries of Justice.
4. Within the meaning of the European Convention of 20 April 1959 on Mutual Assistance in Criminal Matters, Ministry of Justice means, where the Federal Republic of Germany is concerned, the Federal Minister of Justice and the Justice Ministers or Senators of the Federal States.
5. Information laid with a view to proceedings in respect of infringements of the legislation on driving and rest time, in accordance with Article 21 of the European Convention of 20 April 1959 on Mutual Assistance in Criminal Matters or with Article 42 of the Benelux Treaty on Extradition and Mutual Assistance in Criminal Matters of 27 June 1962, as amended by the Protocol of 11 May 1974, may be sent by the legal authorities of the requesting Contracting Party directly to the legal authorities of the requested Contracting Party.

CHAPTER 3 APPLICATION OF THE NON BIS IN IDEM PRINCIPLE

Article 54

A person who has been finally judged by a Contracting Party may not be prosecuted by another Contracting Party for the same offences provided that, where he is sentenced, the sentence has been served or is currently being served or can no longer be carried out under the sentencing laws of the Contracting Party.

Article 56

If further proceedings are brought by a Contracting Party against a person who has been finally judged for the same offences by another Contracting Party, any period of deprivation of liberty served on the territory of the latter Contracting Party on account of the offences in question must be deducted from any sentence handed down. Account will also be taken, to the extent that national legislation permits, of sentences other than periods of imprisonment already undergone.

Article 57

1. Where a Contracting Party accuses an individual of an offence and the competent authorities of that Contracting Party have reason to believe that the accusation relates to the same offences as those for which the individual has already been finally judged

by another Contracting Party, these authorities shall, if they deem it necessary, request the relevant information from the competent authorities of the Contracting Party in whose territory judgment has already been delivered.

2. The information requested shall be provided as soon as possible and shall be taken into consideration as regards further action to be taken in the proceedings in progress.
3. At the time of ratification, acceptance or approval of this Convention, each Contracting Party will nominate the authorities which will be authorized to request and receive the information provided for in this Article.

Article 58

The above provisions shall not preclude the application of wider national provisions on the "non bis in idem" effect attached to legal decisions taken abroad.

CHAPTER 4 EXTRADITION

Article 59

1. The provisions of this Chapter are intended to supplement the European Convention of 13 September 1957 on Extradition as well as, in relations between the Contracting Parties which are members of the Benelux Economic Union, Chapter I of the Benelux Treaty on Extradition and Mutual Assistance in Criminal Matters of 27 June 1962, as amended by the Protocol of 11 May 1974, and to facilitate the implementation of these agreements.
2. Paragraph 1 shall not affect the application of the broader provisions of the bilateral agreements in force between Contracting Parties.

CHAPTER 5 TRANSFER OF THE EXECUTION OF CRIMINAL JUDGMENTS

* * *

CHAPTER 6 NARCOTIC DRUGS

Article 70

1. The Contracting Parties shall set up a permanent working party to examine common problems relating to the combating of offences involving narcotic drugs and to draw up proposals, where necessary, to improve the practical and technical aspects of co-operation between the Contracting Parties. The working party shall submit its proposals to the Executive Committee.
2. The working party referred to in paragraph 1, the members of which are nominated by the relevant national authorities, shall include representatives of the police and of the customs authorities.

Article 71

1. The Contracting Parties undertake as regards the direct or indirect sale of narcotic drugs and psychotropic substances of whatever type, including cannabis, and the possession

of such products and substances for sale or export, to take, in compliance with the existing United Nations Conventions (+), all measures necessary for the prevention and punishment of the illicit traffic in narcotic drugs and psychotropic substances.

2. The Contracting Parties undertake to prevent and to punish by administrative and penal measures the illegal export of narcotic drugs and psychotropic substances, including cannabis, as well as the sale, supply and handling of such products and substances, without prejudice to the relevant provisions of Articles 74, 75 and 76.
3. To combat the illegal importation of narcotic drugs and psychotropic substances, including cannabis, the Contracting Parties shall strengthen the checks on the movement of persons and goods and of means of transport at their external borders. Such measures shall be drawn up by the working party provided for in Article 70. This working party shall consider *inter alia* the reassignment of some of the police and customs staff released from internal *border* duty, as well as recourse to modern drug-detection methods and sniffer dogs.
4. To ensure compliance with this Article, the Contracting Parties shall specifically maintain surveillance on places known to be used for drug trafficking.
5. The Contracting Parties shall do all in their power to prevent and combat the negative effects of the illicit demand for narcotic drugs and psychotropic substances of whatever kind, including cannabis. The measures adopted to this end shall be the responsibility of each Contracting Party.

(+) Single Conventions on Narcotic Drugs of 1961 as amended by the 1972 Protocol amending the 1961 Single Convention on Narcotic Drugs; the 1971 Convention on Psychotropic Substances; the United Nations Convention of 20 December 1988 on Illicit Traffic in Narcotic Drugs and Psychotropic Substances.

Article 72

The Contracting Parties shall, in accordance with their constitution and their national legal system, ensure that legislation is enacted to permit the seizure and confiscation of assets deriving from illicit traffic in narcotic drugs and psychotropic substances.

Article 73

1. The Contracting Parties undertake, in accordance with their constitution and their national legal system, to take measures to allow monitored deliveries to take place in the illicit traffic in narcotic drugs and psychotropic substances.
2. In each individual case, a decision to allow monitored deliveries will be taken on the basis of prior authorization by each of the Contracting Parties concerned.
3. Each Contracting Party shall retain responsibility for and control over the operation on its own territory and shall be empowered to intervene.

Article 74

With respect to legal trade in narcotic drugs and psychotropic substances, the Contracting Parties agree to transfer inside the country, wherever possible, checks conducted at the border and arising from obligations under the United Nations Conventions listed in Article 71.

CHAPTER 7 FIREARMS AND AMMUNITION

Article 77

1. The Contracting Parties undertake to bring into line with the provisions of this Chapter their national laws, regulations and administrative provisions relating to the purchase, possession, sale and surrender of firearms and ammunition.
2. This Chapter covers the purchase, possession, sale and surrender of firearms and ammunition by natural and legal persons; it does not cover their supply to the central and territorial authorities, the armed forces or the police, nor the purchase or possession by them of firearms and ammunition nor the manufacture of firearms and ammunition by public undertakings.

* * *

TITLE 4 THE SCHENGEN INFORMATION SYSTEM

CHAPTER 1 SETTING UP OF THE SCHENGEN INFORMATION SYSTEM

Article 92

1. The Contracting Parties shall set up and maintain a joint information system; hereinafter referred to as the Schengen Information System, consisting of a national section in each of the Contracting Parties and a technical support function. The Schengen Information System shall enable the authorities designated by the Contracting Parties, by means of an automated search procedure, to have access to reports on persons and objects for the purposes of border checks and controls and other police and customs checks carried out within the country in accordance with national law and, in the case of the single category of report referred to in Article 96, for the purposes of issuing visas, the issue of residence permits and the administration of aliens in the context of the application of the provisions of this Convention relating to the movement of persons.
2. Each Contracting Party shall set up and maintain, for its own account and at its own risk, its national section of the Schengen Information System, the data file of which shall be made materially identical to the data files of the national sections of each of the other Contracting Parties using the technical support function. To ensure the rapid and effective transmission of data as referred to in paragraph 3, each Contracting Party shall observe, when creating its national section, the protocols and procedures which the Contracting Parties have jointly established for the technical support function. Each national section's data file shall be available for the purposes of automated search in the territory of each of the Contracting Parties. It shall not be possible to search the data files of other Contracting Parties' national sections.
3. The Contracting Parties shall set up and maintain jointly and with joint liability for risks, the technical support function of the Schengen Information System, the responsibility for which shall be assumed by the French Republic; the technical support function shall be located in Strasbourg. The technical support function shall comprise a data file which ensures that the data files of the national sections are kept identical by the on-line transmission of information. The data file of the technical support function

shall contain reports on persons and objects where these concern all the Contracting Parties. The data file of the technical support function shall contain no data other than those referred to in this paragraph and in Article 113(2).

CHAPTER 2 OPERATION AND UTILIZATION OF THE SCHENGEN INFORMATION SYSTEM

Article 93
The purpose of the Schengen Information System shall be in accordance with this Convention to maintain public order and security, including State security, and to apply the provisions of this Convention relating to the movement of persons, in the territories of the Contracting Parties, using information transmitted by the system.

Article 94

1. The Schengen Information System shall contain only the categories of data which are supplied by each of the Contracting Parties and are required for the purposes laid down in Articles 95 to 100. The Contracting Party providing a report shall determine whether the importance of the case warrants the inclusion of the report in the Schengen Information System.

* * *

CHAPTER 3 PROTECTION OF PERSONAL DATA AND SECURITY OF DATA UNDER THE SCHENGEN INFORMATION SYSTEM

Article 102

1. The Contracting Parties may use the data provided for in Articles 95 to 100 only for the purposes laid down for each type of report referred to in those Articles.
2. Data may be duplicated only for technical purposes, provided that such duplication is necessary for direct searching by the authorities referred to in Article 101. Reports by other Contracting Parties may not be copied from the national section of the Schengen Information System in other national data files.
3. In connection with the types of report provided for in Articles 95 to 100 of this Convention, any derogation from paragraph 1 in order to change from one type of report to another must be justified by the need to prevent an imminent serious threat to public order and safety, for serious reasons of State security or for the purposes of preventing a serious offence. The prior authorization of the reporting Contracting Party must obtain for this purpose.
4. Data may not be used for administrative purposes. By way of derogation, data included in accordance with Article 96 may be used, in accordance with the national law of each of the Contracting Parties, only for the purposes of Article 101 (2).
5. Any use of data which does not comply with paragraphs 4 to 7 shall be considered as a misuse in relation to the national law of each Contracting Party.

Article 103
Each Contracting Party shall ensure that, on average, every tenth transmission of personal data is recorded in the national section of the Schengen Information System by the data file

managing authority for the purposes of checking the admissibility of searching. The recording may be used only for this purpose and shall be deleted after six months.

* * *

Treaty on European Union and Final Act, done at Maastricht, February 7, 1992

TITLE 6: PROVISIONS ON COOPERATION IN THE FIELDS OF JUSTICE AND HOME AFFAIRS

ARTICLE K

Co-operation in the fields of justice and home affairs shall be governed by the following provisions.

ARTICLE K.1

For the purposes of achieving the objectives of the Union, in particular the free movement of persons, and without prejudice to the powers of the European Community, Member States shall regard the following areas as matters of common interest:

1. asylum policy;
2. rules governing the crossing by persons of the external borders of the Member States and the exercise of controls thereon;
3. immigration policy and policy regarding nationals of third countries;
   a. conditions of entry and movement by nationals of third countries on the territory of Member States;
   b. conditions of residence by nationals of third countries on the territory of Member States, including family reunion and access to employment;
   c. combating unauthorized immigration, residence and work by nationals of third countries on the territory of Member States;
4. combating drug addiction in so far as this is not covered by 7 to 9;
5. combating fraud on an international scale in so far as this is not covered by 7 to 9;
6. judicial co-operation in civil matters;
7. judicial co-operation in criminal matters;
8. customs co-operation;
9. police co-operation for the purposes of preventing and combating terrorism, unlawful drug trafficking and other serious forms of international crime, including if necessary certain aspects of customs co-operation, in connection with the organization of a Union-wide system for exchanging information within a European Police Office (Europol).

ARTICLE K.2

1. The matters referred to in Article K.1 shall be dealt with in compliance with the European Convention for the Protection of Human Rights and Fundamental Freedoms of 4 November 1950 and the Convention relating to the Status of Refugees of 28 July 1951 and having regard to the protection afforded by Member States to persons persecuted on political grounds.

2. This Title shall not affect the exercise of the responsibilities incumbent upon Member States with regard to the maintenance of law and order and the safeguarding of internal security.

ARTICLE K.3

1. In the areas referred to in Article K.1, Member States shall inform and consult one another within the Council with a view to co-ordinating their action. To that end, they shall establish collaboration between the relevant departments of their administrations.
2. The Council may:
   - on the initiative of any Member State or of the Commission, in the areas referred to in Article K.1(1) to (6);
     - on the initiative of any Member State, in the areas referred to Article K1(7) to (9):
       (a) adopt joint positions and promote, using the appropriate form and procedures, any co-operation contributing to the pursuit of the objectives of the Union;
       (b) adopt joint action in so far as the objectives of the Union can be attained better by joint action than by the Member States acting individually on account of the scale or effects of the action envisaged; it may decide that measures implementing joint action are to be adopted by a qualified majority;
       (c) without prejudice to Article 220 of the Treaty establishing the European Community, draw up conventions which it shall recommend to the Member States for adoption in accordance with their respective constitutional requirements.

Unless otherwise provided by such conventions, measures implementing them shall be adopted within the Council by a majority of two-thirds of the High Contracting Parties.

Such conventions may stipulate that the Court of Justice shall have jurisdiction to interpret their provisions and to rule on any disputes regarding their application, in accordance with such arrangements as they may lay down.

ARTICLE K.4

1. A Co-ordinating Committee shall be set up consisting of senior officials. In addition to its co-ordinating role, it shall be the task of the Committee to;
   - give opinions for the attention of the Council, either at the Council's request or on its own initiative;
     - contribute, without prejudice to Article 151 of the Treaty establishing the European Community, to the preparation of the Council's discussions in the areas referred to in Article K.1 and, in accordance with the conditions laid down in Article 100d of the Treaty establishing the European Community, in the areas referred to in Article 100c of that Treaty.
2. The Commission shall be fully associated with the work in the areas referred to in this Title.
3. The Council shall act unanimously, except on matters of procedure and in cases where Article K.3 expressly provides for other voting rules.

Where the Council is required to act by a qualified majority, the votes of its members shall be weighted as laid down in Article 148(2) of the Treaty establishing the European

Community, and for their adoption, acts of the Council shall require at least fifty-four votes in favour, cast by at least eight members.

ARTICLE K.5
Within international organizations and at international conferences in which they take part, Member States shall defend the common positions adopted under the provisions of this Title.

ARTICLE K.6
The Presidency and the Commission shall regularly inform the European Parliament of discussions in the areas covered by this Title. The Presidency shall consult the European Parliament on the principal aspects of activities in the areas referred to in this Title and shall ensure that the views of the European Parliament are duly taken into consideration.

The European Parliament may ask questions of the Council or make recommendations to it. Each year, it shall hold a debate on the progress made in implementation of the areas referred to in this Title.

ARTICLE K.7
The provisions of this Title shall not prevent the establishment or development of closer co-operation between two or more Member States in so far as such co-operation does not conflict with, or impede, that provided for in this Title.

* * *

Notes and Questions

1. The Maastricht Treaty includes justice and home affairs cooperation within the mainstream framework of the European Commission (EC). EU Members must view as "common interest" their policies on immigration, asylum, and external borders; strategies to fight international fraud and drug addiction; judicial cooperation in civil and criminal matters; and customs cooperation (Art. K.1–K.8). At the senior official level, the treaty creates a coordinating committee of permanent representatives (Art K.4). A K4 Committee was established in anticipation of the post-Maastricht body, and three steering groups have been established under its auspices, dealing with customs and policing, immigration, and judicial cooperation, respectively.

The EU and the Council of Europe offer prototypes for criminal justice cooperation at a regional level, including in the case of the EU among countries participating in free trade agreements, customs unions, and economic integration.

2. The Maastricht Treaty includes provisions covering the adoption of joint positions and international conventions across the range of justice and home affairs policies (Art. K.3). Because of the EU's large number of members – currently twenty-seven states – its ability to develop common foreign policy positions is important. As a result, in international organizations such as the World Bank Group, the United Nations, and the OECD, the EU has the ability to control or strongly influence policymaking and implementation. Perhaps even more importantly, the EU has signed many of the most important international criminal and enforcement law treaties. As a result, the EU has an international obligation to implement the provisions of these treaties.

3. Over time, justice and home affairs has assumed wider institutional authority within the EU over an increasing scope of policies. The authority of the Council of Ministers is

now recognized in this field (Art. K.3). At the senior official level, it will be assisted by a new coordinating committee of permanent representatives (Art. K.4). A K4 Committee was established in anticipation of the post-Maastricht body, and as mentioned earlier, three steering groups have been established under its auspices, dealing with customs and policing, immigration, and judicial cooperation.

4. With respect to terrorism, drugs, and fraud, a network of institutions provide for policy consultation. At the legal level, various international agreements exist under the United Nations and the Council of Europe for mutual recognition and assistance in police and criminal justice policy; there are also an increasing number of crime prevention measures within EC law. These provide an important supplement to the Maastricht Treaty (e.g., the July 1991 Directive on Money Laundering). For example, on June 26, 2007, the European Court of Justice upheld the European Council Directive 91/308/EEC on anti-money laundering,[6] as amended by Directive 2001/97/EC of the European Parliament and of the Council of December 4, 2001 (Directive 91/308),[7] and it ruled against bar associations contesting the directive.[8] The bar associations argued unsuccessfully that the obligations of reporting on and incriminating clients exceeded mere infringement of professional secrecy, to the extent that they wholly destroyed the attorney-client relationship.[9]

5. As the EU Trevi Ministers' organized crime initiatives show, as international coordination of criminal activity increases, it becomes more varied. Consider the phenomenon of "narco-terrorism." The links between terrorism and wider criminal activity and organization are generally very strong within the European Communities. Examples include the relationship between Mafia organizations and terrorist movements in Italy and the extensive involvement of the Irish Republican Army in smuggling, extortion, armed robbery, and commercial and construction frauds. As such activities assume international dimensions, the international community must consider how to effectively combat criminals without unduly restricting state perceptions of their particular security interests.[10]

6. The EU has a special organization, the Task Force for the Coordination of Fraud Prevention, charged with fighting fraud against the EU. The European Anti-Fraud Office (OLAF) has replaced the Task Force and has authority to investigate and prosecute fraud involving community funds. The European Parliament notes the tendency of member states to treat fraud against the EU as less serious than fraud against individual states, a clear case of the nation-state retaining top priority.

7. The key issues concerning European police cooperation in Europe include (1) the level of crime in Europe, (2) the likely impact of changes in the system of border controls within the EC, (3) the difficulties attendant to the policing of the EC because of the diversity of policing organizations that exist within the member states, and (4) the experiences of existing agencies for cooperation (e.g., Europol, Eurojust). Some scholars argue that policy formulation in this field is based on scant information and an inadequate examination of the issues. They advocate the need for police organizations,

[6] OJ 1991 L 166, p. 77.

[7] OJ 2001 L 344, p. 76.

[8] *Order des barreaux francophones et germanophone v. Conseil des Ministres*, European Court of Justice (Grand Chamber), Case C-305/05, June 26, 2007.

[9] For more information *see* Bruce Zagaris, *European Court of Justice Rules against Attorney Professional Secrecy*, 23 INT'L ENFORCEMENT LAW REP. 340 (Sept. 2007).

[10] For insightful discussion of the interaction of integration and policing in Europe, *see* Neil Walker, *European Integration and European Policing: A Complex Relationship in* POLICING ACROSS NATIONAL BOUNDARIES 29–33 (Malcolm Anderson & Monica den Boer eds., 1994).

governments, the EC, and academic research institutions to collect and analyze EC crime statistics. Indeed, law enforcement agencies are still confused concerning the role and capabilities of existing cooperative agreements.[11]

8. Evolving legislation that gives cross-border operational powers to member state police forces offers insight into macro-level enforcement cooperation in the EU. The EU has developed a series of agreements on investigations, arrests, detentions, and interrogations. Discussions on harmonization, streamlining, and compatibility in these areas should occur at the highest level, because the highly sensitive issue of national sovereignty cross-cuts all discussion in this area and requires macro-level political agreements in contrast to cooperative arrangements at an interpersonal or subnational organizational level. "Hot pursuit" across borders is an example of an issue that can be decided only at the macro level because it impinges on sensitive issues of sovereignty and requires national legislation.

Firearms control offers another example of macro-level cooperation. Because EU members have historically had different policies concerning the carrying and use of firearms, harmonization has required high-level agreements. In 1991, the EU passed the Directive on Firearms, harmonizing EU policy on this issue.

Finally, consider macro-level cooperation on the transfer of police intelligence across national boundaries. This sort of police cooperation requires harmonization of data-protection laws and ministerial-level agreements. To some degree, this has occurred under the terms of the 1981 Council of Europe Data Protection Convention. All EC states have signed the 1981 convention, although they have not all given effect to its terms.

9. At the meso level, which is between the micro and macro levels, issues are mainly concerned with the operational structures, practices, procedures, and design of the enterprises of the police and other law enforcement agencies. It is of decisive importance that the layout of the infrastructure (transport, communication, and power distribution systems) and the sector policies, especially regarding education, research, and technology, are oriented toward competitiveness.

One important meso-level concern involves communications between police forces. Issues in this area include compatibility of police information systems, common databases, and coordination and access to information such as criminal intelligence. The dynamic growth in information technology and the police use of computers make this area extremely important.

10. European police cooperation at the micro level involves the investigation of specific offenses and the prevention and control of particular forms of crime. Cooperation at this level occurs primarily in connection with specific crime issues, such as drug trafficking, terrorism, organized crime, and environmental crime. Liaison officers are seconded from one country to work with their counterparts in another, especially in the fields of terrorism, drugs, and football hooliganism.

11. Although considerable opportunities exist for micro-level initiatives and many are already being implemented, police networks already exist between officers of different countries. Successful networks tend to be established at the meso level, and, indeed, many micro-level instances of cooperation depend on effective meso-level arrangements.[12]

[11] For more background on the issues and the need for better analysis of them, *see* John Benyon et al., *Understanding Police Cooperation in Europe: Setting a Framework for Analysis in* POLICING ACROSS NATIONAL BOUNDARIES, *supra* note 10 at 47.

[12] *Id.* at 52–55.

12. European integration has vastly improved the extradition process making it more routine and effective. The EU has instituted the European Arrest Warrant (EAW), which is designed to facilitate the surrender of persons charged with crimes within the EU; it dispenses with some of the normally required procedures for extradition. The facts described in an EAW must, at a minimum, comprise the essential elements of the punishable conduct so that the executing state can ascertain whether the principle of *ne bis in idem* (the principle against trying a person more than once for the same offense) is being violated. The "specialty rule," under which a country can only try a relator for the offenses for which he or she was surrendered, requires a precise description of the individual offenses. However, the form sheet is not suited for listing a multitude of offenses, especially when there are both listed offenses and other offenses, which must be punishable in both legal systems. Although the EU is still working out some implementation issues, the use of an EAW has eliminated some of the lengthy and more cumbersome extradition procedures. For background *see* Bruce Zagaris, *European Union Provides Recommendations on Implementing the European Arrest Warrant*, 21 INT'L ENFORCEMENT L. REP. 94 (Mar. 2005), citing Council of European Union, *Recommendations of the Conference "First Practical Experiences with the European Arrest Warrant,"* 14619/04, Brussels, Nov. 17, 2004.

13. European integration has led to a convergence of adversarial and inquisitorial criminal justice systems. Because all EU criminal justice systems must operate in accordance with the European Convention on Human Rights, the systems are increasingly being harmonized. *See, e.g.*, Christopher Harding, Phil Fennell, Nico Jörg, & Bert Swart, CRIMINAL JUSTICE IN EUROPE: A COMPARATIVE STUDY (Clarendon Press, 1995). There are also several European institutions that deal with criminal enforcement, including the European Court of Human Rights, the Court of Justice of the European Communities, the European Committee on Crime Problems, and Europol.

14. New EU accession countries must undergo audits of their criminal justice systems and then have a two- to- three-year period to meet EU standards. The EU has warned some countries previously proposed for membership, such as Bulgaria and Romania, that they needed to bolster their anticorruption measures to meet the timetable for admission. Even after their admission the EU has threatened sanctions against them for failure to meet anticorruption standards. *See* George Parker, Christopher Condon, & Theodor Troev, *Bulgaria and Romania Warned on Corruption*, FIN. TIMES, June 27, 2007. What measures can be used to compel accession countries to comply with international and European criminal justice requirements? Consider the EU's efforts to compel the former members of Yugoslavia to comply with the requests of the International Criminal Tribunal for War Crimes in the Former Yugoslavia.

15. As discussed later, an important aspect of Western European integration in relation to international criminal cooperation and criminal justice harmonization is that it provides a model for other economic integration groups. This is especially relevant insofar as the European Union and its members participate in international organizations such as the Organization of American States and Inter-American Development Bank.

III. Western Hemisphere and Economic Integration

In the Western Hemisphere efforts to harmonize criminal justice systems have occurred in the areas of cooperation in procedural and substantive criminal law foreign police assistance, and administration of justice programs. The predominant power of the United

States has allowed it to assert a leadership role in making and implementing policy, often in the context of national, bilateral, and regional security.[13]

A. *The Organization of American States*

1. Criminal Enforcement Cooperation and Criminal Justice

Much of the international criminal and enforcement cooperation and criminal justice harmonization in the Western Hemisphere takes place under the auspices of the Organization of American States (OAS). Within the OAS, the Inter-American Judicial Committee (IAJC) undertakes much of the legal advisory work. The IAJC, the OAS's advisory body on juridical matters, helps promote the progressive development and codification of international law and studies juridical problems related to the integration of regional developing countries. It has eleven members, whom the General Assembly elects for a period of four years from panels of three candidates presented by the member states. To facilitate an equitable geographical representation, no two members of the committee can be from the same state.

The 1970 entry into force of the revised OAS Charter created new mechanisms with important implications for international enforcement cooperation. In 1979, the Inter-American Court of Human Rights established links to the OAS General Assembly. In 1986, the OAS created the Inter-American Drug Abuse Control Commission (CICAD)[14] and upgraded the Inter-American Defense Board (IADB).[15]

Since 1997, the Organization of American States has also convened regular meetings of ministers of justices and attorneys general (Reunión Extraordinaria de los Ministros de Justicia de las Américas, or REMJA). These meetings provide a forum for wide-ranging discussions on all aspects of international enforcement cooperation and criminal justice in the region, presaging more dynamic regional cooperation on criminal matters.[16] Although REMJA exists within the OAS framework, it is not an organic body or an agency of the OAS like other bodies concerned with international criminal and enforcement cooperation such as CICAD or the Inter-American Committee against Terrorism (CICTE).[17]

REMJA has focused on single crime issues, such as cybercrime; prison and penitentiary policy; and the training of judges, prosecutors, and judicial officers, thereby improving international criminal cooperation.[18] It has helped promote law enforcement cooperation throughout the hemisphere. Since REMJA's creation, OAS members have ratified and begun to implement universal and regional international cooperation instruments. Many REMJA members have participated in its information exchange network. The group also focuses its attention on specific issues, including human trafficking.[19]

[13] For additional background on international criminal and enforcement cooperation and criminal justice harmonization in the Western Hemisphere, *see* Bruce Zagaris, *Developments in the Institutional Architecture and Framework of International Criminal and Enforcement Cooperation in the Western Hemisphere*, 37 U. Miami Inter-Am. L. Rev. 421, 421–516 (2006).

[14] For the history of CICAD, *see* http://www.cicad.oas.org/EN/Main/AboutCICAD/history.htm.

[15] Zagaris, supra note 13 at 454.

[16] *Id.* at 472. *See also* David P. Warner, *Law Enforcement Cooperation in the Organization of American States: A Focus on REMJA*, 37 U. Miami Inter-Am. L.Rev. 387, 387–420 (2006).

[17] *Id.* at 400.

[18] Zagaris, *supra* note 13 at 476–80.

[19] Warner, *supra* note 16 at 408–10.

Because REMJA is neither a standing OAS agency or entity nor a treaty-based structure, its viability is wholly dependent on OAS institutions such as the Permanent Council. The Council drafts and approves REMJA's agenda, promotes and tracks its conclusions and recommendations, and directs and observes its components. Looking toward the future, REMJA's continued dynamism would seem to require a more sound legal basis and adequate staffing and funding.[20] The success of the various REMJA initiatives also depends on countries deciding to support its initiatives, as Canada has done with REMJA's information exchange network.[21] The establishment of a Committee on the Americas' Crime Problem, emulating the European Committee on Crime Problems, would be an even bolder step. For more on this idea, *see* the Notes and Questions section.

2. The Inter-American Human Rights System

The Inter-American human rights system has two distinct legal sources: the first from the Charter of the OAS and the second from the American Convention on Human Rights. For the relevant treaties and related text, reports, judicial opinions, and historical documents on the OAS system, *see* T. Buergenthal & R. Norris, Human Rights: The Inter-American System (4 vols., 1982–87).

The Inter-American Human Rights Commission (IAHRC) conducts on-site investigations of the human rights conditions of a country when it receives numerous individual communications or other credible evidence, usually from NGOs, that a government may be committing large-scale violations of human rights.[22] It also adjudicates individual petitions. However, the petition system has two critical limitations. First, because the petitions are directed against states that are not parties to the American Convention on Human Rights, the Inter-American Court of Human Rights has no contentious jurisdiction to deal with them. Second, the IAHRC sends its decisions to the General Assembly, but it has no interest in acting on the decisions. Noncompliance by states with these decisions in these cases (e.g., especially by the United States) deprives the system of its effectiveness.[23]

Despite the limits in the jurisdiction of the Court and the Commission's powers, they have dealt with a variety of cases concerning state liability for failure to investigate, prosecute, and punish gross human rights violations and other crimes. *Velásquez Rodríguez v. Honduras*, Inter-Am. Ct. H.R.,Ser.C No. 4 (Judgment of July 29, 1988). The system has also adjudicated cases of police practices, such as eavesdropping, search and seizure, and the exclusionary rule (*e.g., García Pérez v. Peru*, Inter-Amer. Cmr. H.R. Rept. No. 1/95, Case 11.006, Inter-Am. Cm. H.R. 71, OEA/Ser.L/V/II.88, Doc. 9 rev. (1995) (the army's seizure of papers from former and current Peruvian president Dr. Alan García, and court access for determining the lawfulness of his arrest and continuing detention; *e.g., Suárez Rosero v. Ecuador*, Inter-Am. Ct. H.R., Judgment of 12 Nov. 1997) (initial arrest and detention of the defendant for drug trafficking was arbitrary). They have also adjudicated a variety of cases of criminal trial due process protection, such as judicial and jury impartiality and the right to a speedy trial (*e.g., Firmenich v. Argentina*, Inter-Amer. Cmn. H.R., Resolution 17/89, Report Case 10037 (13 Apr. 1989), Annual Report of the Inter-American Commission on Human Rights, OEA/Ser.L/V/II.76 (10 Sept. 1989) (whether the duration

[20] *Id.* at 410–13.
[21] *Id.* at 416–17.
[22] T. Buergenthal, International Human Rights 136 (1988).
[23] *Id.* at 143.

between detention and trial after arrest in and extradition from Brazil was reasonable). They have also adjudicated issues relating to capital punishment (*e.g.*, *Pinkerton and Roach v. U.S.*, Resolution No. 3/87, Case 9647, Inter-Amer. Cmn. H.R., Annual Report of the 1986–1987 Inter-American Commission on Human Rights 147, OEA/Ser.L/V/II/71, doc 9 rev 1 (1987) (whether the death penalty in the United States for crimes committed by minors violates the right to life and right to equality before the law).

Notes and Questions

1. The Inter-American human rights system, unlike the European, has not been able to enforce its decisions. For instance, in the *Soering* case the United States and Commonwealth of Virginia gave assurances that the death penalty would not be applied to a relator who was the subject of an extradition request to the United Kingdom. In contrast, the United States and other countries in the Americas do not abide by the decisions of the Inter-American system on the death penalty. Does this completely nullify the value of the Inter-American system with respect to violations of human rights in criminal cases?

2. What, if any, precedential value do decisions of regional human rights systems have on national jurisprudence? *See, e.g.*, *Stanford v. Kentucky*, 492 U.S. 361, 290 (Brennan, J. dissenting). *See* discussion in Martin & Wilson, THE RIGHTS INTERNATIONAL COMPANION TO CRIMINAL LAW & PROCEDURE *supra*, at 328–29.

3. In the *García Pérez v. Peru* case, the IACHR called for the application of the exclusionary rule. What precedential value can such a decision have not on only national courts but also on international criminal courts? *See* discussion in Martin & Wilson, *supra*, at 193–94.

B. *The North American Free Trade Agreement (NAFTA)*

NAFTA's only criminal and enforcement provisions govern intellectual property and customs laws. This is despite the fact that during the ratification process some members of Congress threatened to vote against ratification because of the perceived lack of Mexican cooperation with U.S. extradition requests. Critics of the bill argued that a number of such cases involved serious crimes committed by Mexican nationals in the United States who then fled back across the border.

These concerns notwithstanding, the George H. W. Bush administration opposed the inclusion of regulatory provisions and mechanisms in nontrade areas. The Clinton administration, meanwhile, conditioned support for ratification on the inclusion of side agreements on labor and the environment, which did not include criminal or enforcement provisions.

Trade Negotiations and Agreements

Part Six: Intellectual Property

Chapter Seventeen

Article 1701: Nature and Scope of Obligations

1. Each Party shall provide in its territory to the nationals of another Party adequate and effective protection and enforcement of intellectual property rights, while ensuring

that measures to enforce intellectual property rights do not themselves become barriers to legitimate trade.

2. To provide adequate and effective protection and enforcement of intellectual property rights, each Party shall, at a minimum, give effect to this Chapter and to the substantive provisions of:
   a. the Geneva Convention for the Protection of Producers of Phonograms Against Unauthorized Duplication of their Phonograms, 1971 (Geneva Convention);
   b. the Berne Convention for the Protection of Literary and Artistic Works, 1971 (Berne Convention);
   c. the Paris Convention for the Protection of Industrial Property, 1967 (Paris Convention); and
   d. the International Convention for the Protection of New Varieties of Plants, 1978 (UPOV Convention), or the International Convention for the Protection of New Varieties of Plants, 1991 (UPOV Convention).

If a Party has not acceded to the specified text of any such Conventions on or before the date of entry into force of this Agreement, it shall make every effort to accede.

3. Annex 1701.3 applies to the Parties specified in that Annex.

Article 1702: More Extensive Protection
A Party may implement in its domestic law more extensive protection of intellectual property rights than is required under this Agreement, provided that such protection is not inconsistent with this Agreement.

Article 1703: National Treatment
1. Each Party shall accord to nationals of another Party treatment no less favorable than that it accords to its own nationals with regard to the protection and enforcement of all intellectual property rights. In respect of sound recordings, each Party shall provide such treatment to producers and performers of another Party, except that a Party may limit rights of performers of another Party in respect of secondary uses of sound recordings to those rights its nationals are accorded in the territory of such other Party.

***

Article 1704: Control of Abusive or Anticompetitive Practices or Conditions
Nothing in this Chapter shall prevent a Party from specifying in its domestic law licensing practices or conditions that may in particular cases constitute an abuse of intellectual property rights having an adverse effect on competition in the relevant market. A Party may adopt or maintain, consistent with the other provisions of this Agreement, appropriate measures to prevent or control such practices or conditions.

Article 1705: Copyright

1. Each Party shall protect the works covered by Article 2 of the Berne Convention, including any other works that embody original expression within the meaning of that Convention. In particular:
   (a) all types of computer programs are literary works within the meaning of the Berne Convention and each Party shall protect them as such; and

(b) compilations of data or other material, whether in machine readable or other form, which by reason of the selection or arrangement of their contents constitute intellectual creations, shall be protected as such.

The protection a Party provides under subparagraph (b) shall not extend to the data or material itself, or prejudice any copyright subsisting in that data or material.

* * *

Article 1706: Sound Recordings

1. Each Party shall provide to the producer of a sound recording the right to authorize or prohibit:
   (a) the direct or indirect reproduction of the sound recording;
   (b) the importation into the Party's territory of copies of the sound recording made without the producer's authorization;
   (c) the first public distribution of the original and each copy of the sound recording by sale, rental or otherwise; and
   (d) the commercial rental of the original or a copy of the sound recording, except where expressly otherwise provided in a contract between the producer of the sound recording and the authors of the works fixed therein.

Each Party shall provide that putting the original or a copy of a sound recording on the market with the right holder's consent shall not exhaust the rental right.

2. Each Party shall provide a term of protection for sound recordings of at least 50 years from the end of the calendar year in which the fixation was made.
3. Each Party shall confine limitations or exceptions to the rights provided for in this Article to certain special cases that do not conflict with a normal exploitation of the sound recording and do not unreasonably prejudice the legitimate interests of the right holder.

Article 1707: Protection of Encrypted Program Carrying Satellite Signals
Within one year from the date of entry into force of this Agreement, each Party shall make it:

(a) a criminal offense to manufacture, import, sell, lease or otherwise make available a device or system that is primarily of assistance in decoding an encrypted program-carrying satellite signal without the authorization of the lawful distributor of such signal; and
(b) a civil offense to receive, in connection with commercial activities, or further distribute, an encrypted program-carrying satellite signal that has been decoded without the authorization of the lawful distributor of the signal or to engage in any activity prohibited under subparagraph (a).

Each Party shall provide that any civil offense established under subparagraph (b) shall be actionable by any person that holds an interest in the content of such signal.

Article 1708: Trademarks

* * *

Article 1709: Patents

* * *

Article 1710: Layout Designs of Semiconductor Integrated Circuits

* * *

Article 1711: Trade Secrets

* * *

Article 1712: Geographical Indications

* * *

Article 1713: Industrial Designs

1. Each Party shall provide for the protection of independently created industrial designs that are new or original. . . .

Article 1714: Enforcement of Intellectual Property Rights: General Provisions

1. Each Party shall ensure that enforcement procedures, as specified in this Article and Articles 1715 through 1718, are available under its domestic law so as to permit effective action to be taken against any act of infringement of intellectual property rights covered by this Chapter, including expeditious remedies to prevent infringements and remedies to deter further infringements. Such enforcement procedures shall be applied so as to avoid the creation of barriers to legitimate trade and to provide for safeguards against abuse of the procedures.
2. Each Party shall ensure that its procedures for the enforcement of intellectual property rights are fair and equitable, are not unnecessarily complicated or costly, and do not entail unreasonable timelimits or unwarranted delays.
3. Each Party shall provide that decisions on the merits of a case in judicial and administrative enforcement proceedings shall:
   (a) preferably be in writing and preferably state the reasons on which the decisions are based;
   (b) be made available at least to the parties in a proceeding without undue delay; and
   (c) be based only on evidence in respect of which such parties were offered the opportunity to be heard.
4. Each Party shall ensure that parties in a proceeding have an opportunity to have final administrative decisions reviewed by a judicial authority of that Party and, subject to jurisdictional provisions in its domestic laws concerning the importance of a case, to have reviewed at least the legal aspects of initial judicial decisions on the merits of a case. Notwithstanding the above, no Party shall be required to provide for judicial review of acquittals in criminal cases.
5. Nothing in this Article or Articles 1715 through 1718 shall be construed to require a Party to establish a judicial system for the enforcement of intellectual property rights distinct from that Party's system for the enforcement of laws in general.

6. For the purposes of Articles 1715 through 1718, the term "right holder" includes federations and associations having legal standing to assert such rights.

Article 1715: Specific Procedural and Remedial Aspects of Civil and Administrative Procedures

1. Each Party shall make available to right holders civil judicial procedures for the enforcement of any intellectual property rights provided in this Chapter. Each Party shall provide that:
   (a) defendants have the right to written notice that is timely and contains sufficient detail, including the basis of the claims;
   (b) parties in a proceeding are allowed to be represented by independent legal counsel;
   (c) the procedures do not include imposition of overly burdensome requirements concerning mandatory personal appearances;
   (d) all parties in a proceeding are duly entitled to substantiate their claims and to present relevant evidence; and
   (e) the procedures include a means to identify and protect confidential information.
2. Each Party shall provide that its judicial authorities shall have the authority:
   (a) where a party in a proceeding has presented reasonably available evidence sufficient to support its claims and has specified evidence relevant to the substantiation of its claims that is within the control of the opposing party, to order the opposing party to produce such evidence, subject in appropriate cases to conditions that ensure the protection of confidential information;
   (b) where a party in a proceeding voluntarily and without good reason refuses access to, or otherwise does not provide relevant evidence under that party's control within a reasonable period, or significantly impedes a proceeding relating to an enforcement action, to make preliminary and final determinations, affirmative or negative, on the basis of the evidence presented, including the complaint or the allegation presented by the party adversely affected by the denial of access to evidence, subject to providing the parties an opportunity to be heard on the allegations or evidence;
   (c) to order a party in a proceeding to desist from an infringement, including to prevent the entry into the channels of commerce in their jurisdiction of imported goods that involve the infringement of an intellectual property right, which order shall be enforceable at least immediately after customs clearance of such goods;
   (d) to order the infringer of an intellectual property right to pay the right holder damages adequate to compensate for the injury the right holder has suffered because of the infringement where the infringer knew or had reasonable grounds to know that it was engaged in an infringing activity;
   (e) to order an infringer of an intellectual property right to pay the right holder's expenses, which may include appropriate attorney's fees; and
   (f) to order a party in a proceeding at whose request measures were taken and who has abused enforcement procedures to provide adequate compensation to any party wrongfully enjoined or restrained in the proceeding for the injury suffered because of such abuse and to pay that party's expenses, which may include appropriate attorney's fees.
3. With respect to the authority referred to in subparagraph 2(c), no Party shall be obliged to provide such authority in respect of protected subject matter that is acquired or

ordered by a person before that person knew or had reasonable grounds to know that dealing in that subject matter would entail the infringement of an intellectual property right.

4. With respect to the authority referred to in subparagraph 2(d), a Party may, at least with respect to copyrighted works and sound recordings, authorize the judicial authorities to order recovery of profits or payment of pre-established damages, or both, even where the infringer did not know or had no reasonable grounds to know that it was engaged in an infringing activity.
5. Each Party shall provide that, in order to create an effective deterrent to infringement, its judicial authorities shall have the authority to order that:
   (a) goods that they have found to be infringing be, without compensation of any sort, disposed of outside the channels of commerce in such a manner as to avoid any injury caused to the right holder or, unless this would be contrary to existing constitutional requirements, destroyed; and
   (b) materials and implements the predominant use of which has been in the creation of the infringing goods be, without compensation of any sort, disposed of outside the channels of commerce in such a manner as to minimize the risks of further infringements.

In considering whether to issue such an order, judicial authorities shall take into account the need for proportionality between the seriousness of the infringement and the remedies ordered as well as the interests of other persons. In regard to counterfeit goods, the simple removal of the trademark unlawfully affixed shall not be sufficient, other than in exceptional cases, to permit release of the goods into the channels of commerce.

6. In respect of the administration of any law pertaining to the protection or enforcement of intellectual property rights, each Party shall only exempt both public authorities and officials from liability to appropriate remedial measures where actions are taken or intended in good faith in the course of the administration of such laws.
7. Notwithstanding the other provisions of Articles 1714 through 1718, where a Party is sued with respect to an infringement of an intellectual property right as a result of its use of that right or use on its behalf, that Party may limit the remedies available against it to the payment to the right holder of adequate remuneration in the circumstances of each case, taking into account the economic value of the use.
8. Each Party shall provide that, where a civil remedy can be ordered as a result of administrative procedures on the merits of a case, such procedures shall conform to principles equivalent in substance to those set out in this Article.

Article 1716: Provisional Measures

1. Each Party shall provide that its judicial authorities shall have the authority to order prompt and effective provisional measures:
   a. to prevent an infringement of any intellectual property right, and in particular to prevent the entry into the channels of commerce in their jurisdiction of allegedly infringing goods, including measures to prevent the entry of imported goods at least immediately after customs clearance; and
   b. to preserve relevant evidence in regard to the alleged infringement.

* * *

Article 1717: Criminal Procedures and Penalties

1. Each Party shall provide criminal procedures and penalties to be applied at least in cases of willful trademark counterfeiting or copyright piracy on a commercial scale. Each Party shall provide that penalties available include imprisonment or monetary fines, or both, sufficient to provide a deterrent, consistent with the level of penalties applied for crimes of a corresponding gravity.
2. Each Party shall provide that, in appropriate cases, its judicial authorities may order the seizure, forfeiture and destruction of infringing goods and of any materials and implements the predominant use of which has been in the commission of the offense.
3. A Party may provide criminal procedures and penalties to be applied in cases of infringement of intellectual property rights, other than those in paragraph 1, where they are committed willfully and on a commercial scale.

Article 1718: Enforcement of Intellectual Property Rights at the Border

1. Each Party shall, in conformity with this Article, adopt procedures to enable a right holder, who has valid grounds for suspecting that the importation of counterfeit trademark goods or pirated copyright goods may take place, to lodge an application in writing with its competent authorities, whether administrative or judicial, for the suspension by the customs administration of the release of such goods into free circulation. No Party shall be obligated to apply such procedures to goods in transit. A Party may permit such an application to be made in respect of goods that involve other infringements of intellectual property rights, provided that the requirements of this Article are met. A Party may also provide for corresponding procedures concerning the suspension by the customs administration of the release of infringing goods destined for exportation from its territory.
2. Each Party shall require any applicant who initiates procedures under paragraph 1 to provide adequate evidence:
   (a) to satisfy that Party's competent authorities that, under the domestic laws of the country of importation, there is prima facie an infringement of its intellectual property right; and
   (b) to supply a sufficiently detailed description of the goods to make them readily recognizable by the customs administration.

The competent authorities shall inform the applicant within a reasonable period whether they have accepted the application and, if so, the period for which the customs administration will take action.

3. Each Party shall provide that its competent authorities shall have the authority to require an applicant under paragraph 1 to provide a security or equivalent assurance sufficient to protect the defendant and the competent authorities and to prevent abuse. Such security or equivalent assurance shall not unreasonably deter recourse to these procedures.
4. Each Party shall provide that, where pursuant to an application under procedures adopted pursuant to this Article, its customs administration suspends the release of goods involving industrial designs, patents, integrated circuits or trade secrets into free circulation on the basis of a decision other than by a judicial or other independent authority, and the period provided for in paragraphs 6 through 8 has expired without

the granting of provisional relief by the duly empowered authority, and provided that all other conditions for importation have been complied with, the owner, importer or consignee of such goods shall be entitled to their release on the posting of a security in an amount sufficient to protect the right holder against any infringement. Payment of such security shall not prejudice any other remedy available to the right holder, it being understood that the security shall be released if the right holder fails to pursue its right of action within a reasonable period of time.

5. Each Party shall provide that its customs administration shall promptly notify the importer and the applicant when the customs administration suspends the release of goods pursuant to paragraph 1.
6. Each Party shall provide that its customs administration shall release goods from suspension if, within a period not exceeding 10 working days after the applicant under paragraph 1 has been served notice of the suspension, the customs administration has not been informed that:
   (a) a party other than the defendant has initiated proceedings leading to a decision on the merits of the case, or
   (b) a competent authority has taken provisional measures prolonging the suspension,
   (c) provided that all other conditions for importation or exportation have been met. Each Party shall provide that, in appropriate cases, the customs administration may extend the suspension by another 10 working days.
7. Each Party shall provide that if proceedings leading to a decision on the merits of the case have been initiated, a review, including a right to be heard, shall take place on request of the defendant with a view to deciding, within a reasonable period, whether these measures shall be modified, revoked or confirmed.
8. Notwithstanding paragraphs 6 and 7, where the suspension of the release of goods is carried out or continued in accordance with a provisional judicial measure, Article 1716(6) shall apply.
9. Each Party shall provide that its competent authorities shall have the authority to order the applicant under paragraph 1 to pay the importer, the consignee and the owner of the goods appropriate compensation for any injury caused to them through the wrongful detention of goods or through the detention of goods released pursuant to paragraph 6.
10. Without prejudice to the protection of confidential information, each Party shall provide that its competent authorities shall have the authority to give the right holder sufficient opportunity to have any goods detained by the customs administration inspected in order to substantiate the right holder's claims. Each Party shall also provide that its competent authorities have the authority to give the importer an equivalent opportunity to have any such goods inspected. Where the competent authorities have made a positive determination on the merits of a case, a Party may provide the competent authorities the authority to inform the right holder of the names and addresses of the consignor, the importer and the consignee, and of the quantity of the goods in question.
11. Where a Party requires its competent authorities to act on their own initiative and to suspend the release of goods in respect of which they have acquired prima facie evidence that an intellectual property right is being infringed:
   (a) the competent authorities may at any time seek from the right holder any information that may assist them to exercise these powers;
   (b) the importer and the right holder shall be promptly notified of the suspension by the Party's competent authorities, and where the importer lodges an appeal against

the suspension with competent authorities, the suspension shall be subject to the conditions, with such modifications as may be necessary, set out in paragraphs 6 through 8; and

(c) the Party shall only exempt both public authorities and officials from liability to appropriate remedial measures where actions are taken or intended in good faith.

12. Without prejudice to other rights of action open to the right holder and subject to the defendant's right to seek judicial review, each Party shall provide that its competent authorities shall have the authority to order the destruction or disposal of infringing goods in accordance with the principles set out in Article 1715(5). In regard to counterfeit goods, the authorities shall not allow the re-exportation of the infringing goods in an unaltered state or subject them to a different customs procedure, other than in exceptional circumstances.
13. A Party may exclude from the application of paragraphs 1 through 12 small quantities of goods of a noncommercial nature contained in travellers' personal luggage or sent in small consignments that are not repetitive.
14. Annex 1718.14 applies to the Parties specified in that Annex.

Article 1719: Cooperation and Technical Assistance

1. The Parties shall provide each other on mutually agreed terms with technical assistance and shall promote cooperation between their competent authorities. Such cooperation shall include the training of personnel.
2. The Parties shall cooperate with a view to eliminating trade in goods that infringe intellectual property rights. For this purpose, each Party shall establish and notify the other Parties by January 1, 1994 of contact points in its federal government and shall exchange information concerning trade in infringing goods.

Notes and Questions

1. Many of the policy issues and prospects for future cooperation under NAFTA can be gleaned from the current status of U.S.-Mexico criminal cooperation. Since NAFTA has gone into effect, the surge in the exchange of people, goods, and capital between the United States and Mexico and generally throughout the Americas has signaled its success in bringing people and economies closer.[24] The Enterprise for Americas Initiative, the explosion of free trade and economic integration throughout the Americas, and peace in Central America have facilitated commercial liberalization and economic integration.

At the same time, the liberal movement of persons, goods, and capital enables criminal elements to operate more easily. The concomitant criminal threats include illegal movement of criminals and illegal aliens; transnational corruption of judges and other government officials and agents; contraband in the form of illicit trafficking of narcotics, stolen cultural property, stolen planes and vehicles, and endangered species; kidnapping and ransom of executives and high-net-worth individuals; environmental crimes; money laundering; tax evasion; and piracy and other intellectual property violations.

[24] A revised version of the discussion in this Notes and Questions section was presented on a number of occasions in a paper entitled "International Criminal and Enforcement Cooperation in the Americas in a Post-NAFTA Transition Period with Special Attention to Investing in Mexico" at the American Conference Institute's program Doing Business in Mexico.

In the short term, free trade and economic integration facilitate these crimes. As a result, although governments and well-meaning private sector leaders contemplate economic integration, they should also consider the need to strengthen international criminal cooperation. NAFTA already strengthens intellectual property enforcement. At the request of the Clinton administration, side agreements on environment and labor were concluded. However, these do not have enforcement provisions as do the IP provisions. In the long term, however, NAFTA is likely to strengthen criminal and law enforcement cooperation among its members.

In the years since NAFTA has taken effect, Mexico and the United States have enjoyed significant enforcement cooperation successes: the taking effect of the Mutual Assistance in Criminal Matters Treaty,[25] a bilateral narcotics agreement,[26] a tax information exchange agreement, a prisoner transfer agreement, a convention on the recovery and return of stolen cultural property, and a convention on the recovery and return of stolen vehicles and aircraft. The Mexican government has also assumed an increasingly active but little noticed role in regional criminal policy, especially in the narcotics arena.

On an institutional level, meetings between attorneys general of the border states of the two countries and cooperation among customs, environmental, and intellectual property enforcement officials are gaining momentum. The outcome has been further exchanges of enforcement personnel, translations and studies of each other's laws, discussions and joint operations, harmonization of laws and procedures, an overall enhanced understanding of each other's laws and culture, and establishment of a mutual confidence.

Still, the relationship between the two countries has strains; for example, the diplomatic protests by the government of Mexico over kidnapping of its citizens by the U.S. and state governments.[27] Mexico protested the U.S. Supreme Court decision, *United States v. Alnarez Machain*, affirming jurisdiction despite the forcible kidnapping with DEA involvement of Mexican citizens in Mexico by agents of the U.S. government.[28] Mexico has also expressed concerns over U.S. violations of international human rights law due to the imposition of capital punishment against Mexican citizens; the Mexican government has filed *amicus curiae* briefs in such cases and negotiated a protocol to the extradition treaty. Continued violence against Mexican migrants has also resulted in

[25] For provisions of the MLAT, *see* DEVELOPMENTS IN MEXICAN-U.S. LAW ENFORCEMENT COOPERATION: WHAT THE PRACTITIONER NEEDS TO KNOW 33–40 (Bruce Zagaris ed., ABA Criminal Justice Section, April 20, 1990).

[26] For background on the narcotics cooperation agreement between Mexico and the United States, *see* Bruce Zagaris, *Mexico and the U.S. Conclude Narcotics Cooperation Agreement*, 5 INT'L ENFORCEMENT L. REP. 87 (Mar. 1989), reprinted in DEVELOPMENTS IN MEXICAN-U.S. LAW ENFORCEMENT COOPERATION: WHAT THE PRACTITIONER NEEDS TO KNOW (Bruce Zagaris ed.) 25; for a text of the agreement, *see id.* at 28–32.

[27] *See, e.g., Mexican Government Protests the Kidnapping by the State of Texas of Its Nationals*, 10 INT'L ENFORCEMENT L. REP. 364 (Oct. 1990).

[28] For diplomatic notes from the Mexican Government to the U.S. Department of State, *see* Mexico Secretaria de Relaciones Exteriores, LIMITS TO NATIONAL JURISDICTION DOCUMENTS AND JUDICIAL RESOLUTIONS ON THE ALVAREZ MACHAIN CASE 1992; Note of May 16, 1990 (violation of extradition treaty is denounced and repatriation of Alvarez Machain is requested) 5; Note of July 19, 1990 (formal petition of arrest of Alvarez Machain's kidnappers in order to extradite them) 7; Letter of the Mexico Secretary of Foreign Relations to the U.S. Secretary of State, May 29, 1992 (concern is expressed about the possibility that the U.S. Supreme Court's decision might deny Alvarez Machain's repatriation).

diplomatic protests by the Mexican government.[29] The taking effect of the U.S.-Mexico tax information exchange agreement has caused concern among Mexican investors in the United States.[30] The lack of sufficient cooperation on recovering and returning stolen Mexican cultural property has frustrated the Mexican government. Similarly, the lack of proper control over transborder trafficking of arms has caused the Mexican government to publicly and privately request action by the U.S. government. The violation of the right of detained Mexican nationals to have access to consular assistance, especially in death penalty cases, has led Mexico to bring actions in the International Court of Justice.

Similarly, on the side of the United States, concerns exist about the lack of progress in dealing with narcotics production and transshipment into the United States and narcotics-related corruption in Mexico.[31] The U.S. government has expressed concern about the placement of money from cocaine trafficking into the Mexican financial system.[32] At times, U.S. undercover sting operations have led to prosecutions of Mexican banks and subsequent protests from the Mexican government for conducting intrusive law enforcement operations in Mexico without its permission. The U.S. government and civil society organizations have worked to improve the relative human rights abuses in Mexico, especially of Americans. The U.S. government is concerned about the extent of corruption that deprives Mexican law and its operations of transparency and integrity and has long been a source of tension between it and Mexico. The U.S. intellectual property rights community has focused attention both before and after the negotiation of NAFTA on the lack of enforcement of piracy of CDs, cassettes, and software. Longstanding tension between the United States and Mexico has existed because of the inability of the United States to extradite Mexican nationals, although Mexico has remedied the problem under the Fox and Calderon administrations. The U.S. government has complained about insufficient cooperation in the recovery and return of stolen vehicles and aircraft. The lack of enforcement of environmental issues, such as the Marine Mammal Protection Act, has also led to longstanding U.S. government complaints and litigation.[33]

The U.S. policy of treating narcotics trafficking, money laundering, and even environmental crimes as national security concerns significantly magnifies the policy and diplomatic considerations of transborder crimes. For instance, in 1986, President Reagan's National Security Decision Directive 221 elevated the narcotics trade from a law enforcement matter to a national security matter. In 1989, the Salinas administration reiterated former Mexican President Miguel de la Madrid's pronouncement that drug trafficking was a national security threat.[34]

[29] Bruce Zagaris, *U.S.-Mexico Border Issues Flare Up*, 6 INT'L ENFORCEMENT L. REP. 444 (Dec. 1990) (discussing the filing of seventy-five formal complaints by the Ministry of Foreign Affairs of Mexico over border shootings with the U.S. government between 1985–1990).

[30] Michael J. A. Karlin & Paula Breger, *Exchange of Tax Information between the United States and Mexico*, 6 INT'L ENFORCEMENT L. REP. 69, 72 (Feb. 1990).

[31] *See, e.g.*, U.S. Department of State Bureau for International Narcotics and Law Enforcement Affairs, INTERNATIONAL NARCOTICS CONTROL STRATEGY REPORT xxiii, 140–48 (Mar. 1995).

[32] *Id.* at 498–99.

[33] See, e.g., *Environmental Groups Win Decision Enjoining Imports of Tuna by Mexico and Other Countries, Touching Off Dispute with Mexico*, 6 INT'L ENFORCEMENT L. REP. 376 (Oct. 1990); Sarah Barber, *U.S. Mexico Tuna Fight Moves to GATT while U.S. Appellate Court Gives U.S. Environmentalists a Victory*, 7 INT'L ENFORCEMENT L. REP. 58 (Feb. 1991).

[34] Kate Doyle, *The Militarization of the Drug War in Mexico*, in CURRENT HISTORY 83, 83–84 (Feb. 1993).

The Mexican government has also prioritized safeguarding its sovereignty against illegal incursions by U.S. law enforcement, especially with respect to kidnapping and the protection of Mexican nationals from human rights abuses committed against migrants by U.S. border guards.[35] The Mexican government has succeeded in obtaining a protocol to the extradition treaty whereby the signatory parties undertake not to use kidnapping or other irregular procedures outside the extradition treaty.[36]

In addition to their political, diplomatic, and policy aspects, the number and importance of the transactions in law enforcement create a growing professional and even commercial interest within the private sector. In several law enforcement areas, the U.S. private sector exports hardware, software, and services. In addition, investigative services are needed to engage in due diligence when a company from one country does business in the other; for example, when U.S. firms undertake due diligence in connection with acquisitions or joint ventures in Mexico. Firms providing security equipment and services also are experiencing increased business.[37] U.S. firms that provide physical security protection for executives[38] and security equipment,[39] financial investigation services, crisis management, risk assessment, and related services all have opportunities. Many are forming joint ventures with Mexican and other Latin American partners. Hence, the development of bilateral enforcement cooperation has important implications for businesses and private practitioners.[40]

2. What are the trade-offs between economic integration and enforcement cooperation among all three current NAFTA participants through the current NAFTA provisions and hemispheric institutions? Is the current ad hoc system sustainable? Trade liberalization and economic integration in the Americas will require reconsideration of the economic and enforcement infrastructures.[41]

[35] *See, e.g., Mexico-U.S. Border Flares Up Again*, 7 INT'L ENFORCEMENT L. REP. 385 (Oct. 1985); Cody, *Mexico Protests Alleged Border Aggression by U.S. Agents*, WASH. POST, Oct. 4, 1991, at A22, col. 1; the Mexican Embassy filed at least twenty-four diplomatic notes of protest between 1982 and 1990 with the U.S. State Department on behalf of Mexicans who were killed or seriously injured by INS agents. *See Human Rights Protections for Illegal Aliens on Mexican Border Are Increased*, 8 INT'L ENFORCEMENT L. REP. 287 (July 1992).

[36] For background on the negotiation of the protocol to the extradition treaty, *see U.S. Agrees to Renegotiate Extradition Treaty with Mexico and to Exclude Kidnapping*, 9 INT'L ENFORCEMENT L. REP. 230 (June 1993); *Mexico-U.S. Extradition Treaty Will Be Signed by April 1994*, 10 INT'L ENFORCEMENT L. REP. 51 (Feb. 1994).

[37] *See, e.g., Free Trade and Globalization Give Rise to Growth of International Investigation and Security Firms in the Eastern Hemisphere*, 11 INT'L ENFORCEMENT L. REP. 55 (Feb. 1995).

[38] *See, e.g.*, in Mexico the kidnapping of Banamex President Alfredo Harp Helu in the summer of 1994 and the ransom payment of US $30 million. *Id.*; *see also* David Villano, *To Serve and Protect*, U.S./LATIN TRADE (Dec. 1994).

[39] The Bogota-based Laurel International Risk Management Services opened an office in Colombia mainly to protect oil-drilling equipment from guerrillas. *See Free Trade and Globalization Give Rise*, *supra*, at 56; *Tiptoeing through the Mine Fields*, U.S./LATIN TRADE 142 (Dec. 1994).

[40] For discussions of another leading firm in the Western Hemisphere, Lindquist Avey Macdonald Baskerville, *see* COMBATING FRAUD: NEW CORPORATE RESPONSIBILITIES AND INITIATIVES (conference materials, Oct. 5, 1994, Toronto), esp. Tedd Avey, *The Hidden Cost of Fraud*, *id.*, at 3–14; Hazel de Burgh & Stephen Harney, *Threats to Your Bottom Line*, *id.*, at 45–60; Robert Lindquist & the Hon. Selwyn Richards, *Final Accounting of Johnny "O" Or, How Trinidad Recovered a Crooked Politician's Assets*, *id.*, at 61–76.

[41] For a discussion of the need for a reconsideration and strengthening of mechanisms and infrastructure for enforcement cooperation in the wake of NAFTA, *see* Leslie S. Potter & Bruce Zagaris, *supra*, at 684–90; Bruce Zagaris, *The Transformation of Environment Enforcement Cooperation*, *supra*, at 116–32; Bruce Zagaris & David R. Stepp, *Criminal and Quasi-Criminal Customs Enforcement*, at 37–83.

The traditional approach to enhance enforcement cooperation is to gradually negotiate memoranda of understanding, agreements, and treaties in the various areas of activity. To provide a framework to each of the legal areas covered by the treaties, signatory parties have established commissions to facilitate frequent communication among law enforcement officials. Examples include the bilateral narcotics agreement and MLAT commissions, as well as the Crossborder Environmental Cooperative Enforcement Strategy Work Group.

An important reason for establishing and cooperating with permanent mechanisms such as intergovernmental organizations is that the traditional source of power and major actor in the international arena, the territorial state, is being eclipsed by nonterritorial actors, such as organized crime, intergovernmental organizations, transnational social movements, and multinational corporations.[42] In some countries in the Americas, democracy and the authority of the territorial state are being supplanted by organized crime, including narco-terrorists. The politics of global interdependence are inescapable.

Mexico and the United States may want to consider establishing additional bilateral and regional enforcement mechanisms. They may want to review on a bilateral basis the mechanisms established in the Nordic countries that cut across parliamentarians, criminologists, and ministers responsible for justice. On a regional level, Mexico and the United States may want to consider establishing a Committee on the Americas' Crime Problems, emulating the European Committee on Crime Problems within the Council of Europe. A Committee on the Americas' Crime Problems would meet regularly at a subministerial level to consider all types of crime and propose solutions, including treaties, model legislation, regulations, and other criminal justice means. More than likely, it would be established under an existing regional institution, such as the Organization of American States. Unless our governments take a comprehensive approach to criminal justice in the Americas, nonstate actors, such as narco-terrorists and other organized criminals, will identify and exploit the gaps in the international criminal cooperation regime.[43]

Indeed, the private sector also has an important stake in the development of a proper enforcement regime, because the integrity of economic markets and sectors must be assured. A properly constructed enforcement cooperation regime will have a role for responsible private sector groups consistent with the legal and culture systems of the U.S., Mexican, and Canadian governments.

There are many lessons for the private sectors of all three NAFTA signatories. Because the Mexican legal system does not have as much transparency and formality as the U.S. or Canadian systems, North American investors need to learn about the Mexican enforcement system and how it operates in practice. In some cases, such as enforcement of intellectual property protection, North American firms must determine the best means of enforcing NAFTA standards. In some cases, enforcement has led to a confrontation with the informal economy. For decades, the informal economy has provided an important and, from a Mexican and Latin American perspective, efficient outlet for many sectors of

[42] *See, e.g.*, Scott Carlson & Bruce Zagaris, *International Cooperation in Criminal Matters: Western Europe's International Approach to International Crime*, 15 Nova L. Rev. 551, 552 (1991).

[43] For discussion of better use of the OAS and regional organizations in international criminal cooperation, *see* Bruce Zagaris & Constantine Papavizas, *Using the Organization of American States to Control International Narcotics Trafficking and Money Laundering*, 57 Rev. Int'l de Droit Penal 118 (1986).

the formal economy. In the context of cries of social injustice emanating from Chiapas, Mexicans (and eventually North Americans) are sensitive to overly severe enforcement that has harsh consequences for the informal sector, because its participants are already socially disadvantaged. Overly harsh enforcement of the informal sector can make its participants disappear into the illegal economy, a phenomenon that will have adverse consequences for the entire region. Instead of working in factories with environmental or labor standards under the minimum requirements, such persons, who are making the transition from the lower to middle classes, will be tempted to engage in trafficking of arms, illegal drugs, illegal persons, products, and money.

North American investors must listen carefully and work with their Mexican counterparts to help educate Mexican businesses and the informal sector on the best way to provide a transition to the new rules (e.g., intellectual property enforcement). Rather than bring criminal actions, one method to increase compliance is to initiate or work with nonprofit organizations and trade associations having the same goals – for example, North American environmental organizations have cooperated with their counterparts in trying to change the practices and attitudes of Mexican businesses. By continuing to work with those groups, the North American governments, and NAFTA institutions, North American businesses can try to provide for more transparency in Mexican laws and procedures. Once their laws have more transparency, North American businesses can have a better opportunity to participate in the rule-making that affects their competitors and themselves.

There will be a time of transition during the foreseeable future in which Mexico will be creating new institutions to comply with NAFTA and adjusting the practices of existing agencies and courts to it. The dislocation and shock of new competition brought to Mexico, both to its informal sector and small businesses, as NAFTA has been implemented, will continue to create tensions and subject North American businesses to enforcement difficulties. Just as important, the lack of funding for NAFTA institutions has brought tension over the obligations of NAFTA and the lack of mechanisms to fulfill them.

In the short term, the best way to prepare for potential enforcement problems is to conduct research using local intelligence services and even private investigative firms. Before investing, North American firms should conduct sufficient assessment of the various regulatory requirements. For instance, the new intercompany pricing audits of the Mexican Hacienda's Office of International Tax Counsel warrant attention. By reviewing policy statements, regulations, and consulting tax advisers both in Mexico and in the home country, North American firms should gain a better knowledge of and the ability to prepare for current and new regulatory requirements.

The continuing restructuring of some Mexican agencies in substantive areas such as customs, tax, environmental, and human rights policy, in combination with the uncertainties of a more informal regulatory environment, the dislocations brought about by NAFTA, and Mexican politics, requires careful investor planning. In the long run, harmonization is inevitable. However, until harmonization occurs, North American businesses need to reconcile and adjust to legal and cultural enforcement differences. The absence of organizational sanctions, RICO, the death penalty for corporations, civil forfeiture, and lengthy sentences may not be all that bad for U.S. businesses accustomed to a more draconian regime.

3. What are the strategic considerations flowing from criminal enforcement cooperation and the dynamic nature of criminal and quasi-criminal enforcement of national law

in doing business under NAFTA? In particular, lawyers and specialists have had greatly increased roles in interpreting specialized areas of the law, such as those dealing with the environment, intellectual property, customs, trade, and the interaction between civil and criminal law.

4. What, if any, enforcement areas within NAFTA are especially ripe for linkage (e.g., customs and tax enforcement, trade, and narcotics)?

5. To what extent can state enforcement mechanisms help supplement the lack of institutional mechanisms and provisions on a supranational level?

6. To what extent can the private sector help fill gaps in enforcement services (e.g., hijackings of trucks in delivering goods from the ports on the Caribbean coast to Mexico City, personal security for executives, due diligence in anti-money laundering, and environmental problems)?

7. The U.S. private sector has challenged the inadequate implementation of Mexican criminal enforcement of its intellectual property laws. *See, e.g.*, Bruce Zagaris, *Leading U.S. Intellectual Property Rights Trade Association Threatens NAFTA Trade Complaint against Mexico*, 11 INT'L ENFORCEMENT L. REP. 454 (Nov. 1995). However, within several years after NAFTA took effect, the U.S. intellectual property community and the U.S. government signaled that Mexican compliance and enforcement with IPR had improved significantly.

C. *Caribbean Community (CARICOM)*

As a result of the transition from a common market to a single market and economy, the CARICOM heads of governments have agreed to take a number of actions to strengthen their enforcement mechanisms. Some of these steps emulate actions taken by the EU, such as agreeing on a common approach to security with respect to visitors entering CARICOM and implementing a CARICOM Arrest Warrant Treaty and a CARICOM Maritime and Airspace Agreement.

COMMUNIQUE ISSUED AT THE CONCLUSION OF THE TWENTY-EIGHTH MEETING OF THE CONFERENCE OF HEADS OF GOVERNMENT OF THE CARIBBEAN COMMUNITY (CARICOM), 1–4 JULY 2007, NEEDHAM'S POINT, BARBADOS

Crime and Security

The Conference agreed in principle on the implementation of several measures designed to strengthen security arrangements within CARICOM. These measures, which will build on those arrangements established for CWC 2007, include the creation of a Virtual Single Domestic Space facilitated through a voluntary regime of a CARICOM Travel Card with facial and fingerprint biometrics. This Travel Card will allow CARICOM Nationals (with the exception of some of those on the CARICOM Watchlist) and Nationals of Third Countries legally resident within the participating Member States, expedited passage through airports in participating States without having to be subjected to passport examination. Further consultations will be held so that an Implementation Plan can be finalised for approval by the Bureau of the Conference of Heads of Government.

Other measures to be finalised by September 2007 include a CARICOM Maritime and Airspace Agreement and a CARICOM Arrest Warrant Treaty. The Maritime and Airspace

Agreement for CARICOM Member States will allow Member States to make best use of available resources in order to provide surveillance of the maritime environment; while the Arrest Warrant will put in place a legal mechanism to effect surrender of suspected persons and fugitives across borders. In the first instance, the focus will be on providing coverage for the maritime environment shared by Trinidad and Tobago, Barbados, Grenada, St. Vincent and the Grenadines and Saint Lucia.

A COMMUNITY FOR ALL: DECLARATION ON FUNCTIONAL COOPERATION, ISSUED BY THE HEADS OF GOVERNMENT OF THE CARIBBEAN COMMUNITY ON THE OCCASION OF THE TWENTY-EIGHTH MEETING OF THE CONFERENCE, 1–4 JULY 2007, NEEDHAM'S POINT, BARBADOS

WE, the Heads of Government of the Caribbean Community (CARICOM), meeting at Needham's Point, Barbados, 1–4 July, 2007 on the occasion of the 28th Regular Meeting of the Conference of Heads of Government of CARICOM;

11. Crime and Security – 'Securing our Community'

Aware that the security of our people is our highest responsibility and deeply committed to reducing vulnerability to crime and other threats to security within national borders and in our shared economic space, as well as to those emanating from beyond,

We:

Agree to build on the security arrangements successfully implemented for Cricket World Cup 2007 in order to enhance the well-being of the region's citizens and preserve the safety and security of our countries;

Further agree to accelerate the process of intelligence-sharing and human resource development and to develop other relevant bilateral and multilateral security arrangements to supplement limited national resources;

Resolve to develop regional law enforcement instruments which will facilitate a coordinated approach to the scourge of organised crime, international terrorism and financial crimes.

Notes and Questions:

1. CARICOM has a difficult task: trying to achieve criminal and enforcement cooperation to plug gaps that are occurring as a result of the single economic market. One positive element is that it has many models from which to choose because of the evolving EU experiments. The EU also has provided technical and financial assistance to CARICOM on justice and home affairs issues.

2. The establishment of the Association of Caribbean Commissioners of Police (ACCP) is one tangible result of Caribbean economic integration. Since its formation in 1986, the ACCP has achieved significant accomplishments in facilitating coordination and cooperation in response to the regional crime situation. The ACCP's goals are as follows: (a) develop and maintain a professional organization committed to the improvement of policing in the region; (b) promote, foster, and encourage high professional and ethical standards in pursuit of policing objectives; (c) support and advance the just and reasonable interests and aspirations of its members; (d) influence the development of laws, procedures, and practices that will advance the effectiveness of policing in the region; (e) negotiate and secure funding from individuals and organizations supportive of the

goals of the Association; (f) engage in formal relations with any organization, institution, or state agency for the welfare and benefit of the Association and/or its members; (g) take an active interest in the promotion of the development of young people regionally and internationally; (h) arrange conferences, workshops, and seminars for the purpose of sharing information and experiences of benefit to law enforcement; and (i) take all necessary steps to ensure that the Association is sufficiently funded in order to meet its obligations and to ensure that the funds are effectively managed and properly accounted for. Since its establishment, the ACCP has grown in stature and influence in law enforcement regionally and internationally, as CARICOM has given the ACCP responsibility to lead in developing the law enforcement agenda. Regional and international agencies have consulted the ACCP on matters relating to law enforcement. For more background *see* Bruce Zagaris, *Association of Caribbean Commissioners of Police Strengthen Regional Law Enforcement Standards and Cooperation*, 22 INT'L ENFORCEMENT L. REP. 164 (Apr. 2006).

3. The ACCP faces a number of sustainability issues, especially in the context of increasing levels of crime in the region, the region's potential as a staging ground for anti-U.S./Western attacks, and the creation of the Caribbean Single Market and Economy, which will facilitate the prospect of transnational crime in the region. *See* Zagaris, *id*; CARIBBEAN SECURITY IN THE AGE OF TERROR 497 (Ivelaw Griffith ed., 2004).

4. International organizations, such as the UN and the World Bank, have played important roles in efforts to strengthen the Caribbean criminal justice systems. For instance, on May 4, 2007, the UN Office on Drugs and Crime and the Latin America and Caribbean Region of the World Bank issued a report stating that crime and violence are creating a major obstacle to investment, undermining growth, threatening human welfare, and impeding social development in the Caribbean. The report made a series of recommendations for regional and national action. *See, e.g.*, Bruce Zagaris, *World Bank Calls for Improved Criminal Justice Planning in the Caribbean*, 23 INT'L ENFORCEMENT L. REP. 275 (July 2007).

IV. Asia

In Asia, the Asia-Pacific Economic Cooperation (APEC), although only a proposed FTA, is already fostering criminal and enforcement cooperation mechanisms. The current scope of cooperation is limited to certain areas, including counterterrorism, anticorruption, and cybercrime.

APEC Approves Counter-Terrorism and Anti-Corruption Enforcement Cooperation Measures

REPRINTED FROM 20 INT'L ENFORCEMENT L. REP. 17 (JAN. 2004)

by Bruce Zagaris

On October 21, 2003, during the 11th Asia-Pacific Economic Cooperation (APEC) Economic Leaders' Meeting in Bangkok, the delegates adopted a series of counter-terrorism and other enforcement (e.g., anti-corruption and cyber-crime) measures as part of the theme of "World of Differences: Partnership for the Future."

Under the theme of enhancing human security, APEC leaders agreed that transnational terrorism and the proliferation of weapons of mass destruction pose direct and profound challenges to APEC's vision of free, open, and prosperous economies. The leaders agreed to dedicate APEC to the mission of ensuring the security of its people. In that regard, they committed to take all essential actions to: dismantle, fully and without delay, transnational terrorist groups that threaten the APEC economies; eliminate the danger posed by the proliferation of weapons of mass destruction and their means of delivery by strengthening international non-proliferation regimes, adopting and enforcing effective export controls, and taking other legitimate and appropriate measures against proliferation.[44]

APEC leaders also agreed to:

- Strengthen joint efforts to reduce terrorist threats against mass transportation and address the threat posed by terrorists' acquisition and use of Man-Portable Air Defense Systems (MANPADS) against international aviation by committing to (a) adopt strict domestic export controls on MANPADS, (b) secure stockpiles, (c) take domestic action to regulate production, transfer, and broker, (d) prohibit transfers to non-state end-users, and (e) exchange information in support of these efforts. The leaders agreed to continue efforts to strengthen domestic controls on MANPADs and to review its progress next year at the APEC meeting in Chile.
- Increase and better coordinate APEC's counter-terrorism activities, where appropriate, through effective collaboration, technical assistance and capacity building, and cooperation between APEC's Counter Terrorism Task Force, the Counter Terrorism Action Group (CTAG) of the G-8, the United Nations Security Council Counter Terrorism Committee and other relevant international, regional, and functional organizations.
- Implement the APEC Action Plan on SARS and its Health Security Initiative to help APEC prevent and respond to regional health threats, including nationally-occurring infectious disease and bio-terrorism. APEC welcomed the establishment by Singapore and the U.S. of a Regional Emerging Disease Intervention (REDI) Center. APEC encouraged the Life Sciences Innovation Forum to complete its strategic plan by 2004.
- Establish a regional trade and financial security initiative within the Asian Development Bank, to support projects that enhance port security, combat terrorist finance, and achieve other counter-terrorism goals.
- Support implementation of the Advance Passenger Information (API) System pathfinder initiative and efforts to explore development of a regional movement alert system to protect air travelers.
- Accelerate the implementation of the Energy Security Initiative by endorsing its Implementation Plan and, as appropriate, a new Action Plan to enhance regional and global energy security.[45]

On counter-terrorism, the leaders reaffirmed APEC's resolve in fighting terrorism and noted the need to address both the symptoms and the root causes of terrorism, since this is a problem that undermines trade and investment that are APEC's main goals.[46]

[44] APEC, 2003 *Leaders' Declaration, Bangkok Declaration on Partnership for the Future*, Bangkok, Thailand, Oct. 1, 2003 (http://ww.apecsec.org.sg/content/apec/leaders_declarations/2003.html).

[45] *Id.*

[46] APEC, 2003 *Leaders' Declaration, Chair's Summary of Discussions at Retreats I and II, 11th APEC Economic Leaders' Meeting*, Bangkok, 20–21 Oct. 2003 (http://www.apecsec.org.sg/content/apec/leaders_declarations/2003/retreat_summary.html).

Economic ministers expressed a commitment to ongoing work in blocking the cross-border movement of equipment, funds, and people involved in transnational terrorist activities while simultaneously enhancing the free flow of legitimate travelers, trade and investment.

To minimize the potential abuse of alternative remittance systems for terrorism financing purposes, the Ministers noted the Finance Ministers' agreement on the need to explore how alternative remittance systems operate and in some cases, how the formal financial systems can be strengthened to provide more attractive and accessible remittance services.[47]

Under the theme of promoting trade and investment liberalization a resolution obligates the member countries to fight corruption, which it characterized as a major obstacle to social and economic development, by working in 2004 to develop specific domestic actions to combat it. The APEC member countries pledged to promote transparency by implementing its general and area-specific transparency standards through its Transparency by 2005 Strategy.

Ministers welcome the TEL's Report to Leaders and Ministers on Actions of the Telecommunications and Information Working Group to Address Cybercrime and Cybersecurity, which showed the work undertaken to implement the APEC Cybersecurity Strategy, and urged APEC fora and economies to continue their efforts to implement. The Ministers welcomed the Cybercrime Legislation and Enforcement Capacity Building Project and its first meeting held in Thailand in 2003. The Ministers called for additional work by APEC fora and economies to develop laws and procedures to facilitate the investigation and prosecution of transnational cybercrime. Ministers took notice of the efforts economies have made to share information about security threats and to help each other in international cybercrime investigations, and welcomed APEC efforts to promote the development of an international network of Computer Emergency Response Teams ("CERTs"). They also agreed to continue to support the work done by APEC fora and economies to promote security and technical guidelines, raise public awareness about computer security threats, and promote cybersecurity training and education.[48]

The significance of the adoption of counter-terrorism and anti-corruption measures is that, until now, APEC has been primarily a trade group. The weight given to security concerns in the summit statement reflected U.S. priorities. The U.S. and its allies believe the extension of APEC's remit to include counter-terrorism will help make it the "premier summit" for the Asia-Pacific region, potentially surpassing the Association of South East Asian Nations (ASEAN) and its associated meetings with other Asian states, such as China and Japan.[49]

The inclusion of international enforcement cooperation measures indicates the interaction of globalization, free trade and economic integration with transnational crime and hence, the need for free trade and economic integration organizations to compensate for the facilitation of the use of free trade and economic liberalization by criminals with mechanisms to prevent such uses and investigate and prosecute criminals when they take advantage of new breakthroughs to facilitate free trade and economic integration. Normally, the more that an organization makes the transition from free trade to a customs union and a single economic market, the more opportunities for transnational crime and the more potential for criminal justice measures. For instance, the attainment of the Single Economic Market in

[47] APEC, 2003 15th APEC Ministerial Meeting, Joint Statement Summary of Key Issues (http://www.apecsec.org.sg/content/apec/ministerial_statements/annual_ministerial/2003_15th_apec_ministerial.html).

[48] *Id.*

[49] Victor Mallet & Amy Kazmin, *Summit Approves New Anti-Terror Schemes*, FIN. TIMES, Oct. 22, 2003, at 8, col. 3.

the European Community included the responsibilities and authorities for the EU to make justice and home affairs policies.

V. A Hypothetical

You are a White House fellow assigned to the National Security Council. The new administration is overwhelmed by transnational crime from other parts of the Western Hemisphere. The administration suffers from budgetary constraints and wants to restrain unilateral mechanisms for international criminal and enforcement cooperation in the region. It directs you to prepare a paper recommending potential ways that the U.S. government can galvanize the region to more effectively cope with transnational crime in both the short and long term. Would your recommendations be different if the agency for which you worked was the Department of Justice, Department of State, or Homeland Security? If so, how would your approach and potential recommendations differ?

Instead of the United States, this hypothetical can use Mexico, Canada, Brazil, the CARICOM Secretariat (or the Organization of East Caribbean States, a subgroup within CARICOM), or a key CARICOM country such as Trinidad & Tobago, Jamaica, or Barbados. This could be a group assignment for members of a class to present and defend their ideas.

How would your answer be different if you were assigned to the European Union or a constituent organization such as the Justice and Home Affairs Council? The EU gives significant technical and financial assistance on justice and home affairs issues in the Caribbean.

VI. *Additional Reading*

A. *Books*

Peter Andreas, Border Games: Policing the U.S.-Mexico Divide (Cornell Univ. Press 2000).

Hervé Boullanger, La Criminalité Économique en Europe (Economic Crime in Europe) (2002).

Caribbean Security in the Age of Terror 497 (Ivelaw Griffith ed., 2004).

The Challenge of Integration: Europe and the Americas (Peter H. Smith ed., North-South Center 1993).

La Criminalite Economique et Financiere en Europe (Economic and Financial Crime in Europe (Paul Ponsaers & Vincenzo Ruggiero eds., L'Harmattan 2002).

Ivelaw Lloyd Griffith, Drugs and Security in the Caribbean: Sovereignty under Siege (Penn. State Press 1997).

Christopher Harding, Phil Fennell, Nico Jörg, & Bert Swart, Criminal Justice in Europe: A Comparative Study (Clarendon Press 1995).

Policing across National Boundaries (Malcolm Anderson & Monica den Boer eds., Pinter Publishers 1994).

Strategies of the EU and the US in Combating Transnational Organised Crime (Brice De Ruyver, Gert Vermuelen, & Tom Vander Beken eds., Institute for International Research on Criminal Prolicy, University of Ghent, Maklu, Antwerpen-Appeldoorn 2000).

Strategies and Security in U.S.-Mexican Relations Beyond the Cold War (John Bailey & Dergio Aguayo Quezada eds., Center for U.S.-Mexican Studies at U. of California, San Diego 1996).

B. *Articles and Book Chapters*

Ethan Nadelmman, *Harmonization of Criminal Justice Systems, in* The Challenge of Integration: Europe and the Americas 247 (Peter H. Smith ed., North-South Center 1993).

David P. Warner, *Law Enforcement Cooperation in the Organization of American States: A Focus on REMJA*, 37 U. Miami Inter-Am. L.Rev. 387, 387–420 (2006).

Bruce Zagaris, *Addendum: Revenge of the Tequila; Crime Gathers Momentum in U.S.-Mexico Relations*, 3 S.W. J.L. Trade Am. 85–99 (1996).

Bruce Zagaris, *International Criminal and Enforcement Cooperation in the Americas in a Post-NAFTA Transition Period with Special Attention to Investing in Mexico*, 62 pp., Investing in Mexico, American Conference Instit., Mar. 9–10, 1995, and Mar. 15, 1996, 3 S.W. J.L. Trade Am. 1–84 (1996).

Bruce Zagaris, *The Amparo Process in Mexico* 6 U.S.-Mex. L.J. 61–69 (1998).

Bruce Zagaris, *Some Positive Aspects of U.S.-Mexico National Security and International Enforcement: Subnational Cooperation and The Arizona-Sonora Experiment in*, Public Security and Democratic Governance: Challenges to Mexico and the United States (Georgetown University Press 2001).

Bruce Zagaris, *Association of Caribbean Commissioners of Police Strengthen Regional Law Enforcement Standards and Cooperation*, 22 Int'l Enforcement L. Rep. 164 (Apr. 2006).

Bruce Zagaris, *Developments in the Institutional Architecture and Framework of International Criminal and Enforcement Cooperation in the Western Hemisphere*, 37 U. Miami Inter-Am. L.Rev. 421, 421–516 (2006).

Bruce Zagaris & Alvaro Aguilar, *Enforcement of Intellectual Property Protection between Mexico and the U.S.: Dynamic Entertainment and a Precursor of Criminal Enforcement for Western Hemispheric Integration?*, 5 Fordham Intell. Prop. Media & Ent. L.J. 41–124 (Aug. 1994).

Bruce Zagaris & Lisa Stacy Koenig, *Facilitating Futures Trading across the Rio Grande: The Commodity Futures MOU between Mexico and the U.S.* (w.), 3 Latin Am. L. & Bus. Rep. 28–32 (Oct. 1995).

Bruce Zagaris & Julia Padierna Peralta, *Mexico-United States Extradition and Alternatives: From Fugitive Slaves to Drug Traffickers–150 Years and beyond the Rio Grande's Winding Courses*, 12 Am.U. J. Int'l L. & Pol'cy 519–627 (1997).

Bruce Zagaris & Leslie S. Potter, *Toward a Common U.S.-Mexican Cultural Heritage: The Need for a Regional Americas Initiative in the Recovery and Return of Stolen Cultural Property*, 5 Transnat'l Law. 627–90 (Fall 1992).

Bruce Zagaris & J. Resnick, *The Mexico-U.S. Mutual Legal Assistance in Criminal Matters Treaty: Another Step toward the Harmonization of International Law Enforcement*, 14 Ariz. J. Int'l & Comp. L. 1–96 (1997).

Bruce Zagaris & Juan Soldevila, *Tax Eagles Soar across the Rio Grande: Tax Enforcement Cooperation Increases between Mexico and the United States*, 2 Mex. Trade & L. Rep. 1119 (Nov. 1994).

Bruce Zagaris & Maureen T. Walsh, *The United States-Mexico Treaty on the Execution of Penal Sanctions: The Case for Reevaluating the Treaty and Its Policies in View of NAFTA and Other Developments*, 2 S.W. J.L. Trade Am. 385–450 (Fall 1995).

C. *Primary Sources*

International and European Criminal Law: Essential Texts on International and European Criminal Law (Gert Vermeulen ed., 1st ed., Oct. 2000, Maklu, Antwerpen-Appeldoorn) (principal policy documents and multilateral legal instruments on international and European criminal law, with a special focus on initiatives aimed at combating international or organized crime).

D. *Web Sites*

Council of Europe, http://legal.coe.int.
Organization of American States, http://www.oas.org/juridco.
European Union, http://europa.eu.int.

Index